Orestes T Doe

The Record of Births, Marriages, and Deaths in the Town of Franklin

Orestes T Doe

The Record of Births, Marriages, and Deaths in the Town of Franklin

ISBN/EAN: 9783742809704

Manufactured in Europe, USA, Canada, Australia, Japa

Cover: Foto ©ninafisch / pixelio.de

Manufactured and distributed by brebook publishing software (www.brebook.com)

Orestes T Doe

The Record of Births, Marriages, and Deaths in the Town of Franklin

THE RECORD

OF

BIRTHS, MARRIAGES AND DEATHS

IN THE

TOWN OF FRANKLIN,

FROM 1778 TO 1872.

EDITED BY
ORESTES T. DOE,
TOWN CLERK.

FRANKLIN, MASS.:
PRINTED AT THE OFFICE OF THE FRANKLIN SENTINEL.
1898.

INTRODUCTION.

In 1897 the town voted to raise $550 for the purpose of printing its records of Births, Marriages and Deaths. The Town Clerk prepared the copy for the printer, which was a long and tedious work for which no compensation was paid. Albert H. Martin, Esq., has assisted the Clerk in preparing this copy very materially, for a very small compensation.

In 1863 a committee was appointed at the annual meeting to ascertain the condition of the town records and reports thereon. Mr. Horatio Stockbridge was chairman of this committee, which reported that the births, deaths and marriages from 1778 to 1844 were in small books, with no title pages, and entries made there without order or system. The record of a birth that occurred in 1778 might be followed by a birth that occurred in 1815. The record of the report of this committee may be found in Book 3, Page 170 of the Town Records.

In consequence of the report of this committee, the records of births, marriages and deaths were copied and the originals lost or destroyed, probably. Your Clerk has made diligent inquiry for these original books, but has not found any person who has any recollection of ever seeing them; however, Franklin is very fortunate to have a copy of these original records. There are many towns in New England which have no records of these very important events, and now, after having this book printed, these records will be perpetuated.

The Clerk arranged these records in the order of their date, and has kept as near a copy of the records as space would permit; and whenever bad spelling appears in this book, the reader can safely assume that it is the fault of the record and not of the printer.

I hope that the town will continue to make appropriations for the purpose of printing the records of the town meetings from the time of its incorporation to the time when the town began to print its annual reports, as these records contain the most accurate historical information that can be obtained.

This town was a part of Wrentham until 1778. Where a record is dated prior to 1778 the event took place when Franklin was a part of Wrentham, where another record of the same event may be found.

THE INDEX.

A separate index has been made for each division of the book, that is, for the Births, Marriages and Deaths, each one being complete in itself. Both the surnames and the christian names have been arranged in alphabetical order in each index. Many of the surnames have different methods of spelling, and not infrequently are incorrectly spelled; the plan adopted in the index in such cases has been to combine all the different methods of spelling the same name under the method standing first in the alphabetical order, with reference to this name when any of the other methods are reached in their proper order. To this rule there is but one exception in which the christian names are grouped under the second method of spelling the surname with a cross reference from the first method. Cases where no christian names are given are indexed under their surnames by a ——— placed at the beginning of the christian names. In a great many instances the christian names have been incorrectly spelled; but in compiling the index, no liberties have been taken with the christian names and no assumptions have been made as to what they ought to be, as in the case of some of the surnames: on the contrary, they have been indexed strictly as they appear upon the Records, without regard to what may be the correct spelling. The following are a few examples of this: What should be Jemima may appear as Mima, or Amelia may appear as Melia, or Sarah as Sally; Harriet may be spelled Hariet; what should be Louisa or Louise may, by a mistake in the Record, appear as Louis, or vice versa; Catherine and Katherine are indexed under C and K respectively; Francis and Frances are used indiscriminately for both males and females, and so in a few other instances. On page 163, line 2, is found the record of the death of an infant utterly destitute of any name, and having no parents named on the Record. This infant could not be indexed at all; but with this exception, it is thought that every name has been included in the index under some method of spelling.

TOWN CLERK.

CORRECTIONS.

Page 18, line 3. Change Millie Heaton to *Mille* Heaton.
Page 19, line 38. Change H. Cleveland Fisher to H. *Cleaveland* Fisher.
Page 23, line 47. Change Salvanus S. Cook to *Silvanus* S. Cook.
Page 26, line 8. Change T. C. Combs to T. C. *Coombs*.
Page 26, next to last line. David Whitney Bullard should read David *Whiting* Bullard.
Page 27, line 15. Change Marcetta Lathua to *Marietta* Lathua.
Page 28, line 16. Change Fliza Thayer to *Eliza* Thayer.
Page 28, line 22. Change Elezer T. Bullard to *Eleazer* T. Bullard.
Page 30, line 10. Change C. Fisher Daniels to C. *Fisk* Daniels.
Page 31, line 41. Change C. Muller to C. *Miller*.
Page 32, line 39. Change Sylvanius W. F. to *Sylvanus* W. F.
Page 32, line 42. Change I. Francis Harding to I. *Frances* Harding.
Page 43, line 3. Change E. Augustus Wales to E. *Augusta* Wales.
Page 45, line 7. Change P. Amantha Cook to P. *Cemantha* Cook.
Page 59, No. 10. Change M. A. Rahala to M. A. *Kahala*.
Page 61, No. 30. Change E. Eldon King to E. *Eldora* King.
Page 65, No. 11. Change James Wales to *Jennie* Wales.
Page 68, No. 50. Change Olive S. Daniels to *Oliver* S. Daniels.
Page 73, No. 41. Insert ——— *King* in blank space.
Page 76, No. 16. Change James Lemon to James *Lennon*.
Page 77, No. 23. Change Willard F. Metcalf to *Millard* F. Metcalf.
Page 78, No. 23. Insert ——— *Wadsworth* in blank space.
Page 79, No. 3. Change Bichardsan to *Richardson*.
Page 85, No. 23. Insert ——— *Adams* in blank space.
Page 85, No. 27. Insert ——— *Newell* in blank space.
Page 85, No. 29. Insert ——— *Batchelder* in blank space.
Page 93, line 1. Change Solomon Hawes to Solomon *Hewes*.
Page 96, line 23. Change Joseyh Kingsbury to *Joseph* Kingsbury.
Page 97, line 1. Change Elisha Stevens to Elisha *Sevens*.
Page 100, line 16. Change Julia Brownell to *Julian* Brownell.
Page 102, line 27. Change Dr. John C. Metcalf to Dr. John *G.* Metcalf.
Page 103, line 27. Change Dory Mumle to Dory *Mumler*.
Page 103, line 31. Change Hanan Metcalf to *Hanan* Metcalf.
Page 107, line 3. Change John Govis to John *Goins*.
Page 108, line 31. Change David Wright to David *Wight*.
Page 110, line 19. Change George I. Partridge to George *F. Patridge*.
Page 112, line 20. Otis Metcalf to Otis *F.* Metcalf.
Page 113, line 7. Change Olive Randall to *Oliver* Randall.
Page 114, line 6. Change Mary T. Bullard to Mary *F.* Bullard.
Page 114, line 12. Change Eliza F. Feel to Eliza F. *Teel*.
Page 114, line 15. Change Enoch Bowen to Enoch *Bowers*.
Page 116, line 1. Change June 27, 1749 to June 27, *1849*.
Page 125, line 2. Change Lizzie A. Scott to Lizzie *R.* Scott.
Page 127, line 7. Change W. H. Robbie to W. H. *Roblie*.
Page 132, line 26. Change Eva A. Newell to *Evie* A. Newell.
Page 139, line 11. Change Lemuel E. Bumpus to Lemuel *F.* Bumpus.
Page 143, line 45. Change Jeremiah Mackeny to *Jemima* Mackeny.
Page 144, line 33. Change Hipzibah Lethbridge to *Hipsabah* Lethbridge.
Page 145, line 4. Change Mary Blake to Mary *Baker*.
Page 146, line 10. Change Harry Fisher to *Harvey* Fisher.
Page 146, line 32. Change Lydia Heaton to *Lynda* Heaton.
Page 149, line 56. Change James Fisher, 2y, 25d to James Fisher, *25y, 2d*.
Page 150, line 6. Change Abigail Allen to Abigail *Metcalf*.
Page 152, line 9. Change Luisa Tucker to *Loiusa* Tucker.
Page 154, line 41. Change Pelatian Fisher to *Pelatiah* Fisher.
Page 155, line 13. Change Mrs. John Pierce to *Mr.* John Pierce.

CORRECTIONS.

Page 156, line 1. Change Horace Freeman Whiting to Horace *Trueman* Whiting.
Page 156, line 55. Change Mrs. Sarah Fiske to Mrs. Sarah *Fisher*.
Page 164, line 10. Change Frances O. Wales to *Francis* O. Wales.
Page 177, line 15. Change M. R. Richardson to M. *K.* Richardson.
Page 177, line 19. Change Louisa Knapp to *Louis* Knapp.
Page 178, line 2. Change Susan Lawrence to *Susanna* Lawrence.
Page 186, last line. Change E. E. Crosby to E. E. *Crossley*.
Page 192, line 26. Change Maria H. Coombs to *Marion* H. Coombs.

Franklin Town Records.

BIRTHS IN FRANKLIN.

Births Registered Prior to Jan'y 1, 1845.

DATE OF BIRTH.	NAME, IF ANY.	SEX.	NAME OF PARENTS.
Mar. 15, 1778.	Elihu White.	M	William & Jerusha.
Jan. 23, 1777.	Abigail Dean.	F	Eben'r & Abigail.
Feb. 7, 1777.	Lewis Slocomb.	M	Billa & Jerusha.
Jan. 10, 1778.	Luther Kingsbury.	"	Aaron & Elizabeth.
Nov. 10, 1777.	Jabez Pond.	"	Asa & Judith.
May 26, 1778.	Fardanand Lethbridge.	"	Samuel & Sarah.
Jan. 13, 1778.	Aaron Clay.	"	Aaron & Lois.
April 14, 1776.	Nathanael Emmons.	"	Rev. Nathanael & Deliverance.
June 23, 1777.	Diodate Johnson Emmons.	"	" " "
Sept. 20, 1777.	Loui Sayles.	F	Elisha & Katherine.
Aug. 1, 1776.	Colburn Hartshorne.	M	Ebenezer & Lydia.
April 10, 1778.	Ebenezer Hartshorne.	"	" " "
Aug. 9, 1777.	Lois Metcalf.	F	Levi & Lois.
Feb. 27, 1778.	Paul Clark.	M	Samuel & Esther.
Mar. 15, 1778.	Samuel Allen.	"	Abijah & Abigail.
Mar. 12, 1778.	Poly Lethbridge.	F	Richard & Jerusha.
June 15, 1778.	Matilda Kingsbury.	"	Stephen & Abigail.
Oct. 27, 1778.	Eunite Daniels.	"	Seth & Eunite.
Oct. 28, 1778.	Bass Bowditch.	M	Jonathan & Mary.
Sept. 26, 1778.	Milletiah Bullard.	F	Elijah & Mileah.
May 23, 1772.	Anna Pond.	"	Oliver & Anna.
Aug. 1, 1774.	Metcalf Pond.	M	" " "
Nov. 16, 1777.	Samuel Metcalf Pond.	"	" " "
Dec. 24, 1778.	Eunice Mann.	F	Nathan & Eunice, Jr.
Aug. 22, 1778.	Susanna Richardson.	"	Silence Smith.
May 1, 1778.	Asa Williamas.	M	Marbe Dake & Joanna.
Jan. 19, 1778.	Abigail Richardson.	F	Elisha & Abigail.
Oct. 11, 1778.	Luther White.	M	Timothy & Edi.
Mar. 8, 1778.	Franklin Clark.	"	Dyer & Rachel.
Dec. 31, 1778.	Clarinda Ware.	F	Phineas & Susanna.
April 21, 1777.	Samuel Partridge Hawes.	M	Jonathan & Mary.
June 9, 1778.	Larnard Wright.	"	Seth & Joanna.
April 24, 1778.	Elisabeth Wood.	F	David & Hannah.
Jan. 8, 1779.	Julia Slocomb.	"	Billa & Jerusha.
Oct. 3, 1771.	Lucinda Adams.	"	Thaddeus & Rachel.
May 12, 1773.	Abigail Adams.	"	" " "
Jan. 22, 1775.	Thaddeus Adams.	M	" " "
Oct. 25, 1777.	Rachel Adams.	F	" " "
Jan. 31, 1779.	Whiting Metcalf.	M	James & Abigail, Jr.
Oct. 7, 1778.	Poly Ware.	F	Oliver & Betty.
Sept. 17, 1779.	Joel Gould.	M	Joseph & Kezia.
Jan. 3, 1779.	Samuel Morse.	"	Samuel & Sarah, Jr.

DATE OF BIRTH.	NAME, IF ANY.	SEX	NAME OF PARENTS.
April 7, 1779.	Nathan Heaton.	M	Isaac & Thankfull, Jr.
Mar. 15, 1779.	Noah Heaton.	"	Noah & Abigail.
Feb. 7, 1779.	Daniel Adams.	"	John & Neomy, Jr.
June 7, 1779.	Samuel Robinson.	"	Benjamin & Hipsabeth.
April 12, 1779.	Abigail Dean.	F	Ichabod & Chloe.
April 6, 1775.	Eunice Whiting.	"	Pelatiah & Hannah.
Nov. 12, 1777.	Pelatiah Whiting.	M	" "
Feb. 24, 1779.	Eliab Fisher.	"	Joseph & Susa.
July 28, 1760.	Hette Aldis.	F	John & Esther.
Sept. 24, 1771.	Eunice Aldis.	"	" "
Mar. 3, 1773.	Sara Aldis.	"	" "
May 28, 1779.	Nancy Thurston.	"	Abijah & Rachel.
Aug. 23, 1779.	Baruch Pond.	M	Asa & Judith.
Feb. 3, 1777.	Willard Metcalf.	"	Bille & Patta.
Nov. 3, 1778.	Polly Metcalf.	F	" "
July 6, 1779.	Salla Richardson.	"	Eli & Mahetabel.
Sept. 21, 1776.	Israel Lee.	M	Joseph & Jemima.
Sept. 18, 1778.	Sarah Lee.	F	" "
Sept. 19, 1779.	Abigail Rockwood.	"	Elisha & Eunice.
Sept. 16, 1779.	Salla Metcalf.	"	Levi & Lois.
Dec. 7, 1779.	Harmon Clap.	M	Aaron & Lois.
April 7, 1778.	Joseph Millard.	"	Joseph & Thankfull.
Aug. 15, 1779.	Jesse Ware.	"	Jesse & Kezia.
Nov. 14, 1779.	Alibeaus Partridge.	"	Elisha & Sarah.
Jan. 2, 1780.	Moses Ware.	"	Eli & Thaymer.
Feb. 17, 1780.	Eldod Man.	"	Elias & Mary.
Oct. 31, 1779.	Clayrasa Cook.	F	Stephen & Elizabeth.
April 18, 1780.	Molly Hills.	"	Ziba & Molly.
Sept. 11, 1779.	Name Pond.	"	Elijah & Mehetable.
Dec. 5, 1779.	Lydia Ellis.	"	Timothy & Sarah.
April 21, 1780.	Jemima Man.	"	Nathan & Eunice, Jr.
May 10, 1780.	Cali Williams.	"	Marbe Dake & Joanna.
Aug. 28, 1779.	Lois Metcalf.	"	Samuel & Lois.
Mar. 24, 1779.	Nathan Gillmore.	M	William & Mary.
Sept. 18, 1779.	Susanna Lethbridge.	F	Richard & Jerusha.
Aug. 25, 1780.	Judson Metcalf.	M	Hanan & Mary.
Mar. 28, 1780.	Esther Clark.	F	Samuel & Esther.
June 23, 1780.	Meletiah Adams.	"	Moses & Abigail.
Oct. 12, 1780.	Amasa Ware.	M	Billy & Sarah.
Oct. 3, 1780.	Hannah Partridge.	F	Joshua & Hannah.
Dec. 16, 1779.	Mary Allen.	"	Abijah & Abigail.
Sept. 30, 1780.	Martha Emmons.	"	Rev. Nath'l & Martha.
Sept. 20, 1780.	Thankfull Millard.	"	Joseph & Thankfull.
Dec. 6, 1780.	Nama Lethbridge.	"	Samuel & Sarah.
Aug. 23, 1770.	Esther Hills.	"	Ephraim & Abigail.
Mar. 29, 1772.	Ichabod Hills.	M	" "
Jan. 24, 1774.	Jonah Hills.	"	" "
May 21, 1775.	Beulah Hills.	F	" "
Aug. 27, 1776.	Jemima Hills.	"	" "
Dec. 21, 1777.	Micah Hills.	M	" "
Aug. 24, 1779.	Nabe Hills.	F	" "
June 15, 1780.	Arial Sayles.	M	Elisha & Catharine.
Dec. 10, 1780.	Jonathan Bowditch.	"	Jonathan & Mary.
Nov. 21, 1780.	Nance Richardson.	F	Elisha & Abigail.
Sept. 25, 1779.	Esther Baker.	"	Abigail & Esther.
Dec. 18, 1780.	Philo Slocomb.	M	Billa & Jerusha. (Oct. 25, 1780)
July 5, 1780.	Horatio Kingsbury.	"	Stephen & Abigail.
Feb. 23, 1778.	Jonathan Wails.	"	Jonathan & Olive.
Mar. 11, 1781.	Otis Wails.	"	" "
Mar. 31, 1781.	Oliver Richardson.	"	Daniel & Lydia.
April 19, 1776.	Elisabeth Daniels.	F	Nathan & Elisabeth, Jr.

FRANKLIN TOWN RECORDS—BIRTHS. 11

DATE OF BIRTH.	NAME, IF ANY.	SEX.	NAME OF PARENTS.
Feb. 9, 1778.	Cyrus Daniels.	M	Nathan & Elisabeth, Jr.
Oct. 14, 1779.	Dorcas Daniels.	F	" "
Mar. 2, 1781.	Julia Fisher.	"	Joseph & Susa.
April 12, 1781.	James Fisher.	M	Peter & Joanna.
Jan. 12, 1782.	David Daniels.	"	Nathan & Elisabeth, Jr.
April 28, 1781.	Seneca Man.	"	Elias & Mary.
April 19, 1777.	Ebenezer Day.	"	David & Mercy.
April 24, 1779.	David Day.	"	" "
April 13, 1781.	Jonathan Day.	"	" "
Feb. 6, 1780.	Lois Wood.	F	David & Hannah.
June 20, 1781.	Caleb Thurston.	M	Abijah & Rachel.
June 6, 1781.	Alesford Metcalf.	"	James & Abigail, Jr.
Mar. 23, 1781.	Solomon Blake.	"	Solomon & Sibel.
April 21, 1781.	Betsy Dean.	F	Ichabod & Chloe.
April 8, 1781.	Hannah Adams.	"	Nathaniel & Hannah.
Mar. 3, 1773.	Rhoda Pond.	"	Hezekiah & Loes.
Nov. 6, 1775.	Prise Pond.	"	" "
Mar. 7, 1778.	Abigail Pond.	"	" "
Feb. 12, 1781.	Jeremiah Metcalf Pond.	M	" "
Feb. 3, 1781.	Envira Ware.	F	Phineas & Susanna.
Aug. 31, 1781.	Sanford Ware.	M	Jesse & Kezia.
Dec. 3, 1781.	Marcus Robbins.	"	Aquila & Elizabeth.
Nov. 22, 1781.	Silence Wood.	F	David & Hannah.
Oct. 25, 1781.	Calley Pond.	"	Robert & Olive, Jr.
Feb. 23, 1781.	Cyrus Adams.	M	John & Noamy, Jr.
May 29, 1779.	Mehetabele Partridge.	F	Eleazer & Lois.
Sept. 10, 1780.	Kezia Partridge.	"	" "
May 27, 1782.	Eleazer & } Partridge. Ithamer	M "	" "
May 26, 1782.	Esther Man.	F	Elias & Mary.
July 14, 1782.	Perez Fisher.	M	Peter & Joanna.
Aug. 30, 1782.	Chloe Man.	F	Nathan & Eunice.
April 28, 1782.	Kezia Hawes.	"	Ichabod & Sarah.
Sept. 10, 1782.	Stephen Kingsbury.	M	Stephen & Abigail.
Oct. 24, 1782.	Nanna Billings.	F	Enoch & Nanna.
Oct. 11, 1782.	Mary Bowditch.	"	Jonathan & Mary.
Mar. 25, 1782.	Levi Ellis.	M	Timothy & Sarah.
Jan. 16, 1780.	Edene Pond.	F	Dr. Elisha & Olive.
Feb. 1, 1782.	Olive Pond.	"	" " "
July 23, 1782.	Hannah Morse.	"	Samuel & Sarah.
Dec. 4, 1782.	Samuel Clark.	M	Samuel & Esther.
Sept. 11, 1782.	Lewis Robbins.	"	Josiah & Sarah.
Sept. 9, 1780.	Nance Gilmore.	F	James & Elizebeth.
Oct. 30, 1782.	Mary Rockwood.	"	Samuel & Sally.
April 11, 1777.	Amos Partridge.	M	Lieut. Amos & Meletiab.
Jan. 1, 1779.	Pairle Partridge.	F	" " "
Jan. 19, 1781.	Apollos Partridge.	M	" " "
Aug. 27, 1782.	David Partridge.	"	" " "
Feb. 21, 1783.	John Pond, Jr.	"	Benjamin & Katharine, 3d.
July 20, 1782.	Richard Sayles.	"	Elisha & Katharine.
Dec. 30, 1782.	Deliverance Emmons.	F	Rev. Nath'l & Martha.
Nov. 9, 1774.	John Partridge Allen.	M	John & Abigail.
Dec. 13, 1776.	Asa Allen.	"	" "
Mar. 11, 1779.	Simeon Allen.	"	" "
Mar. 10, 1783.	Ellera Allen.	"	" "
Feb. 15, 1783.	Warren Ware.	"	Phinehas & Susanna.
Jan. 11, 1783.	William Lethbridge.	"	Richard & Jerusha.
Sept. 2, 1781.	Ruth Pond.	F	Malchiah & Ruth.
April 29, 1783.	Sinai & } Heaton. Syntha	" "	Isaac & Thankfull.
Jan. 19, 1783.	Peter Adams.	M	John & Neomy, Jr.

FRANKLIN TOWN RECORDS—BIRTHS.

DATE OF BIRTH.	NAME, IF ANY.	SEX.	NAME OF PARENTS.
May 23, 1783.	Baruch Richardson.	M	Daniel & Lydia.
June 30, 1783.	Julete Bullard.	F	John & Rachel.
Dec. 16, 1777.	James Gilmore.	M	David & Joanna.
Jan. 10, 1782.	Pashance Gilmore.	F	" "
June 5, 1782.	David Baker.	M	Abijah & Esther.
Feb. 22, 1783.	Daniel Thurston.	"	Daniel & Susanna, Jr.
Aug. 5, 1783.	Sabara Partridge.	F	Joshua & Hannah.
Aug. 24, 1783.	Cyrus Dean.	M	Ebenezer & Abigail, Jr.
July 20, 1783.	Willis Fisher.	"	Joseph & Susa.
Oct. 18, 1783.	Benjamin Rockwood.	"	Elisha & Eunice.
Feb. 18, 1783.	Oliver Dean.	"	Seth & Edene.
Nov. 29, 1783.	Polly Mann.	F	Elias & Mary.
Oct. 3, 1783.	Martin Pond.	M	Roberh & Olive.
Nov. 15, 1783.	Clauduis Drusus Haward.	"	Soloanes & Olive.
Dec. 14, 1783.	Ebenezer Partridge Wood.	"	David & Hannah.
April 28, 1783.	Llewis Guild.	"	Samuel & Ruth.
Mar. 17, 1774.	Elisabath Smith.	F	James & Betty.
Sept. 5, 1776.	Molly Smith.	"	" "
Dec. 11, 1778.	James Smith.	M	" "
Mar. 14, 1781.	Elias Smith.	"	" "
April 23, 1783.	Sarah Smith.	F	" "
Mar. 10, 1784.	Salla Whiting.	"	Asa & Mary, Jr.
Mar. 26, 1784.	Abigail Allen.	"	Abijah & Abigail.
Nov. 10, 1782.	Joanna Hills.	"	Leonard & Margaret.
Mar. 22, 1784.	Elias Hills.	M	" "
Dec. 24, 1783.	Salla Rockwood.	F	Timothy & Sarah.
Oct. 5, 1783.	Ichabod Dean.	M	Ichabod & Chloe.
Dec. 9, 1781.	Asa Pond.	"	Asa & Judith.
April 20, 1784.	Perez Pond.	"	" "
April 29, 1784.	Joshua Lawrence.	"	Amos & Hannah.
May 20, 1784.	Paul Dexter Pond.	"	Paul & Calla.
Sept. 7, 1784.	Eliphoz Lawrence.	"	Joseph & Anna.
Aug. 5, 1784.	Jemima Richardson.	F	Elisha & Abigail.
Sept. 20, 1784.	David Thurston.	M	Abijah & Rachel.
Mar. 19, 1781.	Timothy Addams.	"	Thaddeus & Rachel.
Oct.14 or 15,1784	Almera Woodward.	F	James & Lois.
Sept. 6, 1784.	John Fisher.	M	Jason & Mary.
Dec. 6, 1784.	Sophey Bowditch.	F	Jonathan & Mary.
May 31, 1784.	Lewis Fisher.	M	Peter & Joanna.
Jan. 9, 1785.	Allenar Legg.	F	Joshua & Esther.
April 26, 1784.	John Crooks.	M	John & Beriah.
April 28, 1784.	Luther Ellis.	"	Timothy & Sarah.
Sept. 26, 1784.	Sarah Ware.	F	Eli & Thamer.
Jan. 10, 1782.	Sanford Gillmore.	M	William & Mary.
April 23, 1776.	Hannah Cushing.	F	Perez & Ruth.
Feb. 21, 1778.	Pyam Cushing.	M	" "
July 17, 1780.	Marques Delefyette Cushing.	"	" "
Aug. 7, 1783.	David Cushing.	"	Capt. Perez & Ruth.
Jan. 31, 1785.	Enoch Billings.	"	Enoch & Nanna.
April 26, 1783.	Ede Hills.	F	Ziba & Molly.
Feb. 7, 1785.	Luke Thurston.	M	Daniel & Susanna.
Jan. 30, 1785.	Rachel Wales.	F	Jonathan & Olive.
Nov. 7, 1784.	Elijah Richardson.	M	Daniel & Lydia.
Aug. 12, 1783.	Mary Metcalf.	F	Asa & Ruth.
May 2, 1784.	Williams Emmons.	M	Rev. Nath'l & Martha.
Oct. 16, 1784.	Theron Metcalf.	"	Hanan & Mary.
Jan. 25, 1785.	Olive Clark.	F	Samuel & Esther.
July 26, 1785.	Polly Pond.	"	Benjamin & Catharine, 3d.
Mar. 25, 1785.	Harvey Ware.	M	Phinehas & Susanna.
Feb. 5, 1785.	Eliab Metcalf.	"	James & Abigail.
Sept. 14, 1784.	Claracy Lethbridge.	F	Samuel & Sarah.

FRANKLIN TOWN RECORDS—BIRTHS.

DATE OF BIRTH.	NAME, IF ANY.	SEX	NAME OF PARENTS.
Jan. 11, 1785.	Tryphena Dean.	F	Seth & Edena.
June 28, 1785.	Richard Lethbridge.	M	Richard & Jerusha.
Nov. 28, 1783.	Nancy Adams.	F	Nethaniel & Hannah.
Sept. 28, 1785.	Salle Heaton.	"	Isaac & Thankfull.
Nov. 7, 1785.	Phylete Bullard.	"	John & Rachel.
Nov. 23, 1785.	Joseph Lawrence.	M	Joseph & Anna.
Jan. 1, 1785.	Harvey Colman.	"	Job & Anna.
Oct. 26, 1784.	Hannah Rockwood.	F	Samuel & Sally.
Nov. 10, 1785.	Sarah Emmons.	"	Rev. Nath'l & Martha.
July 9, 1785.	Synthe Mann.	"	Nathan & Eunice.
July 16, 1785.	Avilda Sayls.	"	Elisha & Catharine.
Dec. 31, 1785.	Sally Heaton.	"	Samuel & Huldah.
Oct. 24, 1785.	Elone Lewitt.	"	Peter & Susanna.
Mar. 31, 1786.	Betty Darling.	"	Eli & Rebeccah.
Jan. 6, 1786.	Jerusha Fairbanks.	"	Asa & Juleta, Jr.
July 22, 1786.	Hephzibah Bacon Richardson.	"	Daniel & Lydia.
Oct. 10, 1786.	Elvira Woodward.	"	James & Lois.
Nov. 11, 1786.	Ezra Daniels.	M	Nathan & Sarah.
Jan. 17, 1786.	Olive Pond.	F	Robert & Olive, Jr.
Nov. 24, 1783.	Ichabod Haws.	M	Ichabod & Sarah.
Mar. 29, 1786.	Abel Haws.	"	" " "
Nov. 24, 1786.	Amor Bacon Gay.	"	Thomas & Mary.
Aug. 12, 1785.	Maxcy Fisher.	"	Joseph & Susa.
April 4, 1786.	Asa Metcalf.	"	Asa & Ruth.
Sept. 23, 1786.	Prudence Ferery Metcalf.	F	Eliel & Silence.
Oct. 20, 1786.	Judith Pond.	"	Asa & Judith.
Mar. 28, 1786.	John Farrington.	M	Eliphelet & Jemima.
Aug. 1, 1785.	Nathan Partridge.	"	Eleazer & Lois.
June 5, 1786.	Anna Baker.	F	Abijah & Esther.
Mar. 31, 1785.	Samuel Adams.	M	John & Naomi.
Nov. 11, 1786.	Olive Gillmore.	F	Robert & Olive.
Feb. 18, 1787.	Rosilinda Mann.	"	Elias & Mary.
Oct. 2, 1786.	Mary Whiting.	"	John & Charlotte.
Jan. 20, 1787.	Olive Rockwood.	"	Benjamin & Anna.
Oct. 12, 1786.	Abial Kingsbury.	"	Benjamin & Olive.
Jan. 21, 1787.	Polly Williams.	"	Samuel & Abigail.
July 24, 1784.	Lucy Harding.	"	Elesha & Ruth.
Feb. 5, 1787.	Paul Thurston.	M	Daniel & Susanna.
Mar. 30, 1787.	Jason Fisher.	"	Jason & Mary.
May 14, 1787.	Rebeccah Mann.	F	Thomas & Rebeccah.
Oct. 20, 1787.	Catharine Pond.	"	Benjamin & Catharine, Jr.
May 26, 1787.	Peter Fisher.	M	Peter & Joanna.
Sept. 30, 1787.	Alfred Ware.	"	Lt. Phinehas & Susanna.
July 23, 1787.	Ebenezer Ward Adams.	"	Ward & Olive.
Oct. 7, 1786.	Saben Lethbridge.	"	Samuel & Sarah.
Aug. 20, 1787.	Elisha Partridge Pratt.	"	Jeremiah & Miriam.
June 14, 1787.	Joel Daniels.	"	Joel & Mary.
Jan. 28, 1788.	Luke Daniels.	"	Nathan & Sarah.
Oct. 17, 1787.	Malehiah Pond.	"	Malehiah & Ruth.
Feb. 2, 1787.	Fisher Adams.	"	Nathaniel & Hannah.
April 15, 1784.	Betsy Pond.	F	Eli & Hulda.
July 5, 1787.	Lucinda Pond.	"	" "
Jan. 19, 1788.	Betsy Richardson.	"	Daniel & Lidia.
Feb. 2, 1788.	Nathan Mann.	M	Nathan & Eunice.
Mar. 18, 1786.	Sydney Whiting.	"	Asa & Mary, Jr.
Aug. 5, 1787.	Erastus Emmons.	"	Rev. Nath'l & Martha.
Jan. 30, 1788.	Lyman Bullard.	"	John & Rachel.
Mar. 22, 1788.	Jerusha Lethbridge.	F	Esq. Richard & Jerusha.
Mar. 25, 1787.	Asa Rockwood.	M	Timothy & Sarah.
July 31, 1788.	Joseph Woodward.	"	James & Lois.
May 5, 1786.	Mary Fisher.	F	Levi & Mary.

FRANKLIN TOWN RECORDS—BIRTHS.

DATE OF BIRTH.	NAME, IF ANY.	SEX.	NAME OF PARENTS.
Dec. 20, 1787.	Ruth Fisher.	F	Levi & Mary.
Nov. 2, 1788.	Abijah Fisher.	M	Timothy & Hannah.
May 18, 1785.	Sally Gilmore.	F	David & Molly, Jr.
Oct. 26, 1787.	Rufus Gillmore.	M	" " "
Aug. 23, 1787.	Sally Coleman.	F	Job & Nanny.
Jan. 9, 1788.	Abigail Bacon.	"	Joseph & Chloe.
June 22, 1788.	Robert Pond.	M	Robert & Olive, Jr.
April 19, 1788.	Silvea Ware.	F	Jesse & Kezia.
Mar. 17, 1788.	George Fisher.	M	Joseph & Susa.
April 10, 1788.	Julitta Fairbanks.	F	Asa & Julitta, Jr.
Oct. 7, 1788.	Olive Morse.	"	Jason & Olive.
Dec. 4, 1788.	Eleazer Hills Lawrence.	M	Joseph & Anna.
Mar. 15, 1788.	John Abby.	"	Joseph & Hannah.
June 18, 1788.	Amariah Daniels, Jr.	"	Amariah & Elizabeth.
April 4, 1789.	Benjamin Pond, 3d.	"	Benjamin & Catharine, Jr.
Dec. 3, 1788.	Samuel Lethbridge, 3d.	"	Samuel & Sarah, Jr.
Mar. 22, 1789.	Charlotte Whiting.	F	John & Charlotte.
Nov. 9, 1788.	Julette Thurston.	"	Abijah & Rachel.
June 3, 1788.	Rena Richardson.	"	Seven & Esther.
Aug. 11, 1787.	Abigail Kingsbury.	"	Lt. Stephen & Abigail.
Dec. 8, 1786.	Meranda Ellis.	"	Timothy & Sarah.
Feb. 9, 1789.	Elihu Ellis.	M	" "
Oct. 26. 1787.	Stephen Lewitt.	"	Peter & Susanna.
June 1, 1789.	Sally Daniels.	F	Nathan & Sarah, Jr.
Feb. 5, 1783.	William Slocum.	M	Billa & Jerusha.
June 13, 1789.	Harvey Metcalf.	"	Nathan & Patty.
Dec. 3, 1788.	Thomas Stanley Mann.	"	Thomas & Rebecca.
July 7, 1789.	Sally Fisher.	F	Levi & Mary.
Aug. 12, 1789.	Lidia Richardson.	"	Daniel & Lidia.
May 19, 1788.	Eliab Richardson.	M	Amasa & Lidia.
July 16, 1788.	Sara Haws.	F	Ichabod & Sarah.
Aug. 11, 1789.	David Fisher.	M	Moses & Mary.
Jan. 19, 1781.	Apollos Partridge.	"	Amos & Meletiah.
Aug. 27, 1782.	David Partridge.	"	" "
Sept. 21, 1784.	Elisabeth Partridge.	F	" "
Jan. 21, 1788.	Rhoda Partridge.	"	" "
Mar. 29, 1786.	Lurana Gillmore.	"	Israel & Meletiah.
Mar. 1, 1790.	Abigail Lethbridge.	"	Esq. Richard & Jerusha.
Dec. 25, 1789.	Mary Fisher.	"	Jason & Mary.
Mar. 2, 1790.	Hariot Fisher.	"	Eleazer & Susanna, Jr.
April 10, 1790.	Silvester Dean.	M	Esq. Seth & Edene.
April 26, 1789.	Apollos Pond.	"	Apollos & Julittea.
Feb. 6, 1790.	Rufus Putnam Gay.	"	Thomas & Mercy.
April 2, 1790.	Hermon Heaton.	"	Isaac & Thankfull, Jr.
Nov. 12, 1789.	Philander Ware.	"	Phinehas & Susanna.
Oct. 3, 1790.	Whiting Fisher.	"	Timothy & Hannah.
Aug. 17, 1790.	Elisha Richardson.	"	Elisha & Abigail.
Oct. 19, 1790.	Hannah Lawrence.	F	Cephas & Esther.
Aug. 30, 1790.	Milton Metcalf.	M	Calven & Eunice.
Feb. 12, 1790.	Betsy Mann.	F	Elias & Mary.
May 28, 1790.	Edward Gay.	M	Timothy & Submittea.
May 24, 1789.	Huldah Heaton.	F	Samuel & Huldah.
Oct. 26, 1788.	Robert Gillmore, Jr,	M	Robert & Olive.
Mar. 23, 1790.	James Gillmore, Jr.	"	" "
June 9, 1790.	Ransom Lawrence.	"	Joseph & Anna.
July 5, 1789.	Olive & } Kingsbury.	F	Benjamin & Olive.
" "	Benjamin }	M	
Aug. 13, 1791.	Nathan Daniels, 4th.	"	Nathan & Sarah, Jr.
July 16, 1791.	Daniel Pond.	"	Benjamin & Catharine, Jr.
Oct. 21, 1787.	Naomi Adams.	F	John & Naomi, Jr.
Oct. 23, 1789.	James Adams.	M	" "

FRANKLIN TOWN RECORDS—BIRTHS.

DATE OF BIRTH.	NAME, IF ANY.	SEX	NAME OF PARENTS.
Mar. 13, 1791.	Polly Morse.	F	Levi & Keturah.
June 25, 1787.	Nancy Pierce.	"	John & Mary.
Sept. 12, 1790.	John Pierce, Jr.	M	" "
June 15, 1791.	Delea Richardson.	F	Ezekiel & Lidia.
July 16, 1791.	Julia Lawrence.	"	David & Lois, Jr.
Jan. 6, 1792.	Hephzibah Lethbridge.	"	Esq. Richard & Jerusha.
July 6, 1791.	Justin Pond.	M	Timothy & Rachel.
Oct. 9, 1791.	Joanna Fisher.	F	Peter & Joanna.
Aug. 29, 1790.	Lewis Pond.	M	Robert & Olive.
July 1, 1791.	Julia Fisher.	F	Moses & Mary.
Jan. 23, 1791.	Nathaniel Fisher, Jr.	M	Lewis & Abigail.
Sept. 10, 1791.	Melenda Metcalf.	F	Dea. Jonathan & Mary.
Oct. 5, 1790.	Darius Briggs, Jr.	M	Darius & Elizabeth.
Dec. 24, 1791.	Patty Mann.	F	Nathan & Eunice.
April 14, 1791.	Polly Hartshorn.	"	David & Mary.
Mar. 19, 1792.	Nancy Hills.	"	Jason & Polly.
Nov. 18, 1788.	Rebeca McLaine Whiting.	"	Asa & Mary.
Mar. 16, 1790.	Sene Bullard.	"	John & Rachel.
Aug. 6, 1786.	Lucius Taylor.	M	James & Salome.
Mar. 17, 1788.	Benjamin Taylor.	"	" "
Aug. 2, 1789.	James Taylor.	"	" "
Nov. 18, 1791.	Melea Taylor.	F	" "
Sept. 25, 1791.	Caroline Fairbanks.	"	Capt. Asa & Julitta, Jr.
Mar. 15, 1792.	Daniel Richardson.	M	Daniel & Lydia.
Oct. 29, 1780.	Marquis Metcalf.	"	Billa & Patty.
Dec. 19, 1783.	Patta Metcalf.	F	Billa & Patta.
May 9, 1788.	Eben Metcalf.	M	" "
Mar. 8, 1790.	William Metcalf.	"	" "
Sept. 12, 1791.	Peggy Metcalf.	F	Titus & Peggy.
Oct. 14, 1790.	Jason Morse.	M	Jason & Olive.
Feb. 16, 1790.	Peter Linett.	"	Peter & Susanna.
April 9, 1792.	Nathan Lawrence.	"	Cephas & Esther.
Jan. 31, 1788.	Elijah Dalphon Farrington.	"	Eliphalet & Jemima.
May 18, 1790.	Dolly Ware Farrington.	F	" "
Mar. 2, 1792.	Fradrack Farrington.	M	" "
July 20, 1789.	Elvira Metcalf.	F	Asa & Melea.
Jan. 25, 1792.	Melea Metcalf.	"	" "
Jan. 12, 1792.	Julitta Metcalf.	"	Capt. James & Abigail.
Oct. 24, 1788.	Levina Sayles.	"	Elisha & Catharine.
Mar. 1, 1791.	Willard Sayles.	M	" "
June 20, 1790.	Elizabeth Woodward.	F	James & Lois.
May 21, 1792.	Austin Woodward.	M	" "
May 5, 1792.	Polly Boyd.	F	Bethuel & Sukey.
June 3, 1792.	William Gilmore.	M	William & Nancy.
Nov. 7, 1790.	Joseph Fisher.	"	Joseph & Susa.
June 25, 1792.	Herman Fisher.	"	" "
April 10, 1792.	Susanna Metcalf.	F	Calvin & Eunice.
June 20, 1792.	Persis Metcalf.	"	Doct. Paul & Persis.
July 26, 1792.	Isaac Heaton.	M	Isaac & Thankfull, Jr.
Mar. 24, 1788.	Achsa Metcalf.	F	Hanan & Mary.
Aug. 23, 1792.	Samuel Biram Fisher.	M	Eleazar & Susa.
July 6, 1792.	John Bullard.	"	John & Rachel.
Jan. 24, 1792.	Nahum Thurston.	"	Daniel & Susanna.
Sept. 14, 1792.	Jemima Fisher.	F	Jason & Polly.
Nov. 11, 1791.	Willard Pond.	M	Benajah & Mary.
Dec. 29, 1792.	Susa Ware.	F	Phinehas & Susa.
Sept. 25, 1792.	Sukey Morse.	"	Levi & Ketura.
Dec. 26, 1792.	James Bailey.	M	Phillips & Abigail.
Oct. 20, 1777.	Esther Guild.	F	Eben'r & Lydia.
June 29, 1781.	Lucy Guild.	"	" "
May 23, 1783.	John Guild.	M	" "

FRANKLIN TOWN RECORDS—BIRTHS.

DATE OF BIRTH.	NAME, IF ANY.	SEX	NAME OF PARENTS.
Jan. 23, 1786.	Eben'r Guild, Jr.	M	Eben'r & Lydia.
Oct. 7, 1791.	Timothy Guild.	"	" "
Feb. 10, 1791.	Sena Metcalf.	F	Nathan & Patty.
April 5, 1785.	Abijah Clark.	M	Abijah & Melatiah.
Nov. 26, 1792.	Melatiah Clark.	F	" "
Nov. 2, 1792.	Ezekiel Richardson.	M	Ezekiel & Lydia.
Dec. 16, 1792.	Kezia Pond.	F	Barzillai & Melesent.
July 19, 1783.	Sarah Pond.	"	" "
April 6, 1787.	Mary Pond.	"	" "
Jan. 15, 1791.	Melesent Pond.	"	" "
Aug. 16, 1792.	Prudy Lawrence.	"	Daniel & Betsey.
Feb. 4, 1793.	John Whiting, Jr.	M	John & Charlotte.
Feb. 8, 1785.	Phebe Guild.	F	Samuel & Ruth.
Nov. 17, 1786.	Betsey Guild.	"	" "
Dec. 30, 1789.	Cyrus Guild.	M	" "
Aug. 6, 1792.	Samuel Guild, Jr.	"	" "
Aug. 31, 1752.	Abijah Hawes.	"	Josiah & Maria.
Oct. 6, 1754.	Matthias Hawes.	"	" "
Oct. 27, 1756.	Mary Hawes.	F	" "
Mar. 9, 1759.	Joab Hawes.	M	" "
Jan. 28, 1761.	Jemima Hawes.	F	" "
April 17, 1763.	Beriah Hawes.	"	" "
May 22, 1765.	Levi Hawes.	M	" "
July 12, 1786.	Lewis Harding.	"	Elisha & Ruth.
Nov. 2, 1792.	Isabella Taylor.	F	James & Salome.
Mar. 22, 1793.	Whiting Adams.	M	William & Elizabeth.
July 9, 1792.	Harvey Morse.	"	Jason & Esther.
April 18, 1793.	Palmy Lawrence.	F	Cephas & Esther.
May 18, 1787.	Eunice Lawrence.	"	Joseph & Anna.
Aug. 18, 1792.	Anna Lawrence.	"	" "
Dec. 23, 1792.	Stephen Mann.	M	Thomas & Rebecha.
Jan. 31, 1793.	Willard Kingsbury.	"	Benjamin & Olive.
April 13, 1793.	Sabra Adams.	F	John & Naomi.
June 29, 1786.	Collins Braley.	M	Solomon & Esther.
May 9, 1788.	Nancy Braley.	F	" "
Feb. 3, 1791.	Lydia Braley.	"	" "
July 26, 1793.	Hiram Pond.	M	Benjamin & Catharine.
Mar. 11, 1793.	Nancy Fisher.	F	Moses & Mary.
Jan. 4, 1790.	*Marcus Richardson.	M	Ziba & Huldah.
May 12, 1791.	Susanna Richardson.	F	" "
April 19, 1793.	Moses Richardson.	M	" "
June 17, 1793.	Polly Metcalf.	F	Deac. Jonathan & Mary.
Feb. 10, 1789.	Laureta Pond.	"	Asa & Judith.
Nov. 27, 1783.	Ferdinand Legg.	M	Abner Legg & his wife.
Jan. 4, 1786.	Julia Legg.	F	" " "
Sept. 14, 1793.	John Warren Blake.	M	Whiting & Polly.
July 1, 1793.	George Payson Ellis.	"	Daniel & Anna.
Sept. 13, 1793.	Olive Daniels.	F	Nathan & Sarah.
Feb. 4, 1785.	Maxcy Allen.	M	Abijah & Abigail.
May 12, 1787.	Marena Allen.	F	" "
May 27, 1789.	Abijah Allen.	M	" "
May 29, 1793.	Cyrus Allen.	"	" "
July 30, 1792.	Abigail Pond.	F	Oliver & Mima, Jr.
Oct. 8, 1787.	Abigail Wood.	"	Holland & Abigail.
Oct. 14, 1793.	Horatio Wood.	M	" "
May 2, 1790.	Kezia Daniels.	F	Joel & Mary.
Jan. 13, 1793.	Cynthia Daniels.	"	" "
Oct. 23, 1793.	Susanna Linett.	"	Peter & Susanna.
July 18, 1793.	Harmon Pond.	M	Timothy & Rachel.
Dec. 21, 1793.	Eliel Metcalf White.	"	Elijah & Betsey.
Aug. 23, 1792.	Joseph Gillmor.	"	Joseph & Lucy.

*Born in Medway.

FRANKLIN TOWN RECORDS—BIRTHS. 17

DATE OF BIRTH.	NAME, IF ANY.	SEX.	NAME OF PARENTS.
Dec. 29, 1792.	Lewis Whiting Fisher.	M	Lewis & Abigail.
Sept. 26, 1793.	Arbe Bullard.	"	John & Rachel.
Feb. 17, 1794.	Esther Morse.	F	Jason & Esther.
Feb. 24, 1790.	Molly Gillmore.	"	David & Molly, Jr.
Aug. 30, 1793.	David Gillmore.	M	" " "
Nov. 9. 1793.	Samuel Allen Kingsbury.	"	Capt. Stephen & Abigail.
Nov. 12, 1793.	Abigail Fairbanks.	F	Capt. Asa & Julitta.
Aug. 31, 1793.	Amos Fisher, Jr.	M	Amos & Lois.
Aug. 31, 1790.	Joseph Adams.	"	Moses & Chloe.
April 18, 1787.	Hiram Knapp.	"	Moses & Peggy.
April 11, 1789.	Peggy Knapp.	F	" "
Oct. 6, 1791.	Alfred Knapp.	M	" "
Dec. 24, 1793.	Melville Knapp.	"	" "
July 9, 1789.	Merinda Pond.	F	Eli & Huldah.
Feb. 19, 1792.	Asa Aldis Pond.	M	" "
Nov. 12, 1772.	Rachel Clark.	F	John & Ruth.
April 11, 1790.	Sabra Richardson.	"	Seva & Esther.
Feb. 16, 1792.	Rosa Richardson.	"	" "
Mar. 26, 1791,	Abigail Fisher.	"	Levi & Mary.
Sept. 5, 1793.	*Rena Fisher.	"	" "
Nov. 22, 1792.	Roxeena Pond.	"	Benajah & Mary.
Oct. 15, 1793.	Alvin Blake.	M	Abraham & Chloe, Jr.
May 1, 1792.	Joseph Pierce, Jr.	"	John & Mary.
Aug. 28, 1778.	†Levina Sayles.	F	Daniel & Eunice.
May 18, 1780.	†Selah Sayles.	"	" "
Jan. 30, 1782.	†Anna Sayles.	"	" "
Feb. 10, 1784.	†Stephen Sayles.	M	" "
Dec. 11, 1785.	†Josiah Sayles.	"	" "
Mar. 6, 1788.	†Uvilda Sayles.	F	" "
Feb. 29, 1792.	†Daniel Sayles, Jr.	M	" "
Dec. 22, 1785.	Alpheus Adams.	"	Thadeus & Rachel.
April 20, 1792.	Warren Barrons.	"	William & Sarah.
Aug. 9, 1780.	John Gowen, Jr.	"	John & Lydia.
Mar. 1, 1794.	Betsey Fisher.	F	Daniel C. & Larana.
May 1, 1794.	Mary Hawes.	"	Levi & Pamela.
Feb. 23, 1794.	Seth Lawrence Hartshorn.	M	David & Mary.
May 11, 1794.	Ebenezer Lawrance.	"	Joseph & Anna.
Sept. 5, 1794.	Lewis Hills.	"	Jason & Molly.
July 30, 1794.	Olivia Metcalf.	F	Calvin & Eunice.
Sept. 16, 1794.	Artemas Metcalf.	M	Asa & Melea.
Sept. 17, 1794.	Harvey Woodward.	"	James & Lois.
Oct. 7, 1794.	Almon Lawrence.	"	Cephas & Esther.
Sept. 14, 1794.	Seth Daniels.	"	Joseph & Susa.
July 22, 1794.	Alexander Metcalf Fisher.	"	Caleb & Sally.
June 5, 1794.	Lois Morse.	F	Levi & Ketura.
Nov. 17, 1794.	Rufus Miller.	M	Jesse & Vina.
Sept. 27, 1794.	Timothy Lealand Pond.	"	Timothy & Rachel.
July 15, 1794.	Philo Thurston.	"	Daniel & Susanna.
April 23, 1794.	Mehetable Richardson.	F	Sceva & Esther.
July 20, 1794.	Junia Metcalf.	M	Nathan & Patty.
June 13, 1794.	Timothy Rockwood, Jr.	"	Timothy & Sarah.
Dec. 28. 1794.	Frederic Fisher, Jr.	"	Eleazer & Susanna, Jr.
Feb. 3, 1794.	Aaron Merryfield.	"	Moses & Margaret.
July 24, 1794.	Bartholomy Foster Taylor.	"	James & Salome.
Sept. 18, 1794.	Sena Pond.	F	Jem Otis & Sally.
Sept. 10, 1794.	John Sayles.	M	Daniel & Eunice.
Jan. 9, 1794.	Polly Barrons.	F	William & Sarah.
June 23, 1774.	Barnum Clark.	M	John & Relief, Jr.
July 26, 1777.	Baxter Clark.	"	" " "
Dec. 24, 1781.	Relief Clark.	F	" " "
May 1, 1785.	John Clark, 3d.	M	" " "

* Mr. Elisha Bullard, the husband of Rena Fisher, says that she was born on the 5th of February, 1793, instead of September. Feb. 20, 1880, A. A. Russegue. Town Clerk.
† Born in Smithfield.

FRANKLIN TOWN RECORDS—BIRTHS.

DATE OF BIRTH.	NAME, IF ANY.	SEX.	NAME OF PARENTS.
May 7, 1788.	Nathan Clark.	M	John & Relief, Jr.
Nov. 20, 1791.	Lynda Heaton.	F	Samuel & Huldah.
Mar. 13, 1794.	Millie Heaton.	"	" "
Mar. 21, 1796.	Olive Heaton.	"	" "
May 14, 1794.	Patty Fisher.	"	Asa & Rachel.
Mar. 2, 1795.	William Makepeace, Jr.	M	Wm. & Mary.
Nov. 8, 1752.	Moses Hawes.	"	Joseph & Hannah.
Dec. 26, 1754.	Susa Hawes.	F	" "
June 3, 1756.	Joseph Hawes, Jr.	M	" "
April 17, 1759.	Abigail Hawes.	F	" "
July 26, 1761.	Amos Hawes.	M	" "
June 6, 1766.	Peter Hawes.	"	" "
Aug. 8, 1767.	Meletiah Everitt Hawes.	F	" "
May 16, 1763.	Elihu Pond.	M	Benjamin & Mary.
April 11, 1764.	Polly Pond. (wife of Elihu)	F	Col. John Boyd & ———
	Rouina Pond.		Elisha & Polly.
Sept. 17, 1769.	*Jemima Pond. (2d wife of Elihu)	"	Elisha Cutlar.
Mar. 17, 1790.	Polly Boyd Pond.	"	Elihu & Jemima.
Dec. 17, 1795.	Almira Ellis.	"	Daniel Ellis & his wife.
Feb. 5, 1794.	Timothy Perry, Jr.	M	Timothy & Thankfull.
April 6, 1796.	Patience Perry.	F	" "
Dec. 31, 1801.	Joel Perry.	M	" "
Nov. 27, 1784.	Solomon Wright.	"	Seth & Joanna.
Jan. 22, 1783.	Mary Dean.	F	Paul Dean & Jerusha.
Aug. 14, 1782.	Luther Going.	M	John & Lydia.
April 12, 1795.	Abigail Metcalf.	F	Billy & Patty.
Aug. 21, 1795.	Virgil Hewes.	M	Solomon & Sally.
April 23, 1795.	Lydia Guild.	F	Eben'r & Lydia.
June 23, 1795.	Zenas Edward Robinson.	M	Amariah & Rebecha.
Feb. 24, 1795.	Elias Watts Mann.	"	Elias & Mary.
Mar. 16, 1795.	John McWails.	"	John & Ruth.
Mar. 17, 1795.	Sally White.	F	Nathan & Susanna.
Oct. 22, 1795.	Meranda Pond.	"	Benjm. & Catharine, Jr.
Sept. 22, 1795.	Henry Pond.	M	Benajah & Mary.
July 24, 1795.	Asa Fairbanks, 3d.	"	Capt. Asa & Julitta, Jr.
May 8, 1795.	Thomas Richardson.	"	Daniel & Lydia.
Mar. 26, 1795.	Nancy Metcalf.	F	Deac. Jonathan & Mary.
June 6, 1795.	Henry Daniels.	M	David & Lucy.
April 17, 1795.	Daniel Sanford Lawrence.	"	Daniel & Betsey.
Sept. 1, 1795.	Harvey & } Fisher.	"	
Sept. 1, 1795.	Harlow }	"	Lewis & Abigail.
Oct. 19, 1795.	Betsey Daniels.	F	Nathan & Sarah.
July 6, 1795.	Jonathan Adams.	M	Moses & Chloe.
Oct. 16, 1795.	Polly Lawrence.	F	Ozias & Mary.
Nov. 27, 1795.	Esther Lawrence.	"	Cephas & Esther.
Jan. 7, 1795.	Eunice Adams.	"	John & Eunice.
Nov. 6, 1795.	Charles Robert Blake.	M	Abraham & Chloe, Jr.
Oct. 28, 1795.	Nathaniel Fisher.	"	Jason & Mary.
Dec. 9, 1795.	Abigail Harding Metcalf.	F	Jeremiah & Bathsheba.
May 8, 1795.	Israel Pierce.	M	John & Mary.
Sept. 22, 1795.	Asa Whiting, Jr.	"	Joseph & Polly, Jr.
Jan. 20, 1795.	Theodore Turner Kingsbury.	"	Benjamin & Olive.
Aug. 24, 1795.	William White.	"	Nathan & Susanna.
Feb. 1, 1795.	Harvey Turner.	"	Calvin & Olive.
Dec. 31, 1791.	Aaron Morse.	"	Darius & Peda.
Aug. 4, 1793.	Moses Morse.	"	" "
April 15, 1796.	Darius Morse.	"	" "
Sept. 13, 1798.	Aaron Morse.	"	" "
May 1, 1795.	John Aldis Ware.	"	Amariah & Eunice.
June 29, 1798.	Frederick A. Ware.	"	" "
Jan. 27, 1797.	Lucy Morse.	F	Jason & Miriam.

* Born in Medway.

FRANKLIN TOWN RECORDS—BIRTHS.

DATE OF BIRTH.	NAME, IF ANY.	SEX.	NAME OF PARENTS.
Jan. 29, 1796.	Elisha Harding.	M	Asa & Comfort.
Mar. 8, 1796.	Nathan Whiting.	"	John & Charlotte.
Jan. 20, 1796.	Julius Fisher.	"	Daniel Cowel & Lurana.
Feb. 28, 1796.	Paul Metcalf.	"	Titus & Eunice.
Mar. 17, 1796.	Willard Fisher.	"	Caleb & Sally.
April 26, 1796.	Senaca Hills.	"	Jason & Polly.
July 13, 1796.	Abijah Thurston Miller.	"	Jesse & Nina.
April 6, 1796	Clary Fisher.	F	Joseph & Susa.
Aug. 6, 1796.	Armeliah Lawrence.	"	Joseph & Anna.
Aug. 26, 1796.	Lysander Blake Hills.	M	Joseph & Deborah, Jr.
Mar. 11, 1796.	Manly Lincoln.	"	William & Patty.
April 18, 1796.	Phinehas Ware.	"	Eli & Tama.
Oct. 5, 1796.	Polly Whiting.	F	Joseph & Polly, Jr.
May 21, 1796.	Moses Fisher, Jr.	M	Moses & Mary.
May 23, 1796.	Salome Taylor.	F	James & Salome.
Aug. 2, 1796.	Fisher Daniels.	M	Joseph & Susanna.
Aug. 16, 1796.	Abigail Fisher.	F	Levi & Mary.
Oct. 28, 1796.	Mary Metcalf.	"	Billy & Patty.
May 15, 1796.	Jem Otis Pond.	M	Jem Otis & Sally.
Oct. 30, 1796.	Electa Metcalf.	F	Capt. James & Abigail.
June 24, 1796.	Sally Lethbridge.	"	Samuel & Sally.
Oct. 31, 1796.	Nathan White.	M	Nathan & Susanna.
April 27, 1796.	Mary Gay.	F	Timothy & Submit.
Oct. 25, 1796.	Asa Richardson.	M	Daniel & Lydia.
May 4, 1796.	Horace Mann.	"	Thomas & Rebecca.
Jan. 2, 1796.	Lois Clark.	F	Abijah & Melatiah.
Oct. 21, 1796.	Meranda Richardson.	"	Seva & Esther.
Aug. 20, 1796.	Nabby Sayles.	"	Daniel & Eunice.
Aug. 18, 1796.	Polly Knapp.	"	Major Moses & Peggy.
Feb. 1, 1797.	Olive Turner.	"	Calvin & Olive.
Mar. 21, 1796.	Olive Heaton.	"	Samuel & Huldah.
Aug. 7, 1796.	Silvia Pond.	"	Timothy & Rachel.
Nov. 15, 1796.	Jarvis Pond.	M	Wm. & Polly.
Dec. 3, 1796.	David Wood Daniels.	"	David & Lucy.
Nov. 23, 1796.	Nathan Austin Fisher.	"	Asa & Rachel.
Dec. 16, 1796.	Olive Richardson.	F	Ezekiel & Lydia.
Feb. 9, 1797.	Abigail Gay.	"	Thomas & Mary.
April 13, 1797.	Harman Cleveland Fisher.	M	Timothy & Dorcas, Jr.
June 26, 1797.	Olive Metcalf.	F	Nathan & Patty.
Aug. 22, 1797.	Sally Bacon.	"	Thomas & Ruth.
Nov. 2, 1797.	Timothy Gay, Jr.	M	Timothy & Submit.
April 30, 1797.	Levi Fisher Morse.	"	Levi & Keturah.
Nov. 11, 1797.	Clarinda Pond.	F	Cutlar & Hannah.
July 11, 1797.	Meranda Blake.	"	Calvin & Melea.
Dec. 24, 1797.	Julia Metcalf.	"	Calvin & Eunice.
April 6, 1797.	Abigail Hawes.	"	Levi & Pamela.
Sept. 21, 1797.	Abigail Richardson.	"	John Wilkes & Matilda.
July 12, 1797.	Mayo Pond.	M	Oliver & Jemima.
Sept. 25, 1797.	Alfred Allen.	"	Abijah & Abigail.
Jan. 1, 1797.	Chloe Fales Adams.	F	James & Sarah.
June 26, 1797.	Lois Adams.	"	John & Eunice.
Aug. 2, 1797.	Betsey Willard Boyd.	"	William & Betsey.
Nov. 9, 1797.	Jonson Thurston.	M	Daniel & Susanna.
Aug. 26, 1797.	Alfred Cook.	"	Whipple & Lucy.
Oct. 15, 1798.	Amasa Cook, Jr.	"	Amasa & Patty.
Feb. 15, 1798.	Nathan Otis Gillmore.	"	Nathan & Nancy.
Jan. 27, 1798.	Goldsbury Pond, Jr.	"	Goldsbury & Prissilla.
Jan. 31, 1798.	Betsey Pond Hills.	F	Jason & Molly.
April 18, 1798.	Nathan Clark Pond.	M	Nathan & Rachel.
Feb. 22, 1798.	Artemas Metcalf.	"	Abijah & Sarah.
Jan. 17, 1798.	Harlow Lawrence.	"	Daniel & Besey.

FRANKLIN TOWN RECORDS—BIRTHS.

DATE OF BIRTH.	NAME, IF ANY.	SEX.	NAME OF PARENTS.
June 14, 1798.	Virgil Hammond Hewes.	M	Solomon & Sarah.
July 31, 1798.	Hannah Fisher.	F	Timothy & Dorcas.
July 7, 1798.	Jesse Miller.	M	Jesse & Nina.
Jan. 6, 1798.	Lewis Leprilete Miller.	"	Nath'l & Hannah.
Jan. 9, 1798.	Nathan Rockwood.	"	Timothy & Sarah.
July 9, 1798.	Partridge Pond.	"	Ichabod & Sarah.
Oct. 31, 1798.	Polly Guild.	F	Samuel & Ruth.
Mar. 9, 1798.	Jotham Parkhurst.	M	Moses & Catharine.
May 20, 1798.	John Fairbanks Pond.	"	Barzillai & Melesent.
Aug. 8, 1798.	Artimas Gilbert Metcalf.	"	Jeremiah & Bathsheba.
Aug. 4, 1798.	Julia Maria Daniels.	F	Joseph & Susa.
April 22, 1798.	Joseph Whiting, 4th.	M	Joseph & Polly, Jr.
June 4, 1798.	Samuel Heaton, Jr.	"	Samuel & Huldah.
Nov. 23, 1798.	Ward Adams.	"	Nehemiah & Mary.
Nov. 7, 1798.	Susanna White.	F	Nathan & Susanna.
Dec. 15, 1798.	Elisha Hubbard.	M	Joshua & Sally.
Dec. 16, 1799.	Jarvis Harlow Hills.	"	Joseph & Deborah, Jr.
Nov. 28, 1798.	Amanda Pond.	F	Timothy & Rachel.
Feb. 16, 1798.	Pliny Daniels.	M	David & Lucy.
Nov. 19, 1798.	Patty Whiting Boyd.	F	Willard & Betsey.
Nov. 7, 1798.	Susanna White.	"	Nathan & Susanna.
May 18, 1798.	Polly Makepeace.	"	Wm. & Mary.
May 11, 1798.	Aurela Perry.	"	Simeon & Sybbel.
Dec. 6, 1798.	Caleb Blake Kingsbury.	"	Capt. Benjm. & Olive.
Mar. 12, 1798.	Cyntha Pond.	"	Benajah & Mary.
July 30, 1798.	Lydia Bishop Mann.	"	Thomas & Rebecca.
Dec. 28, 1798.	William Foster.	M	Elias & Rhoda.
April 16, 1798.	Julia Guild.	F	William & Waitstill.
July 9, 1798.	Juliana Sayles.	"	Daniel & Eunice.
Aug. 11, 1798.	Hiram Pond.	M	Jem Otis & Sally.
Feb. 28, 1798.	Lucinda Ware Force.	F	Amariah & Kezia.
Jan. 16, 1799.	Thomas Bacon Adams.	M	James & Sarah.
Jan. 22, 1799.	Asa Whiting Lawrance.	"	Cephas & Esther.
Mar. 26, 1799.	Nathan Metcalf, Jr.	"	Nathan & Patty.
Mar. 5, 1799.	John Mason Adams.	"	John & Eunice.
Aug. 22, 1799.	Hannah Whiting.	F	John & Charlotte, Esq.
May 7, 1799.	Bathsheba Metcalf.	"	Samuel & Mary.
Sept. 11, 1799.	Francis Blake.	M	Abraham & Chloe, Jr.
July 24, 1799.	Charles Martel Fisher.	"	Jason & Mary.
	Hannah Fales Miller.	F	Jesse & Vina.
June 18, 1799.	Eunice Fisher.	"	Moses & Mary.
Jan. 9, 1800.	Clementinie Sabins Lethbridge.	"	James & Susa.
Dec. 29, 1799.	George Washington Knapp.	M	Major Moses & Peggy.
June 21, 1799.	John Calvin Metcalf.	"	Calvin & Eunice.
Jan. 17, 1799.	Jemime White.	F	Jonathan & Melea.
Sept. 28, 1799.	Harriot Byron Torry.	"	John & Sally.
June 16, 1799.	Joseph Morse.	M	Jason & Meriam.
Jan. 19, 1800.	Willard Pierce.	"	Isaac & Nabby.
Mar. 14, 1800.	Warren Hills.	"	Jason & Molly.
May 7, 1799.	Hannah Metcalf.	—	Jonathan & Mary.
April 6, 1800.	Adin Fisher.	M	Timothy & Dorcas.
Nov. 3, 1800.	Levi Pond.	"	Ichabod & Sarah.
April 30, 1800.	Chloe Adams.	F	Moses & Chloe.
June 2, 1800.	Elias Metcalf.	M	Timothy & Abigail.
Mar. 3, 1800.	Austin Blake.	"	Robert & Abigail, Jr.
Oct. 21, 1800.	James Adams, Jr.	"	James & Sarah.
April 10, 1800	Charlottee Sabins Kingsbury.	F	Aaron & Polly.
July 29, 1800.	Hannah Pond.	"	Oliver & Mime.
Aug. 30, 1800.	Daniel Cowel Fisher, Jr.	M	Daniel C. & Lurana.
Oct. 15, 1800.	Erasmus Pond.	"	Goldsbury & Prissilla.
July 2, 1800.	Rachel Pond.	F	Nathan & Rachel.

FRANKLIN TOWN RECORDS—BIRTHS. 21

DATE OF BIRTH.	NAME, IF ANY.	SEX	NAME OF PARENTS.
Aug. 2, 1800.	James Preston Pond.	M	Robert & Olive, Jr.
Nov. 12, 1800.	Joseph Miller, Jr.	"	Jesse & Nina.
April 9, 1800.	Bathsheba Jones.	F	John & Sarah.
Sept. 11, 1800,	George Washington Blake.	M	Abraham & Chloe, Jr.
Feb. 21, 1801.	Sukey Sumner Hawes.	F	Solomon & Sarah.
April 12, 1801.	Benjamin Guild.	M	Samuel & Ruth.
May 18, 1801.	Nathan Hawes.	"	Jonathan & Sarah.
Jan. 30, 1786.	*Betsey Harding.	F	Esq. James & Abigail.
Aug. 24, 1788.	Nabby Harding.	"	" " "
Dec. 19, 1790.	Joseph Harding.	M	Esq. James & Abigail.
Oct. 30, 1794.	Ruth Guild.	F	Samuel & Ruth.
Mar. 19, 1797.	Rachel Guild.	"	" "
Oct. 17, 1797.	Grace Pond.	"	William & Polly.
Nov. 19, 1799.	William Pond.	M	" "
Jan. 29, 1795.	Willard Pond.	"	Robert & Olive, Jr.
Sept. 14, 1797.	Sally Pond.	F	" " "
Feb. 13, 1797.	Adams Jones.	M	John & Sarah.
Jan. 1, 1799.	Timothy Ellis Jones.	"	" "
Jan. 24, 1794.	Nancy Clark.	F	Ensign Dyar & Nancy.
Mar. 17, 1796.	Lanson Clark.	M	" " "
May 19, 1799.	Laura Clark.	F	" " "
Aug. 9, 1801.	Adaline Clark.	"	" " "
July 21, 1801.	Increase Sumner Pond.	M	Oliver N. & Esther.
Feb. 14, 1799.	Anson Lawrence.	"	Ozias & Mary.
Oct. 10, 1797.	Abigail Whiting Fisher.	F	Lewis & Abigail.
Sept. 9, 1800.	Artemas Adams.	M	John & Eunice.
Oct. 24, 1800.	Sumner Pond.	"	Jem Otis & Sally.
July 20, 1797.	Betsey White.	F	Elijah & Betsey.
Aug. 31, 1799.	Elijah White, Jr.	M	" "
Oct. 4, 1801.	Betsey White.	F	" "
April 18, 1800.	William White.	M	Jonathan & Melea.
July 2, 1800.	Rachel Pond.	F	Nathan & Rachel.
Sept. 29, 1800.	Nathaniel Emmons Fisher.	M	Lewis & Abigail.
May 26, 1800.	David Heaton.	"	Samuel & Huldah.
Aug. 17, 1800.	Unity Mira Daniels.	F	Joseph & Susa.
Oct. 2, 1798.	Melinda Clark.	"	Paul & Phebe.
Jan. 20, 1797.	Charles Perrigo.	M	James & Comfort.
Nov. 17, 1800.	Clarinda Perrigo.	F	" "
Sept. 25, 1800.	William Bradbury Boyd.	M	Willard & Betsey.
June 29, 1799.	Nancy Partridge.	F	Aaron & Abigail.
Aug. 17, 1789.	†Sally Cook.	"	Jirah & Patience.
Aug. 24, 1793.	‡Samuel Cook.	M	" "
Jan. 8, 1798.	Galen Cook.	"	" "
June 13, 1800.	Pliny Cook.	"	" "
April 3, 1794.	§Erastus Richardson.	"	Amasa & Lydia.
Jan. 30, 1801.	George Preston Cleaveland.	"	Samuel & Lona.
Feb. 26, 1801.	Anna Warren White.	F	Nathan & Polly.
Oct. 21, 1801.	Lucy Daniels.	"	David & Lucy.
April 2, 1801.	Elizabeth Metcalf.	"	Billy & Patty.
Jan. 29, 1801.	Charles Fisher.	M	Fred'k Fisher & Chloe Lindly.
June 18, 1801.	Sukey Whiting.	F	Seth & Olive.
May 3, 1801.	Daniel Penniman Clark.	M	Paul & Phebe.
Dec. 16, 1801.	Mason Wails.	"	Otis & Jemima.
Oct. 23, 1801.	Perlina French Thurston.	F	Caleb & Levisa.
Oct. 17, 1801.	George LaMont Makepeace.	M	William & Mary.
Jan. 22, 1802.	Ruth Adams Whiting.	F	Joseph & Ruth.
Dec. 24, 1801.	Ruth Wails.	"	Jonathan & Hannah, Jr.
May 31, 1802.	Alanson Merrifield.	M	Marcus & Juda.
June 28, 1802.	Nathaniel Whiting.	"	John & Charlottee, Esq.
Mar. 4, 1802.	Robert Blake, Jr.	"	Robert & Abigail.
April 12, 1802.	Polly Boyd.	F	Willard & Betsey.

* Born in Dorchester.   † Born in Smithfield.   ‡ Born in Bellingham.   § Born in Uxbridge.

DATE OF BIRTH.	NAME, IF ANY.	SEX.	NAME OF PARENTS.
May 13, 1802.	Harvey Hills.	M	Jason & Molly.
July 23, 1802.	Lydia Pond.	F	Benjamin & Lydia, Jr.
Aug. 23, 1802.	Johnson Ellis Richardson.	M	Timothy & Nancy.
July 1, 1802.	George Washington Morse.	"	Jason & Meriam.
Aug. 12, 1802.	Michael Metcalf.	"	Nathan & Patty.
Aug. 14, 1802.	Elkanah Miller.	"	Jesse & Vina.
April 28, 1803.	Lucinda Brick.	F	Jonathan & Polly.
Nov. 13, 1803.	Aldis Allen.	M	Samuel & Sarah.
Jan. 17, 1803.	Hannah Wales.	F	Jonathan & Hannah.
Feb. 3, 1803.	James Metcalf, 3d.	M	Willard & Lucy.
May 1, 1803.	Lucy Baker Fisher.	F	Daniel C. & Lurana.
Sept. 25, 1803.	Hannah Cleavland.	"	Bela Cleaveland & Anna Baker.
Feb. 17, 1802.	Abigail Jones.	"	John & Sarah.
Sept. 22, 1803.	Cyntha Pond.	"	Otis & Margret.
May 31, 1803.	Eliza Tilestone Fisher.	"	Caleb & Sarah.
Nov. 20, 1801.	Leander Partridge Cobb.	M	Luther & Rachel.
April 12, 1803.	Luther Cobb, Jr.	"	"
Mar. 12, 1800.	Jairons Whiting.	"	Joseph & Polly, Jr.
Mar. 19, 1802.	Sally P. Whiting.	F	" " "
Dec. 3, 1803.	Lucy Whiting.	"	" " "
Mar. 22, 1804.	Nancy Guild.	"	Samuel & Ruth.
Jan. 18, 1804.	Allen Partridge.	M	Phinehas & Abigail.
Feb. 10, 1804.	Oliver Ellis Adams.	"	Nehemiah & Mary.
Feb. 25, 1803.	Thomas Jefferson Daniels.	"	Cyrus & Polly.
April 15, 1803.	Eliza Lawrence.	F	Daniel & Betsey.
May 1, 1804.	Sarah Fairbanks.	"	Capt. Asa & Juletta, Jr.
Oct. 28, 1803.	Orion Smith Kingsbury.	M	Asa & Huldah.
Dec. 17, 1803.	Abijah Whiting Metcalf.	"	Whiting & Betsy.
April 21, 1804.	Elias Ware Hills.	"	Jason & Molly.
June 5, 1804.	Irena Fisher.	F	Jason & Mary.
July 13, 1804.	Addison Cleavland.	M	Samuel & Lona.
Sept. 14, 1804.	Esther Baker Warfield.	F	John & Esther.
Dec. 4, 1802.	Mary Dawson Metcalf.	"	William Pitt & Susanna.
Dec. 30, 1804.	Dexter Ward Daniels.	M	Cyrus & Polly.
Sept. 3, 1804.	Harriot Harding.	F	Asa & Comfort.
April 28, 1803.	Hiram & } Allen.	M	John P. & Mehitable.
April 28, 1803.	Almira }	F	
April 6, 1803.	Otis Wails.	M	Otis & Jemima.
Dec. 4, 1803.	Susanna Hawes.	F	Jonathan & Sally.
Nov. 11, 1799.	Bathsheba Crane Metcalf.	"	Jeremiah & Bathsheba.
Dec. 25, 1802.	Mary Robinson Metcalf.	"	" "
Nov. 25, 1804.	Joseph Harding Metcalf.	M	" "
Oct. 28, 1803.	Abigail Clap Daniels.	F	David & Lucy.
July 23, 1804.	Abigail Whiting.	M	Peter & Anna, Jr.
May 1, 1803.	Waldo Cutler Perry.	"	Simeon & Sybbel.
Nov. 15, 1785.	Amos Adams.	"	William & Elizabeth.
Oct. 4, 1804.	Eben Hubbard.	"	Joshua & Sarah.
Oct. 16, 1800.	John Haven Richardson.	"	John Wilks & Matilda.
April 15, 1803.	Eli Pond, Jr.	"	Eli & Hannah.
Jan. 22, 1804.	Sally & } Miller.	F	Jesse & Vina.
Jan. 22, 1804.	Nancy }	"	
Feb. 27, 1804.	Eliza Ann Richardson.	"	Timothy & Nancy, Jr.
Jan. 21, 1805.	Benjamin Davis Pond.	M	Benjamin & Lydia, Jr.
Feb. 25, 1805.	Timothy Ellis, Jr.	"	Timothy & Deborah.
Oct. 28, 1803.	*Preston Ellis.	"	" "
Jan. 18, 1800.	Preston Hawes.	"	Levi & Pamela.
Dec. 14, 1804.	Josiah Hawes.	"	" "
Jan. 17, 1804.	Juline Pond.	F	Goldsbury & Prucilla.
Mar. 20, 1801.	Jatham Clark Cutler.	M	Samuel & Lucy.
Mar. 16, 1804.	John Hudson Cutler.	"	" "
Oct. 17, 1804.	Eliza Guild Wood.	F	Cooledge & Phebe.

* Born in Bellingham.

DATE OF BIRTH.	NAME, IF ANY.	SEX.	NAME OF PARENTS.
Mar. 28, 1805.	John Fisher Adams.	M	Cyrus & Polly.
Dec. 6, 1803.	Ellis Perry.	"	Arnold & Betsey.
April 9, 1805.	Allen Metcalf.	"	Willard & Lucy.
June 21, 1790.	Willard Wails.	"	James & Abigail.
Mar. 25, 1793.	James Wails, Jr.	"	" "
Oct. 16, 1796.	Olive Fairbanks Wails,	F	" "
Nov. 16, 1802.	Clarissa Thayer.	"	Martin & Patty.
Feb. 21, 1805.	Adaline Thayer.	"	" "
Jan. 15, 1802.	Lucinda Gary.	"	John & Polly.
Aug. 7, 1803.	Louisa Gary.	"	" "
Feb. 4, 1805.	Nancy Gary.	"	" "
Jan. 7, 1804.	Jonathan Wails Thayer.	M	Benjamin & Rachel.
June 23, 1805.	Fanny Hawes.	F	Jonathan & Sally.
Dec. 11, 1804.	Patty Metcalf.	"	Nathan & Patty.
Aug. 11, 1805.	James Harvey Hewes.	M	Solomon & Sarah.
Mar. 14, 1789.	Mehitabel Rockwood.	F	Benjamin & Anna.
July 28, 1791.	Benjamin Rockwood, Jr.	M	" "
Mar. 15, 1794.	Jerusha Rockwood.	F	" "
April 2, 1797.	Seth & } Rockwood.	M	" "
April 2, 1797.	Samuel }	"	
Aug. 11, 1805.	Polly Wails.	F	Otis & Jemima.
April 5, 1800.	Nahum Ward Daniels.	M	David & Lucy.
Mar. 31, 1805.	Hannah Daniels.	F	" "
April 18, 1799.	Miranda Cook.	"	Whipple & Lucy.
Feb. 11, 1801.	Winslow Cook.	M	" "
Nov. 9, 1802.	Whipple Cook, Jr.	"	" "
Oct. 5, 1804.	Betsey Cook.	F	" "
Jan. 23, 1805.	Nancy Richardson Adams.	"	Daniel & Nancy.
Aug. 16, 1805.	Adaline Fisher.	"	Timothy & Dorcas, Jr.
Aug. 24, 1805.	Julia Thurston.	"	Caleb & Levisa.
Dec. 8, 1800.	Esther Ware.	"	Amariah & Eunice.
Feb. 28, 1805.	Hannah A. Ware.	"	" "
May 6, 1805.	Mary Clark.	"	Paul & Phebe.
Mar. 11, 1788.	Johanna Wright.	"	Seth & Johanna.
Oct. 22, 1802.	Mary Pond.	"	Benajah & Mary.
Aug. 23, 1805.	Benajah Pond, Jr.	M	" "
Aug. 30, 1805.	Abijah Richardson Baker.	"	David & Jemima.
Dec. 22, 1804.	Mariantinette Pond.	F	Robert & Olive.
Oct. 30, 1805.	Julim Laureal Miller.	M	Phillip & Lephe.
Oct. 2, 1802.	Sally Clark.	F	Nathan & Nancy.
July 22, 1804.	Nathan Clark, Jr.	M	" "
Nov. 25, 1805.	Eliza Partridge Daniels.	F	Cyrus & Polly.
Feb. 6, 1806.	William Pitt Metcalf, Jr.	M	William P. & Susanna.
Jan. 23, 1805.	Olive Gillmore Hills.	F	Joseph & Deborah, Jr,
Oct. 28, 1805.	Albert Cleaveland.	M	Bela & Hannah,
Feb. 20, 1806.	Abigail Harding Partridge.	F	Phinehas & Abigail.
Sept. 8, 1804.	Salvanus Scott Cook.	M	Jerah & Patience.
Jan. 5, 1806.	Esther Pond.	F	Oliver N. & Esther.
May 11, 1802.	Sabra White.	"	Jona. & Melea.
Dec. 7, 1803.	Japheth White.	M	" "
Nov. 15, 1805.	Willis Merrifield.	"	Marcus & Lydia.
Oct. 28, 1805.	Roxana Blake.	F	Robert & Abigail.
Sept. 12, 1800.	*Lucy Harding Morse.	"	James & Olive.
Mar. 26, 1803.	*James Hewins Morse.	M	" "
July 8, 1779.	Olive Harding.	F	Elisha & Ruth.
Oct. 14, 1806.	Lucy Fisher.	"	John & Lucy.
Oct. 3, 1806.	Sukey Guild.	"	John & Lois.
July 27, 1806.	Polly Hills.	"	Jason & Molly.
Mar. 25, 1806.	David Fisher.	M	Levi & Mary.
Jan. 9, 1806.	Lyman Pond.	"	Jeremiah M. & Polly.
Mar. 30, 1806.	Alfred Pond.	"	Nathan & Rachel.

* Born in Bellingham.

FRANKLIN TOWN RECORDS—BIRTHS.

DATE OF BIRTH.	NAME, IF ANY.	SEX.	NAME OF PARENTS.
Jan. 12, 1806.	Sally Boyd.	F	Bethuel & Sukey.
Nov. 29, 1806.	Nancy Melinda Clark.	"	Paul & Nancy, 2d.
Jan. 21, 1807.	Fisher Metcalf.	M	Timothy & Abigail.
Jan. 30, 1803.	Polly White.	F	Nathan & Polly.
Feb. 20, 1806.	Lyman Partridge White.	M	" "
Jan. 7, 1807.	Samuel Pond.	"	William & Polly.
Mar. 21, 1801.	Jonathan Metcalf, Jr.	"	Dea'n Jonathan & Mary.
July 14, 1803.	Eliel Metcalf.	"	" "
Oct. 10, 1805.	Caroline Metcalf.	"	" "
Aug. 20, 1806.	John Bridges Combs.	"	Oded & Polly.
May 4, 1806.	Joel Guild.	"	Samuel & Ruth.
Nov. 15, 1807.	Asa Cutler Kingsbury.	"	Asa & Huldah.
Sept. 20, 1808.	Albert Metcalf.	"	Dea'n Jonathan & Mary.
Nov. 25, 1808.	Marquis Metcalf Crooks.	"	John & Patty.
Oct. 6, 1808.	Isaac Erving Heaton.	"	Nathan & Sally.
Nov. 8, 1808.	Mary Ann Adams.	F	William & Mary, Jr.
Oct. 15, 1808.	Abigail Hubbart.	"	Joshua & Sarah.
Nov. 1, 1808.	Samuel Guild Cutler.	M	Samuel & Lucy.
Oct. 19, 1808.	Addison Clark Lawrence.	"	Eliphaz & Susanna.
July 17, 1808.	Julitta Metcalf Bates.	F	Lyman & Jerusha.
Jan. 12, 1807.	Charlotte Baker.	"	David & Jemima.
July 6, 1804.	Sibyl Adams.	"	Thomas & Olive.
May 12, 1803.	Gillmore Pond.	M	Jemotis & Sally.
May 1, 1807.	Sally Pond.	F	Jemotis & Sally.
Feb. 23, 1809.	Caroline Morse.	"	Jason & Mariam.
Aug. 28, 1808.	Smith Fisher.	M	Perez & Mary.
Oct. 7, 1809.	Caroline Hills.	F	Jason & Molly.
May 23, 1809.	David Baker Fisher.	M	Daniel C. & Sarah.
May 10, 1809.	Mille Farrington Wood.	F	Levi & Joanna.
May 4, 1799.	Calvin Turner, Jr.	M	Calvin & Olive.
July 28, 1803.	Miranda Turner.	F	" "
Sept. 20, 1804.	Joseph Jones Clark.	M	Simeon & Betsey.
Jan. 10, 1808.	Preston Hawes Clark.	"	" "
June 8, 1802.	Oliver Dean Boyd.	"	Willard & Betsey.
Mar. 18, 1804.	Amos Hawes Boyd.	"	" "
Mar. 28, 1806.	Juliana Boyd.	F	" "
May 27, 1808.	Abigail Fisher Boyd.	"	" "
Jan. 10, 1810.	Mary Clark Partridge.	"	Eleazer & Mary.
Dec. 11, 1809.	Abigail Sumner Gay.	"	Amos B. & Loammi.
Sept. 1, 1806.	Nancy Fisher.	"	Caleb & Sally.
Aug. 1, 1780.	Elias Baker.	M	John & Molly.
Feb. 5, 1782.	Rhoda Baker.	F	" "
June 5, 1784.	Polly Baker.	"	" "
Oct. 5, 1788.	Julia Baker.	"	" "
Aug. 28, 1790.	Olive Harding Baker.	"	" "
May 16, 1809.	John Ellis Baker.	M	Elias & Sally.
Nov. 25, 1809.	Henry Johnson Pond.	"	William & Polly.
Feb. 19, 1810.	John Edmund Guild.	"	John & Lois.
Mar. 25, 1809.	Amos Shumway Adams.	"	Thomas & Olive.
June 27, 1809.	Sarah Bacon Adams.	F	James & Lucy, Esq.
Nov. 27, 1800.	Erastus Clark.	M	Samuel & Hannah.
Oct. 29, 1800.	*Sally Nelson.	F	Francis & Zilpah.
Dec. 24, 1791.	Eli Milton Richardson.	M	Amasa & Lydia.
July 30, 1809.	Sally Anjalina Smith.	F	Luther & Sally.
Feb. 10, 1810.	Elisabeth Adams.	"	Amos & Betsey.
Sept. 10, 1801.	John George Metcalf.	M	Dr. Wm. P. & Susanna.
Nov. 20, 1809.	Ferdinand Holton Miller.	"	Philip W. & Lephe.
Dec. 15, 1808	Nancy Mann Richardson.	F	Timothy & Nancy.
Sept. 17, 1809.	Deborah Fairbanks Ellis.	"	Timothy & Deborah.
May 12, 1810.	Eliza Bezely.	"	Edward & Charlotte.
Aug. 6, 1810.	Charlotte Fisher.	"	Timothy & Dorcas, Jr.

* Born in Clinton, N. Y.

FRANKLIN TOWN RECORDS—BIRTHS. 25

DATE OF BIRTH.	NAME, IF ANY.	SEX.	NAME OF PARENTS.
Aug. 5, 1800.	Silas Thayer Norcross.	M	Asa & Silvia.
Jan. 30, 1808.	Asa Greenwood Norcross.	"	" "
Aug. 10, 1809.	Silvia Norcross.	F	" "
Jan. 7, 1810.	Levi Clark Fisher.	M	Levi & Susanna.
Feb. 7, 1810.	Elisabeth Gillmore Pond.	F	Jemotis & Sally.
April 9, 1807.	Mary Ann Gowen.	"	Asa & Mary.
Sept. 13, 1804.	John Warren Miller.	M	Dr. Nath'l & Hannah.
Aug. 13, 1810.	Saphony Alexander Thurston.	F	Caleb & Levisa.
Nov. 27, 1798.	Melia Fisher.	"	Eleazer & Susanna.
Nov. 1, 1809.	Joseph Whiting Metcalf.	M	Whiting & Betsey.
July 13, 1810.	Mary Mann Walker.	F	Isaac & Mary.
July 21, 1808.	Eliza Whiting.	"	Joseph & Polly, 2d.
May 22, 1810.	Susanna Candon Lethbridge.	"	James & Susanna.
Oct. 12, 1810.	James Dawson Clark.	M	Simeon & Betsey.
Mar. 18, 1806.	Caroline Boyden.	F	James & Pamelia.
Oct. 12, 1808.	Betsey Boyden.	"	" "
July 1, 1810.	Sally Hawes.	"	Jonathan & Sally.
May 7, 1811.	Eliza Maria Thurston.	"	Daniel & Bathsheba.
Aug. 2, 1808.	Horatio Kingsbury Clark.	M	Nathan & Nancy.
Dec. 24, 1810.	Theron Edmund Clark.	"	" "
Mar. 15, 1810.	Lucretia Burr Ware.	F	Eleazer & Sally.
July 20, 1807.	Stephen Howard Corbett.	M	Nath'l & Huldah.
Oct. 19, 1810.	Washington Pierce.	"	John & Mary.
Oct. 14, 1807.	Paul Baxter Clark.	"	Paul & Phebe.
Jan. 30, 1811.	Milton Metcalf Fisher.	"	Willis & Caroline.
Sept. 14, 1807.	Joseph Blake Whiting.	"	Peter & Anna.
June 5, 1809.	Peter Whiting. 3d.	"	" "
Jan. 1, 1811.	Stephen Mann Blake.	"	Robert & Abigail.
Nov. 22, 1810.	Charles Metcalf.	"	Willard & Lucy.
May 27, 1811.	Edward Bullard.	"	Jonathan & Polly.
Aug. 4, 1810.	Abigail Baker.	F	David & Jemima.
Mar. 18, 1811.	Nancy Thurston.	"	David & Miranda.
Nov. 11, 1809.	Eliza Pitman Pond.	"	Jeremiah M. & Polly.
Dec. 6, 1803.	Rhoda Morse.	"	Darius & Peda.
Mar. 10, 1806.	Lydia Morse.	"	" "
Mar. 8, 1808.	Levi Morse.	M	" "
Jan. 20, 1810.	Obed Daniels Morse.	"	" "
May 29, 1810.	Ichabod Hawes Wood.	"	Eben'r P. & Sally.
June 16, 1810.	Alonzo Hills Wood.	"	Levi & Joann.
Jan. 25, 1811.	Clarissa Ann Boyden.	F	James & Pamela.
Mar. 11, 1811.	Emily Partridge.	"	Timothy & Genett.
Oct. 17, 1809.	Nabby Ware.	"	David & Betsey.
May 27, 1811.	Elvira Ware.	"	" "
Mar. 2, 1807.	Betsey Ware.	"	" "
Aug. 2, 1807.	George Stillman Cutler.	M	Samuel & Lucy.
Nov. 14, 1807.	Jabez Fisher Lawrence.	"	Ozias & Mary.
May 25, 1805.	David Gage Colburn.	"	Western & Anna.
July 3, 1803.	Eleanor Blake Richardson.	F	Amasee & Lydia.
July 8, 1797.	*Meranda Pond.	"	Eli & Hannah.
Oct. 29, 1806.	Milletiah Pond.	"	Benjamin & Lydia. Jr.
Sept. 17, 1791.	Prentice Pond.	M	Solomon P. & Tryphena.
Oct. 17, 1796.	Kezia Gould Pond.	"	" "
Oct. 12, 1805.	Caroline Goldsbury Pond.	F	" "
April 17, 1807.	Gilbert Dean Metcalf.	M	Whiting & Betsey.
Sept. 12, 1807.	Willis Wales.	"	Otis & Jemima.
Sept. 21, 1807.	Warren Wood.	"	Ebenezer P. & Sarah.
Nov. 13, 1807.	Ezekiel Austin Thayer.	"	Martin & Patty.
Nov. 28, 1807.	Levina Miller.	F	Jesse & Levina.
Nov. 20, 1806.	George Lowel Richardson.	M	Timothy & Nancy, Jr.
June 30, 1807.	Roxey Metcalf.	F	Nathan & Patty.
Oct. 24, 1806.	Ezekiel Hall Clark.	M	Nathan & Nancy.

* Born in Holliston.

FRANKLIN TOWN RECORDS—BIRTHS.

DATE OF BIRTH.	NAME, IF ANY.	SEX	NAME OF PARENTS.
Dec. 8, 1807.	Nancy Metcalf.	F	Willard & Lucy.
Oct. 17, 1807.	Nancy Fales Gillmor.	"	William & Nancy.
Mar. 4, 1807.	Daniel Peter Whiting, Jr.	M	Joseph & Ruth, 3d.
Mar. 27, 1808.	Persis Ware.	F	David & Betsey.
Sept. 2, 1807.	Lysena Clark Smith.	"	Luther & Sally.
Dec. 13, 1807.	Susanna Morse Blake.	"	Solomon & Hannah, Jr.
Feb. 14, 1808.	Joseph Thomas Bacon.	M	Dea. Joseph & Ruth.
Jan. 1, 1808.	Theophilus Clark Combs.	"	Oded & Polly.
May 12, 1807.	Joel Nelson Blake.	"	Robert & Abigail.
Sept. 13, 1807.	Warren Fisher.	"	Pelatiah & Irene.
July 19, 1807.	Hannah Cutler Pond.	F	Cutlar & Hannah.
Dec. 27, 1807.	Nathan Ware.	M	Amariah & Eunice.
June 24, 1807.	Simeon Ellis.	"	Timothy & Deborah.
Aug. 19, 1808.	Preston Woodward.	"	James & Lois.
Nov. 7, 1806.	Fanny Woodward.	F	" "
April 20, 1808.	Elihu White, Jr.	M	Elihu & Achsa.
Dec. 22, 1807.	Albert Adams.	"	Alpheus & Achsah.
Mar. 6, 1808.	Harriot Thurston.	F	Caleb & Levisa.
June 9, 1806.	Lucy Cook.	"	Whipple & Lucy.
April 14, 1790.	*Nahum Sayles.	M	Daniel & Eunice.
Aug. 27, 1800.	Ariel Sayles.	"	" "
Feb. 14, 1802.	Oren Sayles.	"	" "
Aug. 26, 1806.	Eliza Ann Dean.	F	Ichabod & Betsey, Jr.
April 17, 1808.	Julia Adams Dean.	"	" "
Mar. 17, 1800.	David Morse Gay.	M	Timothy & Submit.
May 28, 1803.	Nancy Gay.	F	" "
Dec. 28, 1806.	Nelson Gay.	M	" "
Feb. 12, 1802.	Clarissa Ann Pond.	F	Timothy & Rachel.
Oct. 26, 1805.	Lyman Partridge Pond.	M	" "
April 10, 1808.	Mary Sumner Thurston.	F	Daniel & Bathsheba.
April 11, 1808.	Theron Clement Hills.	M	Joseph & Deborah, Jr.
Sept. 17, 1808.	Loisa Guild.	F	John & Lois.
Sept. 25, 1802.	Albert Early Daniels.	M	Joseph & Susanna.
Oct. 24, 1804.	Caroline Melita Daniels.	F	" "
Oct. 26, 1806.	Willis George Daniels.	M	" "
Oct. 6, 1808.	Susan Fisher Daniels.	F	" "
Aug. 17, 1804.	John Day Clark.	M	Ens'n Dyar & Nancy Clark.
Feb. 9, 1807.	Mary Hawes Clarke.	F	" " " "
Sept. 2, 1808.	William Emmerson Clark.	M	" " " "
Sept. 5, 1800.	Elona Richardson.	F	Timothy & Nancy, Jr.
Sept. 22, 1805.	Almira Hart Kingsbury.	"	Asa & Huldah.
May 10, 1811.	Abigail Daniels Dean.	"	Ichabod & Betsey, Jr.
May 14, 1798.	Adela Pond.	"	Oliver N. & Esther.
Feb. 23, 1800.	Nathaniel Ogden Pond.	M	" " "
Oct. 10, 1807.	Spencer Atkinson Pratt.	"	Dr. Spencer & Elisabeth.
Oct. 23, 1811.	George Washington Whiting.	"	Joseph & Polly, 2nd.
Jan. 12, 1811.	Abner Gilbert Fuller.	"	Abner and Lydia.
Sept. 22, 1811.	Abigail Richardson Metcalf.	F	Nathan & Abigail.
April 10, 1811.	Orrella Thayer.	"	Martin & Patty.
April 30, 1811.	Caleb Mason Guild.	M	John & Lois.
Nov. 1, 1811.	Brainard Heaton.	"	Nathan & Sally.
May 28, 1810.	Olive Morse.	F	James & Olive.
Oct. 20, 1811.	Jemima Wales.	"	Otis & Jemima.
Dec. 31, 1810.	Sally Baker.	"	Elias & Sally.
Jan. 15, 1812.	David Thurston Morse.	M	Darius & Peda.
Oct. 4, 1811.	Ira Allen.	"	Ichabod & Olive.
July 11, 1811.	Horatio Kingsbury Gowen.	"	Asa & Mary.
Sept. 20, 1811.	Mary Ida Fisher.	F	Esq. James & Calley.
Jan. 20, 1812.	David Fisher.	M	Levi & Susanna.
July 9, 1811.	David Whitney Bullard.	"	Jonathan & Polly.
Nov. 1, 1811.	Nathaniel Morrill.	"	Isaac & Julia.

* Born in Smithfield.

FRANKLIN TOWN RECORDS—BIRTHS. 27

DATE OF BIRTH.	NAME, IF ANY.	SEX	NAME OF PARENTS.
June 30, 1812.	Chloe Guild.	F	Samuel & Ruth.
Jan. 11, 1812.	Charlotte Bacon Gay.	"	Amos Bacon & Loammi B.
Jan. 23, 1791.	Nathaniel Fisher.	M	Lewis & Abigail, Esq.
Dec. 29, 1792.	Lewis Whiting Fisher.	"	" " "
Sept. 1, 1795.	Harlow & } Fisher.	"	" " "
Sept. 1, 1795.	Harvey }	"	
Oct. 10, 1797.	Nabby Whiting Fisher.	F	" " "
Sept. 29, 1800.	Nathaniel Emmons Fisher.	M	" " "
Oct. 10, 1802.	Maria Ann Fisher.	F	" " "
Aug. 7. 1804.	Caroline Fisher.	"	" " "
Jan. 23, 1807.	John Hancock Fisher.	M	" " "
Jan. 28, 1809.	Walter Harris Fisher.	"	" " "
Aug. 10, 1813.	Abigail Ursula Fisher.	F	" " "
May 3, 1810.	Susanna Lawrence.	"	Eliphaz & Susanna.
May 1, 1812.	Marcetta Lathua.	"	" "
Feb. 22, 1812,	Ruth Mariah Richardson.	"	Elisha & Ruth.
Mar. 9, 1812.	Lydia Blake Whiting.	"	Peter & Anne.
Feb. 29, 1812.	Horatio Kingsbury.	M	Stephen & Olive.
May 7, 1812.	*Emeline Copps Mann.	F	Nathan & Margarett, Jr.
Jan. 3, 1811.	Richardson Thayer.	M	Asa & Abigail.
July 17, 1812.	Asa Clark Thayer.	"	" "
Aug. 16, 1801.	Ebenezer Torrey.	"	John & Sally.
June 5, 1804.	Sally Richardson Torrey.	F	" "
Aug. 2, 1806.	John Torrey, Jr.	M	" "
Oct. 30, 1812.	Ebenezer Torrey Metcalf.	"	William P. & Susanna.
Nov. 22, 1808.	Calley Dexter Pond.	F	Paul D. & Huldah.
June 27, 1811.	Elbridge Pond.	M	" "
Oct. 22, 1812.	Artemus Warren Gowen.	"	Luther & Elvira.
Aug. 20. 1811.	Jesse Miller, Jr.	"	Jesse & Vina.
Aug. 6, 1810.	Sydney Sandford Whiting.	"	Sidney & Olive.
June 18, 1811.	Elisabeth Whiting.	F	" "
Jan. 9, 1810.	†Louisa Fisher.	"	Preston & Huldah.
Sept. 6, 1811.	Charles Lovell Fisher.	M	" "
May 17, 1809.	Rachel Johnson Miller.	F	Jesse & Vina.
Mar. 18, 1812.	Fisher Hartshorn Harding.	M	Lewis & Irene.
Feb. 11, 1806.	Fisher Adams Kingsbury.	"	Ebenezer A. & Mary.
Aug. 24, 1808.	Ebenezer Lawton Kingsbury.	"	" " "
Dec. 6, 1767.	Lewis Fisher.	"	Lieut. Nathaniel.
Feb. 28, 1769.	‡Abigail Fisher, wife of Lewis.	F	Capt. Lewis Whiting.
Mar. 1, 1811.	Mary Fisk Kingsbury.	"	Ebenezer A. & Mary.
June 1, 1812.	William Maddison Adams.	M,	William & Mary, Jr.
Aug. 14, 1811.	Emaline Betsey Metcalf.	F	Whiting & Betsey.
Jan. 16, 1812.	Levi Williams Wood.	M	Levi & Anna.
Jan. 23, 1813.	Lurana Fisher.	F	Daniel C. & Betsey.
Oct. 22, 1810.	§Edward Davis Jones.	M	Edward & Mary.
Sept. 22, 1812.	Jemima Leland Daniels.	F	Luke & Jemima.
Oct. 13, 1807.	Laura Allen.	"	Ellery & Experience.
April 29, 1810.	Abigail Partridge Allen.	"	" " "
Mar. 7, 1812.	Fidelia Allen.	"	" " "
Mar. 30, 1813.	Stephen Wilkes Richardson.	M	John Wilkes & Matilda.
Feb. 25, 1813.	Joseph Milton Whiting.	"	Joseph & Ruth, Jr.
Jan. — 1812.	Harriot Saphrona Thurston.	F	Caleb & Levisa.
Dec. 6, 1812.	George Edwards Boyd.	M	Willard & Betsey.
Aug. 10, 1813.	Abigail Ursula Fisher.	F	Lewis & Sula C., Esq.
Aug. 7, 1813.	Erastus Darwin Miller.	M	Dr. Nathaniel & Hannah.
Dec. 1, 1800.	Laura Metcalf.	F	Samuel & Mary.
Oct. 10, 1802.	Miletiah Metcalf.	"	" "
Sept. 10, 1804.	Samuel Metcalf, Jr.	M	" "
Nov. 28, 1805.	Mary Ann Metcalf.	F	" "
Aug. 19, 1807.	Hiram Metcalf.	M	" "
Dec. 25, 1809.	Laura Metcalf.	F	" "

*Born in Walpole.   † Born in Smithfield.   ‡ Born in Wrentham. They were married April 7, 1790.   § Born in N. Providence.

FRANKLIN TOWN RECORDS—BIRTHS.

DATE OF BIRTH.	NAME, IF ANY.	SEX	NAME OF PARENTS.
July 16, 1812.	Miranda Newman Metcalf.	F	Samuel & Mary.
Aug. 17, 1813.	Erastus Rockwood.	M	Asa & Julia.
Oct. 31, 1813.	Timothy Agustus Warren Partridge.	"	Tim E. & Gennette.
Jan. 11, 1812.	Lewis Blake.	"	Robert & Abigail.
June 30, 1810.	Adaline Jane Gillmore.	F	William & Molley.
Oct. 24, 1812.	Abigail Charlotte Gillmore.	"	William & Molley.
Dec. 19, 1813.	Mary Ann Rockwood.	"	Benjm. & Hannah.
May 2, 1813.	Susan Hancock.	"	Amos & Betsey.
Dec. 5, 1812.	Emerson Adams.	M	Alphens & Achsah.
Jan. 9, 1814.	Horace Austin Wood.	"	Levi & Anna.
April 5, 1812.	Daniel Brintnell Thurston.	"	Daniel & Bathsheba.
May 17, 1813.	Asa Metcalf Baker Fuller.	"	Asa & Hepzibah.
Mar. 8, 1813.	William Fisher Fuller.	"	Abner & Lydia.
July 25, 1813.	Juletta Richardson.	F	Elisha & Ruth.
May 4, 1813.	George Nelson Fisher.	M	Jason & Mary, Jr.
Dec. 18, 1806.	Eliza Thayer.	F	James & Sally.
Sept. 13, 1808.	Fisher Daniels Thayer.	M	James & Sally.
Aug. 3, 1810.	Asa Clark Thayer.	"	James & Sally.
Sept. 12, 1812.	Sally Thayer.	F	James & Sally.
Jan. 6, 1813.	Mary Dahm Jones.		Edward & Mary.
Mar. 11, 1813.	Sarah Hawkins Fisher.	F	Maxcy & Persis.
Jan. 24, 1814.	Elezer Thompson Bullard.	M	Joseph & Julia.
June 14, 1812.	Alden Bradford Cleaveland.	"	Nathan & Polly.
July 22, 1810.	Betsey Ann Daniels.	F	Amariah & Anne, Jr.
Mar. 23, 1812.	William Henderson Daniels.	M	" " "
Feb. 10, 1814.	Amos Fisher Daniels.	"	" " "
Nov. 19, 1812.	Mary Ann Daniels.	F	Joel & Philena.
Oct. 17, 1813.	Deborah Burril Thayer.	"	Capt. Davis & Betsey.
April 15, 1813.	George Perkins Fisher.	M	Lieut. Willis & Caroline.
Jan. 14, 1814.	Nancy Allen Metcalf.	F	Willard & Lucy.
May 3. 1811.	Austin Davis Pond.	M	Martin & Annie.
July 31, 1813.	William Henry Pond.	"	Martin & Annie.
Nov. 7, 1813.	George Warren Blake.	"	Solomon & Hannah.
Mar. 12, 1811.	Martha Phipps.	F	William & Fanny.
Oct. 31, 1812.	William Phipps, Jr.	M	William & Fanny.
Dec. 24, 1812.	Julia Maria Boyden.	F	James & Pamelia.
April 11, 1814.	Pamelia Thayer.	"	Martin & Patty.
July 3, 1812.	Sabin Ware.	M	Eleazer & Sarah.
Jan. 12, 1814.	Gilbert Clark Knapp.	"	Hiram & Lois.
Sept. 17, 1809.	Deborah Fairbanks Ellis.	F	Timothy & Deborah.
Sept. 22, 1811.	Rhoda Partridge Ellis.	"	" " "
Feb. 1. 1813.	Maria Bloomfield Ellis.	"	" " "
May 28, 1814.	Charles Lewis Harding.	M	Lewis & Irene.
April 3, 1811.	Peter Adams.	"	James & Lucy, Esq.
April 27, 1814.	Charles Alfred Wails.	"	Otis & Jemima.
Oct. 12, 1812.	Sarah Ann Sayles.	F	Caleb & Rhoda.
April 10, 1814.	Gilbert Rhodney Thurston.	M	Daniel & Bathsheba.
May 30, 1814.	Caroline Lawrence.	F	Eliphaz & Susanna.
Jan. 5, 1815.	Mary Adaline Fisher.	"	Jason & Mary, Jr.
May 27, 1812.	Chandler Leville Scott.	M	Otis & Mahetabel.
May 17, 1814.	Charles Harrison Scott.	"	Otis & Mahetabel.
May 1, 1791.	*Otis Scott.	"	David & Sarah.
July 4, 1814.	Erastus Lovel Metcalf.	"	Preston & Lucretia.
May 3, 1814.	Samuel Tirrel Gillmor.	"	William & Molly.
May 28, 1814.	Jemima Aldana Adams.	F	William & Mary.
July 6, 1812.	Harriot Wales.	"	Willard & Sally.
June 9, 1814.	George French Wales.	M	Willard & Sally.
Jan. 4, 1815.	Asa Pond.	"	Jeremiah M. & Polly.
Dec. 14, 1814.	Rhoda Baker.	F	Elias & Sally.
Feb. 28, 1815.	Delia Emmons Bacon.	"	Dea. Joseph & Ruth.
Nov. 18, 1814.	Adella Robbins Gillmore.	"	James & Irene, Jr.

* Born in Bellingham.

FRANKLIN TOWN RECORDS—BIRTHS. 29

DATE OF BIRTH.	NAME, IF ANY.	SEX.	NAME OF PARENTS.
Aug. 19, 1814.	Mary Clark.	F	Samuel & Hannah.
July 6, 1815.	Elizabeth Maria Pratt.	"	Dr. Spencer & Elizabeth.
Feb. 3, 1814.	Evelina Villers Thayer.	"	Maj. Davis & Betsey.
Sept. 17, 1815.	Elbridge Preston Hartshorn.	M	Preston & Ann.
Dec. 20, 1815.	Polly Wright.	F	Solomon & Polly.
Feb. 8, 1815.	Hervey Wilton Morse.	M	Hervey & Betsey.
July 3, 1815.	Jemima Jane Baker.	F	David & Jemima.
June 9, 1815.	Louisa Marena Gowen.	"	Maj'r Asa & Mary.
Oct. 23, 1815.	Julitta Richardson Partridge.	"	Nathan & Sally.
Nov. 13, 1814.	Susanna Fisher.	"	Levi & Susanna.
Nov. 24, 1815.	Nathaniel Hawes.	M	Jonathan & Sally.
Mar. 21, 1816.	Dianthe Partridge.	F	Phinehas & Abigail.
Oct. 21, 1815.	Lucy Cutler Guild.	"	John & Lois.
Oct. 24, 1815.	Davis Thayer.	M	Capt. Asa & Abigail.
April 22, 1815.	Emelina Meleta Richardson.	F	Eli M. & Melita.
April 24, 1816.	Willard Adams Ware.	M	David & Betsey.
June 5, 1806.	Lucy Cook.	F	Whipple & Lucy.
June 3, 1808.	Maxcy Cook.	M	Whipple & Lucy.
April 9, 1810.	Charles Madison Cook.	"	Whipple & Lucy.
June 12, 1812.	Milton Cook.	"	Whipple & Lucy.
Aug. 19, 1815.	Elbridge Gerry Cook.	"	Whipple & Lucy.
Dec. 23, 1814.	Olive Metcalf Ware.	F	Eleazer & Sarah.
Jan. 6, 1816.	Asa Phillips Rockwood.	M	Asa & Julia.
May 5, 1816.	Walter Harris Gay.	"	Amos B. & Locine.
May 9, 1816.	Abigail Bacon Fisher.	F	Lieut. Willis & Caroline.
Mar. 17, 1816.	William Curtis Harding.	M	Lewis & Irene.
Aug. 10, 1816.	George Metcalf Gowen.	"	Luther & Elvira.
Nov. 10, 1815.	Martha Warren Phipps.	F	William & Fanny.
Aug. 3, 1816.	Caleb Warner Sayles.	M	Caleb & Rhoda.
Aug. 28, 1816.	Oliver Gilbert Fisher.	"	Oliver & Thankfull.
Oct. 20, 1816.	Davis Thayer.	"	Maj'r Davis & Betsey.
Oct. 28, 1816.	Eunice Susan Thurston.	"	Daniel & Bathsheba.
Mar. 26, 1816.	Abigail Laurinda Metcalf.	F	Nathan & Abigail.
Aug. 10, 1816.	Sarah Maria Pond.	"	Willard & Sally.
Mar. 31, 1816.	Stephen Burton Fuller.	M	Abner & Lydia.
Dec. 22, 1816.	Sylvia Pond Partridge.	F	Eleazer & Mary.
April 1, 1816.	Dorcas Allen.	"	Samuel & Polly.
July 2, 1814.	Bulkley Adams Harding.	M	Jonathan & Nancy.
Mar. 22, 1814.	Calista Allen.	F	Ellery & Experience.
Dec. 10, 1816.	Martha Allen.	"	Ellery & Experience.
Dec. 29, 1816.	Waldo Suarrow Miller.	M	Phillips W. & Lephe.
Feb. 26, 1816.	Emilia Knapp.	F	Hiram & Lois.
Aug. 1, 1816.	Cynthia Plau Mann.	"	Nathan & Margaret, Jr.
April 24, 1817.	Abigail Thayer Thurston.	"	Caleb & Levisa.
Oct. 10, 1816.	Clarissa Day Richardson.	"	Elisha & Ruth.
Jan. 17, 1817.	John Warren Fisher.	M	Jason & Mary, Jr.
April 20, 1817.	Frelove Fairbanks Wales.	F	Otis & Jemima, Jr.
Sept. 2, 1798.	Amelia Hawes.	"	Moses & Polly.
Sept. 30, 1810.	Hiram Abiff Daniels.	M	Joseph & Susanna.
Mar. 9, 1813.	Martha Carpenter Daniels.	F	Joseph & Susanna.
May 25, 1817.	Harriot Louisa Daniels.	"	Joseph & Susanna.
Jan. 12, 1815.	Darvin Joseph Daniels.	M	Joseph & Susanna.
April 15, 1816.	Nathan Adams.	F	Amos & Betsey.
June 10, 1817.	Layton Jenks Adams.	"	Amos & Betsey.
Mar. 5, 1816.	James Allen Boyden.	"	James & Pamelia.
Aug. 21, 1817.	Joseph Newel Bullard.	"	Joseph & Julia.
Oct. 1, 1807.	Lewis Daniels.	"	David & Lucy.
April 12, 1809.	Mary Clap Daniels.	F	David & Lucy.
April 19, 1815.	Lowell Cleaveland.	M	Nathan & Polly.
May 17, 1813.	Emeline Fisher.	F	Perez & Polly.
June 16, 1817.	Moses Everett Thomson.	M	Moses & Betsey.

FRANKLIN TOWN RECORDS—BIRTHS

DATE OF BIRTH.	NAME, IF ANY.	SEX.	NAME OF PARENTS.
April 22, 1816.	Jairus Lawrence.	M	Eliphur & Susanna.
June 9, 1817.	David Parker Baker.	"	David & Jemima.
Oct. 26, 1815.	John Richardson Pond.	"	Martin & Ami.
June 23, 1817.	Henry Bowen Pond.	"	Martin & Ami.
Jan. 24, 1818.	Julian Rockwood.	F	Asa & Julia.
Mar. 19, 1817.	Lucy Maria Adams.	"	James & Lucy, Esq.
July 1, 1818.	Elias Anson Partridge.	M	Nathan & Sally.
Feb. 16, 1817.	Harrot Newell Richardson.	F	Eli M. & Melita.
July 4, 1815.	Arnold Rawson Pond.	M	Paul D. & Huldah.
July 19, 1817.	Charles Fisher Daniels.	"	Luke & Jemima.
April 28, 1817.	Melinda Fisher.	F	Levi & Susanna.
June 25, 1818.	Mercey Bacon Gay.	"	Amos B. & Loami.
Dec. 5, 1817.	Sylvia Lucretia Knapp.	"	Hiram & Lois.
Oct. 16, 1817.	Gillmore Miller.	M	Jesse & Vina.
April 27, 1817.	Alfred Harding Metcalf.	"	Whiting & Betsey.
July 22, 1818.	Elisha Fisher Richardson.	"	Elisha & Ruth.
Sept. 3, 1818.	Gilbert Hartshorn.	"	Seth L. & Lydia.
May 11, 1818.	Elinor Fisher.	F	Jason & Mary, Jr.
June 17, 1813.	Susan Fisher.	"	Preston & Huldah.
Aug. 1, 1818.	Nancy Maria Fisher.	"	Preston & Huldah.
Feb. 21, 1815.	Matilda Emily Fisher.	"	Preston & Huldah.
Jan. 4, 1818.	George Warren Harding.	M	Lewis & Irene.
Feb. 26, 1818.	Horace Augustus Richardson.	"	Ezekiel & Chloe, Jr.
Jan. 3, 1818.	Richardson Metcalf.	"	Nathan & Abigail.
May 15, 1818.	Harriot Emily Mann.	F	Nathan & Margaret, Jr.
Oct. 1, 1818.	George Newell Thurston.	M	Daniel & Bathsheba.
Dec. 27, 1812.	Nancy Clark.	F	Nathan & Nancy.
Sept. 25, 1815.	Charles Willard Clark.	M	Nathan & Nancy.
Jan. 8, 1818.	Dyar Gilbert Clark.	"	Nathan & Nancy.
Sept. 15, 1817.	Charlotte Louisa Gillmore.	F	James & Irene.
April 2, 1818.	Gardner Adams.	M	Alpheus & Achsah.
June 9, 1816.	Abigail Blake.	F	Robert & Abigail.
Feb. 24, 1818.	Charles Fisher Blake.	M	Robert & Abigail.
Oct. 1, 1817.	Abigail Hills Heaton.	F	Nathan & Sally.
Oct. 7, 1818.	Harriot Francis Gillmore.	"	Joseph & Maria.
Feb. 27, 1816.	Nancy Cutler Fuller.	"	Moses & Elizabeth.
June 22, 1818.	Elizabeth Cutler Fuller.	"	Moses & Elizabeth.
June 6, 1817.	Eliza Jane Fisher.	"	Peter & Mary, Jr.
April 12. 1818.	Almira Lawrence.	"	Elephaz & Susanna.
Mar. 21, 1819.	Esther Adams.	"	Amos & Betsey.
Dec. 24, 1818.	George Robert McLane Gillmore.	M	Lt. Robert & Rebeca.
Nov. 3, 1818.	Charles Willis Fisher.	"	Willis & Caroline.
Aug. 8, 1793.	Elihu Pond, Senior.	"	Elihu & Jemima.
May 23, 1795.	Elihu Pond, Jr.	"	Elihu & Jemima.
Aug. 29, 1798.	Emily Pond.	F	Elihu & Jemima.
April 15, 1800.	Edwards Pond.	M	Elihu & Jemima.
June 10, 1802.	Joseph Park Pond.	"	Elihu & Jemima.
May 10, 1805.	Caroline Pond.	F	Elehu & Jemima.
Dec. 14, 1809.	James Sullivan Pond.	M	Elehu & Jemima.
Dec. 13, 1811.	Elizabeth Pond.	F	Elehu & Jemima.
May 2, 1819.	Clarissa Prentis Partridge.	"	Phinehas & Abigail.
Jan. 19, 1819.	Lucinda Adams Gillmore.	"	Joseph & Sarah, Jr.
May. 14, 1819.	Preston Willard Fisher.	M	Preston & Huldah.
Aug. 30, 1819.	Mary Allen.	F	Ellery & Experience.
Sept. 2, 1819.	William Henry Wales.	M	Otis & Jemima.
Dec. 2, 1819.	Charles Gowen.	"	Luther & Elvira.
Apr. 12, 1817.	*Maria Angenette Scott.	F	Otis & Mehitabel.
Aug. 6, 1819.	*Julia Ann Scott.	"	Otis & Mehitabel.
Sept. 19, 1819.	Charles Richmond Fisher.	M	Daniel C. & Betsey.
Mar. 11, 1817.	Henry Orville Ellis.	"	Timothy & Abigail.
Feb. 14, 1819.	Abigail Hunt Ellis.	F	Timothy & Abigail.

* Born in Bellingham.

FRANKLIN TOWN RECORDS—BIRTHS. 31

DATE OF BIRTH.	NAME, IF ANY.	SEX.	NAME OF PARENTS.
July 17, 1816.	Horace Preston Metcalf.	M	Preston & Lucretia.
Sept. 30, 1818.	Timothy Augustus Metcalf.	"	Preston & Lucretia.
Sept. 28, 1815.	George Leonard Wood.	"	Levi C. & Joanna.
June 19, 1817.	Asa Whiting Wood.	"	Levi C. & Joanna.
July 18, 1819.	Susanna Torry Wood.	F	Levi C. & Joanna.
Aug. 23, 1819.	Susan Ruggles.	"	Josiah & Sukey.
July 25, 1815.	Austin Metcalf.	M	Samuel & Mary.
July 13, 1817.	Harriot Metcalf.	F	Samuel & Mary.
Sept. 7, 1815.	Wsllard Clark Whiting.	M	Peter & Anna.
Nov. 22, 1819.	George Newell Fuller.	"	Asa & Hepzibah.
Sept. 3, 1819.	Melissa Blake Hills.	F	Lysander B. & Elizabeth.
Nov. 21, 1818.	Emeline Ware,	"	Alfred & Jemima.
Oct. 26, 1817.	Albert Gillmore.	M	Wm. & Molly.
June 5, 1819.	Olive Maria Gillmore.	F	Wm. & Molly.
Jan. 23, 1820.	Julia Bullard.	"	Joseph & Julia.
Sept. 3, 1819.	John Haven Kingsbury.	M	Capt. Steven & Olive.
July 1, 1818.	Gilbert Adams Ware.	"	David & Betsey.
Dec. 14, 1819.	Elbridge Gerry Ware.	"	David & Betsey.
Sept. 9, 1819.	George Washington Fisher.	"	Oliver & Thankfull.
Sept. 10, 1819.	Jane Maria Pond.	F	Capt. Benajah & Sybil.
Jan. 21, 1819.	John Richardson Thompson.	M	Moses & Betsey.
Aug. 15, 1819.	James Partridge Gillmor.	"	James & Rena.
April 10, 1815.	Louisa Jane Fisher.	F	Capt. Maxey & Persis.
June 23, 1817.	Joseph Warren Fisher.	M	Capt. Maxey & Persis.
June 27, 1819.	Susan Fisher.	F	Capt. Maxey & Persis.
Feb. 9, 1818.	Otis Torry Parkhurst.	M	Horace & Mary Ann.
Aug. 26, 1819.	Horace Hamilton Parkhurst.	"	Horace & Mary Ann.
Dec. 19, 1818.	Samuel Morse Bullard.	"	Cephas & Sukey.
Jan. 17, 1818.	Erastus Guild.	"	Cyrus & Amy.
Feb. 15, 1819.	Charlotte Gillmore Richardson.	F	Eli M. & Meleta.
Dec. 27, 1818.	Sarah Pond.	"	Justin & Ruth.
Jan. 1, 1820.	Justin Eli Pond.	M	Justin & Ruth.
Feb. 4, 1820.	Leusia Maria Hills.	F	Lewis & Anna.
Sept. 25, 1819.	James Thomas Voax Woodward	M	Austin & Mary Ann.
Sept. 28, 1819.	Susan Knapp.	F	Alfred & Eleanor.
Feb. 8, 1820.	Eliza Ann Harding.	"	Lewis & Irene.
Mar. 24, 1820.	Abijah Thurston Rockwood.	"	Asa & Julia.
June 15, 1820.	Maria Thurston.	"	Caleb & Lovica.
Aug. 7, 1820.	Asa Partridge.	M	Phinehas & Polly.
Sept. 15, 1820.	Augustus Mowry Blake.	"	Ira & Laura.
Aug. 20, 1819.	Charlotte Muller.	F	Jesse & Vina.
May 2, 1820.	Marshal Gardner Merrifield.	M	Aaron & Mary.
April 20, 1820.	Hiram Knapp.	"	Hiram & Lois.
Sept. 10, 1819.	Henry Martin Green.	"	Martin & Lois.
June 3, 1820.	Eliza Jane Daniels.	F	Luke & Jemima.
May 19, 1818.	Huldah Pond.	"	Paul D. & Huldah.
Feb. 7, 1820.	Wellington Pond.	M	Paul D. & Huldah.
Dec. 12, 1820.	Harriot Hills.	F	Seneca & Maria.
June 15, 1820.	Edward H. Robbins Gillmore.	M	Robert & Rebekah G.
Nov. 11, 1820.	Charles Willis Fisher.	"	Willis & Caroline.
July 6, 1817.	Nancy Williams Harding.	F	Lewis & Mary, 2d.
Nov. 12, 1800.	George Leprilette Lawrence.	M	Daniel & Betsey.
Oct. 8, 1819.	Eliab Metca'f Pond.	"	Jeremiah M. & Polly.
Sept. 3, 1821.	Thomas Pinkney Gay.	"	Amos B. & Loami.
Sept. 18, 1820.	Hiram Thurston.	"	Daniel & Bathsheba.
Sept. 24, 1819.	Juliana Metcalf.	F	Nathan & Abigail.
Dec. 24, 1820.	William Tyler Richardson.	M	Eli M. & Melita.
Mar. 21, 1819.	Esther Adams.	F	Amos & Betsey.
April 7, 1821.	Julia Adams.	"	Amos & Betsey.
July 25, 1821.	George Hartshorn.	M	Seth L. & Lydia.
Feb. 28, 1821.	Lorinda Ann Guild.	F	Cyrus & Ami.

FRANKLIN TOWN RECORDS—BIRTHS.

DATE OF BIRTH.	NAME, IF ANY.	SEX	NAME OF PARENTS.
Jan. 22, 1821.	Erastus Adams.	M	Alpheus & Achsah.
Dec. 27, 1817.	Charles Edwin Thayer.	"	Martin & Patty.
Dec. 15, 1819.	Mary Bassett Partridge.	F	Nathan & Sally.
April 30, 1822.	Horace Gowen.	M	Luther & Elvira.
Oct. 3, 1820.	Julia Ann Pierce.	F	John & Julia.
Feb. 19, 1822.	Mareah Abbot Fisher.	"	Whiting & Esther.
Jan. 5, 1822.	John Wheeler Partridge.	M	Phinehas & Polly.
Oct. 25, 1821.	Julia Baker.	F	David & Jemima.
Aug. 24, 1821.	Hermon Maxey Fisher.	M	Maxey & Persis.
Dec. 31, 1820.	Peruda Adaline Thompson.	F	Moses & Betsey.
May 14, 1821.	Sylvia Pond.	"	Timothy L. & Abigail.
Aug. 5, 1820.	Eleanor Amanda Haskell.	"	Samuel & Amanda.
Dec. 8, 1821.	Amos Turner Lawrence.	M	Eliphaz & Susanna.
Aug. 17, 1822.	Horace Smith Morse.	"	Joseph & Sally.
Feb. 24, 1820.	William Makepeace Thayer.	"	Davis & Betsey.
June 6, 1822.	Betsey Ann Thayer.	F	Davis & Betsey.
July 23, 1822.	Ithamar Partridge.	M	Nathan & Sally.
Dec. 15, 1820.	Eliza Ann Fisher.	F	Weston & Margarett.
Aug. 18, 1822.	Edwin Allen Fisher.	M	Weston & Margarett.
June 7, 1821.	Lowell Gillmore.	"	Joseph & Maria.
Jan. 25, 1822.	Henry Thurston.	"	Daniel & Bathsheba.
June 25, 1820.	Otis Fisher Metcalf.	"	Preston & Lucretia.
April 21, 1822.	Lucretia Metcalf.	F	Preston & Lucretia.
Jan. 28, 1822.	George Sylvester Rawson.	M	Isaac G. Diana.
July 12, 1822.	Horatio Hunting.	"	Dr. Amory & Mary.
Mar. 6, 1822.	Nancy Maria Harding.	F	Lewis & Irene.
Oct. 3, 1822.	Matilda Hawes Knapp.	"	Alfred & Eleanor.
Sept. 15, 1810.	Lois Bailey Hitchcock.	"	Thomas Z. & Betsey.
Mar. 7, 1822.	Joann Hopkins Fisher.	"	Oliver & Thankfull.
Aug. 23, 1823.	Electa Bullard.	"	Joseph & Julia.
April 5, 1819.	William Warren Metcalf.	M	William & Sally.
Mar. 9, 1823.	Caroline Fairbanks Fisher.	F	Willis & Caroline.
Feb. 22, 1823.	William Russell Lincoln.	M	Manly & Fidelia.
Sept. 20, 1822.	Joseph Gillmor Hills.	"	Lewis & Anna.
July 28, 1822.	Albert Milton Richardson.	"	Eli Milton & Melita.
Nov. 6, 1821.	James Rockwood.	"	Asa & Julitta.
Dec. 12, 1822.	Alfred Thurston.	"	Daniel & Bathsheba.
April 13, 1819.	William Williams Farrington.	"	David & Chloe.
May 4, 1821.	Sylvanius Warren Farrington.	"	David & Chloe.
Nov. 20, 1823.	James Morse.	"	Levi F. & Tryphena.
Sept. 6, 1823.	Erasmus Pond Fisher.	"	Oliver & Thankfull.
Feb. 6, 1824.	Irene Francis Harding.	F	Lewis & Irene.
Mar. 23, 1823.	Herman Blake Miller.	M	Elkanah & Issabell.
Sept. 2, 1823.	Mary Hartshorn.	F	Seth L. & Lydia.
Nov. 10, 1823.	Sally Putnam Partridge.	"	Phinehas & Polly.
May 8, 1818.	Henry Newel Boyden.	M	James & Pamela.
Oct. 5, 1820.	Hannah Boyden.	F	James & Pamelia.
Nov. 27, 1812.	Ebenezer Ellis Warfield.	M	John & Esther.
May 20, 1816.	Abijah Baker Warfield.	"	John & Esther.
Mar. 28, 1819.	Harriot Atwood Warfield.	F	John & Esther.
Feb. 25, 1822.	Polly Adeline Wood.	"	Levi & Joanna.
Oct. 6, 1823.	Benjamin Blake.	M	David P. & Polly.
Sept. 20, 1822.	William Lewis Fisher.	"	James & Lydia.
April 6, 1823.	George Leland Pond.	"	Timothy Leland & Abigail.
April 8, 1823.	Abigail Crane Woodward.	F	Harvey & Meranda.
Aug. 2, 1823.	Paul Metcalf Fisher.	M	Capt. Maxey & Persis.
Nov. 9, 1821.	Charlotte Sophia Ellis.	F	Timothy & Abigail.
Feb. 13, 1820.	Caroline Blake.	"	Robert & Abigail.
Oct. 1, 1821.	Harriot Elvira Woodward.	"	Austin & Mary Ann.
Sept. 9, 1823.	Joseph Addison Woodward.	M	Austin & Mary Ann.
Mar. 4, 1824.	Mary Wadsworth.	F	Seth & Olive.

FRANKLIN TOWN RECORDS—BIRTHS.

DATE OF BIRTH.	NAME, IF ANY.	SEX	NAME OF PARENTS.
Nov. 24, 1819.	Mary Jane Morse.	F	Henry & Betsey.
Jan. 15, 1824.	Lucius Quintus Cincinatus Morse.	M	Henry & Betsey.
June 4, 1824.	Eliza Eveline Holbrook Hattien.	F	Willard & Eliza.
Aug. 8, 1819.	Erasmus B. Metcalf.	M	Whiting & Betsey D.
Feb. 3, 1822.	Charles Edwards Metcalf.	"	Whiting & Betsey D.
Mar. 5, 1823.	Emerson Newel Bullard.	"	Elisha & Rena, Jr.
Feb. 20, 1823.	Clarisa Bullard.	F	Elisha & Rena, Jr.
Oct. 12, 1823.	Austin Judson Blake.	M	Austin & Waittee.
July 6, 1820.	Olive Daniels Ware.	F	Samuel & Olive, Jr.
Mar. 8, 1824.	Samuel Gilbert Ware.	M	Samuel & Olive, Jr.
Dec. 27, 1812.	Nancy Clark.	F	Nathan & Nancy.
Sept. 25, 1815.	Willard Clark.	M	Nathan & Nancy.
Jan. 8, 1818.	Dyar Gilbert Clark.	"	Nathan & Nancy.
July 18, 1819.	Alfred Clark.	"	Nathan & Nancy.
Dec. 30, 1822.	Gilbert Clark.	"	Nathan & Nancy.
May 10, 1824.	Nathaniel Horace Fisher.	"	Nathaniel & Loisa.
Mar. 1, 1824.	Albert Banbridge Cummings.	"	Benjamin & Lydia.
May 1, 1822.	Lydia Ellis Pond.	F	Justin & Ruth D.
Sept. 29, 1824.	Timothy Pond.	M	Justin & Ruth D.
May 5, 1824.	Abigail Mary Richardson.	F	Elisha & Ruth.
July 12, 1824.	Martha Whiting.	"	Asa & Betsey W.
Nov. 4, 1814.	Susan Matilda Fisher.	"	William B. & Sukey.
Oct. 19, 1822.	Caroline Pond.	"	Edwards & Charlotte.
Dec. 6, 1823.	Isabel Pond.	"	Edwards & Charlotte.
July 20, 1824.	Sally Walker Johnson.	"	Willard & Permela.
April 19, 1824.	Artemas Brown Bullard.	M	Cephas & Sukey.
Feb. 5, 1824.	Charlotte Amanda Gillmor.	F	Joseph & Maria.
May 30, 1824.	George Warren Richardson.	M	Eli M. & Melita.
Jan. 14, 1825.	Mary Park Blake.	F	David P. & Polly.
Feb. 9, 1824.	Charles Sewall Fisher.	M	Charles M. & Olive.
April 9, 1824.	William Albert Heaton.	"	Samuel & Tirzah.
July 20, 1823.	*James Gillmor Pierce.	"	Israel & Eliza Ann.
April 17, 1823.	Sarah Jane Fisher.	F	Whiting & Esther.
June 20, 1823.	Sabin Hubbard.	M	Elisha & Amelia.
Oct. 22, 1821.	Lucinda Allen.	F	Ellery & Experience.
Aug. 31, 1822.	Charles Leeds Dunbar.	M	Charles & Patience.
Dec. 1, 1824.	Susanna Matilda Dunbar.	F	Charles & Patience.
Nov. 2, 1824.	Achsah Metcalf Adams.	"	Alpheus & Achsah.
Oct. 22, 1821.	Lucinda Allen.	"	Ellery & Experience.
Mar. 23, 1821.	†Mary Metcalf.	"	Pelatiah & Abigail.
Oct. 2, 1822.	†Charles Herman Metcalf.	M	Pelatiah & Abigail.
Dec. 27, 1824.	Eleanor Amelia Metcalf.	F	Pelatiah & Abigail.
Oct. 6, 1806.	Mary Ann Dunbar.	"	Simeon Dunbar & wife.
May 7, 1809.	James Clark Dunbar.	M	Simeon Dunbar & wife.
Mar. 18, 1813.	John Allen Dunbar.	"	Simeon Dunbar & wife.
Aug. 16, 1819.	William Lewis Dunbar.	"	Simeon Dunbar & wife.
Jan. 27, 1814.	Nathaniel Davis Kingsbury.	"	Capt. Adams & Polly.
May 22, 1816.	Clarisa Elizabeth Kingsbury.	F	Capt. Ebenezer A. & Polly.
Mar. 23, 1818.	Polly Fisher Kingsbury.	"	Capt. Ebenezer A. & Polly.
Mar. 12, 1821.	Abner Ellis Kingsbury.	M	Capt. Ebenezer A. & Polly.
April 16, 1823.	Charlotte Helen Kingsbury.	F	Capt. Ebenezer A. & Polly.
Dec. 17, 1822.	Elmira Frelove Wales.	"	Otis & Jerusha, Jr.
Nov. 25, 1824.	Joanna Alden Wales.	"	Otis & Jerusha, Jr.
May 4, 1825.	Mary Jane Blake.	"	Robert & Sally, Jr.
Nov. 22, 1823.	Sarah Ann Gillmor.	"	Joseph & Sally, Jr.
Oct. 25, 1824.	Juliana Metcalf Pond.	"	Jolusborough & Julia Ann, Jr.
Nov. 24, 1822.	Edmund Hunting.	M	Dr. Amory & Mary C.
Nov. 7, 1824.	Albert Greene Gillmor.	"	Capt. Robert & Rebecha.
Sept. 5, 1825.	Mary Fisher Bullard.	F	Elisha & Rena, Jr.
May 17, 1825.	Alfred Daniels Pond.	M	Jeremiah M. & Polly.
June 13, 1825.	Julia Ann Richardson.	F	Eli M. & Melita.

* Born in North Carolina. † Born in Smithfield.

FRANKLIN TOWN RECORDS—BIRTHS.

DATE OF BIRTH.	NAME, IF ANY.	SEX.	NAME OF PARENTS.
July 28, 1825.	Erastus Emmons Baker.	M	David & Jemima.
Jan. 27, 1824.	Adeline Metcalf.	F	Preston & Lucretia.
Dec. 28, 1825.	Alfred Metcalf.	M	Preston & Lucretia.
May 12, 1824.	Betsey C. Greenwood.	F	Joseph & Betsey.
July 15, 1825.	Asa Bullard.	M	Joseph & Julia.
April 21, 1818.	Adaline Allen.	F	Stephen & Betsey.
Dec. 29, 1819.	Emily Allen.	"	Stephen & Betsey.
Dec. 23, 1821.	Edwin Francis Allen.	M	Stephen & Betsey.
Oct. 9, 1823.	Charlotte Jane Allen.	F	Stephen & Betsey.
May 22, 1825.	Hiram George Allen.	M	Stephen & Betsey.
Feb. 20, 1825.	Joel Johnson Morse.	"	Stillman P. & Anna.
July 23, 1822.	George Ithamar Partridge.	"	Nathan & Sally.
Aug. 7, 1824.	Harriet Maria Partridge.	F	Nathan & Sally.
Feb. 5, 1826.	Joseph Warren Bullard.	M	Cephas & Sukey.
Aug. 17, 1825.	Lois Anngenette Green.	F	Martin & Lois.
Sept. 3, 1825.	John Hiram Hall.	M	Leonard & Lamira.
Mar. 17, 1824.	Susanna Bailey Rockwood.	F	Asa & Julia.
July 29, 1825.	Mary Ann Taft Thayer.	"	Nathaniel & Caroline.
June 29, 1825.	Mary Louisa Fisher.	"	Nathaniel & Louisa.
Feb. 5, 1820.	Joseph Hawes Fisher.	M	Peter & Mary, Jr.
Dec. 23, 1821.	James Ferdinand Fisher.	"	Peter & Mary, Jr.
Dec. 19, 1825.	Lewis Leprilete Fisher.	"	Peter & Mary, Jr.
July 23, 1925.	Betsey Whiting Metcalf.	F	Whiting & Betsey.
May 25, 1826.	Abigail Blake.	"	David P. & Polly.
Jan. 11, 1823.	William Henry Claflin.	M	Jeremiah & Roxcena.
Oct. 6, 1824.	*Calvin Samuel Claflin.	"	Jeremiah & Roxcena.
June 2, 1826.	Squire Geo. Warren Lafayette Daniels.	"	Amariah & Anna, Jr.
Mar. 17, 1822.	Charles Willard Gillmor.	"	James & Rena, 2d.
Sept. 2, 1824.	Francis Henry Gillmor.	"	James & Rena, 2d.
Oct. 7, 1825.	Calvin G. Boyden,	"	James & Pamela.
Aug. 28, 1823.	Artemas Barden.	"	David & Julia.
April 4, 1826.	Charles Edson Morse.	"	Harvey & Betsey.
April 19, 1826.	Charlotte Partridge.	F	Phinehas & Polly.
July 5, 1826.	Julia Ann Partridge.	"	Eleazar & Hannah.
Jan. 28, 1825.	George Lincoln Morse.	M	George W. & Patty.
Sept. 26, 1826.	Matilda Kingsbury Richardson.	F	John H. & Louisa.
Aug. 22, 1826.	Ellen Maria Fisher.	"	Willis & Caroline.
Sept. 8, 1826.	Louisa Franklin Morse.	"	Levi F. & Tryphena.
Aug. 8, 1826.	James Fisher Hawkins.	M	Aaron C. & Esther.
Oct. 18, 1814.	Rachel Emeline Fisher.	F	Richard & Hannah.
Jan. 28, 1825.	Bathsheba Thurston.	"	Daniel & Bathsheba.
Dec. 23, 1825.	Asa Allen.	M	Ellery & Experience.
Jan. 21, 1827.	Samuel Augustus Morse.	"	Stillman P. & Anna.
Aug. 2, 1827.	Manly DeValence Lincoln.	"	Manly & Fidelia.
July 29, 1824.	†Julia Aurelia Lincoln.	F	Manly & Fidelia.
Mar. 31, 1826.	William Edwin Hubbard.	M	Elisha & Amelia.
Feb. 25, 1824.	William Ellis Gillmor.	"	George A. & Sarah.
Oct. 14, 1826.	Caroline Ormelia Gillmor.	F	George A. & Sarah.
April 10, 1826.	Thomas Jefferson Daniels.	M	Nathan & Roxana.
July 28, 1826.	Elias Pinckney Wood.	"	Levi & Joanna.
Oct. 29, 1825.	Edmond Fisher Pond.	"	Timothy L. & Abigail.
July 13, 1826.	Julia Sequestra Knapp.	F	George W. & Clarissa.
Sept. 23, 1820.	Eliza Phipps.	"	William & Fanny.
April 19, 1823.	Harriet Newel Phipps.	"	William & Fanny.
Oct. 16, 1825.	Jenner Lewis Sweeting Pratt.	M	Dr. Spencer & Jane W.
May 3, 1824.	Elias Addison Paine.	"	Joseph Addison & Lucy.
Sept. 10, 1826.	Marena Allen.	F	Cyrus & Sally.
May 29, 1826.	Joseph H. Wardsworth,	M	Seth & Olive.
June 24, 1829.	Mariah Richardson Fisher.	F	Capt. Maxcy & Persis.
Feb. 19, 1827.	Olive Rebekah Gillmor.	"	Capt. Robert & Rebekah G.
Jan. 3, 1826.	George Dean Heaton.	M	Samuel & Tirzah.

* Born in Canton.   † Born in Roxbury.

FRANKLIN TOWN RECORDS—BIRTHS. 35

DATE OF BIRTH.	NAME, IF ANY.	SEX.	NAME OF PARENTS.
April 15, 1827.	Gilbert Clark Fisher.	M	Adin & Mary.
July 16, 1827.	William Rockwood.	"	Asa & Julia.
April 19, 1827.	Mary Ann Fuller.	F	Moses & Mary.
May 5, 1827.	Emeline Bullard.	"	Elisha & Rena, Jr.
May 19, 1818.	Huldah Pond.	"	Paul D. & Huldah.
Feb. 7, 1821.	Wellington Pond.	M	Paul D. & Huldah.
Jan. 5, 1824.	Polly Hill Pond.	F	Paul D. & Huldah.
Jan. 31, 1827.	Samuel Willis Pond.	M	Paul D. & Huldah.
Aug. 30, 1820.	Charles Adams Daniels.	"	Joseph & Susannah.
Nov. 4, 1827.	Julia Hartshorn.	F	Seth L. & Lydia.
Aug. 11, 1793.	*James Fisher.	M	John & Hannah.
Aug. 9, 1826.	Eliza Fisher.	F	James & Lydia.
Mar. 4, 1807.	Daniel Peter Whiting.	M	Joseph & Ruth.
Feb. 21, 1827.	Albert Rockwood Fisher.	"	Philo & Ann.
April 22, 1827.	Joseph Hills Daniels.	"	Lieut. Albert E & Olive.
June 12, 1826.	Hannah Marion Pond.	F	Nelson & Hannah.
Aug. 12, 1827.	†Adelia Maria Pond.	"	Nelson & Hannah.
Oct. 2, 1827.	Albert Richardson Pond.	M	Timothy L. & Abigail.
Dec. 13, 1827.	Hannah Jane Rockwood.	F	Nathan & Hannah.
April 17, 1827.	Horace Truman Whiting.	M	Capt. Jairus & Mary.
Oct. 21, 1822.	Sabin Allen Daniels.	"	Henry & Mary.
April 16, 1824.	Henry Metcalf Daniels.	"	Henry & Mary.
Feb. 3, 1827.	Eliza Daniels.	F	Henry & Mary.
Eeb. 28, 1825.	Lewis Adrean Guild.	M	Cyrus & Amy.
Aug. 9, 1827.	Elvira Louisa Guild.	F	Cyrus & Amy.
Feb. 10, 1828.	George Brown Partridge.	M	Phinehas & Polly.
Oct. 2, 1826.	Edmond Sanford Pond.	"	James Preston & Sukey.
——22, 1828.	Olive Celestina Pond.	F	James Preston & Sukey.
May 31, 1828.	Alvira Wood Jourdan.	"	Charles & Milla F.
Sept. 17, 1825.	Josephine Aurela Perry.	"	Waldo C. & Julia.
Oct. 4, 1828.	Seth Rockwood Hills.	M	Ellist & Peggy.
May 12, 1827.	Lewis Thurston.	"	Daniel & Bathsheba.
July 13, 1828.	Orlando Sweet Engley.	"	John & Lucy.
Jan. 8, 1826.	William Henry Fisher.	"	Weston & Margarette.
Nov. 12, 1828.	Laura Matilda Blake.	F	Ira & Laura.
Sept. 10, 1825.	*William Turner Haskell.	M	Samuel & Amanda.
Sept. 10, 1827.	Clarrinda Pond Haskell.	F	Samuel & Amanda.
Sept. 3, 1828.	Pruda Maria Bullard.	"	Joseph & Julia.
Dec. 5, 1828.	Charles Henry Bemis.	M	Henry & Nancy.
May 9, 1828.	Samuel Andrew Blake.	"	David P. & Polly.
Mar. 16, 1814.	John Brooks Whiting.	"	Sidney & Olive.
Dec. 12, 1815.	James Munro Whiting.	"	Sidney & Olive.
Mar. 12, 1820.	Jane Whiting.	F	Sidney & Olive.
Feb. 5, 1829.	Clarisa Ann Buffington.	"	William & Margarett.
June 22, 1827.	Harriet Rachel Blake.	"	Robert & Sally, Jr.
Mar. 2, 1827.	Mary Meranda Merrifield.	"	Aaron & Ruth.
Oct. 30, 1827.	John Allen.	M	Ellery & Experience.
Dec. 21, 1827.	Harriet Metcalf Fisher.	F	Capt. Maxey & Persis.
Jan. 20, 1828.	Herman Miller Blake.	M	Herman R. & Nancy.
Aug. 19, 1827.	Harriet Maria Pond.	F	Hiram & Joanna.
Sept. 5, 1717.	Mary Whiting.	"	Sidny & Olive.
Nov. 13, 1828.	Matilda Maria Ware.	"	David & Betsey.
April 15, 1819.	‡Eliza Ann Ray.	"	James & Selina.
April 1, 1821.	§Sarah Anjuline Ray.	"	James & Selina.
Nov. 5, 1823.	Horace Warren Ray.	M	James & Selina.
April 16, 1826.	Amanda Malvina Ray.	F	James & Selina.
Oct. 4, 1828.	Amanda Malvina Ray, 2d.	"	James & Selina.
Oct. 8, 1808.	Abel Pond.	M	Timothy & Rachel.
Nov. 4, 1812.	Gilbert C. Pond.	"	Timothy & Rachel.
April 21, 1829.	Eliza Jane Partridge.	F	Eleazar & Hannah.
Feb. 27, 1829.	Levina Miller Ware.	"	Daniel A. & Levina.

* Born in Medway. † Born in Uxbridge. ‡ Born in Bellingham. § Born in Wrentham.

FRANKLIN TOWN RECORDS—BIRTHS.

DATE OF BIRTH.	NAME, IF ANY.	SEX	NAME OF PARENTS.
July 3, 1826.	Melancey Maria Blake.	F	Austin Blake & Wattee D.
Mar. 28, 1827.	Abigail Clarinda Allen.	"	Amos H. & Abigail.
Nov. 25, 1825.	William Henry Woodward.	M	Austin & Mary.
Sept. 17, 1827.	Elizabeth Preston Woodward.	F	Austin & Mary.
June 20, 1829.	Alfred Allen Woodward.	M	Austin & Mary.
Oct. 9, 1829.	Charles Addison Richardson.	"	Elisha & Harriet.
Aug. 9, 1825.	Elsie Colwell Woodward.	F	Preston & Elizabeth.
July 23, 1829.	Rena Bullard.	"	Elisha & Rena, Jr.
June 2, 1829.	Sarah Ann Fisher.	"	James & Lydia.
Nov. 8, 1829.	Lois Blake.	"	David P. & Polly.
Oct. 8, 1829.	Louisa Marion Thurston.	"	Daniel & Bathsheba.
Feb. 10, 1822.	Sarah Wightman.	"	George & Tryphena.
Jan. 3, 1823.	Horace Wightman.	M	George & Tryphena.
April 5, 1828.	William Barnard, Jr.	"	William & Sally.
Nov. 14, 1829.	Abigail Haven Richardson.	F	John H. & Louisa.
Dec. 30, 1822.	Gilbert Clark.	M	Nathan & Nancy.
Mar. 3, 1825.	Abigail Hawes Clark.	F	Nathan & Nancy.
Mar. 16, 1827.	Thomas Edwin Whiting.	M	Asa & Betsey.
Sept. 22, 1828.	William Boyd Whiting.	"	Asa & Betsey.
Feb. 16, 1830.	Sarah Maria Cook.	F	Samuel & Maria Cook.
Feb. 2, 1829.	Lucy Gilbert Daniels.	"	Nathan & Roxana.
April 13, 1829.	Lucy Ann Fisher.	"	Lt. Philo & Ann.
Oct. 16, 1827.	Mary Hawes.	"	Josiah & Esther.
May 19, 1829.	Esther Adams Hawes.	"	Josiah & Esther.
June 4, 1822.	Silas Penniman.	M	Nathan & Roxeena.
June 7, 1828.	Charles Penniman.	"	Nathan & Roxeena.
June 28, 1829.	Hannah Penniman.	F	Nathan & Roxeena.
Dec. 31, 1820.	William Claflin King.	M	John & E———
Aug. 8, 1823.	{ John Adams King.	"	John & E———
Aug. 8, 1823.	{ George Washington King.	"	John & E———
April 6, 1826.	Albert Newel King.	"	John & E———
May 25, 1829.	Charles Jackson King.	"	John & E———
Mar. 21, 1816.	Elmira Diantha Partridge.	F	Phenehas & Abigail.
Aug. 11, 1827.	Waldo Daniels.	M	Fisher & Unice.
Dec. 1, 1829.	Sarah Jane Fuller.	F	Moses & Mary.
Mar. 20, 1830.	Catharine Fisher Bullard.	"	Cephas & Sukey.
Aug. 2, 1829.	George Daniels Kingsbury.	M	Fisher & Caroline.
Feb. 5, 1828.	James Emers Fales.	"	James D. & Mary.
May 16, 1826.	James Emerson Fales.	"	James D. & Mary.
Nov. 27, 1829.	Alexander Metcalf Fisher.	"	Willard & Betsey.
June 7, 1829.	Ellen Mariah Daniels.	F	Capt. Albert E. & Olive.
Nov. 12, 1828.	Sarah Smith Ware.	"	Samuel & Sally.
April 2, 1829.	Alby Miranda Bacon.	"	Joseph T. & Mary Ann.
July 23, 1830.	Thomas Metcalf Bacon.	M	Joseph T. & Mary Ann.
Aug. 16, 1826.	Harriet A. Pond.	F	Lt. Increase S. & Clarinda.
April 12, 1831.	Nathaniel O. Pond.	M	Lt. Increase S. & Clarinda.
Nov. 4, 1829.	Betsey Rebekah McL. Gillmor.	F	William & Betsey.
Oct. 30, 1830.	Mathan Miller Rockwood.	M	Nathan & Hannah.
Feb. 14, 1831.	Harriet Keith Partridge.	F	Eleazar & Hannah.
Feb. 2, 1831.	Charles Partridge.	M	Phinehas & Polly.
April 25, 1830.	Warren Fisher Norcross.	"	Asa G. & Irene.
Oct. 27, 1830.	Lewis Gillmor Miller.	"	Joseph & Catharine.
Jan. 17, 1831.	William Elleot Hills.	"	Elleot & Peggy.
Oct. 31, 1829.	Benjamin Haden Guild.	"	Joel & Eliza.
Aug. 13, 1830.	William Davis Gillmore.	"	Capt. Robert & Rebeekah.
Feb. 3, 1831.	Emeline Whiting Metcalf.	F	Abijah W. & Joanna.
Sept. 30, 1829.	Jairus Bradford Whiting.	M	Jairus & Mary H.
July 31, 1829.	John Laurel Torry.	"	Samuel & Eunice.
Oct. 7, 1821.	*George Baxter Torry.	"	Samuel & Eunice.
Mar. 27, 1822.	Francis Wheeler Pond.	"	Malchiah & Mary J.
Feb. 22, 1822.	Martha Washington Aldana Pond.	F	Malchiah & Mary J.

* Born in Boston.

FRANKLIN TOWN RECORDS—BIRTHS.

DATE OF BIRTH.	NAME, IF ANY.	SEX.	NAME OF PARENTS.
Dec. 6, 1819.	Mary Jane Pond.	F	Malchiah & Mary J.
July 17, 1829.	Malchiah Addison Pond.	M	Malchiah & Mary J.
April 28, 1817.	Juliann Daniels.	F	Ezra & Abigail.
Nov. 2, 1818.	Clarissa Marie Daniels.	"	Ezra & Abigail.
Mar. 22, 1820.	Benjamin Franklin Daniels.	M	Ezra & Abigail.
Sept. 10, 1822.	Almira Augusta Daniels.	F	Ezra & Abigail.
—— 28, 1824.	Caroline Matilda Daniels.	"	Ezra & Abigail.
Sept. 22, 1826.	Sophia Phidella Daniels.	"	Ezra & Abigail.
April 5, 1830.	Henry Smith Daniels.	M	Ezra & Abigail.
Jan. 12, 1830.	Nathaniel Hammon Pond.	"	Justin & Ruth.
June 21, 1830.	Charlotte Maria Pond.	F	Gillmor & Rachel.
May 25, 1828.	Liberty Warren Burr.	M	Liberty & Sarah.
Sept. 10, 1831.	Sarah Orrilla Burr.	F	Liberty & Sarah.
Jan. 31, 1829.	Lucinda Wood.	"	Robert & Mary.
Feb. 20, 1831.	Owen Wood.	M	Robert & Mary.
Nov. 1, 1830.	Elial Metcalf.	"	Preston & Lucretia.
Oct. 1, 1827.	Metcalf Gilmore.	"	James & Rena, 2d.
Dec. 11, 1828.	Edwin Ruthvien Lincoln.	"	Manly & Phidelia.
July 8, 1830.	Franklin Hamilton Lincoln.	"	Manly & Phidelia.
Dec. 17, 1826.	Eliza Hunting.	F	Dr. Amory & Mary C.
Feb. 21, 1832.	Juliet Hunting.	"	Dr. Amory & Mary C.
April 7, 1831.	Walter Hartshorn.	M	Seth L. & Lydia.
Sept. 22, 1829.	George Otis Pond.	"	Paul D. & Huldah.
Oct. 15, 1828.	Lewis Henry Hawes.	"	Nathan & Sylvia.
Aug. 8, 1832.	Mary Jane Hawes.	F	Nathan & Sylvia.
July 25, 1832.	Eliza Ann Blake.	"	Robert & Sally, Jr.
Dec. 30, 1831.	Rosanna Pitman Whiting.	"	Capt. Jairus & Mary.
Aug. 27, 1831.	Edward Hawes.	M	Josiah & Esther.
Mar. 9, 1832.	Sally Pond.	F	Gillmore Pond & Rachael.
June 9, 1832.	Sarah Jane Rockwood.	"	Nathan & Hannah F.
Feb. 28, 1831.	Julia Frances Fisher.	"	Lt. Willis & Caroline.
Nov. 5, 1831.	Martha Bullard.	"	Elisha & Rena, Jr.
Aug. 17, 1831.	Cephas Holbrook Richardson.	M	Eli M. & Melita.
July 12, 1831.	Arvilla Adams Engley.	F	John & Lucy Engley.
April 16, 1830.	Ellen Maria Buffington.	"	William & Margaret.
May 15, 1832.	Sarah Jane Buffington.	"	William & Margaret.
June 3, 1832.	Susan Adelia Gillmore.	"	Capt. Robert & Rebekah.
May 1, 1832.	Joseph Kimball Pierce.	M	Israel & Almira.
Mar. 25, 1832.	James Edson Ware.	"	Alfred & Jemima.
Nov. 19, 1832.	Martha Miller Metcalf.	F	Abijah W. & Joanna W.
Nov. 19, 1830.	Gilbert Fuller.	M	Abner & Lydia.
Jan. 3, 1831.	Nathaniel Harmon Pond.	"	Justin & Ruth.
April 3, 1832.	Alvin Davis Pond.	"	Justin & Ruth.
Mar. 10, 1831.	Ellen Matilda Woodward.	F	Austin & Mary Ann.
Mar. 2, 1833.	Caroline Louisa Woodward.	"	Austin & Mary Ann.
April 7, 1832.	Louisa Jane Smalley.	"	Rev. Elom & Louisa J.
April 17, 1830.	Martha Emmons Fisher.	"	Capt. Maxcy & Persis.
June 24, 1832.	Nancy Fisher.	"	Capt. Maxcy & Persis.
Feb. 12, 1833.	Marshall Warren Fisher.	M	Adin & Mary.
Oct. 12, 1831.	Nancy Meranda Blake.	F	Hermon R. & Nancy.
April 28, 1833.	Frances Ann Esty.	"	Martin & Hannah.
June 17, 1833.	Ellen Maria Gay.	"	Timothy & Julia.
June 10, 1833.	Edwin Partridge.	M	Phinehas & Polly.
Oct. 6, 1833.	Albert Dean Richardson.	"	Elisha & Harriet.
Nov. 23, 1833.	William Hills.	"	Eliot & Peggy.
May 26, 1833.	Abigail Hawes.	F	Josiah & Esther.
Dec. 2, 1833.	Oramel Bradley Blake.	M	Ira & Laura.
May 11, 1818.	Ellen Maria Fisher.	F	Jason & Mary, Jr.
Dec. 3, 1831.	George Bacon.	M	Joseph T. & Mary Ann.
Aug. 24, 1833.	Ellen Bacon.	F	Joseph T. & Mary Ann.
Oct. 26, 1833.	Alexander Gillmore Pond.	M	Gillmore Pond & Rachael.

FRANKLIN TOWN RECORDS—BIRTHS.

DATE OF BIRTH.	NAME, IF ANY.	SEX.	NAME OF PARENTS.
Aug. 10, 1833.	*Susan Malinda Pond.	F	James P. & Sukey.
May 4, 1833.	†Frances Elizabeth Smith Gray.	"	Smith & Pamelia.
Mar. 16, 1834.	Caroline Elizabeth Blake.	"	David P. & Polly.
May 23, 1834.	Nancy Louisa Bemis.	"	Henry & Nancy.
Dec. 21, 1829.	George Lewis Blake.	M	Hermon R. & Nancy.
Oct. 12, 1831.	Nancy Maranda Blake.	F	Hermon R. & Nancy.
July 20, 1833.	Julia Ann Blake.	"	Hermon R. & Nancy.
Oct. 24, 1832.	‡Henry Fisher.	M	James & Lydia.
July 20, 1834.	Martin Cook.	"	John & Mary.
Nov. 23, 1833.	Alfred John Pierce.	"	Israel & Elmira.
Dec. 12, 1833.	Elbridge Moulton Phipps.	"	William & Fanny.
June 6, 1834.	Calvin Claflin.	"	Jeremiah & Lois.
Aug. 10, 1834.	Sarah Matilda Blake.	F	Robert & Sally, Jr.
April 2, 1831.	Susan Fisher Kingsbury.	"	Fisher A. & Caroline.
May 24, 1834.	George Daniels Kingsbury.	M	Fisher A. & Caroline.
Oct. 12, 1835.	George Fisher Morse.	"	Levi F. & Tryphena.
June 21, 1834.	William Henry Fisher.	"	William & Sarah Ann.
June 15, 1833.	Albert Mory Morse.	"	Amos H. & Mary Jane.
Dec. 4, 1803.	Mary Elizabeth Metcalf.	F	Dr. William P. & Susanna.
Feb. 6, 1806.	William Torry Metcalf.	M	Dr. William P. & Susanna.
Oct. 30, 1812.	Ebenezer Torry Metcalf.	"	Dr. William P. & Susanna.
Feb. 19, 1833.	Abigail Laurinda Metcalf.	F	Michael & Sally.
Nov. 9, 1834.	Sewell Fisher.	M	Willard & Betsey.
Mar. 6, 1834.	Sarah Eda Jones.	F	Timothy E. & Eda.
Jan. 12, 1834.	Elial Fisher.	M	Capt. Maxcy & Persis.
April 27, 1824.	Jane Elizabeth Pond.	F	Hiram & Joann.
May 22, 1831.	James Hiram Pond.	M	Hiram & Joann.
May 19, 1833.	Amory Pond.	"	Hiram & Joann.
July 28, 1835.	Rachel Maranda Pond.	F	Gillmore & Rachel.
April 27, 1833.	§Sarah Eliseheth Dunn.	"	Alexander & Caroline.
Aug. 1, 1835.	Caroline Pamelia Dunn.	"	Alexander & Caroline.
Nov. 23, 1828.	Mary Ann Gillmore Hall.	"	Horace B. & Mary Ann.
Oct. 10, 1830.	Abigail Charlotte Hall.	"	Horace B. & Mary Ann.
July 22, 1833.	Jane Elizabeth Hall.	"	Horace B. & Mary Ann.
Jan. 8, 1835.	Mary Ann Bancroft Gillmore.	"	Capt. Robert & Rebekah.
Jan. 26, 1834.	Elon Erastus Engley.	M	John & Lucy.
May 18, 1836.	William Haven Daniels.	"	Henry & Mary.
April 21, 1818.	Adaline Allen.	F	Stephen & Betsey.
Dec. 29, 1819.	Emily Allen.	"	Stephen & Betsey.
Dec. 23, 1821.	Edwin Frances Allen.	M	Stephen & Betsey.
Jan. 31, 1827.	Hiram Hazard Allen.	"	Stephen & Betsey.
July 17, 1828.	Jane Amanda Allen.	F	Stephen & Betsey.
June 16, 1830.	Frederick Allen.	M	Stephen & Betsey.
April 7, 1832.	James Allen.	"	Stephen & Betsey.
Oct. 13, 1835.	Willard Augustus Allen.	"	Stephen & Betsey.
April 6, 1835.	Calvin Milton Hawes.	"	Josiah & Esther.
Feb. 28, 1836.	Mary Richardson.	F	Stephen & Eliza.
May 14, 1832.	Nancy Maria Gillmore.	"	Philander S. & Nancy.
Mar. 15, 1834.	William Smith Gilmore.	M	Philander S. & Nancy.
April 16, 1836.	Joseph Hills Gilmore.	"	Philander S. & Nancy.
July 23, 1822.	Mary Maria Whiting.	F	Joseph & Zeolide, 2d.
July 10, 1824.	William Eustis Whiting.	M	Joseph & Zeolide, 2d.
Sept. 17, 1831.	Zeolide Elizabeth Whiting.	F	Joseph & Zeolide, 2d.
April 29, 1836.	Almira Lovering Pond.	"	Alfred & Louisa.
Aug. 19, 1835.	Susan Malinda Blake.	"	Hermon R. & Nancy.
April 6, 1828.	George Allen.	M	Cyrus & Sally.
June 6, 1831.	Cyrus Milton Allen.	"	Cyrus & Sally.
Oct. 7, 1836.	Thomas Bacon Allen.	"	Cyrus & Sally.
Sept. 29, 1834.	Harriet Adaline Daniels.	F	Nathan & Roxana.
Oct. 19, 1827.	Charlotte Daniels.	"	David W. & Hannah.
Dec. 28, 1829.	Edwin Daniels.	M	David W. & Hannah.

* Born in Waldoborough, Me.   † Born in Bellingham.   ‡ Born in Medway.   § Born at Alna, Me.

FRANKLIN TOWN RECORDS—BIRTHS.

DATE OF BIRTH.	NAME, IF ANY.	SEX	NAME OF PARENTS.
Oct. 17, 1836.	Sarah Amelia Metcalf.	F	Michael & Sally.
Aug. 16, 1834.	Edwin Lafayette Gay.	M	Wilkes & Deborah B.
Nov. 15, 1835.	Henry Wilks Gay.	"	Wilkes & Deborah B.
Mar. 28, 1837.	Susan Maria Hills.	"	Eliot & Peggy.
Sept. 17, 1836.	Sarah Fisher.	F	Willard & Betsey R.
Sept. 20, 1834.	Marshall Greenwood Norcross.	M	Asa G. & Irene.
May 25, 1837.	Josephine Norcross.	F	Asa G. & Irene.
Jan. 31, 1837.	Ellen Malinda Clark.	"	Capt. Paul B. & Abigail.
July 12, 1837.	Maria Louisa Fay.	"	Chester & Sally Ann.
Aug. 8, 1837.	Mary Richardson.	"	Stephen W. & Eliza B.
Nov. 6, 1837.	George Nelson Metcalf.	M	Abijah W. & Joanna W.
Aug. 26, 1837.	Bradford Fisher Morse.	"	Amos H. & Mary Jane.
Jan. 7, 1834.	Olive Whiting.	F	Sidney & Olive.
Oct. 21, 1837.	Augustus Edwin Adams.	M	Newell & Abigail.
Dec. 24, 1837.	Edwin Calvin Pond.	"	Calvin & Elizebeth.
April 18, 1833.	Jane A. Daniels.	F	Albert E. & Olive G.
April 6, 1836.	Mary L. Daniels. }	"	Albert E. & Olive G.
April 6, 1836.	Martha E. Daniels. }	"	Albert E. & Olive G.
Feb. 20, 1834.	Maria W. Bullard.	"	Silas & Adeline.
May 14, 1837.	Mary C. Bullard.	"	Silas & Adeline.
April 7, 1838.	Erastus Daniels Rockwood.	"	Erastus & Mary.
Sept. 6, 1837.	Asa Terrel Perry.	"	Asa D. & Rhachuel.
Sept. 22, 1838.	Emeline Hannah Perry.	"	Asa D. & Rhachuel.
Dec. 25, 1838.	Ann Frances Gay.	"	Wilkes & Deborah B.
Dec. 31, 1828.	Joshua George Hubbard.	M	Elisha & Amelia.
Nov. 24, 1837.	Elizebeth Amelia Hubbard.	F	Elisha & Amelia.
Jan. 11, 1836.	Harriet Bowditch Hall.	"	Horace B. & Mary Ann.
Oct. 8, 1838.	George Gardner Hall.	M	Horace B. & Mary Ann.
April 1, 1838.	Martha Norcross.	F	Asa G. & Irene.
July 19, 1838.	George Allen Kingsbury.	M	Horatio & Adeline
Mar. 6, 1839.	Eldana Melinda Gay.	F	Timothy & Julia
Oct. 3, 1826.	Julia Ann Wales.	"	Otis & Jerusha, Jr.
Sept. 3, 1830.	Jonathan Wales.	M	Otis & Jerusha, Jr.
June 22, 1832.	Abigail Adams Wales.	F	Otis & Jerusha, Jr.
Feb. 28, 1834.	John Davis Wales.	M	Otis & Jerusha, Jr.
Mar. 15, 1836.	Mary Holbrook Wales.	F	Otis & Jerusha, Jr.
Aug. 5, 1838.	Oen Otis Wales.	M	Otis & Jerusha, Jr.
May 13, 1838.	George Wood.	"	Robert & Mary.
Dec. 12, 1838.	George Gardner Phipps.	"	William & Mary C.
Sept. 8, 1839.	John Warren Richardson.	"	Stephen W. & Eliza B.
Dec. 20, 1838.	Julia Eliza Hawes.	F	Josiah & Esther.
Oct. 3, 1839.	Louisa Darwin Miller.	"	Dr. Erasmus D. & Louisa.
July 15, 1839.	Michael Edmund Metcalf.	M	Michael & Melia.
Oct. 25, 1838.	Edmond Tyler Fisher.	"	Adin & Mary.
Sept. 29, 1833.	George Shaw Leonard.	"	Hartford & Betsey.
Jan. 6, 1836.	Mary Louisa Leonard.	F	Hartford & Betsey.
Feb. 12, 1836.	Francis Ann Blake.	"	Elias & Mary Ann, Jr.
Nov. 11, 1839.	Wm. Adelbert E. Blake.	M	Elias & Mary Ann, Jr.
May 23, 1825.	Alfred G. Metcalf.	"	William Metcalf & wife.
Nov. 29, 1836.	Emily Harris Fisher.	F	Walter H. & Emily.
June 8, 1839.	Walter Merrifield Fisher.	"	Walter H. & Emily.
Feb. 23, 1840.	Wm. Henry Pond.	"	Calvin & Eliza J.
Mar. 25, 1824.	Harriet S. Pond.	F	Martin Pond and wife.
Oct. 31, 1827.	Eliza Jane Pond.	"	Martin Pond and wife.
Dec. 11, 1830.	Ellen Pond.	"	Martin Pond and wife.
Oct. 4, 1835.	George E. Hartshorn.	M	Edmond & Susan.
July 16, 1839.	Olive A. Hartshorn.	F	Edmond & Susan.
Feb. 11, 1836.	Maria H. Kingsbury.	"	Fisher A. & Caroline M.
Oct. 2, 1839.	Emery E. Kingsbury.	M	Fisher A. & Caroline M.
Nov. 26, 1838.	Edwin A. Cleaveland.	"	Lowell B. & Melinda S.
Sept. 20, 1834.	Isabella Jane Adams.	F	Simeon P. & Harriet B.

FRANKLIN TOWN RECORDS—BIRTHS.

DATE OF BIRTH.	NAME, IF ANY.	SEX.	NAME OF PARENTS.
Feb. 6, 1838.	Hellen Frances Adams.	F	Simeon P. & Harriet B.
June 6, 1839.	Louisa R. Gillmore.	"	George McL. & Emeline L.
Oct. 12, 1839.	Daniel W. Whiting.	M	Willard C. & Charlotte.
Nov. 27, 1837.	Harriet F. Guild.	F	Loring C. & Harriet.
Oct. 13, 1839.	Charles E. Guild.	M	Loring C. & Harriet.
July 18, 1833.	Samuel S. Cook.	"	Samuel & Maria.
July 23, 1840.	Gardner A. Dean.	"	Luther & Amelia.
Oct. 23, 1840.	Sarah Hellen Warfield.	F	Ebenr. E. & Sarah.
July 17, 1839.	Emeline Gay.	"	David & Mary Ann.
June 10, 1829.	Charles Melvine Nason.	M	George W. & Hannah C.
Oct. 26, 1832.	Wm. Emmons Nason.	"	George W. & Peacy B.
Jan. 11, 1834.	George Warren Nason.	"	George W. & Peacy B.
Dec. 28, 1835.	James Henry Nason.	"	George W. & Peacy B.
Oct. 23, 1837.	Jesse Leonard Nason.	"	George W. & Peacy B.
Sept. 10, 1836.	Albert A. Blake.	"	Charles G. & Lorenda.
July 16, 1838.	Harriet L. Blake.	F	Charles G. & Lorenda.
Dec. 10, 1840.	Henry A. Blake.	M	Charles G. & Lorenda.
Dec. 22, 1834.	Weston Fisher.	"	Weston & Margaret.
Nov. 19, 1836.	Lucy Cobb Fisher.	F	Weston & Margaret.
July 7, 1840.	Thomas W. Fisher.	M	Weston & Margaret.
Mar. 14, 1836.	Mary Eliza Miller.	F	Jesse & Susan, Jr.
July 30, 1827.	William A. Dean.	M	Ichabod & Hannah.
Sept. 18, 1828.	Hannah M. Dean.	F	Ichabod & Hannah.
July 26, 1830.	George W. Dean.	M	Ichabod & Hannah.
Oct. 9, 1832.	Charlotte F. Dean.	F	Ichabod & Hannah.
Aug. 19, 1835.	Charles I. Dean.	M	Ichabod & Hannah.
June 16, 1837.	Hannah M. Dean.	F	Ichabod & Hannah.
Dec. 22, 1838.	Betsey Fisher.	"	Willard & Betsey R.
Nov. 25, 1839.	George Fisher.	M	Willard & Betsey R.
Mar. 26, 1840.	Abigail Maria Kingsbury.	F	Horatio & Adelia.
Nov. 23, 1840.	George W. Hills.	M	Elliot & Peggy.
Aug. 4, 1832.	Charlotte F. Lincoln.	F	Manly & Fidelia.
Oct. 3, 1840.	Herbert Lafayette Lincoln.	M	Manly & Fidelia.
July 25, 1841.	—— —— Rand.	"	James S. & Sylvia.
Dec. 5, 1840.	Francis Augusta Cleaveland.	F	Lowell B. & Melinda.
Dec. 19, 1840.	William Henry Pond.	M	Alfred & Louisa.
May 21, 1840.	Clara Fisher.	F	Maxey & Abigail.
May 15, 1841.	—— Fisher.	M	Maxey & Abigail.
June 30, 1834.	John L. Miller.	"	John Warren Miller and wife.
Feb. 10, 1838.	Francis G. Miller.	"	John Warren Miller and wife.
Aug. 17, 1840.	Lewis L. Miller.	"	John Warren Miller and wife.
July 15, 1841.	Adalade M. Gillmore.	F	George R. & Emeline.
July 17, 1841.	George Walter Claflin.	M	Jeremiah & Lucy Ann.
Feb. 15, 1836.	*George Warren Haywood.	"	Ira & Elizabeth.
Nov. 29, 1840.	Albert OrVille Bacon.	"	James & Mary Ann.
May 2, 1841.	Charles Herbert Gay.	"	Wilkes & Deborah, Jr.
Jan. 4, 1842.	—— —— Whiting.	"	Joseph M. & Clarissa.
Feb. 18, 1841.	Geo. Alexander Norcross.	"	Rufus & Marinda.
July 2, 1841.	Nancy Melvina Gay.	F	David & Mary Ann
Mar. 14, 1840.	Isabel B. Guild.	"	William & Ruth.
Aug. 10, 1835.	Elizabeth E. Guild.	"	William & Ruth.
Jan. 13, 1842.	Charles H. Guild.	M	Charles & Elizabeth.
Feb. 18, 1837.	Erastus W. Pond.	"	Gillmore & Rachel.
April 7, 1840.	Susan B. Pond.	F	Gillmore & Rachel.
Jan. 7, 1842.	James Francis Adams.	M	Peter & Clarissa.
April 12. 1841.	William Stephen Richardson.	"	Stephen W. & Eliza B.
Oct. 23, 1837.	Francis S. Hills.	"	Harvey & Abigail.
Feb. 12, 1842.	Hannah B. Miller.	F	John W. & Emily.
——————	Henry D. Hartshorn.	M	Gilbert & Eleanor.
Sept. 6, 1841.	Mary Jane Fisher.	F	Smith & Mary.
Oct. 13, 1840.	Caroline Amelia Blake.	"	Robert Blake, Jr., and wife.

* Born in Plainfield, N. H

FRANKLIN TOWN RECORDS—BIRTHS.

DATE OF BIRTH.	NAME, IF ANY.	SEX.	NAME OF PARENTS.
Jan. 29, 1842.	Timothy Ellis Gay.	M	Timothy & Julia.
Nov. 23, 1839.	Horace G. Miller.	"	Gillmore & Rhoda.
May 7, 1840.	Jesse T. Miller.	"	Gillmore & Rhoda.
Feb. 17, 1842.	George A. A. Blake.	"	Elias & Mary Ann.
July 13, 1841.	Albert Davis Nason.	"	Geo. W. & Peacey.
Oct. 9, 1834.	Sarah Jane Jordan.	F	Alfred & Sarah L.
Nov. 10, 1836.	Albert Lewis Jordan.	M	Alfred & Sarah L.
Jan. 14, 1838.	Edwin Arnold Jordan.	"	Alfred & Sarah L.
Jan. 5, 1841.	Alfred Harris Jordan.	"	Alfred & Sarah L.
— —, 1842.	Thomas Nilson Graham.	"	David & Lydia.
Aug. 7, 1842.	Granville Morse.	"	Levi & Tripena.
June 6, 1842.	Nathan Clark.	"	Alfred & Polly.
Dec. 23, 1842.	Georgiana Parker Miller.	F	Dr. E. D. & Louisa.
Jan. 5, 1842.	Harriet Maria Richardson.	"	Wm. T. & E. Maria.
April 4, 1836.	Addison N. Pond.	M	Hiram & Joam.
Jan. 24, 1842.	Almira Louisa Pond.	F	Hiram & Joam.
May 11, 1842.	George R. Thompson.	M	John R. & Mary Jane.
June 26, 1842.	Harriet A. Fisher.	F	Walter H. & Emely.
Nov. 24, 1832.	Edwin King.	M	John & Ereptia.
Dec. 1, 1834.	Harriet King.	F	John & Ereptia.
June 17, 1839.	Mary King.	"	John & Ereptia.
Oct. 11, 1841.	Elizabeth L. Clark.	"	Erastus & Elizabeth.
May 30, 1842.	Angelia Josephine Morse.	"	Horace S. & Eliza Jane.
Jan. 31, 1843.	Mary Elizabeth Warfield.	"	Ebenr. E. & Sarah.
July 10, 1843.	Charles Richardson Adams.	M	Peter & Clarissa D.
Feb. 12, 1843.	Charles C. Metcalf.	"	Erasmus B. & Ann S.
Aug. 30, 1843.	Lucius Adelbert Morse.	"	George W. & Esther.
Aug. 24, 1840.	John Edwin Pierce.	"	John & Caroline.
Mar. 21, 1842.	Elmira W. Inman.	F	Seth & Elmira.
Mar. 21, 1843.	Harriet Elizabeth Metcalf.	"	Mitchael & Melia.
Nov. 2, 1843.	Cornelia Aregelia Norcross.	"	Rufus Norcross and wife.
Nov. 13, 1836.	Geo. Washington Pierce.	M	Washington & Nancy G.
Nov. 23, 1839.	Charles Stillman Pierce.	"	Washington & Nancy G.
July 15, 1842.	Addison Daniels Pierce.	"	Washington & Nancy G.
Sept. 18, 1840.	Israel Ferdinand Pierce.	"	Israel & Almira.
Aug. 13, 1843.	Susan Almira Pierce.	F	Israel & Almira.
April 23, 1843.	Martha Laura Gillmore.	"	Philander S. & Nancy.
Nov. 7, 1823.	Lycurgus Sayles.	M	Oren W. Sayles & wife.
Oct. 14, 1825.	Joana Sayles.	F	Oren W. Sayles & his wife.
June 10, 1828.	Latinus V. Sayles.	M	Oren W. Sayles & his wife.
Sept. 28, 1830.	George L. Sayles.	"	Oren W. Sayles & his wife.
Nov. 10, 1832.	Olive A. Sayles.	F	Oren W. Sayles & his wife.
Jan. 8, 1835.	Catherine A. Sayles.	"	Oren W. Sayles & his wife.
June 9, 1839.	Smith O. Sayles.	M	Oren W. Sayles & his wife.
Nov. 25, 1841.	Thomas Wilson Door Sayles.	"	Oren W. Sayles & his wife.
Oct. 15, 1838.	Rufus Albert Fisher.	"	Frederick & Sarah.
Aug. 24, 1843.	Arabella Jane Morse.	F	Amos H. & Mary Jane.
Aug. 20, 1843.	George Albert Green Gillmore.	M	Geo. R. McL. & Emeline.
June 11, 1843.	Amelia Bassett Partridge.	F	Geo. I. & Harriet.
Nov. 12, 1843.	Harriet Jane Pond.	"	Calvin & Eliza.
Feb. 22, 1844.	Phebe Louisa Blake.	"	Elias & Mary Ann.
June 18, 1843.	Harriet Adelade Elizabeth Hill.	"	Elliot & Peggy.
Aug. 23, 1843.	Evelyn Eliza Fisher.	"	David & Nancy.
Feb. 17, 1842.	Louisa Amelia Ware.	"	David & Betsey.
Sept. 11, 1839.	George Lowell Blake.	M	Barnum & Harriet.
Jan. 11, 1841.	Adelaid Maria Blake.	F	Barnum & Harriet.
Mar. 28, 1843.	Louisa Eveline Blake.	"	Barnum & Harriet.
April 2, 1842.	Edmond Joel Rockwood.	M	Erastus & Mary Ann.
Dec. 17, 1843.	Ada Francis Daniels.	F	Albert E. & Olive.
Oct. 23, 1843.	Ellen Maria Green.	"	Jobe & Mary Ann.
Oct. 23, 1843.	Mary Ann Fisher.	"	Adin & Mary.

FRANKLIN TOWN RECORDS—BIRTHS.

DATE OF BIRTH.	NAME, IF ANY.	SEX.	NAME OF PARENTS.
Sept. 3, 1843.	Henrietta T. Scott.	F	Charles & Maria.
Jan. 18, 1844.	Leander Darwin Sargeant.	M	Charles A. Sargeant & wife.
Jan. 20, 1844.	Charles C. Lawrence.	"	Leonard P. Lawrence & wife.
Feb. 23, 1844.	Adalaid E. Lawrence.	F	Abijah E. Lawrence & wife.
Feb. 28, 1836.	Daniel C. Covell.	M	David Covell & wife.
Jan. 9, 1844.	Lucy A. Covell.	F	David Covell & wife.
Feb. 14, 1844.	Clarissa Kimball.	"	Jonas Kimball & his wife.
Dec. 16, 1836.	Emily Kimball.	"	Jonas Kimball & his wife.
Mar. 21, 1839.	Edmond Kimball.	M	Jonas Kimball & his wife.
Mar. 9, 1842.	Susan Kimball.	F	Jonas Kimball & his wife.
Sept. 6, 1834.	Maria B. Adams.	"	Oren W. & Hannah.
July 5, 1836.	Lowell W. Adams.	M	Oren W. & Hannah D.
Nov. 18, 1837.	Alvin B. Adams.	"	Oren W. & Hannah D.
Feb. 23, 1839.	William W. Adams.	"	Oren W. & Hannah D.
Oct. 6, 1840.	Henry C. Adams.	"	Oren W. & Hannah D.
Mar. 18, 1844.	Louisa Maria Pond.	F	George R. & Clarissa.
July 26, 1844.	Jane Menerva Bullard.	"	Saml. M. & Harriet A.
Oct. 28, 1843.	Abby Fisher.	"	Willard & Betsey R.
May 21, 1845.	Henry B. Richardson.	M	Stephen W. & Eliza.
Jan. 27, 1842.	Abigail Olive Wales.	F	Amos A. & Rhoda F.
Oct. 24, 1834.	Agustus Hiram Newell.	M	Hiram & Clarissa.
April 27, 1840.	Ellen Frances Newell.	F	Hiram & Clarissa.
May 4, 1842.	Olney Pierce Newell.	M	Hiram & Clarissa.
Mar. 23, 1844.	Clarence Edgar Barton.	"	Nathan R. & Louisa, shoemaker
Oct. 9, 1843.	Catherine Elizabeth Shepardson	F	John & Mary, Farmer.
Feb. 12, 1844.	James Dyer Harris.	M	Elisha & Betsey, Laborer.

I hereby certify that the foregoing is a true copy of the original record, which has been transcribed from Page 12 to Page 60, by the direction of the town.

Franklin, March 1st, 1864.

A. A. RUSSEGUE, Town Clerk.

Number of Births in Franklin for the Year next preceding May 1st, 1845.

(Residence of Parents Franklin unless otherwise indicated.)

No.	NAME (IF ANY.)	SEX.	DATE OF BIRTH.	NAME OF PARENTS.	OCCUPATION OF FATHER.	INFORMANT.
1	George Albert Green Gillmore	M	August 6, 1844	George R. & Emeline	Bonnet Presser	The Father
2	George Henry Hills	M	Sept. 27, "	Harvey & Abigail	do	"
3	Ellen Augustus Wales	F	Dec. 5, "	William & Mary R.	Laborer	School Committee
4	Samuel Harris Jordan	M	Oct. 18, "	Alfred Jordan	Farmer	"
5	Laura Ann Blake	F	" 21, "	Augustus M. & Deborah	Carpenter	"
6	Lydia Adaline Whiting	"	" 6, "	Daniel P. & Adaline	Miller	"
7	Josephine Ellen Whiting	"	Sept. 27, "	Joseph M. & Clarissa	Farmer	"
8	Allison Sargeant Brown	M	Jan. 7, "	Leonard & Susan	Shoe Maker	"
9	Eldora A. Follett	"	Sept. 4, 1844	Willard & Lydia	Farmer	"
10	Abby Adams	"	Apr. 23, 1845	Peter & Clarissa	Do	"
11	Evelyn Amelia Dunton	"	" 25, "	Joel & Lavina	Sawyer	"
12	Edgar Knapp Ray	M	July 17, 1844	James P. & Susan	Cotton Goods Manuf.	"
13	Merriam Adams	F	Apr. 5, 1845	Orin Adams	Cabinet Maker	"
14	Edward Augustus Blake	M	Nov. 24, 1844	Barnum & Harriett	Bonnet Manufacturer	"
15	Sarah Jane Ely	F	Aug. 25, "	David & Abigail	Merchant	"
16	Evelyn Cleaveland	"	" 21, "	Lowell Cleaveland	Carpenter	"
17	Leoma Gay	"	July 10, "	Walter H. Gay	Farmer	"
18	Edmund Clark Dean	M	June 13, "	Luther & Maria A.	Tailor	"
19	Anna Frances Atwood	F	Aug. 8, "	Jonathan F. & Anna	Bonnet Manufacturer	"
20	Isadora Susan Gay	"	Mar. 2, 1845	Wilkes & Deborah B.	Do	"
21	Mary Josephine Hartshorn	"	June 17, 1844	Edmund & Susan	Carpenter	"
22	Susan Emily Foster	"	June 28, "	Elisha & Louisa	Farmer	"
23	Sarah Louisa Jordan	"	Sept. 1, 1844	George & Sarah	Carpenter	"
24	Lucelia Adalaid Daniels	"	Aug. 11, "	Fisher & Anna	Farmer	"
25	Ethnah Elvera Blake	"	Mar. 19, 1845	William & Lydia	Do	"
26	Mary Louisa Fisher Brown	"	Feb. 2, "	James O. & Nancy	Do	"
27	Edmund Francisca Partridge	M	" 2, "	George I. Partridge	Do	"
28	Ugene R. Cole	"	" 9, "	Nathan & Lucy	Do	"
29	Levi Lewis Gay	"	Mar. 26, "	David M. Gay	Do	"
30	Sarah Ann Kingsbury	F	May " 1844	Nathaniel D. & Sarah	Blacksmith	"
31	Emma Eugene Ware	"	Apr. 29, "	Gilbert Ware		"

Number or Births in Franklin for the Year next preceding May 1st, 1845.—(Continued.)

No.	NAME (IF ANY.)	SEX	DATE OF BIRTH.	NAME OF PARENTS.	OCCUPATION OF FATHER.	INFORMANT.
32	Henry Bullard Richardson	M	June —, 1844	Stephen W. & Eliza	Box Maker	School Committee
33		"	June —, "	Samuel & Amanda Haskell	Farmer	" "
34	Victoria Lawrence	F	June 24, "	Hellen, father's name not known		" "
35	Ruth Heaton	"	Dec. —, "	Wm. A. & Nancy		" "
36	John Woods Brown	M	July 12, 1824	James O. & Nancy	Shoe Maker	" "
37	Jabez Allen Brown	"	Dec. 12, 1825	" "	"	" "
38	Aelsah Emeline Brown	F	Dec. 19, 1828	" "	"	" "
39	Julia Brown	"	Sept. 10, 1832	" "	"	" "
40	Wm. Henry Brown	M	Oct. 5, 1834	" "	"	" "
41	Edward Osgood Brown	"	Apl. 22, 1838	" "	"	" "
42	Hellen Augusta Brown	F	Aug. 10, 1843	" "	"	" "
43	Mary Louisa Fisher Brown	"	Feb. 2, 1845	" "	"	" "
44	Benj. Haven Guild	M	Oct. 31, 1829	Joel Guild & Eliza	Laborer	" "
45	Mary Elizabeth Guild	F	July 24, 1833	" "	"	" "
46	Martha Louisa Guild	"	Dec. 27, 1838	" "	"	" "
47	Joseph Grafton Guild	M	Sept. 4, 1842	" "	"	" "
*	Jerome Starkweather Daniels	"	May 5, 1845	Chas. F. & Eliza P.	Bonnet Presser	The Father

* Born in Upon.

Number of Births in Franklin during the Year preceding May 1st, 1846, was Forty One.

No.	NAME (IF ANY.)	SEX	DATE OF BIRTH.	NAME OF PARENTS.	OCCUPATION OF FATHER.	INFORMANT.
1	Frederic Newell	M	Aug. 8, 1845	Twin sons of Hiram and Clarissa Newell, his wife	Boat Maker	School Committee
2	Francis Newell	"	" "		"	do
3	Nancy Lavilla Allen	F	Sept. 30, "	Amos H. & Eliza P.	Farmer	do
4	Ellen Josephine Heaton	"	Aug. 22, "	Samuel & Persis	do	" "
5	Sayles	M	Dec. 9, "	Orin & Almira	do	" "
6	Joseph Whiting	"	Jan. 9, 1846	Daniel P. & Adaline B.	Miller	" "
7	Mary Louisa Rockwood	F	Feb. 3, "	Erastus & Louisa M.	Shop Keeper	" "
8	Merry Richardson Clark	"	April 4, "	Paul B. & Abigail A.	Farmer	" "
9	Flora Augusta Kingsbury	"	May 13, 1845	Fisher A. & Caroline	do	" "
10	Frances Zebiah Ware	"	Sept. 30, "	William D. & Almira	Cotton Manufacturer	

FRANKLIN TOWN RECORDS—BIRTHS. 45

Number of Births in Franklin during the Year preceding May 1st, 1846, was Forty One.—(Continued.)

No.	NAME (IF ANY.)	SEX.	DATE OF BIRTH.	NAME OF PARENTS.	OCCUPATION OF FATHER.	INFORMANT.
11	James Ervin Ware	M	October 22, 1845	Benja. B. & Sally	Cotton Manufacturer	School Committee
12	Mary Arabella Sewar Gillmore	F	Sept. 21, "	George R. M. & Emeline	Bonnet Presser	"
13	Metcalf Everett Pond	M	Oct. 26, "	Goldsburg, Jr. & Julia Ann	Farmer	"
14	Amos Sanford Wales	"	April 28, 1846	Amos & Rhoda F.	do	"
15	—— Rockwood	"	Dec. 9, 1845	Abijah T. & Sarah	Bonnet Presser	"
16	Lydia Avy Green	F	Jan. 21, 1846	Job, Jr. & Mary Avy	Farmer	"
17	Philena Amantha Cook	"	April 29, "	Elias & Orinda G.	Wheel Wright	"
18	—— Foster	M	Mar. 18, "	Elisha &	Farmer	"
19	Jane Dudley	F	April 28, "	Sumner & Elizabeth	Cotton Manufacturer	"
20	*William Gardner White	M	July 29, 1845	Adam H. & Nancy N.	Boot Maker	"
21	John Rollins Mann	"	July 8, "	Jonathan & Marietta	Physician	"
22	Caroline Anstice Gillmore	F	Aug. 4, "	Edward R. & Susan E.	Merchant	"
23	Adalin A. Agusta Ballou	"	Aug. 28, "	Thurston & Caroline	Yeoman	"
24	Edward Appleton Adams	M	Oct. 2, "	Ezekiel & Susan	Cabinet Maker	"
25	Alonzo Robinson Claflin	"	Oct. 21, "	Jeremiah & Lucy Ann	House Wright	"
26	Mary Emily Munroe	F	June 26, "	Charles & Emely	Painter	"
27	Persis Maria Blake	"	June 9, "	Charles G. & Lorinda	Yeoman	"
28	Edwin Merrill Pierce	M	July 17, "	Washington & Nancy	Mason	"
29	George Henry Scott	"	Feb. 16, 1846	George W. & Lucy Ann	Labourer	"
30	Jacob Edward Wiggin	"	Jan. 23, "	Shepherd & Joan	Mechanic	"
31	George Warren Daniels	"	Dec. 29, 1845	Wm. H. & Abigail	Labourer	"
32	Frank Eugene Hartshorn	"	Dec. 25, 1845	Edmund & Susan M.	House Wright	"
33	Edward Agustus Norcross	"	Dec. 20, "	Rufus & Marinda	Farmer	"
34	Charles Edward Barton	"	April 27, 1846	Nathan R. & Louisa	Shoe Maker	"
35	Sarah Adeline Smith	F	March 12, "	Joseph Howard & Sarah	Labourer	"
36	Georgiana Emily Smith	"	May 19, 1845	Timothy & Emely	do	"
37	Martha Jane Fisher	"	Oct. 19, "	Walter H. & Emely	Farmer	"
38	Anna Frances Metcalf	"	Jan. 16, 1846	Erasmus B. & Anna S.	do	"
39	Mary Shepherd Harris	"	April 22, "	Elisha & Betsey	Labourer	"
40	Mary Ella Isadora Marsh	"	Sept. 24, 1845	Lewis H. & Mary B.	do	"
41	George Seth Partridge	M	July 8, 1844	Seth & Laura Ann	Farmer	Father

* Born in Medway.   † Born in Walpole.

FRANKLIN TOWN RECORDS—BIRTHS.

Number of Births in Franklin during the Year next preceding May 1st, 1847, was Fifty Two.—Registered June 12th, 1847.

No.	NAME (IF ANY.)	SEX.	DATE OF BIRTH.	NAME OF PARENTS.	OCCUPATION OF FATHER.	INFORMANT.
1	Frances Orinda Wales	F.	Aug. 17, 1846	Wm. H. & Mary R.	Farmer	School Committee
2	Anna Frances Adams	"	Sept. 6, 1846	Orrin & Hannah	Farmer	" "
3	George Ellis Emerson	M	July 16, 1846	Ellis P. & Mary S.	Carpenter	" "
4	Edmund Francis Howard	"	March 11, 1847	Amos & Alvira	Laborer	" "
5	James Francis Ray	"	March 1, 1847	James P. & Susan R.	Manufacturer	" "
6	Maria Amelie Dean	F.	Nov. 27, 1846	Luther & Maria A.	Tailor	" "
7	Susan Maria Daniels	"	April 9, 1847	Amos F. & Lucretia C.	Laborer	" "
8	*Sarah Caroline Gurney	"	Jan. 3, 1847	Wm. & Caroline D.	Tailor	" "
9	Abigail Ann Hart	"	Oct. 3, 1846	Chas. E. & Julia Ann	Shoe Maker	" "
10	‡Samuel Agustus Bullard	M	Jan. 8, 1847	Samuel & Harriet A.	Pianoforte Maker	" "
11	‡Mary Shepherd Harris	F.	April 16, 1847	Elisha R. & Betsey	Laborer in Factory	" "
12	Emma Henrietta Tufts	"	Dec. 23, 1846	Charles & Sophia	Carriage Maker	" "
13	Theron Gilbert Gillmore	M	April 22, 1847	Philander S. & Nancy	Laborer	" "
14	Abba Isabella Hills	F.	April 19, 1847	Harvey & Mary	Bonnet Presser	" "
15	Evelina Eadora Metcalf	"	Sept. 16, 1846	Alfred G. & Charlotte	Farmer	" "
16	Alice Isadora Metcalf	"	July 10, 1846	Otis G. & Lucy Maria	Carpenter	" "
17	Martha Atkins Pond	"	Nov. 8, 1846	Gillmore & Rachael L.	Bonnet Presser	" "
18	Nancy Maria Kimball	"	June 3, 1846	Jonas & Abia	Stone Cutter	" "
19	George Sumner Corbett	M	April 2, 1847	James S. & Mary A.	Bonnet Presser	" "
20	George Samuel Pond	"	Sept. 20, 1846	George R. & Clarissa M.	Laborer	" "
21	Lucius Osborne Rockwood	"	Jan. 15, 1847	Abijah T. & Sarah M.	Bonnet Presser	" "
22	Cyrus Herbert Snow	"	Oct. 16, 1846	Cyrus B. & Catherine M.	Bonnet Manufacturer	" "
23	Francis Alonzo Russegne	"	Jan. 24, 1847	Alpheus A. & Mary	Merchant	" "
24	Francis Irwin Barden	"	Dec. 4, 1846	Thomas A. & Susan E.	Merchant	" "
25	Francis Atwood	"	Aug. 20, 1846	J. Francis & Anna M.	Bonnet Manufacturer	" "
26	Edward Howe Miller	"	Dec. 7, 1846	John W. & Hannah	Farmer	" "
27	Walter Hawes Allen	"	Feb. 18, 1847	Amos H. & Eliza	Farmer	" "
28	Ann Eliza Clark	"	Oct. 11, 1846	Alfred & Eliza	Farmer	" "
29	Mary E. Kingsbury	"	May 26, 1846	Nathl. D. & Sarah	Farmer	" "
30	Elisha Hopkins	"	Nov. 15, 1846	Elisha &	Weaver	" "
31	William Hamilton	"	July 25, 1846	Alexd. & Sophronia	Dresser in Factory	" "

* Born in Providence, R. I.   † Born in Boston.   ‡ Born in Dedham.

Number of Births in Franklin during the Year next preceding May 1st, 1847, was Fifty Two.—Registered June 12th, 1847.—(Continued.)

No.	NAME (IF ANY.)	SEX	DATE OF BIRTH.	NAME OF PARENTS.	OCCUPATION OF FATHER.	INFORMANT.
32	Charles Eugene Richardson	M	Sept. 11, 1846	Howard & Mary	Laborer	School Committee
33	Edith Minerva Jorden	"	May 27, 1846	George A. & Sarah L.	Carpenter	" "
34	Ella Agusta Ware	"	April 6, 1847	Lyman S. & Susan	Carpenter	" "
35	Amelia Wilmarth Brown	"	Oct. 31, 1846	Leonard & Susan	Shoe Maker	" "
36	Josephine Cook	"	Sept. 1, 1846	Winslow & Ruth	Farmer	" "
37	Charles Elliot Stockbridge	"	Dec. 29, 1846	Horatio & Data A.	Farmer	" "
38	Herbert Willis Nye	M	Jan. 28, 1847	Caleb T. & Sophia B.	Merchant	" "
39	Henry Wm. Ny-	"	Aug. 16, 1846	William & Eliza	Farmer	" "
40	Susan A. Inman	F	Jan. 6, 1847	Seth & Catherine	Boat Builder	" "
41	Mary A. Metcalf	"	March 16, 1847	Horace P. & Nancy A.	Shoe Maker	" "
42	Eudora Frances Hills	"	Dec. 1, 1845	Sanford & Mary C.	Bonnet Presser	" "
43	——— Richardson	M	Aug. 11, 1846	Stephen M. & Mary B.	Box Maker	" "
44	Alonzo R. Miller	"	Sept. 22, 1846	Gillmore & Sarah B.	Farmer	" "
45	Adeline N. Pierce	F	Dec. 11, 1846	Washington & Nancy G.	Mason	" "
46	*Henry S. Brown	M	Oct. 6, 1846	Allen J. & Sylvina	Merchant	" "
47	James M. A. Blake	"	July 30, 1846	Elias & Mary Ann	Carpenter	" "
48	Albert James Gillmore	"	May 31, 1846	James & Hannah	Farmer	" "
49	Emily Jane Rhodes	F	Feb. 7, 1847	Wm. F. & Alice A.	Bonnet Presser	" "
50	†Louisa Ann Holmes	"	July 17, 1846	Ebenz. N. & Nancy W.	Laborer	" "
51	Sewell Rollins Mann	M	April 29, 1847	Jona. & Marietta R.	Physician	" "
52	——— Newell	F	Nov. 15, 1846	Arnold & Eliza	Boat Maker	" "

* Born in Providence, R. I.   † Born in Slatersville.

Births in Franklin during the Year next preceding May 1st, 1848.—Registered May 26th, 1848.

No.	NAME (IF ANY.)	SEX	DATE OF BIRTH.	NAME OF PARENTS.	OCCUPATION OF FATHER.	INFORMANT.
1	Nahum Fisher Metcalf	M	March 24, 1848	Otis F. & Lucy M.	Carpenter	
2	*Ellen Maria Adams	F	Nov. 14, 1847	Ezekiel & Susan F.	Cabinet Maker	
3	Nelson Erwin Newell	M	April 30, 1848	Nelson C. & Amanda	Bonnet Manufacturer	
4	Sarah Maria Gordan	F	May 27, 1847	Addison & Ann E.	Laborer	
5	——— Ware	F	March 6, 1848	Elbridge G. & Eliza	Thread Manufacturer	

* Born in Bellingham.

FRANKLIN TOWN RECORDS—BIRTHS.

Births in Franklin during the Year next preceding May 1st, 1848.—Registered May 26th, 1848.—(Continued.)

No.	NAME (IF ANY.)	SEX	DATE OF BIRTH	NAME OF PARENTS	OCCUPATION OF FATHER	INFORMANT
6	Walter Fernando Partridge	M	Feb. 11, 1848	George L. & Harriet	Farmer	
7	Charageene Harding Whiting	F	Oct. 2, 1847	Joseph M. & Clarisa	Farmer	
8	Mary Cushman	"	April 10, 1848	John & Mary	Labourer	
9	Ella Jane Richardson	"	Oct. 15, 1847	Howard & Mary	Labourer	
10	John Lewis Fisher	M	Feb. 4, 1848	Walter H. & Emely	Farmer	
11	Alice Maria Adams	F	Sept. 19, 1847	Peter & Clarissa	Farmer	
12	Joseph Lewis Gay	M	Jan. 18, 1848	David M. & Mary A.	Labourer	
13	Eugene Preston Newell	M	Sept. 22, 1847	Hiram & Clarissa	Labourer	
14	—— Adams	M	March 18, 1848	Orin W. & Hannah	Labourer	
15	Martha Briggs Whiting	F	Nov. 20, 1847	Daniel P. & Adeline	Miller	
16	Ella Agusta Ware	F	June 1, 1847	Lyman S. & Susan	Carpenter	
17	Elizabeth Janette Wiggins	F	Nov. 9, 1847	Shepherd & Joanna E.	Labourer	
18	George Washington Barrows } Twins	M	Feb. 10, 1848	Sabin & Harriet	Labourer	
19	Emeline Lucretia Barrows }	F	" " "	" "	"	
20	Abby Maria Gay	F	Aug. 30, 1847	Walter H. & Sally	Labourer	
21	Mary Fisher	F	June 27, 1847	Willard & Betsey	Farmer	
22	Charles Hamilton Heaton	M	Nov. 10, 1847	Samuel & Persis	Farmer	
23	Willard Ellis Scott	M	Oct. 4, 1847	Willard & Deborah	Farmer	
24	Charles Scott	M	June 19, 1847	Charles & Sarah	Carpenter	
25	Abby Jane Green	F	June 22, 1847	Daniel & Abby Jane	Labourer	
26	Caroline Hart	F	April 1, 1848	Charles E. & Julia	Shoe Maker	
27	Alexander Ezra Hart	M	June 27, 1847	Alexander & Caroline	Boot Maker	
28	Edward Wilson Wescott	M	Dec. 16, 1847	Jerome & Almira	Carpenter	
29	Mary —— Cleveland	F	May 1, 1847	Lowell B. & Melinda	Carpenter	
30	—— Hartshorn } Twins	M	July 26, 1847	Edmund & Susan M.	Carpenter	
31	—— Hartshorn }	M	" " "	" "	"	
	Preston Clark Nason	M	Nov. 29, 1847	George W. & Peacy	Farmer	

Births in Franklin from May 1st, 1848, to December 31st, 1848.—Registered Jan'y, 1849.

NO.	NAME (IF ANY.)	SEX	DATE OF BIRTH.	NAME OF PARENTS.	OCCUPATION OF FATHER.	FATHER'S BIRTHPLACE.	MOTHER'S BIRTHPLACE.
1	Thomas Mee	M	May 10, 1848	Michael & Maria	Labourer	Ireland	Ireland
2	Marion Adelia Kingsbury	F	June 4, "	Horatio & Adelia	Farmer	Franklin	Franklin
3	*Harriet Maria Dorr	"	June 16, "	David S. & Helen	Labourer	Sutton	Winslow, Me.
4	—Nye	"	June 18, "	Caleb T. & Sophia	Trader	New Braintree	Franklin
5	Ezra Warren Kelsey	M	July 6, "	Giles C. & Mary Ann	Labourer	Whiting, Vt.	Upton
6	Julia Etta Rockwood	F	July 8, "	Abijah T. & Sarah M.	Bonnet Presser	Franklin	Wrentham
7	Ellen Frances Jordon	"	Aug. 3, "	Alfred & Sarah L.	Farmer	Coventry. R. I.	Barn-table
8	*Eliza Ann Cummings	"	Aug. 7, "	Jeremiah & Mary A.	Labourer	Ireland	Ireland
9	John Quincy Robinson	M	Aug. 11, "	John & Hannah	Painter		Grafton, N. H.
10	Isolin Frances Thayer	F	Aug. 29, "	Nathl. & Caroline	Bonnet Presser	Franklin	Uxbridge
11	Henry Fisher Daniels	M	Sept. 3, "	Amos F. & Lucredia C.	Labourer		Berkley
12	Midvina Viana Scott	F	Sept. 5, "	Chas. & Amanda M. R.	Blacksmith	Wrentham	Franklin
13	—Metcalf	M	Sept. 8, "	Michael & Amelia	Farmer	Franklin	"
14	Edward Cary Ware	"	Sept. 20, "	Benja. B. & Sally D.	Thread Manuf.	Wrentham	Easton
15	Alfred Clark, Jr.	"	Sept. 26, "	Alfred & Polly	Labourer	Franklin	Franklin
16	William Franklin Robinson	"	Oct. 1, "	Wm. F. & Jane I.		Ireland	Boston
17	Emeline Frances Smith	F	Oct. 23, "	Timothy & Emily	Factory Labourer	Stoughton	Scituate
18	Cornelia Elizabeth Briggs	"	Oct. 25, "	Hiram E. & Deborah A.	Farmer	Mansfield	Attleboro
19	Charles Henry Hamilton	M	Oct. 25, "	Alexander & Saphrona	Labourer	Scituate, R. I.	Scituate, R. I.
20	Mary Jane Pierce	F	Oct. 29, "	Washington & Nancy	Mason	Franklin	Wrentham
21	Laura Josephine Burr	"	Nov. 19, "	Edmund & Emeline A.	Box Maker	Bellingham	Holliston
22	William Henry Newell	M	Nov. 27, "	Arnold J. & Eliza Ann	Boat Builder	Cumberland. R. I.	Cumberland, R. I.
23	Job Herbert Green	"	Nov. 27, "	Job & Mary H.	Labourer	Smithfield, R. I.	Weelheet
24	†Violetta Paolina Richardson	F	Nov. 28, "	Howard & Mary	"	Attleborough	Orem, Me.
25	Adin B. Fairbanks	M	Nov. 29, "	Joel & Elizabeth	"	Jefferson. Me.	Weymouth
26	Mary Louisa Blake	F	Dec. 2, "	Charles G. & Lorinda	Farmer	Franklin	Bellingham
27	Gilbert Adams Wales	M	Dec. 11, "	Otis & Jerusha H.	"		
28	Bernice May Allen	F	Dec. 13, "	Amos H. & Eliza C.	"	Union, Me.	Smithfield, R. I.
29	Engene Morse Rockwood	M	Dec. 15, "	Erastus & Louisa	Trader	Franklin	Natick
30	Clarissa Mary Bassett	F	Dec. 18, "	Oscar M. & Susan M.	"	"	Mendon
31	Elizabeth Agusta Pond	"	Dec. 24, "	Justin E. & Polly M.	Shoe Maker		Attleborough

* Born in Medway. † Born in Boston. ‡ Born in Blackstone.

Births in the Town of Franklin during the Year 1849.—Registered Jan'y 25th, 1850.

No.	NAME (IF ANY.)	SEX	DATE OF BIRTH.	NAME OF PARENTS.	OCCUPATION OF FATHER.	FATHER'S BIRTHPLACE.	MOTHER'S BIRTHPLACE.
1	James Edwin Wales	M	Jan. 30, 1849	Wm. & Mary Rebecca	Farmer	Franklin	Caroline, N. Y.
2	Walter Scott Stockbridge	"	Feb. 12, "	Horatio & Data Ann		Uxbridge	Uxbridge
3	Charles Henry Whitney	"	Feb. 20, "	Silas & Ann H.	Labourer	Medway	Pawtucket
4	Marianna Wales	F	Feb. 26, "	Amos A. & Rhoda	"	Bellingham	Rome, Me.
5	Hannah Frances Hazard	"	Mar. 8, "	Charles C. & Betsey		Portsmouth, R. I.	Attleboro
6	Frances Elizabeth Tufts	"	April 3, "	Charles C. & Sophia H.	Painter	Medford	Cambridge
7	Caroline Eliza Marden	"	April 14, "	William & Eliza	Boat Builder	Nova Scotia	Belchertown
8	Martha Kimball	"	April 25, "	Moses & Mary	Labourer	Medway	Mansfield
9	Theodore Asa Pond	M	June 3, "	Asa & Sabra P.	"	Franklin	Milford
10	Jonathan Edwards Mann	"	June 3, "	Jonathan & Marietta	Carpenter	Randolph	Newburyport
11	Ella Augusta Hills	F	June 7, "	Sanford & Mary C.	Physician	Franklin	Alstead, N. H.
12	Ellen Augusta Blake	"	June 11, "	Willard N. & Mehitable	Bonnet Presser	Medway	Harwich
13	Ellen Maria Holmes	"	June 11, "	Charles H. & Alvira	Boot Maker	Nantucket	Fairfield, Me.
14	George Lewis Richards	M	June 17, "	Amos & Mary	Labourer	Winslow, Me.	England
15	John Whiting Metcalf	"	June 28, "	Erasmus B. & Ann S.	"	Franklin	Medway
16	Bradford Henri Pond	"	July 27, "	Alexd. D. & Lucinda L.	Farmer	"	Wrentham
17	Warren Coffee	†	Aug. 5, "	Warren & Ruth	Boot Maker		
18	Charles Frances Fisher	M	Aug. 16, "	Smith & Mary	Labourer	Smithfield, R. I.	Franklin
19	Eugene Hawes	"	Aug. 25, "	Nathl. & Eliza Ann	Farmer	Franklin	Franklin
20	Emma Frances Ware	F	Aug. 26, "	Elias & Harriet G.	Boat Builder	"	Cumberland, R. I.
21	Arravesta Follett } Twins	"	Aug. 28, "	Willard & Lydia C.	"	Cumberland, R. I.	Pawtucket, R. I.
22	Arravilla Follett	"	Aug. 28, "	Willard & Lydia C.	"	"	Pawtucket
23	Herbert Wallace Metcalf	M	Aug. 29, "	Otis & Lucy Maria	Carpenter	Franklin	Franklin
24	Almira White	F	Sept. 7, "	Adam H. & Nancy	Boot Maker		Dedham
25	——— Williams	"	Sept. 12, "	George & Maria	Labourer	Wrentham	Brewer, Me.
26	Alfred Peck Newell	M	Sept. 20, "	Hiram & Clarisa	Boat Builder	Cumberland, R. I.	Cumberland, R. I.
27	Francis Uriah Brayman	"	Sept. 20, "	Wanton & Mary	Labourer	Exeter, R. I.	Shrewsbury
28	William Henry Ware	"	Sept. 22, "	Lyman S. & Susan T.	Carpenter	Milford	Franklin
29	Zachariah Colvin	"	Sept. 28, "	Caleb & Mary	Labourer	Scituate, R. I.	Mendon
30	Emma Jane Maxey	F	Sept. 29, "	Milton & Abigail D.	"	Wrentham	Easton
31	Ella Georgette Daniels	"	Oct. 11, "	Waldo & Helen G.		Franklin	Wrentham

* Born in Holliston.   † Mulatto.

Births in the Town of Franklin during the Year 1849.—Registered Jan'y 25th, 1850.—(Continued.)

NO.	NAME (IF ANY.)	SEX	DATE OF BIRTH.	NAME OF PARENTS.	OCCUPATION OF FATHER.	FATHER'S BIRTHPLACE.	MOTHER'S BIRTHPLACE.
32	*Jeremiah Cummings	M	Oct. 16, 1849	Jeremiah & Mary A.	Labourer	Ireland	Ireland
33	Adelbert Davis Thayer	"	Oct. 27, "	Davis, Jr. & Mary	Trader	Franklin	Franklin
34	—— Miller	F	Oct. 27, "	Gillmore & Sarah F.	Farmer	"	Newbury, Me.
35	Ella Iantha Blake	"	Nov. 17, "	George & Abby M.	Labourer	"	Wrentham
36	William Francis Woolford	M	Nov. 22, "	Wm. & Maria		England	Framingham
37	Wm. Edmund Richardson	"	Dec. 5, "	Wm. T. & Ellen M.	Bonnet Presser	Franklin	Pawtucket, R. I.
38	Martha Ariana Caroline Hart	F	Dec. 10, "	Alexd. L. & Martha A.	Boot Maker	Boston	Franklin
39	Margaret Murphy	"	Dec. 18, "	Andrew & Julia	Farmer	Ireland	Ireland
40	—— Cleveland	M	Dec. 26, "	Lowell B. & Melinda	Carpenter	Franklin	Douglas
	Irena Amanda Bullard	F	Feb. 14, "	Samuel M. & Harriet A.	Stair Builder	"	Franklin

Births in the Town of Franklin during the Year 1850.—Registered Jan'y. 1851.

NO.	NAME (IF ANY.)	SEX	DATE OF BIRTH.	NAME OF PARENTS.	OCCUPATION OF FATHER.	FATHER'S BIRTHPLACE.	MOTHER'S BIRTHPLACE.
			1850				
1	Herbert Eugene Hamilton	M	Jan. 17	George & Maria	Labourer	Scituate, Mass.	Strong, Me.
2	Albretto Erastus Richardson	"	Feb. 3	Howard & Mary	Labourer	Attleboro	Bangor, Me.
3	Hannah Jane Adams	F	Feb. 4	Ezekiel & Susan	Cabinet Maker	Bellingham	Franklin
4	Herbert Alden Jorden	M	Feb. 15	Gilbert C. & Emely	Carpenter	Coventry, R. I.	Western N'w York
5	†Eugene Gilbert Fisher	"	March 8	Gilbert C. & Sally A.	Farmer	Franklin	Walpole
6	Carlos Franklin Kelsey	"	March 28	Alexd. & Saphrona	Boot Maker	Whiting, Vt.	Franklin
7	Edward Francis Hamilton	"	March 31	Benja. B. & Betsey	Manufacturer	Scituate, Ms.	Scituate, Ms.
8	Elizabeth Adelaid Ware	F	April 17	Chas. E. & Julia A.	Boot Maker	Portsmouth, N. H.	Easton
9	Susan Maria Hart	"	April 22	Aaron & Ruth	Farmer	Wrentham	Franklin
10	Emma Frances Merrifield	"	May 1	Joseph & Ann	Farmer	Cumberland, R. I.	Cumberland, R. I.
11	—— Weatherhead	"	May 8	Charles & Amanda	Blacksmith	Wrentham	Uxbridge
12	Estella Amanda Scott	"	May 26	Walter H. & Sally A.	Labourer	Franklin	Franklin
13	Lucina Pinkney Gay	"	May 27	James A. & Lucena	Boot Maker	Franklin	Cumberland, R. I.
14	Adelaide Louisa Guild	"	July 10	Cyrus B. & Victoria M.	Bonnet Presser	Bridgewater	Utica, N. Y.
15	‡Ruth Alice Snow	"	July 17	Benja. H. & Mary	Boot Maker	Medway	Pittston, Me.
16	Aldana Elizabeth Chamberlain	"	July 19	Wm. F. & Alice A.	Bonnet Presser	Wrentham	Boston
17	†Edmund Francis Rhodes	M	July 26	Walter H. & Emely	Farmer	Franklin	Wrentham
18	George Henry Fisher	"	July 27				"

* Born in Hopkinton.   † Born in Dover, N. H.   ‡ Born in Wrentham

FRANKLIN TOWN RECORDS—BIRTHS.

Births in the Town of Franklin during the Year 1850.—Registered Jan'y, 1851.—(Continued.)

NO.	NAME (IF ANY.)	SEX	DATE OF BIRTH.	NAME OF PARENTS.	OCCUPATION OF FATHER.	FATHER'S BIRTHPLACE.	MOTHER'S BIRTHPLACE.
			1850				
19	Janette Phipps Daniels	F	July 31	Charles F. & Eliza	Farmer	Franklin	Franklin
20	Estelle Louisa Pond	"	Aug. 3	Henry E. & Louisa	Labourer	Dedham	Newport, R. I.
21	Nathaniel Emmons Adams	M	August 4	Peter & Clarissa	Farmer	Franklin	Franklin
22	Henry Elmore Bussegue	"	August 11	Alpheus A. & Mary	Merchant	Benson, Vt.	Whiting, Vt.
23	George Edwin Gay	"	August 12	Thomas & Ellen	Labourer	Franklin	Holley, N. Y.
24	Mary Rourk	F	Sept. 2	James & Mary	"	Ireland	Ireland
25	Dennis Sullivan	M	Sept. 8	John & Ellen	"	"	"
26	Alfred Knapp Ray	"	Sept. 26	James P. & Susan	Manufacturer	Mendon	Franklin
27	Caroline Matilda Daniels	F	October 5	Amos F. & Lucretia	Labourer	Franklin	Berkley
28	Rosanna Farley	"	October 12	Peter & Mary	"	Ireland	Ireland
29	Herbert Lawrence	M	October 16	Amos F. & Harriet	"	Franklin	N. Kingston, R. I.
30	Adelbert Osmond Cook	"	Nov. 21	John M. & Elvira			Landaff, N. H.
31	—— Bullard	F	Dec. 10	Silas & Adeline	Farmer	Holden	Franklin
32	—— Blake	M	Dec. 12	Augustus M. & Melissa	Carpenter	Franklin	"

Births in the Town of Franklin during the Year 1851.—Registered Jan'y, 1852.

NO.	NAME (IF ANY.)	SEX	DATE OF BIRTH.	NAME OF PARENTS.	OCCUPATION OF FATHER.	FATHER'S BIRTHPLACE.	MOTHER'S BIRTHPLACE.
			1851				
1	Thomas Wall	M	Jan. 18	Thomas & Ellen	Labourer	Ireland	Ireland
2	—— Briggs	"	Jan. 24	Hiram E. & Deborah A.	Farmer	Mansfield	Attleboro
3	Nancy Jane Whiting	F	Jan. 30	James M. & Nancy J.		Wrentham	Wrentham
4	Edward Perryman	M	Feb. 24	Luke & Elizabeth	Labourer	Ireland	New Brunswick
5	Mary Rebecca Wales	"	March 4	Wm. H. & Mary R.	Farmer	Franklin	Ohio, N. Y.
6	Flavius Ballou Whiting	M	March 20	Joseph B. & Phila	"	"	Cumberland, R. I.
7	Oramel Nason	"	March 21	Chas. M. & Sylvia A.	Labourer	"	Franklin
8	Ella Maria Metcalf	F	March 25	Otis F. & Lucy M.	Carpenter	"	Attleboro
9	Vesta Almira Pond	"	April 2	Justin E. & Polly M.	Boot Maker	"	Appleton, Me.
10	Adelbert Alvah Metcalf	M	April 10	Alvah & Harriett	Miller	Appleton, Me.	Tannton
11	Edward Engine Hunt	"	May 16	Edward & Rebecca	Boot Maker	Tannton	Ireland
12	Richard O'Neal	"	May 28	Nicholas & Maria	Labourer	Ireland	
13	Engine Cummings	"	June 9	Jeremh. & Mary A.			Medway
14	Mary Gilbert Metcalf	F	July 1	Alfred H. & Susan	Farmer	Franklin	Plymouth, Me.
15	Anna Agusta Gay	"	July 25	Samuel E. & Sarah			

FRANKLIN TOWN RECORDS—BIRTHS.

Births in the Town of Franklin during the Year 1851.—Registered Jan'y, 1852.—(Continued.)

NO.	NAME (IF ANY.)	SEX	DATE OF BIRTH.	NAME OF PARENTS.	OCCUPATION OF FATHER.	FATHER'S BIRTHPLACE.	MOTHER'S BIRTHPLACE.
			1851				
16	Ella Jane Hart	F	July 31	Daniel W. & Harriet S.	Boot Maker	Boston	Franklin
17	—— Ward	M	Aug. 22	Edward L. & Mary F.	"	Wilton, Me.	"
18	Alfred Almond Jorden	"	Aug. 30	Alfred & Sarah	Labourer	Coventry, R. I.	Barnstable
19	Edwin Newell	"	Sept. 12	Arnold J. & Eliza	Boot Maker	Cumberland	Cumberland, R. I.
20	Charles Granville Hazard	"	Sept. 14	Charles & Betsey	Boot Maker	Portsmouth, N. H.	Attleboro
21	Gerrard Fitzpatrick	"	Sept. 16	John L. & Elizabeth A.	Farmer	Ireland	Ireland
22	Martha Emeline Green	F	Sept. 22	Job & Mary A.	Labourer	Smithfield, R. I.	Weellfleet
23	*Hendrick Sanford Hills	M	Sept. 22	Sanford & Mary	Bonnet Presser	Franklin	Alstead, N. H.
24	Abby Melvina Colvin	F	Sept. 27	Wm. & Charlotte	Boot Maker	Sutton	Northfield
25	Ada A. Hawes	"	Sept. 30	Nathl. & Elvira A.	Boot Maker	Franklin	Cumberland, R. I.
26	Walter Scott Bassett	M	Oct. 29	Oscar M. & Susan M.	Bonnet Manuf.	Dunbarton, N. H.	Mendon
27	Alice Iantha Jorden	F	Oct. 30	George A. & Sarah J.	Carpenter	Coventry, R. I.	Utica, N. Y.
28	George Richardson Metcalf	M	Nov. 9	Richardson & Harriet N.	Farmer	Franklin	Upton
29	Hellen McCarty	F	Dec. 2	Eugine & Mary	Labourer	Ireland	Ireland

Births in the Town of Franklin during the Year 1852.

NO.	NAME (IF ANY.)	SEX	DATE OF BIRTH.	NAME OF PARENTS.	OCCUPATION OF FATHER.	FATHER'S BIRTHPLACE.	MOTHER'S BIRTHPLACE.
			1852				
1	Nathan Rockwood Miller	M	Jan. 4	Gillmore & Sarah F.	Farmer	Franklin	Newburg, Me.
2	Henry Eugene Noyes } Twins	F	Jan. 25	Henry & Mary	Inn Holder	Newport, Vt.	Langdon, Vt.
3	Hellen Emergene Noyes }	F	Jan. 25	Henry & Mary	"	"	"
4	Ida Delma Blake	"	Jan. 25	George L. & Abby M.	Boot Maker	Franklin	Wrentham
5	—— Clark	"	Feb. 2	Paul B. & Abigail	Farmer	"	Medway
6	Eliza Alice Pond	"	Feb. 19	Addison M. & Eliza A.	Boot Maker	"	Brewster
7	Daniel Sheen	M	Feb. 23	John & Hannah	Labourer	Ireland	Ireland
8	Viola Antonette Snow	F	March 8	Cyrus B. & Victoria M.	"	Bridgewater	Pittston, Me.
9	Carabel Adams	"	March 9	Peter & Clarissa	Farmer	Franklin	Franklin
10	Martha Lavina Penniman	"	March 14	Daniel & Charlotte	"	"	Medway
11	Almeda Elizabeth Hamilton	"	March 16	Alexd. & Sophronia	Labourer	Scituate, R. I.	Scituate, R. I.
12	George Bridgely Whiting	M	March 24	Daniel P. & Lydia	Miller	Franklin	Norton
13	William Franklin Ferren	F	April 18	Charles & Charlotte	Farmer	Concord, N. H.	Orange

*Hendrick Sanford Hills has been changed to Alberton Metcalf Hills by direction of the parents.   Franklin, February 29, 1876.
A. A. RUSSEGUE, Town Clerk.

Births in the Town of Franklin during the Year 1852.—(Continued.)

NO.	NAME (IF ANY.)	SEX	DATE OF BIRTH.	NAME OF PARENTS.	OCCUPATION OF FATHER.	FATHER'S BIRTHPLACE.	MOTHER'S BIRTHPLACE.
			1852				
14	Mary Murphy	F	April 20	John & Eliza	Farmer	Ireland	Ireland
15	Harriet Agusta Lawrence	"	April 23	Amos & Harriet	Labourer	Franklin	No. Kingston
16	Erastus Gardner Adams	M	April 26	Erastus & Mary G.	Painter	"	Dunbarton, N. H.
17	William Andrew Sullivan	"	April 27	William & Bridget	Labourer	Ireland	Ireland
18	Ellen Maria Aldana Pond	F	April 29	Malchiah & Ellen M.	Farmer	Franklin	Portland, Me.
19	Elmond Leander Bemis	M	April 30	Charles H. & Eveline C.	Carriage Maker	"	Franklin
20	George Hamilton	"	May 2	William & Jane	Boot Maker	Scituate, R. I.	Winslow, Me.
21	Julia Arabella Freeman	F	May 18	James M. & Amanda	Boot Manuf.	Norton	Wrentham
22	Grace Maria Hardy	"	May 26	David S. T. & Maria	Jeweller	Medway	New York
23	Mary Maria Riley	M	May 28	John & Margaret	Labourer	Ireland	Ireland
24	Packard	M	May 29	Almond Packard & Hannah Dupee	Farmer	Pavis, Me.	No. Kingston
25	Francis Herbert Fisher	"	May 29	Adin & Mary	"	Franklin	Franklin
26	Henry Adams	"	June 15	Albert & Susan D.	"	"	Windsor, Vt.
27	Francis Stephen Coombs Adams	"	June 23	Stephen F. Coombs & Julia	Labourer	Bellingham	Medway
28	Mary Ann Granger	F	June 26	Edmund & Catherine	"	Ireland	Ireland
29	George Samuel Kilburn	M	June 29	Warren & Betsey	Bonnet Presser	Shrewsbury, Vt.	Medway
30	Carrie Annetta Bullard	F	July 1	Samuel M. & Harriet	Stair Builder	Franklin	Franklin
31	Esmeyeld Richardson	"	July 4	Howard & Mary	Labourer	Attleboro	Ormand, Me.
32	Burlingame	M	July 18	Smith & Abby C.	Carpenter	Cumberland, R. I.	Franklin
33	Frank Eldon Ware	"	July 22	Benja. B. & Sally	Manufacturer	Franklin	Easton
34	Joseph Jackman Hart	"	July 24	John M. & Sarah	Boot Maker	Boston	Fall River
35	Earl Bradford Guild	"	July 24	James A. & Lucena	"	Wrentham	Utica, N. Y.
36	Henry O'Brine	"	July 26	Patrick & Margaret	Labourer	Ireland	Ireland
37	John Ingraham	"	July 29	William & Mary	"	"	"
38	Susan Elizabeth Marrs	F	August 4	John & Eliza	Boot Maker	"	Tolland, Ct.
39	George Mayo Standish	M	August 25	George & Harriet	Labourer	Foxboro	Walpole
40	Ann Jane Murphy	F	September 14	Patrick & Ann	Boot Maker	Ireland	Ireland
41	Aline Lervda Dorr	"	September 15	David S. & Hellen	Labourer	Sutton	Winslow, Me.
42	Hannah Elizabeth Shay	"	Sept. 22	Michael & Abby	Physician	Ireland	Ireland
43	Dana Scammel	M	October 4	Lucius L. & Ann W.	Painter	Bellingham	Charlestown
44	Ephraim Robinson	"	October 7	John K. & Hannah	Carpenter	Ireland	Grafton, N. H.
45	Rosina Hoyt } Twins	F	October 8	Jesse & Betsey	"	Enfield, N. H.	New York
46	Rosetta Hoyt }	"	October 8	Jesse & Betsey			

Births in the Town of Franklin during the Year 1852.—(Continued.)

NO.	NAME (IF ANY.)	SEX	DATE OF BIRTH.	NAME OF PARENTS.	OCCUPATION OF FATHER.	FATHER'S BIRTHPLACE.	MOTHER'S BIRTHPLACE.
			1852				
47	Emma Eliza Nye	F	October 18	William & Eliza	Farmer	New Braintree	Franklin
48	Annie Amanda Brown	"	October 23	Leonard & Mahitable	Boot Maker	Cumberland, R. I.	Wrentham
49	Abby Harding Metcalf	"	Nov. 4	Alfred H. & Susan	Farmer	Franklin	Medway
50	William Henry Karr	M	Nov. 5	John & Mary	Boot Maker	Ireland	Ireland
51	Ellen Frances Metcalf	F	Nov. 8	Otis F. & Lucy M.	Carpenter	Medway	Franklin
52	—— Conger	"	Nov. 9	Craige & Jane	"	Matuchin, N. J.	Westboro
53	Joseph Henry Penniman	M	Nov. 14	Luke & Elizabeth	Labourer	Ireland	Ireland
54	George Murphy	"	Nov. 17	George & Ellen	"	"	"
55	Abbot Sequard Pond	"	November 18	Erasmus & Adela	Physician	Franklin	Franklin
56	Janette Eliza Whiting	F	November 18	Wm. E. & Betsey Ann	Bonnet Presser	"	"
57	Charles Lyman Stewart	M	November 21	Charles W. & Mary H.	Merchant	Sudbury, Vt.	Orwell, Vt.
58	Marietta Batridge Gay	F	November 27	Thomas & Paulina	Boot Maker	Franklin	Enfield, N. H.
59	Albert Barton Daniels	M	November 27	Joseph H. & Sarah S.	Merchant	"	Bellingham
60	Clara Maria Corbin	F	November 29	Nelson & Nancy M.	Mason	Dudley	Wrentham
61	—— Clark	"	Dec. 2	George A. & Lois	Boot Maker	Milford	Franklin
62	—— Rockwood	M	Dec. 20	Abijah T. & Sarah	Bonnet Presser	Franklin	Wrentham
63	—— Cook	F	Dec. 22	Marcena & Louisa	Boot Maker	Wrentham	Cumberland, R. I.
64	—— Titetson	M	Dec. 25	Abraham & Hannah	Labourer	Ashford, Ct.	Charlotte, Me.

Births in the Town of Franklin during the Year 1853.

			1853				
1	Laura Melissa Daniels	F	Jan. 10	Amos & Lucretia	Labourer	Franklin	Burkley
2	Henry Castello	M	Jan. 16	John & Margarett	"	Ireland	Ireland
3	Frank Pierce Marsh	"	Feb. 19	Lewis H. & Margaret	Bonnet Presser	Cumberland, R. I.	Franklin
4	Alice Jennette Lincoln	F	March 22	Manly D. & Eliza B.	Blacksmith	Franklin	Wrentham
5	Lavina Frances Wales	"	March 26	Wm. H. & Julia	Farmer	"	Pelham
6	Harriet Frances Gay	"	April 17	Walter H. & Sally Ann	Labourer	"	Cumberland, R. L
7	Eveline Elizabeth Morse	"	April 27	Aaron H. & Deborah	Bon't Manufact'r	Worcester	Franklin
8	Susan Joanna Wiggin	"	May 11	Shepherd & Joanna	Box Maker	Derry, N. H.	Essex
9	Wm. Sternes DeWitt	M	May 28	Alexd. F. & Martha	Tailor	Franklin	Walpole
10	William Sumner Metcalf	"	June 5	Alfred G. & Charlotte	Farmer	"	Franklin
11	Mary Lucy King	F	June 16	Warren & Julia A.	Mason	Rehoboth	"

Births in the Town of Franklin during the Year 1853.—(Continued).

NO.	NAME (IF ANY.)	SEX.	DATE OF BIRTH.	NAME OF PARENTS.	OCCUPATION OF FATHER.	FATHER'S BIRTHPLACE.	MOTHER'S BIRTHPLACE.
			1853				
12	Wilber Blossom Woodman	M	June 16	William & Sarah	Painter	Kennebunk, Me.	Conway, N. H.
13	*Wm. Clarence Thomas	"	June 19	George H. & Elizabeth	Bonnet Presser	Cumberland, R. I.	Franklin
14	George Earnest Metcalf	"	June 29	Alvah & Harriet	Box Maker	Appleton, Me.	Montville, Me.
15	Joseph Lawrence Larkin	"	July 4	John & Mary Ann	Labourer	Ireland	Ireland
16	John Warren Jorden	"	July 6	Alfred & Mary	"	Coventry, R. I.	Barnstable
17	Violette Pauline Ware	F	July 16	Arival P. & Maryann		Wrentham	Winslow, Me.
18	Edward Herbert Ward	M	July 31	Edward & Mary	Farmer	Milton	Franklin
19	Girtrude Darling Pond	F	August 30	Eliab M. & Isabel		Franklin	"
20	Alice Leonora Tolman	"	Sept. 16	Wm. & Clementina	Butcher	Sharon	Gardner, Me.
21	Susan Edna Gordon	"	Sept. 16	Peter & Ellen		Ireland	Ireland
22	——Newell	M	Sept. 24	Hiram & Clarissa	Boot Maker	Cumberland, R. I.	Cumberland, R. I.
23	——Gay	F	Sept. 24	Samuel E. & Sarah	Boot Maker	Franklin	Newport, Me.
24	Frances Lavina Hart	"	October 1	Daniel & Harriet	Farmer	Boston	Franklin
25	Harriet Louisa Barileu	"	October 1	Artemas & Louisa	Boot Maker	Franklin	Walpole
26	Thomas Sullivan	M	October 3	William & Bridget	Labourer	Ireland	Ireland
27	Issadora Underhill	F	October 4	Richard & Emeline	R. R. Master	Peirmont, N. H.	Peirmont, N. H.
28	Martha Ella Earle	"	October 11	Samuel & Martha	Labourer	New Braintree	Claremont, N. H.
29	——Gilmore	"	October 15	Philander S. & Nancy	Farmer	Franklin	Franklin
30	Wm. Allison Chase	M	October 23	Hiram & Matilda	Boot Maker	Medway	Slatersville, R. I.
31	Malinda Harris	F	October 26	Elisha & Betsey	Labourer	Burrillville, R. I.	Norton
32	——Hamilton	M	October 26	Wm. & Jane	"	Scituate, R. I.	Scituate, R. I.
33	Laura Eveline Daniels	F	Nov. 1	Benj. F. & Laura	Boot Maker	Franklin	Brewer, Me.
34	Hettia Ann Darling	"	Nov. 11	George & Mary	"	Ireland	Ireland
35	William Henry Pond	M	Nov. 22	Alexl. & Lucinda		Clayton, N. Y.	Wrentham
36	——Frost	F	Dec. 12	Wm. O. & Caroline	Boat Maker	Cumberland, R. I.	Roxbury
37	†——Lockwood	M	Dec. 14	Erastus & Louisa	Manufacturer	Franklin	Natick
38	Henry Granger	"	Dec. 27	Edmund & Catherine	Labourer	Ireland	Ireland
39	Adin Sargeant Hubbard	"	April 4	Sabin & Almira	Carpenter	Franklin	Hubbardston
40	Myron R. Underhill	"	Oct. 4	Richard & Emeline C.	R. R. Employe	Franklin	

* Born in Buffalo, O. † I am fully satisfied that No. 37 is an error, and should be stated as in No. 40. This last record (40) so far as to date of birth is taken from the family Bible of Richard Underhill.

A. A. RUSSEGUE, Town Clerk. Sept., 1854.

Births in the Town of Franklin during the Year 1854.

NO.	NAME (IF ANY.)	SEX	DATE OF BIRTH.	NAME OF PARENTS.	OCCUPATION OF FATHER.	FATHER'S BIRTHPLACE.	MOTHER'S BIRTHPLACE.
			1854				
1	Julia Murphy	F	Jan. 1	Andrew & Julia	Farmer	Ireland	Ireland
2	Emma Sobriety Adams	"	Jan. 5	Seneca & Julia A.	"	Bellingham	Medway
3	Alice Robinson	"	Jan. 10	John K. & Hannah	Painter	Ireland	Grafton, N. H.
4	——Fisher	"	Jan. 14	Gilbert & Emely	Laborer	Franklin	Walpole
5	Mary Agusta Baker	"	Jan. 15	Erastus E. & Abby	Bonnet Presser	"	Franklin
6	Hannah Frances Adams	"	Jan. 21	Orin & Hannah	Cabinet Maker	"	Newport, R. I.
7	Henry Metcalf Bacon	M	Jan. 24	George & Julia A.	Farmer	"	Henniker, N. H.
8	Isabella Ida Hartshorn } Twins	F	Feb. 6	Edmund & Susan	Laborer	Walpole	Milford
9	Arrabella Ada Hartshorn	"	Feb. 6	Edmund & Susan	"	"	"
10	Ellen Murphy	"	Feb. 16	Patrick & Ann	"	Ireland	Ireland
11	William Francis Ray	M	March 2	Francis B. & Susan B.	Manufacturer	Mendon	Franklin
12	Ella Maria Fisher	F	March 2	Walter H. & Emely M.	Farmer	Franklin	Wrentham
13	Hannah Mntcha	"	March 4	Daniel & Mary	Laborer	Ireland	Ireland
14	Willie Oscar Nason	M	March 24	Chas. M. & Sylvia	Farmer	Franklin	Cumberland, R. I.
15	Ellis Scott	"	March 31	George & Lucy	Laborer	Bellingham	Medway
16	Emma Frances Freeman	F	March 31	James M. & Mary	Boot Manuf.	Mendon	Kingston, R. I.
17	Alvah Morrison Merrill	M	April 13	John M. & Mary	Clergyman	Salem, N. H.	Franklin
18	Edward Sanford Hills	"	April 13	Sanford & Mary	Bonnet Presser	Franklin	Alstead, N. H.
19	Lanar Sullivan	F	April 14	John & Ellen	Laborer	Ireland	Ireland
20	Mary Emony Cook	"	April 20	Lucian & Sarah	Boot Maker	Foxboro	Sherburne
21	Alton Alden Jorden	M	April 22	George A. & Sarah	Carpenter	Coventry, R. I.	Utica, N. Y.
22	Wm. Metcalf Cleveland	"	April 25	Lowell & Melinda		Franklin	Sutton
23	John Murphy	"	April 30	John & Eliza	Laborer	Ireland	Ireland
24	——Whiting	"	May 1	James C. & Nancy	Farmer	Wrentham	Wrentham
25	William Buckley	"	May 1	Daniel & Julia	Laborer	Ireland	Ireland
26	Elizabeth Miller Robinson	F	May 7	George & Jane	Painter	"	Scotland
27	Janette Marion Morse	"	May 8	Aaron H. & Deborah	Bonnet Manuf.	Framingham	Franklin
28	Emma Grace Luthera Dean	"	May 10	Luther & Maria	Tailor	Claremont, N. H.	Hartford, Ct.
29	Margaret Erwin	"	May 15	Thomas & Ellen	Laborer	Ireland	Ireland
30	Dennis Murphy	M	May 20	Timothy & Julia	"	"	"
31	Benja. Andrew Hart	"	May 26	John & Sarah	Boot Maker	Boston	Fall River
32	Julia Featherston	F	May 29	James & Bridget	Laborer	Ireland	Ireland
33	Jenny Lind Gorden	"	May 30	Addison & Ann	"	Charlton	Bellingham

Births in the Town of Franklin during the Year 1854.—(Continued.)

NO.	NAME (IF ANY.)	SEX	DATE OF BIRTH.	NAME OF PARENTS.	OCCUPATION OF FATHER.	FATHER'S BIRTHPLACE.	MOTHER'S BIRTHPLACE.
34	——— Lewis } Twins	M	1854 June 5	——— & Mary Lewis			Wrentham
35	——— Lewis } Twins	"	June 5	——— & Mary Lewis			"
36	Julia Costello	F	June 6	James & Mary	Laborer	Ireland	Ireland
37	Sanford Cary Hardy	M	June 8	Sanford & Maria	Pedler	Wrentham	Portsmouth, N. H.
38	Leonard Brown	M	June 8	Leonard & Mehitable	Boot Maker	Cumberland, R. I.	Wrentham
39	Ellen Hollerin	F	June 8	Timothy & Joanna	Laborer	Ireland	Ireland
40	Josephine Bosworth	"	June 8	Nathl. Bosworth & Mary J. McCarty	Pedler	Bellingham	Bennington, Vt.
41	Lowell Maddison Wiswall	M	July 4	Lowell & Melinda	Boot Maker	Medway	Canton
42	Mary Adams	F	July 9	Albert & Susan	Daguerratypist	Franklin	Windsor, Vt.
43	John Edward Aull	M	Aug. 4	John & Ellen	Mason	St. John, N. B.	Franklin
44	——— Gillmore	F	Aug. 5	Gilbert H. & Elizabeth	Farmer	Franklin	Pittsfield, N. H.
45	——— Clark*	M	Aug. 21	Paul B. & Abby	Laborer	"	Medway
46	Josephene S. Winn	F	Aug. 27	Otis & Lydia		Sag Harbor	New Bedford
47	Elizabeth Esther Perriman	F	Sept. 3	Luke & Elizabeth	Physician	New Brunswick	New Brunswick
48	Hellen Stearns Scammell	"	Sept. 6	Lucius L. & Ann	Laborer	Bellingham	Charleston
49	Agnes Murphy	"	Sept. 10	George & Ellen		Ireland	Ireland
50	——— Pond	"	Sept. 16	Addison & Eliza	Box Maker	Franklin	Brewster
51	Marietta Whiting	"	Sept. 18	Daniel P. & Lydia	Boot Maker	Attleboro	Norton
52	Maryeth Maranda Martin	"	Oct. 3	Wm. H. & Maranda	Carpenter	Meclmin, N. Y.	Franklin
53	——— Conger	M	Oct. 3	Craig M. & Jane	Boot Maker	Bellingham	Westboro
54	George Frederic Thompson	M	Oct. 15	David W. & Mary	Bon't Manuf.	Dunbarton, N. H.	Smithfield, R. I.
55	Elizabeth Maria Bassett	F	Jan. 4	Oscar M. & Susan M.	Laborer	Bridgewater	Blackstone
56	——— Snow	"	Oct. 16	Cyrus B. & Victoria	Farmer	Burrilville, R. I.	Pittston, Me.
57	Athena M. Inman	"	Oct. 20	Seth & Catherine	Painter	Ireland	Bellingham
58	——— Robinson	"	Oct. 30	John K. & Hannah	Bonnet Presser	London, Eng.	Grafton, N. H.
59	Charles Augustus Thomas	"	Nov. 24	James & Elizabeth	Laborer	London, Eng.	London, Eng.
60	——— Black	M	Dec. 1	John & Margaret	Clerk	Ireland	Ireland
61	Henry Larkin	F	Dec. 6	Curtis & Carrie	Laborer	Holliston	Boston
62	——— Mann	M	Dec. 6	John & Mary	Farmer	Ireland	Ireland
63	——— Metcalf	F	Dec. 22	William & Sarah		Chesterfield, N.H.	Winthrop, Me.
64	Lucy Caroline Coolcdge	"	Dec. 23	Richardson & Harriet		Franklin	Providence, R. L.
		"	Dec. 25	Joseph & Martha		Sherburne	Franklin

*Stillborn.

Births in the Town of Franklin during the Year 1854.—(Continued.)

NO.	NAME (IF ANY.)	SEX	DATE OF BIRTH.	NAME OF PARENTS.	OCCUPATION OF FATHER.	FATHER'S BIRTHPLACE.	MOTHER'S BIRTHPLACE.
			1854				
65	Henry Granger	M	Dec. 27	Edward & Catherine	Laborer	Ireland	Ireland
66	Cheney	"	Dec. 29	Lyman S. & Lizzie	Clerk	Essex, N. Y.	Stark, Me.

Births in the Town of Franklin during the Year 1855.—T. C. Hills, Registrar.

NO.	NAME (IF ANY.)	SEX	DATE OF BIRTH.	NAME OF PARENTS.	OCCUPATION OF FATHER.	FATHER'S BIRTHPLACE.	MOTHER'S BIRTHPLACE.
			1855				
1	James G. W. Salley	M	Jan. 8	James & Susan	Farmer	Mexico, Me.	Franklin
2	William Henry Wales	"	Jan. 19	William H. & Julia	"	Franklin	Pelham
3	George W. Treen	"	Jan. 21	James & Sarah	Laborer	Cumberland, Nov.	Wrentham
4	Harriet Almira Bartlett	F	Jan. 26	Amos & Adeline	Boot Maker	Attleboro	Franklin
5	Matilda Earle Pond	"	Jan. 31	Henry E. & Louisa	Bonnet Bleacher	Dedham	Newport, R. I.
6	Abby Maria Adams	"	Jan. 31	Peter & Clarissa	Farmer	Franklin	Franklin
7	James Herbert Blake	M	Feb. 5	Seth & Mary	Carriage Maker	Dover	Conway, N. H.
8	Isabella A. Williams	F	March 4	Lewis & Huldah	Boot Maker	Wrentham	Mendon
9	Arthur Lewis Fisher	M	March 9	John H. & Nancy	Farmer	Franklin	Franklin
10	Mary Ann Rahala	F	April 3	James & Margaret	Laborer	Ireland	Ireland
11	George Dwight Metcalf	M	April 4	Alfred H. & Susan	Farmer	Franklin	Medway
12	(Amended) Loui A. Dean	"	April 9	George W. & Ellen	Bonnet Presser	"	Franklin
13	Sarah Lucina Farnum	F	April 11	Albert & Sarah	Boot Maker	Ashford, Ct.	Cumberland, R. I.
14	Willis Eugene Marston	M	April 30	James & Bulah	Farmer	Newfield, Me.	Peru, Me.
15	Maryann Sullivan	F	May 1	William & Bridget	Laborer	Ireland	Ireland
16	Joseph Herbert Baker	M	May 6	Erastus E. & Abby M.	Bonnet Presser	Franklin	Franklin
17	Nathan Anson Daniels	"	May 7	Thomas J. & Celia Ann	Farmer	"	Medway
18	Margarette Murphy	F	May 11	Timothy & Julia	Laborer	Ireland	Ireland
19	Ellen Elizabeth Pierce	"	May 24	Washington & Nancy	Mason	Franklin	Wrentham
20	Ready Clinton Newell	M	May 26	Arnold J. & Eliza	Boat Maker	Cumberland, R. I.	Cumberland, R. L.
21	Ida Darling	F	May 31	Alfred C. & Hannah	Carpenter	Wrentham	Wrentham
22	Edward McFarland	M	June 7	Hugh & Celia	Laborer	Ireland	Ireland
23	Ida Marian Daniels	F	June 30	Waldo & Hellen	Teacher	Franklin	Walpole
24	Oliver Dean Gay	M	July 8	Saml. S. & Sarah	Farmer	"	Newport, Me.
25	Mary Anna Metcalf	F	July 11	John & Mary	Laborer	Sherburne	Franklin
26	James Hollarin	M	Aug. 7	Timothy & Joanna	"	Ireland	Ireland
27	Gardner Fisk Daniels	"	Aug. 15	Chas. F. & Eliza	Farmer	Franklin	Franklin

Births in the Town of Franklin during the Year 1855.—(Continued.)

NO.	NAME (IF ANY.)	SEX	DATE OF BIRTH.	NAME OF PARENTS.	OCCUPATION OF FATHER.	FATHER'S BIRTHPLACE.	MOTHER'S BIRTHPLACE.
			1855				
28	Carrie Mitchel Tolman	F	Aug. 16	Samuel & Caroline	Bonnet Presser	Sharon	Freeport, Me.
29	John Quincy Adams	M	Aug. 21	Erastus & Mary	"	Franklin	Dunbarton, N. H.
30	Wm. Henry Farris	F	Aug. 24	Daniel & Elvira	Sawyer	Vasselboro, Me.	Hope, Me.
31	Ellen Frances Thayer	F	Aug. 25	Smith W. & Lacinda	Boot Maker	Douglas	Winslow, Me.
32	Catherine Shelian	"	Sept. 3	John & Hannah	Laborer	Ireland	Ireland
33	George Granger	M	Sept. 10	Edmund & Catherine	"	"	"
34	Rhoda Ann Ware	F	Oct. 7	David & Betsey	Farmer	Franklin	Hopkinton
35	Harriet Phipps Richardson	"	Oct. 10	Charles & Mary Jane	Clerk	"	Westfield
36	William Joseph Whiting	M	Oct. 12	Wm. E. & Betsey Ann	Bonnet Presser	"	Franklin
37	Edgar Austin Thomas	"	Oct. 13	Geo. H. & Elizabeth	"	Cumberland, R. I.	Wrentham
38	Charles Henry Corbin	"	Nov. 9	Nelson & Nancy	Mason	Dudley	"
39	Thomas Henry Murphy	"	Nov. 18	Patrick & Ann	Laborer	Ireland	Ireland
40	James Desmond	"	Nov. 21	Jeremiah & Mary	"	"	Wrentham
41	——— Jorden	F	Dec. 19	Geo. A. & Lavina	Carpenter	Coventry	Wrentham
42	Theodore Parker Farr	M	Dec. 19	Parker R. & Ahby	Bonnet Presser	Chesterfield, N.H.	Cumberland, R. I.
43	——— Hart	"	Dec. 28	Michael & Margarette	Laborer	Ireland	Ireland

Births in the Town of Franklin during the Year 1856.—T. C. HILLS, Registrar.

NO.	NAME (IF ANY.)	SEX	DATE OF BIRTH.	NAME OF PARENTS.	OCCUPATION OF FATHER.	FATHER'S BIRTHPLACE.	MOTHER'S BIRTHPLACE.
			1856				
1	——— Flinn	F	Jan. 21	John & Jane	Laborer	Ireland	Hudson, N. Y.
2	Jane Augusta Brown	"	Jan. 25	George F. & Ellen M.	Clerk	Medway	Franklin
3	Isabelle Louisa Fisher	"	Jan. 30	Walter H. & Emely	Farmer	Franklin	Wrentham
4	Ann Burkley	"	Feb. 10	Daniel & Julia	Laborer	Ireland	Ireland
5	Adelbert Merrill Nason	M	Feb. 19	George W. & Hettie, Jr.	"	Franklin	Lunenburg
6	Thomas Garvin	"	Feb. 29	Thomas & Hannah	"	Ireland	Ireland
7	Ervin Loyd Hill	"	March 31	Lewis & Harriet	Box Maker	Elmon, Vt.	Bellingham
8	Harriet Zeolide Thompson	F	April 11	George & Joanna	Boot Maker	Sumner, Me.	Swansey
9	Sarah Ann Riley	"	April 27	John & Margarett	Laborer	Ireland	Ireland
10	Margarett Ryan	"	May 9	James M. & Ellen	"	"	"
11	——— Clark	"	May 13	Horatio & Lucy	Boot Maker	Canada	Franklin
12	George Meaker Russegue	M	May 24	Alpheus A. & Mary	Merchant	Benson, Vt.	Whiting, Vt.
13	Thomas Costello	"	June 12	Thomas & Mary	Laborer	Ireland	Ireland

Births in the Town of Franklin during the Year 1856.—(Continued.)

No.	NAME (IF ANY.)	SEX.	DATE OF BIRTH.	NAME OF PARENTS.	OCCUPATION OF FATHER.	FATHER'S BIRTHPLACE.	MOTHER'S BIRTHPLACE.
			1856				
14	Margarett Sullivan	F	June 19	Dennis & Margaret	Laborer	Ireland	Ireland
15	Adelia Amelia Ballou	"	June 24	Darwin T. & Nancy	Farmer	Cumberland, R. I.	Franklin
16	Herbert Brooks Bacon	M	July 7	George W. & Julia	Bonnet Presser	Franklin	"
17	George Arthur Wiggin	"	July 11	Shepherd & Almira	Box Maker	Wolfsboro, N. H.	"
18	—— Hawes	"	July 17	Nathaniel & Eliza	Boat Maker	Franklin	Cumberland, R. I.
19	William Henry Allen	"	July 20	C. Milton & Sarah	Bonnet Presser	"	Southboro
20	George Otis Winn	"	July 28	Otis & Lydia S.	Laborer	Utica, N. Y.	New Bedford
21	Frank B. Cheney	"	July 30	Lyman S. & Lizzie	Clerk	Essex, N. Y.	Stark, Me.
22	Jessie Caroline Ballou	F	Aug. 13	George W. & Eliza	Boot Maker	Cumberland, R. I.	Medway
23	Wm. Archibald Laing	M	Aug. 16	Robert & Nancy	Tailor	Halifax, N. S.	Franklin
24	Leroy Armond Darling	"	Aug. 20	Alfred O. & Hannah	Carpenter	Wrentham	Wrentham
25	Emery Wolford	"	Sept. 1	William & Martha	Farmer	Ireland	Framingham
26	George Conger	"	Sept. 10	Craig M. & Jane	Carpenter	Mechuin, N. Y.	Westboro
27	—— Brown	F	Sept. 13	Leonard & Malitta	Boot Maker	Cumberland, R. I.	Wrentham
28	Wm. Albert Bartlett	M	Sept. 14	Amos & Adeline	"	Wrentham	Franklin
29	George Oliver Capron	"	Sept. 16	Newton & Cornelia	Merchant	Cumberland, R. I.	"
30	Elizabeth Eldon King	F	Sept. 22	Warren & Julia	Laborer	Rehoboth	"
31	Nellie Elizabeth Metcalf	"	Sept. 25	Otis F. & Maria	Carpenter	Franklin	"
32	Ellen Murphy	"	Sept. 29	George & Ellen	Laborer	Ireland	Ireland
33	Nathan Cleveland Nye	M	Oct. 7	Caleb T. & Sophia	Merchant	New Braintree	Franklin
34	—— Bacon	"	Oct. 7	Thomas & Emely	Teacher	Franklin	"
35	Charlotte Lavina Thayer	F	Oct. 15	Joseph & Eliza	Clergyman	Mendon	Heath
36	Mary Ann Conoley	"	Oct. 27	Patrick & Mary	Laborer	Ireland	Ireland
37	John Halferin	M	Nov. 3	Timothy & Joanna	"	"	"
38	—— Stewart	"	Nov. 3	Charles W. & Mary	Merchant	Stafford, Vt.	Orwell, Vt.
39	Edward Larkin	"	Nov. 4	John & Mary	Laborer	Ireland	Ireland
40	—— Vannet	F	Nov. 28	Albert & Sarah	"	Cumberland, R. I.	Westford
41	Carrie Ellen Staples	"	Nov. 29	Amos & Ellen	"	Cumberland	Wrentham
42	George Eugene Hart	M	Nov. 20	Daniel W. & Harriet	Boot Maker	Boston	Franklin
43	—— Miller	F	Dec. 4	Hermon B. & Mary	Farmer	Franklin	
44	—— Blake	"	Dec. 7	Seth & Mary	Carriage Maker	Dover	Conway, N. H.

Births in the Town of Franklin during the Year 1857.—Registered Jan'y 17th, 1858.

NO.	NAME (IF ANY.)	SEX	DATE OF BIRTH.	NAME OF PARENTS.	OCCUPATION OF FATHER.	FATHER'S BIRTHPLACE.	MOTHER'S BIRTHPLACE.
			1857				
1	Hannah Gertrude Snow	F	Jan. 17	Cyrus B. & Victorie	Merchant	Bridgewater	Pittston, Me.
2	— Remick	"	Feb. 2	Wm. & Catherine	Boot Maker	Paris, Me.	Ireland
3	Sarah Elizabeth Darling	"	Feb. 5	Jesse & Mary	"	New York	"
4	Artemas Barden	M	Feb. 7	Artemas & Hannah L.	Farmer	Franklin	Walpole
5	Catherine Costello	F	Feb. 8	Patrick & Ann	Laborer	Ireland	Ireland
6	William Loren Daniels	M	Feb. 11	Amos & Lucretia	Farmer	Franklin	Barkley
7	William J. Walker	"	Feb. 21	Wm. J. Walker & Maria Kingsbury	Carpenter	Boston	Franklin
8	Mary Ann McParland	F	March 1	Hugh & Celia	Laborer	Ireland	Ireland
9	William Edda Clark	M	March 21	William & Ellen	"	Medway	Franklin
10	Clarence Decatur Lincoln	"	April 4	Manly D. & Eliza	Boot Maker	Franklin	Wrentham
11	Violetta Amanda Wales	F	April 10	William & Julia	Blacksmith	Franklin	Bellingham
12	Edwin Morrison	M	April 10	Seth & Maria	Farmer		Medway
13	Mary Frances Gibson	F	April 14	Cornelius & Mary	Bonnet Presser	Melrose	Auburn
14	Mary Evelyn Morse	"	May 4	Monroe & Emely	Laborer	Hopkinton	Goshen, N. Y.
15	Catherine Sullivan	"	May 22	William & Bridget	Clerk	Framingham	Ireland
16	Calesta Coffee	"	May 26	Warren & Ruth	Laborer	Ireland	Wrentham
17	David Erastus Baker	M	May 30	Erastus E. & Abby M.	Farmer	Wrentham	Franklin
18	Samuel Robertson Marsh	"	May 31	Lewis H. & Sophia	"	Franklin	Roxbury, Vt.
19	Annie Maria Emerson	F	June 1	Ellis P. & Mary	Carpenter	Smithfield, R. I.	Attleborough
20	— Royals	"	June 9	Justin & Lydia	Laborer	Dedham	Wrentham
21	Josephene Francis Bassett	"	June 20	Oscar M. & Susan M.	Clerk	Medford	Blackstone
22	Earnest Ballou Marden	M	June 23	George & Susan	Carpenter	Dunbarton, N. H.	Cumberland, R. I.
23	Nellie Fisher	F	June 24	Marshall & Ellen	"	Freedom, Me.	Cumberland
24	Millard Nason	M	June 25	William E. & Mary	Bonnet Presser	Franklin	"
25	Harriet Agusta Frost	F	July 2	Wm. & Caroline	Boat Maker	Cumberland	Charlton
26	Isabelle French Whiting	"	July 9	Peter & Lydia	Box Maker	Franklin	Boston
27	Marcella Woodward	"	July 11	Marcellus & Sarah	Farmer	Whitefield, Me.	Norton
28	Sarah Granger	"	July 13	Edmund & Catherine	Laborer	Ireland	Franklin
29	Jeremiah Buckley	M	July 14	Daniel & Julia	"	"	Ireland
30	Fanny Robinson	F	July 17	George & Jane	Painter	"	Scotland
31	Frances Abby Shay	"	July 25	Michael & Abby	Laborer	"	Ireland
32	— Robinson	M	July 27	John & Hannah	Painter	"	Grafton, N. H.
33	Sarah Louisa Webb	F	July 27	Wm. & Harriet	Boot Maker	Norton	Dedham

Births in the Town of Franklin during the Year 1857.—(Continued.)

NO.	NAME (IF ANY.)	SEX	DATE OF BIRTH.	NAME OF PARENTS.	OCCUPATION OF FATHER.	FATHER'S BIRTHPLACE.	MOTHER'S BIRTHPLACE.
			1857				
34	George Stanley Paine	M	July 28	Stephen & Sarah	Carpenter	Burrilville	Cumberland
35	Edgar C. Dean	"	Aug. 27	George & Ellen	Boot Maker	Franklin	Franklin
36	Caroline Ada Clark	F	Aug. 29	Joseph & Elizabeth	Farmer	Attleboro	Attleboro
37	—— Ferguson	"	Sept. 4	John & Margaret	Laborer	Ireland	Ireland
38	—— Dougherty	"	Sept. 8	Edward & Mary	"	"	"
39	Charles Edmund Walker	M	Sept. 9	Wm. J. & Susan	Carpenter	Boston	Franklin
40	Arthur Wilmot Razee	"	Sept. 12	Amos & Abby	Tailor	Bellingham	Ware
41	Edward Agustus Wiggin	"	Sept. 14	Shepard & Almira	Box Maker	Wolfsboro, N. H.	Franklin
42	—— Thompson	"	Sept. 17	David & Mary	Laborer	Vermont	Burrilville, R. I.
43	Elenor Castello	F	Sept. 21	John & Margaret	"	Ireland	Ireland
44	Eva Frances Harris	"	Sept. 24	Elisha & Betsey		Burrilville	Norton
45	Winneford Cook	"	Sept. 24	Lucian & Sarah	Boot Maker	Bellingham	Sherborn
46	Mary Eliza Murphy	"	Sept. 28	Patrick & Ann	Laborer	Ireland	Ireland
47	Ida Janette Holmes	"	Oct. 3	Rufus & Mary	"	Nova Scotia	Scotland
48	Ada Cordelia Pitman	"	Oct. 9	John & Cordelia	Painter	Portsmouth, N. H.	Franklin
49	—— Mann	M	Oct. 9	William & Sarah	Farmer	Chesterfield, Me.	Winthrop, Me.
50	Manning Adelbert Follett	"	Oct. 11	James & Ann Eliza	Boot Maker	Attleboro	Cumberland, R. I.
51	Frank Agustine Wilkinson	"	Oct. 21	Willard & Fanny	Laborer	Cumberland, R. I.	Westboro
52	—— Ballou	"	Oct. 27	Darwin T. & Nancy	Farmer	"	Bellingham
53	Herbert Adams	"	Oct. 28	Peter & Clarissa	"	Franklin	Franklin
54	Martin McRue	"	Nov. 9	Patrick & Bridget	Laborer	Ireland	Ireland
55	—— Briggs	F	Nov. 13	Hiram E. & Deborah	Farmer	Mansfield	Attleboro
56	Grace Mabell Breck	"	Nov. 14	Elias & Julia	Laborer	Medfield	Agusta, Me.
57	Sarah Ann Woodman	"	Nov. 14	William & Sarah	Farmer	Kennebunk, Me.	Conway
58	Georgeanna King	"	Nov. 16	George & Lucy Ann	Physician	Rochester	Middleboro
59	—— Whiting	M	Dec. 3	Wm. E. & Betsey Ann	Clerk	Franklin	Franklin
60	Fred Adelbert Adams	"	Dec. 14	James & Sarah	Farmer	Boston	Boston
61	George Wildes Metcalf	"	Dec. 18	Charles & Julia	Bonnet Presser	Wrentham	Franklin
62	—— Whiting	F	Dec. 19	Albert & Vesta	Boot Maker	Charlton	Strong, Me.

DATE OF BIRTH.	NAME (IF ANY.)	SEX.	NAME OF PARENTS.	OCCUPATION OF FATHER.	FATHER'S BIRTHPLACE.	MOTHER'S BIRTHPLACE.	Informant	When Regist'd
Jan. 2, 1848	*Henry Fisher Pond	M	Henry E. & Loueza B.	Clerk	Dedham	Newport, R. I.	H. E. Pond	1865 Jan. 13
Sept. 22, 1856	Frank Davis Pond	"	"	"	"	"	"	"
Mar. 4, 1861	Grace Sumner Pond	F	"	"	"	"	"	"
Sept. 25, 1858	Freddie Albert Carpenter	M	Chas. H. & Abbie A.	Bon't Blocker	Newfield, Me.	Cumberland, R.I.	C. H. C.	
							A. A. Russegue, Town Clerk.	
Apr. 24, 1842	Charles Edward Monroe	M	Charles D. & Emely	Painter	Shrewsbury, Mass	Walpole, Mass.		
							A. A. Russegue, T. Clerk.	

* Born in Wrentham.

Births Registered in Franklin, Norfolk County, during the Year 1858.—T. C. Hills, Registrar.

(Residence of Parents Franklin unless otherwise indicated.)

NO.	DATE OF BIRTH.	NAME (IF ANY.)	SEX.	NAME OF PARENTS.	OCCUPATION OF FATHER.	FATHER'S BIRTHPLACE.	MOTHER'S BIRTHPLACE.
	1858						
1	Jan. 11	Dennis Sullivan	M	Dennis & Margaret	Laborer	Ireland	Ireland
2	Jan. 12	Charles Partridge Adams	"	Albert & Susan	Farmer	Franklin	Windsor, Vt.
3	Feb. 24	Arthur Addison Pond	"	Addison & Eliza	"	"	Brewster
4	Feb. 26	Ellen Sheen	F	John & Hannah	Laborer	Ireland	Ireland
5	March 21	Arlon Alonzo Ballou	M	Barton & Phila	Carpenter.	Pelham	Cumberland, R. I.
6	March 30	James Edward Newell	"	Albert & Mary	Bon't Presser	Cumberland, R. I.	Waterford
7	April 8	Edith Morse	F	Thomas & Elizabeth	Boot Maker	Framingham	Goshen, N. H.
8	April 15	Ellen Murphy	"	John & Eliza	Farmer	Ireland	Ireland
9	May 7	Herbert Whiting Thayer	M	Davis & Mary, Jr.	Merchant	Franklin	Franklin
10	May 9	Ida Elizabeth Hartshorn	F	George & Ellen	Laborer	"	"
11	May 16	James Wales	"	John & Adelaide	Farmer	"	"
12	May 17	Edna Jane Ware	"	Benja. B. & Sally	Laborer	Wrentham	Easton
13	May 20	Elizabeth E. Cook	"	S. Smith & Emeline	Bon't Presser	Franklin	Wrentham
14	June 1	Olive Miller	"	Hermon B. & Mary	Farmer	"	Franklin
15	June 4	Richard Elbridge Gurney	M	Wm. & Louisa	"	Providence, R. I.	Medway
16	June 15	Medora Anne Daniels	F	Mancy & Harriett	"	Blackstone	Franklin
17	June 18	Catherine Sullivan	"	John & Ellen	Laborer	Ireland	Ireland
18	June 27	Charlotte Levina Miller	"	Gilmore & Sarah	Farmer	Franklin	Newbury, Me.
19	June 30	Ella Brown	"	Albert & Addeline	Bon't Presser	Wrentham	Wrentham
20	July 10	Cora Marion Adams	"	James & Lydia	Farmer	Boston	Boston
21	July 19	Julia Thompson	"	George & Joanna	Boot Maker	Sumner, Me.	Swanzey
22	July 19	{ Ada Marinda Guild	"	James & Lucena	"	Wrentham	Sag Harbor
23	July 19	{ Ida Malinda Guild	"	James & Lucena	"	"	"
24	July 24	Sarah Nellie Corbin	"	Nelson & Nancy	Mason	Wrentham	Wrentham
25	Aug. 1	Jeremiah Desmond	M	Jeremiah & Mary	Laborer	Ireland	Ireland
26	Aug. 5	Annie Mary Gilmore	F	Gilbert H. & Elizabeth	Mason	Franklin	Pittsfield, N. H.
27	Aug. 12	Frank Earnest Cleveland	M	Lowell B. & Melinda	Carpenter	Scotland	Sutton
28	Aug. 12	Hellen Joanna Davidson	F	Wm. & Elizabeth	Dyer	Mendon	England
29	Aug. 22	Jennette F. Freeman	"	James & Mary	Boot Manuf.	Matuchen, N. J.	Kingston, R. I.
30	Aug. 24	Carrie Elizabeth Conger	"	Craig M. & Jane	Carpenter	Benson, Vt.	Framingham
31	Sept. 3	Willie Alpheus Russegue	M	Alpheus A. & Mary	Merchant		Whiting, Vt.

Births Registered in Franklin, Norfolk County, during the Year 1858.—(Continued.)

No.	DATE OF BIRTH.	NAME (IF ANY.)	SEX	NAME OF PARENTS.	OCCUPATION OF FATHER.	FATHER'S BIRTHPLACE.	MOTHER'S BIRTHPLACE.
	1858						
32	Sept. 7	Sarah Emeline Metcalf	F	Erasmus B. & Ann	Farmer	Franklin	England
33	Sept. 8	James McFarland	M	Hugh & Celia	Laborer	Ireland	Ireland
34	Sept. 19	—— Fisher	F	Gilbert & Emely	Teamster	Franklin	Walpole
35	Sept. 23	Florabelle Crosley	"	Reuben & Mary	Stable Keeper	Franklin	Franklin
36	Oct. 2	—— Wadsworth	"	Joseph H. & Abby	Merchant	"	"
37	Oct. 23	—— Metcalf	"	Saml. & Eliza J.	Clerk	"	"
38	Oct. 23	—— Metcalf	"	Saml. & Eliza J.	"	"	"
39	Oct. 25	Jennie Elizabeth Hills	"	Sanford & Mary	Don't Presser	Franklin	Alstead, N. H.
40	Oct. 30	George Marshall Fisher	M	Marshall & Ellen	"	"	Cumberland, R. I.
41	Oct. 30	Merry Bay Scott	F	Charles & Amanda	Blacksmith	Wrentham	Franklin
42	Nov. 2	Timothy Holferin	M	Timothy & Joanna	Laborer	Ireland	Ireland
43	Dec. 4	Lucella Frances Farr	F	Parker A. & Abby	Don't Presser	Chesterfield, N.H.	Cumberland, R. I.
44	Dec. 14	Nellie M. Wolford	"	Wm. & Martha	Farmer	England	Framingham
45	Dec. 25	—— Marston	M	James & Beulah	Carpenter	Newfield, Me.	Peru, Me.
46	Dec. 31	Bessie M. Blake	F	Oramel B. & Grace	Boot Maker	Franklin	Brookville, Me.
	Feb. 22	Ellen Maria Adams	"	Wm. W. & Mary A.			——, Me.

Births Registered in Franklin, Norfolk County, Mass., during the Year 1859.

No.	DATE OF BIRTH.	NAME (IF ANY.)	SEX	NAME OF PARENTS.	OCCUPATION OF FATHER.	FATHER'S BIRTHPLACE.	MOTHER'S BIRTHPLACE.
	1859						
1	Jan. 3	George N. Salley	M	James & Susan	Boot Maker	Mexico, Me.	Franklin
2	Jan. 6	Marcellas Woodward	"	Marcellas & Sarah	Teacher	Whitefield, Me.	
3	Jan. 31	Nathan Amos Staples	"	Amos & Eliza	Farmer	Cumberland, R. I.	Wrentham
4	Feb. 11	Emily Frances Morse	F	Munroe & Emely	Don't Presser	Framingham	Goshen, N. H.
5	Feb. 11	Ellen Frances Adams	"	Asa & Olive	Boot Maker	Bellingham	New York
6	Feb. 13	Adelbert Morris Thomas	M	James & Elizabeth	Don't Presser	England	England
7	Feb. 14	Charles Gay	"	Henry & Marion	Clerk	Franklin	Haverhill, N. H.
8	Feb. 18	Madora Chamberlain	F	Lucius & Bethiah	Boot Maker	Coventry, Ct.	Harwich
9	Feb. 20	Edward Francis Daniels	M	Wheaton & Harriett	Farmer	Franklin	Franklin
10	March 8	Herbert Eugene Bartlett	"	Wm. & Adeline	Boot Maker	Attleborough	"
11	March 8	Charles Walter Laing	"	Robert & Nancy	Tailor	Halifax, N. S.	New Braintree
12	March 15	Charlene Daniels	F	Amos & Lucretia	Farmer	Franklin	Buckley
13	March 18	Mary Ann Corbett	"	John & Ann	Boot Maker	Ireland	Ireland

Births Registered in Franklin, Norfolk County, Mass., during the Year 1859.—(Continued.)

No.	DATE OF BIRTH.	NAME (IF ANY.)	SEX.	NAME OF PARENTS.	OCCUPATION OF FATHER.	FATHER'S BIRTHPLACE.	MOTHER'S BIRTHPLACE.
	1859						
14	March 31	Charles G. Lincoln	M	Russell & Deborah	Laborer	Franklin	Howe, Me.
15	April 5	Wm. Henry Greene	"	Nelson & Mary A.	"	Wrentham	England
16	April 16	George B. Remick	"	Wm. & Catherine	Boot Maker	Green, Me.	Ireland
17	May 1	Eleanor Jennetie Clark	F	Asa & Havilla	"	Medway	Cleyton, N. Y.
18	May 3	Susan Follen	"	Thomas & Ellen	Laborer	Ireland	Ireland
19	May 5	Elisha Joseph Harris	M	Elisha & Betsey	"	Burrillville, R. I.	Norton
20	May 21	Ellis Gilmore	"	Wm. D. & Harriet	Bon't Presser	Franklin	Wrentham
21	May 27	Harriet Eliza Morse	F	Aaron H. & Deborah	Bt. Manuf.	Framingham	Franklin
22	May 29	Austin Metcalf Baker	M	Erastus E. & Abby	Farmer	Franklin	"
23	May 28	—— McCue	"	Patrick & Bridget	Laborer	Franklin	"
24	June 10	Wm. Crowningshield	"	James & Hannah	Farmer	Ireland	Ireland
25	June 16	Susan E. Young	F	Wm. & Mary	Laborer	Cumberland, R. I.	Wrentham
26	June 17	Addison Richard Thayer	M	Wm. M. & Rebecca	Clergyman	Attleboro	New Brunswick
27	June 18	Adelbert Wales	"	Wm. & Julia	Farmer	Franklin	Dover
28	June 23	Lillian A. Paine	F	Stephen & Sarah	Carpenter	Burrillville, R. I.	Bellingham
29	July 10	Ellen Josephine Hartshorn	"	George & Ellen	Laborer	Franklin	Cumberland, R. I.
30	July 23	Catherine Murphy	"	Patrick & Ann		Ireland	Franklin
31	Aug. 7	William E. King	M	George & Lucy Ann	Physician	Rochester	Ireland
32	Aug. 8	—— Hill	F	Lewis & Harriet	Box Maker	Elmon, Vt.	Middleborough
33	Aug. 9	Walter Earnest Jorden	M	George A. & Sarah	Carpenter	Coventry, R. I.	Bellingham
34	Aug. 10	George Anna Dean	F	George & Ellen	Boot Maker	Franklin	Utica, N. Y.
35	Sept. 2	Evelyn E. Hilton	"	Wm. & Betsey	"	Acton	Franklin
36	Sept. 7	Jesse Darling	M	Jesse & Mary	"	Cleyton, N. Y.	Bellingham
37	Sept. 11	John Riadon	"	John & Joanna	Laborer	Ireland	Ireland
38	Sept. 21	William Teehan	"	Michael & Julia	"	Brookfield	"
39	Sept. 23	Frederic Clarence Clark	"	Wm. & Ellen	Boot Maker	Medway	Franklin
40	Sept. 29	Maybelle Morse	F	Albert & Jennie	Bon't Presser	Franklin	Essex, Ct.
41	Sept. 29	Cora Jane Daniels	"	Nahum & Silvia A.	Farmer	Blackstone	Blackstone
42	Oct. 1	Mary C. Clark	"	Joseph & Elizabeth	"	Franklin	Attleborough
43	Oct. 1	Thomas Hollihan	M	John & Margarett	Laborer	Ireland	Ireland
44	Oct. 2	Archabald Robinson	"	George & Jane	Painter	"	Scotland
45	Oct. 6	—— Whiting	"	Peter & Lydia	Farmer	Franklin	Norton
46	Oct. 9	Willie Austin Cotton	"	Daniel C. & Abby	Tin Manuf.	Holden, N. H.	Wareham

Births Registered in Franklin, Norfolk County, Mass., during the Year 1859.—(Continued.)

NO.	DATE OF BIRTH.	NAME (IF ANY.)	SEX	NAME OF PARENTS.	OCCUPATION OF FATHER.	FATHER'S BIRTHPLACE.	MOTHER'S BIRTHPLACE.
	1859						
47	Oct. 13	Rolla Williams	M	Lewis & Huldah	Boot Maker	Wrentham	Mendon
48	Oct. 18	Maud Louise Richardson	F	Albert & Louisa	Reporter	Franklin	Warehouse Point, Ct.
49	Oct. 22	—— Fuller	"	Wm. & Mira	Stable Keeper	Medway	Upton
50	Nov. 3	Olive Sanford Daniels	M	Maney & Harriet	Farmer	Blackstone	Franklin
51	Nov. 11	Daniel Warren Taft	"	Daniel F. & Ann Eliza	Laborer	Uxbridge	Mendon
52	Nov. 14	—— Whiting	F	Joseph M. & Clarissa	Box Maker	Franklin	Norton
53	Nov. 15	Agnez Cook	"	Lucian & Sarah	Boot Maker	Cumberland, R. I.	Sherborn
54	Nov. 21	—— Hill	M	Wm. & Susan	"	Franklin	Foxboro
55	Nov. 30	—— Daniels	"	Waldo & Ellen	Teacher		Walpole
56	Dec. 5	Abby Howard	F	Appollas & Caroline	Farmer	Bridgewater	Lynn, N. H.
57	Dec. 7	—— Smith*	M	J. Warren Smith & Maria Menard	Clerk	Boston	Blue Hill, Me.
58	Dec. 12	Ellen Laura Wiggin	F	Shepherd & Almira	Box Maker	Wolfsboro	Franklin

* Stillborn.

Births Registered in the Town of Franklin during the Year 1860.—T. C. Hills, Registrar.

NO.	DATE OF BIRTH.	NAME (IF ANY.)	SEX	NAME OF PARENTS.	MAIDEN NAME OF MOTHER.	OCCUPATION OF FATHER.	FATHER'S BIRTHPLACE.	MOTHER'S BIRTHPLACE.
	1860							
1	Jan. 2	Georgeda Idella Adams	F	Gardner & Eunice	Darling	Clerk	Franklin	Cumberland, R.I.
2	Jan. 11	Michael Henry Sullivan	M	Dennis & Margaret	Mitchell	Laborer	Ireland	Ireland
3	Jan. 20	Irene Millard Pike	F	Alonzo G. & Martha T.	Cram	Farmer	Wilmington	Boston
4	Jan. 27	Michael Edward Shay	M	Michael & Ably	Sullivan	Laborer	Ireland	Ireland
5	Feb. 25	Mary Isabelle O'Riley	F	James & Mary	Williams	"	"	Scotland
6	March 2	Frederic Weston Joslin	M	John & Elizabeth	Foster	Spinner	Cumberland, R.I.	Plainfield, N. J.
7	April 5	Fred Holbrook Greene	"	Henry M. & Maggie M.	Webster	Bon't Manuf.	Franklin	Franklin
8	April 7	Erastus Lovell Metcalf	"	Otis F. & Lucy M.	Daniels	Carpenter	"	Hadley
9	April 7	Mabel Harriet Morse	F	Bradford L. & Evelyn S.	Blake	Bon't Presser	"	Attleboro
10	April 9	Gracie Mary Emerson	"	Elias P. & Mary S.	Balcom	Carpenter	Dedham	Cumberland, R.I.
11	April 14	Charles Henry Partridge	M	George I. & Harriet	Hancock	Boot Maker	Franklin	Walpole
12	April 19	Susan Fisher DeWitt	F	Alexd. F. & Martha E.	Jillett	Tailor	"	

Births Registered in the Town of Franklin during the Year 1860.—(Continued.)

NO.	DATE OF BIRTH.	NAME (IF ANY.)	SEX	NAME OF PARENTS.	MAIDEN NAME OF MOTHER.	OCCUPATION OF FATHER.	FATHER'S BIRTHPLACE.	MOTHER'S BIRTHPLACE.
	1860							
13	April 20	Winnie McCue	F	Patrick & Bridget	McAlister	Farmer	Ireland	Ireland
14	April 28	John Dennie	M	Michael & Sarah	Devoy	Shoe Maker	"	Franklin
15	April 28	——Day*	"	Joseph & Elsie	Woodward	Bon't Presser	Paxton	Windsor, Vt.
16	May 2	Susie Merrill Adams	F	Albert & Susan	White	Farmer	Franklin	Westboro
17	May 6	Willard Lincoln Wilkinson.	M	Willard B. & Fanny	Green	Boot Maker	Cumberland, R.I.	Ireland
18	May 8	Ellen Connolly	F	Patrick & Mary	Slattery	Farmer	Ireland	Douglas
19	May 9	Walter Leroy Nason	M	Wm. E. & Mary J.	Albee	"	Franklin	Franklin
20	May 17	Charles Francis Nye	"	Cleb T. & Sophia B.	Cleveland	Merchant	New Braintree	England
21	May 28	Josephene Fletcher	F	Joseph & Ann	Marshall	Weaver	England	Ireland
22	June 4	Eliza Jane Sullivan	"	Wm. & Bridget	Gellon	Farmer	Ireland	Franklin
23	June 7	Jessie Harriet Benson	"	Stephen & Lizzie	Scott	Clerk	Mendon	Ireland
24	June 15	Francis Buckley	M	Daniel & Julia	Fitz Jerald	Laborer	Ireland	
25	June 16	James Haggarty	"	Patrick & Mary	Meenine	"	"	Franklin
26	June 20	Arthur Leslie Ruggles	"	Albion L. & Martha L.	Gilmore	Tinsmith	Medway	Goshen, N. H.
27	June 27	Mabel Ermina Morse	F	Thomas D. & Sarah E.	Lewis	Bon't Presser	Natick	Franklin
28	July 2	Welton Adelbert Pond	M	Eliab M. & Isabella I.	Lawrence	Farmer	Franklin	"
29	July 4	Albert William Rockwood†	"	Wm. & Matilda	Blake	"	"	Ireland
30	July 24	Margaret Hollerin	F	Timothy & Margaret	Warren	Laborer	Ireland	Grafton
31	July 29	Lillie Agusta Mitchell	"	C. L. & Sarah G.		Bon't Manuf.	Sangerville, Me.	Medway
32	July 30	Paul Eugene Gurney	M	Wm. A. & Louise M.	Adams	Farmer	Providence, R. I.	Waine, Me.
33	Aug. 2	Alice Metcalf	F	Chas. A. & Elizabeth	Hight	Bon't Presser	Winthrop, Me.	Ireland
34	Aug. 3	Jeremiah McCarty	M	Eugene & Mary	McCarty	Farmer	Ireland	Holliston
35	Aug. 4	Estella Maria Paine	F	Adin B. & Cynthia L.	Eames	Boot Maker	Bellingham	
36	Aug. 13	Arthur Warren Kilburne	M	Warren A. & Mary A.	Black	Bon't Presser	Shrewsbury	
37	Aug. 16	Lydia Thompson Cook	F	Messena A. & Louise A.	Newell	Boot Maker	Wrentham	Cumberland, R.I.
38	Aug. 17	Cora Isabelle Cleveland	"	Lowell B. & Melinda S.	Metcalf	Bon't Br'k Maker	Franklin	Douglas
39	Aug. 25	John Larkin	M	John & Mary	Dorcey	Farmer	Ireland	Ireland
40	Aug. 26	Flora Augusta Blake	F	Albert A. & Rowena A.	Morrill	"	Franklin	Newport, Me.
41	Aug. 28	Michael Murphy	M	John & Eliza	Hickey	Bon't Presser	Ireland	Ireland
42	Sept. 1	Charles Henry Jorden	"	Henry A. & Josephene S.	Guild	Painter	Franklin	Foxboro
43	Sept. 7	Seth Albert Blake	"	Seth & Mary J.	Emerson	Farmer	Dover	Conway, N. H.
44	Sept. 21	Joanna Desmond	F	Jereh. & Catherine	Warren	"	Ireland	Ireland
45	Sept. 24	Sarah Marcella Woodward	"	Marcellas & Sarah A.	Ware	Teacher	Whitefield, Me.	Franklin

* Stillborn.   † Should read Elbert William Rockwood.

Births Registered in the Town of Franklin during the Year 1860.—(Continued.)

NO.	DATE OF BIRTH.	NAME (IF ANY.)	SEX	NAME OF PARENTS.	MAIDEN NAME OF MOTHER.	OCCUPATION OF FATHER.	FATHER'S BIRTHPLACE.	MOTHER'S BIRTHPLACE.
	1860							
46	Sept. 30	Philip Hews McParland	M	Hugh & Celia M.	Doherty	Laborer	Ireland	Ireland
47	Oct. 1	Frank Smith	"	Calvin & Nettie S.	Stearns	Clerk	Dorchester	Killingly, Ct.
48	Oct. 13	Elizabeth Sarah Davidson	F	Wm. E. & Elizabeth		Dyer	Scotland	England
49	Oct. 21	—— Hill	"	Albert H. & Charlotte A.	White	Boot Maker	Bellingham	Franklin
50	Nov. 18	Ada Frances Corbin	"	Otis & Julia	West	Farmer	Attleboro	Wrentham
51	Dec. 12	Mary Alice Robinson	"	Robert & Eunice		Carpenter	Ireland	Newburyport
52	Dec. 13	Josephene Gilbert Knapp	"	Gilbert G. & Lucinda	Godard	Bo't Manuf.	Franklin	Athol
53	Dec. 31	Ernest Eugene Hubbard	M	Sabin & Almira	Sargeant	Carpenter		Hubbardston

Births Registered in the Town of Franklin, Norfolk County, Mass., during the Year 1861.—T. C. Hills, Registrar.

NO.	DATE OF BIRTH.	NAME (IF ANY.)	SEX	NAME OF PARENTS.	MAIDEN NAME OF MOTHER.	OCCUPATION OF FATHER.	FATHER'S BIRTHPLACE.	MOTHER'S BIRTHPLACE.
	1861							
1	Jan. 1	Earnest Munroe Morse	M	M. Munroe & Emely F.	Lewis	Don't Presser	Natick	Goshen, N. H.
2	Jan. 14	Mitty Sarah Joselyn	F	Adam & Mary E.	Billings	Boot Maker	Cumberland, R.I.	Thompson, Ct.
3	Jan. 20	William Warren Hill	M	Isaac & Marrion	Abbe	Box Maker	Montpelier, Vt.	Milford
4	Jan. 21	Mary Martha Pond	F	Addison M. & Eliza A.	Small	Farmer	Franklin	Brewster
5	Feb. 1	Welcom Farnum Adams	M	Lyman & Sarah E.	Tolman	Soldier	Bellingham	Foxboro
6	Feb. 7	Elroy Wales Rockwood	"	Erastus D. & Abby O.	Wales	Farmer	Franklin	Franklin
7	Feb. 12	Ada Louise Corbin	F	Nelson & Nancy M.	Ruggles	Mason	Dudley	Wrentham
8	March 2	Nellie Carrie Grow	"	Nathl. S. & Jane	Whiting	Laborer	Hartford, Ct.	Franklin
9	March 8	Fred Edwin Pond	M	Edwin J. & Emely V.	Potter	Music Teacher	Franklin	Providence, R. I.
10	March 9	Elmer Ellsworth Wales	"	Davis & Adelaide B.	Whiting	Farmer	"	Franklin
11	March 20	Nellie Adelaide Daniels	F	Mahlon M. & Sylvia A.	Alexander	"		Mendon
12	March 20	—— Robinson*	M	John K. & Mary E.	Clark	Painter	Mendon	Middleboro
13	March 28	Wm. Henry Adams	"	Wm. W. & Mary A.	Wood	Boot Maker	Ireland	Bucksport, Me.
14	April 17	Joseph Wadsworth	"	Joseph H. & Abigail L.	Metcalf	Merchant	Franklin	Franklin
15	May 3	James Henry Garvin	"	James & Ellen	Fitzgerald	Laborer		Ireland
16	May 19	Julia Gracie Evelyn Springer	F	Wm. A. & Julia	Breck	Boot Maker	Ireland	Springfield, Me.
17	May 20	Ellen Eliza Cook	"	Abner & Julia V.	Cook	Farmer	Augusta, Me.	Bellingham
18	May 21	Abner James Colvin	M	Henry J. & Lydia O.	Fisk	Carder	Franklin	Thompson, Ct.
19	June 20	—— Lincoln†	"	Wm. R. & Deborah	Tracy	Don't Presser	Blackstone	Rome, Me.

* Stillborn. † Stillborn.

Births Registered in the Town of Franklin, Norfolk County, Mass., during the Year 1861.—(Continued.)

NO.	DATE OF BIRTH.	NAME (IF ANY.)	SEX	NAME OF PARENTS.	MAIDEN NAME OF MOTHER.	OCCUPATION OF FATHER.	FATHER'S BIRTHPLACE.	MOTHER'S BIRTHPLACE.
	1861							
20	June 29	Michael Murphy	M	Patrick & Ann	Hamlin	Laborer	Ireland	Ireland
21	July 1	Daniel Sullivan	"	Michael & Margaret	Shay	"	"	"
22	July 6	Ellen Hullihan	F	John & Margaret	McCarty	"	"	"
23	July 10	Jeremiah Reardon	M	John & Ann	Warren	"	"	"
24	July 11	Edith Martha Grant	F	Joseph & Sarah C.	Comstock	Farmer	Cumberland, R.I.	Wrentham
25	July 20	John James Corbett	M	John and Ann	O'Gara	"	Ireland	Ireland
26	July 24	Phillip Jones	"	Wm. C. & Catherine	Owens	"	Green, Me.	"
27	July 30	Cornelius Shehan	"	John & Harmora	Cornelly	Laborer	Ireland	"
28	Oct. 5	Alden Mann	"	Wm. & Sarah B.	Metcalf	Farmer	Chesterfield, N.H.	Winthrop, Me.
29	Aug. 10	Lucy Ann Hill	F	Robert R. & Lucy A.	Adams	Nail Maker	Providence, R.I.	Franklin
30	Aug. 19	Elmor Ellsworth Crossley	M	Reuben & Mary F.	Hills	Stable Keeper	Tarriffville, Ct.	"
31	Aug. 24	Anna Maria Daniels	F	Mancy & Harriet	Baker	Farmer	Blackstone	"
32	Aug. 24	Laura Emely Blake	"	Oramel B. & Grace F.	Shepardson	Carpenter	Franklin	Brooksville, Me.
33	Aug. 31	Lucy Rachael Bartlett	"	Wm. A. & Harriet A.	Daniels	Farmer	Attleboro	Franklin
34	Sept. 22	Jane Stewart	"	Robert D. & Martha	Hood	Wheelwright	Nova Scotia	Nova Scotia
35	Sept. 25	John Elmer Ogden	M	John E. & Louise B.	Gilmore	Soldier	Seekonk	Franklin
36	Oct. 5	Margaret Lizzie Sullivan	F	John & Elizabeth	Nanglon	Laborer	Ireland	Ireland
37	Oct. 7	Caroline Cook	"	Milton & Louise	Cook	Farmer	Franklin	Bellingham
38	Oct. 15	Alfred Farrington Gilmore	M	Wm. D. & Harriet M.	Farrington	Don't Presser	"	Wrentham
39	Oct. 17	John Coughlin	"	Daniel & Margaret	Skenecks	Laborer	Ireland	Ireland
40	Oct. 17	Charles Fisher	"	Gilbert C. & Emely J.	Keith	Farmer	Franklin	Walpole
41	Nov. 1	—— DeWitt	"	Horace S. & Harriet E.	Alby	Stabler	"	Bucksport, Me.
42	Nov. 6	Aldis Maxey Allen	"	C. Milton & Sarah M.	Williams	*.*	"	Southboro
43	Nov. 12	—— Whiting	F	Daniel P. & Lydia A.	Briggs	Farmer	"	Norton
44	Nov. 22	—— Hill	M	William & Susan A.	White	"	"	Foxboro
45	Dec. 6	—— Metcalf	"	Sam'l. W. & Eliza J.	Partridge	Clerk	Wrentham	Franklin
46	Dec. 20	—— Harris	"	Elisha R. & Betsey	Shepardson	Farmer	Burrillville, R.I.	Norton
47	Dec. 22	—— Wales	F	Wm. H. & Julia A.	Bosworth	"	Franklin	Pelham
48	Dec. 26	—— Gilmore	"	James P. & Hannah	Thompson	Don't Presser	"	Wrentham
49	Dec. 30	—— Guild	M	Wm. H. & Mary A.	Ware	Laborer	"	Medway

. Don't Frame Maker.

Births Registered in the Town of Franklin, Norfolk County, Mass., during the Year 1862.

NO.	DATE OF BIRTH.	NAME (IF ANY.)	SEX.	NAME OF PARENTS.	OCCUPATION OF FATHER.	FATHER'S BIRTHPLACE.	MOTHER'S BIRTHPLACE.	INFORMANT.
	1862							
1	Jan. 2	Aider A. Pond	F	Eliab M. & Isebella I.	Farmer	Franklin	Franklin	Father
2	Jan. 21	Annie Laurie Adams	"	Erastus & Mary G.	Painter	"	Dumbarton, Vt.	"
3	Feb. 20	Joseph Emerson Clark	M	Joseph W. & Elizabeth C.	Machinest	"	Attleborough	"
4	Feb. 12	Ada Lousea Adams	F	William G. & Lillian A.			Salem, N. H.	Grandfather
5	Feb. 2	Ada E. Dean	"	George W. & Ellen E.		Boston	Franklin	Father
6	March 5	Mary Ann Dolan	"	John & Elizabeth	Boot Maker	Franklin	Ireland	"
7	March 5	Mary Eliza Thayer	"	Davis, Jr. & Mary M.	Manufacturer	Ireland	Franklin	"
8	April 29	Harict Gilmore Miller	"	Gilmore & Sarah F.	Farmer	Franklin	Newburg, Me.	Father
9	May 1	Emma Francis Sullivan	"	Dennis & Margaret	Laborer		Ireland	"
10	May 15	Lydia Ballou Brown	"	Leonard & Meheta	Farmer	Ireland	Wrentham	"
11	May 24	Bradly Mortimer Rockwood	M	William & Laura M.	Sawyer	Cumberland	Franklin	"
12	May 29	Norman H. Briggs	"	Hiram E. & Deborah A.	Farmer	Franklin	Attleborough	"
13	June 3	Mary Leola Daniels	F	Lucius W. & Sarah H.		Mansfield	Franklin	"
14	June 6	Everett Marsh Green	M	Henry M. & Margaret M.	***	Franklin	Plainfield, N. J.	"
15	June 9	Ella Gertrude Nason	F	Jesse L. & Hellen M.	Grocery Clerk	"	Brewer, Me.	"
16	June 12	Patrick Connelly	M	Patrick & Mary	Farmer		Ireland	"
17	June 17	Thomas L. Hagerty	"	Patrick & Mary.	Laborer	Ireland	Dover, Mass.	
18	July 7	Emma Lucinda Thayer	F	Wm. M. & Rebecca W.	Clergyman	Franklin	England	"
19	July 16	Fanny Emely Davidson	"	William & Elizabeth	Dyer	Scotland	Franklin	"
20	Aug. 18	Burnside Winfield Scott	M	Charles H. & Amanda M.	Blacksmith	Wrentham	Cumberland, R.I.	
21	Aug. 27	Charles I. Hancock	"	Francis E. & Hannah M.	Boot Maker	Cumberland, R.I.	Ireland	
22	Sept. 9	Patrick Lennon	"	Thomas & Margarett	Laborer	Ireland	Southborough	
23	Sept. 13	Malon E. Wilkinson	"	Willard B. & Fanny S.	Boot Maker	Cumberland	Middleborough	"
24	Sept. 20	Frances Eddy King	F	George & Lucy Ann	Physician	Rochester, Mass.	Walpole	"
25	Sept. 23	Emeline Ann Gilmore	"	George R. & Emeline L.	Bon't Presser	Franklin	Franklin	"
26	Nov. 2	Ellis S. Lawrence	"	Willard S. & Elizabeth	Boot Maker	Milford	Appleton, Me.	
27	Nov. 7	——— Wadsworth	M	George M. & Emeline M.	Farmer	Franklin	Nova Scotia	"
28	Nov. 11	George Edwin Stewart	"	Robert B. & Martha	Wheelright	Nova Scotia	Killingly, Ct.	
29	Dec. 26	——— Smith	F	Calvin B. & Nettie S.	Bon't Blocker	Dorchester	Ireland	"
30	Nov. 20	Abby A. Foley	"	Thomas & Ellen	Farmer	Ireland	"	
31	Oct. 9	Margarett Clara Larkin	"	John & Mary	Laborer	"	"	

*** Straw Goods Manufacturer.

FRANKLIN TOWN RECORDS—BIRTHS.

Births Registered in the Town of Franklin, Norfolk County, Mass., during the Year 1862.—(Continued.)

NO.	DATE OF BIRTH.	NAME (IF ANY.)	SEX	NAME OF PARENTS.	OCCUPATION OF FATHER.	FATHER'S BIRTHPLACE.	MOTHER'S BIRTHPLACE.	INFORMANT.
32	Jan. 26	Albert Dean Richardson	M	Albert D. & Mary Eliza	Reporter	Franklin	Warehouse Point	
33	" 16	Charles Frederick Whiticker	"	James G. & Matilda D.	Carpenter	"	Wheelock	
34	June 9	Mabel E. Howard	F	Apollos W. & Caroline W.	Farmer	No. Bridgewater	Lime, N. H.	
35	March 22	Adie Congor	"	Craig M. & Jane M.	Carpenter	New Jersey	Westborough	
36	March 14	George Matherson Webb	M	Wm. H. & Hariet F.	Boot Maker	Easton	Dedham	
37	June 27	Julia Allice Fitzpatrick	F	John L. & Elizabeth A.	Marble Work'r	Ireland	Boston	
38	" 27	Anna M. Williams	"	Lewis F. & Huldah D.	Boot Maker	Wrentham	Mendon	
39	Sept. 21	Daniel Burkley	M	Daniel & Julia	Labourer	Ireland	Ireland	
40	Oct. 21	Mary Amanda Mills	F	Albert H. & Charlotte A.	Farmer	Bellingham	Franklin	
41	Nov. 25		"	Warren W. & Julia A.	Mason	Rehoboth	"	
42	Nov. 30	Anna Felce	"	Patsey & Hannah	Labourer	Ireland	Ireland	
43	Dec. 23	— Staples	M	Amos W. & E. Ellen	Farmer	Cumberland	Wrentham	
44	" 29, '51	William Isaac Perkins	"	Stover & Rachel	Laborer	Penobscot, Me.	Brooklyn, N. Y.	
45	Oct. 28, '58	Mary Darcy Larkin	F	John & Mary	"	Ireland	Ireland	
46	June 24, "	Charles Higgerty	M	Patrick & Mary	"	"	"	
47	Jun 10, "	Frank A. Everett	"	Alfred F. & Maria W.	Cordwainer	North Adams	Franklin	
48	Mar. 11, "	Elvira Ballou Brown	F	Leonard & Meheta B.	Franklin	Cumberland, R.I.	Wrentham	
49	May 6, '59	John James Stewart	M	Robert B. & Martha	Wheelright	Nova Scotia	Nova Scotia	
50	Feb. 28, '60	Hariet E. Staples	F	Amos W. & E. Ellen	Farmer	Cumberland, R.I.	Wrentham	
51	Apr. 23, '61	Ella Hills	"	Lewis W. & Hariet A.	Box Maker	Vermont		
52	Oct. 20, '61	Ellsworth Nahum Daniels	M	Thomas J. & Mary E.	Laborer	Franklin	Sharon	
53	Sep. 17, '61	Martha Fransena Woolford	F	Wm. & Martha	Farmer	England	Framingham	
54	July 2, '61	Wilton A. Pond	M	Eliab M. & Isabella L.	"	Franklin	Franklin	
55	Jan. 30, '61	Louesa Adelaid Metcalf	F	Alfred G. & Charlott A.				

Births Registered in Franklin in the Year 1863.—(The informants during the year 1863 were the parents.)

NO.	DATE OF BIRTH.	NAME (IF ANY.)	SEX	NAME OF PARENTS.	MAIDEN NAME OF MOTHER.	OCCUPATION OF FATHER.	FATHER'S BIRTHPLACE.	MOTHER'S BIRTHPLACE.
1	Nov. 17, '62	Jenny Parker Baker	F	Erastus E. & Abby M.	Bacon	Farmer	Franklin	Franklin
2	Dec. 14, '62	Celia McParland	"	Hugh & Celia	Doherty	Labourer	Ireland	Ireland

FRANKLIN TOWN RECORDS—BIRTHS.

Births Registered in Franklin in the Year 1863.—(Continued.)

No.	DATE OF BIRTH.	NAME (IF ANY.)	SEX	NAME OF PARENTS.	MAIDEN NAME OF MOTHER.	OCCUPATION OF FATHER.	FATHER'S BIRTHPLACE.	MOTHER'S BIRTHPLACE.
3	Dec. 27, '62	Walter Addison Staples	M	Amos W. & Ellen E.	Lawrence	Farmer	Cumberland, R.I.	Wrentham
4	Jan. 7, '63	George Alfred Eaton	"	George B. & Ellen M.	Daniels	Engineer	Boston	Medway
5	" 13, "	Eugene Ellsworth Everett	"	Alfred F. & Margette	Bullard	Boot Maker	Bennington, Vt.	Franklin
6	" 31, "	Harriet F. Sullivan	F	Wm. & Bridgett	Galon	Labourer	Ireland	Ireland
7	Feb. 4, "	Nannona Granger	"	George & Nelly	Coauny	"	"	Springfield
8	" 15, "	Estella Robler	"	Wm. H. & Aurelia	Adams	Machinist	New Brunswick	Winstead, Ct.
9	Feb. 26, "	George Anna Briggs	"	Richard A. & Ann Eliza	Joslyn	Labourer	Providence, R.I.	Ireland
10	" 27, "	Eugene McCarty	M	Eugene & Mary	"	Labor	Ireland	Franklin
11	Mar. 2, "	Arthur Orenzo Miller } Twins	"	Herman B. Mary W.	Wadsworth	Blacksmith	Franklin	
12	" "	& Alice Oretia do.	F					
13	" 18, "	Carrie Matilda Hills	"	Frank S. & Martha E.	Lincoln	Bon't Presser	Medway	Washington, Me.
14	" 19, "	Lyons B. Condon	M	Benjamin & Milly	Harding	Boot Cutter	Northbridge	Yarmouth, N.S.
15	" 28, "	Walter Elmer Daniels	"	Maury M. & Hariet N.	Baker	Farmer	Blackstone	Franklin
16	April 7, "	Jeremiah Hodherin	"	Timothy & Joanna	Warren	"	Ireland	Ireland
17	" 8, "	—— Hulihan	F	John & Margaret	McCarty	Labourer	"	Wrentham
18	" 8, "	Lucy Maribel King	"	Wm. F. & Laura Ann	Lawrence	Farmer	Wrentham	Franklin
19	" 8, "	Frank Wheaton Daniels	M	Josephus W. & Hariet E.	King	"	Franklin	Bellingham
20	" 13, "	Ellis Levi Cook	"	Abner & Julia E.	Cook	"	Wrentham	Ireland
21	May 11, "	Margaret O. Riely	F	James & Margaret	Williams	Labourer	Ireland	Norton
22	" 23, "	Joseph F. Gifford	M	Milly A. & Julia F.	Ames	Farmer	Fall River	Ireland
23	June 10, "	Patrick Murphey	"	John & Eliza	Hickey	Carpenter	Ireland	Foxboro
24	" 26, "	Clarence Edmond Jordon	"	Henry A. & Josephine S.	Guild	Painter	Franklin	Conway, N.H.
25	July 9, "	Hattie Woodman	F	William & Sarah	Benison	Engineer	Kennebunk, Me.	Auburn
26	" 11, "	Lyman Henry Gibson	M	Amelius & Mary	Boyden	Boot Maker	Hopkinton	Ireland
27	" 28, "	Jesse Darling	"	Jesse & Mary	Meiee	Labourer	Clayton, N.Y.	
28	" 30, "	John Hews	"	Patrick & Lizzie	Tollan		Ireland	
29	" 31, "	Thomas Clarry	"	Michael K. & Mary	Loftus		"	
30	Aug. 17, "	Edward Allen Gilmore	"	Geo. H. & Martha J.	Bordon	Farmer	Providence	Hopkinton
31	Sept. 1, "	—— Fisher	"	Sewell & Angie M.	Blanchard		Franklin	Prospect, Me.
32	" 4, "	Edna Eliza Marsh	F	Lewis H. & Sophia	Robertson	Bo't Bleacher	Smithfield, R.I.	Roxbury, Vt.
33	" 15, "	—— Richardson	"	Albert D. & Mary L.	Pease	Reporter	Franklin	Warehouse Pt., Ct.
34	" 15, "	Flora Gertrude Hartshorn	"	George & Hellen	Pickering	Labourer	"	Franklin
35	Oct. 3, "	David Barrus	M	Charles A. & Marion W.	Coombs	Mariner	Boston	Bellingham

FRANKLIN TOWN RECORDS—BIRTHS. 75

Births Registered in Franklin in the Year 1863.—(Continued.)

NO.	DATE OF BIRTH.	NAME (IF ANY.)	SEX	NAME OF PARENTS.	MAIDEN NAME OF MOTHER.	OCCUPATION OF FATHER.	FATHER'S BIRTHPLACE.	MOTHER'S BIRTHPLACE.
36	Oct. 7	Frank Ellsworth Miller	M	Alonzo R. & Hannah E.	Cole	Boot Maker	Franklin	Beverly
37	" 7	Catherine Marion Riadon	F	John & Joanna	Warren	Labourer	Ireland	Ireland
38	" 9	Hattie Adelia Daniels	"	Lucius W. & S. Hellen	Warfield	Farmer	Franklin	Franklin
39	" 15	Ida Jane Adams	"	Charles H. & Lucinda	Stratton	Boot Maker	"	Sherburn
40	" 17	Mary Elizabeth Snida	"	Thomas & Jane	Calehan	Labourer	Ireland	Ireland
41	Nov. 15	Laura L. Pond	"	James H. & Mary Ann	Fisher	Wire Manuf.	Franklin	Franklin
42	Dec. 5	Minna Emeline Allen	"	Thomas B. & Martha M.	Metcalf	Farmer	"	"
43	" 9	John Ryon	M	Edmond & Mary	Haley	Labourer	Ireland	Ireland
44	" 10	Clark	"	Joseph W. & Caroline J.	Briggs	Machinist	Franklin	Attleboro
45	" 13	Emery Woolford	"	William & Martha	Stratton	Farmer	England	Framingham
46	" 26	Dugen	"	Daniel & Mary	Murry	Labourer	Bangor, Me.	Ireland
47	Nov. 3	Jenny Gilmore Hills	F	Joseph G. & Maryann B.	Gilmore	Trader	Monmonth, Me.	Franklin
	Apr.14 '57	Charles Edward Morrison	M	Seth & Sarah Maria	Barnard	Bon't Presser	Wrentham	Waldoboro, Me.
	Feb. 12 '63	John Murry Fisher		Weston & Margarett	Levenseller	Farmer	"	Medway
	June 1 '43	Lucia A. Stockbridge	F	Horatio J. & Ixta Ann	Kempton	"	Uxbridge	Uxbridge

Births Registered in Franklin, in the County of Norfolk, for the Year 1864.

NO.	DATE OF BIRTH.	NAME (IF ANY.)	SEX	NAME OF PARENTS.	OCCUPATION OF FATHER.	FATHER'S BIRTHPLACE.	MOTHER'S BIRTHPLACE.	INFORMANT.
	1864							
1	Jan. 24	Albert Erastus Rockwood	M	Edmond J. & Abbie W.	Teamster	Franklin	Bellingham	C. F. Daniels
2	Feb. 5	Ida Barton	F	Francis & Hannah	Laborer	Wrentham	Ireland	"
3	" 17	Nettie Metcalf Blake	"	Wm. A. & Eliza J.	Bootmaker	Franklin	Franklin	"
4	" 25	Ellen Maria Pond	"	Addison & Eliza	Farmer	"	Brewster	"
5	" 25	Patrick Francis Murphy	M	Patrick & Ann	Laborer	Ireland	Ireland	"
6	March 4	Mary Feely	F	Patrick & Hannah	"	"	"	"
7	March 31	Ella Hortense Carpenter	"	Chas. H. & Abbie A.	Bon't Blocker	Newfield, Me.	Cumberland, R.I.	"
8	April 5	Herbert Edmond Sally	M	James & Susan	Laborer	Mexico, Me.	Franklin	"
9	April 14	Walter Francis Blake	"	Oranel B. & Grace F.	Carpenter	Franklin	W. Brooksville, Me.	"
10	May 7	Frederic Nelson Cass	"	Anson & Charlotte	Laborer	Bellingham	Springfield, Ill.	"

Births Registered in Franklin, in the County of Norfolk, for the Year 1864.—(Continued.)

NO.	DATE OF BIRTH.	NAME (IF ANY.)	SEX	NAME OF PARENTS.	OCCUPATION OF FATHER.	FATHER'S BIRTHPLACE.	MOTHER'S BIRTHPLACE.	INFORMANT.
	1864							
11	May 20	Adelbert Hartwell Morse	M	Aaron H. & Deborah	Manufacturer	Worcester	Franklin	C. F. Daniels
12	" 25	Jane Elizabeth Davidson	F	William & Elizabeth	Dyer	Scotland	England	"
13	" 28	—— Hill	M	William & Susan	Boot Maker	Franklin	Foxboro	C. F. D.
14	June 4	—— Richardson	"	John W. & Almira	Farmer	"	Medway	"
15	" 12	Elmer Jerome Thayer	"	Lapeolate M. & Ellen	Cordwainer	Douglas	Nova Scotia	"
16	" 23	James Lemon	"	Thomas & Margarett	Laborer	Ireland	Ireland	"
17	" 30	Annie Leonora Crooks	F	Marcus D. & Angelia	Mechanic	Bellingham	Richmond, N. H.	"
18	July 11	Lyman Henry Gibson	M	Cornelius & Mary C.	Engineer	Hopkinton	Auburn	"
19	July 20	—— Adams	"	William G. & Lilian A.	Artist	Boston	Salem	"
20	" 22	James Buckley	"	Daniel & Julia	Laborer	Ireland	Ireland	"
21	" 25	Minnie Ann Remick	F	Wm. & Catherine	Boot Maker	Ireland	"	"
22	Aug. 3	Margarett Connelly	"	Patrick & Mary	Laborer	Gardner, Me.	"	"
23	" 8	Mary E. Conlin	"	Daniel & Ann	"	Ireland	"	"
24	" 12	Ida Bradon	"	Chas. & Marion	"	"	Milford	"
25	" 24	Hattie Mabel Cobb	"	Henry & Betey	"	Hopkinton	Yarmouth	"
26	Sept. 1	Ellen Lynch	"	Edward & Mary	Boot Maker	Mansfield	Ireland	"
27	" 3	Frederick Gorton	M	John A. & Emeline C.	Laborer	Ireland	Greenfield, N. H.	"
28	" 15	Mary Emmons Mann	F	William & Sarah B.	Farmer	Charlton	Windrop, Me.	"
29	Sept. '64	Freddie Albert Carpenter				Chesterfield, x.n.		
29	Oct. 6	—— Hood	"	James & Annett	Blacksmith	Nova Scotia	Canton	"
30	" 12	Josephine M. Claflin	"	James & Dorras	Boot Maker	Scotland	Nova Scotia	"
31	" 14	Eliza Jane Sullivan	"	Dennis & Margarett	Laborer	Ireland	Ireland	"
32	" 25	Franklin Everett Howard	M	Apollos & Caroline	Farmer	No. Bridgewater	Lime, N. H.	"
33	" 25	Margarett McParland	F	Hugh & Celia	Laborer	Ireland	Ireland	"
34	Nov. 2	—— King	"	Warren & Julia	Mason	Rehoboth	Franklin	"
35	Nov. 9	Lawrence H. Larkin	M	John & Mary	Laborer	Ireland	Ireland	"
36	" 13	Mary Elizabeth Smeedy	F	Thomas & Jane	"	"	"	"
37	" 17	—— Everett	M	Alfred F. & Maria W.	Boot Maker	Bennington, Vt.	Franklin	"
38	" 28	Marion Roseline Pierce	F	Ferdinand J. & Oceanna A.	Farmer	Franklin	Cumberland, R.I.	"
39	Dec. 13	Emery Woolford	M	Wm. & Martha	"	England	Framingham	"
40	" 22	—— Corlin	F	Otis & Julia Ann	"	Dudley	Rehoboth	"
41	" 29	—— King	M	George & Lucy Ann	Surgeon	Rochester	Middletown	"

* Born in Bellingham.

Births Registered in Franklin, in the County of Norfolk, for the Year 1865.—A. A. RUSSEGUE, Registrar.

NO.	DATE OF BIRTH.	NAME (IF ANY.)	SEX	NAME OF PARENTS.	OCCUPATION OF FATHER.	FATHER'S BIRTHPLACE.	MOTHER'S BIRTHPLACE.
	1865						
1	Jan. 4	Clara Anna Fairbanks	F	John L. & Eliza	Bon't Presser	Boston	Cumberland, R. I.
2	" 22	Matilda Gertrude Knapp	"	Gilbert C. & Lucinda	Farmer	Franklin	Athol
3	March 5	Charles Frances Hill	M	Isaac & Mariam	Box Maker	Montpelier, Vt.	Milford, Mass.
4	" 7	— Daniels	F	Mancy M. & Hariet N.	Farmer	Blackstone	Franklin
5	" 19	Walter Eugene Cook	M	Milton & Lonesa A.	"	Franklin	Bellingham
6	" 23	Frank Sherelin Hills	"	Joseph E. & Mary A. B.	Trader	Attleboro	Franklin
7	April 22	Carrie Howard Young	F	William S. & Mary	Farmer	No. Carolina	St. Johns, N. B.
8	" 22	Wynn	"	Wm. H. & Sarah J.	Painter	Franklin	Charlestown, Mass
9	May 6	Julian Burbank Bacon	"	Geo. W. & Julia	Farmer	Coventry, R. I.	Manchester, N. H.
10	" 12	Emma Frances Jordon	"	Douglass B. & Elizabeth G.	Laborer	Piermont, N. H.	Mendon, Mass.
11	" 31	John Alonzo Davis	M	John A. & Martha P.	Painter	Ireland	Haverhill, Mass.
12	June 9	Timothy Feely	"	Patrick & Hannah	Laborer	Maine	Ireland
13	July 9	Jennie C. Woodman	F	Wm. & Sarah	Painter	Wayland	So. Kenison
14	" 18	Lillian Frances Sherman	"	Edward H. & Clara H.	Straw Maker	Franklin	Wayland
15	" 29	Ernest Darwin Daniels	M	Lucius W. & S. Hellen	Farmer	"	Franklin
16	Aug. 7	Mabel Fisher	F	Marshall W. & Ellen F.	Bon't Maker	"	Cumberland, R. I.
17	" 14	Hariet Ada Sargent	"	Asa & Susan C.	Mechanic	"	Franklin
18	" 26	Jenny Lonsea Gilmore	"	William D. & Hariet M.	Carpenter	Greenfield, N. H.	Wrentham
19	" 29	Wm. H. Gould	M	Wm. H. & Nancy J.	Boot Maker	Ireland	Goshean, N. H.
20	Sept. 17	Michael S. Lavan	"	Michael & Hannah	Bon't Presser	"	Ireland
21	" 24	Minnie Mary Corbin	F	Daniel O. & Ann B.	"	Sea Conk	Franklin
22	April 2	Mary Blanchard Fisher	"	Sewell & Angie Maria	Farmer	Franklin	Prospect, Me.
23	Sept. 29	Willard Fisher Metcalf	M	John & Mary	"	E. Medway	Franklin
24	Oct. 11	John Collins Healy	"	Timothy J. & Catherine	Laborer	Ireland	Ireland
25	" 24	George Dean	"	Chas. L. & Adelaid C.	Machinest	Franklin	Boston
26	Nov. 9	Etta Amelia Barney Corbin	F	Henry E. & Caroline A.	Block Maker	Wrentham	Rehoboth
27	" 9	Lawrena Nigh Larkin	M	John & Mary	Farmer	Ireland	Ireland
28	" 3	Charlotte Abby Canney	F	Wm. N. & Mary A. B.	Dyer	Farmington, N. H.	Ireland
29	" 18	Bridget Sexton	"	John & Bridget	Harness Maker	Ireland	Wrentham
30	" 26	Walter Leroy Cass	M	Anson L. & Charlotte	Farmer	Richmond, N. H.	Ireland
31	" 30	Lizzie Anna Hood	F	James & Annette	Blacksmith	Pieta, Nova Scotia	Springfield, Ill.
32	Dec. 3	Emma Lonesa Franklin	"	Hartford H. & Julia E.	Farmer	Cumberland, R. I.	Canton, Mass.
33	" 11	Frank Gifford	M	Jtily A. & Matilda F.	Bon't Presser	Fall River	Taunton

Births Registered in Franklin, in the County of Norfolk, for the Year 1865.—(Continued.)

NO.	DATE OF BIRTH.	NAME (IF ANY.)	SEX.	NAME OF PARENTS.	OCCUPATION OF FATHER.	FATHER'S BIRTHPLACE.	MOTHER'S BIRTHPLACE.
	1865						
34	July 8	Peter McMann, Jr.	M	Peter & Margarett	Laborer	Ireland	Ireland
35	" 1	Myrtie Elmina Joslin	F	Adam & Mary E.	Boot Maker	Cumberland	Woodstock, Ct.
36	Sept. 30	Sarah Murphy	"	George & Ellen	Laborer	Ireland	Ireland
37	August 7	Martha Emma Walker	"	John H. & Emily J.	Clerk	Vermont	Wrentham

Births Registered in Franklin during the Year 1866.—A. A. RUSSEGUE, Registrar.

NO.	DATE OF BIRTH.	NAME (IF ANY.)	SEX.	NAME OF PARENTS.	OCCUPATION OF FATHER.	FATHER'S BIRTHPLACE.	MOTHER'S BIRTHPLACE.
	1866						
1	Dec. 9	Mabel Frances Nason	F	Albert D. & Ann F.	Travelling Agent	Franklin	Franklin
2	February 26	Millard Lincoln Farr	M	Parker R. & Abba F.	*	Westmoreland, N. H.	Cumberland, R. I.
3	Aug. 17	Elmer Lugene Morse	"	Granville & Catherine E.	Horseler	Franklin	Franklin
4	Jan. 2	Henry Pelton Fisher	"	Henry E. & Mary J.	†	Medway	Johnston, R. I.
5	April 30	Henry Edwin Young	"	William & Emely A.	Dyer	England	England
6	Oct. 23	Eliza Jane Fairbanks	F	David & Eliza A.	Carpenter	Jefferson, M. E.	Medway
7	July 17	Everett Lincoln Hubbard	M	Sabin & Almira S.		Franklin	Oxford
8	March 18	Annie Loweza Morse	F	Thos. D. & Sarah E.	Bonnet Presser	Franklin	Lempster, N. H.
9	October 3	Charles Bradley Blake	M	Oranel B. & Grace F.	Carpenter	Natick	West Brookville, Me.
10	May 21	Julius Thurston Rockwood	"	William & Laura M.	Trader	Franklin	Franklin
11	April 22	Anson Fisher Barton	"	Francis & Hannah	Mechanic	"	Ireland
12	Feb. 1	Frederick Palmer Chapman	"	Elisha P. & Elizabeth J.	Farmer	Wrentham	Oro Prato, Brazil
13	Feb. 20	Emma Grace Pierce	F	John E. & Hope T.	Bonnet Presser	Brooklyn, Conn.	Woonsocket
14	Jan. 16	Elizabeth Smith Bassett	"	Charles S. & Abbie G.	Straw Manuf.	Franklin	Phillipston
15	Feb. 13	Ella Jane White	"	Thomas S. & Sarah A.	Farmer	Barre	Franklin
16	Feb. 22	Sarah Jane Hancock	"	Francis E. & Hannah M.	Machinest	Mansfield	
17	Sept. 28	Elizabeth Ann Mann	"	Alexander & Hellen P.	Mason	Cumberland	
18	March 4	Patrick Ford	M	John & Celia	Farmer	Scotland	Scotland
19	July 15	Esther Matilda King	F	Warren & Julia A.	Mason	Ireland	Ireland
20	July 12	Phillip Doherity	M	William & Bridget	Laborer	Franklin	Franklin
21	April 29	Annie Maria Sullivan	F	Dennis & Margaret	Farmer	Ireland	Ireland
22	Sept. 19	Bertha Atwood Stockbridge	"	Frank M. & Emely A.	"	Cumberland	Cumberland
23	Dec. 5		M	Joseph H. & Abbie L.		Franklin	Franklin

* Hat & Bonnet Presser. † Hat & Bonnet Presser.

FRANKLIN TOWN RECORDS—BIRTHS.

Births Registered in Franklin during the Year 1866.—(Continued.)

No.	DATE OF BIRTH.	NAME (IF ANY.)	SEX.	NAME OF PARENTS.	OCCUPATION OF FATHER.	FATHER'S BIRTHPLACE.	MOTHER'S BIRTHPLACE.
24	July 18, 1866	Frank Ellsworth Gay	M	Frank B. & Mary A.	Farmer	Natick	St. Johns
25	March 10, "	Charles Sniddly	"	Thomas & Jane S.	Laborer	Ireland	Ireland
26	Sept. 13, "	Harriet Talcott Wyckoff	F	William A. & Ada L.	Clerk	Albany, N. Y.	Rockville, Conn.
27	March 25, "	William Eardon	M	John & Joanna	Laborer	Ireland	Ireland
28	Sept. 18, "	John Gorden	"	John & Susan	Boot Maker	"	"
29	Aug. 15, "	David Addison King	"	Wm. F. & Susan	Farmer	Wrentham	Wrentham
30	Dec. 12. "	Ella M. Thayer	F	Merick P. & Harriet H.	Boot maker	Douglass	Milford
31	Nov. 11, "	Margaret Lannon	"	Thomas & Margaret	Laborer	Ireland	Ireland
32	March 11, "	Cora Almira Briggs	"	Richard A. & Ann Eliza	"	Providence, R. I.	Franklin
33	Dec. 5, "	Daniel Buckley	M	John & Honorah	"	Ireland	Ireland
34	May 16, "	Mary Ann Sullivan	F	Daniel & Julia	"	"	"
35	Oct. 19, "	Manerva Ann Wales	"	Wm. H. & Julia A.	Farmer	Franklin	Franklin
36	Dec. 24, "	Clinton M. Clark	M	Wm. S. & Ellen M.	Boot Maker	Medway	"
37	Dec. 16, "	Arthur Llewellyn Lincoln	"	Wm. R. & Deborah D.	Bo n't Bleacher	Franklin	Rome, Me.
38	Aug. 1, "	Nellie Colburn Darling	F	Mayo C. & Susie A.	Butcher	Bellingham	Franklin
39	Aug. 26, 1863	Thomas Francis Ford	M	John & Celia	Farmer	Ireland	Ireland
40	April 14, 1858	Charles Edward Morrison	"	Seth & Maria	Laborer	Foxboro	Medway
41	Jan. 3, 1866	James Patrick Sulliven	"	William & Bridget	"	Ireland	Ireland
42	Aug. 14, "	Mary Ophelia Pelton	F	Geo. A. & Catherine S.	Clergyman	Stockbridge	Bromson
43	Jan. 11, "	Walter Lyman King	M	George & Lucy A.	Physician	Rochester	Middleboro
	Jan. 24, 1861	Frank Nelson Adams	"	Albin B. & Lydia A.	Boot Maker	Franklin	Newport, R. I.

Births Registered in Franklin, Norfolk County, in the Year 1867.—A. A. Resseure, Registrar.

No.	DATE OF BIRTH.	NAME (IF ANY.)	SEX.	NAME OF PARENTS.	OCCUPATION OF FATHER.	FATHER'S BIRTHPLACE.	MOTHER'S BIRTHPLACE.
1	Jan. 2, 1867	Henry Deforge	M	Eli & Rosele	Laborer	Canada	Canada
2	Jan. 6, "	Bessie Jane Cobb	F	Henry G. & Betcy T.	Carpenter	Easton	Yarmouth
3	Jan. 7, "	Mary Richardson	"	John W. & Elmira	Farmer	Franklin	Medway
4	Jan. 7, "	Bridget Scofield	"	Daniel & Bridget	Laborer	Ireland	Ireland
5	Jan. 21, "	Mary Lizzie Allen	"	Thomas B. & Martha M.	Farmer	Franklin	Franklin
6	" 23, See Below	Hartwell Adelbert Caswell	M	Andrew A. & Susan F.	Carpenter	Taunton	Milford
7	Jan. 26, 1867	Claracy Ann Robenson	F	James & Delia M.		Iowa	Hopkinton
8	Feb. 19, 1865	Martha Almira Shepard	"	Addison S. & Harriet M.	Farmer	Wrentham	Franklin

Births Registered in Franklin, Norfolk County, in the Year 1867.—(Continued.)

No.	DATE OF BIRTH.	NAME (IF ANY.)	SEX	NAME OF PARENTS.	OCCUPATION OF FATHER.	FATHER'S BIRTHPLACE.	MOTHER'S BIRTHPLACE.
9	Feb. 21, 1867	John Sherman Prue	M	Peter & Elizabeth E.	Boot Maker	Canada	Maine
10	March 9, 1866	Mary Jane Darling	F	Jesse & Mary		Clayton, N. Y.	Ireland
11	March 19, 1867	Catherine Sexton	"	John & Bridget	Laborer	Ireland	"
12	March 24, "	Ellen Frances Smiddy	"	Thomas & Jane	Harness Maker		
13	March 25, "	Lillian Frances Hill	"	William & Susan A.	Laborer		Foxboro
14	April 2, "	Emma Josephine Adams	"	Henry C. & Lydia A.	Farmer	Franklin	Newport, R. I.
15	April 7, "	Joanna Maria Feeley } Twins	"	Patrick & Hannah	Shoemaker	"	Ireland
16	April 7, "	Julia Maria Feeley }	"		Laborer	Ireland	"
17	April 10, "	John Thomas O'Brien	M	Thomas & Elizabeth L.	"	New Brunswick	New Brunswick
18	April 11, "	Franklin Dexter Pierce	"	John E. & Hope T.	Boot Maker	Franklin	Woonsocket, R. I.
19	April 18, "	George Edmond Rich	"	Lemuel F. & Margaret	Carpenter	Isoborough, Me.	Ireland
20	April 28, "	Lillian Mabel Witherell	F	Naaman W. & Carrie E.		Attleborough	Franklin
21	May 12, "	Hattie Mabel Turner	"	Thadus M. & Hattie E.	Merchant	Medfield	Sherborn
22	May 13, "	Harriett Eliza Bassett	"	Chas. S. & Abby G.	Straw Manuf.	Barre	Phillipstown
23	May 21, "	Frank Herbert Fisher	M	Gilbert C. & Emilie J.	Expressman	Franklin	Walpole
24	May 22, "	James Crowley	"	Cornelius & Rosana	Boot Maker	Ireland	New York
25	May 26, "	Sarah Ellen Colgan	F	John & Catherine	Laborer	"	Ireland
26	May 31, "	Bridget McParland	"	Hugh & Celia	"	"	"
27	June 3, "	Timothy Lynch	M	Edward & M.	"	"	"
28	June 6, "	Eva Augusta Corbin	F	Sylvanus & Clara A.	Boot Maker	Rehoboth	Providence, R. I.
29	June 12, "	Joseph Daniel Shay	M	Michael & Abby	Blacker	Ireland	Ireland
30	June 23, "	Harville Albert Caswell } Twins	"	Andrew A. & Susan F.	Laborer	Taunton	Milford
31	June 23, "	Hartwell Adelbert Caswell }	"	"	Carpenter	"	"
32	June 26, "	Jamie Hood	F	James & Annet	Blacksmith	Nova Scotia	Canton
33	June 28, "	William Hoyle Adams	M	William G. & Lillian A.	Inventor	Boston	Salem
34	June 29, "	Mary Ann Walker	F	John H. & Emma J.	Clerk	Whiting, Vt.	Wrentham
35	July 21, "	Abbie Ella Nowell	"	Albert J. & Betcy W.	Farmer	Franklin	Franklin
36	July 27, "	Lena Mary Gifford	"	Hily A. & Julia F.	Laborer	Fall River	Norton
37	Aug. 17, "	Addie Mary Shepard	"	Addison S. & Hariet M.	Farmer	Wrentham	Franklin
38	Aug. 2, "	Edgar Atwood Young	M	William & Emely A.	Dyer	England	England
39	Aug. 5, "	Charles Arthur Cobb	"	Charles M. & Georiana	Don't Presser	Mansfield	Milton
40	Sept. 3, 1864	Hatty Ann Stewart	F	Robert M. & Marfia	Wheelright	Nova Scotia	Nova Scotia
41	Sept. 19, 1867	Frederick Thomas Foley	M	Thomas & Ellen	Farmer	Ireland	Ireland

Births Registered in Franklin, Norfolk County, in the Year 1867.—Continued

NO.	DATE OF BIRTH.	NAME (IF ANY.)	SEX	NAME OF PARENTS.	OCCUPATION OF FATHER.	FATHER'S BIRTHPLACE.	MOTHER'S BIRTHPLACE.
42	Oct. 3, 1867	William Henry Stewart	M	Robert B. & Martha	Wheelright	Nova Scotia	Nova Scotia
43	Nov. 4, "	Oscar Jefferson Daniels	"	Thomas J. & Mary E.	Farmer	Franklin	Canton
44	" 12, "	Eleanor Dorcas Pond	F	Saml. W. & Dorcas B.	"	"	Noridge Walk, Me.
45	" 12, "	Annie M. Cotton	"	Daniel C. & Abbie	Tin Smith	Holderness, N. H.	Wareham
46	" 16, "	James Darling	M	Jesse & Mary	Boot Maker	Clayton, N. Y.	Ireland
47	" 19, "	Julia Fitzgerald	F	John & Catherine	Laborer	Ireland	"
48	" 21, "	Mary Healey	"	Timothy J. & Catherine	Teamster	"	"
49	" 21, "	Margaret McParland	"	Hugh & Celia	Printer	"	"
50	" 30, "	Annie Randall Lombard	"	Solmon T. & Anna J.	Farmer	Truro	Wrentham
51	Dec. 4, "	King	"	George & Lucy A.	Physician	Rochester	Middleboro
52	" 13, "	*Enely Smith Holbrook	"	Amasa L. E. & Mary A.	Farmer	Sutton	Westport
53	" 17, "	Cornelius Daniel Sullivan	M	Daniel & Julia	Laborer	Ireland	Ireland
54	" 21, "	Mary Ellen Falnan	F	Wm. & Mary	"	"	"
55	March 26, 1864	Elton Orlando Clark	M	†Alvin H. & Charlotte M.	Mechanic	Bellingham	Bellingham
56	Dec. 3, "	Charles R. Hill	"	Robert R. & Lucy	Nailor	Sharpsburg, M. D.	Franklin
57	Sept. 9, 1865	Margaret Ella O'Brien	F	Timothy & Elizabeth J.	Laborer	New Brunswick	New Brunswick
58	Jan. 12, 1866	Alice Augusta Clark	"	†Alvin & Charlotte M.	Mechanic	Bellingham	Bellingham
59	Aug. 25, "	Elizabeth Prue	"	Frank & Josephine	Spinner	Canada	Canada
60	Sept. 15, "	Ella Frances Prue	"	Paul & Agnes	"	"	Ireland
61	" 18, "	Thomas O'Brien	M	Patrick & Mary C.	Laborer	Ireland	"
62	Oct. 17, "	William James Haggerty	"	Patrick & Mary	"	"	"
63	Nov. 8, "	James Martin Kelly	"	Michael & Mary F.	"	"	"
64	Dec. 25, "	Mary Irene Hosie	F	George S. & Hannah B.	Bonnet & Hat	Paisley, Scotland	Maine
65	Jan. 29, 1867	Ellen Tracy Burns	"	Michael & Ellen	Boot Maker	Ireland	Ireland
66	March 23, "	William Patrick Clary	M	Michael & Mary	"	"	"
67	May 25, 1865	Ellen Jane Clary	F		"	"	"
68	April 10, 1867	Alvah Chapman Wadsworth	M	George M. & Emeline M.	Farmer	Franklin	Appleton, Me.
69	Dec. 14, "	Albert James Riley	"	James & Mary	"	Ireland	Ireland
70	May 14 "	Cate J. Sullivan	F	Dennis & Margaret	"	"	"

* Born in New Bedford.   † Residence in Bellingham.

Births Registered in Franklin, Norfolk County, for the Year 1868.—A. A. Kingsbury, Registrar.

NO.	DATE OF BIRTH.	NAME (IF ANY.)	SEX.	NAME OF PARENTS.	OCCUPATION OF FATHER.	FATHER'S BIRTHPLACE.	MOTHER'S BIRTHPLACE.
	1868						
1	Jan. 6	Charley Albert Staples	M	Amos W. & E. Ellen	Laborer	Cumberland, R.I.	Wrentham
2	" 8	James Gordon	"	Bartholomew & Ellen Ford	Boot Maker	Ireland	Ireland
3	" 31	Freddie Elbridge Cook	"	Barton F. & Silvina Mary	Farmer	Franklin	Bayvest, N. B.
4	Feb. 4	Nannie Jane Ford	F	John & Celia	Laborer	Ireland	Ireland
5	" 17	Carrie Eva Hills	"	Joseph G. & Mary A. B.	Merchant	Franklin	Franklin
6	" 13	Fred Valentine Cornelius Gibson	M	Cornelius & Mary C.	Mechanic		Auburn, Mass.
7	" 13	Hellen Lousi Morse	F	Chas. H. & Lizzie M.	Machinist		Franklin
8	" 7	Hannah Feely	"	Dennis & Julia (McHugh)	Laborer	Ireland	Ireland
9	March 4	Freddie Ellsworth Hubbard	M	Sabin & Mary (Sargent)	Laborer	Franklin	Oxford
10	" 31	Marion Gertrude Gurney	F	William A. & Louisa	Carpenter	Providence	Medway
11	April 25	Edgar Adelbert Gay	M	Frank B. & Mary Ann (Wier)	Farmer	Natic	New Brunswick
12	" 26	Mary Ann Doherty	F	William & Bridget (Donnelly)	Laborer	Ireland	Ireland
13	May 8	Ada Eldora Gifford	"	Stephen I. & Mary	Bleacher	Dartmouth, Mass	Tiverton, R. I.
14	June 11	Joseph H. Sullivan	M	Dennis & Margaret (Mitchell)	Farmer	Ireland	Ireland
15	" 20	Ellen Maria Fairbanks	F	David & Eliza Ann (Barton)	Carpenter	Jefferson, Me.	Medway
16	" 21	Emma Louisa Corbett	"	George S. & Louesa J. (Weatherhead)	Boo't Blocker	Franklin	Cumberland, R.I.
17	" 24	John Winthrop Tory	M	John W. and Clara A. (Hall)	Station Agent	Sutton	Medway
18	" 28	Charles Feely	"	Patrick & Hannah	Laborer	Ireland	Ireland
19	July 8	Mary Francis Wales	F	Ellen Auguster			Franklin
20	" 13	William Davidson Mann	M	Alexander & Hellen N.	Mason	Scotland	Scotland
21	" 16	Charles Lennon	"	Thomas & Margaret (McAdams)	Laborer	Ireland	Ireland
22	Aug. 6	Eva Murdock	F	William & Louisa V.	Blacksmith	Novia Scotia	Nova Scotia
23	" 13	Flora Arletta Brown	"	Ezekiel P. & Hannah J.	Farmer		Wrentham
24	Sept. 4	Edgar Franklin Hill	M	William & Lucy (Fairbanks)		Franklin	Hopkinton
25	" 11	Joanna Connors	F	Daniel & Mary	Laborer	Ireland	Ireland
26	" 15	George Edward Prue	M	Paul & Bridget A.	Mule Spinner	L. Canada	"
27	" 5	Daniel Coughlin	"	Daniel & Ann (Shank)	Laborer	Ireland	"
28	Oct. 11	James Henry Sexton	"	John & Bridget	Harness Maker		"
29	Nov. 7	Elizabeth Agnes Coffield	F	Daniel & Bridget	Weaver		
30	" 14	Francis P. Maguire	M	Bernard & Mary J.	Mason		Washington, N.H
31	" 11	Henry Morton Howard	F	Apollos E. & Caroline W.	Farmer	No. Bridgwater	Lyme, N. H.
32	Dec. 1, '67	Ardher Adams Dean	M	Chas. I. & Adalaide C.	Machinest	Franklin	Boston
33	" 8, '68	Sarah Metcalf Allen	F	Thomas B. & Martha M.	Farmer		Franklin

FRANKLIN TOWN RECORDS—BIRTHS. 83

Births Registered in Franklin, Norfolk County, for the Year 1868.—(Continued.)

NO.	DATE OF BIRTH.	NAME (IF ANY.)	SEX.	NAME OF PARENTS.	OCCUPATION OF FATHER.	FATHER'S BIRTHPLACE.	MOTHER'S BIRTHPLACE.
	1868						
34	Dec. 21	Mary Elizabeth Dugan	F	Daniel & Mary (Murray)	Laborer	Bangor, Me.	Ireland
35	"	Celina Praxide Lucier	"	Augustine & Marie		Canada East	Canada East

Births Registered in Franklin, County of Norfolk, for the Year 1869.—A. A. Bussegue, Registrar.

NO.	DATE OF BIRTH.	NAME (IF ANY.)	SEX.	NAME OF PARENTS.	OCCUPATION OF FATHER.	FATHER'S BIRTHPLACE.	MOTHER'S BIRTHPLACE.
	1869						
1	Jan. 28	Frederick J. Thayer	M	Laprelate M. & Alice (Hood)	Cordwainer	Douglass	New Anan, N. S.
2	Jan. 21	William Stephen Richardson	"	John W. & Elmira L. (Mason)	Farmer	Franklin	Medway
3	Jan. 24	William Edward Keefe	"	Arthur & Julia E. (McHugh)	Teamster	Ireland	Ireland
4	Feb. 25	William P. Riley	"	Peter & Bridget (Flood)	Laborer	Franklin	Franklin
5	March 14	Annie Dette Chilson	F	James O. & Melansa M. (Heaton)	Butcher	Bellingham	Wrentham
6	March 9	Wendell Bennet Lombard	M	Sobaon T. & Annie J. (Bennet)	Printer	Truro	Ireland
7	March 22	Patrick Feely	"	Dennis & Julia (McHugh)	Laborer	Ireland	Ireland
8	March 16	Henry & Edwin Prue, Twins	"	Joseph & Gustine (Belmont)		Canada	Canada
9	March 4	Casmere Prue	"	Frank & Jessie L. (Lemont)	Spinner	Ireland	Ireland
10	April 1	Henry Snidtly	"	Thomas & Jane (Callahan)	Laborer	Ireland	Ireland
11	April 22	Mary Elizabeth Warren	F	William S. & Catherine J. (McCarthy)	Artist	New York	New York
12	May 23	Minnie Adele Cobb	"	Henry G. & Betsey T. (Newcomb)	Carpenter	Easton	Yarmouth
13	May 8	Hattie E. King	"	George & Lucy A. (Eddy)	Physician	Rochester	Middleborough
14	May 18	Gertrude Wales	"	William H. & Julia A. (Bosworth)	Farmer	Franklin	Pelham
15	June 2	Martha Ella Wadsworth	"	Joseph H. & Abbie L. (Metcalf)			Franklin
16	June 2	Melvin Augustus Adams	M	Lyman & Violetta (Ware)	Laborer	Gloucester, R. I.	Ireland
17	June 2	John Henry Greenwood	"	Levi & Ellen	"	Thomaston, Vt.	Franklin
18	July 24	Charles Francis Lesure	"	John F. & Mary Jane (Fisher)	Bootmaker	Medway	Franklin
19	July 16	Charles Kingsbury Shepardson	"	Thaddeus H. & Annie E. (Fales)	Carpenter	Brooksville, Me.	Medfield
20	July 16, 1868	Hellen Augustus Fisher	F	Henry E. & Mary J. (Patterson)	Hat Presser	Medway	Johnston, R. I.
21	July 21	John Francis Foster	M	William & Sarah A. (Carfield)	Laborer	Scotland	Ireland
22	Aug. 9	Lewis Addison Edward Blake	"	George A. A. & Elizabeth A. (Jencks)	Boot Maker	Franklin	Cumberland, R.I.
23	Aug. 7	Mary Ford	F	John & Celia (McFarland)	Laborer	Ireland	Ireland
24	Aug. 26	Alice Elizabeth Gould	"	William H. & Nancy J. (Lewis)	Carpenter	Greenfield, N. H.	Goshean, N. H.
25	Aug. 16	Marrietta Hood	"	James & Annett (Bartlett)	Blacksmith	Nova Scotia	Canton
26	Aug. 21	Anna Mabel Rockwood	"	Edmond, Jr. & Arbie W. (Cook)	Teamster	Franklin	Bellingham
27	Aug. 8	Caroline Torrey	"	John F. & Clara A. (Hall)	R. R. Agent	Sutton	Medway

Births Registered in Franklin, in the County of Norfolk, for the Year 1869.—(Continued.)

No.	DATE OF BIRTH.	NAME (IF ANY.)	SEX.	NAME OF PARENTS.	OCCUPATION OF FATHER.	FATHER'S BIRTHPLACE.	MOTHER'S BIRTHPLACE.
	1869						
28	Sept. 11	Frederick Newhall Bassett	M	Chas. S. & Abbie G. (Biggelow)	Straw Mfr.	Barre	Philipston
29	Sept. 1	Ella Baker Daniels	F	Maury M. & Mary E. (Kingston)	Farmer	Franklin	New Brunswick
30	Sept. 4	Austin Fletcher Benson	M	Heman C. & Eliza D. (Fletcher)	Manufacturer	Orleans	Mendon
31	Sept. 27	Chauncey Fuller Gilmore	"	Albert J. & Anna S. (Scamilton)	Farmer	Franklin	Providence, R. I.
32	Sept. 2	Jeremiah Sullivan	"	Daniel & Julia (Buckley)	Laborer	Ireland	Ireland
33	Sept. 29	Irving Wadsworth Gould	"	Joseph P. & Marianna (Wales)		Boston	Franklin
34	Sept. 28	Margarett Feeley	F	Patrick & Hannah (McHugh)		Ireland	Ireland
35	Oct. 24	Anna Rosetta Birch	"	Lemuel F. & Margaret M.	Carpenter	Isleborough, Me.	Attleborough
36	Nov. 13	Nellie Decta Clark	"	Joseph M. & Elizabeth C. (Briggs)	Machinist	Franklin	Franklin
37	June 22, 1867	Mary Ann Daniels	"	Maury M. & Harriet N. (Baker)	Farmer	"	England
38	June 13, "	*Albert Henry Bonsell	M	William H. & Sarah A. (Aiken)	Bleacher	England	Franklin
39	June 13, 1866	Edward Lester Gowen	"	Horace M. & Sarah M. (Cole)	Manufacturer	Franklin	Natick
40	Aug. 21, "	Effie Jane Morley	F	James T. & Nancy J. (Blake)	Boot Maker	Boston	Roxbury, Mass.
41	Dec. 27, "	Lizzie Maud Weatherhead	"	Charles E. & Sarah E. (Rook)	Straw Presser	Franklin	South Parris, Me.
42	Nov. 2, 1869	Ernest Walter Day	M	Joseph P. & Georgia E. (Brett)	Hat Blocker	Paxton	Ireland
43	Mch. 31, "	Edward Burns	"	John & Catherine (Owens)	Farmer	Ireland	

* Born in Cambridgeport.

Births Registered in Franklin for the Year 1870.

No.	DATE OF BIRTH.	NAME (IF ANY.)	SEX.	NAME OF PARENTS.	OCCUPATION OF FATHER.	FATHER'S BIRTHPLACE.	MOTHER'S BIRTHPLACE.
	1870						
1	Jan. 15	Edwin N. Hollbrook	M	Milton F. & Melissa B.	Mechanic	Medway	Bellingham
2	Jan. 22	Adelaid Fonseena Gay	F	Francis B. & Mary A.	Farmer	Franklin	Natick
3	Feb. 13	Abbie Maria Allen	"	Cyrus M. & Sarah M.	"	"	Southboro
4	Feb. 7	Adelaid Frances Stockbridge	"	Francis M. & Emely A.	"	Cumberland	Cumberland
5	Feb. 22	George Edwin Staples	M	Amos W. & Ellen E.	"		Wrentham
6	March 26	Mary Margaret Burns	F	John & Catherine		Ireland	Ireland
7	March 15	Eddy Lincoln Morse	M	Thomas D. & Sarah E.	Boot Maker	Natick	Lempster, N. H.
8	April 4	Charles Dean	"	Chas. L. & Adelaid C	Machinest	Franklin	Boston
9	April 12	Margaret Lynch	F	Edward & Mary	Boot Maker	Ireland	Ireland

Births Registered in Franklin for the Year 1870.—(Continued.)

No.	DATE OF BIRTH.	NAME (IF ANY.)	SEX.	NAME OF PARENTS.	OCCUPATION OF FATHER.	FATHER'S BIRTHPLACE.	MOTHER'S BIRTHPLACE.
	1870						
10	April 25	Henrietta Catherine Dunton	F	Chas. H. & Mary B.	Boot Maker	Franklin	Norridgwalk, Me.
11	May 1	George M. Bent		George O. & Whellmere B.	Carpenter	Framingham	Natick
12	May 7	James Timothy Healey		Timothy & Cathrine	Teamster	Ireland	Ireland
13	May 11	Welcome Earnest Scott		Willard E. & Florrilla A.	Farmer	Franklin	Somers, Conn.
14	May 14	Frank Davidson		R. H. & Annie M.	Laborer	St. Johns, N. B.	Boothbay, Me.
15	May 31	Hellen Agnes Mann	F	Alexander R. & Hellen P.	Mason	Scotland	Scotland
16	June 3	Daniel Herbert Young	M	William & Emely A.	Dyer	England	England
17	June 5	Medora Abbie Rockwood	F	Erastus D. & Abbie O.	Farmer	Franklin	Franklin
18	June 13	Willie Hall Partridge	M	Joseph H. & Monerva A.	Mason	Medway	Wrentham
19	July 22	Charles Andrew Jordan		Edwin A. & Eliza J.	Farmer	Franklin	Eden, Me.
20	July 22	Bridget Doherty	F	William & Bridget	Laborer	Ireland	Ireland
21	Aug. 10	Francis Thomas Riley	M	Peter & Bridget	Mechanic	"	"
22	Aug. 13	Timothy Feeley		Dennis & Julia	Laborer	"	"
23	Aug. 17	Bertha Florence Morse	F	Moses & Catherine S.	Farmer	Maine	Martha's Vineyard
24	Aug. 21	William Warren King		Major M. & Emely F.	Machinist	Natick	Goshen, N. H.
25	Aug. 23	Sarah Elizabeth Sullivan	M	Wm. F. & Laura A.	Farmer	Wrentham	Wrentham
26	Aug. 29		F	Dennis & Margaret.	"	Ireland	Ireland
27	Sept. 2			Albert J. & Betsey W.		Franklin	Franklin
28	Sept. 5	Claretha Hannah Elizabeth Nason		Chas. M. & Sylvia A.	Stone Mason	West Gardner, Me.	Holes, N. H.
29	Sept. 18		"	Ira F. & S. Lizzie	Blacksmith	Cumberland	Bellingham
30	Sept. 24	Lillie May Capron		Sanford T. & Lucina	Livery Stable	Rochester	Middleboro
31	Sept. 29	Theodore Dexter King	M	George & Lucy A.	Physician	Wrentham	Franklin
32	Oct. 14	Louis Addison Shepard	"	Addison S. & Hariet M.	Farmer	Framingham	Roxbury
33	Oct. 14	Anna Louisa Darling	F	Nathan E. & Abbie M.	Butcher	Franklin	Medway
34	Nov. 2	Blanche Lillian Gowen	"	Horace M. & Sarah M.	Manufacturer	Nova Scotia	Nova Scotia
35	Nov. 6	Clarence Frank Murdock	"	William & Louisa V.	Blacksmith	Ireland	Ireland
36	Nov. 15	Daniel McParland	M	Hugh & Celia	Laborer	"	"
37	Nov. 19	Margaret Ann Burns	F	Michael & Ellen M.	Boot Maker	Wrentham	Wrentham
38	Nov. 30	Etta Ophelia Watkins		John P. & Julia A.	Machinist	St. Johns, N. B.	Cumberland, R. I.
39	Nov. 30	Charles Andrew Dunn	M	William E. & Sarah E.	Carpenter	Ireland	Ireland
40	Dec. 28	Phillip H. McClusky		Hugh & Bridget	Painter	"	"
41	Dec. 25	Abby Gordon	F	Bartholomew & Ellen	Boot Maker		
42	Dec. 13	George J. Davidson	M	John H. & Addie P.	Merchant Tailor	Scotland	New Ipswich, N.H.

Births Registered in Franklin for the Year 1870.—(Continued.)

NO.	DATE OF BIRTH.	NAME (IF ANY.)	SEX	NAME OF PARENTS.	OCCUPATION OF FATHER.	FATHER'S BIRTHPLACE.	MOTHER'S BIRTHPLACE.
43	Nov. 12, 1868	Harry Archibald Bent	M	Geo. O. & Wheilmere B.	Carpenter	Framingham	Natick
44	Dec. 21, "	George Warren Fuller	"	Geo. N. & Harriet M.	Farmer	Franklin	Leicester
45	Feb. 25, 1869	William Patrick Riley	"	Peter & Bridget	Mechanic	Ireland	Ireland
46	Sept. 9, 1869	Francis Albert Bacon	"	Albert O. & Ann E.	Farmer	Franklin	Bellingham
47	Oct. 9, "	Anna Josephine Cook	F	Joseph W. & Polly J.		Wrentham	Woonsocket, R. I.
48	Oct. 19, "	Amy Estelle Cooper	"	Pliny E. & Ellen J.	Machinest	South Canton	Franklin
49	Nov. 14, "	George Henry Thorn	M	James H. & Mary B.	Farmer	Boston	Beverly

Births Registered in Franklin as follows in 1871.—A. A. Rosseere, Registrar.

NO.	DATE OF BIRTH.	NAME (IF ANY.)	SEX	NAME OF PARENTS.	OCCUPATION OF FATHER.	FATHER'S BIRTHPLACE.	MOTHER'S BIRTHPLACE.
	1871						
1	Jan. 17	Francis Kelly	M	Michael & Mary	Laborer	Ireland	Ireland
2	Feb. 17	Willard Melville Gaeyman	"	Ezra & Caroline E.	Farmer	Bellville, N. J.	Carver, Mass.
3	Feb. 28	George Randolph Russell	"	Thomas J. & Jennie M.	Laborer	Cumberland, R. I.	Blackstone
4	March 29	Batha Idilla Hood	F	James & Annette	Blacksmith	Nova Scotia	Canton
5	April 4	Henry E. Watkins	M	Henry & Ida E.	Laborer		
6	April 6	Herbert J. Lincoln	"	William M. & Sarah E.	Farmer	Providence, R. I.	Rome, Me.
7	April 17	Thomas Joseph Lennon	"	Thomas & Margaret	Laborer	Ireland	Ireland
8	April 27	George Harry Weston	"	Edward G. & Della	"	Norfolk, Va.	Newbern, N. C.
9	May 14	Alice Ann Maria Foster	F	George W. & Amelia L.	Farmer	Franklin	Lynn
10	June 1	Eddie Jefferson Darling	M	Mayo C. & Lucy Ann	Butcher	Bellingham	Franklin
11	June 10	Ellen Galvin	F	James & Ellen	Laborer	Ireland	Ireland
12	June 25	Willie Almon Cook	M	Joseph W. & Polly	Farmer	Wrentham	Woonsocket, R. I.
13	July 8	Isadora Carr	F	*William W. & Caroline H.	Carder	State New York	Union, Me.
14	July 14	Julia Sullivan	"	Daniel & Julia	Laborer	Ireland	Ireland
15	July 17	Lillia Mary Briggs	"	Richard A. & Ann E.		Providence, R. I.	Winstead, Ct.
16	July 18	Levi Howard Tower	M	Jason & Mary E.	Farmer	Cumberland	N. B.
17	July 22	Frank Smith Cook	"	Smith S. & Ann J.		Franklin	Westboro
18	July 26	Frederick Henry King.	"	Frederick A. B & Catherine L.	Carpenter	So. Paris, Me.	Boston
19	Sept. 12	Daniel Edward Sullivan	"	John & Elizabeth	Farmer	Ireland	Ireland
20	Sept. 30	Albert Horace Goss	"	Ashley & Laura Ann	Rail Reading	Randolph, Vt.	Randolph, Vt.
21	Oct. 2	Mary Eliza Doherty.	F	Michael & Annie	Laborer	Ireland	Ireland

* Residence Fall River.

FRANKLIN TOWN RECORDS—BIRTHS.

Births Registered in Franklin as follows in the Year 1871.—(Continued.)

NO.	DATE OF BIRTH.	NAME (IF ANY.)	SEX.	NAME OF PARENTS.	OCCUPATION OF FATHER.	FATHER'S BIRTHPLACE.	MOTHER'S BIRTHPLACE.
	1871						
22	Oct. 6	Harriet Ellen Shepardson	F	Thaddeus H. & Annie E.	Carpenter	Brookville, Me.	Medfield
23	Oct. 8	Augustus Blele	M	Blini & Cordalia	Laborer	Montreal	Montreal, Canada
24	Oct. 20	Florence Clatlin	F	*Calvin & Isabella J.	Merchant	Franklin	Franklin
25	Oct. 22	Anna Eudora Blake	"	George A. A. & Elizabeth A.	Boot Maker	"	Cumberland, R. I.
26	Oct. 23	Adelaide Cooper	"	Pliny E. & Ella J.	Machenest	Canton	Franklin
27	Oct. 28	Thomas Francis Johnson	M	Thomas & Julia	Wool Sorter	Ireland	Ireland
28	Nov. 16	Ellen Elizabeth Corbett	F	John & Johanna	Farmer	"	"
29	Nov. 19	Michael Cullin	M	Garret & Bridget	Laborer	"	"
30	Dec. 20	Arthur Bent	"	George O. & Willına W.	Carpenter	Framingham	Natick
31	June 11, 1869	Annie R. Fisher	F	Daniel W. & Mary E.	Farmer	Wrentham	Providence, R. I.
32	April 2, 1870	Walter Cook	M	Samuel S. & Ann J.	"	Franklin	Westboro
33	Dec. 6, "	James Joseph Colgan	"	John & Catherine	Laborer	Ireland	Ireland
34	Aug. 11, 1871	Nellie Sullivan	F	Daniel & Julia	"	"	"
35	Aug. 28, "	Joseph Yousoo	M	Frank & Lonesa	"	Canada	Canada
36	Aug. 7, "	Ada Edwina Serres Metcalf	F	†Edwin S. & Ada Emily	Musician	Washington, Vt.	Bangor, Me.
37	June 6, "	Mary Grace Nickolson	"	‡Donold & Martha M.	Stenographer	England	Boylston

* Residence New York City. † Residence Boston. ‡ Residence New York and Boylston.

MARRIAGES.

FRANKLIN TOWN RECORDS—Marriages Registered in Franklin Prior to May 1, 1844.

DATE OF MARRIAGE.	GROOM. NAME.	RESIDENCE.	BRIDE. NAME.	RESIDENCE.	BY WHOM MARRIED.
April 23, 1778	James Metcalf, Jr.	Franklin	Abigail Harding		*Rev. Nathaniel Emmons
May 7, 1778	Ziba Hills		Molly Newton		" "
June 3, 1778	Elisha Rockwood		Eunice Clark		" "
June 11, 1778	Joshua Legg		Esther Smith		" "
July 20, 1778	Joseph Pond		Margaret Pond		" "
Nov. 5, 1778	Asa Daniels		Eunice Fisher		" "
Nov. 12, 1778	Jeremiah Ruggles		Ketturah Daniels		" "
Jan. 14, 1779	Aaron Farrington	Franklin	Saphrona Weatherhead	Cumberland, R.I.	Peter Darling, J. P.
Jan. 28, 1779	Elisha Partridge		Sarah Fales		
April 1, 1779	Asa Whiting, Jr.		Mary Gilmore		
May 3, 1779	Jeremiah Crocker, Free Negro		Rose Hager (Free Negro)		Jabez Fisher, J. P.
May 6, 1779	Elias Mann		Mary Ware		
Oct. 21, 1779	Hanan Metcalf		Mary Allen		
Dec. 22, 1779	Ebenezer Lawrence		Mrs. Mary Harding		
Feb. 3, 1780	John Baker		Molly Harding	Franklin	
June 1, 1780	Asa Fuller		Meletiah Metcalf	"	
Oct. 12, 1780	Robert Pond, Jr.		Olive Richardson	"	
Nov. 6, 1780	Nathan Wight		Jarusha Metcalf	"	
Dec. 7, 1780	John Merifield		Molly Metcalf	"	
Dec. 22, 1780	Joseph Hills		Esther Ellis	"	
Dec. 22, 1780	Aquila Robbins		Elizabeth Thurston	Wrentham	
Jan. 13, 1781	Benjamin Witmarsh		Eunice Darling	Franklin	
May 25, 1781	Elias Ware		Debby Groves	Medway	
May 30, 1781	Samuel Rockwood		Sally Richardson	Franklin	
Aug. 2, 1781	Timothy Puffer		Sally Lethbridge	"	
Aug. 9, 1781	Abner Legg		Lavina Pond	"	
Oct. 29, 1781	Ezra Harvey		Esther Haws		
April 18, 1782	William Adams		Elisabeth Whiting		

* Congregational Clergyman.

FRANKLIN TOWN RECORDS—MARRIAGES.

DATE OF MARRIAGE.	GROOM.		BRIDE.		BY WHOM MARRIED.
	NAME.	RESIDENCE.	NAME.	RESIDENCE.	
May 23, 1782	Seth Dean	Franklin	Edena Pond	Franklin	
Sept. 18, 1782	Barzilla Pond	"	Meletent Fairbanks	"	
Oct. 17, 1782	Leonard Hills	"	Margarette Williams	"	
Nov. 6, 1782	Asa Metcalf	"	Ruth Clark	"	
Nov. 21, 1782	Eliab White	Bellingham	Rachel Adams	"	
Dec. 5, 1782	Abijah Clark	Franklin	Jemima Haws	"	
Dec. 19, 1782	Peter Darling	"	Meletiah Pond	"	
Jan. 31, 1783	Jones Hills	"	Perry Robinson	"	
Feb. 6, 1783	Billy Mann	"	Jeensha Ballard	"	
July 3, 1783	Gaius Smith	Rehoboth	Molly Thurston	"	
Nov. 13, 1783	Titus Metcalf	Franklin	Olive Fisher	"	
Nov. 27, 1783	John Fisher	"	Pegge Fisher	"	
Dec. 18, 1783	James Woodward	"	Mary Fisher	"	
July 2, 1784	Moses Adams	"	Lois Ellis	"	
Jan. 22, 1784	Joseph Lawrence	"	Chloe Wright	"	
April 15, 1784	Samuel Williams	Wrentham	Anna Hills	"	
May 13, 1784	Charles Harris	Douglass	Abigail Hills	"	Stephen Metcalf, J. P.
May 20, 1784	Noah Hills	Medfield	Meletiah Hawes	"	
June 17, 1784	David Lovel	Franklin	Esther Baker	"	
Oct. 29, 1784	Benjamin Clark	"	Silence Battle	"	
Nov. 4, 1784	Lievett Peter	Croyden	Esther Jones	"	
Nov. 18, 1784	Edward Hall	Franklin	Susanna Richardson	Grafton	
Nov. 23, 1784	Asa Fairbanks	"	Abagail Pond	Franklin	
Dec. 1, 1784	David Gilmore, Jur.	"	Julitha Metcalf	"	
Mar. 18, 1785	William Williams	Medway	Molly Robbins	"	
Mar. 31, 1785	John Whiting	Franklin	Susanna Pond	"	
June 1, 1785	Jesse Daniels	"	Charlotte Whiting	"	
June 9, 1785	Levi Fisher	"	Susanna Hawes	"	
Oct. 13, 1785	Eli Darling	"	Mary Clark	"	
Nov. 15, 1785	Robert Gilmore	"	Rebach Pond	"	
Nov. 29, 1785	Joel Daniels	"	Olive Robbins	"	
Dec. 1, 1785	Timothy Gay	"	Mary Daniels	"	
Dec. 27, 1785	Simeon Partridge	"	Submit Blackman	"	
			Aebsah Metcalf	"	

DATE OF MARRIAGE.	GROOM.		BRIDE.		BY WHOM MARRIED.
	NAME.	RESIDENCE.	NAME.	RESIDENCE.	
Jan. 12, 1786	Thomas Gay	Franklin	Mary Bacon	Franklin	Rev. Nathaniel Emmons
Jan. 23, 1786	Nathan Daniels, Jr.	"	Sarah Smith	Walpole	"
Feb. 16, 1876	James Taylor	"	Salome Partridge	Franklin	"
March 2, 1786	Annariah Daniels	Hopkinton	Elizabeth Clark	"	"
March 9, 1786	Ebenezer Siload	Franklin	Rhoda Fisher	Wrentham	"
April 13, 1786	Amos Ware	"	Rachael Pond	Franklin	"
May 12, 1786	Benjamin Rockwood	"	Anna Bullard	"	"
Sept. 7, 1786	John Pierce	Greenwich	Mary Gilmore	"	"
Oct. 9, 1786	Solomon Tonn	Franklin	Lois Butler	"	"
Oct. 12, 1786	Jason Morse	"	Olive Blake	"	"
Oct. 16, 1786	Jeremiah Pratt	"	Miriam Partridge	"	"
Oct. 26, 1786	David McLane	Medway	Rebecah Gilmore	"	"
Jan. 11, 1787	Ebenezer Thompson	Franklin	Forada Richardson	"	"
April 3, 1787	Anasa Richardson	"	Lydia Richardson	"	"
April 12, 1787	Simeon Daniels	"	Abigail Daniels	"	"
April 19, 1787	Joseph Heaton	"	Kesia Holmes	"	"
April 29, 1787	Samuel Fisher	"	Rena Dean	"	"
Sept. 5, 1787	Seeva Richardson	"	Esther Hixon	"	"
Oct. 11, 1787	Moses Parcus	Walpole	Catherine Hucker	"	"
Oct. 18, 1787	Aaron Fisher	Franklin	Rachael Fisher	"	"
Nov. 22, 1787	Nathan Pond	Wrentham	Lucretia Thurston	"	"
Jan. 31, 1788	Timothy Fisher	Franklin	Hannah Whiting	"	"
March 12, 1788	Asa Metcalf	"	Melia Ware	Holliston	"
March 17, 1788	Samuel Blake	"	Eunice Rockwood	Franklin	"
June 18, 1788	Apollos Pond	"	Juletta Daniels	"	"
Sept. 4, 1788	David Hartshorn	"	Mary Lawrence	"	"
Sept. 18, 1788	Nathan Metcalf	Boston	Patty Metcalf	Boston	"
Sept. 21, 1788	Thomas Revere	Franklin	Rebekah Lovering	Franklin	"
Nov. 6, 1788	Moses Fisher	Alstead	Mary Hixon	"	"
Dec. 17, 1788	Lt. Hezekiah Fisher	Medfield	Dinah Pond	"	"
Jan. 22, 1789	Cyrus Kingsbury	Lebanon	Philete Partridge	"	"
May 24, 1789	Amos Boyden	Franklin	Susanna Kingsbury	"	"
Sept. 22, 1789	Rev. Walter Harris		Jemima Fisher	"	"
Oct. 13, 1789	Amos Harding		Hannah Baker	"	"

FRANKLIN TOWN RECORDS—MARRIAGES.

DATE OF MARRIAGE.	GROOM. NAME.	RESIDENCE.	BRIDE. NAME.	RESIDENCE.	BY WHOM MARRIED.
Oct. 15, 1789	Nathaniel Thayer	Franklin	Rhoda Fisher	Medway	Rev. Nathaniel Emmons
Oct. 15, 1789	Daniel Fisher	"	Lorana Fisher	Franklin	"
Nov. 11, 1789	Jabez Ware	"	Hannah Allen	"	"
Nov. 12, 1789	Calvin Metcalf	"	Eunice Adams	"	"
Nov. 26, 1789	Cephas Lawrence	"	Esther Whiting	"	"
Dec. 17, 1789	Lewis Farrington	"	Sarah Morse	"	"
Jan. 20, 1790	Jesse Hills	Bellingham	Abigail Fisher	"	"
Feb. 5, 1790	Nathan Clark	Franklin	Sabra Metcalf	"	"
Feb. 5, 1790	Amos Richardson	Wrentham	Eunice Pond	"	"
April 28, 1790	Darius Briggs	Franklin	Elizabeth Gilmore	"	"
June 3, 1790	Eli Taft	Upton	Esther Adams	"	"
Sept. 16, 1790	John Fales	Attleboro	Phebee Gilmore	"	"
Nov. 17, 1790	Levi Morse	Franklin	Katurah Fisher	"	"
Feb. 17, 1791	Jason Blake	"	Lydia Holbrook	Wrentham	"
Feb. 17, 1791	Bethuel Boyd	"	Sukey Whiting	"	"
Mar. 10, 1791	Sylvester Partrige	"	Sarah Collins	Franklin	"
Mar. 24, 1791	David Lawrence, Jr.	"	Lois Pond	"	"
May 27, 1790	Walden Morse	Sharon	Hannah Brown	"	Jabez Fisher, J. P.
May 15, 1791	Abner Wight	Milford	Huldah Pond	"	Rev. Nathaniel Emmons
Oct. 12, 1791	Jason Hills	Franklin	Molly Grover	"	"
Jan. 5, 1792	Joseph Haws, Jr.	"	Hannah Whiting	"	"
Mar. 26, 1792	Jesse Robbins	Hopkinton	Ruth Pierce	"	"
April 16, 1792	Samuel Goddard	Keene, N. H.	Kesia Pond	"	"
April 28, 1792	William Bennet	Franklin	Mary Daniels	"	"
May 27, 1792	Willing Blake	"	Molly Lindley	"	"
July 12, 1792	Timothy Fisher, Jr.	Medway	Rhoda Morse	"	"
Nov. 22, 1792	Jasper Adams	Hopkinton	Emma Rounds	Walpole	Jabez Fisher, J. P.
Nov. 29, 1792	Joseph Morse	Franklin	Olive Fairbanks	Franklin	Rev. Nathaniel Emmons
Jan. 1, 1793	Levi Hawes	Alstead	Carmelia Clark	"	"
Jan. 27, 1793	Samuel Richardson	Franklin	Kezia Partrige	"	"
Feb. 14, 1793	William Lincoln	Leicester	Patty Tiffany	"	"
Feb. 27, 1793	Silas Armsby	Franklin	Elizabeth Kingsbury	"	"
June 20, 1793	Abraham Blake, Jr.	"	Chloe Blake	"	"
July 10, 1793	Dyer Clark, Jr.	"	Nancy Day	"	"

FRANKLIN TOWN RECORDS—MARRIAGES.   93

DATE OF MARRIAGE.	GROOM. NAME.	RESIDENCE.	BRIDE. NAME.	RESIDENCE.	BY WHOM MARRIED.
Sept. 4, 1793	Solomon Hawes	Franklin	Sally Hammond	Franklin	Rev. Nathaniel Emmons
Sept. 4, 1793	Joseph Daniels	"	Susa Fisher	"	"
Nov. 7, 1793	Jem Otis Pond	"	Sally Gilmore	"	"
Nov. 20, 1793	Amariah Ware	"	Eunice Alden	"	"
Nov. 20, 1793	Caleb Fisher	"	Sally Cushing	"	"
Dec. 12, 1793	Daniel Ide	Medway	Sally Clark		"
Dec. 19, 1793	Jesse Miller	Franklin	Vina Thurston		"
Jan. 30, 1794	Samuel Blake	Wrentham	Lois Partridge		"
Feb. 20, 1794	Abijah Metcalf	Franklin	Sarah Blake		"
March 12, 1794	Aaron Harr	Sherborn	Beriah Kingsbury		"
April 16, 1794	William Makepeace	Bellingham	Mary Whiting		"
April 16, 1794	David Daniels	Franklin	Lucy Wood		"
May 8, 1793	Titus Metcalf		Eunice Lawrence		"
May 7, 1794	George Allen	Albany	Emice Haven		"
Sept. 2, 1794	Jabez Newel	Cumberland	Jerusha Cook		"
Nov. 6, 1794	Obadiah Allen Thayer	Wrentham	Abigail Adams		"
Dec. 31, 1794	Elias Partridge	Franklin	Abigail Chase	Sutton	"
Jan. 7, 1795	Willard Boyd		Betsy Whiting	Wrentham	"
Jan. 15, 1795	Ozias Lawrence		Mary Fisher	Franklin	"
Feb. 5, 1795	Olney Titus	Wrentham	Abigail Gilmore		"
April 30, 1795	Calvin Blake	Franklin	Meletiah Pond		"
May 4, 1795	Aaron Blackington	Attleboro	Sally Aldis		Jabez Fisher, Esq., J. P.
May 28, 1795	Timothy Fisher, Jr.	Franklin	Dorcas Cleavland	Medfield	Rev. Nathaniel Emmons
Sept. 24, 1795	Nathan Pond	"	Rachael Clark	Franklin	"
Feb. 9, 1796	James Adams	Parris	Sarah Bacon		"
Feb. 10, 1796	Joel Robinson	Wrentham	Lucy Thompson		"
Feb. 18, 1796	Dea. Phillip Blake	Attleboro	Beriah Lawrence		"
March 4, 1796	Benjamin Foster	Franklin	Hannah Ware		"
Oct. 5, 1797	Nathan Gilmore	Holliston	Nancy Fisher		"
Oct. 9, 1797	Jeremiah Leland	Franklin	Sarah Hawes		"
Nov. 9, 1797	Capt. Joseph Hills	"	Betty Pond		"
Jan. 1, 1798	Timothy Richardson, Jr.	"	Nancy Mann		"
Sept. 20, 1798	Seneca Aldridge	"	Rachael Adams		Doct. Nathaniel Emmons
Oct. 10, 1798	William Gilmore	"	Molly Hills		"

FRANKLIN TOWN RECORDS—MARRIAGES.

DATE OF MARRIAGE.	GROOM. NAME.	GROOM. RESIDENCE.	BRIDE. NAME.	BRIDE. RESIDENCE.	BY WHOM MARRIED.
Nov. 29, 1798	John Torry, Jun'r	Franklin	Sally Richardson	Franklin	Doct. Nathan'l Emmons
Jan. 6, 1799	Rev. John Bowers Preston	Rupert	Polly Haven	"	"
Jan. 10, 1799	Benjamin Partrige	Bellingham	Milcha Pond	"	"
Jan. 16, 1799	Apollos Gilmore	Walpole, N. H.	Susanna Reed	Sherburn	"
Jan. 31, 1799	Eben'r Kollock	Franklin	Mary Smith	Franklin	"
Jan. 31, 1799	David Thompson	"	Betsy Clark	"	"
Mar. 12, 1799	Ebenezer Alden	Middleboro	Patience Gilmore	"	"
April 4, 1799	Diodat Bradshaw	Wrendam	Mary Whiting	Wrentham	"
April 11, 1799	Robert Blake	"	Abigail Blake	Franklin	"
April 11, 1799	Aaron Partrige	Bellingham	Abigail Pond	"	"
April 25, 1799	Larnel Thayer	Franklin	Polly Parnel		"
Aug. 29, 1799	James Morse	"	Olive Harding		"
Sept. 5, 1799	Timothy Adams	"	Betsy Payson		"
Oct. 24, 1799	Benjamin Parnel	"	Sarah Kollock		"
Nov. 25, 1799	Ebenezer Blake	"	Ede Pond		"
Nov. 28, 1799	Nathan Adams	"	Julia Richardson		"
Jan. 16, 1800	Seth Bacon	"	Mehetable Morse	Franklin	"
Mar. 19, 1800	Thadeus Hastings, of the Plantation Cathd Barretstown	Walpole	Nancy Thurston	Franklin	"
April 3, 1800	Jesse Nason	Franklin	Hannah Clark		"
April 3, 1800	Willard Fairbanks	Bellingham	Susanna Lethbridge		"
Aug. 14, 1799	Caleb Adams	Franklin	Widow Melatiah Holbrook		John Whiting, J. P.
Dec. 19, 1799	Welcome Scott	"	Phebe Freeman		"
Aug. 30, 1798	Elias Foster	"	Rhoda Ware		"
Mar. 13, 1800	John Partridge Allen	"	Mehetable Wakefield		John Whiting, Esq., J.P.
May 8, 1800	Moses Hill	Medway	Lydia Whiting		*
Sept. 25, 1800	William Scott	Bellingham	Selah Sayles		Doct. Nathan'l Emmons
Nov. 17, 1800	Samuel Cushing	Franklin	Dorcas Daniels		"
Nov. 17, 1800	Seth Whiting	"	Olive Ware		"
Jan. 1, 1801	Asa Partridge	Holliston	Polly Richardson		"
Jan. 1, 1801	Ames Bullard	"	Galley Pond		"
Jan. 1, 1801	Macy Adams	Franklin	Clarinda Ware		"
Jan. 14, 1801	Prince Baylies	"	Patience Swazey	Attleboro	"
Feb. 4, 1801	Joseph Whiting, 3d	"	Ruth Bacon	Franklin	"
Feb. 22, 1801	James Dowson	Boston	Mary Torry		"

* Nathan Putnam, Esq., J. P., Worcester County.

FRANKLIN TOWN RECORDS—MARRIAGES. 95

DATE OF MARRIAGE.	GROOM.		BRIDE.		BY WHOM MARRIED.
	NAME.	RESIDENCE.	NAME.	RESIDENCE.	
Sept. 1801	Jonathan Wails, Jr.	Franklin	Hannah Albe	Franklin	Rev. Nathaniel Emmons
Oct. 1, 1801	Peter Daniels	Providence	Abigail Dean	"	"
Oct. 8, 1801	Eli Messenger	No. Providence	Martha Blake	"	"
Oct. 12, 1801	Otis Wails	Franklin	Jemima Albe	"	"
Oct. 29, 1801	Horace Cook	Wrentham	Leuretia Bates	Bellingham	"
Nov. 23, 1801	Dr. Spencer Pratt	Foxborough	Elizabeth Wood	Franklin	"
Nov. 26, 1801	Benja. Pond, Jur.	Franklin	Lydia Ellis	"	Doct. Nathnl Emmons
Nov. 26, 1801	Nathan Clark	"	Nancy Payson	"	"
Dec. 17, 1801	Jacob Briggs	"	Nancy Gilmor	"	"
Jan. 26, 1802	Thomas Bear	Mansfield	Jenny Spear	"	"
Jan. 28, 1802	Stuthael Fales	Franklin	Thankful Miller	"	"
March 11, 1802	Nahum Holbrook	Walpole	Susanna Rockwood	"	"
April 7, 1802	Asa Gowen	Bellingham	Polly Allen	"	"
April 28, 1802	Martin Thayer	Franklin	Patty Thayer	"	"
May 8, 1803	Lyman White	"	Hannah Cushing	"	"
June 1, 1803	Abel Ellis	"	Rachel Woodward	"	"
Aug. 11, 1803	Arnold Perry	Sutton	Betsey Harding	"	"
Sept. 28, 1803	Benja. Thayer, Jur.	Franklin	Rachel Wails	"	"
Sept. 29, 1803	Peter Whiting, Jur.	"	Anna Sayles	"	"
Oct. 12, 1803	Peter Thayer	"	Abigail Blake	"	"
Dec. 22, 1803	Ichabod Dean, Jur.	"	Betsey Adams	"	"
Dec. 28, 1803	Cyrus Adams	"	Mary Hawes	"	"
Jan. 17, 1804	Capt. Joseph Bacon	Barrein, Vt.	Ruth Heaton	"	"
Feb. 12, 1804	Warren Keith	Franklin	Jemima Merrifield	"	"
March 29, 1804	Daniel Adams	Westborough	Nancy Richardson	"	"
April 17, 1804	Benja. Whiting	Franklin	Sibbel Blake	Mendon	"
April 18, 1804	Nathaniel Albe	Bellingham	Sena Penniman	Bellingham	"
May 10, 1804	Joseph Rockwood	Franklin	Anna Chilson	Franklin	"
May 23, 1804	Bela Cleaveland	"	Hanna Adams	Bellingham	"
Oct. 4, 1804	John Wails	"	Abigail Adams	Franklin	"
Nov. 29, 1804	David Baker	"	Jemima Richardson	"	"
Feb. 7, 1805	Daniel Thurston	Upton	Bathsheba Brintnell	"	"
March 7, 1805	Job Carpenter	Wrentham	Unity Daniels	"	"
Aug. 28, 1804	Samuel Pond		Catharine Smith		John Whiting, Esq.

DATE OF MARRIAGE.	GROOM.		BRIDE.		BY WHOM MARRIED.
	NAME.	RESIDENCE.	NAME.	RESIDENCE.	
May 9, 1805	Esq'r James Harding	Franklin	Lois Bacon	Franklin	Rev. Doct. Nath'l Emmons
May 16, 1805	Lyman Bates	Bellingham	Jerusha Fairbanks	"	"
June 3, 1805	John W. Adams	Medfield	Amy Ballou	"	"
Oct. 10, 1805	Jason Fisher	Franklin	Olive Smith	"	"
Oct. 13, 1805	Jeremiah M. Pond	"	Polly Morse	"	"
Nov. 3, 1805	William Slocomb	"	Selah Cushing	"	"
Jan. 2, 1806	John Guild	"	Lois Round	"	Doct. Nath'l Emmons
Jan. 9, 1806	Paul Clark, Jur.	"	Nancy Peck	"	"
Feb. 12, 1806	David Ware	"	Betsey Adams	Bellingham	"
Mar. 30, 1806	Eleazer Partridge, Jur.	"	Mary Fisher	Franklin	"
May 18, 1806	James Thayer	"	Sally Daniels	"	"
June 25, 1806	Ebenezer Partridge Wood	"	Sarah Hawes	"	"
Nov. 2, 1806	Thomas Bliss	Boston	Mary Payson	"	"
Nov. 6, 1806	Soloman Blake, Jur.	Franklin	Hannah Morse	Wrentham	"
Nov. 27, 1806	Elias Baker	"	Sally Ellis	Franklin	"
Jan. 15, 1807	Alpheus Adams	Packersfield, N.H	Aclsah Partridge	"	"
Feb. 7, 1807	Mare Basset	Franklin	Katherine Kingsbury	"	"
June 10, 1807	Perez Fisher	"	Mary Perry	"	"
June 25, 1807	Abijah Clark, Jur.	"	Peggy Knap	"	"
Aug. 13, 1807	Timothy Partridge	Providence	Genette Groves	"	"
Aug. 30, 1807	Dr. Amos Allen	Franklin	Alveil Kingsbury	"	"
Oct. 13, 1807	Jonathan Wells	Worcester	Charlotte Brick	"	"
Nov. 22, 1807	Joseyh Kingsbury	Wrentham	Esther Thurston	"	"
Nov. 26, 1807	Asa Ware. Jur.	Douglass	Rena Richardson	"	"
Jan. 6, 1808	Asa Hills	Bellingham	Rhoda Baker	"	"
Feb. 22, 1808	John Adams	Leominster	Perssis Wheeler	"	"
Feb. 3, 1808	Elijah Richardson	Franklin	Polly Baker	"	"
April 14, 1808	John Crooks	Waldoborough	Patty Metcalf	"	"
May 22, 1808	Samuel Morse	Franklin	Olive Pond	"	"
June 9, 1808	William Adams, Jur.	"	Mary Fisher	"	"
June 16, 1808	Daniel C. Fisher	"	Sarah Wood	"	"
June 16, 1808	James Adams	*	Lucy Fairbanks	"	"
Dec. 4, 1808	Rufus Gillmore		Julitta Fairbanks	"	"
Jan. 1, 1809	Eli Richardson, Jur.	Franklin	Chloe Lindley	"	"

*Of the first Range, No. 2 in the Co. of Hancock.

DATE OF MARRIAGE.	GROOM.		BRIDE.		BY WHOM MARRIED.
	NAME.	RESIDENCE.	NAME.	RESIDENCE.	
Jan. 1, 1809	Elisha Stevens	Roxbury	Abigail Lethbridge	Franklin	Doct. Nath'l Emmons
Mar. 23, 1809	Henry Campbell	Oxford	Sarah Blake	"	"
Mar. 28, 1809	Eliakim Morse	Franklin	Lucinda Pond	"	"
Feb. 23, 1809	Edmond Payson	Boston	Julia Lawrence	"	Elisha Pond, J. P.
Nov. 26, 1809	John Stricklin	Barre	Sibyl Adams	Medway	"
Sept. 19, 1811	Richard Mann	Mendon	Susanna Parkhurst	Franklin	James Adams, Esq., J. P.
Nov. 21, 1811	Samuel Davis	Cumberland	Polly Witherell	Wrentham	"
April 6, 1809	Amos Adams	Franklin	Betsey Follett	Franklin	Doct. Nath'l Emmons
April 13, 1809	Levi Fisher	"	Sussanna Clark	"	"
April 16, 1809	Amos B. Gay	"	Loami B. Herrick	"	"
April 20, 1809	Leland Frank	Wrentham	Huldah Heaton	"	"
Sept. 5, 1809	David Thurston	Franklin	Miranda Ellis	"	"
Nov. 2, 1809	Sidney Whiting	"	Olive Morse	"	"
Nov. 28, 1809	Elijah Holbrook	Bellingham	Betsey Ide	"	"
Jan. 10, 1810	Elijah Wheelock	Attleborough	Nancy Harding	"	"
Feb. 8, 1810	Lt. Willis Fisher	Franklin	Caroline Fairbanks	"	"
Feb. 11, 1801	William Lethbridges	"	Annie Mann	"	"
June 12, 1810	Asa Darling	Medway	Julia Thayer	"	"
June 14, 1810	William Paine	Bellingham	Ruth Wilbar	"	"
June 28, 1810	Nathan Metcalf	Franklin	Abigail Richardson	"	"
Nov. 29, 1810	John Alley	New Bedford	Rosalinda Mann	"	"
Jan. 24, 1811	Luke Thurston	Franklin	Olive Clark	"	"
Feb. 24, 1811	Nathan Cleveland	"	Polly Battles	"	"
April 4, 1811	Asa Fuller	"	Hepzebah Blake	"	"
April 25, 1811	Elisha Richardson	"	Ruth Fisher	"	"
May 23, 1811	Lewis Harding	"	Irene Hartshorn	"	"
Sept. 5, 1811	Benjamin Rathbourn	East Hartford,Ct	Joanna Wright	"	"
Sept. 22, 1811	Ebenezer Guild, Ju'r	Franklin	Hepzibah Russel	"	"
Nov. 7, 1811	Nathan Place	Cumberland	Cynthia Mann	"	"
Nov. 21, 1811	Enoch Blandine	Franklin	Mille Lincoln	"	"
Dec. 3, 1811	Luther Gowen	"	Elvira Metcalf	"	"
Dec. 8, 1811	Maxcy Fisher	"	Persis Metcalf	"	"
Jan. 16, 1812	Lewis Fisher, Esq.	"	Sula C. Bacon	"	"
Jan. 26, 1812	David Barden	"	Julia Baker	"	"

FRANKLIN TOWN RECORDS—MARRIAGES.

DATE OF MARRIAGE.	GROOM.		BRIDE.		BY WHOM MARRIED.
	NAME.	RESIDENCE.	NAME.	RESIDENCE.	
Feb. 2, 1812	Otis Scott	Franklin	Mehitabel Richardson	Franklin	Doct. Nathl. Emmons
April 16, 1812	Joseph Bullard	"	Julia Thompson	"	" "
April 27, 1812	Nahum Pike	Westborough	Rachel Thurston	"	" "
April 27, 1812	Peter Lewitt, Jur.	Franklin	Lucy Russel	"	" "
April 7, 1813	Cyrus Guild	"	Olive Haskel	Cumberland	" "
May 18, 1812	Ransom Lawrence	Walpole, N. H.	Betsy Grant	Franklin	" "
June 16, 1812	Jason Fisher, Jur.	Franklin	Mary Rich	"	" "
July 1, 1812	Leonard Hyde	Roxbury	Jerusha Lethridge	"	" "
Oct. 1, 1812	Harvey Hayford	Franklin	Prudence Laurence	"	" "
Oct. 20, 1812	Spooner Alden	*	Nancy Peirce	"	" "
Nov. 26, 1812	Asa Rockwood	Franklin	Julia Thurston	"	" "
Dec. 30, 1812	James Morse	"	Clarissa Bullard	"	" "
Jan. 14, 1813	James Gillmore, 2d	Wrentham	Rena Partridge	"	" "
March 11, 1813	Stephen A. Clark	Franklin	Olive Heaton	"	" "
May 20, 1813	Hiram Knapp	"	Lois Clark	"	" "
Aug. 26, 1813	Leander Simpson	Wrentham	Mrs. Susanna Lethbridge	"	" "
Nov. 25, 1813	Alson Pond	Franklin	Abigail Cornelia Patch	"	" "
March 10, 1814	Lemuel Scott	Mansfield	Ruth Guild	"	" "
March 20, 1814	Phineas Cline	Wrentham	Betsey Hodges	"	" "
April 22, 1814	Preston Ware	Franklin	Jerusha Wright	"	" "
June 29, 1814	Willard Pond	"	Sally Hills	"	" "
July 14, 1814	Levi Ellis	Dedham	Delia Richardson	"	" "
July 28, 1814	Willard Gay, Esq.	Franklin	Martha Emmons	"	" "
Nov. 24, 1814	Eli Pond	Cumberland	Mrs. Ruth Bullard	Holliston	" "
Dec. 1, 1814	Alfred B. Lee	Franklin	Lydia Guild	Franklin	" "
Jan. 12, 1815	Nathan Partridge	Colerain	Sally Bassett	"	" "
Feb. 7, 1815	Calvin Pennell	Medway	Rebeca Mann	"	" "
April 12, 1815	Rev. Jacob Ide	Franklin	Mary Emmons	"	" "
Nov. 16, 1815	Peter Fisher, Jur.	"	Mary Hawes	"	" "
Nov. 23, 1815	Dea. James Metcalf	"	Mrs. Olive Gilmore	"	" "
Nov. 30, 1815	Melville Knapp	"	Clarinda Pond	"	" "
Dec. 21, 1815	Alfred Ware	Walpole, N. H.	Jemima Fisher	"	" "
Jan. 16, 1816	Henry Rice		Polly Morse	"	" "

* Plantation No. 2, First Range.

FRANKLIN TOWN RECORDS—MARRIAGES.

DATE OF MARRIAGE.	GROOM. NAME.	RESIDENCE.	BRIDE. NAME.	RESIDENCE.	BY WHOM MARRIED.
Jan. 18, 1816	Morse Ellis	Medway	Almira Woodward	Franklin	Doct. Nath'l Emmons
April 3, 1816	Isaac Sawin	Dedham	Melatiah Everett	"	"
April 4, 1816	Joseph Harding	Franklin	Matilda Butterworth	"	"
April 25, 1816	Capt. Samuel Allen	Medway	Julitta Metcalf	"	"
July 4, 1816	Alfred Knapp	Franklin	Eleanor Hawes	"	"
Sept. 5, 1816	Justin Pond	"	Ruth Davis Perry	"	"
Oct. 3, 1816	Jarvis Deane	Salisbury, Vt.	Nancy Torrey	"	"
Oct. 8, 1816	Major Joel Robinsson	Paris	Sally Heaton	"	"
Oct. 29, 1816	Oliver Gridley, Jur.	Franklin	Sally Lethbridge	"	"
Feb. 20, 1817	Nathan Place	Cumberland	Beriah Crooks	"	"
June 16, 1817	Joseph Gillmor, Jur.	Franklin	Sarah Shaw	"	"
June 19, 1817	Samuel Ware, Jur.	"	Sally Daniels	"	"
June 26, 1817	Joel Adams	"	Lois Ware	"	"
Sept. 4, 1817	Cephas Holbrook	Bellingham	Polly Knapp	"	"
Sept. 21, 1817	Benjamin Hathaway	Savoy	Betsey Edwards	"	"
Oct. 9, 1817	Seth L. Hartshorn	Franklin	Lydia Paddock	"	"
Oct. 23, 1817	Piam Bullard	"	Lucy Morse	"	"
Nov. 6, 1817	Samuel Haskill, Jur.	Bellingham	Amanda Pond	"	"
Nov. 27, 1817	Samuel Payson	Holliston	Adela Pond	"	"
Dec. 4, 1817	Cephas Bullard	Franklin	Susa Morse	"	"
Dec. 18, 1817	Joseph Gillmor	"	Maria Dilburr	"	"
Feb. 18, 1818	Philo Thurston	"	Julia M. Daniels	"	"
March 20, 1818	Lt. Robert Gillmor	"	Rebecca Gillmore McLane	Wrentham	"
March 20, 1818	William Adams	"	Huldah Nickleson	Franklin	"
April 2, 1818	Cyrus Guild	"	Annie Pierce	"	"
April 6, 1818	Rufus Miller	"	Sena Metcalf	"	"
Aug. 14, 1817	*David Horton	"	†Susan Raymond	"	Lewis Fisher, Esq., J. P.
May 17, 1816	Isaac Harrington	"	Lucy Raymond	"	"
March 1, 1818	Shepherd Perkins	Holliston	Elsa Daniels	"	Joseph Bacon, Esq., J. P.
April 19, 1818	Cushman Thayer	Mendon	Miranda Pond	"	Doct. Nath'l Emmons
May 12, 1818	Duty Sayles	Cumberland	Nancy Butterworth	"	"
July 20, 1818	Calvin Sampson	Roxbury	Hepzibah Lethbridge	"	"
Aug. 27, 1818	John Pushee	Franklin	Hannah Devrant	"	"

* Late of Rehoboth. † Late of Middleborough.

FRANKLIN TOWN RECORDS—MARRIAGES.

DATE OF MARRIAGE.	GROOM.		BRIDE.		BY WHOM MARRIED.
	NAME.	RESIDENCE.	NAME.	RESIDENCE.	
Sept. 23, 1818	Weston Fisher	Franklin	Margaret Levenseller	Franklin	Doct. Nath'l Emmons
Oct. 22, 1818	Aaron Merrifield	"	Mary Thayer	"	"
Oct. 21, 1818	William Jackson	"	Anna Pratt	"	"
Nov. 11, 1818	George W. Lawton	Bellingham	Cynthia Pond	"	"
Dec. 3, 1818	Austin Woodward	Franklin	Mary Ann Vox	"	"
Dec. 17, 1818	Lysander B. Hills	"	Elizabeth Lambert	"	"
Jan. 7, 1819	John Nutter	"	Polly Whiting	"	"
Feb. 7, 1819	Samuel B. Fisher	"	Melia Metcalf	"	"
April 8, 1819	Elisha Bullard	"	Rena Fisher	"	"
April 22, 1819	Lewis Hills	"	Anna Lawrence	"	"
Sept. 1, 1819	Samuel Fichen	Chelmsford	Lois Blake	"	"
Sept. 7, 1819	Dr. Elisha Harding	Franklin	Amelia Hawes	"	"
Oct. 3, 1819	Simeon Powers	Croyden, N. H.	Miriam Partridge	"	"
Nov. 1, 1819	Phinehas Partridge	Franklin	Polly Wheeler	"	"
Nov. 3, 1819	Seneca Hills	"	Maria Richardson	"	"
Nov. 18, 1819	John Pierce, Jur.	"	Julia Brownell	"	"
Nov. 23, 1819	Caleb B. Kingsbury	"	Natalia Walker	Medway	"
Dec. 23, 1819	James G. Green	"	Cynthia Pond	Franklin	"
April 2, 1820	Calvin Dean	"	Eliza Hewett	"	"
May 7, 1820	Andrew Simmonds	Norton	Lucy Becket	"	James Adams, Esq., J. P.
April 9, 1820	Jabez Wright	Franklin	Mehitabel Rockwood	"	Doct. Nath'l Emmons
April 26, 1820	Seth Holbrook	Bellingham	Chloe Fairbanks Wales	"	"
April 27, 1820	Timothy L. Pond	Franklin	Abigail Fisher	"	"
May 5, 1820	Pelatiah Metcalf	Smithfield, R. I.	Abigail Hawes	"	"
June 7, 1820	Alexander C. Witt	Franklin	Mary Makepeace	"	"
June 7, 1820	Archibald C. Witt	"	Patty Fisher	"	"
Sept. 12, 1820	Samuel Millard	Attleboro	Eleanor Richardson	"	"
Dec. 7, 1820	James P. Pond	Franklin	Sukey Whiting	"	"
Dec. 18, 1820	Henry Daniels	"	Mary Metcalf	"	"
April 3, 1821	Edward Gay	"	Hannah Allen	"	"
April 5, 1821	Dea. Jesse Metcalf	Hope, Me.	Betsey Mann	"	"
April 14, 1821	George Cheever	Attleborough	Abigail Kingsbury	"	"
May 17, 1821	Simeon Fuller	Medway	Nancy Hartshorn	"	"
Oct. 15, 1821	Addison Metcalf	Winthrop, Me.	Chloe F. Adams	"	"

FRANKLIN TOWN RECORDS—MARRIAGES.   101

DATE OF MARRIAGE.	GROOM.		BRIDE.		BY WHOM MARRIED.
	NAME.	RESIDENCE.	NAME.	RESIDENCE.	
Nov. 12, 1821	Austin Blake	Franklin	Watee D. Perham	Upton	Doct. Nathaniel Emmons
Nov. 22, 1821	Charles Dunbar	"	Padience Perry	Franklin	"
Dec. 6, 1821	Erasmus Pond	"	Ruth M. Snow	"	"
Feb. 10, 1822	Nathan Penniman	"	Roxy Nichols	"	"
Mar. 4, 1822	Manly Lincoln	"	Fidelia Fearlum	"	"
Mar. 18, 1822	Charles Allen	"	Nancy Gay	"	"
Mar. 21, 1822	Joseph F. Gilmor	"	Sally P. Whiting	"	"
April 17, 1822	Samuel Cook	"	Joann Smith	"	"
April 25, 1822	Nathan Rockwood	"	Hannah F. Miller	"	"
May 1822	James Wales, Jr.	"	Sylvia Scott	"	"
June 2, 1822	Levi F. Morse	"	Tryphena Foster	"	"
June 25, 1822	Harvey Woodward	"	Miranda Ware	Paxton	"
Aug. 29, 1822	Abijah Clark, Jr.	"	Susan Wadsworth	Franklin	"
Sept. 12, 1822	Charles M. Fisher	"	Olive Boyden	"	"
Sept. 15, 1822	Alfred Woodward	"	Carline M. Wright	"	"
Oct. 31, 1822	Seth Wadsworth	"	Olive Metcalf	"	"
Nov. 26, 1822	Dr. Spencer Pratt	Barre	Jane Wheeler	"	"
Nov. 28, 1822	Morris Lincoln	Franklin	Susan Thayer	"	"
Dec. 4, 1822	David P. Blake	"	Polly B. Pond	"	"
Dec. 5, 1822	John H. Richardson	"	Louisa Pike	"	"
Jan. 1, 1823	Frederick A. Ware	"	Sarah Morse	"	"
Jan. 13, 1823	Nathan Daniels, Jr.	"	Roxana Thayer	"	"
April 10, 1823	Luther Gowen	"	Polly Hartshorn	"	"
April 17, 1823	Jarvis H. Hills	Wrentham	Phila Brown	"	"
May 1, 1823	Samuel Fales, 2d	Pawtucket	Mary H. Hills	"	"
Dec. 5, 1822	Jedediah Phipps	Franklin	Rhoda Morse	"	"
May 8, 1823	Willard Johnson	"	Parmelia Clark	"	"
May 22, 1823	Asa Whiting	"	Betsy W. Boyd	"	"
Sept. 30, 1823	Nathaniel Fisher	"	Louiza Blanchard	"	"
Oct. 8, 1823	Fisher Daniels	"	Eunice Adams	"	"
Oct. 12, 1823	Preston Woodward	Westborough	Elisabeth Nason	"	"
Nov. 6, 1823.	Asa B. Furbush	Mansfield	Mary Fisher	"	"
Nov. 13, 1813	Willard Hatten	Franklin	Eliza Thayer	"	"
Nov. 20, 1823	Rufus Basset		Mary Smith	"	"

DATE OF MARRIAGE.	GROOM. NAME.	RESIDENCE.	BRIDE. NAME.	RESIDENCE.	BY WHOM MARRIED.
Feb. 12, 1824	Elijah Nason	Franklin	Mary Rockwood	Franklin	Doct. Nath'l Emmons
May 13, 1824	Robert Blake, Jr.	"	Sally Miller	"	"
July 3, 1823	Samuel Heaton	"	Turzah Carlton	"	Rev. Abial Fisher, Jr.*
Nov. 2, 1823	James O. Brown	"	Nancy Guild	"	Rev. Silas Hall†
May 31, 1824	George Washington Morse	"	Patty Lincoln	"	Doct. Nath'l Emmons
June 3, 1824	Julius Fisher	"	Mary W. Horton	"	"
June 17, 1824	Herman Blake	"	Nancy Miller	"	"
July 22, 1824	Elliot Hills	"	Peggy Rockwood	"	"
Dec. 16, 1824	Dr. Jacob Kittereclge	Dover, N. H.	Lucinda Gridley	"	"
Jan. 18, 1825	Waldo C. Perry	Franklin	Juliann Boyd	"	"
Nov. 4, 1824	Aaron C. Hawkins	Cumberland	Esther Fisher	"	Mr. John Allen‡
March 3, 1825	Hopkins Shipy	Franklin	Bathsheba Inman	"	"
March 10, 1825	John Woods	"	Persis Johnson	"	"
Aug. 9, 1818	Elihu Pond, Jr.	"	Rachel Fuller	"	Lewis Fisher, Esq., J. P.
May 1, 1825	Michael Metcalf	"	Sally Clark	"	Doct. Nath'l Emmons
May 24, 1825	Amory B. Cook	Wrentham	Mary Hawes	Wrentham	"
May 25, 1825	Eli Pond, Jr.	Sutton	Mariah Bullard	Franklin	"
Aug. 28, 1825	George Hall	Wrentham	Molia Fisher	"	"
Sept. 1, 1825	Capt. Joel Hills	Belfast, Me.	Abigail Hawes	"	"
Oct. 4, 1825	Cyrus Allen	Franklin	Sarah Bacon	"	"
Oct. 9, 1825	Martin C. Forrist	Foxborough	Prudence Chamberlain	"	"
Nov. 16, 1825	Capt. Joseph Merian	Framingham	Alice Thayer	"	"
Nov. 24, 1825	Lucius Messenger	Medway	Lucretia Woodward	"	"
Dec. 29, 1825	Albert E. Daniels	Franklin	Olive G. Hills	"	"
Jan. 5, 1826	Thomas Thain	"	Maranda Cook	"	"
Feb. 26, 1826	Increase Sumner Pond	"	Clarinda Allen	"	"
March 16, 1826	Dr. John C. Metcalf	"	Abigail Holbrook	"	"
April 5, 1826	David Daniels	"	Hannah Partridge	"	"
April 13, 1826	Adin Fisher	Walpole	Mary Clark	"	"
April 27, 1826	William Buffington	Franklin	Mrs. Margaret Mann	"	"
May 4, 1826	Job Broady	"	Mrs. Anna Jackson	"	"
May 25, 1826	Amos H. Allen	"	Abigail Daniels	"	"
June 1, 1826	Thomas Stanton	Newton	Betsey Boyden	"	"

* Bellingham. † Attleborough. ‡ Wrentham.

FRANKLIN TOWN RECORDS—MARRIAGES.

DATE OF MARRIAGE.	GROOM.		BRIDE.		BY WHOM MARRIED.
	NAME.	RESIDENCE.	NAME.	RESIDENCE.	
Dec. 25, 1825	Capt. Ichabod Dean	Franklin	Hannah Fisher	Franklin	Rev. Adin Ballou, Milford
June 29, 1825	Rev. William Bowen	Haverhill	Charlotte Emeline Weeden	"	Rev. John Allen, Wrentham
July 23, 1826	Jairius Whiting	Franklin	Mary Cheney	"	Doct. Nath'l Emmons
Aug. 23, 1826	Hiram Clark	Croyden, N. H.	Adeline Fisher	"	"
Nov. 30, 1826	Josiah Hawes	Franklin	Esther Taft	"	"
Mar. 25, 1827	George W. Nason	"	Hannah C. Pond	"	"
April 1, 1827	Hiram Cook	Mendon	Betsy Ware	"	"
Aug. 19, 1827	Hezekiah Hawkins	Franklin	Sarah Reading Carleton	"	James Adams, Esq., J. P.
Jan. 24, 1828	Horace B. Hall	"	Mary Ann W. Gillmore	"	Rev. Nathan Holman
April 16, 1829	John Wilson Metcalf	Wrentham	Caroline Fayette Pratt	"	Rev. Adin Ballou
June 19, 1828	Daniel Addison Ware	"	Levina Miller	"	Rev. Elisha Fisk, Wrentham
Sept. 18, 1828	Daniel Merrill Hancock	"	Rachel Johnson Miller	"	"
Oct. 22, 1828	David Farrington	Franklin	Charlotte Casper	"	"
Jan. 22, 1829	Benjamin Dore	Wrentham	Susan Lawrence	"	"
Mar. 2, 1828	Hyman Brunswick	Boston	Emeline H. B. Voax	"	"
Mar. 2, 1828	John Torry	Sutton	Caroline Fisher	"	Rev. Moses Thacher, Wrentham
July 13, 1828	Thomas Goldthwart, Jr.	Northbridge	Abigail Skinner	"	"
Oct. 21, 1828	Samuel Fisher	Providence, R. I.	Harriet Tiffany	"	"
Feb. 22, 1829	Lewis Thompson	Franklin	Polly Sweet	"	"
April 5, 1829	Asa G. Norcross	"	Irine Fisher	"	"
May 31, 1829	Richard Whitaker	Providence	Mary Ann Gillmor	"	"
June 10, 1829	Nathan Horr	Franklin	Betsy Fuller	"	Rev. Adin Ballou, Milford
May 7, 1829	Benjamin W. Ripley	Milford	Lucy Cook	"	"
May 7, 1829	Nathan Comestock, Jr.	Wrentham	Betsey Cook	"	"
July 3, 1829	John Robertson	Medway	Eliza M. Thurston	"	Rev. E. Smalley, Franklin
Sept. 15, 1829	Sullivan Sweet	Marlborough, Conn.	Caroline Tillinghest	"	"
Oct. 18, 1829	John J. Fisher	Franklin	Dory Munle	"	"
Oct. 27, 1829	Dr. John W. Tenney	Sutton	Eliza J. Fisher	"	"
Oct. 29, 1829	William Hills	Wrentham	Marietta L. Lawrence	"	"
Nov. 23, 1829	Simeon Lesure	Franklin	Abigail Pond	"	"
Feb. 18, 1830	Hanan Metcalf	"	Prudence Keith	"	"
Mar. 18, 1830	Elisha Foster	"	Sarah Lane	"	"
April 29, 1830	Amos H. Allen	"	Mary W. Simons	"	"
June 1, 1830	Rev. Asa Hixon	Oakham	Charlotte Baker	"	"

DATE OF MARRIAGE.	GROOM. NAME.	GROOM. RESIDENCE.	BRIDE. NAME.	BRIDE. RESIDENCE.	BY WHOM MARRIED.
Sept. 2, 1830	Willis Wales	Franklin	Esther B. Warfield	Franklin	Lewis Fisher, Esq., J. P.
Dec. 17, 1827	William Gilhmore, 2d	"	Betsey Clark	"	Rev. Stephen Gano*
Dec. 30, 1830	Preston Ellis	"	Samantha Partridge	"	Calvin Newton†
Dec. 22, 1830	Theron C. Hills	"	Hannah D. Snow	"	Rev. Adin Ballou†
Nov. 25, 1830	Timothy Gay	"	Julia Barden	"	Rev. E. Smalley
Dec. 26, 1830	Randall T. Brayton	Killingley, Conn.	Fanny Claflin	"	"
Feb. 8, 1831	Levi Williams	Franklin	Pamela Boyden	"	"
Feb. 24, 1831	Amos Adams	"	Sally Partridge	"	"
Dec. 1, 1831	William Lindley	"	Sukey P. Cook	"	Rev. Adin Ballou†
June 9, 1831	George W. Nason	"	Peacy B. Cook	"	Rev. E. Smalley
June 27, 1831	Charles Hawes	Wrentham	Susan Guild	"	"
July 27, 1831	Alexander Dunn	Bangor, Me.	Caroline Boyden	"	"
Oct. 27, 1831	Edwin Eaton	North Bridgewater	Abigail P. Allen	"	"
Dec. 22, 1831	Philander Gilmore	Franklin	Nancy Clark	"	"
Jan. 19, 1832	Alfred Pond	"	Louisa Fisher	"	"
March 6, 1832	Sylvester Clark	Uxbridge	Rhoda Baker	"	"
April 16, 1832	Emerson Fales	Holliston	Deborah Snow	"	"
April 17, 1832	Wilkes Gay, Jr.	Franklin	Miranda Thurston	"	"
Oct. 5, 1829	Jemotis Pond	"	Betsey Wood	"	"
May 2, 1832	Lewis Young	Dorchester	Caroline Morse	"	Wm. Makepeace, Jr., J.P.
May 9, 1832	Calvin Smith	Franklin	Nancy Melinda Clark	"	Rev. E. Smalley
Aug. 9, 1832	John Pierce	Wrentham	Eliza Whiting	"	"
Sept. 11, 1832	Edwin E. Blake	Franklin	Lydia Morse	"	"
Sept. 16, 1832	Jedediah Phipps	Medway	Julia M. Boyden	"	"
Sept. 20, 1832	Elias Dupee	Franklin	Nancy Cleaveland	"	"
Oct. 1, 1832	Reuben Cook	East Sudbury	Chloe A. Twitchell	"	"
Nov. 29, 1832	Edwin A. Roby	Franklin	Adeline J. Gilmore	"	"
Dec. 18, 1832	Silas Bullard	Holliston	Nancy Thurston	Medway	"
March 13, 1833	Stephen Metcalf, Jr.	Franklin	Lucretia Whipple	Franklin	"
March 16, 1823	Obadiah Adams, Jr.	Wrentham	Susan P. Smith	"	"
April 18, 1833	Daniel Whiting	Franklin	Rhoda Foster	"	"
	Amos A. Wales	"	Sarah Fairbanks	"	"
	Elias Metcalf				

* Providence, R. I. † Bellingham. ‡ Mendon.

FRANKLIN TOWN RECORDS—MARRIAGES.

DATE OF MARRIAGE.	GROOM. NAME.	RESIDENCE.	BRIDE. NAME.	RESIDENCE.	BY WHOM MARRIED.
Nov. 25, 1833	Dr. Shadrach Atwood	Bellingham	Ruth M. Pond	Franklin	Rev. Adin Ballou, Mendon
May 8, 1833	Ezekiel Adams	Providence	Maria Brick	"	Rev. E. Smalley
June 6, 1833	Jeremiah Burnam	Milford, N. H.	Abigail Whiting	"	"
Aug. 29, 1833	Marshall P. Wilder	Dorchester	Abigail Baker	"	"
Sept. 16, 1833	Daniel C. Fisher, Jr.	Franklin	Silvia D. Wood	"	"
Oct. 30, 1833	Camillas Hall, 2d	Providence	Jemima Wales	"	"
Nov. 21, 1833	William Aldrich	Wrentham	Nancy M. Gillmore	"	"
Nov. 28, 1833	Simeon P. Adams	Franklin	Harriet B. Wood	"	"
Mar. 27, 1834	Lyman P. Ware	Wrentham	Clarissa Boyden	"	"
July 2, 1834	Alpheus C. Grant	Milford	Hannah A. Wiggin	"	Rev. Stephen Cutler, Mendon
May 12, 1834	Elias Blake, Jr.	Wrentham	Mary Ann Adams	"	Rev. E. Smalley
May 22, 1834	Daniel Arnold, Jr.	Bellingham	Jane Martin	"	"
Aug. 13, 1834	Elias Baker	Franklin	Hannah Foster	"	"
Nov. 27, 1834	Erastus Rockwood	"	Mary Ann Daniels	"	"
Dec. 29, 1834	Lyman P. White	"	Meranda E. Pond	"	"
Jan. 1, 1835	Levi L. Harwood	Sherburn	Ann P. Hills	"	"
Mar 2, 1835	Ira Heywood	Plainfield, N. H.	Elizabeth C. N. Woodward		"
April 2, 1835	Emerson Adams	Franklin	Abigail Blake		Wm. Makepeace, Jr., J. P.
Mar. 8, 1835	Alonzo H. Wood	Wrentham	Abigail B. Glidden	Wrentham	George Makepeace, Esq., J. P.
Dec. 14, 1834	Gordon Rawson	Lowell	Sarah Cummings		"
Feb. 26, 1835	Jedediah Phipps	Franklin	Martha C. Hills	Hubbardston, Vt.	Rev. Joseph T. Massey
Nov. 19, 1835	William G. Whipple	"	Mary Cleaveland	Franklin	John C. Newell, Wrentham
Jan. 10, 1836	David Covill	Bellingham	Lucy L. Engley	"	Wm. Makepeace, Jr., J. P.
Jan. 21, 1836	Jonas Kimball	Franklin	Nancy M. Pettis		
May 5, 1835	David Ely		Abigail T. Thurston		Rev. E. Smalley
June 11, 1835	David Cheney	Lisbon, Me.	Nancy Gillmore		"
Aug. 2, 1835	Leonard A. Arnold	Cumberland	Abigail C. Gillmore		"
Aug. 10, 1835	Wm. F. Fuller	Franklin	Prudence Clark		"
Sept. 29, 1835	Luther Blake	"	Polly B. Blake	Medway	"
Oct. 8, 1835	Elijah Clark	Medway	Mary A. Kingsbury	Franklin	"
Oct. 12, 1835	John H. Fisher	Franklin	Belenda Adams		"
Nov. 19, 1835	Joel G. Partridge	Medway	Emeline M. Richardson		"
Nov. 19, 1835	Horatio Kingsbury	Franklin	Adelia R. Gilmore		"

* Bellingham.

FRANKLIN TOWN RECORDS—MARRIAGES.

DATE OF MARRIAGE.	GROOM. NAME.	RESIDENCE.	BRIDE. NAME.	RESIDENCE.	BY WHOM MARRIED.
Dec. 3, 1835	Charles G. Blake	Franklin	Lovrinda A. Ballou	Franklin	Rev. E. Smalley
March 28, 1836	Apollos Wilmarth	"	Aldana L. Adams	"	"
April 25, 1836	Charles T. Clark	"	Adeline Clark	"	"
May 26, 1835	Wm. Whittemore	Hubbardston	Martha W. Phipps	"	Rev. Doct. N. Emmons §
March 31, 1837	Walter H. Gay	Franklin	Sally N. Hawkins	"	Willis Fisher, Esq., J. P.
May 5, 1836	Elihu Pond, Esq.	"	Marena Allen	"	Rev. E. Smalley
June 22, 1836	Benjamin Foster	"	Mary Ann W. Cook	"	"
Sept. 1, 1836	Caleb Fisher	"	Achsah Metcalf	"	"
Oct. 20, 1836	Asa D. Perry	"	Mrs. Rachel E. Fisher	"	"
Feb. 21, 1837	Mortimer Blake	"	Harriet L. Daniels	"	"
April 6, 1837	Gilbert A. Ware	Grafton	Janitt Shields	"	"
April 19, 1837	Samuel Metcalf, Jr.	Franklin	Della E. Bacon	"	"
June 7, 1837	Ezekiel Adams	Providence	Susan Fisher	"	"
June 18, 1837	Moses Kimball	Franklin	Mary Hatten	"	"
Sept. 4, 1837	Nathan Pond	"	Olive Marsh	"	"
Oct. 24, 1837	Thomas Kideler	"	Nancy Fisher	Holliston	"
Nov. 29, 1837	James Coolidge	"	Ruth Butler	Franklin	"
Jan. 1, 1838	Ebinezer E. Warfield	"	Helen B. Whiting	Medfield	Rev. Henry Gifford
March 1, 1838	Levi Blake	"	Louisa Barden	Franklin	Rev. E. Smalley
March 21, 1838	Warrin J. Ballou	Cumberland	Almira Lawrence	"	"
April 26, 1838	Erastus L. Metcalf	Franklin	Emeline Fisher	"	"
May 3, 1838	Leonard Brown	Mendon	Susan Sergeant	"	"
June 21, 1838	Ebenezer W. Robinson	Freestown	Sarah B. Adams	"	"
June 27, 1838	John Cushing	Medway	Sarah Maria Pond	"	"
Sept. 6, 1838	James S. Corbet	Franklin	Abigail Bassett	"	Rev. John Parker *
Dec. 6, 1838	Barnum Blake	"	Harriet F. Gillmore	"	Jon. E. Forbush †
Nov. 8, 1838	Abiram W. Wales	"	Olive M. Ware	"	Rev. J. T. Massey ‡
Nov. 29, 1838	Theodore S. Bemis	"	Persis Hills	"	"
Nov. 15, 1838	Willard C. Whiting	"	Charlotte Miller	"	"
Feb. 19, 1839	Adams Daniels	Medway	Abby Fisher	"	Rev. T. D. Southworth
April 2, 1839	Jonathan Pond, Jr.	Franklin	Eliza J. Fisher		"
April 2, 1839	Wm. Gaskell	"	Abigail Hubbard		"
April 25, 1839	Jeremiah Claflin	"	Lucy Ann Robinson		"

* Holliston.   † West Wrentham.   ‡ Bellingham.   § Congregational Clergyman.

FRANKLIN TOWN RECORDS—MARRIAGES. 107

DATE OF MARRIAGE.	GROOM.		BRIDE.		BY WHOM MARRIED.
	NAME.	RESIDENCE.	NAME.	RESIDENCE.	
Oct. 23, 1839	Charles E. Gates	Walpole	Harriet S. Wales	Franklin	Benj. H. Davis, Wrentham
Dec. 25, 1782	Timothy Rockwood	Franklin	Sarah Philips	Bellingham	Rev. Noah Alden*
Jan. 14, 1786	John Govis		Mary Cook		" "
Jan. 20, 1791	Jesse Holbrook	Bellingham	Clarissa Hixon	Franklin	" "
March 26, 1795	Joseph Ellis	Franklin	Abigail Pratt	Bellingham	" "
May 7, 1795	Luther Cobb	Bellingham	Rachel Clark	Franklin	" "
Nov. 4, 1795	Phineas Holbrook	"	Polly Waller	"	" "
May 13, 1770	Amariah Holbrook		Molley Wright		
April 20, 1798	Duty Allen	Franklin	Betsey Briggs	Mansfield	Rev. Roland Green†
July 25, 1785	Samuel Metcalf	"	Mary Clark	Paxton	Rev. Daniel Grovesner‡
Nov. 5, 1786	George Adams	"	Hannah Pettee	Foxborough	Rev. Thomas Kindell§
April 17, 1783	John Gilmore	"	Mary Cook	"	
May 1, 1796	Samuel Guild	"	Ruth Morse	Wrentham	Rev. Joseph Benn‖
Jan. 14, 1798	Simon Cutler	"	Lydia Grant	"	Rev. William Williams‖
July 3, 1798	Amasa Cook	"	Patty Heaton	"	
July 5, 1786	Samuel Holbrook	Wrentham	Mary Fisher	Franklin	Rev. John Cleaveland‖
Jan. 10, 1787	Ward Adams	Franklin	Olive Daggett	Wrentham	Rev. David Avery‖
Dec. 24, 1793	Amos Hawes	"	Meletiah Everett	"	
Sept. 25, 1794	Calvin Turner	"	Olive Ballard	Dedham	Rev. Jabez Chickering¶
Sept. 9, 1789	Jeremiah Metcalf	"	Bathsheba Crane	Oxford	Rev. Elias Dudley, Oxford
Oct. 20, 1790	Jno. Kingsbury	"	Rebecca Ayers	Brookfield	Rev. Joseph Appleton 1
June 27, 1793	Nathaniel Adams	"	Zebiah Holbrook	Sharon	Rev. Philip Curtis, Sharon
Oct. 16, 1788	Elijah White	"	Betsey Wiswell	Holliston	Rev. Timothy Dickinson 2
Feb. 21, 1792	Amos Fisher	"	Lois Hill	Sherburn	Rev. Elijah Brown 3
Sept. 23, 1797	Otis Pond	"	Cynthia Sparhawk	"	
Dec. 18, 1797	Nathan Woodward	"	Anna Armsby	Sutton	Rev. Edmond Mills, Sutton
Nov. 17, 1797	Darius Pond	"	Persis Armsby	"	" "
Oct. 20, 1785	Solomon Gay	"	Cloe Daniels	Franklin	Samuel Barrett, Esq. 4
June 28, 1792	Benjamin Kingsbury	"	Olive Blake	Wrentham	Rev. George Morey 5
Nov. 7, 1793	Darius Morse	"	Esperance Adams	Franklin	Seth Ballard, Esq. 5
Nov. 16, 1794	Asa Harding	"	Comfort Boyden	Walpole	Rev. George Morey 5
Jan. 5, 1796	Joseph Whiting	"	Polly Page	"	" "
	Jason Morse		Miriam Smith		

* Bellingham. † Mansfield. ‡ Paxton. § Foxborough. ‖ Wrentham. ¶ Dedham. 1 Brookfield. 2 Holliston. 3 Sherborn. 4 Boston. 5 Walpole.

FRANKLIN TOWN RECORDS—MARRIAGES.

DATE OF MARRIAGE.	GROOM.		BRIDE.		BY WHOM MARRIED.
	NAME.	RESIDENCE.	NAME.	RESIDENCE.	
May 30, 1789	Royal Ellis	Franklin	Sally Turner	Walpole	Seth Bullard, Esq.*
Oct. 17, 1792	Augustus Neel	Mendon	Betsey Clark	Franklin	Rev. Caleb Alexander†
Aug. 28, 1788	Jonathan Stockwell, Jr.	Douglas	Polly Smith	"	Rev. Isaac Stone, Douglas
May 4, 1794	Timothy Blake	Franklin	Julia Dean	Shrewsbury	Rev. Joseph Sumner‡
Nov. 25, 1784	Joshua Slocomb	"	Lucy Dunn	Northbridge	John Crane, Northbridge
July 5, 1780	Amos Lawrence		Hannah Daniels	Medway	Rev. N. Bucknam§
Oct. 25, 1780	Daniel Richardson	Medway	Lydia Baron	Franklin	"
May 1, 1781	Benjamin Pond, 3d	Franklin	Catherine Cutler	Medway	Rev. David Sanford§
June 21, 1781	Billings Fairbanks	"	Abigail Fisher	Franklin	"
Jan. 14, 1782	Ichabod Hawes	Medway	Sarah Pond	"	"
Aug. 22, 1785	Asa Adams	Natick	Martha Metcalf	"	"
May 1, 1786	Jeremiah Parker	Whiting	Hannah Pond		"
Jan. 26, 1787	James Richardson	Franklin	Hannah Hayward	Medway	Rev. Nathan Bucknam§
Jan. 9, 1788	Seth Fisher		Lydia Ellis		Rev. David Sanford§
May 29, 1788	Joel Hawes	Medway	Phila Thayer	Franklin	"
Oct. 18, 1789	Ziba Richardson	Franklin	Huldah Thompson	Medway	Rev. Benjamin Green§
Feb. 2, 1791	Paul Metcalf	"	Persis Richardson	"	Rev. David Sanford§
Nov. 3, 1790	Jonathan Metcalf	"	Mary Adams		"
Nov. 3, 1790	Timothy Pond	"	Rachel Adams		"
Sept. 20, 1791	Benajah Pond		Mary Pond	Franklin	"
Jan. 27, 1892	Oliver Pond		Mine Pond	"	"
Feb. 9, 1792	Elisha Sanford	Medway	Hannah Metcalf	"	"
Nov. 25, 1793	Simeon Clark	Franklin	Sally White	Medway	"
April 24, 1794	Nathan White	"	Susanna Cutler	"	"
Jan. 21, 1796	William Pond	"	Polly Hide	"	"
April 26, 1796	Thomas Baron	"	Ruth Adams		"
Sept. 29, 1796	John Jones	Medway	Sarah Ellis	Franklin	Abijah Richardson, Esq., J.P.
Jan. 19, 1797	Goldsbury Pond	Franklin	Priscilla Fisher	"	"
Nov. 15, 1788	Nahum Hayward	Medway	Berijah Plimpton	Medway	Rev. David Sanford§
April 24, 1799	James Fales	"	Hannah Daggett	Franklin	"
Nov. 6, 1799	David Wright	Franklin	Hepzibah Hixson		"
Nov. 25, 1784	Joshua Slocomb	Douglas	Lucy Dunn	Northbridge	Rev. John Crane‖
Aug. 28, 1788	Jonathan Stockwell		Polly Smith	Franklin	Rev. Isaac Stone, Douglas

* Walpole. † Mendon. ‡ Shrewsbury. § Medway. ‖ Northbridge.

FRANKLIN TOWN RECORDS—MARRIAGES.

DATE OF MARRIAGE.	GROOM.		BRIDE.		BY WHOM MARRIED.
	NAME.	RESIDENCE.	NAME.	RESIDENCE.	
Oct. 17, 1792	Augustus Neel	Mendon	Betsey Clark	Franklin	Rev. Caleb Alexander*
March 5, 1794	John Adams	Franklin	Eunice Monlton	Dover	Rev. Benja. Cary, Dover
March 31, 1839	Gillmore Miller	"	Rhoda T. Clark	Wrentham	John E. Forbush†
April 21, 1839	George R. Gillmore	"	Eneline L. Barrows	Franklin	"
May 2, 1839	Jesse Miller	"	Nancy Hancock	Wrentham	"
Nov. 13, 1839	Daniel Lozell	Bellingham	Amey Guild	Franklin	"
Jan. 1, 1840	Lorenzo Miller	Rhode Island	Laretta W. Darling	"	Rev. T. D. Southworth
April, 1840	Elbridge Howe	Franklin	Olive Gillmore		"
"	Ebenezer E. Warfield	"	Sarah Morse		"
"	James A. Guild	"	Lucina Winn		"
"	Stephen C. Johnson	"	Juliana Metcalf		"
"	Charles E. Slocom	"	Abigail B. Fisher		"
"	Luther Ellis	"	Arathuse Wilson		"
"	William Gillmore	"	Chloe D. Perham		"
"	Joel E. Hunt	"	Emelia Knapp		"
"	Asa Harding	"	Mrs. Abigail Bassett		"
"	Gardner Adams	"	Eunice Darling		"
"	James Bigelow	"	Lucy Adams		"
March 31, 1841	Erasmus B. Metcalf	"	Anna S. Downe	Uxbridge‡	David A. Grosvenor†
April 28, 1841	Seth Inman	"	Elmira White	Franklin	Rev. Jacob Ide, Medway
June 3, 1841	Erastus Clark	"	Elizabeth Lawrence	"	
June 26, 1841	Abijah M. Pond	"	Melissia H. Woodward	"	Luther Bailey, Medway
	Jairus B. Lawrence	"	Maria B. Smith	"	Rev. T. D. Southworth
	Zenas Skinner	"	Anjinette Blake	"	"
	Daniel Penniman	"	Charlotte Pond	"	"
	Smith Fisher	"	Mary Clark	"	"
	James S. Rand	"	Sylvia L. Knapp	"	"
	Gilbert Hartshorn	"	Eleanor A. Haskell	"	"
	Charles E. Hart	"	Julia A. Daniels	"	"
	Lewis H. Marsh	"	Mary B. Morse	"	"
	John R. Thompson	"	Mary L. Blake	"	"
	Samuel Alexander	"	Betsey Ingley	"	"
	Peter Adams	"	Clarissa Richardson	"	"

* Mendon. † Wrentham. ‡ Uxbridge.

From May 1, 1840, to May 1, 1841, no other date.

FRANKLIN TOWN RECORDS—MARRIAGES.

DATE OF MARRIAGE.	GROOM. NAME.	RESIDENCE.	BRIDE. NAME.	RESIDENCE.	BY WHOM MARRIED.
Nov. 3, 1841	Wm. Fletcher	Franklin	Huldah Tiffany	Franklin	Rev. T. D. Southworth
Dec. , 1841	Lyman S. Ware	"	Susan Wood	"	S. C. Hewitt*
May 4, 1841	Wm. G. Whipple	"	Julia A. Lincoln	"	"
May 25, 1841	Sabin Holbrook	"	Maria Phips	"	Rev. T. D. Southworth
May 30, 1841	Samuel M. Bullard	"	Harriet A. Warfield	"	"
June 10, 1841	David Ware, Jr.	"	Betsey Pettis	"	"
Aug. 16, 1841	Charles Gowen	"	Harriet Phipps	"	"
Aug. 26, 1841	Richardson Metcalf	"	Mary A. Baker	"	"
Sept. 5, 1841	Horace S. Morse	"	Eliza Jane Daniels	"	"
Sept. 7, 1841	Elias Metcalf	"	Mrs. Nancy Cleaveland	"	"
Oct. 20, 1841	Nathan McKean	"	Mrs. Susan Hubbard	"	"
Nov. 4, 1841	Charles F. Daniels	"	Eliza Phipps	"	"
Dec. 2, 1841	Abit H. Balcom	"	Sabil M. Chase	"	"
Dec. 26, 1841	Nathan Ware	"	Elvira Hawes	"	"
Dec. 30, 1841	George A. Jordan	"	Sarah L. Winn	"	"
Jan. 16, 1842	James P. Gillmore	"	Hannah T. Thompson	"	"
April 19, 1842	George L. Partridge	"	Harriet Hancock	"	"
Oct. 30, 1842	Wm. T. Richardson	"	Ellen M. Gay	"	"
May 24, 1842	Hartford H. Franklin	"	Julia E. Guild	"	B. H. Davis, Attleboro
June 6, 1842	Joseph A. Paine	"	Amelia C. Buffington	"	Rev.Tertius D.Southworth
June 8, 1842	Daniel H. Forbes	"	Jemima J. Baker	"	"
Sept. 25, 1842	Joseph Moses	"	Julia A. Hardy	"	"
Oct. 23, 1842	Edward R. H. Gillmore	"	Susan E. Brown	"	"
Nov. 24, 1842	Augustus M. Blake	"	Mewlissia Hills	"	"
Dec. 1, 1842	Ellis P. Emerson	"	Mary S. Balcom	"	"
Mar. 5, 1843	Hiram Partridge	"	Betsey A. Daniels	"	"
April 18, 1843	Jerome Wescott	"	Almira Ballou	"	"
May 31, 1843	Caleb L. Coolidge	"	Lucinda Allen	"	Rev. Jacob Ide, Medway
Aug. 3, 1843	James P. Ray	Phila., Pa.	Susan Knapp	"	Wm. R. G. Miller, Milford
Aug. 20, 1843	J. Francis Atwood	Franklin	Anna M. Pond	"	Rev. Adin Ballou, Milford
May 4, 1843	Abijah T. Rockwood	"	Sarah M. Peck	"	Elisha Fisk, Wrentham
June 4, 1843	Willard Scott	"	Deborah F. Ellis	"	Rev. T. D. Southworth
	Elias Whiting	Seekonk	Mrs. Chloe D. Gillmore		

* West Wrentham

FRANKLIN TOWN RECORDS—MARRIAGES.

DATE OF MARRIAGE.	GROOM.		BRIDE.		BY WHOM MARRIED.
	NAME.	RESIDENCE.	NAME.	RESIDENCE.	
June 13, 1843	Abijah B. Warfield	Franklin	Sarah E. Nichols	Franklin	Rev. T. D. Southworth
June 28, 1843	George B. Pond	"	Clarissa Norcross	"	"
June 30, 1843	Saml. W. Grant	"	Mary H. Pond	"	"
Sept. 28, 1843	Jacob Kittridge	"	Elizabeth Pond	"	"
Oct. 25, 1843	Wm. Nye		Eliza Daniels	"	"
Nov. 30, 1843	Abijah Cook	Bellingham	Mrs. Roxana Penniman	"	"
March 17, 1844	Henry M. Daniels	Franklin	Susan Nye	"	"

I hereby certify that the foregoing is a true copy of the original record, and that the same has been transcribed by direction of the town.

Franklin, March 1, 1864.

Attest. A. A. RUSSEGUE,
Town Clerk.

Marriages in Franklin during the Year next preceding May 1, 1845 and 1846.

Single and First Marriage unless otherwise stated. Residence of Parents Franklin unless otherwise stated.

NAME AND SURNAME OF GROOM AND BRIDE.	AGE	OCCUPATION.	DATE OF MARRIAGE.	BY WHOM MARRIED.	PLACE OF BIRTH.	Residence at Time of Marriage.	NAME OF PARENTS.
Benjamin G. Seekel	24	Carpenter	July 7, 1844	Benjamin Wood		Providence, R.I.	Hiram
Jane E. Pond	20	Seamstress		Upton, Ms., Minister	Franklin	"	
Edward F. Dickerson	32	†	Aug. 1, 1844	Tartus D. Southworth		Canucant, O.	Eli M. & Melita Rockwood
*Harriet N. Winslow	28	§		Minister, Franklin	Franklin	"	
James D. Miller	24	$	Oct. 31, 1844	"		Boston	Lewis, Esq.
Harriet M. Patridge	20	Seamstress		"		Franklin	
Harlow Fisher	49	Labourer	Feb. 25, 1845	"		"	
*Ruth Scott	50	"		"		"	
†Erastus Richardson	50	Physician	April 13, 1845	"	Franklin	Eastport, Me.	Amasa & Lydia
Mary Shumway		House Keeper		"	Oxford	Franklin	
†Stephen W. Richardson	22	Yeoman	Feb. 5, 1845	D. Sanford, Medway	Franklin	"	Wilkes
Mary Bullard		House Keeper		Minister	Medway	"	
Eliab M. Pond		Yeoman	Feb. 11, 1845	"	Franklin	"	Leonard
Isabella I. Lawrence		Straw Sewer		"	"	"	
Bowers S. Chase		Fact'y Labourer	May 1, 1845				
Fanny Bradford							
†Seth Inman	49	Farmer	April 16, 1845	Jacob Ide		Franklin	Philip & Eleuthire
Catherine A. Partridge	22			Minister, Medway		"	Preston & Lucretia
Otis Metcalf	25	Carpenter	May 25, 1845	"		"	Nahum & Lucy
Lucy M. Daniels	21						

Marriages in Franklin during the year next preceding May 1, 1846, was eight.

Albert M. Richardson		School Teacher	May 30, 1845	T. D. Southworth		Franklin	Eli M. & Melita
Eliza W. Allen		Seamstress		Minister, Franklin		"	
Ebenezer N. Holmes		Farmer	Sept. 17, 1845	"		"	
Nancy Whitney		Straw Sewer				"	
Ezekiel W. Clark		Trader	Sept. 18, 1845	"		Paris, Me.	
Sarah T. Robinson		Straw Sewer				Franklin	
William M. Thayer		‡	Oct. 19, 1845	"		"	Davis & Betsey
Rebecca W. Richards		Straw Sewer				"	

* Widow.   † Widower.   ‡ Minister of the Gospel.   § Polisher of Piano Fortes.   1 Medway.

Marriages in Franklin during the Year next preceding May 1, 1846—Continued.

NAME AND SURNAME OF GROOM AND BRIDE.	AGE	OCCUPATION.	DATE OF MARRIAGE.	BY WHOM MARRIED.	PLACE OF BIRTH.	Residence at Time of Marriage	NAME OF PARENTS.
Caleb T. Nye		Store Keeper	Nov. 24, 1845	T. D. Southworth Minister, Franklin	Franklin	Franklin	Nathan & Nancy
Sophia B. Cleveland		Straw Sewer		"	"	"	Elisha
Elisha F. Richardson		Gardener	Dec. 4, 1845	"	"	"	Samuel
Olive D. Ware		Straw Sewer		"	"	"	
Andrew Grover		Boot Maker	April 22, 1846	"	"	Wrentham	
Almira C. Gould		Fact'y Laborer		"	"	Easton	
Olive Randall			Nov. 4, 1845	Peter Adams		Franklin	
Sarah A. Whittemore				J. P., Franklin		"	
Charles W. Ladd	23	Bon't Presser	April 5, 1846	Jacob Ide, Medway Minister	Roxbury	"	Asa & Betsey 1
Abby H. Clark	21	Straw Sewer			Franklin		Nathan & Nancy

Marriages in Franklin during the Year next preceding May 1, 1847 and 1848. Registered June 2, 1847.

NAME AND SURNAME OF GROOM AND BRIDE.	AGE	OCCUPATION.	DATE OF MARRIAGE.	BY WHOM MARRIED.	PLACE OF BIRTH.	Residence at Time of Marriage	NAME OF PARENTS.
*David Thompson	75	Farmer	Sept. 24, 1846	T. D. Southworth Minister, Franklin		Walpole, N. H.	David & Lucy 2
Esther Clark	65	House Work			Franklin	Franklin	Samuel & Olive
Oscar M. Bassett	23	Merchant	Oct. 1, 1846	"		"	Rufus 3
Susan M. Scott	18	Straw Sewer				"	Saul B. & Susan P.
Alexander Hart	27	Shoe Maker	Nov. 2, 1846	David Sanford Minister, Medway		"	Chas. C. & Ann
Caroline M. Daniels	22	Straw Sewer			Franklin	"	Ezra & Abigail
William E. Hubbard	20	Carpenter	Nov. 11, 1846	T. D. Southworth Minister, Franklin		"	Elisha & Amelia
Martha W. Chilson	20	Straw Sewer				Bellingham	Orren & Deadama 4
Gilbert B. George	23	Clerk	Nov. 19, 1846	David Sanford Minister, Medway		Roxbury	Jacob & Abigail 1
Helen C. Kingsbury	20	Straw Sewer			Franklin	Franklin	Adams & Polly
James Cutler, Jr.	27	Shoe Maker	Nov. 4, 1845	T. D. Southworth Minister, Franklin	Holliston	Holliston	James & Nancy 5
Louisa F. Morse	20	Straw Sewer	Nov. 16, 1846	"	Franklin	Franklin	Levi & Triphena
*John Park		Carpenter				Brookline	
Ellen Chamberlain							
Horace N. Adams	20	Boot Maker	Nov. 26, 1846	"	Franklin	Medway	Nathan & Roxana 6
Julia A. Wales	20	Straw Sewer				Franklin	Otis & Jerusha
Hiram Chase	21	Fact'y Laborer	March 4, 1847	Edward G. Sears Minister, N. Wrentham		"	Slade & Lurana
Matilda Small	24						Josiah & Deborah
Sabin Hubbard	23	Carpenter	March 24, 1847	T. D. Southworth Minister, Franklin	Franklin	"	Elisha & Amelia
Almira Sargent	21	Straw Sewer					Asa & Polly

* Widower.   1 Roxbury.   2 Walpole, N. H.   3 Foxboro.   4 Bellingham.   5 Holliston.   6 Medway.

Marriages in Franklin during the Year next preceding May 1, 1847 and 1848.—(Continued.)

NAME OF GROOM AND BRIDE.	AGE	OCCUPATION.	DATE OF MARRIAGE.	BY WHOM MARRIED.	PLACE OF BIRTH.	Residence at Time of Marriage.	NAME OF PARENTS.
Arival P. Ware	23	Carpenter	April 4, 1847	E. G. Sears, North Wrentham, Mass.		Medway, Mass.	Amherst & Lucinda 1
Mary A. Richardson	22	†				Franklin	Howard & Mary

Marriages in Franklin during the Year next preceding May 1, 1848 was Fourteen.—Registered June 6, 1848.

NAME OF GROOM AND BRIDE.	AGE	OCCUPATION.	DATE OF MARRIAGE.	BY WHOM MARRIED.	PLACE OF BIRTH.	Residence at Time of Marriage.	NAME OF PARENTS.
Henry E. Pond	23	‡	May 13, 1847	T. D. Southworth	Dedham	Franklin	Eliphalet & Ann 2
Louisa B. Loufflorough	23	‡		Minister of Franklin			Wade & Mary
John Metcalf	26	Shoe Maker	May 20, 1847	" "	Medway	Medway	Daniel & Clarissa 1
Mary T. Ballard	21	Straw Sewer			Franklin	Franklin	Elisha & Rena
Simeon Taylor, Jr.	29	§	June 10, 1847	Edward G. Sears		Boston	Simeon & Sibil 3
Nancy M. Harding	25	Straw Sewer		N. Wrentham	Franklin	Franklin	Lewis & Irena
Giles C. Kelsey	17	Shoe Maker	Sept. 6, 1847	Jacob Ide			Chas. C. & Sally 4
Sally Ann Warren	17	‖		Minister, Medway			Franklin & Polly
*Timothy E. Jones	48	Farmer	Aug. 16, 1847	David Metcalf, J. P.	Franklin		John & Sarah
Eliza F. Fee‖	24	House Work		Bellingham			Gersham & Eliza
Agustus H. Ballard	19	Carpenter	Sept. 16, 1847	T. D. Southworth			Hermon & Prudence
Maryann G. Hall	18	Straw Sewer		Minister, Franklin			Horace B. & M. A.
Enoch Bowen	23	Boot Maker	Oct. 6, 1847	Edward C. Rogers		Medway	Gardner J. & Betsey
Joanna A. Wales	22	Straw Sewer		Minister, W. Wrentham	Franklin	Franklin	Otis & Jerusha
Obadiah K. Johnson	21	Merchant	Oct. 7, 1847	T. D. Southworth		Cumberland, R.I.	Ruel & Betsey
Elizabeth C. Ware	21	Straw Sewer		Minister, Franklin	Franklin	Franklin	Willard & Anna
*John Drake	40	Farmer	Oct. 5, 1847	Abner Mason		Bellingham	John & Rebecca
Mary C. Grant	22	House Work		Minister of Medway		Medway	Rhodes & Martha
Edward H. Hixon	21	Shoe Maker	Oct. 6, 1847			Franklin	Reuben & Polly 1
Abigail Blake	21	Straw Sewer				Franklin	David P. & Polly
Darwin T. Briggs	24	Writing Master	Feb. 6, 1848	T. D. Southworth	Franklin	Providence, R. I.	Tyler & Joanna
†Almira B. Heath	22	Straw Sewer		Minister, Franklin		Franklin	Michael & Melia
*Alexander L. Hart	28	Boot Maker	April 6, 1848	David Sanford			Chas. C. & Ann
Martha A. Pond	24	House Work		Minister, Medway	Franklin		Malakial & Mary
Willard N. Blake	26	Shoe Maker	April 6, 1848	T. D. Southworth	"		Harvey & Betsey 1
Mehitable J. Cahoon	18	‡		Minister, Franklin			Joseph & Hannah 5
*Barnard Moore	27	Stone Cutter	April 12, 1848	D. Sanford		Medway	Otis & Susan
‖Mary H. Grant	24	House Work		Minister, Medway	Franklin	Franklin	Paul D. & Huldah Pond

* Widower. ‖ Widow. † Adopted daughter. ‡ Laborer in factory. § Piano Forte Maker. 1 Medway. 2 Dedham. 3 Boston. 4 Whiting. 5 Harwich.

FRANKLIN TOWN RECORDS—MARRIAGES. 115

Marriages in Franklin from May 1, 1848 to December 31, 1848.—Registered Dec. 25, 1849.

NAME OF BRIDE AND GROOM.	AGE.	OCCUPATION.	DATE OF MARRIAGE.	BY WHOM MARRIED.	PLACE OF BIRTH.	Residence at Time of Marriage	NAME OF PARENTS.
*Hiram Metcalf	40	Boot Maker	June 21, 1848	Jacob Ide, D.D.	Franklin	Blackstone	Sam'l & Mary C.
Melinda Fisher	31	Straw Sewer		Minister, Medway	"	Franklin	Levi & Susan
Alexander Thayer	21	Fact'y Laborer	June 25, 1848	T. D. Southworth	"	"	Sylvanus & Olive
Mary E. Hallet	20	"		Minister, Franklin	"	"	Henry & Hopey
Hanson E. Dickinson	30	Merchant	Aug. 14, 1848	" "	Granby	Granby	Erastus & Olive 1
Julia Ann Richardson	23	Straw Sewer		" "	Franklin	Franklin	Eli M. & Melita
Preston M. Farrington	23	Bon't Presser	Aug. 20, 1848	" "	Wrentham	"	Nathan & Julia
Caroline Thayer	21	Straw Sewer		" "	Franklin	"	Nath'l & Caroline
Edson Dana Hammond	22	Merchant	Oct. 8, 1848	" "	New York	New York	Paul & Abigail 2
Louisa Marion Thurston	19	Straw Sewer		" "	Franklin	Franklin	Daniel & Bathsheba
Alexander D. Pond	21	Boot Maker	Oct. 11, 1848	" "	"	"	Justin & Ruth
Lucinda L. Scott	20	Fact'y Laborer		" "	"	"	Lemuel & Ruth
Emerson N. Ballard	28	Farmer	Oct. 12, 1848	Jacob Ide, D.D.	Franklin	"	Elisha & Rena
Susan J. Partridge	23	House Work		Minister, Medway	Medway	"	Philip & Atthena
Waldo Daniels	21	Farmer	Oct. 15, 1848	T. D. Southworth	Franklin	"	Fisher & Eunice
Helen R. Gilmore	22	House Work		Minister, Franklin	Medfield	"	Marcus & Atarah 3
George N. Barber	24	Boot Maker	Nov. 15, 1848	Jacob Ide, D.D.	Medway	Medway	Asahel & Harriet 4
Mary A. Fuller	32	Straw Sewer		Minister, Medway	Franklin	Franklin	Moses & Mary
*Davis Thayer, Jr.	52	Merchant	Nov. 30, 1848	T. D. Southworth	"	"	Davis & Betsey
Mary N. Whiting	26	Straw Sewer		Minister, Franklin	"	Providence, R. I.	Joseph & Zealde
William R. Lincoln	25	Bon't Presser	Dec. 24, 1848	" "	"	Franklin	Manly & Fidelia
Deborah D. Tracy	22	Dress Maker			Rowe, Me.		Benja. & Sarah 5

Marriages in Franklin during the Year next preceding January 1, 1849.—Registered Jan. 10, 1850.

James T. Pebbles	28	Shoe Mann'f	Jan. 1, 1849	Abner Mason	Natick	Natick	John & Lucretia 6
Nancy L. Messenger	19	House Work		Minister, Medway	"	"	Edward & Peggy H. 6
Isreal W. Taylor	28	Cordwainer	Jan. 11, 1849	T. D. Southworth			Seth & Sally 7
Sarah J. Fisher	20	Straw Braider		Minister, Franklin	Franklin	Franklin	Weston & Susan
Gilbert C. Fisher	22	Farmer	April 15, 1849	" "	"	"	Adin & Mary
Emily J. Keith	19	House Work		" "	"	"	Charles & Nancy
James La Croix	25	Farmer	June 14, 1849	" "	Medway	Medway	William & Jamima 4
Mary S. Hodgers	23	Straw Sewer		" "	Franklin	Franklin	Willard & Mary

* Widower. 1 Granby. 2 New York. 3 Medfield. 4 Medway. 5 Rowe, Me. 6 Natick. 7 Lyman, Me.

Marriages in Franklin during the Year next preceding January 1, 1849.—(Continued.)

NAME OF BRIDE AND GROOM.	Age.	OCCUPATION.	DATE OF MARRIAGE.	BY WHOM MARRIED.	PLACE OF BIRTH.	Residence at Time of Marriage.	NAME OF PARENTS.
*Cyrus B. Snow	36	Merchant	June 27, 1849	T. D. Southworth	Bridgewater	Franklin	Cyrus & Ruth
Victoria M. Scott	19	House Work		Minister, Franklin	Pittston, Me.	"	Daniel & Ruth 1
David P. Baker	32	Merchant	June 28, 1849	"	Franklin	"	David & Jemima 2
Angenette L. Green	23	Straw Sewer		"	"	"	Martin & Lois
*Hartford Leonard	53	Blacksmith	June 28, 1849	David Sanford	Foxboro	"	Jacob & Milly 3
†Joanna W. Metcalf	46	Straw Sewer		Minister, Medway	Franklin	"	Jabez & Martha Norton
William E. Whiting	25	Bon't Presser	July 3, 1849	T. D. Southworth	"	"	Joseph & Zealide
Betsey Ann Thayer	27	Straw Sewer		Minister, Franklin	"	"	Davis & Betsey
*Obed B. Thayer	26	Shoe Maker	Sept. 13, 1849	Joseph Thayer	Mendon	Mendon	Otis & Mercy 4
Orinda H. Cook	22	Straw Braider		Minister, Webster	Franklin	Franklin	Elias & Orinda
George W. Seavey	20	Clerk	Sept. 20, 1849	T. D. Southworth	"	§	David & Betsey 2
Ellen M. Woodward	18	Straw Braider		Minister, Franklin	"	Franklin	Austin & Lucy
*Edwin Thompson	40	Clergyman	Oct. 9, 1849	David Sanford	Lynn	Walpole	Wm. & Eunice 5
Louisa J. Fisher	34	House Work		Minister, Medway	Franklin		Maxcy & Persis
*Willard Fisher	53	Farmer	Dec. 12, 1849	T. D. Southworth	"	Franklin	Caleb & Sally
Clarissa Bullard	26	Straw Sewer		Minister, Franklin	"	"	Elisha & Iiena

Marriages in Franklin during the Year next preceding January 1, 1850 and 1851.— Registered January, 1851.

NAME OF BRIDE AND GROOM.	Age.	OCCUPATION.	DATE OF MARRIAGE.	BY WHOM MARRIED.	PLACE OF BIRTH.	Residence at Time of Marriage.	NAME OF PARENTS.
			1850.				
Robert Shurtleff	22	Farmer	March 31	T. D. Southworth	Carver	Franklin	Luther & Hannah
Betsey Alley	26			Minister, Franklin	Franklin	"	John & Rosalinda
Rufus Chapin	22	Shoe Manu'r	May 12	John Dwight	Milford	Cincinnati, O.	Rufus & Lydia
Julia F. Fisher	19			Minister, Medway	Franklin	Franklin	Willis & Caroline
Alvah Metcalf	26	Sawyer	May 30	T. D. Southworth	Appleton, Me.	"	Junia & Melinda
Harriet Vose	22			Minister, Franklin	"	"	Alek & Harriet
Edwin Ainsworth	35	Post Master	May 30	"	Claremont, N. H.	Claremont, N. H.	Walter & Catherine
Mary M. Earle	22				New Braintree	Franklin	William & Sophia
Asa White	23		June 4	Jacob Ide	Whiting, Vt.	Medway	Nathan & Lucinda
Lydia A. Partridge	18			Minister, Medway	Walpole	Franklin	Seth & Laura A.
*Granville McCallam	43	Cotton Spinner	June 5	E. L. Messenger	Scotland	Smithfield, R. I.	Gilbert & Margaret
Abby Grant	42			Bap. Minister, Medway	Wrentham	"	Rhodes & Martha
George F. Kingman	28	Merchant	June 13	David Sanford	Mansfield	New Bedford	Henry & Nancy
Betsey W. Metcalf	24			Minister, Medway	Franklin	Franklin	Whiting & Betsey

* Widower. † Widow. ‡ Sash and Blind Maker. § Newton Lower Falls. 1 Pittston, Me. 2 Hollistom. 3 Foxboro. 4 Mendon. 5 Lynn.

Marriages in Franklin during the Year preceding January 1, 1850 and 1851.—(Continued.)

NAME OF BRIDE AND GROOM.	AGE.	OCCUPATION.	DATE OF MARRIAGE.	BY WHOM MARRIED.	PLACE OF BIRTH.	Residence at Time of Marriage.	NAME OF PARENTS.
			1850				
John S. Walker	25	Manufacturer	June 20	T. D. Southworth Minister, Franklin	Maryland	Medway	Dean & Rebecca
Ellen Hoyt	26	Labourer			Boston	Franklin	William & Ellen E.
*Charles M. Nason	21		July 4	Wm. J. Breed Minister, Prov., R. I.	Franklin		George W. & Hannah C.
Sylvia A. Newell	19				Cumberland, R.I.		Hiram & Clarissa
J. George Hubbard	21	School Teacher	Aug. 15	T. D. Southworth Minister, Franklin	Franklin		Elisha & Amelia
Emely C. Farrington	22				Wrentham		Nathan & Julia
Artemas Barden	26	Farmer	Aug. 15	" "	Franklin		David & Julia
Julia A. Farrington	28				Wrentham		Nathan & Julia
Charles H. Benis	21	CarriageMaker	Aug. 18	" "	Franklin		Henry & Nancy
Evelyn C. Jorden	17				"		Charles & Milla
Erasmus A. Pond	22	Merchant	Aug. 19	Samuel Hunt Minister, Franklin	Newton		Goldsbury & Julia A.
Adelia M. Morse	20				Franklin		George W. & Esther
Samuel E. Gay	25	Farmer	Oct. 3	T. D. Southworth Minister, Franklin	Newport, Me.		Willard & Mary
Sarah A. Webber	30				Franklin		David & Nancy
†Michael Metcalf	48	Farmer	Nov. 11	C. H. Force, Minister, Central Falls	Fall River	CentralFalls,R.I.	Nathan & Patty
†Hannah Sunderland	42			S. S. Bradford,Minister, Pawtucket	Medford		William & Ruth
*Agustine B. Boyle	24	Boat Builder	Nov. 18		Wrentham	New Bedford	John P. & Mary
Lydia E. Darling	19					Franklin	Silas & Phila

Marriages in Franklin during the Year 1851.—Registered Jan., 1852.

			1851				
†Alexd. L. Hart	31	Boot Maker	Jan. 1	D. Sanford	Boston	Franklin	Charles C. & Ann L.
Mary J. Pond	31				Franklin		Malchaih & Mary J.
Manly D. Lincoln	24	Blacksmith	Jan. 15	T. D. Southworth Minister, Franklin	Wrentham	Wrentham	Manly & Fidelia
Eliza B. Fisher	18				Medway	Franklin	Francis & Charlotte
George M. Underwood	19	Boot Maker	Jan. 19	"	Franklin		Horace & Mercy
Sarah G. Pond	19				Dunham, Canada	Natick	Gilmore & Raelhael
Wm. G. Clark	24	Cordwainer	Jan. 25	Samuel Hunt Minister, Franklin	Franklin	Franklin	John B.
Achsah Fisher	18				Wrentham		Weston & Susan
†Alfred Ware	64	Carpenter	Jan. 28		Wrentham		Samuel & Mehitabel
Bebee Draper	54				Attleboro		Josiah & Mary

* Married in Providence, R. I.   † 2d Marriage.   ‡ 3d Marriage.   § Married in Central Falls, R. I.   ¶ Minister Village Ch., Medway.

Marriages in Franklin during the Year 1851.—(Continued.)

NAME OF BRIDE AND GROOM.	Age.	OCCUPATION.	DATE OF MARRIAGE.	BY WHOM MARRIED.	PLACE OF BIRTH.	Residence at Time of Marriage.	NAME OF PARENTS.
			1851.				
George H. Thomas	23	Boot Maker	April 8	Samuel Hunt Minister, Franklin	Cumberland, R.I.	Franklin	Philip & Sarah
Elizabeth P. Woodward	23		April 8	"	Franklin	"	Austin & Mary A.
Erastus E. Baker	25	Farmer			"	"	David & Jemima
Abby M. Bacon	22				"	"	Joseph T. & Mary A.
William H. Martin	20	Boot Maker	May 3	T. D. Southworth Minister, Franklin	Attleboro	"	Wm. & Harriet
Maranda R. Pond	16				Franklin	"	Gilmore & Racheal
Ebenr. S. Vose	21	Carpenter	Oct. 20	Willis Fisher Justice of the Peace	Montville, Me.	"	Alexd. & Belinda
Betsey A. Ware	20				"	"	Guy W. & Matilda

Marriages in Franklin during the Year preceding January 1, 1852.

NAME OF BRIDE AND GROOM.	Age.	OCCUPATION.	DATE OF MARRIAGE.	BY WHOM MARRIED.	PLACE OF BIRTH.	Residence at Time of Marriage.	NAME OF PARENTS.
			1852.				
Robert J. Laing	26	Tailor	April 5	Samuel Hunt Minister, Franklin	Halifax, N. S.	Franklin	†Archd. & Mary A.
Nancy S. Earle	21				Braintree	"	William & Sophia
Alexd. Chase	24	Boot Maker	June 28	John Lovejoy, Minister Woonsocket, R. I.	Medway	"	Mason & Lurana
Almira Black	23				Cumberland, R.I.	Cumberland, R.I.	George & Polly
*Wm. H. Wales	32	Farmer	Sept. 2	Samuel Hunt Minister, Franklin	Franklin	Franklin	Otis & Jemima
*Julia A. Armington	27				Bellingham	"	†Rufus&Mary Bosworth
Francis L. Hutchings	23	Carpenter	Sept. 7	"	Oxford, Me.	Cambridge	William
Francis A. Shaw	22				Bethel, Me.	"	Levi & Clarissa
*John H. Fisher	45	Bon't Presser	Sept. 7	"	Franklin	Franklin	Lewis & Abigail
Nancy E. Thayer	21					"	Nathaniel & Nancy
William P. Shaw	27	Carpenter	Sept. 7	"	Bethel, Me.	"	Levi & Clarissa
Dorcas V. L. Hooper	27				Mahew, Miss.	"	William & Vina
William D. Higgins	24	Boot Maker	Sept. 14	†Joseph B. Breed	Charlotte, Me.	"	John & Abigail
Rebecca Hamilton	22	"			Cohasset	"	Silas
Theopilas M. Greenlaw	23	"	Sept. 14	†Joseph B. Breed	Charlotte, Me.	"	Zadock & Lydia
Caroline N. Higgins	26					"	John & Abigail
George W. Bacon	21	Farmer	Nov. 9	Samuel Hunt Minister, Franklin	Franklin	"	Joseph T. & Mary A.
Julia A. Brooks	21				Henniker, N. H.	"	Pascal P. & Almira
J. W. M. Pherson	57	Stone Mason	Nov. 25	"	Scotland	"	Barnard & Elizabeth M.
Patty Metcalf	47				Franklin	"	Nathan & Patty

* Second Marriage.   † Baptist Minister, Woonsocket.   ‡ Boston.

Marriages in Franklin during the Year preceding January 1, 1852.—(Continued.)

NAME OF BRIDE AND GROOM.	AGE.	OCCUPATION.	DATE OF MARRIAGE.	BY WHOM MARRIED.	PLACE OF BIRTH.	Residence at Time of Marriage	NAME OF PARENTS.
			1852				
Robert H. Ware	20	Carpenter	Dec. 16	Samuel Hunt, Minister, Franklin	Sherburne	Milton	Albert R. & Joanna D.
Abby A. Cutting	20			"	Enfield	Franklin	David & Lucy
*Artemas Barden	29	Farmer	Dec. 30	"	Franklin	"	David & Julia
Hannah L. Guild	25				Walpole		Leonard & Hannah

Marriages in Franklin during the Year 1853.

NAME OF BRIDE AND GROOM.	AGE.	OCCUPATION.	DATE OF MARRIAGE.	BY WHOM MARRIED.	PLACE OF BIRTH.	Residence at Time of Marriage	NAME OF PARENTS.
			1853				
*Warren N. King	25	Mason	Jan. 16	Samuel Hunt, Minister, Franklin	Rehoboth	Franklin	David & Lucy
Julia A. Blake	19			"	Franklin	"	Hermon R. & Nancy
Eliphalet Eames	26	Boot Maker	March 8	"	Framingham	Framingham	Jonathan & Susan
Mary Elizabeth Guild	19			"	Franklin	Wrentham	Joel & Eliza
*Samuel Hunt	43	Minister	April 11	Jacob Ide, Minister 2d Ch., Medway	Attleboro	Franklin	Richard & Ann
Warren A. Richardson	36	Spinner	April 23	Willis Fisher, J. P. in Franklin	Franklin	"	Willis & Caroline Fisher
Susan Hefford	17				Milford	"	Howard & Mary
John K. Allen	21	Sash Maker	May 16	Samuel Hunt, Minister, Franklin	Medfield	"	John & Cynthia
*Eliza Mason	21			"	Pawtucket	Pawtucket, R. I.	Charles & Waity
Francis B. Ray	30	Manufacturer	May 25	"	"	New York, N. Y.	Wm. & Rachael Booth
Susan B. Rockwood	29			"	Mendon	Franklin	Joseph & Lydia
William P. Shepherd	26	Clerk in Store	May 25	"	Franklin	"	Asa & Julia
Emeline W. Metcalf	22			"	Foxboro	Foxboro	Lewis & Olivia
Francis M. Blake	27	Boot Maker	June 12	Daniel Sweet, Minister, Johnston, R. I.	Franklin	Franklin	Abijah & Joanna
Maria E. Converse	19			J. O. Means, Minister 1st Ch., Medway	Eastford, Ct.	Johnston, R. I.	Harvey & Betsey
Lucian A. Cook	27	Boot Maker	June 25	John Boyden, Uv. Minister, Woonsocket	Cumberland	Franklin	Horace & Almira
Sarah Hooker	24				Sherburne	Sherborne	Silas & Joanna
Charles H. Carpenter	24	Bon'l Presser	June 30		Newfield, Me.	Franklin	Zibeon & Mary
Abby A. Ballou	20				Cumberland, R.I.	"	Isaac & Sally
Seneca A. Greenwood	28	Boot Maker	July 3	Joseph T. Massey, Bapt. Minister, Bellingham	Southboro	Medway	Thurston & Caroline
Maria B. Adams	18				Newport, R. I.	Franklin	Seneca & Martha
George H. Robinson	22	Painter	Sept. 4	J. M. Merrill, M. E. Minister, Franklin	Ireland	"	Orrin W. & Hannah D.
Jane Robinson	22			"	"		Wm. & Fanny Arch'd

* Second Marriage.

FRANKLIN TOWN RECORDS—MARRIAGES.

Marriages in Franklin during the Year 1853.—(Continued.)

NAME OF BRIDE AND GROOM.	AGE.	OCCUPATION.	DATE OF MARRIAGE.	BY WHOM MARRIED.	PLACE OF BIRTH.	Residence at Time of Marriage.	NAME OF PARENTS.
			1853.				
*Leonard F. Everett	44	Farmer	Oct. 19	Samuel Hunt, Minister, Franklin	Westminster	Sutton	Pelatiah & Dorcas
*Hannah Mann	42				Smithfield	Blackstone	Elisha & Hannah Hopkins

Marriages in Franklin during the Year preceding January, 1854.

NAME OF BRIDE AND GROOM.	AGE.	OCCUPATION.	DATE OF MARRIAGE.	BY WHOM MARRIED.	PLACE OF BIRTH.	Residence at Time of Marriage.	NAME OF PARENTS.
			1854.				
*Henry M. Phetteplau	40	Machinist	Jan. 5	J. T. Massey, Baptist Minister, Bellingham	Smithfield, R. I.	Smithfield, R. I.	Asahel & Nancy
Joanna Sayles	26				Franklin	Franklin	Orrin & Almira
George M. Walker	24	Clerk	Feb. 1	Sam'l Hunt, C. T. Minister, Franklin	Whiting, Vt.	Buffalo	Whitfield & Patty
Martha M. DeWitt	26				Franklin	Franklin	Archd. & Patty
*Orlando J. Davis	27	Boot Maker	Feb. 6	Sam'l Hunt, Minister, Franklin	Calais, Vt.	Milford	John
Berthenia E. Wheeler	22				"	"	Shepherd
Benj. F. Rice							Nath'l & Ann
Roxana Boynton	25	Mechanic	Feb. 12	J. M. Merrill, M. E. Minister, Franklin	Lancaster	Clinton	Wm. & Candice
†Silas Adams	53	Farmer	April 19	Sam'l Hunt, C. T. Minister, Franklin	Grafton, N. H.	Franklin	Samuel & Chloe
*Harriet E. Spaulding	44				Bellingham	Bellingham	Wm. & Ann M. Hasley
George W. Ballou	22	Boot Maker	April 27	P. Crandon, M. E. Minister, Woonsocket	Boston	Franklin	Thurston & Caroline
Eliza J. Daniels	16				Cumberland	Medway	Willard & Elizabeth
George W. Dean	23	Boot Maker	May 11	John Boyden, Uv. Minister, Woonsocket	Medway	Franklin	Ichabod & Hannah
Ellen E. Darling	19				Franklin	"	Alfred & Electa
*Stephen A. Coombs	56	Farmer	May 23	Sam'l Hunt, C. T. Minister, Franklin	Bellingham	Bellingham	Jesse & Sarah
*Olivia S. C. Grant	44				New Braintree	Franklin	Wm. & Sophia Earle
Hugh McParland	30	Laborer	Aug. 7	J. Brady, R. C. Minister, Woonsocket	Ireland	"	Edward & Mary
Celia Dougharty	24				"	"	Foley & Mary
*Alfred O. Darling	27	Carpenter	Sept. 6	Francis Smith, Minister, Providence, R. I.	Franklin	Wrentham	Alfred & Electa
Hannah A. Cook	20				Wrentham	Franklin	Abner & Betsey
Wm. H. Woodward	28	Merchant	Sept. 14	Sam'l Hunt, C. T. Minister, Franklin	Franklin	"	Austin & Mary A.
Martha J. Farrington	23				Wrentham	"	Nathan & Julia
*Joseph Dunbar	44	Cabinet Maker	Oct. 8	J. M. Merrill, M. E. Minister, Franklin	Hingham	Hingham	Amos & Rachael
†Sally B. Adams	60				Northbridge	Franklin	Simeon & Abigail Bassett
Hartford P. Leonard	32	Trader	Oct. 17	Sam'l Hunt, C. T. Minister, Franklin	Foxboro	"	Hartford & Betsey
Mary A. Whitaker	22				Brooklyn, C.	"	Richard & Mary A.

*2d Marriage.   †3d Marriage.

Marriages in Franklin during the Year preceding January 1, 1854.—(Continued.)

Name of Bride and Groom	Age	Occupation	Date of Marriage	Place of Birth	By Whom Married	Residence at Time of Marriage	Name of Parents
			1854				
Osmyn A. Stanley	32	Carpenter	Oct. 19		D. P. Harriman, Minister, Burrillville, R.I.	Franklin	John & Juliet
Harriet A. Harris	20					Burrillville, R.I.	Eleazer & Harriet
George E. Wallace	27	Carpenter	Nov. 28	Dalton, N.H.	Dan'l Heath, J. P., Freeman, Me.	Franklin	Ira & Kezia
Adaline B. Mayo	26			Freeman, Me.		Freeman, Me.	Isiah & Sarah

Marriages in Franklin during the Year 1855.

Name of Bride and Groom	Age	Occupation	Date of Marriage	Place of Birth	By Whom Married	Residence at Time of Marriage	Name of Parents
			1855				
*James B. Wilson	57	Manufacturer	Feb. 8	New Braintree	D. Sanford, C. T.	Medway	James & Jane
Harriet N. Pond	29			Franklin	Minister, Medway	Franklin	Hiram & Joanna
Parker R. Farr	23	Bon't Presser	April 5	Chesterfield, N.H.	John Boyden, Uv.	"	Russel & Sarah
Ably E. Alexander	22			Cumberland, R.I.	Minister, Woonsocket	"	Welcome & Alpha
George F. Brown	25	Clerk	April 16	Medway	Henry W. Beecher	"	Artemas & Patience
Ellen M. Daniels	25			Brookline, L.I.	Minister, Brookline, L.I.	Franklin	Albert E. & Olive G.
Thomas M. Bacon	24	Teacher	May 9		D. Sanford, C. T.	"	Joseph T. & Mary A.
Emely J. Thayer	21			Medway	Minister, Medway	"	Nathaniel & Caroline
Anson D. Dolliff	23	Carpenter	July 31	Baptist Belmont, Me.	J. B. Breed,	"	Thomas W. & Sarah C.
Abby Wales	22			Franklin	Minister, Woonsocket	"	Otis & Jerusha
George R. Lewis	20	Boot Maker	Aug. 16	Gibson, Me.	P. Wood, M. E.	"	James W. & Ruth
Caroline Greene	19			Uxbridge	Minister, Franklin	"	Ezaak & Mary
†Marshall P. Wilder	56	Merchant	Sept. 8	Rindge, N.H.	Asa Hixon, C. T.	Dorchester	Samuel L.
Julia Baker	33			Franklin	Minister, Franklin	Franklin	David & Jemima
*Rensælaer Patch	33	R. R. Repairer	Sept. 26	Northfield	Samuel Hunt, C. T.	Framingham	Jonathan & Sally
Merena Allen	29			Franklin	Minister, Franklin	Franklin	Cyrus & Sally
*George H. Frost	31	Produce Dealer	Nov. 28	Dedham	"	Boston	John & Fanny
Susan M. Pond	22			Franklin		Franklin	James P. & Susan
Calvin M. Smith	22	Clerk	Nov. 29	Dorchester	Geo. Brancroft, M.E.	"	Calvin & Caroline
A. Janette Stearns	20			Killingly, Ct.	Minister, Woonsocket	Blackstone	Shepherd & Bethiah

Marriages in Franklin during the Year 1856.

Name of Bride and Groom	Age	Occupation	Date of Marriage	Place of Birth	By Whom Married	Residence at Time of Marriage	Name of Parents
			1856				
Amos W. Staples	24	Farmer	Jan. 1	Cumberland, R.I.	P. Wood. M. E.	Cumberland, R.I.	Lyman & Sally
Eliza E. Lawrence	19			Wrentham	Minister, Franklin	Wrentham	Addison

* Second Marriage. † Third Marriage.

Marriages in Franklin during the year 1856.—(Continued.)

NAME OF BRIDE AND GROOM.	Age.	OCCUPATION.	DATE OF MARRIAGE.	BY WHOM MARRIED.	PLACE OF BIRTH.	Residence at Time of Marriage	NAME OF PARENTS.
			1856.				
John D. Wales	21	Carpenter	Feb. 14	‡Joseph T. Massey	Franklin	Franklin	Otis & Jerusha
Adelaid B. Whiting	20				Mendon	"	Joseph B. & Phila B.
William Hill	22	Boot Maker	March 15	P. Wood, M. E. Minister, Franklin	Franklin	Franklin	Elliot & Peggy
Susan A. White	19				Foxboro	Foxboro	Eli & Peggy
William D. Gilmore	25	Bon't Presser	April 10	Samuel Hunt, C. T. Minister, Franklin	Franklin	Franklin	Robert & Rebecca
Harriet M. Farrington	21				Wrentham	"	Nathan & Julia
Marcellus A. Woodward	32	Farmer	April 26	" "	Whitefield, Me.	Medway	Alfred & Caroline
Sarah A. Ware	27				Franklin	Franklin	Samuel & Sarah
*Roxana Buxton	66	Miller	May 11	" "	Wrentham	Medway	William & Patience
*William Williams	50				Smithfield, R. I.	Smithfield, R. I.	Eben'r & Mary Darling
Mayo C. Darling	26	Butcher	May 22	Joseph Thayer U. Minister,So.Franklin	Bellingham	Bellingham	Jefferson B. & Joanna
Lucy A. Cook	24				Franklin	Franklin	Elias & Orinda
Samuel S. Cook	23	Bon't Presser	June 16	John Boyden, U'v. Minister,Woonsocket	Franklin	"	Samuel & Maria
Emeline White	19				Wrentham	"	Jason W. & Laurena
Wm. E. Wood	24	Jeweler	June 17	M. P. Webster, M. E. Minister, Franklin	London, N. H.	Wrentham	William & Sarah
Medora A. Metcalf	18				Hope, Me.	Franklin	Moses G. & Melia
Benj. W. Whiting	35	Farmer	June 24	Samuel Hunt, C. T. Minister, Franklin	Wrentham	Wrentham	Eliphalet & Esther
Mary C. Metcalf	27				Winthrop, Me.	Franklin	Joseph & Chloe F. A.
†Wilson C. Ballon	24		Aug. 5	" "	Wrentham	Wrentham	Caleb & Sally
Bridget McGee	18				Ireland	"	Arthur & Mary
Ward Adams	58		Sept. 1	" "	Franklin	Franklin	Nehemiah & Mary
Hannah Blake	52				Warren, Me.	"	Willing & Polly
Charles H. Sanger	26	Bon't Bleacher	Nov. 27	" "	Templeton	Framingham	Obediah & Betsey
Eliza A. Bullard	24				Franklin	Franklin	Cephas & Sukey
George W. House	29	Boot Maker	Dec. 11	M. P. Webster, M. E. Minister, Franklin	Williamstown, Vt.	Blackstone	Wm. J. & Susan
Eliza L. Bates	19				Pawtucket, R. I.	Franklin	John & Emeline
J. Wheaton Daniels	24	Farmer	Dec. 31	Samuel Hunt, C. T. Minister, Franklin	Franklin	"	Fisher & Ann
Harriet E. King	21				Franklin	"	John & Erepta

*2d Marriage.   ‡Baptist Minister, Bellingham.

†This name should read Caleb W. Ballou; this name is taken from the family record.

May 10, 1881.

A. A. RUSSEGUE, Town Clerk.

Marriages in Franklin during the Year 1857.

NAME OF BRIDE AND GROOM.	AGE.	OCCUPATION.	DATE OF MARRIAGE.	BY WHOM MARRIED.	PLACE OF BIRTH.	Residence at Time of Marriage	NAME OF PARENTS.
			1857				
Addison H. Pickering	22	Boot Maker	Feb. 21	Joseph Thayer	Franklin	Medway	Simon & Elizabeth
Harriet A. Griffin	22			Union. Franklin	Roxbury	"	William
*Luke Daniels	68	Farmer	April 12	Samuel Hunt, C. T.	Franklin	Franklin	Nathan & Sarah
*Amelia T. Hubbard †	60			Minister Franklin	Dedham	"	Hezekiah & Elizabeth
Albert H. Hill	25	Boot Maker	May 18	Jacob Ide, C. T.	Bellingham	Bellingham	Henry & Hannah
Charlotte A. White	21			Minister, Medway	Franklin	Franklin	Lyman P. & Miranda E.
William A. Gurney	22	Farmer	July 5	Edward B. Hall. Min-	Providence, R. I.	"	William & Caroline
Louise M. Adams	18			ister. Providence,R.I.	Milford	"	James
Oramel B. Blake	23	Carpenter	Sept. 4	Mortimer Blake.C.T.	Franklin	"	Ira & Laura
Grace F. Shepardson	21			Minister, Taunton	W. Brookfield, Me.	"	Thadeous & Harriet S.
Joseph H. Wadsworth	31	Merchant	Sept. 10	Wm. M. Thayer, C.T.	Franklin	"	Seth & Olive M.
Abby L. Metcalf	22			Minister, Franklin	"	"	Michael & Sally
*William H. Wales	38	Farmer	Oct. 21	Erastus Rockwood	"	"	Otis & Jemima
*Julia A. Armington †	31			J. P., Franklin	Bellingham	"	Rufus & Mary
Edwin H. King	24	Bon't Presser	Oct. 22	Samuel Hunt, C. T.	Franklin	"	John & Erepta
Martha E. Daniels	21			Minister, Franklin	"	"	Albert E. & Olive G.

Marriages Registered in the Town of Franklin, County of Norfolk, during the Years 1858 and 1859.—T. C. HILLS, Registrar.

DATE OF MARRIAGE.	NAME OF BRIDE AND GROOM.	Residence at Time of Marriage	AGE	OCCUPATION.	PLACE OF BIRTH.	NAME OF PARENTS.	BY WHOM MARRIED.
1858.							
Jan. 1	*John Kingsbury	Medfield	72	Farmer	Medfield	Amos & Molly	D. Sanford, C. T.
	*Ellen Miria Pond	"	43		Portland, Me.		Minister, Medway
Jan. 27	Erastus D. Rockwood	Franklin	20	"	Franklin	Erastus & Mary	Joseph Massey, Bapt.
	Abbie O. Wales	"	16		"	Amos A. & Rhoda	Minister, Bellingham
Feb. 3	William S. Young	"	28	"	New Brunswick	Nelson	Andrew N. Adams Uv.
	Mary Murphy	"	21			John	Minister, Franklin

* Second Marriage. † Maiden Name Turner. ‡ Maiden Name Bosworth.

FRANKLIN TOWN RECORDS—MARRIAGES.

Marriages Registered in the Town of Franklin, County of Norfolk, during the Years 1858 and 1859.—(Continued.)

DATE OF MARRIAGE.	NAME OF BRIDE AND GROOM.	Residence at Time of Marriage.	AGE.	OCCUPATION.	PLACE OF BIRTH.	NAME OF PARENTS.	BY WHOM MARRIED.
1858.							
Feb. 24	William D. Smith	Wrentham	41	Farmer	Wrentham	Samuel & Polly	S. Hunt, C. T. Minister, Franklin
	Adeline M. Linkfield	Franklin	21		N. Providence, R. I.	Benj. & Maria	
April 1	John B. Clark	Worcester	35	Merchant	Marlboro	Benj. & Lucy	Sam'l Hunt, C. T. Minister, Franklin
	Martha Norcross	Franklin	20		Franklin	Asa G. & Irene	
June 1	*Ossian Sumner	Providence, R. I.	30	Druggist	Ashford, Ct.	Samuel & Sally	Joseph T. Massey
	Kate A. Sayles	Franklin	23		Franklin	Oren & Almira	
Sept. 23	Charles Wilson	"	35	Laborer	Callais, Me.	George & Jane	§
	Maria H. Kingsbury	"	22		Franklin	Fisher A. & Caroline	
Sept. 30	Benjamin Frost	"	45	Boat Maker	"	Peter & Eliza	A. N. Adams, Uv. Minister, Franklin
	Susan Clark	"	28		"	Abijah & Susan	
Nov. 10	Henry W. Gay	"	23	Clerk	Haverhill, N. H.	Wilks & Deborah	Wm. M. Thayer, C. T. Minister, Franklin
	Marion L. Pillsbury	"	21		Crowden, N. H.	Stephen & Mary A.	
Dec. 12	Hermon F. Clark	"	28	Bon't Presser	Cumberland, R.I.	Hiram & Adeline	"
	Carrie N. Ballou	"	22		Wrentham	Warren J. & Caroline	
Dec. 19	Hiram Ware	Wrentham	31	Farmer	Foxboro		A. N. Adams, Uv. Minister, Franklin
	Nancy Kemp	Foxboro	25		Franklin		
Dec. 29	William Rockwood	Franklin	30	Farmer	"	Asa & Julia	Mortimer Blake, C. T. Minister, Franklin
	Laura M. Blake	"	30			Ira & Laura	

Marriages in the Town of Franklin during the Year 1859.

1859.							
March 31	Calvin Claflin	Franklin	24	Clerk	Franklin	Jeremiah & Lois	Wm. M. Thayer, C. T. Minister, Franklin
	Isabella J. Adams	"	24		"	Simeon P. & Harriet	
March 16	*Joel Daniels	"	71	Farmer	"	Joel & Mary	"
	Jemima L. Daniels	"	47		"	Luke & Jemima	
May 12	Sylvester E. Howard	"	23	Boot Maker	Milford	Amos & Elvira	D. Sanford, C. T. Minister, Medway
	Mary E. Whiting	"	18		Matlee Island	Aaron & Mary	
May 22	*Willis Fisher, Esq.	"	75	Farmer	Franklin	Joseph & Susan	Samuel Hunt, C. T. Minister, Franklin
	*Mahitable Wright	"	70		"	†	
June 5	John C. Metcalf	Ashland	27	Box Maker	Appleton, Me.	Junia & Melinda	‡
	Sarah Metcalf	Franklin	24		Franklin	Michael & Sally	

* Second Marriage.   † Benjamin & Mehitable Rockwood.   ‡ Baptist Minister, Bellingham.   § S. Hunt & Wm. M. Thayer, C. T. Ministers, Franklin.

Marriages in the Town of Franklin during the Year 1859.—(Continued.)

DATE OF MARRIAGE.	NAME OF BRIDE AND GROOM.	Residence at Time of Marriage.	Age	OCCUPATION.	PLACE OF BIRTH.	NAME OF PARENTS.	BY WHOM MARRIED.
1859.							
July 28	Stephen S. Benson	Franklin	45	Bock Keeper	Mendon	Henry S. & Lydia	Franklin Davis, C. T.
	Lizzie A. Scott	"	25		Franklin	Saul B. & Susan	Minister, N. Wrentham
August 30	Isaac Hill	"	21	Box Maker	Montpelier, Vt.	Wm. & Maria	Jacob Ide, C. T.
	Miliam Abb	"	24		Milford	Charles & Mary	Minister, Medway
Sept. 20	George A. Tobine	"	21	Farmer	Bridgewater, N. H.	George W. & Mary	Wm. M. Thayer, C. T.
	Ellen F. Newell	"	19		Franklin	Hiram & Clarissa	Minister, Franklin
Oct. 17	Caleb C. Munroe	Worcester	23	Spinner	Scituate, R. I.	David & Mary A.	Andrew N. Adams
	Mary A. Lake	Franklin	21		Woonsocket, R.I.	George & Fanny	Uv. Minister, Franklin
Nov. 24	Jedediah Southworth	Stoughton	21	Carpenter		Albert & Harriet	"
	Francelia E. Richards	Winslow, Me.	20			Jere'h & Sarah	

Marriages registered in the Town of Franklin, County of Norfolk, during the Year 1860.—T. C. Hills, Registrar.

DATE OF MARRIAGE.	NAME OF BRIDE AND GROOM.	Residence at Time of Marriage.	Age	OCCUPATION.	PLACE OF BIRTH.	NAME OF PARENTS.	BY WHOM MARRIED.
1860.							
April 15	*Frederic Augustus Ware	Franklin	61	Farmer	Franklin	Amariah & Eunice	A. N. Adams, Uv.
	†Ann Maria Pond	"	38		Framingham	Roswell & Ann Bent	Minister, Franklin
April 27	Alvin B. Adams	"	22	Boot Maker	Franklin	Oren W. & Hannah D.	"
	Lydia Ann Dolley	"	19		Providence, R. I.	George & Mary	
May 26	Horace S. DeWitt	"	29	Stable Keeper	Franklin	Arch'd & Patty	
	Hattie E. Alby	"	21		Bucksport, Me.	Robert & Sarah	
May 26	Nathaniel G. Johnson	"	30	Boot Maker	Holliston	Nathaniel & Eunice	Massena Goodrich
	Louise N. Bemis	"	26		Franklin	Henry & Nancy	†
June 23	Jesse L. Nason		22	Clerk		George W. & Peacey	Edward N. Kirk
	Hellen M. Thompson	Ellsworth, Me.	22		Ellsworth, Me.	Elbridge & Hellen	Minister, Boston
June 24	†Samuel Cross	Franklin	41	Weaver	England	William & Alice	A. N. Adams, Uv.
	†Eliza Marden	"	40		Bellingham	Lewis & Lydia Coles	Minister, Franklin
July 16	William A. Springer	Medway	23	Boot Maker	Augusta, Me.	Tillinghast & Elona	Wm. M. Thayer, C. T.
	Julia Breck	Franklin	20		Springfield, Me.	Elias & Julia	Minister, Franklin
July 17	Horatio A. Jorden	"	21	Brakeman	Wrentham	Charles & Milla	Samuel Hunt. C. T.
	Sarah J. Chamberlain	"	20		Franklin	Benja. & Harriet	Minister, Franklin
Sept. 9	*Elbridge Hayward	Milford	44	Carpenter	Farmington, Me.	Amariah & Hannah	David Sanford, C. T.
	Nellie C. Hardy	Franklin	24		Medway	Eliphalet D. & Eunice M.	Minister, Medway

* Third Marriage.   † Second Marriage.   ‡ Uv. Minister, N. Providence, R. I.

FRANKLIN TOWN RECORDS—MARRIAGES.

Marriages Registered in the Town of Franklin, County of Norfolk, during the Year 1860.—(Continued.)

DATE OF MARRIAGE.	NAME OF GROOM AND BRIDE.	Residence at Time of Marriage	OCCUPATION.	AGE	PLACE OF BIRTH.	NAME OF PARENTS.	BY WHOM MARRIED.
1860							
Oct. 6	*John K. Robinson	Franklin	Painter	40	Ireland	John & Jane K.	Wm. M. Thayer, C.T. Minister, Franklin
	Mary R. Clark	"		27	Plymouth	Robert R. & Deborah	
Oct. 7	Frank S. Hills	"	Bon't Presser	22	Franklin	Harvey & Abigail	Joseph Kellock, Bapt. Mins'r, Rockland,Me.
Oct. 31	Martha E. Lincoln	Washington, Me.		22	Washington, Me.	Nathaniel & Matilda	Samuel Hunt, C. T. Minister, Franklin
	Amos P. Woodward	Franklin	Farmer	22	Franklin	Austin & Mary A.	
	Charlotte M. Thayer	"		24	"	Nath'l & Caroline	
Nov. 6	Joseph Grant	Wrentham	"	24	Cumberland,R.I.	Samuel & A'pha	
	Sarah Comstock	"		24	Wrentham	Nathan & Betsey	
Nov. 12	*Thomas J. Daniels	Franklin	"	32	Franklin	Nathan & Roxanna	David Richards, M.E. Minister, Holliston
	Mary E. Billings	"		27	Stoughton	Dudley & Aehsa	
Dec. 5	*Francis J. Adams	Westboro	"	38	Holliston	Stephen & Catherine	Samuel Hunt, C. T. Minister, Franklin
	Nancy A. Richardson	Franklin		34	Franklin	Elisha & Ruth F.	

Marriages Registered in the Town of Franklin, County of Norfolk, during the Year 1861.—T. C. Hills, Registrar.

DATE OF MARRIAGE.	NAME OF GROOM AND BRIDE.	Residence at Time of Marriage	OCCUPATION.	AGE	PLACE OF BIRTH.	NAME OF PARENTS.	BY WHOM MARRIED.
1861							
March 11	James G. Whitaker	Franklin	Carpenter	23	Franklin	Richard & Mary A.	Baron Stow, Baptist Minister, Boston
	Matilda D. Whiting	Holliston	Straw Sewer	28	Wheelock, Vt.	Newhall & Elizabeth	
May 26	George M. Wadsworth	Franklin	Farmer	25	Franklin	Seth & Olive	R. Carver, C. T. Minister, S. Franklin
	Emeline M. Metcalf	"	Straw Sewer	20	Appleton, Me.	Junia & Melinda	
June 2	*Winslow Cook	"	Farmer	60	Franklin	Whipple & Lucy	N. R. Wright, Uv. Minister, Franklin
	Lydia H. Tower	"	House Work	44	Cumberland,R.I.	Jason & Philenia	
June 9	Asahel F. Lovett	Medway	Farmer	24	Medway	Asahel P. & Eliza	"
	Olive A. Hartshorn	Franklin	Straw Sewer	22	Franklin	Edmund & Susan M.	
June 13	John L. Fairbanks	"	Bon't Presser	34	Boston	George S. & Ann	"
	Eliza Pond	"	Straw Sewer	24	Cumberland,R.I.	Lyman & Claramond	
June 19	Homer V. Snow	"	Bon't Presser	23	Mendon	Cyrus B. & Catherine	E.C. Messinger, Bapt. Minister, Medway
	Harriet A. Pillsbury	"	Straw Sewer	21	Piermont, N. H.	Stephen & Mary A.	
July 2, 1860	William Francis King	Wrentham	Farmer	20	Wrentham	David & Lucy	Samuel Hunt, C.T. Minister, Franklin
	Laura Annie Lawrence	Wrentham	Straw Sewer	18		Addison C. & Olive	
Aug. 31	William Gardner Adams	Franklin	Machinest	18	Boston	Gardiner & Eunice	John Boyden, Uv. Min. Cumberland,R.I
	Lillian Augusta Holt	"	Straw Sewer	17	Concord, N. H.	Jeremiah & Catherine	W

* Second Marriage.

FRANKLIN TOWN RECORDS—MARRIAGES. 127

Marriages Registered in the Town of Franklin, County of Norfolk, during the Year 1861.—(Continued.)

DATE OF MARRIAGE.	NAME OF BRIDE AND GROOM.	Residence at Time of Marriage	OCCUPATION.	AGE	PLACE OF BIRTH.	NAME OF PARENTS.	BY WHOM MARRIED.
1861							
Sept. 1	James Collins	Franklin	Laborer	38	Ireland	Andrew & Mary	M. Carroll, R. C. Priest, Foxboro
	Joanna Lorden	"	Housework	35	"	James & Mary	
Sept. 3	Lucius W. Daniels	"	Farmer	22	Franklin	Fisher & Ann E.	Wm. M. Thayer, C.T. Minister, Franklin
	*Nellie S. Warfield	"	Straw Sewer	20	"	Eben'r & Sarah	
Sept. 10	†Eliphalet D. Hardy	"	Farmer	67	Bradford	Henry & Rachael	Wm. W. Cowell, J.P. Wrentham
	Lydia Harris	"	Housework	59	Cumberland, R.I.	§	
Sept. 20	Wm. Henry Robbie	Walpole	Machinest	23	Prince Edward's Isl.	John & Mary Ann	Wm. M. Thayer, C.T. Minister, Franklin
	Aurelia Eunice Adams	Franklin	Straw Sewer	17	Springfield	Gaither & Eunice	
Sept. 30	Thomas R. Shields	"	Seaman	22	Winterport, Me.	Rodger & Esther	Samuel Hunt, C.T. Minister, Franklin
	Amelia J. Small	"	Straw Sewer	19	"	Allen & Louise	
Oct. 27	Daniel Dugan	"	Laborer	23	Bangor, Me.	Charles & Mary Ann	M. Carroll, R. C. Priest, Foxboro
	Mary Murray	"	Housework	24	Ireland	Morris & Bridget	

Marriages Registered in the Town of Franklin, County of Norfolk, during the Year 1862.—A. A. RUSSEGUE, Registrar.

DATE OF MARRIAGE.	NAME OF BRIDE AND GROOM.	Residence at Time of Marriage	OCCUPATION.	AGE	PLACE OF BIRTH.	NAME OF PARENTS.	BY WHOM MARRIED.
1862							
April 3	John H. Walker	Champaigne, Ill.	Railroad Man	23	Whiting, Vt.	Whitfield & Martha	Jacob Ide, Pastor 2d Ch. Medway
	Emma Jane Whittier	Franklin	Straw Sewer	25	Wrentham	Reuben & Mary Ann	
April 29	Thomas B. Allen	"	Farmer	29	Franklin	Cyrus & Sally B.	D. Sanford Clergyman
July 14	Martha M. Metcalf	"	Operator	32	Swanzey, Mass.	John & Chloe	Gideon Cole, Pastor Bapt. Ch. Wrentham
	‡John M. Bryant	Cumberland, R.I.		44	Franklin	Joseph & Sarah S.	
July 4	Lucinda A. Gilmore	Franklin	Farmer	25	"	Alfred & Sarah L.	‡David H. Ela, Cumberland, R. I.
	Albert L. Jordon	"		16		Geo. W. & Julia C.	
Aug. 16	Clara D. Thompson	"	Laborer	26	Palmer, Mass.	Nathaniel P. & Maria	Adin Ballou, Minister, Hopedale, Mass.
	Joseph C. Jacobs	"		21	Blackstone, Mass	Benjamin & Alpha	
Aug. 18	Sarah A. Dyer	"	Don't Presser	22	Franklin	Elias & Mary Ann	J.T. Tucker, Minister 1st Parish, Holliston
	Wm. A. Blake	"		17		Eliab M. & Isabella I.	
Sept. 6	Eliza I. Pond	"	Farmer	25	Woonsocket,R.I.	Horatio J. & Data Ann	John Boyden,Clergyman, Cumberland
	Francis M. Stockbridge	"		19	Cumberland,R.I.	Simeon & Della	
Oct. 30	Emely A. Stedman			74	Sutton, Mass.	Stephen & Hannah	Gideon Cole Clergyman
	†Jonathan Cole	Cumberland, R.I.		62	Rehoboth,Mass.	George & Ann Weden	
Nov. 24	†Charlotte E. Bowen	Wrentham			Wrentham	George & Miranda	S. W. Squires Minister, Franklin
	John E. Grant	"		24	Cumberland,R.I.	Nath'l & Eliza Ann	
	Elvira S. Hawes	Franklin		23			Pastor M.E. Ch.

* Should be Sarah Hellen. † 2d Marriage. ‡ 3d Marriage. § Christopher Harris & Thankful Alexander. ‖ Abijah Metcalf & Joanna W. Leonard.

Marriages registered in the Town of Franklin, County of Norfolk, in the Year 1863.—A. A. RESSEGUE, Registrar.

DATE OF MARRIAGE.	NAME OF BRIDE AND GROOM.	Residence at Time of Marriage	AGE	OCCUPATION.	PLACE OF BIRTH.	NAME OF PARENTS.	BY WHOM MARRIED.
Feb. 22, 1863	George H. Gilmore	Franklin	33	Farmer	N.Providence,R.I	George A. & Sally S.	W. S. McKensie, Clerg. Providence, R. I.
	Martha J. Bordon	Wrentham	24	"	Hopkinton		
Dec. 31, 1863	Henry A. Bliss	Franklin	20	"	N.Providence,R.I	Josiah E. & Caroline	David H. Ela, pastor M.E.Ch.Woonsocket,R.I.
	Frances J. Montgomery	"	20	"	Harvard	James & Mary J.	Samuel Hunt, Congl. Clergyman, Franklin
July 2, 1860	William F. King††		20	"	Wrentham	David & Lucy	
	Laura Ann Lawrence	Wrentham	18			Addison C. & Olive	†Theodore Cook
Nov. 3, 1860	William H. Guild	Franklin	20	Boot Maker	Franklin	James A. & Lucena P.	
	Mary A. Ware	Wrentham	18	Labourer	Medway	William D. & Almira	†Michael McCabe
Jan. 7, 1863	*Edmond Doherety	Franklin	50		Ireland	John & Mary	
	Margaret Knox	"	38		"	Patrick & Bridgett	
Jan 20, 1863	George H. Chapin	Sherburn	22	Clerk	Uxbridge	B. Taft & M. O. Chapin	Samuel Hunt, Congl. Clergyman, Franklin
	Hellen S. Cleaviland	Franklin	20		Franklin	Lowell B. & Melinda S.	
Feb. 5, 1863	James H. Pond	"	31	Farmer	"	Hiram & Joanna M.	§Wm. M. Thayer
	Mary Ann Fisher	"	19		"	Adin & Mary	
May 5, 1863	George A. A. Blake	"	21	Boot Maker	"	Elias & Mary Ann	Gideon Cole, Baptist Clergyman, Wrentham
	Mary A. S. Gilmore	"	17	Parents' Consent	"	Geo. R. & Emeline	
April 8, 1863	Edmond J. Rockwood	"	21	Farmer	"	Erastus & Mary A.	Geo. W. Stacy Clergyman, Milford
	Abby W. Cook	"	19	"	Bellingham	Albert & Olive C.	
April 21, 1863	*Nathan Staples	"	58		Cumberland,R.I.	Ezekiel & Dorcas	†Michael McCabe
	Bridget Darcy	"	39		Ireland	Hugh & Mary	
May 1, 1863	Laprelate M. Thayer	"	41	Boot Maker	Douglass	Sylvenas & Olive	T. E. St. John, Clergyman, Worcester
	Allice Hood	"	23		Nova Scotia	John & Ellen	
June 7, 1863	Edmond M. Metcalf	"	23	Fireman	Franklin	Michael & Melia	David H. Ela, Pastor M. E. Ch., Woonsocket.
	Fanny A. Luke	"	19		Woonsocket,R.I.	George W. & Fany W.	
June 27, 1863	Anson L. Cass	Boston	22	Farmer	Richmond, N. H.	Jarvis & Rachael	§William M. Thayer
	Charlotte H. Monroe	Franklin	22		Springfield, Ill.	Edward & Mary	
Oct. 4, 1863	William B. Cadmus	Dedham	22	Clerk	Boston	Wm. H. & Levina Y.	A. Æ. Ellsworth‖
	Hariet E. Metcalf	Franklin	20		Franklin	Michael & Amelia	
Oct. 15, 1863	Addison S. Shepard	"	35	Farmer	Wrentham	Chickery & Relief	§Wm. M. Thayer
	*Hariet M. Wilson	"	36		Franklin	Hiram & Joanna Pond	
Oct. 27, 1863	Daniel O. Corbin	"	19	Don't Presser	Sea Konk	Otis & Nancy	Josephus W. Horton Clergyman, Swanzey
	Anna B. Newell	"	17		Franklin	Arnon J. & Eliza	

* Second Marriage. † Clergyman, Smithfield, R. I. ‡ Catholic Pastor, Woonsocket, R. I. § Cong'l Clergyman, Franklin. ‖ Pastor Cong'l Church, Milford, Mass. ¶ Stephen & Phebe Bordon (Gordon.) †† See page 126.

Marriages Registered in Franklin, County of Norfolk, during the Year 1863.—(Continued.)

DATE OF MARRIAGE.	NAME OF BRIDE AND GROOM.	Residence at Time of Marriage	Age	OCCUPATION.	PLACE OF BIRTH.	NAME OF PARENTS.	BY WHOM MARRIED.
1863							
Nov. 6	John P. Watkins	Franklin	24	Boot Maker	Hopedale in Milford	Emery & Emily	Adin Ballon, Minister, Hopedale
	Julia Corbin	"	26		Wrentham	Otis & Thankful	
Aug. 4	*Joseph E. Shepardson	"	39	Manufacturer	Smithfield, R. I.	James & Esther	Edward G. Thurber Min., Walpole, Mass.
	Hellen G. Cole	"	23		"	Erastus & Hannah	
Dec. 15	Martin V. Tingly	Bellingham	25	Boot Maker	Bellingham	Chas. W. & Margaret L.	Alfred A. Ellsworth Clergyman, Milford
	Lizzie M. Adams	Franklin	21		"	Erastus & Mary E.	
Nov. 26	Timothy Healy	"	20	Laborer	Ireland	John & Joanna	†Michael McCabe
	Catherine Collins	"	21		"	John & Joanna	

Marriages Registered in Franklin, County of Norfolk, during the Year 1864.

DATE OF MARRIAGE.	NAME OF BRIDE AND GROOM.	Residence at Time of Marriage	Age	OCCUPATION.	PLACE OF BIRTH.	NAME OF PARENTS.	BY WHOM MARRIED.
1864.							
Jan. 3	James O. Adams	Franklin	33	Bon't Presser	Nova Scotia	William & Mary	Wm. M. Thayer Clergyman
	*Mary Ann Potter	"	36		England	Abel & Susan Walker	
Jan. 7	Ferdinand I. Pierce	"	23	Boot Maker	Franklin	Israel & Almira	S. W. Squire, Minister of the Gospel
	Oscanna A. Scott	"	19		Cumberland, R.I.	Lewis & Hariet	
Jan. 28	Henry Merchant	Pawtucket, R. I.	19	Seaman	Pawtucket, R. I.	Alexander & Thankful	"
	Lucy Jane Clark	Franklin	27	Publisher	Franklin	John & Rebecca	
Feb. 2	Howard M. Ticknor	West Roxbury	25		Boston	William D. & Emeline S.	Samuel Hunt Clergyman
	Hellen Francis Adams	Franklin	33	Blacksmith	Franklin	Simeon P. & Harriet B.	
March 3	James Hood	"	21		Nova Scotia	John & Ellen	S. W. Squire Min. of the Gospel
	Annet Bartlett	"	21	Farmer	Canton	George & Rebecca	
March 8	Granville Morse	"	20		Franklin	Levi F. & Triphena	Daniel Rounds Pastor Baptist Ch.
	Catherine E. Shepardson	"	34		"	John & Mary	
April 5	Alfred W. Pond	"	15	Engineer	Medway	Malihiah & Mary	John Boyden Clergyman
	Elizabeth Baldwin	Attleboro	35	Baker	Franklin	Elijah & Louesa	
April 16	Orlando S. Engley	Medway	20	Farmer	Medway	John & Lucy	Samuel Hunt Clergyman
	Abbie Jane Albee	Medfield	25		"	Geo. W. & Charlotte	
April 6	Erastus O. Clark	Franklin	26		Bellingham	John C. & Eliza Ann	Wm. M. Thayer Clergyman
	Lydia Armington	"	27	Farmer	"	George W. & Elizabeth	
May 10	James O. Chilson	So. Bellingham	20		Franklin	Orin & Diadama	"
	Melansa G. M. Heaton	Franklin				Samuel & Tirzah	

*Second Marriage. † Catholic Pastor, Woonsocket, R. I.

Marriages in Franklin during the Year 1864.—(Continued.)

DATE OF MARRIAGE.	NAME OF BRIDE AND GROOM.	Residence at Time of Marriage	AGE.	OCCUPATION.	PLACE OF BIRTH.	NAME OF PARENTS.	BY WHOM MARRIED.
1864.							
May 20	*Richard D. Bethell	Cumberland, R.I.	63	Farmer	Thornton, N. H.	Stephen & Hannah	Wm. M. Thayer Clergyman
	*Susan Maine	"	45		Plattsburg, N. Y.	James & Cynthia Phillips	
June 8	*Charles Beckwith	Niantic, Ct.	36	Broker	Providence, R. I.	Alonzo S. & Laura M.	S. J. Horton, assisted
	Hannah B. Miller	Franklin	22		Franklin	John W. & Emily M.	by Dr. Ide, clergyman
July 21	*James C. Sloan	"	49	Boot Maker	Roxbury, Mass.	Ambros H. & Martha	S. W. Squire, Minister of the Gospel
	*Mary E. Joslyn	"	25		Southbridge	Geo. B. & Phebe Gordon	
Aug. 30	Barnum C. Pierce	Wrentham	21	Spinner	Valley Falls, R.I.	Barnum B. & Esther B.	Samuel Hunt Clergyman
	Martha E. Foster	Franklin	18		Newton	Francis & Martha	
Sept. 22	John Edwin Pierce	"	24	Farmer	Franklin	John & Caroline	Wm. M. Thayer Clergyman
	Hope T. Borden	"	21		Woonsocket, R.I.	Stephen & Phebe	
Oct. 13	Emmerson F. Warren	Medway	25	Boot Maker	Franklin	Franklin & Polly	B. A. Edwards Clergyman
	Luthera Smith	"	23		Medway	Sewell & Julia	
Oct. 31	Cyrus R. Crane	Rutland, Vt.	28	Provo Marshall	Middlebury, Vt.	Cillian & Cynthia	S. W. Squire, Minister of the Gospel
	Juline O. Pond	Franklin	21		Franklin	Goldsbury & Julia A.	
Nov. 12	Lucean B. Brown	Wrentham	31	Overseer	Plainfield, Ct.	George & Emire	"
	*Amanda Pratt	"	20		Grafton	Chas. & Sarah Watson	
Nov. 23	Positonius L. Miller	Franklin	30	Farmer	Camden	Ferdinand & Lucia	D. Sandford Clergyman
	Agnes Dillings	"	25		Nova Scotia	Thomas & Eliza	
Nov. 24	Owen E. Ballou	Milford	22	Box Maker	Wrentham	Barton & Phebe	S. W. Squire, Minister of the Gospel
	*Aurelia E. Robbe	Franklin	20		Springfield	Gardner & Eunice Adams	
Nov. 24	Lyman C. Darling	Milford	25	Teamster	Bellingham	Welcome B. & Alpha	Adin Ballou, Minister of the Gospel
	Louesa M. Whiting	Franklin	23		Franklin	Joseph B. & Phila	
Dec. 8	*Levi F. Morse	"	67	Farmer	"	Levi & Katurah	Ebenezer Burgess Clergyman
	Susan M. Fisher	"	45		"	Maxey & Perces	
Dec. 28	Albert I. Nowell	"	25	"	"	Armon, Jr. & Eliza	"
	Betsy W. Clark	"	22		"	Paul B. & Abbie A.	

Marriages registered in Franklin, County of Norfolk, during the Year 1865.—A. A. Ressegue, Registrar.

1865.							
Jan. 1	Samuel Sawyer	Franklin	28	Bon't Presser	Saco, Me.	Henry & Hannah	S. W. Squire, Minister of the Gospel
	Caroline M. Lawrence	Wrentham	25		Wrentham	Adeline C. & Olive	

* Second Marriage.

Marriages Registered in Franklin, County of Norfolk, during the Year 1865.—(Continued.)

DATE OF MARRIAGE.	NAME OF BRIDE AND GROOM.	Residence at Time of Marriage	AGE	OCCUPATION.	PLACE OF BIRTH.	NAME OF PARENTS.	BY WHOM MARRIED.
1865							
Jan. 2	George A. Crooks	Bellingham	34	Farmer	Bellingham	Joel and Ester	S. W. Squire, Minister of the Gospel
	Ellen A. Cook	Wrentham	34		Wrentham	Avery & Charlotte	
Jan. 4	Olney P. Newell	Franklin	22	"	Franklin	Hiram & Clarisa	†Adin Ballon. Minister of the Gospel
	†Elizabeth L. Lawrence	Medway	22			Erastus & Elizabeth	
Jan. 8	†Asa Sargent, Jr.	Franklin	56	"	Hubardston	Asa & Polly	E. Burgess, Clergyman, So. Franklin
	†Susan Frost	"	35			Abijah & Susan Clark	
Jan. 7	†John F. Lasure	Medway	23	Boot Maker	Medway	Simeon & Abbie	S. W. Squire, Minister of the Gospel
	Mary J. Fisher	Franklin	23		Franklin	Smith & Mary C.	
Jan. 17	Edmond T. Fisher	"	26	Farmer	"	Adin & Mary	Jacob Ide, Pastor 2d Ch., Medway
	Kittie Armington	"	20		Oxford	George & Elizabeth	
Jan. 18	John F. Torry	"	27	"	Sutton	John & Caroline	Johnathan Edwards
	Clarra Hall	"	18		Medway	Tillotson H. & Lucinda	Cong'l Pastor, Dedham
Feb. 15	William S. Ward	"	29	Don't Presser	Ware	Reuben & Paraside	D. Sanford, Clergyman. Medway
	†Ada Fuller§	"	30		Franklin	Oliver & Lucinda	
Feb. 12	†Samuel S. Cook	"	31	Farmer	Franklin	Samuel & Maria	J. W. Willett, Clergyman, Cumberland, R.I
	Anna J. Kelly	"	28		Westboro	Edward & Mary	
April 19	Albert J. Gilmore	"	19	"	Franklin	James & Fanny H.	John Boyden, Clergyman, Cumberland, R.I
	Anna S. Swanitton	Wrentham	23		Providence, R. I.	John & Mary	
June 8	†Charles E. Nichols	Franklin	49	"	Smithtown, L. I.	Paul & Laurana	S. W. Squire, Minister of the Gospel
	†Caroline P. Cole	"	46		Lebanon, N. H.	Clark & Mary J. Aldrich	
July 12	Henry Mayshaw	Wrentham	22	Boot Maker	Canada	Maynard & Mary	Wm. M. Thayer, Clergyman, Franklin
	Ellen B. Vose	"	18		Wrentham	Lewis & Ellen	
Aug. 31	Geo. A. Stearns	Blackstone	22		Barre	Shepard & Bertha	S. W. Squire, Minister of the Gospel
	Addie M. Barber	"				Eital & Hannah	
Sept. 21	Wm. R. Pickering	Franklin	23	Boot Maker	Milford	Simon & Elizabeth	*Charles W. Wilder
	Hattie L. Phillips.	Fitchburg	23		Fitchburg	Geo. W. & Mary	
Sept. 15	Samuel H. Jordon	Franklin	19	Farmer	Franklin	Alfred & Sarah L.	John Boyden, Clergyman, Woonsocket, R.I
	Alice J. Thompson	"	17		Wrentham	Geo. W. & Joanna	
Oct. 18	Warren Butman	Wrentham	23	"	Franklin	John & Maria	S. W. Squire, Minister of the Gospel
	Julia A. Cook	"	17		Woonsocket	Ruben & Julia A.	
Nov. 30	†Lyman Adams	Franklin	45	"	Bellingham	John & Rosanna	D. Sanford, Cong'l Clergyman, Medway
	Christiana Adams	Bellingham	21		"	Sabin & Mary A.	

† Second Marriage.　‡ Hopedale in Milford.　§ Maiden Name Duggles.　¶ Pastor M. E. Church, W. Medway.

FRANKLIN TOWN RECORDS—MARRIAGES.

Marriages Registered in Franklin, County of Norfolk, during the Year 1865.—(Continued.)

DATE OF MARRIAGE.	NAME OF BRIDE AND GROOM.	Residence at Time of Marriage	AGE	OCCUPATION.	PLACE OF BIRTH.	NAME OF PARENTS.	BY WHOM MARRIED.
1865.							
Dec. 6	William M. Coney Ophelia H. Scott	Franklin "	25 23	Laborer	Wrentham Franklin	Albert & Celinda Sanl B. & Susan	†Adin Ballou,
Dec. 28	Edmund F. Partridge Emma S. Curtis	Wrentham Concord, N. H.	21 18	Bon't Blocker	" Boston	Geo. I. & Hariet William & Emily	Geo. A. Pelton Clergyman, Franklin
Sept. 7	*Nelson C. Newell ‡Adaline A. Barrows	Franklin Wrentham	58 35	Farmer	Cumberland,R.I. Wellington, Ct.	Jabez & Jerusha D. B. & Arminda Reed	John Boyden Clergyman

Marriages Registered in Franklin, County of Norfolk, during the Year 1866.—A. A. RUSSEGUE, Town Clerk.

1866.							
Feb. 11	Joshua G. Follett Susan A. Pierce	Wrentham "	25 22	Farmer	Wrentham Franklin	Jenks & Betcy Israel & Almira	Geo. A. Pelton Clergyman, Franklin
Feb. 28	Lucien B. Newell *Mardie E. Flanders	Franklin Bodowinham	25 25	Bon't Bleacher	Cumberland,R.I. Bodowinham	Nelson C. & Amanda Reubin & Philena Blake	§Geo. S. Weaver
March 11	Charles E. Clark Nettie M. Folsom	Franklin Wrentham	21 22	Clerk	Milford Natick	Charles W. & Elvira Aaron & Adeline	S. W. Squire Clergyman, Franklin
March 29	Addison Pickering *Rebecca W. Leland	Holliston "	30 24	Mechanic	Pawtucket, R. I. Franklin	Simeon & Elizabeth Rhodes & — Green	
April 13	Henry C. Adams *Lydia A. Adams	Franklin "	25 25	Soldier	Franklin Newport, R. I.	Oren W. & Hannah Nelson & Mary Dowley	John Boyden, Clergyman, Woonsocket R.I. "
April 21	John Martin *Mary Ann Clegg	" "	30 32	Weaver	Canada Scotland	John & Lucy James & Mary Ross	"
June 9	Alfred J. Pierce Susie A. Fuller	" St. Albans, Me.	32 25	Boot Maker	Franklin WestGardner,Me	Israel & Almira James & Susan	Geo. A. Pelton Clergyman, Franklin
June 20	Thomas E. H. Grantham Ella G. Canny	Toronto, C. W. Franklin	26 20	Merchant	Toronto, C. W. Wrentham	John & Ann M. Wm. N. & Mary A. B.	
July 6	*Fenner Darling Sarah M. Southwick	Blackstone "	36 26	Engineer Bon't Bleacher	Cumberland Appleton, Me.	Anson & Amey Nadan & Sarah	†Adin Ballou
Aug. 25	Eli J. Linniken Eva A. Newell	Franklin "	21 28	Butcher	Franklin Worcester	Robert & Rachael Arnon J. & Eliza	‡Lucius M. S. Haynes
Oct. 22	David W. Corson Hannah M. Allen	" "	31		Franklin Millbury	William W. & Almira Chas. & Martha	S. W. Squire Clergyman, Franklin

* Second Marriage. † Minister of the Gospel, Hopedale, Milford. ‡ Pastor First Baptist Church, Oswego, N. Y. § Pastor Universalist Ch., Lawrence.

FRANKLIN TOWN RECORDS—MARRIAGES. 133

Marriages Registered in Franklin, County of Norfolk, during the year 1866.—(Continued.)

DATE OF MARRIAGE.	NAME OF BRIDE AND GROOM.	Residence at Time of Marriage	AGE	OCCUPATION.	PLACE OF BIRTH.	NAME OF PARENTS.	BY WHOM MARRIED.
1866							
Nov. 8	William W. Curtis	Holliston	22	Mechanic	Worcester	Nathaniel & Hariet	S. W. Squire, Minister of the Gospel, Franklin
	Annie R. Pickering	Franklin	18		Franklin	Simon & Elizabeth	
Nov. 15	George N. Fuller		46	Farmer		Asa & Hepzibah	A. H. Coolige, Pastor 1st Cong. Ch., Leicester
	Hariet M. Craig	Holliston	26		Leicester	John, Jr. & Harriet	
Nov. 15	Elijah F. Hawes	Wrentham	21	Bm't Presser	Wrentham	Ebenezer & Laura B.	H. D. L. Webster, Clergyman, Franklin
	Ellen F. Ballou	Franklin	22			Barton & Phebe	
Nov. 14	Preston C. Nason		18	Clerk	Franklin	George W. & Peary B.	"
	Jennie Potter		17		Boston	James C. & Mary A.	
Nov. 21	Sylvenus W. Corbin		19	Blocker	Rehoboth	Otis & Nancy	Geo. A. Pelton, Clergyman, Franklin
	Clarra A. Linsey	Bath, Me.	19		Providence, R. I.	Augustus & Sarah	
Nov. 24	Sanford T. Capron	Franklin	38	Manufacturer	Cumberland, R.I.	Oliver & Silence	John Boyden, Clergyman, Woonsocket
	Lucina A. Daring	Bellingham	23		Bellingham	Welcome B. & Alpha	
Nov. 29	William E. Plummer	Franklin	26	Bleacher	Monmouth, Me.	Joseph H. & Hannah	§John C. Perry
	Martha A. Gilmore	Monmouth, Me.	"		"	John O. & Hariet	
Dec. 5	Asa M. Franc'en	Attleboro	29	Machinest	Woonsocket, R.I.	James & Elvira	Geo. A. Pelton, Clergyman, Franklin
	Mary E. Green	Franklin	25		Franklin	Job & Mary	
Nov. 27	Henry S. Adams	Attleborough	38	Painter	R. I.	Ralph W. & Elizabeth	H. D. L. Webster, Clergyman, Franklin
	Charlotte E. Allen	W. Medway	21		Medway	George W. & Charlotte	
Dec. 22	Peter Price	Franklin	28	Boot Maker.	Canada	Paul & Almira	A. A. Russegue, Justice of the Peace
Dec. 23	Lizzie E. Sampson	"	27		Bodoinham, Me.	Rufus & Mary	S. W. Squire, Clergyman, Franklin
	Charles H. Blake	Wrentham	31	Mechanic	Wrentham	Edwin E. & Eliza	
Dec. 25	*Martha L. Russell †	Franklin	27		Strong, Me.	Joshua & Betcy	Wm. Phipps, Clergyman, Paxton
	George A. Brown		23	Straw Worker	†	E. P. & Sarah J.	
Dec. 30	Lucy A. Harrington	Paxton	21		Paxton	Simon & Alonie	Wm. H. Fitzpatrick, Clergyman, Milford
	James McBearmont	Franklin	25	Laborer	Ireland	Cornelius & Ellen	
	Rosa McMullen	Milford	22		"	Thomas & Susan	

Marriages Registered in Franklin, County of Norfolk, in the Year 1867.—A. A. Russegue, Registrar.

1867							
Dec. 29	*William Woodman	Franklin	40	Painter	Kenebunkport, Me.	James & Eliza	Sam.E.Herrick, Clergyman,Chelsea,Mass.
	Susan H. Swift	"	37		Winslow, Me.	Joseph & Mehitable	

* Second Marriage.　† Maiden Name Wormwell.　‡ Head of Wallace Bay, N. S.　§ Pastor M. E. Ch., Monmouth, Me.

Marriages Registered in Franklin, County of Norfolk, in the Year 1867.—(Continued.)

DATE OF MARRIAGE.	NAME OF BRIDE AND GROOM.	Residence at Time of Marriage	AGE	OCCUPATION.	PLACE OF BIRTH.	NAME OF PARENTS.	BY WHOM MARRIED.
1867.							
Jan. 14	*George W. Bacon	Franklin	35	Bleacher	Franklin	Joseph T. & Mary A.	George A. Pelton
	*Emily J. Bacon	"	33		"	Nath'l & Caroline Thayer	Clergyman
Feb. 10	Allen E. Dart	Wrentham	23	"	Wrentham	Thomas & Betsy	S. W. Squire
	Cobb		19		Boston	Hermon & Lucy	Clergyman
Feb. 13	Melzar W. Allen	Walpole	26	Twine Maker	Winthrop, Me.	Lemuel & Adeline	George A. Pelton
	Martha Metcalf	Franklin	25	Teacher	Wrentham	Joseph A. & Chloe	Clergyman
April 17	Charles M. Aldrich	Wrentham	20	Book Keeper	"	Artemas & Jane T.	"
	Hariet A. Fisher	Franklin	24		Franklin	Walter H. & Emely M.	
May 1	Barton F. Cook	"	23	Farmer	"	Milton & Louesa M.	A. F. Herick
	Silvina M. Brown	"	20		"	E. P. & Sarah J.	Clergyman, Holliston
June 1	Frank Perkins	Middleboro	21	Shoe Maker	Middleboro	John C. & Matilda	Wm. M. Thayer
	Nellie M. Clark	Franklin	21		"	Robert & Deborah	Clergyman
June 20	Joseph P. Gould	Boston	21	Carver	Boston	Joseph P. & Louesa H.	D. M. Crane
	Marianna Wades	Franklin	18		Franklin	Amos & Rhoda	Clergyman, Boston
July 3	John B. Whiting	"	52	Farmer	Ireland	Sidney & Olive	S. W. Squire
	Margaret Heany	Wrentham	28	Mechanic	Wrentham	William & Margaret	Clergyman
July 3	Rufus F. White	Franklin	40		Providence, R.I.	Lysander & Susan	A. A. Bussegue
	*Hannah Cony	"	23	Painter	Wrentham	Wm. & Caroline Esty	Justice of the Peace
July 4	Anthony Connor	Wrentham	19	Jeweller	Foxboro	Isaac & Elizabeth	James H. Lyon
Aug. 6	Sarah J. Lawrence	Franklin	21	Laborer		Addison C. & Olive	B. A. Edwards
	George W. Grover	Mt. Vernon, Me.	22	Grocer	Great Falls, N.H.	Charles P. & Emeline	Clergyman, Sharon
Aug. 15	Lizzie A. Henna	Boston	24		Franklin	Thomas B. & Mary	William M. Thayer
	*Charles W. Andrews	Franklin	20	Don't Presser		Elisha & Sarah	Clergyman
Aug. 31	Geo. Anna M. Colvin	"	45	Carpenter	Cumberland, R.I.	Caleb & Mary	"
	George S. Corbett	"	21		Reedfield	James S. & Abigail B.	
Oct. 23	Louesa J. Weatherhead	"	45	Laborer	Augusta, Me.	Horace & Louesa J.	Luther Keene
	*Osmyn A. Stanley	"	21	Laborer	Woonsocket, R.I.	John & Juliet	Clergyman
Nov. 16	*Emma M. Pierce	"	37		Medway	Jefferson & Ruth E.	D. Sanford
	Charles L. Bennet	"	17		Burke, Vt.	Alexander S. & Julia	Clergyman
Nov. 28	Allice L. Scott	"	29	Teacher	Provincetown	Pardon & Julia	W. Spaulding
	†	Provincetown	24			Asahel & Louesa C.	Marblehead
	Sarah Irving Ryder					Ruben & Lucinda	

* Second Marriage.   † Lester Lorenzo Burrington.   ‡ Clergyman, Pawtucket, R.I.

Marriages Registered in Franklin, County of Norfolk, in the Year 1867.—(Continued.)

DATE OF MARRIAGE.	NAME OF BRIDE AND GROOM.	Residence at Time of Marriage.	AGE	OCCUPATION.	PLACE OF BIRTH.	NAME OF PARENTS.	BY WHOM MARRIED.
1867							
Dec. 6	Andrew S. Fuller	Franklin	21	Painter	Woonsocket, R.I.	John & Betsy	S. W. Squire, Clergyman
	Jane Foster	"	18		Medway	Francis & Martha	
Dec. 25	William H. Howe	Milford, N. H.	25	Mechanic	Milford, N. H.	Oliver & Martha W.	Luther Keene, Clergyman
	Ella F. Fisher	Franklin	19		Bellingham	Lewis L. & Sarah H.	

Marriages Registered in Franklin for the Year 1868.—A. A. Russegue, Registrar.

1868							
Jan. 1	*Oliver Dean	Franklin	84	Gentleman	Franklin	Seth & Edena	A. A. Minor, Clergyman, Boston
	*Lonesa C. Hawes	"	52		Wrentham	Joseph & Sally C. Cobb	
Jan. 1	Nathan E. Darling	"	19	Farmer	Framingham	Ellis A. & Susan M.	Luther Kene, Clergyman, Franklin
	Abbie M. Pike	"	18		Roxbury	Alonzo G. & Martha	
Jan. 6	*Nancy M. Daniels	"	32	Farmer	Blackstone	Moses & Amy C. Daniels	Edward A. Lyon, Clergyman, Woonsocket, R.I.
	Mary E. Kingston	"	23		Frederickton, N.B.	John H. & Kate E.	"
Jan. 23	John Newgent	Bellingham	25	Boot Maker	On the Water	John & Eliza	
	*Susan A. Remick	Franklin	23			George & Ann Fisk	
Jan. 29	William Dove	"	30	Boot Maker	Wrentham	Benjamin & Susan	Jacob Ide, Clergyman, Medway
	Kate McDonald	Medway	23		Wallace, N. S.	Daniel & Isabella	
Feb. 10	Joseph L. Gammell	Fitchburg	19	Machinest	Northfield, Vt.	Francis & Nora	S. W. Squire, Clergyman Franklin
	Bella F. Adams	"	25		Salem	Erastus & Mary G.	
Feb. 24	*George O. Bent	Franklin	18	Carpenter	Framingham	Archibald & Fanny H.	John Boyden, Clergyman, Woonsocket
	Wilmer D. Bent	"	31	Carpenter	Thompson, Conn.	George & Mary	
April 2	*Alonzo M. Taft	"	21		Natick	Squire & Mary	James E. Docker Clergyman
	Elmira Holden	Blackstone	28	Brick layer	Cumberland, R.I.	William & Lourea	
April 18	Bernard McGuire	Franklin	21		Ireland	Patrick & Mary	G. L. Dement Clergyman
	Mary J. Graves	"	22	Don't Blocker	E. Washington, N.H.	William & Mary	
April 23	George H. Partridge	"	18		Oldtown, Me.	Joseph H. & Julia A.	D. Sanford
	Alfaretta A. Vose	Wrentham	26	Don't Presser	Wrentham	Weston A. & Abby A.	Clergyman
May 2	Albert E. Follett	Franklin	22		Cumberland, R.I.	Albert & Lonna	†John B. Wheelright
	Addie Partridge	"	34	Carpenter	Parris, Me.	Austin & Sarah	
June 3	Thaddeus H. Shepardson	"	22		Brookville, Me.	Thaddeus & Hariet	Luther Kene, Clergyman, Franklin
	Annie E. Fales				Medfield	Oliver & Mary	

* Second Marriage.   † Ordained Minister, So. Parris, Me.

Marriages Registered in Franklin, County of Norfolk, for the Year 1868.—(Continued.)

DATE OF MARRIAGE.	NAME OF BRIDE AND GROOM.	Residence at Time of Marriage	AGE	OCCUPATION.	PLACE OF BIRTH.	NAME OF PARENTS.	BY WHOM MARRIED.
1868.							
July 2	Edwin R. Rogers	Franklin	22	Barber	East Brewster	Alonzo & Lydia C.	†J.W. Holman
	Estella A. Scott	"	18		Franklin	Chas. H. & Amanda	Pastor
July 22	Daniel Brown	Wrentham	27	Pattern Maker	Ireland	Alexander & Margaret	Wm. M. Thayer
	Hester A. Getchell	Topsfield, Me.	27		Topsfield, Me.	Josiah & Mary	Clergyman
Aug. 12	James W. Wilkinson	Franklin	30	Shoe Maker	Wrentham	Willard B. & Lucy	D. Sanford
	*Fannie A. Blake	"	28		Franklin	Elias & Mary A.	Clergyman, Medway
Aug. 14	William F. Everett	Wrentham	22		Wrentham	Metcalf & Julia B.	"
	Lucia M. Blake	Franklin	19		Boston	Seth & Mary	
Aug. 26	James G. Perrigo	Milford	26	Boot Maker	Wrentham	Caleb & Mary G.	†Adin Ballou
	Nellie J. Heaton	Franklin	23		Franklin	Samuel & Thurstia	
Sept. 1	*Albert H. Dolliver	New York	36	Sail Maker	Boston	Thomas & Maria	D. Sanford
	*Clarra E. Montgomery	"	31		New York	Sam'l H. & Alice F. Crocker	Clergyman, Medway
Sept. 17	Lyman Adams	Franklin	18	Card Striper	Gloucester	Sabin & Mary Ann	Daniel Rounds, Clergyman, No. Wrentham
	Violetta P. Ware	"	15		Franklin	A. P. & Mary Ann	
Nov. 26	John C. Pond	Medway	19	Boot Maker	Medway	Timothy & Eliza J.	Luther Keene
	Mary Emma Fisher	Franklin	18		Franklin	Lewis S. & Sarah	Clergyman, Franklin
Nov. 26	Thomas J. Russell	"	23	Carder	Cumberland, R.I.	Thomas & Harriet M.	John Boyden, Clergyman, Woonsocket R.I.
	Jenna Maria Pierce	Milford	23		Blackstone	Clarendon J. & Emeline D.	
Nov. 26	Joseph G. Guild	Franklin	26	Bon'l Presser	Franklin	Joel & Eliza	Thomas C. Biscoe
	Illeone E. Guild	Uxbridge	22		Uxbridge	Caleb & Julia	Clergyman, Uxbridge
Nov. 26	Albert L. Brock	Franklin	28	Mechanic	Blackstone	Sanford W. & Mary E.	John Boyden, Clergyman, Woonsocket R.I.
	Mary J. Britton	"	18		Dover, Mass.	Joseph & Mary J.	
Nov. 26	Joseph P. Day	"	24	Bon't Blocker	Paxton	Joseph & Elsie C.	John B. Wheelwright
	Georgie E. Brett	"	24		South Parris, Me.	Luther & Mary	Clergyman, So. Parris, Me.
Nov. 23	F. Leslie Metcalf	"	20	Book Keeper	Mendon	John G. & Abigail	Alvah Black, Justice of Peace, Parris, Me.
	Mary A. Woodbury	"	29		Parris, Me.	Asa & Tacy	
Dec. 3	Walter M. Fisher	"	29	Manufacturer	Franklin	Walter H. & Emely M.	Luther Keene
	Allice I. Metcalf	"	27	Teacher	"	Otis F. & Lucy M.	Clergyman, Franklin
Dec. 29	William C. Simmons	Boston	30		Wareham	Charles & Eliza	Edward G. Thurber
	Rebecca Breck	Franklin			Springfield	Elias & Juliaette	Clergyman, Walpole
Dec. 31	Asa R. Rounds	"	24	Sizer	Attleborough	Sylvenas C. & Amanda A.	Luther Keene
	Josephine A. Cook	"	22		Franklin	Winslow & Ruth(Whiting)	Clergyman, Franklin

* Second Marriage.   † First Baptist Society, Franklin.   ‡ Minister of the Gospel, Hopedale, Milford, Mass.

Marriages Registered in Franklin, County of Norfolk, in the Year 1869.—A. A. RUSSEGUE, Registrar.

DATE OF MARRIAGE.	NAME OF BRIDE AND GROOM.	Residence at Time of Marriage	Age	OCCUPATION.	PLACE OF BIRTH.	NAME OF PARENTS.	BY WHOM MARRIED.
1869							
Jan. 9	*Stephen T. Gifford	Franklin	41	Laborer	Dartmouth	William & Sarah	Chas. R. Walker Clergyman
Jan. 10	*Susan S. Watson †	Providence, R.I.	44		Providence, R.I.	Joseph & Mahaly	
	Pliny E. Cooper	Franklin	22	Machinest	Canton	Pliny & Nancy	William M. Thayer Clergyman
	Ella J. Hart		17	"	Franklin	Daniel W. & Hariet S.	
Jan. 20	George F. Wadsworth	Milton	24	"	Dorchester	George & Sophia R.	Albert K. Teele Clergyman, Milton
	Mary J. Miller	Franklin	20		Medway	Herman B. & Mary	
Feb. 2	Charles R. Gowen		22	Laborer	Acworth, N. H.	George M. & Hannah	A. R. Baker, Minister of the Gospel
	‡Kate M. Hills		19		New York	Jarvis H. & Phila B.	
March 28	*John Duffy		45	Farmer	Ireland	Edward & Elizabeth	Philip Gillick, C. Pastor, Attleboro
	*Bridget Staples		45			Hogh & Mary Darcy	
Feb. 14	Charles E. Williams		20	Boot Maker	Franklin	Charles & Mary A.	Joseph T. Massey Clergyman, Bellingham
	Louisa Ware	Wrentham	18		Wrentham	William & Almira G.	
April 8	John C. Heath	Needham	26	Engineer	Troy, Me.	Caleb & Mary F.	D. Sanford Clergyman
	Antionette S. Clark	Medway	25		Medway, Mass.	Sanford & Nancy G.	
July 9	*Emerson W. Hoffses	Franklin	33	Carpenter	Warren, Me.	John G. & Maria M.	George S. Noyes Clergyman, Boston
	Maria Smith		26		Liverpool, N. S.	Jonathan & Birtha	
July 13	Henry Bullard Richardson	Amherst	22	Teacher	Franklin	Stephen W. & Eliza B.	J. L. Jenkins, Clergyman, Amherst
	Mary Elizabeth Lincoln	Providence, R.I.	22		Amherst	Rufus S. & Lydia B.	
July 30	Frederick A. Tillinghast	Providence	35	Painter	Cohoes Falls, N.Y.	John J. & Mary S.	§Richard Eddy
	Susan A. Watson	Franklin	22		Providence, R.I.	Gustavas & Susan S.	
July 24	William G. Hart.		22	Machine Tender	Montville	William & Betsey	Luther Keene Clergyman
	Annie Nottage		17		Hopkinton	Joseph S. & E'iza	
Aug. 12	Willard E. Scott		21	Fireman	Franklin	Willard & Deborah	S. L. Holman, Clergyman, Woonsocket, R.I
	Flora A. Jones	Blackstone	21		Somers	Erwin & Nancy	
Aug. 16	Dennis F. Daily	Franklin	22	Boot Maker	Boston	William & Julia	Samuel Warner Justice of the Peace
	Martha E. Foster		22		Newton U. Falls	Francis & Martha	
Aug. 17	*George R. Marden	Woolwich, Me.	30	Bleacher	Palermo, Me.	James & Lucy	A. A. Miner Clergyman, Boston
	Anna Savage	Franklin	24		Woolwich, Me.	James & Emely	
Aug. 20	*Nathan W. Frail	Brooklyn, N. Y.	45	Carpenter	Hopkinton	Isaac & Sarah	J. Hydesmith, Clergyman, Brooklyn, N.Y.
	*Abbie B. Latinville	Providence, R.I.	30		Wrentham	George & Polly Fairbanks	
Oct. 3	Jonas Kenyon	Providence, R.I.		Laborer	Providence, R.I.	Caleb S. & Mercy	A. A. Russegue Justice of the Peace
	Mary Gilbright				Pascoag, R.I.	Thomas & Catherine	

* Second Marriage.   † Maiden Name Manchester.   ‡ Adopted Daughter.   § Pastor Universalist Church, Franklin.

Marriages Registered in Franklin, County of Norfolk, in the Year 1869.—(Continued.)

DATE OF MARRIAGE.	NAME OF GROOM AND BRIDE.	Residence at Time of Marriage.	AGE	OCCUPATION.	PLACE OF BIRTH.	NAME OF PARENTS.	BY WHOM MARRIED.
1869.							
Oct. 26	William Frank Billings	Milford	22	Teamster	Blackstone	William L. & Eunice	Luther Keene, Clergyman
	Minnie M. Douglass	Franklin	21		Essex, Vt.	Samuel & Almira	
Oct. 28	Edwin A. Jordan	"	31	Farmer	Franklin	Alfred & Sarah	"
	Eliza J. Mayo	"	28		Eden, Me.	Ambrose & Parmelia	
Oct. 31	Eliab P. Ballou	"	23	Carpenter	Wrentham	Barton & Phebe	Adin Ballou, Clergyman, Hopedale, Mass.
	Jane F. Williams	Medway	20		Medway	Nathan A. & Esther B.	
Nov. 14	*Austin Blake	Franklin	69	Farmer	Franklin	Robert & Abigail	Richard Eddy, Clergyman
	Martha M. Tuson	Boston	25		Boston	Edmund & Mary	
Nov. 18	Francis A. Russegue	Franklin	22	Clerk	Franklin	Alpheus A. & Mary	Luther Keene, Clergyman
	Addie A. Dean	"	24		Boston	Bathuel P. & Sarah S.	
Dec. 23	Edwin A. Guild	"	25	Boot Maker	Franklin	James A. & Lucina P.	Daniel Rounds, Clergyman
	Amanda M. Adams	"	25		Woonsocket, R.I.	Sidon & Eliza	
Aug. 22	†John Doyle	"	35	Laborer	Ireland	Edward & Catherine	§Philip Gillick, Clergyman, Attleboro
	Mary Sullivan	"	24		"	John & Ellen	

Marriages Registered in Franklin, in the County of Norfolk, in the Year 1870.— A. A. Russegue, Registrar.

DATE OF MARRIAGE.	NAME OF GROOM AND BRIDE.	Residence at Time of Marriage.	AGE	OCCUPATION.	PLACE OF BIRTH.	NAME OF PARENTS.	BY WHOM MARRIED.
1870.							
Jan. 17	John Howe Davidson	Franklin, Mass.	32	Merchant Tailor	Scotland	James & Ann	‖Mark Trafton
	Pruella Addie Millard	Providence, R. I.	25		New Ipswich	James M. & Laura B.	
Jan. 10	Benjamin C. Thayer	Franklin	30	Farmer	Northborough	Ethan & Serena	S. L. Holman, Clergyman, Woonsocket, R.I
	Ellen F. Jordan	"	26		Franklin	Alfred & Sarah	
Jan. 20	Albert Barton	Medway	26	Mechanic	Medway	Willard & Susan	Luther Keene, Clergyman, Franklin
	Mary Stimpson	"	21		"	John & Martha	
March 10	‡John S. Nottage	Franklin	60	Shoe Maker	Boston	Josiah & Sarah	W. A. Nottage, Clergyman, Westboro
	‡Elizabeth Howard	"	57		Mendon	Ebenezer & Hannah	
April 23	Robert A. Stewart	"	29	Wheel right	Nova Scotia	James & Jenette	S. L. Holman, Clergyman, Woonsocket
	Susan C. Rae	"	20		"	William M. & Elizabeth	
April 30	‡John Picket	"	75	Farmer	Plainfield, Ct.	John & Eunice	J. Merrill, Clergyman, Cambridge, Mass.
	*Huldah Scott	"	74		Putney, Vt.	James & Mary Thurston	
June 22	Daniel H. Rounds	"	22	Carpenter	Attleborough	Sylvens C. & Amanda A.	Luther Keene, Clergyman, Franklin
	A. Arabella Hills	"	23		Franklin	Harvey & Mary	

* Third Marriage. † Second Marriage. ‡ Fourth Marriage. § Registered Feb. 8, 1871, it not having been returned until this day. ‖ M. E. Clergyman, Prov. R. I.

Marriages Registered in Franklin, in the County of Norfolk, in the Year 1870.—(Continued.)

DATE OF MARRIAGE.	NAME OF BRIDE AND GROOM.	Residence at Time of Marriage	AGE	OCCUPATION.	PLACE OF BIRTH.	NAME OF PARENTS.	BY WHOM MARRIED.
1870							
June 28	George Warren Foster	Franklin	29	Farmer	Franklin	Benjamin & Mary Ann	G. L. Holman, Clergyman, Smithfield, R. I.
	Amelia L. Whelden	"	17		Lynn	William & Ann	
Sept. 24	*Jason Tower	"	45	"	Cumberland, R.I.	Jason & Philena	‡Joseph T. Massey
	Mary E. Jardin	"	21		New Castle, N.B.	Richard & Ellen	
Sept. 17	George W. Pierce	"	33	Mason	Franklin	Washington & Nancy	†J. W. Manning, Clergyman, Old South Ch.
	Lizzie Hopkins	Lawrence, Mass.	22		New Portland, Me		William M. Thayer
Nov. 23	Wm. N. Manchester	Franklin	32	Machineest	Tiverton, R. I.	William & Rhoda	Clergyman, Franklin
	*Anna M. Darling	Woonsocket	26		Attleborough	Pliny & Nancy Cooper	Geo. W. Mansfield
Nov. 6	Edward G. Weston	Franklin	21	Laborer	Norfolk, Va.	William & Phillis	M. E. Clergyman
	Della C. Gasken	"	21		Newbern, N. C.	William & Celia	Wm. C. Reed, Clergyman, So. Dennis
Dec. 30	Lemuel E. Bumpus	"	22	Trader	Plymouth	Mark J. & Mary A.	Luther Keene
	Marietta Chase	South Dennis	24		South Dennis	Joshua & Thankful	Clergyman, Franklin
Dec. 20	Nathaniel T. Hubbard	Franklin	44	†	Vernon, Conn.	Nathaniel & Betey T.	Philip Gillick, Clergyman, No. Attleboro
	Mary L. Daniels	"	34		Franklin	Albert E. & Olive G.	
Dec. 25	Francis Ford	"	22	Boot Maker	Ireland	Patrick & Mary	§Frederick C. Newell
	Mary Ann Granger	"	17		Franklin	Edward & Catherine	
Aug. 28	Henry A. Hartshorn	"	23	Trader	"	Edmond & Susan	
	Ida M. Cobb	"	17		Pawtucket, R. I.	Henry G. & Betsey	Philip Gillick, Clergyman, No. Attleboro
Nov. 12	Michael Doherty	"	32	Laborer	Ireland	Philip & Mary	
	Anna Angles	"	25		"	Thomas & Nancy	

Marriages Registered in Franklin, in the County of Norfolk, in the Year 1871.

1871							
Jan. 1	George N. Gaskell	Franklin	23	Carpenter	Bellingham	William & Abigail	Henry C. Leonard
	Ann Eliza Clark	"	23		Franklin	Alfred & Polly	Universalist Clergyman
Jan. 22	Edward Kingsley	"	28	Laborer	Ireland	Philip & Bridget	Philip Gillick
	Rosa McHugh	"	25		"	Thomas & Rosa	Catholic Pastor
Jan. 22	Gerrat Callan	Norfolk	23	Laborer	"	Michael & Ann	"
	Bridget McHugh	Franklin	27			Martin & Mary	
March 2	Henry W. Healy	"	23	Blacksmith	South Weymouth	William & Phebe	S. L. Holman
	Thersa Young	"	23		Cushling, Me	Mhyrus & Lizza	Clergyman

*Second Marriage. †Straw Goods Manufacturer. ‡Clergyman, Bellingham. §Clergyman, Cumberland. R. I.

Marriages Registered in Franklin, County of Norfolk, in the Year 1871.

DATE OF MARRIAGE.	NAME OF BRIDE AND GROOM.	Residence at Time of Marriage	AGE	OCCUPATION.	PLACE OF BIRTH.	NAME OF PARENTS.	BY WHOM MARRIED.
1871 March 7	Dennis Long	Franklin	19	Laborer	Franklin	John & Ellen	S. S. Holman Clergyman
	Lottie Carlow	"	22		St. Johns, N. B.	Dennis & Annie	
March 30	Grainville W. Moulton	"	26	Straw Worker	Framingham	William & Eliza	W. F. Crafts, Justice Peace, Stoneham Mass
	Hattie A. Taylor	"			Weld, Me.	Stephen & C.	
April 23	William E. Britton	Abington	21	Boot Maker	Abington	William & Susan	S. W. Squire Clergyman
	Mary A. Taft	Franklin			Blackstone	Daniel & Ann E.	
May 2	George A. Kingsbury	Norfolk	32	Farmer	Franklin	Horatio & Adelia	D. Sanford Clergyman
	Louesa M. Richardson	"				John H. & Louisa	
May 24	William A. Arnold	"	22	Painter	E. Greenwich, R.I	Christopher H. & Almira	S. W. Squire Clergyman
	Ines E. Pond	Franklin	19		Franklin	Henry & Ann	
May 27	*Oramel B. Blake	"	57	Carpenter	"	Ira & Laura	Mortimer Blake Clergyman
	Mary A. Roix	Belfast, Me.	32		Brookville, Me.	Joseph & Ann Dennet	
Sept. 20	Fremont M. Richardson	Franklin	22	Clerk	Hartland, Me.	Stephen W. & Hariet B.	Wm. Thayer Clergyman
	Henrietta Heaton	"	21		Franklin	William A. & M. A.	
Sept. 21	Charles H. Heaton	"	25	Market Man	Winterport, Me.	Samuel & Tirza	S. W. Squire Clergyman
	Annie M. Couillard	"	32		"	Joshua & Sarah	
Sept. 28	Rufus Albert Fisher	"	33	Farmer	Franklin	Frederick & Sarah N.	J. K. Bragg Clergyman
	Hariet Augustus Lawrence	"	19		"	Amos T. & Hariet W.	
Oct. 19	Charles F. Johnson	"	28	Clerk	Manchester, N.H	George R.& Hepsebeth	Luther Keene Clergyman
	Isoline F. Thayer	"	23		Franklin	Nathaniel & Caroline	
Nov. 5	*James W. Allen	Medway	56	Boot Finisher	Wendell, Me.	Moses Allen & Betsey	S. W. Squire Clergyman
	Mary A. Pond	Norfolk	40		Wrentham	[Freeman	
Nov. 11	*Josiah H. Stubbs	Franklin	50	Engineer	Mansfield	Hollbrook & Mary	Luther Keene Clergyman
	*Ann Webb	"	29		Boston	John & Ann Addie	
Nov. 30	Geo. Albert Adams	"	22	Teacher	Springfield	Gardner & Eunice R.	Wm. M. Thayer Clergyman
	Clara Isabel Gowen	"	22		Franklin	Horace W. & Sarah M.	
Nov. 30	James Frank Woodman	Norfolk	22	Shoe Maker	West Medway	James & Mary A.	M. E. Johnson Clergyman
	*Maria Louesa Rhodes	Franklin	24		Wrentham	Lyman E. & Hariet J.	
Dec. 7	Allen W. Macdougall	"	25	Carpenter	Callis, Me.	Augustus M. & Flora	Charles J. White Clergyman
	Anna A. Gay	"	20		Franklin	Samuel E. & Sarah	
Aug. 10	George H. Ware	"	23	Boot Maker	Medway	William D. & Elizabeth	§Levi Bayer
	Edith Mc E. Vay	Wrentham	20		Manchester, N.H	James & Mary	

* Second Marriage. † Maiden Name Thayer. ‡ Samuel Pond & Catherine Smith. § Rector Trinity Parish, Wrentham.

Marriages Registered in Franklin, County of Norfolk, in the Year 1871.—(Continued.)

DATE OF MARRIAGE.	NAME OF BRIDE AND GROOM.	Residence at Time of Marriage	AGE.	OCCUPATION.	PLACE OF BIRTH.	NAME OF PARENTS.	BY WHOM MARRIED.
1871 Sept. 13	Willard G. Cowell Jennie M. Fisher	Wrentham Norfolk	24 25	Dentist	Wrentham Franklin	William W. & Abbie E. Walter H. & Emely	Luther Keene Clergyman

DEATHS.

Deaths Registered in Franklin Prior to May 1, 1844.

DATE OF DEATH.	NAME OF DECEASED.	SEX.	RELATIONSHIP.
April 25, 1778	Widow of Abial Metcalf	F	
June 22, 1778	†Deliverance Emmons	"	Wife of Rev. Nath'l
April 28, 1778	Phebe Pond	"	
Aug. 20, 1778	*Abigail Pond	"	
Sept. 5, 1778	Jabez Pond	M	Son of Asa & Judith
Sept. 7, 1778	David Morse	"	Son of Sam'l & Sarah, Jr.
Sept. 14, 1778	Susanna Morse	F	Daughter of Sam'l & Sarah, Jr.
Sept. 13, 1778	Elias Hills	M	Son of James & Abigail
Sept. 7, 1778	Nathaniel Emmons	"	Son of Rev. Nath'l
Sept. 8, 1778	Diodate Jonson Emmons	"	Son of Rev. Nath'l
Sept. 19, 1778	Lois Morse	F	Daughter of Sam'l & Sarah, Jr.
Sept. 21, 1778	Amos Daniels	M	Son of Isaac & Margaret
Sept. 23, 1778	Amos Bacon	"	Son of Thomas & Lydia
Sept. 24, 1778	Elizabeth Daniels	F	Daughter of Nathan & Elizabeth
Sept. 29, 1778	—— Blake	"	Daughter of Solomon & Sibbel
Sept. 27, 1778	Peter Addams	M	Son of Peter & Esther
Oct. 3, 1778	Hipsabah Bacon	F	Daughter of Thomas & Lydia
Oct. 5, 1778	Molly Daniels	"	Daughter of Isaac & Margaret
Oct. 16, 1778	Ammariah Lane	M	Son of Zephaniah & Hannah
Oct. 24, 1778	Abigail Dean	F	Daughter of Ebenezer & Abigail
Oct. 31, 1778	†Abigail Bacon	"	Wife of Ensn. Seth
June 21, 1777	Abigail Pond	"	Daughter of Oliver & Anna
Sept. 6, 1775	Metcalf Pond	M	Son of Oliver & Anna
Mar. 27, 1779	†Peda Slocomb	F	Wife of John
Mar. 26, 1779	Caleb Lethbridge	M	Son of Samuel & Sarah
Jan. 14, 1779	William Heaton	"	
July 4, 1773	John Aldis	"	
Aug. 20, 1779	†Mariah Hawes	F	Wife of Josiah
Sept. 20, 1779	David Pond	M	Son of Eben'r & Frelove
Sept. 21, 1779	Joseph Whiting	"	
Oct. 22, 1779	Baruch Pond	"	Son of Asa & Judith
Oct. 27, 1779	†Abigail Hubbard	F	Wife of Joshua
Jan. 9, 1780	The Widow Anna Fisher	"	
Feb. 28, 1780	Eldod Mann	M	Son of Elias & Mary
Dec. 16, 1779	Pennuel Pond	"	Son of Eben'r & Frelove
July 6, 1780	Poly Ware	F	Daughter of Oliver & Betty
Sept. 5, 1780	Abigail Addams	"	Daughter of Moses & Abigail
Sept. 27, 1780	Abijah Baker	M	
Oct. 13, 1780	†Magdalen Daniels	F	Wife of David
Oct. 14, 1780	Timothy Addams	M	
Nov. 10, 1780	†Judith Clark	F	Wife of Benjamin
Feb. 14, 1781	William Mann	M	
Aug. 28, 1778	Beulah Hill	F	Daughter of Ephraim & Abigail
Oct. 18, 1779	Micah Hill	M	Son of Ephraim & Abigail
April 1, 1781	Jeremiah Mackeny	F	
Sept. 24, 1778	Elizabeth Daniels	"	Daughter of Nathan & Elisabeth
May 4, 1781	Dea. Nathan Mann	M	
Sept. 14, 1778	Ebenezer Day	"	Son of David & Mercy
Sept. 16, 1781	Thomas Lawrence	"	
Nov. 22, 1781	Gideon Fairbanks	"	Son of Capt. Asa & Sarah.
Nov. 19, 1781	David Daniels	"	

* Widow.   † Married.

FRANKLIN TOWN RECORDS—DEATHS.

DATE OF DEATH.	NAME OF DECEASED.	SEX.	RELATIONSHIP.
Nov. 25, 1781	Joshua Lawrence	M	
Jan. 15, 1782	Hugh Boyd	"	
Jan. 24, 1782	Theophilus Bacon	"	Son of Seth
Feb. 14, 1782	Julia Partridge	F	Daughter of Eleazar & Lois
Mar. 10, 1782	Caleb Whiting	M	Son of Pelatiah & Hannah
April 25, 1782	Samuel Morse	"	
May 11, 1782	Joshua Hubbard	"	
May 19, 1782	Ruben Lee	"	Son of Joseph & Jemima
June 27, 1779	Mehitable Partridge	F	Daughter of Eleazer & Lois
Dec. 26, 1782	*Jemima Richardson	"	
Jan. 7, 1783	†Elizabeth Daniels	"	Wife of Nathan, Jr.
Jan. 12, 1783	*Mary Whiting	"	
Jan. 29, 1783	Samuel Allen	M	
Feb. 3, 1783	‡Solomon Hewes Pratt	"	
Mar. 25, 1783	Daniel Kingsbury	"	
June 8, 1783	Salla Williams	F	Daughter of Duke & Joanna
July 22, 1783	Benjamin Rockwood	M	
Aug. 2, 1783	†Abigail Adams	F	Wife of Moses
Aug. 8, 1782	David Daniels	M	Son of Nathan & Elizabeth
Nov. 5, 1783	Keziah Hawes	F	Daughter of Ichabod & Sarah
Jan. 5, 1784	Abel Pond	M	Son of Widow Sarah
Jan. 30, 1784	Jerusha Williams	F	Daughter of Marbe Duke & Joanna
June 6, 1784	Thomas Bacon	M	
July 14, 1784	Seneca Mann	"	Son of Elias & Mary
Aug. 6, 1784	Esther Mann	F	Daughter of Elias & Mary
Aug. 7, 1784	John Fisher	M	
Sept. 9, 1784	†Jemima Fisher	F	Wife of Lieut. Nathaniel
Oct. 6, 1784	Elizabeth Partridge	"	Wife of Eben'r
Nov. 27, 1784	Jane Willson	"	
Dec. 3, 1784	†Meletiah Ellis	"	Wife of Joseph
Dec. 6, 1784	Polly Pond	"	Wife of Elihu
Jan. 6, 1785	Deborah Bacon	"	
Jan. 24, 1785	†Hipzibah Lethbridge	"	Wife of Samuel
Feb. 9, 1785	Noah Heaton	M	Son of Lieut. Noah & Abigail
Feb. 26, 1785	†Mehitabel Pond	F	Wife of Ichabod
May 2, 1785	Ichabod Pond	M	
June 24, 1785	Dea. Daniel Thurston	"	
Aug. 3, 1785	John Crooks	"	
Aug. 8, 1785	Mary Hawes	F	Daughter of Josiah
Aug. 9, 1785	Judson Metcalf	M	Son of Hanan & Mary
Sept. 18, 1785	Abigail Hawes	F	Daughter of Joseph & Hannah
Nov. 10, 1785	Seth Daniels	M	
Oct. 10, 1785	Nathaniel Heaton	"	
Nov. 18, 1785	†Lydia Gowens	F	Wife of John
Nov. 30, 1785	Julia Daniels	"	Daughter of Widow Eunite
Sept. 24, 1785	Synthe Heaton	"	Daughter of Isaac & Thankfull, Jr.
Sept. 25, 1785	Sinai Heaton	"	" " "
Feb. 26, 1786	*Mary Fales	"	
Dec. 11, 1785	Elone Lewitt	"	Daughter of Peter & Susanna
July 7, 1786	Abigail Allen	"	Daughter of Abijah & Abigail
July 25, 1786	Asa Clark, Jr.	M	
Oct. 1, 1786	†Mary Bowditch	F	Wife of Jonathan
July 7, 1787	Ruth Metcalf	"	Wife of Asa
Dec. 15, 1787	Benjamin Clark	M	
Jan. 10, 1788	†Abigail Fisher	F	Wife of Lt. Hezekiah
July 21, 1786	Harvey Ware	M	Son of Lt. Phinehas & Susanna
Aug. 10, 1786	Elvirah Ware	F	Daughter of Lt. Phinehas & Susanna
Feb. 3, 1787	Nancy Adams	"	Daughter of Nathaniel & Hannah
Oct. 22, 1788	Mary Adams	"	Wife of Seth
May 28, 1789	Elihu Ellis	M	Son of Timothy & Sarah

* Widow.   † Married.   ‡ Drowned in a well.

FRANKLIN TOWN RECORDS—DEATHS. 145

DATE OF DEATH.	NAME OF DECEASED.	SEX.	RELATIONSHIP.
Feb. 14, 1789	†Mary Ware	F	Wife of Jabez
April 4, 1790	Moses Morse	M	
April 9, 1790	†Hannah Adams	F	Wife of Nath'l
April 18, 1790	Mary Blake	"	Daughter of widow Esther
April 28, 1790	Peggy Partridge	"	Wife of Silvester
May 7, 1790	Nancy Lethbridge	"	Daughter of Samuel
May 21, 1790	Hannah Blake	"	Wife of Asa
May 29, 1790	Dea. Ebenezer Guild	M	
Oct. 11, 1790	†Hannah Fisher	F	Wife of Timothy, Jr.
Nov. 14, 1790	†Olive Morse	"	Wife of Jason
Nov. 28, 1790	Seth Adams	M	
Mar. 23, 1791	Elisha Mann	"	
Feb. 22, 1787	Benjamin Pond	"	
April 22, 1791	John Ferrington	"	
April 29, 1791	†Hannah Ware	F	Wife of Jabez
April 21, 1789	William Gillmor	M	
May 26, 1789	Israel Gillmor	"	
June 4, 1791	Jonathan Wright	"	
Sept. 19, 1786	Lucy Harding	F	Daughter of Elisha & Ruth
June 25, 1791	Nathan & Nathaniel Hawes	M	§Sons of Jonathan & Mary
June 25, 1791	Elisha Harding, Jr.	"	§Son of Elisha & Ruth
June 30, 1791	†Hannah Torrey	F	Wife of John
Aug. 20, 1791	Nathan Daniels	M	
Jan. 28, 1792	George Adams	"	
Nov. 20, 1791	Melea Taylor	F	Daughter of James & Salome
Oct. 29, 1791	†Peggy Metcalf	"	Wife of Titus
April 21, 1792	Harman Heaton	M	Son of Isaac & Thankful
June 10, 1792	‡Eunice Goldsbury	F	
Nov. 8, 1790	Joseph Fisher	M	Son of Joseph & Susa
Oct. 3, 1792	Eliel Metcalf	"	
Aug. 11, 1792	Daniel Pond	"	Son of Benjamin & Catherine, Jr.
Oct. 25, 1792	*Ward Adams	"	
May 13, 1793	†Noami Adams	F	Wife of John Adams, Jr.
May 30, 1793	Ensn. John Adams	M	
May 28, 1791	Eleazar Hills Lawrence	"	Son of Joseph & Anna
July 20, 1793	¶Chloe Thurston	F	
July 25, 1793	†Rhoda Fisher	"	Wife of Timothy, Jr.
Aug. 22, 1793	Jabez Lincoln	M	
Sept. 5, 1793	Abigail Fisher	F	Daughter of Levi & Mary
Oct. 1, 1793	William Ockinton	M	
Oct. 16, 1793	John Adams, Jr.	"	
Oct. 24, 1792	‡Hannah Metcalf	F	
Oct. 26, 1793	David Lawrence	M	
Dec. 4, 1793	Isaac Heaton	"	
Dec. 5, 1793	Seth Lawrence	"	
Dec. 9, 1793	Dr. Paul Metcalf	"	
July 9, 1786	Maxcy Allen	"	Son of Abijah & Abigail
Sept. 19, 1793	Spencer Wood	"	Son of Holland & Abigail
May 23, 1790	Kezia Daniels	F	Daughter of Joel & Mary
Feb. 20, 1794	John Goings	M	Foreigner
July 24, 1793	Hermon Pond	"	Son of Timothy & Rachel
April 19, 1794	†Kezia Blake	F	Wife of Robert
Aug. 15, 1794	†Kezia Gould	"	Wife of Joseph
June 12, 1794	†Lydia Whiting	"	Wife of Peter
Oct. 17, 1794	Aaron Kingsbury	M	
Dec. 21, 1794	†Esther Morse	F	Wife of Jason
Dec. 22, 1794	Asa Whiting	M	
Dec. 25, 1794	Nathaniel Fisher, Jr.	"	Son of Lewis & Abigail

* Died at Shrewsbury, of Small Pox. † Married. ‡ Widow. § Drowned in Beaver Pond.
¶ Hanged herself.

FRANKLIN TOWN RECORDS—DEATHS.

DATE OF DEATH.	NAME OF DECEASED.	SEX.	RELATIONSHIP.
May 12, 1795	*Esther Baker	F	Wife of Abijah
July 5, 1795	Polly Metcalf	"	Daughter of Billy & Patty
Jan. 1, 1795	†Sarah Pond	"	
Oct. 3, 1795	Merinda Pond	"	Daughter of Eli & Huldah
Feb. 6, 1796	Timothy Rockwood, Jr.	M	Son of Timothy & Sarah
Mar. 2, 1796	Ruth Wails	F	Wife of John
Mar. 6, 1796	Hepzebah Ware	"	Daughter of Eli & Tamar
Feb. 17, 1796	Lucretia Doah (died at Boston.)	"	Wife of Nath'l
April 13, 1796	Eben'r Metcalf, Jr.	M	Son of Bille & Patty
May 1, 1796	Harry Fisher	"	Son of Lewis & Abigail
May 14, 1896	*Lydia Bacon	F	Wife of Thomas
July 15, 1796	†Rebecha Wright	"	
Oct. 4, 1796	*—— Daniels	"	Wife of Henry
Oct. 4, 1896	Ebenezer Lawrence	M	
April 20, 1796	Phinehas Ware	"	Son of Eli & Tamar
May 30. 1796	Elisha Pond	"	
Aug. 10, 1796	†Hannah Hawes	F	
Feb. 13, 1797	Abigail Gay	"	Daughter of Thomas & Mary
Jan. 5, 1795.	*Sally Clark	"	Wife of Simeon
Oct. 24, 1794	Sena Pond	"	Daughter of Jem. Otis & Sally
Mar. 14, 1797	Hannah Whiting	"	Wife of Pelatiah
July 8, 1797	Eben'r Lawrence	M	Son of Joseph & Anna
May 26, 1797	Thomas Bacon, Jr.	"	
May 27, 1797	Artemas Metcalf	"	Son of Asa & Melea
July 7, 1797	Roger Braley	"	
Dec. 27, 1797	Julia Metcalf	F	Daughter of Calvin & Eunice
Jan. 27, 1798	*Rebecha Metcalf	"	Wife of Barnabas
Mar. 15, 1798	Elisha Richardson	M	
Feb. 25, 1798	Artemas Metcalf	"	Son of Abijah & Sarah
June 30, 1798	Samuel Morse	"	
July 25, 1798	†Esther Clark	F	
Oct. 3, 1793	Lydia Heaton	"	Daughter of Samuel & Huldah
Nov. 27, 1796	Jarvis Pond	M	Son of Wm. & Polly
May 15, 1799	Capt. Thomas Bacon	"	
Jan. 2, 1799	*Susanna White	F	Wife of Nathan
July 19, 1799	Eunice Hawes	"	
Jan. 14, 1800	Joshua Daniels	M	
Jan. 23, 1800	†—— Morse	F	
Feb. 4, 1800	†Mary Daniels	"	
Feb. 7, 1800	Isaac Heaton	M	
May 14, 1799	Esther Metcalf	F	Daughter of Timothy & Abigail
Nov. 18, 1799	Jesse Miller, Jr.	M	Son of Jesse & Vina
April 8, 1800	William White	"	
Dec. 14, 1800	Oliver Pond	"	
Dec. 22, 1800	Robert Blake	"	
July 1, 1796	Aaron Morse	"	Son of Darius & Pede
Dec. 20, 1795	John Aldis Ware	"	Son of Amariah & Eunice
Feb. 5. 1801	John Clark	"	
July 3, 1798	Adams Jones	"	Son of John & Sarah
Mar. 12, 1801	Oliver Smith, Jr.	"	Son of Oliver & Catherine
Mar. 30, 1801	Dr. Ebenezer Metcalf	"	
April 25, 1801	Samuel Rockwood	"	
Mar. 31, 1797	Lanson Clark	"	Son of Dyar & Nancy, Jr.
Jan. 23, 1799	Betsey White	F	Daughter of Elijah & Betsey
Sept. 6, 1801	Betsey Hills	"	Daughter of Jason & Molly
Sept. 25, 1800	Abigail Whiting Fisher	"	Daughter of Lewis & Abigail
Mar. 12, 1802	Peter Adams, aged 80 y	M	In the 80th year of his age
Nov. 22, 1801	Jesse Ware, Jr.	"	
July 6, 1800	Melinda Clark	F	Daughter of Paul & Phebe

* Married.   † Widow.

FRANKLIN TOWN RECORDS—DEATHS.

DATE OF DEATH.	NAME OF DECEASED.	SEX.	RELATIONSHIP.
Aug. 30, 1802	Nathaniel Whiting	M	Son of John, Esq., & Charlott
Aug. 3, 1803	Dea. James Metcalf	"	
Aug. 5, 1803	Petronella Blake	F	
Nov. 18, 1803	*Jemima Pond	"	Wife of Oliver
Jan. 2, 1804	Dr. Abijah Everett	M	
Dec. 25, 1803	Maxey Allen Gowin	"	Son of Asa & Polly
Mar. 14, 1804	Malciah Pond	"	
Jan. 3, 1797	Betsey Daniels	F	Daughter of Nathan & Sarah
May 19, 1804	Eleazer Fisher	M	
June 14, 1804	*Mary Fisher	F	Wife of Jason
Aug. 29, 1803	Capt. Asa Fairbanks, Jr.	M	
Jan. 18, 1804	Capt. Amos Haws	"	
Nov. 3, 1804	Daniel Adams	"	
Dec. 16, 1804	Timothy Ellis	"	
Dec. 31, 1804	Dexter Ward Daniels	"	Son of Cyrus & Polly
Mar. 20, 1804	*Abigail Harding	F	Wife of James
Jan. 27, 1805	Daniel Penniman Clark	M	Son of Paul & Phebe
Oct. 11, 1804	Millie Clark	F	Daughter of Abijah & Milletiah
Dec. 15, 1802	*Mrs. Chloe Bacon, 41y. 20d.	"	Wife of Capt. Joseph
Oct. 26, 1803	Henry Pond	M	Son of Benajah & Mary
Mar. 19, 1805	The Widow Heaton	F	
May 11, 1802	Eliab Pond	M	Son of Eli
May 20, 1802	Eli Pond	"	
Mar. 8, 1805	*Rebecca Pond†	F	Wife of Robert, late of Franklin
Jan. 31, 1800	Preston Hawes	M	Son of Levi & Pamela
June 28, 1805	Jabez Ware	"	
June 30, 1805	Abial Metcalf	"	†
Aug. 1, 1805	Eunice Metcalf	F	Wife of Dr. John
Oct. 3, 1805	Henry Daniels	M	
Oct. 8, 1805	Vina Fisher	F	Daughter of Timothy
Oct. 21, 1805	Asa Clark	M	
Dec. 9, 1805	Dea. Peter Whiting	"	
Dec. 9, 1805	Olive Gilmor	F	Daughter of Capt. Robert & Olive
Dec. 26, 1805	†Susanna Mann	"	
Feb. 8, 1806	Alexander Reed	M	§
Mar. 30, 1806	Eben Hubbard	"	Son of Joshua & Sarah
April 24, 1806	Samuel Pond	"	
May 4, 1806	Susanna Wright	F	
Aug. 29, 1806	Silena Wood	"	Daughter of David & Hannah
Aug. 30, 1806	†Hepzebah Daniels	"	Widow of Henry, late of Franklin
Sept. 17, 1806	†Elizabeth Thurston	"	Widow of Dea. Daniel, late of Franklin
Oct. 14, 1806	†Mary Fisher	"	Widow of Eleazer, late of Franklin
Oct. 15, 1806	Hon. Jabez Fisher, Esq.	M	
Oct. 22, 1806	Samuel Lethbridge	"	
Dec. 19, 1806	Lieut. James Gilmor	"	
Mar. 25, 1806	David Fisher	"	Son of Levi & Mary
Dec 2, 1806	*Sarah Adams, 38y. 9m.	F	Wife of James
Mar. 3, 1807	†Mary Pond	"	
April 7, 1807	Ithamer Partridge	M	Son of Eleazer & Lois
May 15, 1807	*Lurana Fisher, 41y. 7m.	F	Wife of Daniel C.
June 17, 1807	Charles Fisher	M	‖
Aug. 12, 1807	*Content Scott	F	Wife of Ichabod
Sept. 1, 1807	*Hannah Hawes	"	Wife of Ensn. Joseph
Sept. 6, 1807	Abigail Jones	"	Daughter of John & Sally
Sept. 8, 1807	Dyar Clark	M	
Sept. 27, 1807	†Hannah Dean	F	Widow of Ebenezer, late of Franklin
Sept. 27, 1807	Hannah Daniels	"	Daughter of David & Lucy
Oct. 1, 1807	†Widow Metcalf	"	Widow of Jonathan, late of Franklin

* Married. † Widow. ‡ Relative of the late Dea. James Metcalf. § One of this State's Paupers, died at James Wails.' ‖ Son of Frederick Fisher & Chloe Lindley; drowned in Eli Richardson's mill pond.

FRANKLIN TOWN RECORDS—DEATHS.

DATE OF DEATH.	NAME OF DECEASED.	SEX.	RELATIONSHIP.
Nov. 9, 1807	Abigail Bacon, aged 19y.10m.	F	Daughter of Dea. Joseph & Chloe
Nov. 13, 1807	Joseph Ellis	M	
Nov. 22, 1807	*Margaret Pond	F	
Dec. 21, 1807	Dr. Elisha Pond	M	
Dec. 20, 1807	Caroline Pond	F	Daughter of Elihu & Jemima
May 11, 1806	Allen Metcalf	M	Son of Willard & Lucy
Mar. 31, 1808	†Mrs. Mary Fisher	F	Wife of Levi
April 2, 1808	Miss Mary Ellis	"	
April 2, 1808	*Rebecca Lawrence	"	
April 7, 1808	Billing Fairbanks	M	
April 22, 1808	Kate Clark	F	
July 1, 1807	Simeon Ellis	M	Son of Timothy & Deborah
June 22, 1808	†Mrs. Anna Woodward	F	Wife of Nathan Woodward
July 26, 1808	Mercy Blake	"	‡Daughter of Josiah of Walpole
July 30, 1808	—— Warfield	"	Daughter of John & Esther
July 31, 1808	Horatio Kingsbury, age 28y. 26d.	M	Son of Capt. Stephen & Abigail
Aug. 8, 1808	Mrs. Jonathan Wales	F	
Mar. 16, 1807	Nelson Gay	M	Son of Timothy & Submit
Sept. 24, 1808	Polly Hills	F	Daughter of Jason & Molly
Sept. 30, 1808	Nancy Metcalf	"	Daughter of Willard & Lucy
Oct. 7, 1808	Julia Heaton	"	§Daughter of Samuel & Huldah
Sept. 21, 1800	Elona Richardson	"	Daughter of Timothy & Nancy, Jr.
Oct. 28, 1808	Dolly Mann	"	Daughter of Elisha & Susanna
Nov. 4, 1808	Moses Adams, died at Bellingham	M	
Jan. 20, 1809	†Mrs. Peddy Whiting	F	Wife of Sidney
Feb. 25, 1809	†Mrs. Abigail Fisher, aged 40y.	"	Wife of Capt. Lewis
May 4, 1809	John Richardson	M	
June 20, 1809	Thomas Mann	"	
June 27, 1809	†Mrs. Patty Metcalf	F	Wife of Nathan
June 27, 1809	Lieut. Hez'h Fisher	M	
Aug. 4, 1809	Amos Fisher	"	
Aug. 13, 1809	*Keturah Morse	F	
Aug. 19, 1809	Milton Metcalf	M	Son of Calvin & Eunice
Aug. 30, 1809	†Betsey Richardson	F	Wife of Tim'o.
Sept. 16, 1809	Capt. Stephen Kingsbury	M	
Oct. 7, 1809	Simeon Daniels	"	[lin
Oct. 21, 1809	*Abigail Fairbanks	F	Widow of Billings, late of Frank-
Oct. 29, 1809	Capt. Asa Fairbanks	M	
Oct. 18, 1809	John Franklin Cobb	"	Son of Luther & Rachel
Nov. 7, 1809	‖Major Moses Knap	"	
Nov. 10, 1809	*Esther Adams, aged 76y.	F	Relative of Peter Adams
Nov. 16, 1809	†Mrs. Ruth Ide	"	¶Wife of Daniel
Dec. 3, 1809	James Lethbridge	M	
Dec. 27, 1809	Benjamin Pond	"	
Jan. 2, 1810	*Kezia Woodward	F	
Aug. 31, 1795	Elizabeth Clark	"	Daughter of Dyar & Rachel
Jan. 19, 1810	*Mehitabel Rockwood	"	
Jan. 20, 1810	†Mrs. Sarah Fisher	"	2d Wife of Daniel C.
Jan. 23, 1810	Pelatiah Whiting	M	
Feb. 23, 1810	Lewis Pratt (of Mansfield)	"	Died at Dr. Spencer Pratt's
June 7, 1810	Ephraim Grooves	"	
June 20, 1810	†Mrs. Olive Morse, 30y. 11m. 12d.	F	**Wife of James [of Franklin
July 22, 1810	Stephen Mann, age 17y. 7m.	M	††Son of Thomas & Rebecca, late
July 28, 1810	Joseph Gould	"	
Aug. 9, 1810	Harriot Thurston	F	Daughter of Caleb & Levisa
Aug. 11, 1810	The Widow Guild	"	[Franklin
Aug. 23, 1810	Milatiah Hawes	"	Widow of Capt. Amos, late of

* Widow.   † Married.   ‡ Died at Joseph Hawes,' Jr.   § Adopted child of Asa Gowen
‖ Served his country in the whole of the Revolutionary war.   ¶ Formerly wife of John Clark, late of Franklin.   ** Daughter of Elisha & Ruth Harding.   †† Drowned at Uncas pond.

FRANKLIN TOWN RECORDS—DEATHS.

DATE OF DEATH.	NAME OF DECEASED.	SEX.	RELATIONSHIP.
Aug. 23, 1810	Nancy Fales Gillmor	F	Daughter of William & Nancy
Oct. 12, 1810	Roxy Metcalf	"	Daughter of Nathan & Patty
Nov. 21, 1810	*Mrs. Ruth Harding, 61y. 8m. 6d.	"	Wife of Elisha [N. Pond's
Nov. 23, 1810	Henry Day (of Paxton)	M	Son of Joseph, Died at Oliver
Jan. 1, 1811	Betsey Daniels	F	Daughter of Amariah & Nancy Jr.
Jan. 16, 1811	Clarissa Lethbridge	"	Daughter of Samuel & Sally
Jan. 21, 1811	Susan Adams	"	Daughter of Fisher & Mary
Mar. 25, 1811	Dr. Ferdinand Lethbridge, 33y.	M	Son of Samuel & Sally
April 19, 1811	Saphony Alexander Thurston	F	Daughter of Caleb & Levisa
May 10, 1811	*Mrs. Mary Adams	"	Wife of Fisher
June 7, 1811	Mr. James Woodward	M	
July 20, 1811	Lewis Fisher, 3d	"	Son of Asa & Rachel
July 25, 1811	David Thurston, 26y. 10m. 5d.	"	Son of Abijah & Rachel
Aug. 4, 1811	†Chloe Adams	F	Widow of Moses
Oct. 5, 1811	Horatio Clark	M	Son of Abijah & Peggy
Oct. 29, 1811	Dea. Robert Gilmor	"	
Nov. 9, 1811	†Ruth Rockwood, 91y.	F	
Dec. 18, 1811	Joseph Whiting, 2d	M	
Jan. 19, 1812	George Fechem	"	Died at Mr. Wm. Adams'
Mar. 23, 1812	†Dinah Fisher	F	Widow of Lieut. Hezekiah
Mar. 23, 1812	†Hannah Metcalf	"	Widow of Dr. Michael, deceased
May 7, 1812	John Day Clark	M	Son of Capt. Dyar & Nancy
June 13, 1812	Oliver Pond	"	
June 26, 1812	Daniel Lawrence	"	
July 10, 1812	Abijah Thurston	"	§
Dec. 25, 1794	Nathaniel Fisher	"	Son of Capt. Lewis & Abigail
May 1, 1796	Harvey Fisher	"	Son of Capt. Lewis & Abigail
Sept. 25, 1800	Nabby Whiting Fisher	F	Daughter of Capt. Lewis & Abigail
Feb. 25, 1809	*Abigail Fisher	"	‖Wife of Capt. Lewis
Aug. 3, 1812	Eleazer Thompson	M	
Aug. 27, 1812	*Hannah Greene	F	Wife of Joseph Greene
Sept. 28, 1812	Abigail Richardson Metcalf, 1y. 6d.	"	Daughter of Nathan & Abigail
Nov. 29, 1812	Hannah Rockwood	"	¶Daughter of Sam'l & Sarah
Dec. 16, 1812	*Mrs. Lois Partridge	"	Wife of Eleazer
Oct. 1, 1812	Benjamin Rockwood	M	
June 3, 1813	Deliverence Emmons, 30y. 5m. 4d.	F	Daughter of Rev. Nath'l & Martha
July 7, 1813	*Hannah Pond	"	Wife of Eli
July 9, 1813	William Maddison Adams	M	Son of William & Mary Jr.
July 11, 1813	Susanna Morse Blake, 5y. 6m. 28d	F	Daughter of Solomon & Hannah Jr.
July 13, 1813	Jesse Ware	M	
Aug. 28, 1813	*Mary Gay	F	Wife of Thomas
Sept. 7, 1813	Tryphena Dean	"	Daughter of Seth & Edene
Sept. 29, 1813	Fisher Hartshorn Harding, 1y. 6m	M	Son of Lewis & Irene
Oct. 2, 1813	Sally Thayer, 1y. 20d.	F	Daughter of James & Sally
Oct. 8, 1813	†Esther Clark	"	Widow of Asa, late of Franklin
May 7, 1813	†Jerusha White	"	Widow of Wm., late of Franklin
Nov. 28, 1813	†Miletiah Pond	"	Widow of Elisha, late of Franklin
Mar. 28, 1813	Laura Metcalf	"	Daughter of Samuel & Mary
April 20, 1807	Jonathan Metcalf	M	
Jan. 29, 1814	Warren Fisher	"	Son of Pelatiah & Irene Esq.
Jan. 15, 1814	—— Hastings	"	Son of Jonathan
Mar. 17, 1814	Daniel Adams	"	Son of Daniel
Mar. 19, 1814	Asa Adams	"	Son of Daniel & Christian
April 4, 1814	*Dorcas Holmes	F	Wife of Elijah
May 22, 1814	*Mrs. Timothy Fisher	"	
Oct. 12, 1814	James Fisher, 2y. 25d	M	‡‡Son of Asa & Rachel
Oct. 14, 1814	Martha Phipps	F	Daughter of William & Fanny
Oct. 22, 1814	Susan Blake Morse	"	Daughter of Darias & Peda

* Married. † Widow. § Fell down dead. ‖ Mother of the above deceased children.
¶ Late of Franklin, deceased. ‡‡ Died at Boston.

FRANKLIN TOWN RECORDS—DEATHS.

DATE OF DEATH.	NAME OF DECEASED.	SEX	RELATIONSHIP.
Oct. 25, 1814	Nancy Rawson	F	Daughter of Thomson & Lucy
Nov. 22, 1814	Wm. Henry Pond	M	Son of Martin & Annie
Sept. 12, 1814	*Mrs. Olive Guild	F	Wife of Cyrus
Jan. 6, 1815	Emeline Betsey Metcalf	"	Daughter of Whiting & Betsey
Jan. 16, 1815	Dinah Allen	"	Black woman, died at Dr. Emmons
Feb. 3, 1815	*Abigail Allen	"	Wife of Dea. James
Mar. 10, 1815	Lucy Rawson	"	Daughter of Thomson & Lucy
Mar. 20, 1815	*Mrs. Deborah Ellis	"	Wife of Timothy
May 20, 1815	James Drown, aged 19y. 3m.	M	
June 10, 1815	Capt. Joseph Hills	"	
June 23, 1815	*Mrs. Samuel Heaton	F	
July 16, 1815	*Huldah Clark	"	†Wife of Stephen A.
July 24, 1815	*John Allen	M	
May 2, 1815	†Ruth Braley	F	
Oct. 10, 1815	Miss Huldah Howard	"	[Franklin
Oct. 17, 1815	Elvira Woodward, aged 28y. 7d.	"	Daughter of James, late of
Oct. 21, 1815	Joseph Whiting Metcalf,?7y.11m.20d.	M	Son of Whiting & Betsey
Oct. 29, 1815	Julia Richardson	F	Daughter of Elisha & Ruth
Oct. 31, 1815	Charlott Louisa Thurston	"	Daughter of Caleb & Levisa
Nov. 9, 1815	Pliny Wallis	M	Died at Abijah Baker's, Franklin
28, 1815	Mary Richardson	F	Daughter of Elijah & Polly
Dec. 30, 1815	*Clarissa Ware, aged 24y.	"	Wife of Philander [Franklin
Jan. 11, 1816	†Eunice Blake	"	Widow of Rob't, Jr., late of
Jan. 17, 1816	Mary Fisk Kingsbury	"	Daughter of Eben'r A. & Mary
Feb. 6, 1816	Samuel Lethbridge	M	
Mar. 8, 1816	Capt. Asa Thayer	"	
Mar. 21, 1816	Mrs. Timothy Richardson	F	[Franklin
Mar. 24, 1816	†Sarah Pond	"	Relative of Timothy, late of
Mar. 24, 1816	Davis Thayer	M	Son of Capt. Asa, late of Franklin
Mar. 27, 1816	Evelina Viller Thayer	F	Daughter of Maj. Davis & Betsey
April 8, 1816	Hervey Milton Morse, aged 14m.	M	Son of Hervey & Betsey
April 10, 1816	Mary Adaline Fisher	F	Daughter of Jason & Mary Jr.
April 12, 1816	Syvia Pond	"	Daughter of Timothy & Rachel
April 13, 1816	Harriot Saphrona Thurston	"	Daughter of Caleb & Levisa
May 10, 1816	Timothy Metcalf	M	Town Treasurer
June 3, 1816	Mrs. Gillmor	F	Wife of David
May 30, 1816	Thomas Bear	M	A Black Man
June 5, 1816	Gilbert Puffer, aged 1y. 9m.	"	§Son of Stephen & Sally
June 15, 1816	John Baker	"	Died Suddenly
June 24, 1816	Benjamin P. Ware	"	
July 7, 1816	——— Hamblet		‖Child of Joseph & wife
July 8, 1816	Horace Cook Ray	M	Son of James & Thankfull
July 18, 1816	Peter Whiting	"	[lin, deceased
Aug. 5, 1816	†Hannah Pond	F	Relative of Sam'l, late of Frank-
Aug. 24, 1816	*Mary Pond	"	Wife of Capt. Benajah
Oct. 2, 1816	*Mrs. Mary Adams	"	Wife of William, Jr.
Dec. 20, 1816	*Mrs. Mary Staples	"	¶A Stranger
Feb. 23, 1817	Elisha Harding, 68y. 8m. 23d	M	[of Franklin
Mar. 11, 1817	Olive Baker	F	Daughter of John & Molly, late
Mar. 21, 1817	Willard Adams Ware, 10m. 27d.	M	Son of David & Betsey
Mar. 23, 1817	*Lucy Gilmor	F	Wife of Joseph [Susanna
1817	Betsey Fisher	"	Daughter of Ens. Daniel C. &
July 29, 1817	†Sarah Ellis	"	Widow of Timothy
July 31, 1817	†Anna Pond	"	**Widow of Oliver Pond
Aug. 21, 1817	Chauncy Wallis, aged 24y.	M	Died at Robert Blake's
Sept. 20, 1817	†The Widow Nickerson	F	
Sept. 27, 1817	Mrs. Susanna Ware	"	Wife of Lieut. Phinehas
April 23, 1816	Nathaniel Adams	M	Son of Amos, Jr., & Betsey,

* Married.   † Widow.   ‡ Daughter of Sam'l Heaton.   § Was drowned.   ‖ Died at E. Richardson's factory.   ¶ Died at Joseph Whiting's, Jr.   ** Died very suddenly.

FRANKLIN TOWN RECORDS—DEATHS.

DATE OF DEATH.	NAME OF DECEASED.	SEX.	RELATIONSHIP.
Jan. 18, 1818	*Hannah Lincoln	F	
Feb. 17, 1818	†Molly Baker	"	‡Relative of John
Feb. 18, 1818	Ens. Joseph Hawes, aged 90y.	M	
June 3, 1818	Mr. Eleazer Fisher	"	
June 7, 1818	‡Molly Jackson	F	Wife of Mr. Wm.
June 16, 1818	†Mrs. Rachel Clark	"	‡Relative of Dyar
June 18, 1818	*Mrs. Huldah Pond	"	‡Widow of Eli
June 20, 1818	Mr. Nathan Mann	M	
June 22, 1818	*Sarah Morse	F	
June 22, 1818	†Elizabeth Fuller	"	Wife of Moses
July 12, 1818	Stephen A. Clark	M	
July 17, 1818	Spencer Pratt, aged 69y.	"	Died at Dr. Spencer Pratt's
Aug. 28, 1818	*Mary Daniels, aged 96y.	F	†Relative of Nathan
Sept. 16, 1818	Betsey Tucker	"	Daughter of Ebenezer
Oct. 16, 1818	Mr. Nathan Mann	M	‡Son of Nathan
Oct. 20, 1818	Miss Beriah Hawes	F	
Sept. 5, 1816	Matilda Emely Fisher	"	Daughter of Preston & Huldah
Aug. 1, 1818	Nancy Maria Fisher	"	Daughter of Preston & Huldah
Jan. 26, 1819	Joseph Fisher	M	
Jan. 9, 1819	Charlotte Louisa Gillmor	F	Daughter of James & Irene 2d,
Jan. 27, 1819	Sarah Pond, aged 1m.	"	Daughter of Justin & Ruth
Mar. 16, 1819	Mr. Oliver Ware	M	§
April 9, 1819	†Mrs. Lydia Guild	F	Wife of Ebenezer
April 22, 1819	Eliza Ray	"	Died at Major Cutler Pond's
May 4, 1819	Polly Smith	"	Daughter of Christopher & Dia-
Oct. 12, 1793	Elihu Pond, Senior	M	Son of Elihu & Jemima [dama
May 24, 1819	†Mrs. Abigail Partridge	F	Wife of Phinehas
June 11, 1819	Abigail Hills Heaton	"	Daughter of Nathan & Sally
Sept. 12, 1819	Miliah Daniels	"	
Sept. 16, 1819	Charles Willis Fisher	M	Son of Willis & Caroline
Sept. 24, 1819	Harriet Fisher	F	Daughter of James & Cally
Sept. 25, 1819	Joseph Pierce	M	Son of John & Mary
Nov. 8, 1819	*Widow Fisher	F	‡Relative of Timothy
Dec. 13, 1819	†Mrs. Achsah Partridge	"	Wife of Simeon
Dec. 19, 1819	Charlotte Richardson	"	Daughter of Eli M. & Melita
Dec. 24, 1819	Mrs. —— Lethbridge	"	‡Relative of Samuel, Senior
Dec. 30, 1819	Lois Wood	"	Daughter of David & Hannah
Jan. 15, 1820	Capt. Ebenezer Dean	M	
Jan. 15, 1820	Jacob Ruggles, formerly of Wrentham	"	
Jan. 31, 1820	*Abigail Kingsbury	F	‡Relative of Capt. Stephen
Feb. 11, 1820	*Abigail Richardson	"	‡Relative of John
Feb. 26, 1820	†Polly Hawes	"	Wife of Mr. Moses
Mar. 13, 1820	Major Erastus Emmons	M	Son of Rev. Nathaniel & Martha
Oct. 29, 1817	Albert Gillmor	"	Son of Wm. & Molly
Mar. 25, 1820	†Polly Cleavland	F	Wife of Mr. Nathan
April 8, 1820	Chloe Ray	"	‖
May, 1820	Asa Mann	M	
May 22, 1820	Eunice Susan Thurston	F	Daughter of Daniel & Bathsheba
July 5, 1820	†Diadama Smith	"	Wife of Christopher
July 16, 1820	*Elizabeth Whiting	"	Relict of Asa, Senior
Sept. 26, 1820	Ichabod Dean	M	
Sept. 27, 1820	Julia Thurston	F	Daughter of Lt. Caleb & Levisa
Nov. 6, 1820	Maria Thurston	"	Daughter of Lt. Caleb & Levisa
Nov. 9, 1820	Miss Sarah Hawkens	"	
Dec. 15, 1820	†Peggy Clark	"	Wife of Abijah, Jr.
Feb. 15, 1821	Mr. William Lincoln	M	
Feb. 21, 1821	†Mrs. Polly Cobb	F	Wife of Ebenezer
Feb. 27, 1821	Mrs. Prudence	"	‡Relict of Ebenezer Thompson

* Widow.   † Married.   ‡ Late of Franklin.   § Died at Capt. Benajah Pond's, very suddenly.   ‖ An adopted daughter of James Gillmor & wife.

FRANKLIN TOWN RECORDS—DEATHS.

DATE OF DEATH.	NAME OF DECEASED.	SEX.	RELATIONSHIP.
Mar. 1, 1821	†Mrs. Tamar Ware	F	Wife of Eli
Mar. 16, 1821	Freelove Wales	"	Daughter of Otis & Jemima
Mar. 11, 1821	Aurela Perry	"	Daughter of Simeon & Sybil
Dec. 12, 1820	Harriot Hills	"	Daughter of Ens. Senaca & Maria
April 6, 1821	†Mrs. Elizabeth Pratt	"	Wife of Dr. Spencer
April 16, 1821	Joseph Gillmor, 3d	M	Son of William & Molly
May 18, 1821	James Kingsbury	"	
May 28, 1821	*Letisa Cady	F	Died at James Gillmor's
June 5, 1821	Luisa Tucker	"	‡
June 8, 1821	†Mrs. Patience Farrington	"	Wife of Aaron
June 17, 1821	John Warren Fisher, 4y. 5m.	M	§Son of Jason & Mary
Aug. 11, 1821	Asa Rockwood, Jr.	"	Son of Asa & Julia
Aug. 22, 1821	Mr. Billa Ware	"	[Franklin
Aug. 23, 1821	†Mrs. Keziah	F	Relict of Jesse Ware, late of
Sept. 20, 1821	Mary Thurston	"	Daughter of Daniels & Bathsheba
April 26, 1821	Hiram Thurston	M	Son of Daniel & Bathsheba
July 15, 1821	Thomas Pinkney Gay	"	Son of Amos B. & Loami
Oct. 7, 1821	Layton Jenks Adams	"	Son of Amos & Betsey
Oct. 16, 1821	†Mrs. Unity Daniels	F	Relict of Seth, late of Franklin
Oct. 23, 1821	†Mrs. Chloe Dean	"	Relict of Ichabod " "
Oct. 29, 1821	†Mrs. Mary Metcalf	"	Wife of Dea. Jona.
Nov. 19, 1821	†Mrs. Phebe Baker	"	Wife of Abijah
Dec. 3, 1821	William Gillmor, 3d	M	Oldest son of William & Molly
Dec. 11, 1821	Dyar Clark	"	Son of Nathan & Nancy
Dec. 11, 1821	Molly Grosvenor	F	Died at Levi Hawes'
Jan. 5, 1822	Sally Ray	"	Daughter of James & wife
Oct. 31, 1821	Esther Adams	"	Daughter of Amos & Betsey
Nov. 8, 1821	Julia Adams	"	Daughter of Amos & Betsey
Jan. 17, 1822	Seth Rockwood	M	
Jan. 17, 1822	Samuel Clark	"	
Feb. 21, 1821			of Ebenezer & Polly Cobb
April 20, 1821			of Joseph & Sarah Gillmor Jr.
Oct. 21, 1821	Charlotte Metcalf	F	Daughter of Samuel & Mary
Jan. 28, 1822	Irene Pond	"	Daughter of Hezekiah & Lois
Feb. 25, 1822	Ebenezer Tucker	M	
April 24, 1822	Abial Mann	"	
May 1, 1822	Elvira Gowen	F	‖
Sept. 23, 1822	†Mrs. Joanna Fisher	"	Wife of Peter
Sept. 20, 1822	Jason Fisher	M	
Oct. 9, 1822	Sally Tucker	F	Daughter of Ebenezer & wife
Oct. 14, 1822	Joanna Hopkins Fisher	"	Daughter of Oliver & Thankfull
Sept. 26, 1822	Ebenezer Guild	M	
Oct. 10, 1822	Lucy Cutler Guild	F	Daughter of John & Lois
Nov. 10, 1822	Jonas Brick	M	
April 7, 1822	Mariah Abbot Fisher	F	Daughter of Whiting & Esther
Nov. 24, 1822	Mr. Seth Bacon	M	
Jan. 20, 1822	Henry Thurston	"	Son of Daniel & Bathsheba
Dec. 8, 1822	Mr. Hezakiah Pond		
Dec. 12, 1822	†Mrs. Betsey Ware	F	Wife of Amariah, 2d
Jan. 3, 1823	Miss Sarah Emmons	"	Daughter of Rev. Nath'l & Martha
Jan. 8, 1823	William Jackson	M	
Jan. 23, 1823	Jona. Metcalf, Jr.	"	Son of Dea. Jona. & Mary
April 3, 1823	Eber Pickering	"	¶
April 24, 1823	Capt. Eli Richardson	"	
May 30, 1823	Asa Norcross	"	
June 20, 1823	Silas Hartshorn	"	
Sept. 17, 1823	John Pond	"	

† Married. * Widow. ‡ Died at Aaron Farrington's. ▲ Grand daughter. § The son of Jason & Mary Fisher, Jr. Death occasioned by a cart wheel running over the body. ‖ Daughter of Asa & Melea Metcalf, and consort of Luther Gowens. ¶ Found dead on Wm. Makepeace's. Not seen before since the violent storme March 30, evening.

FRANKLIN TOWN RECORDS—DEATHS.

DATE OF DEATH.	NAME OF DECEASED.	SEX.	RELATIONSHIP.
Sept. 26, 1823	Wm. Henry Kingsbury	M	Son of Asa & wife
Sept. 27, 1823	*Mrs. Rachel Adams	F	Wife of Mr. Thaddeus
Sept. 27, 1823	Horatio Hunting	M	Son of Dr. Amory & Mary
Oct. 5, 1823	Mr. Samuel Pond	"	
Jan. 5, 1824	Mr. Solomon Blake	"	
April 7, 1822	James Rockwood	"	Son of Asa & Julitta
Feb. 6, 1823	*Mrs. Thankfull Miller	F	Wife of Dea. Joseph
Mar. 5, 1823	*Mrs. Patty Metcalf	"	Wife of Mr. Wm. H. Metcalf
Oct. 14, 1823	†Elizabeth Gillmor	"	
Oct. 22, 1823	Julia Ann Pierce	"	Daughter of John & Julia Jr.
Feb. 25, 1824	*Mrs. Mary Burden	"	Wife of Mr. Jepthah
Mar. 25, 1824	Susanna Day Blake	"	‡Daughter of Solomon & Hannah
April 15, 1824	Mrs. Deborah	"	Relict of Dr. Lewis Leprilete,
April 20, 1824	Mr. Abijah Baker	M	[late of Franklin
May 13, 1824	*Mrs. Elizabeth Whiting	F	Wife of Dea. Joseph
June 4, 1824	Mr. Nathaniel Thayer	M	
June 16, 1824	*Mrs. Esther Aldice	F	Relict of John, late of Franklin
July 27, 1824	Miss Rachel Gay	"	
July 29, 1824	*Mrs. Mary Merrifield	"	Wife of Aaron
July 29, 1824	*Mrs. Martha Horton	"	Wife of Mr. Jabez
Aug. 22, 1824	*Mrs. Mary Perry	"	Wife of David
Sept. 1, 1824	Joshua Hubbard	M	
Dec. 11, 1821	Dyar Gilbert Clark	"	Son of Nathan & Nancy
Sept. 25, 1824	Nathaniel Horace Fisher	"	Son of Nathan'l & Loisa
Oct. 3, 1824	Mr. Joseph Hills	"	
Oct. 7, 1824	*Mrs. Betsey Dean	F	Wife of Capt. Ichabod
Dec. 21, 1824	Mr. Timothy Kingsbury	M	
July 30, 1824	George Warren Richardson	"	Son of Eli M. & Melita
Jan. 7, 1825	Mr. Simeon Partridge	"	
Feb. 1, 1825	*Mrs. Patty Morse	F	Wife of George Washington
Feb. 11, 1825	Paul Metcalf Fisher	M	Son of Capt. Maxcy & Persis
Feb. 7, 1825	*Mrs. Betsey Adams	F	Wife of Amos
Feb. 10, 1825	*Mrs. Sally Thayer	"	Wife of James
Mar. 4, 1825	Mr. Alfred Allen	M	[Polly
Jan. 17, 1816	Mary Fisk Kingsbury, aged 5y.	F	Daughter of Capt. Ebenezer &
Feb. 18, 1825	Calista Allen	"	Daughter of Ellery & Experience
June 3, 1825	†Esther Clark	"	
July 16, 1825	Eliza Eveline Holbrook Haltien	"	Daughter of Willard & Eliza
July 21, 1835	‡Mr. Nathan Partridge	M	
Aug. 20, 1825	Mr. David Daniels	"	
Oct. 3, 1825	Miss Esther Fisher	F	
Oct. 22, 1825	Mr. Amos Pond	M	
Nov. 10, 1825	Mr. Amasa Darling	"	
Nov. 19, 1825	†Lydia Morse	F	[Franklin
Jan. 8, 1826	*Mrs. Abigail Dean	"	Relict of Capt. Ebenezer, late of
Jan. 17, 1826	Lieut. Phinehas Ware	M	
Jan. 25, 1826	Mr. Alfred Ware	"	
Jan. 27, 1826	*Mrs. Sarah King	F	Wife of Samuel
Feb. 1, 1826	Miss Hannah Ware	"	‡Daughter of Amariah & Eunice
Feb. 25, 1824	Charlotte Jane Allen	"	Daughter of Stephen & Betsey
Feb. 2, 1826	Hiram George Allen	M	Son of Stephen & Betsey
Mar. 10, 1826	*Mrs. Sybil	F	§Relict of Solomon Blake
Mar. 15, 1826	Nancy R. Adams	"	Daughter of Mr. Daniel & Nancy,
Mar. 16, 1826	Mr. Adams Daniels	M	[late of Franklin
May 9, 1826	*Miss Roxcena Claflin	F	Wife of Jeremiah
June 23, 1826	*Mrs. Maria Hills [Daniels	"	Wife of Capt. Senica
June 20, 1826	Squire Geo. Warren LaFayette	M	Son of Amariah & Anna
July 23, 1826	*Mrs. Betsey	F	§Relict of Capt. Joseph Hills
July 23, 1826	Mr. John Guild	M	

* Married.   † Widow.   ‡ Died suddenly.   § Late of Franklin, deceased.

FRANKLIN TOWN RECORDS—DEATHS.

DATE OF DEATH.	NAME OF DECEASED.	SEX.	RELATIONSHIP.
Oct. 2, 1826	*Mrs. Sally Pond	F	Wife of Jem Otis
Sept. 11, 1826	James Morse	M	Son of Levi F. & Tryphena
Sept. 21, 1826	Artemas Brown Bullard	"	Son of Cephas & Sukey
Sept. 27, 1826	Joseph Warren Bullard	"	Son of Cephas & Sudey
Oct. 7, 1826	Mr. James Ray	"	
Sept. 21, 1826	Albert Green Gillmor	"	Son of Capt. Robert & Rebeckah G.
Oct. 10, 1826	*Mrs. Rachel Gillmor	F	Wife of Mr. David
Oct. 12, 1826	Samuel Gilbert Ware	M	Son of Samuel & Olive, Jr.
Nov. 6, 1826	Miss Abiah Willson	F	
Nov. 7, 1826	Dea Joseph Whiting	M	[late of Franklin
Nov. 21, 1826	*Mrs. Rachel	F	Relict of Mr. Abijah Thurston
Jan. 1, 1827	Mrs. Rebeckah Adams	"	Widow of George
Jan. 3, 1827	Alfred Daniels Pond	M	Son of Jeremiah M. & Polly
Feb. 10, 1827	Mr. Warren Fairbanks	"	
Feb. 1, 1825	Bathsheba Thurston	F	Daughter of Daniel & Bathsheba
Feb. 17, 1827	*Mrs. Mary Metcalf	"	Wife of Hanon
Feb. 22, 1827	Harriet Adams	"	Daughter of Amos
Jan. 22, 1827	Samuel Augustus Morse	M	Son of Stillman P. & Anna
June 16, 1827	Miss Silence Rockwood	F	
April 25, 1827	Miss Electa Thompson	"	
Sept. 1, 1827	Miss Keziah Thompson	"	
June 28, 1827	Thadeus Adams	M	
June 13, 1827	*Mrs. Abigail Allen	F	Wife of Amos H.
Aug. 20, 1827	Mr. Samuel C. Johnson	M	
July 15, 1827	Mr. Jason Hills	"	
July 12, 1827	*Mrs. Joanna Cook	F	Wife of Samuel
June 2, 1827	Mr. Jeremiah M. Pond	M	
Sept. 23, 1827	†Olive Haven	F	
Aug. 30, 1827	*Mrs. Hannah Pond	"	Wife of Major Cutler
June 4, 1827	Mr. Eli Richardson	M	
Sept. 20, 1827	Miss Nancy Fisher	F	
Sept. 10, 1827	Edmond Sandford Pond	M	Son of James P. & Sukey
Sept. 26, 1827	*Mrs. Nancy Adams	F	Relict of Daniel
Oct. 3, 1827	*Mrs. Abigail Richardson	"	Relict of Elisha
Oct. 13, 1827	*Mrs. Ruth Richardson	"	Wife of Elisha
Oct. 14, 1827	*Mrs. Unice Daniels	"	Wife of Fisher
Nov. 21, 1827	*Mrs. Therece Jones	"	Wife of Timothy Ellis
Dec. 2, 1827	*Mrs. Hannah Wood	"	Wife of David
June 14, 1826	Hannah Marion Pond	"	Daughter of Nelson & Hannah
March 28, 1828	William Adams	M	
May 19, 1828	Peletian Fisher, Esq.	"	
May 23, 1828	Mrs. Beriah Blake	F	Wife of Dea. Philip
June 7, 1828	*Mrs. Thankfull	"	Relict of Shubel Fales
July 19, 1828	Mr. Joseph Daniels	M	
July 27, 1828	Col. John Boyd	"	
Aug. 5, 1828	*Mrs. Mehitable Bacon	F	Relict of Ens. Seth
Jan. 1, 1828	Mr. Jabez Lambert	M	
Jan. 3, 1828	Otis Farrington	"	Son of David & wife
Jan. 31, 1828	*Mrs. Sally Eddy	F	Wife of Zachariah
Oct. 20, 1828	*Mrs. Anna Morse	"	Wife of Darius, Jr.
Oct. 17, 1828	Mr. Erasmus Pond	M	
Oct. 11, 1828	Julius L. Miller	"	Son of Philip W. & wife
Oct. 26, 1828	*Mrs. Julia Bullard	F	Wife of Joseph
Nov. 23, 1828	Mr. Timothy Gay	M	
Jan. 20, 1829	Mr. Elias Mann	"	
Feb. 17, 1829	*Mrs. Susanna	F	Relict of Joseph Daniels
March 20, 1829	*Mrs. Sarah Rockwood	"	Wife of Timothy
March 28, 1829	*Mrs. Selina Ray	"	Wife of James. She hung herself
June 12, 1829	Hannah Jane Rockwood	"	Daughter of Nathan & Hannah

*Married. †Widow.

FRANKLIN TOWN RECORDS—DEATHS. 155

DATE OF DEATH.	NAME OF DECEASED.	SEX.	RELATIONSHIP.
June 17, 1829	Lieut. Timothy Pond	M	
Jan. 11, 1830	Mr. Seth Wright	"	
July 12, 1829	Mr. Nathaniel Fisher	"	
Aug. 2, 1829	*Mrs. Martha Emmons	F	Wife of Rev. Nathaniel, D.D.
July 22, 1829	John Ellis Baker	M	Son of Elias & Sally
July 10, 1829	Levi Morse	"	Son of Darius & Experience
July 10, 1829	Mr. Jason Morse	"	
July 10, 1829	Miss Duluna Leshure	F	
Sept. 18, 1829	Mr. David Wood	M	
May 20, 1829	*Mrs. Phebe Clark	F	Wife of Paul
Oct. 22, 1829	Mr. Samuel Ware	M	
June 27, 1829	*Mrs. Mary Mann	F	Relict of Elias Mann
Aug. 28, 1829	Mrs. John Pierce	M	
Nov. 11, 1829	Mr. Seth Whiting	"	
Oct. 29, 1829	Lucana Fisher	F	Daughter of Daniel C. & Betsey
Sept. 11, 1829	Mr. Amariah Daniels, Jr.	M	
Nov. 29, 1829	*Mrs. Hannah Boyd	F	Relict of Col. John Boyd
Sept. 3, 1829	Mr. Elias W. Mann	M	
Jan. 15, 1830	Obed Morse	"	Son of Darius & Experience
Mar. 4, 1830	*Mrs. Rachel Fisher	F	Wife of Asa
Mar. 14, 1830	*Mrs. Elmira Pond	"	Wife of Alfred
April 16, 1830	Dea. James Adams	M	
June 4, 1830	Capt. James Wales	"	
June 11, 1830	*Mrs. Eliza Hills	F	Wife of Lysander B.
Aug. 27, 1830	*Mrs. Hannah Nason	"	Wife of George W.
Aug. 29, 1830	Mr. Asa Metcalf	M	
Oct. 9, 1830	Sally Baker	F	Daughter of Elias & Sally
Nov. 21, 1830	*Mrs. Mabell Williams	"	Wife of Levi
Jan. 15, 1830	Mr. George W. Daniels	M	
Jan. 17, 1830	Mr. Aaron Fisher	"	
April 3, 1830	George D. Kingsbury	"	Son of Fisher & Caroline
Dec. 24, 1829	Alexander Metcalf Fisher	"	Son of Willard & Betsey
Mar. 7, 1831	*Mrs. Cynthia Lawton	F	†Wife of George W.
Mar. 10, 1831	*Mrs. Mahitable	"	Relict of Samuel Ware
Mar. 10, 1831	John Woods, Jr.	M	Son of John & his wife
May 23, 1831	Mr. Darius Morse, Jr.	"	
Aug. 1, 1831	James Kingsbury	"	Son of Asa & wife
July 12, 1831	*Mrs. Sarah	F	Relict of Billy Ware
June 2, 1831	*Mrs. Rhoda Phipps	"	Wife of Jedediah
Oct. 21, 1831	David Gillmor	M	
Dec. 27, 1831	Mr. Joseph Hawes	"	
Dec. 31, 1831	*Mrs. Susanna	F	Relict of Daniel Thurston
Dec. 31, 1831	*Mrs. Abigail	"	Relict of Timothy Metcalf
Jan. 5, 1832	*Mrs. Sally Baker	"	Wife of Elias Baker
Jan. 8, 1832	Mr. Jabez Fisher	M	
Jan. 12, 1832	Willard Gillmor	"	Son of James & Rena, 2d
Dec. 11, 1830	Elial Metcalf	"	Son of Preston & Lucretia
Jan. 17, 1832	Lydia Richardson	F	Daughter of Eli M. & Melita
Feb. 12, 1832	*Mrs. Olive Pond	"	Wife of Robert
Feb. 15, 1832	Calvin Claflin	M	Son of Jeremiah & Lois
Feb. 16, 1832	Mary Jane Adams	F	Daughter of Amos & Sally B.
Feb. 20, 1832	Abijah Allen	M	
Mar. 5, 1832	*Mrs. Milly	F	Relict of Asa Metcalf
Mar. 19, 1832	Salina Fisher	"	Daughter of Lieut. Philo & Anna
April 3, 1832	*Mrs. Mary Allen	"	Wife of Amos H.
April 10, 1832	Edward Hawes	M	Son of Josiah & Esther
April 14, 1832	Ogden Pond	"	Son of Increase Sumner & Clar- [inda
April 30, 1832	Dea. Joseph Miller	"	
May 1, 1832	Walter Hartshorn	"	Son of Seth L. & Lydia

* Married.   † Died at Halifax.

FRANKLIN TOWN RECORDS—DEATHS.

DATE OF DEATH.	NAME OF DECEASED.	SEX.	RELATIONSHIP.
June 14, 1832	Horace Freeman Whiting	M	Son of Capt. Jarvis and Mary
June 21, 1832	*Mrs. Ruth Pond	F	Relict of Malchiah
July 19, 1832	*Mrs. Abigail Allen	"	Relict of Abijah
Sept. 17, 1832	Abigail G. Metcalf	"	
Oct. 4, 1832	George Gardner Phipps	M	Son of William & Fanny
Oct. 15, 1832	William E. Hill	"	Son of Elliot & Peggy
Oct. 19, 1832	*Mrs. Lucy Daniels	F	Relict of David
Dec. 11, 1832	Abigail Laurinda Metcalf	"	Daughter of Nathan & Abigail
Jan. 3, 1833	*Mrs. Abigail Blake	"	Wife of Robert
Jan. 8, 1833	Miss Nancy Clark	"	
Dec. 20, 1832	*Mrs. Jemima Ware	"	Wife of Alfred
Feb. 7, 1833	Mr. David Farrington	M	
March 5, 1833	Miss Susanna Ware	F	
April 1, 1833	*Mrs. Mary Wadsworth	"	
April 18, 1833	Mr. Samuel Watson	M	
May 14, 1833	Miss Clara Fisher	F	
May 23, 1833	*Mrs. Hannah	"	Relict of Joseph Hawes
June 14, 1833	*Mrs. Elizabeth Adams	"	Relict of William [Hannah
June 20, 1833	Hannah Dean	"	Daughter of Capt. Ichabod and
July 8, 1833	*Mrs. Jerusha Lethbridge	"	Wife of Richard
Aug. 18, 1833	*Mrs. Rhoda Clark	"	Wife of Sylvester
Sept. 16, 1833	Eliza Ann Blake	"	Daughter of Robert & Sally, Jr.
Sept. 18, 1833	*Mrs. Milly Clark	"	Wife of Abijah
Sept. 1, 1833	Nancy Stone Wadsworth	"	Daughter of Seth and Olive
Oct. 28, 1833	Julia Baker	"	Daughter of Elias
Jan. 9, 1834	*Mrs. Louisa Claflin	"	Wife of Joseph
Jan. 12, 1834	*Mrs. Lydia Phipps	"	Wife of Jedediah
Sept. 19, 1832	Nancy Fisher	"	Daughter of Capt. Maxey&Persis
Feb. 6, 1834	*Mrs. Susan Cleavland	"	Wife of Albert
Feb. 26, 1834	Mr. David Blake	M	
March 14, 1834	Mr. Elisha Bullard	"	
May 3, 1832	Alfred Metcalf	"	Son of Preston & Lucretia
May 12, 1832	Timothy Augustus Metcalf	"	Son of Preston & Lucretia
March 19, 1834	Mr. Eleazar Partridge	"	
March 27, 1834	*Mrs. Milly Blanden	F	Wife of Enoch Blanden
April 1, 1834	James Edson Ware	M	Son of Alfred [Ann
Oct. 12, 1833	Elen Bacon	F	Daughter of Joseph F. & Mary
June 30, 1834	Henry Cleavland	M	Son of Bela & Hannah
June 5, 1834	Ens. Seth Dean	"	
April 21, 1834	Miss Elizabeth Norcross	F	
April 28, 1834	Miss Beckah Willson	"	
May 30, 1834	Miss Mary Bassett	"	
Oct. 1, 1834	*Mrs. Mary Ann Ballou	"	Wife of Wilber
Oct. 18, 1834	Mr. Christopher Smith	M	
Nov. 29, 1834	*Mrs. Sally Rockwood	F	
Dec. 15, 1834	William Turner Haskell	M	Son of Samuel & Amanda
Jan. 3, 1835	*Mrs. Jemima Pond	F	Wife of Elihu, Esq.
Jan. 3, 1834	*Mrs. Cynthia Watson	"	Wife of ———
March 26, 1835	*Mrs. Persis Fisher	"	Wife of Capt. Maxey
April 11, 1835	*Mrs. Patty DeWitt	"	Wife of Capt. Archibald
April 13, 1835	*Mrs. Eunice Mann	"	
April 15, 1835	*Mrs. Waittu Blake	"	Wife of Austin
May 26, 1835	Miss Olive Barden	"	Daughter of David and Julia
June 17, 1835	Horace Richardson	M	Son of Ezekiel & Chloe, Jr.
Aug. 11, 1835	*Mrs. Sarah Fiske	F	Wife of Caleb
July 20, 1835	*Mrs. Olive	"	Relict of Seth Whiting
Sept. 9, 1835	Mr. Simeon Perry	M	
Oct. 17, 1835	Elial Fisher	"	Son of Capt. Maxey & Persis
Nov. 1, 1835	Mr. Eli Ware	"	

*Married.

FRANKLIN TOWN RECORDS—DEATHS

DATE OF DEATH.	NAME OF DECEASED.	SEX.	RELATIONSHIP.
Nov. 10, 1835	Miss Elizabeth Whiting	F	
Nov. 17, 1835	Mr. Daniel C. Fisher	M	
Feb. 29, 1836	Mr. Nathan Woodward	"	
Mar. 7, 1836	Miss Sarah T. Cooms	F	
Mar. 10, 1836	*Mrs. Betsey Willson	"	Wife of Enoch
Mar. 10, 1836	*Mrs. Nancy Melinda Pierce	"	Wife of John
Mar. 22, 1836	Mr. Peter Fisher	M	
April 26, 1836	Mary Richardson	F	Daughter of Stephen & Elizabeth
May 22, 1836	*Mrs. Mary Fisher	"	Wife of Peter
May 24, 1836	Capt. Timothy L. Pond	M	
Aug. 11, 1836	Mr. Albert Metcalf	"	
Aug. 28, 1836	Julia Ann Rockwood	F	Daughter of Asa & Julia
Sept. 8, 1836	Charles King	M	Son of John & wife
Sept. 3, 1836	Mr. Darius Fisher	"	
Oct. 20, 1836	Mr. Elbridge Pond	"	
June 12, 1836	*Mrs. Martha Whittemore	F	Wife of William
Oct. 3, 1836	Miss Susanna Baily	"	
Nov. 8, 1836	Capt. George P. Cleaveland	M	
Nov. 13, 1836	*Mrs. Charlotte Thurston	F	Wife of Major Lewis
Dec. 11, 1836	Sarah H. Fisher	"	Daughter of Capt. Maxey
Dec. 16, 1836	Dea. Philip Blake	M	
Feb. 23, 1837	Eunice A. Daniels	F	Daughter of Fisher & Ann
Feb. 7, 1837	Mr. Richard Whittacar	M	
Feb. 20, 1837	Mr. Joseph Lawrence	"	
Mar. 5, 1837	*Mrs. Rachel Pond	F	Wife of Nathan
Mar. 11, 1837	Mary Louisa Pond	"	Daughter of Sumner & his wife
April 12, 1828	George Allen	M	Son of Cyrus & Sally
Mar. 19, 1837	*Mrs. Rebekah Mann	F	Relict of Thomas Mann
Sept. 24, 1834	Edwin Lafayette Gay	M	Son of Wilkes & Deborah B.
May 19, 1837	Miss Margaret Pond	F	
July 11, 1837	*Mrs. Mehitable	"	Relict of Eli Richardson
July 24, 1837	Miss Mary Ide	"	Daughter of Kollock & wife
Aug. 16, 1837	David T. Morse	M	Son of Darius & Pidn
Aug. 24, 1837	Mr. Joel Daniels	"	
Nov. 19, 1837	Aaron Morse	"	Son of Darius & Pidn
Nov. 27, 1837	Miss Chloe Ware	F	
Jan. 18, 1838	*Mrs. Sally Metcalf	"	Wife of Michael
Jan. 19, 1838	—— Smalley	"	Daughter of Rev. Elum & Louisa J.
Mar. 5, 1838	*Mrs. Sarah Daniels	"	Wife of Nathan
Mar. 17, 1838	Mr. Amasa Richardson	M	[suddenly
Mar. 17, 1838	*Mrs. Lonely Cleaveland	F	Wife of Capt. Samuel, died very
June 12, 1838	Mr. Amariah Daniels	M	
June 18, 1838	*Mrs. Lois Claflin	F	Wife of Jeremiah
Sept. 21, 1838	Miss Hannah Partridge	"	Died at the Poor House
Sept. 22, 1838	Miss Susan Mann	"	Died at the Poor House
Sept. 27, 1838	Miss Hannah Woodward	"	
Feb. 14, 1839	*Mrs. Molly Gillmor	"	Wife of Mr. William
April 9, 1839	James Harding	M	
May 9, 1839	Dea. Levi Hawes	"	
May 27, 1839	*Mrs. Mary Makepeace	F	Wife of Wm., Esq.
July 12, 1839	Mr. Shaw	M	Recently from Foxboro
Aug. 20, 1839	*Mrs. Sally Ware	F	Wife of Fredase A.
Sept 4, 1839	*Mrs. Pamelia	"	Relict of Dea. Levi Hawes
Sept. 6, 1839	Abijah W. Metcalf	M	
Oct. 13, 1839	*Mrs. Elizabeth Daniels	F	Relict of Mr. Amariah
Oct. 19, 1839	Joel Adams	M	
Oct. 20, 1839	Robert Pond	"	
Sept. 30, 1839	Julia Eliza Hawes	F	Daughter of Josiah & Esther
Nov. 7, 1839	Mrs. Hartshorn	"	Wife of Maj. David

* Married

FRANKLIN TOWN RECORDS—DEATHS.

DATE OF DEATH.	NAME OF DECEASED.	SEX.	RELATIONSHIP.
Sept. 15, 1839	Mary Richardson	F	Daughter of Stephen W. & Eliza B
Nov. 30, 1839	Nathan Pennamin	M	
Dec. 1, 1839	Emeline Ware	F	Daughter of Alfred Ware
Dec. 29, 1839	Solomon Blake	M	
Jan. 26, 1840	Willard Wales	"	
April 19, 1840	William Dean	"	Son of Ichabod & Hannah
April 29, 1840	*Mrs. Hannah Miller	F	Wife of Doct. Nathaniel Miller
May 12, 1840	*Mrs. Prudence Metcalf	"	Wife of Hanon Metcalf
May 24, 1840	*Mrs. Metcalf	"	Wife of Willard Metcalf
May 25, 1840	Lucy Ann Cook	"	Daughter of Winslow & Ruth
June 4, 1840	Peggy Brewster	"	
June 30, 1840	Abraham Cummings	M	
July 9, 1840	Rachel Grant	F	Daughter of William & Catherine
July 29, 1840	George Foster	M	Son of Benjamin & Mary Ann
Aug. 2, 1840	Homer Newell	"	Son of Hiram & Clarissa
Aug. 6, 1840	*Peggy Knapp	F	Wife of Moses
Aug. 21, 1840	Edmond Kimball	M	Son of Jonas & Nancy M.
Sept. 9, 1840	Nancy Redwood	F	
Sept. 12, 1840	Col. Caleb Thurston	M	
Sept. 22, 1840	Rev. Nathaniel Emmons	"	
Oct. 8, 1840	*Mrs. Sarah Metcalf	F	Wife of Elias
Oct. 15, 1840	David Graham	M	Son of David & Lydia
Nov. 9, 1840	*Mrs. Fisher	F	Wife of Richard
Dec. 25, 1840	Dea. Samuel Guild	M	
Feb. 12, 1841	Mr. William Gilmore	"	
April 27, 1840	Miss Joanna Jones	F	
Feb. 19, 1841	Clare Fisher	"	Daughter of Maxcy & Abigail
Feb. 10, 1839	Betsey Fisher	F	Daughter of Willard & Betsey
April 9, 1841	Maj. David Hartshorn	M	
April 17, 1841	Mary Ann Thayer [aged 60y.	F	Daughter of Nathaniel & Caroline
July 3, 1841	Capt. Ebenr. Adams Kingsbury,	M	
July 26, 1841	*Mrs. Woodward, aged 43y.	F	Wife of Austin
July 26, 1841	——— Rand	M	Son of James S. & Sylvia
July 30, 1841	*Mrs. Lydia Richardson, 74y.	F	Wife of Amasa
Aug. 17, 1841	——— Hills, aged 1y.		Child of Elliot & Peggy
Sept. 2, 1841	†Widow Fisher [aged 1y.	F	Died at Nashua, N. H.
Sept. 4, 1841	Francis Augusta Cleaveland,	"	Daughter of Lowell B. & Melinda
Sept. 25, 1841	‡	M	Son of David & Nancy
Sept. 29, 1841	Elizabeth Leonard, aged 21y.	F	Daughter of Hartford & Betsey
Nov. 1, 1841	†Judith Brick, aged 77y	"	
Nov. 7, 1841	*Mrs. Abigail Metcalf, aged 70y.	"	Wife of Hanon
Nov. 15, 1841	Leonard Fisher, aged 76y.	M	
Nov. 24, 1841	Nathan Daniels, aged 94y.	"	
Dec. 1, 1841	Miss Abial Ware, aged 90y.	F	
Dec. 4, 1841	Timothy Rockwood, aged 94y.	M	
Dec. 27, 1841	†Joanna Wright, aged 97y.	F	
Jan. 10, 1842	——— Whiting	M	Son of Joseph M. & Clarissa Ann
Jan. 11, 1842	*Mrs. Anna Rockwood, aged 86y.	F	
Jan. 25, 1842	Oliver Peck, aged 12y.	M	Son of Whipple. Drowned.
Feb. 13, 1842	Mr. Cummings, aged 79y.	"	
March 30, 1842	——— Morse	F	Daughter of Amos H. & wife
April 6, 1842	*Mrs. Elmira Inman	"	Wife of Seth Inman
April 7, 1842	*Mrs. Mary Ann Rockwood, 29y.	"	Wife of Capt. Erastus
April 14, 1842	Ziba Pond, aged 78y.	M	
May 26, 1842	David Ware, aged 64y.	"	
May 28, 1842	†Susan Fisher, aged 90y.§	F	
May 28, 1842	†Clarinda Pond, aged 36y.§	"	
June 1, 1842	Darius Morse, aged 75y.	M	

*Married. †Widow. ‡William Henry Harrison Cheeney. §Cause of death, consumption.

FRANKLIN TOWN RECORDS—DEATHS.

DATE OF DEATH.	NAME OF DECEASED.	AGE. Y. M D.	SEX.	RELATIONSHIP.	CAUSE OF DEATH.
July 22, 1842	Wm. Haven Metcalf	15	Male	Son of Gillmore & Rhoda T.	Old age
Aug. 5, 1842	Jesse T. Miller	8	"	Son of Alfred & Sarah L.	
Aug. 12, 1842	Alfred Harris Jordan	6	"	Son of David & Lydia	
Aug. 17, 1842	Thomas Nilson Graham		"		Dysentery
Oct. 19, 1842	Amariah Ware	77	"		Consumption
Oct. 20, 1842	Justin Pond	50	"		Fever
Oct. 22, 1842	Rachel Bullard	47	Female		Lung Fever
Nov. 16, 1842	Abel Balcom		Male		Consumption
Nov. 18, 1842	Margaret G. Thayer	24	Female	Wife of D., Jr.	Consumption
Dec. 31, 1842	Chloe Gilmore		"	Wife of James	
Dec. 30, 1842	Mrs. Whipple		"	Wife of Comfort	
Mar. 3, 1843	Zopher Skinner	69	Male		Consumption
Mar. 7, 1843	Asa G. Norcross	35	"		Consumption
Mar. 22, 1843	Lucius W. Fisher	2	"		Lung Fever
Mar. 23, 1842	Molly Fairbanks	76	Female		Old age
April 20, 1843	Mr. Joseph Whiting	73	Male		Consumption
April 20, 1843	Mr. James Otis Pond	72	"	Son of Maxcy & Abigail	Old age
May, 1843	Dea. Joseph Bacon		"		
May 24, 1843	Thomas Gay		"		
June 8, 1843	Charlotte Whiting	23	Female	Wife of Willard Whiting	Numb palsy
June 12, 1843	Nathan White	76	Male		Old age
June 13, 1843	Hanon Metcalf	87	"		Disease
July 13, 1843	Mrs. Leviey Thurston	65	Female	Wife of Caleb T.	
July 18, 1843	Eunice Ann Daniels	2	"	Daughter of Fisher	
July 18, 1843	Dea. James Metcalf	86	Male		Old age
July 21, 1843	Mr. Wm. Pond	85	"		Consumption
July 21, 1843	Rhoda Miller	25	Female	Wife of Gillmore	Inflammation
Aug. 10, 1843	—— Whiting		Childe	Child of Willard	
Aug. 19, 1843	Marjua Fisher	13	Female	Daughter of Maxey	Consumption
Aug. 19, 1843	Paul D. Pond	60	Male		Consumption
Aug. 31, 1843	Mrs. Haskell	45	Female	Wife of Samuel	
Sept. 16, 1843	John Wilkes Richardson	08	Male		Consumption
Sept. 29, 1843	Mrs. Mary A. Metcalf	23	Female	Wife of Richardson	
Sept. 30, 1843	Irene Fisher	77	Widow		

FRANKLIN TOWN RECORDS—DEATHS.

DATE OF DEATH.	NAME OF DECEASED.	AGE. Y|M|D.	SEX.	RELATIONSHIP.	CAUSE OF DEATH.
Oct. 6, 1843	—— Skinner	16	Male	Son of Zenas & wife	Dysentery
Oct. 8, 1843	Juletta Fairbanks	83	Widow		Old age
Oct. 23, 1843	Mrs. Fanny Phipps	51	Female, M	Wife of William Phipps	Typhus fever
Oct. 30, 1843	Eleazor Ware	77	Male		Fever
Mar. 29, 1843	Elmira W. Inman		Female	Daughter of Seth & Elmira	
Nov. 23, 1843	Asa Fisher	87	Male		Diseas Applexy
Nov. 23, 1843	Cornelia Angeline Norcross	21	Female	Daughter of Rufus & wife	Croup
Nov. 30, 1843	Louisa Jane Blake	1	"	Daughter of Charles G. & wife	Dropsy on the brain
Nov. 30, 1843	Mrs. Heaton	86	M		Dropsy
Dec. 9, 1843	Lois Woodward	82	Widow		Old age
Jan. 20, 1844	Lucretia Ware	33	Female	Of Caleb S. Taft & wife	Consumption
Feb. 16, 1844	Wellington Pond	26	Male	Son of Paul D.	Consumption
Mar. 4, 1844	Charlotte Davis	21	Female	Daughter of Mr. Davis Died at Dr. S. Atwood's	Disease of the heart Was from Maine
Mar. 9, 1844	Jerusha Ware	67	Female		
April 22, 1844	Willard Pond	51	Male		Disease of the brain
May 22, 1844	Mary Nason	90	Widow	Widow of Nason	Old age
May 17, 1844	—— Allen	4	Female	Daughter of Amos H. & Elizabeth	Consumption
Mar. 11, 1844	Samuel Metcalf	71	Male		
April 18, 1844	Sarah Hubbard	74	Female		

I hereby certify that the foregoing, from page 8 to page 31 inclusive, is a true copy of the original record.

Attest: A. A. RUSSEGUE, Town Clerk.

FRANKLIN, March 1, 1864.

FRANKLIN TOWN RECORDS—DEATHS.

The Number of Deaths in Franklin during the Year next preceding May 1st, 1845, was Thirty Three.
(Place of Interment Franklin unless otherwise indicated.)

NAME OF DECEASED.	SEX AND CONDITION.	AGE. Y|M|D	OCCUPATION.	DATE OF DEATH.	CAUSE OF DEATH.	PLACE OF BIRTH.	NAME OF PARENTS OR HUSBAND.
—— (Allen)	Female	4		May 16, 1844	Consumption	Franklin	Amos H. & Eliza Allen
Mary Nason	Widow	90		May 22, 1844	Old age		
Charlottee Wallace	"	84 4 10	House Keeper	Aug. 19, 1844	Apoplexy	Boston	Joshua & Susan Nash
Sophronia L. Graham	Female	4 19	"	Sept. 3, 1844		Franklin	David & Lydia
Molita Richardson	Married	51	"	Sept. 14, 1844	Typhous Fever	Bellingham	Eli M. Richardson
Peter Daniels	"		Farmer	Sept. 16, 1844	Dropsy		
Eliza B. Richardson	"	29	Domestic	Oct. 17, 1844	Typhous Fever	Medway	Stephen W.
Levi Fisher	"	86	Yeoman	Oct. 22, 1844	Old age	Franklin	
Harriett A. Pond	Female	18 2 12	Straw Sewer	Oct. 20, 1844	Consumption	"	Increase S. & Clarrissa
Elizabeth Littlefield	"	66	Spinster	Oct. 30, 1844	Lung Fever		
Abagail Adams				Nov. 10, 1844	Croup		
Daniel Thurston	Married		Shoe Manuf'r	Nov. 13, 1844	Typhous Fever	"	Daniel and Susan
Infant (Haskell)	Male			Nov. 16, 1844		"	Samuel & Amanda Has-[kell
Lewis Fisher	Married	77	Yeoman	Nov. 28, 1844	Consumption	"	
Olive Fisher	Female			Dec. 2, 1844	Typhous Fever		
Samuel Gillmore	Widower	72	"	Dec. 3, 1844			
May Pierce	Widow	82					
Susan M. Thayer	Single	20 5 26	Straw Sewer	Dec. 11, 1844	Disease of the Brain	"	Davis & Betsey
Sophia Daniels	"	18	"	Jan. 4, 1845	Consumption	"	Ezra Daniels
Clarinda P. Haskell	"	17 4 3	"	Jan. 13, 1845	"	"	Samuel & Amanda
Oliver N. Pond			Husbandry	Jan. 26, 1845			
Merriam Morse	Married	78 3 19	Domestic	Feb. 5, 1845	Mortification	Walpole	Jason Morse
Lizzy A. Snow	Female	2 9		Mar. 13, 1845	Scarlet Fever	Franklin	Cyrus & Catherine
George R. Thompson	Male	2 10 4		Mar. 15, 1845	"	"	John & Mary J.
Wm. T. Hartshorn	"	1 2		Mar. 20, 1845	"	"	Gilbert & Ellen A.
*Ithamar Adams	Married		Yeoman	April 9, 1845	Disease of the Brain		
Mrs. Goldsbury Pond	"	60	Domestic	April 18, 1845	Disease of the Heart	"	Goldsbury Pond
Wilkes Gay	"	75	Laborer	April 21, 1845	Cancer	Dedham	
Horace G. Miller	Male	6 18		June 6, 1844	Quincy	Franklin	Gillmore & ——
Addison D. Pierce	"	2 2		Sept. 17, 1844	Scarlet Fever	"	Washington

*Medway.

FRANKLIN TOWN RECORDS—DEATHS.

NAME OF DECEASED.	SEX AND COND'TION	AGE. Y/M/D	OCCUPATION.	DATE OF DEATH.	CAUSE OF DEATH.	PLACE OF BIRTH	NAME OF PARENTS OR HUSBAND.
Mrs. Abigail Hills	Married	82		May 21	Consumption		Harvey Hills
*Jonathan Metcalf	"	12			Lung Fever		
Gilbert Ruel Ray	Male	11	Yeoman	July 11, 1844	Drowned	Medway	George W. & Eliza Ann

Deaths in Franklin during the year next preceding May 1, 1846, was Twenty-Two.   Informant was Sexton.

NAME OF DECEASED.	SEX AND COND'TION	AGE. Y/M/D	OCCUPATION.	DATE OF DEATH.	CAUSE OF DEATH.	PLACE OF BIRTH	NAME OF PARENTS OR HUSBAND.
Deborah B. Gay	Married	31	Care of Family	May 2, 1845	Disease of the Heart	Franklin	Wilks
Louisa Pond	"		"	May 13, 1845	Consumption	"	Alfred
Sarah H. Robinson	Widow	60	Tailoress	May 17, 1845	Fever	Walpole	
Jesse Nason	Married	70	House Wright	May 24, 1845	Consumption	Unknown	
Hannah Allen	Widow	64	Care of Family	June 29, 1845	Fever	Franklin	
Jemima Baker	Married	60	"	July 26, 1845	Still Born	"	David
Infant of (Ballou)				Aug. 12, 1845	Consumption	"	Albert & —— Ballou
Cynthia Mann	Single	29	Seamstress	Aug. 23, 1845	Unknown	"	Nathan & Margarett
Child of (Fisher)		2		Sept. 7, 1845	Consumption	"	Willard & —— Fisher
Abigail Cunliff	Married	31	Care of Family	Sept. 24, 1845	Cholera Infantum	Unknown	Calvin & Eliza Jane [Pond
Child of (Pond)				Dec. 14, 1845	Unknown	Franklin	
†Robert Ray	Married	90	Farmer	Dec. 14, 1845	Disease of the Heart	Unknown	Joseph & Thankful
Joseph Pitcher	Single	28	‡	Dec. 15, 1845	Unknown	Barnstable	Harvey & Abigail Hills
Child of (Hills)				Dec. 19, 1845	"	Franklin	Abijah & —— Rockwood
Child of (Rockwood)				Dec. 27, 1845			Hartford
Betsey Leonard	Married	47	Care of Family	Mar. 1, 1846	Consumption	Foxboro	Samuel & Amelia
Laura Haskell	Single	16	Straw Braider	Mar. 31, 1846	"	Franklin	Jeremiah & Lucy Ann [Claflin
Child of (Claflin)		5		April 8, 1846	Unknown	"	
David Scott	Widower	90	Farmer	April	"	Unknown	
Matilda H. Knapp	Single	23	Straw Sewer	April	Consumption	Franklin	Alfred & Elenor
Mary Marsh	Married	24	Care of Family	April 26, 1846	Measles	Unknown	Lewis H.
Child of (Ray)				July 28, 1845	Fever	Medway	George W. & Eliza A.
Eliza A. Ray	Married	39	Care of Family	June 8, 1845	Consumption	Franklin	George W.
Phineas Partridge	"	69	Husbandry	Dec. 14, 1845	Typhus Fever	"	
Fisher Thayer	"	55	Manufacturer	April 11, 1846	Dropsy	"	

* Interment, Medway.   † Wrentham records show birth in Wrentham Feb. 15, 1776. Parents, Robert Ray & Mary Richardson.   ‡ Labourer in Factory

FRANKLIN TOWN RECORDS—DEATHS.

Deaths in Franklin during the year next preceding May 1, 1847, was Sixteen.

Informant was Sexton unless otherwise indicated. Place of interment Franklin unless otherwise indicated.

NAME OF DECEASED.	SEX AND CONDITION.	AGE. Y M D	OCCUPATION.	DATE OF DEATH.	CAUSE OF DEATH.	PLACE OF BIRTH.	NAME OF PARENTS OR HUSBAND.
Elihu Pond	Married	83	Husbandry	June 2, 1846	Still Born	Franklin	Joel & Wife
Infant		2		June 30, 1846		Medway	Lyman S. & Susan Ware
Eveline A. Dunton	Female	1		July 8, 1846	Dysentery	Franklin	James [Mann
A child of (Ware)		1		July 15, 1846	Consumption		Jonathan & Marietta
Olive Metcalf	Widow	80	Domestic Work	July 24, 1846	Dysentery		Edm'd&Olive Hartshorn
Child of (Mann)	Male	1		Aug. 13, 1846			Edw.R.&Susan Gillmore
Child of (Hartshorn)		1		Aug. 15, 1846			Nathan Cole
Child of (Gillmore)	Male	1		Aug. 16, 1846			Wife of Ezra
Child of (Cole)		1		Aug. 22, 1846			Wife of David
Mrs. Daniels	Married	58	House Work	Aug. 30, 1846	Dropsy		Wife of John
Mrs. Dean		47	"	Nov. 22, 1846	Bilious Colic		Joseph
Rosalinda Alley		60	"	Nov. 25, 1846	Consumption	Franklin	Justin Pond
Anna Lawrence	Widow	86		Dec. 3, 1846		Freetown	Oliver N.
Widow of (Pond)				Feb. 19, 1847			Wm. F. & Allice
Esther Pond	Widow	78		Feb. 28, 1847		Franklin	Bela
Emma Jane Rhodes	Female	2 22		April 30, 1847			Rev. ———— & Sarah
Hannah Cleveland	Widow	65	Domestic Work	July 21, 1847			
John Alden Robinson	Male	3		Jan. 23, 1847			

Number of Deaths in Franklin during the Year next preceding May 1, 1848, was Twenty-Two.

NAME OF DECEASED.	SEX AND CONDITION.	AGE. Y M D	OCCUPATION.	DATE OF DEATH.	CAUSE OF DEATH.	PLACE OF BIRTH.	NAME OF PARENTS OR HUSBAND.
Charles F. Hart	Married	66	Laborer	July 16, 1847	Consumption	Portsmouth, N.H	Willard
Betsey Fisher	"	42	Care of Family	July 21, 1847	"	Medway	Timothy & Julia
Ellen Gay	Single	14 2 1		Aug. 18, 1847	Dysentery	Franklin	*
Infant child of (Briggs)		14		Aug. 24, 1847			Willard & Betsey Fisher
Infant child of (Fisher)				Aug. 20, 1847			Eliza F. Jones
Child of (Jones)		2 3		Aug. 20, 1847			
Harriet Fisher	Single	57		Sept. 7, 1847	Typhus Fever	Franklin	
Willard Boyd	Married	76		Sept. 26, 1847	Cancer	"	
Caroline M. Hart		25		Oct. 4, 1847	Consumption.	"	Alexd. L.
& Deborah Briggs.							

Informant was Sexton unless otherwise indicated. Place of interment Franklin unless otherwise indicated.

NAME OF DECEASED.	SEX AND COND'TION	AGE. Y M D	OCCUPATION.	DATE OF DEATH.	CAUSE OF DEATH.	PLACE OF BIRTH.	NAME OF PARENTS OR HUSBAND.
Chloe Richardson	Widow	58		Oct. 13, 1847	Paralasys	Norton	Nathan & Hannah
Nathan Rockwood, Jr.	Single	17		Nov. 11, 1847	Inflamation of Bowels	Franklin	
Joseph Ray	Married	56		Dec. 7, 1847	Erysipelas	"	
Chloe Mann	Single	65		Jan. 16, 1848	Consumption	"	
Alfred Pond	Widower	41		Jan. 25, 1848	Erysipelas	"	
Seth Appleby	"	78		Jan. 29, 1848	Dropsy	"	
Ellen Melinda Clark	Female	11		Feb. 18, 1848	Dropsy on Brain	"	Paul B. & A. A.
Enoch Blandin	Widower	78		Mar. 26, 1848	Influenza	"	
Claragene Whiting	Female	6		Mar. 29, 1848	Lung Fever	Norton	Joseph M. & C. A.
Frances O. Wales	"	9		April 8, 1848	Dropsy on Brain	Franklin	Wm. & Mary R.
Henry Farrington	Married	26		April 26, 1848	Consumption	"	
Louis Harding	Widow	83		April 28, 1848	"	"	
Whiting Adams	Single	55		April 30, 1848	"	"	
Harriet S. Gates	Married	35		June 16, 1847	"	"	Charles E.
Harriet Chamberlaine	"	29		June 23, 1847	"	"	Benja.
Abigail Wales	Widow	82		Sept. 18, 1847	"	"	
Ellen E. Chamberlin	Female	5		Jan. 18, 1848	Erysipelas	"	Benja. & Harriet

Deaths in Franklin from May 1, 1848, to December 31, 1848. Registered January, 1849.

*Herbert A. Hartshorn	Male	9 19		May 11, 1848	Lung Fever	Franklin	Edmund and Susan
†Badsheba Thurston	Widow	61		June 7, 1848	Liver Complaint	Foxborough	
*Martha Richards	Female	18 4 20		June 10, 1848	Consumption	Winslow, Me.	Jeremiah & Sarah
†Child of (Nye)				June 18, 1848	"	Franklin	Caleb T. & Sophia Nye.
†Anna Broady	Married	77		June 28, 1848	"	"	John Broady
†Catharine Snow	"	57		July 21, 1848	Scrofula	Holden	Cyrus B. Snow
†Caroline Fisher	Single	27		July 29, 1848	Consumption	Franklin	Willis & Caroline
†Julia Adams	Married	72		Aug. 29, 1848	"	"	Nathan
†Peggy Rockwood	Widow	88		Sept. 3, 1848	"	Mansfield	[Hills
†Margarette Ann Hills	Female	13		Sept. 8, 1848	"	New York	Adopted by Jarvis H.
†Abigail Fairbanks	Single	54		Sept. 8, 1848	Dysentery	Franklin	
†Eliza Phinney	"	17		Sept. 10, 1848	Typhus Fever	"	

*Informant, John Warfield. †Informant, Jason Fisher.

Deaths in Franklin from May 1, 1848, to Dec. 31, 1848.—(Continued.) Place of interment Franklin unless otherwise indicated.

NAME OF DECEASED.	S	AGE. Y M D	OCCUPATION.	DATE OF DEATH.	CAUSE OF DEATH.	PLACE OF BIRTH.	NAME OF PARENTS OR HUSBAND.	INFORMANT.
Dexter F. Wiswell	*M	71		Sept. 10, 1848	Dysentery	Frankfort, Me.		Jason Fisher
Eunice Ware	W	77		Sept. 15, 1848	"			"
Esther Starkie	"	72		Sept. 18, 1848	"			"
Child of (Follett)	M			Sept. 20, 1848	"	Franklin	Willard & Lydia Follett	"
Ira Blake	Mr.	38	Blacksmith	Sept. 20, 1848	"	Wrentham	Philip & ————	"
Child of (Newell)	M	1		Sept. 24, 1848	"	Franklin	Hiram & Clarissa Newell	"
Francis Adora Tufts	F	8		Sept. 25, 1848	"		Charles & Sophia	"
Ann M. Morrifield	Mr.	71		Oct. 5, 1848	Paralysis	Medway	Aaron & Ruth	"
Ruth Snow	"	25		Oct. 11, 1848	Fever	Norton	Cyrus	"
George Ide	"	68		Oct. 11, 1848	Consumption	Wrentham	Kollock & Mary	"
Nathan Clark	"	76		Dec. 5, 1848	Disease of the Liver	Franklin	Asa	"
Polly Partridge		24	Labourer	Dec. 10, 1848	Consumption	Ireland		
Patrick Simmonds		36	"	Dec. 16, 1848	"	Franklin	Samuel	John Warfield
Eben'r E. Warfield		50		Oct. 11, 1848	"	"	John H.	"
*Juletta Allen		50		Dec. 30, 1848	Cancer on Breast	Hopkinton		"
†Louisa P. Richardson		37		Dec. 7, 1848		Swansey		
†Caleb Horton								

Deaths in the Town of Franklin during the Year 1849.—Registered January, 1850.

NAME OF DECEASED.	S	AGE. Y M D	OCCUPATION.	DATE OF DEATH.	CAUSE OF DEATH.	PLACE OF BIRTH.	NAME OF PARENTS OR HUSBAND.	INFORMANT.
John Mitchell	M	91		Jan. 3, 1849	Dropsey on Brain		John & Catherine	J. Fisher
Rhoda Thayer	W	52 14		Jan. 9, 1849	Old Age			
Electa Metcalf	S	1 2		Jan. 13, 1849	Dysentery	Franklin		J. Warfield
Lewis W. Hartshorn	M	67 3 25		Feb. 5, 1849	Cripple from Birth	"	Lewis	
John Snow	Mr.	94	Labourer	Feb. 5, 1849	Fever			J. Fisher
Abijah Clark	Wr.			Mar. 5, 1849	Old Age	Franklin		
Child of (Metcalf)	F	7		April 8, 1849	Water on the Brain	Medway	Michael & Amelia Metcalf	"
Joseph Partridge	Mr.	32	Carpenter	April 23, 1849	Brain Fever	Chelsey		"
Harriet Adams	F	1 6		June 16, 1849	Kick of a horse		Simeon P. & Harriet	"
Joel Dunton	Mr.	42	Labourer	July 1, 1849	Dysentery	Franklin		"
Maddison Blake	M	3 14		Aug. 11, 1849	"		Elias & Mary Ann	"
Timothy Fisher	Mr.	88	Farmer	Aug. 13, 1849	Old Age	Franklin		

*,*M, Male. F, Female. S, Single. Mr., Married. W, Widow. Wr., Widower. * Died in Medway. † Died in Boston.

Deaths in Franklin during the Year 1849.—(Continued). Place of interment Franklin unless otherwise indicated.

NAME OF DECEASED.	S	AGE. Y/M/D	OCCUPATION.	DATE OF DEATH.	CAUSE OF DEATH.	PLACE OF BIRTH.	NAME OF PARENTS OR HUSBAND.	INFORMANT.
Esther Lawrence	S	54		Aug. 25, 1849	Dysentery	Franklin		J. Fisher
Susanna Fisher	W	86 3 27		July 27, 1849	Old Age	Milford		J. Warfield
Irene A. Bullard	F	6 14		Aug. 28, 1849	Consumption	Franklin	Saml. M. & Harriet	"
Anna Brick	Mr.	58 3 21		Aug. 29, 1849	Dropsy	Hopkinton	Silas	"
Amelia Metcalf		37		Aug. 30, 1849	Consumption	Franklin	Michael Metcalf	J. Fisher
Allice Maria Adams	F	2		Sept. 9, 1849	Dysentery	"	Peter & Clarissa	"
Child of (Fisher)	M			Sept. 9, 1849		"	Smith & Mary	"
George Watson	S	21	Laborer	Oct. 1, 1849	Intemperance			
Betsey Hartshorn	W	77 1 16		Oct. 4, 1849	Dropsy	Ireland		J. Warfield
Eli Pond	Mr.	79	Farmer	Oct. 16, 1849	Old Age	Mansfield		J. Fisher
Jonathan E. Mann	M	4 20		Oct. 27, 1849	Consumption	Franklin	Jon'a. & Marietta	"
Anna H. Leland	W	81		Nov. 18, 1849	"	"		
Caroline A. Hart	F	1 8 8		Dec. 8, 1849	Disease of Heart	"	Chas. E. & Julia A.	J. Warfield
Martha A. Hart	Mr.	26 10		Dec. 22, 1849	Fever	"	Alex. L.	J. Fisher
*Charles Gates	M	6		Feb. 28, 1849	Small Pox	Worcester	Charles E.	"
*Charles Gay	S	8		June 11, 1849	Consumption	Franklin	Wilkes & Deborah	"
Elenor Richards	S	19 1 3		Aug. 25, 1849	Dysentery	Winslow, Me	Amos & Mary	J. Warfield
Sarah Richards	F	2 2 19		Aug. 28, 1849	Dropsy	"	Amos & Mary	"
‡Abigail Wales	Mr.	32 8 25		July 31, 1849	Consumption	Bellingham	George	"
‡Child of (Wales)	F	3		Sept. 30, 1849	"	"	George W. & Abigail	J. Fisher
‡Sarah A. Wales	F	19 7 12		Oct. 21, 1849		"	Willard & Sarah	"
§Almira Wescott	Mr.	30		Nov. 11, 1849		Franklin	Jerome	"

Deaths in the Town of Franklin during the Year 1850.—Registered January, 1851.

				1850				
Emely F. Richardson	F	4		Feb. 27	Typhoid Fever	Bellingham	Howard & Mary	John Warfield
Thankful Pitcher	Mr.	80		Mar. 6	Dropsy	Barnstable	Joseph	"
Edwin L. Brown	S	23 7	Shoe Maker	Mar. 24	Consumption	"	Lewis C. & Rosanna	Jason Fisher
Sabin Ware	Mr.	38 9 8	Farmer	April 11	Suicide	Franklin	Eleazer & Olive	"
Andrew Fenno		59	Harness Maker	May 26	Dropsy	Dorchester	Unknown	"
George Fisher	S	37 1 23	R.R.Conductor	June 7	Fever & Ague	Franklin	Willis & Caroline	"
Nathaniel Miller	Mr.	80	Surgeon	June 10	Old Age	Rehoboth	Philip	John Warfield

, M male, F female, S single, Mr. married, W widow, Wr. widower. *Died in Wrentham. †Died in New York. ‡Died in Bellingham. §Died in Medway.
= Interment Cumberland, R.I. * Birthplace Cumberland, R.I.

Deaths in the Town of Franklin during the Year 1850.—(Continued.)

Place of interment Franklin unless otherwise indicated.

NAME OF DECEASED.	S	AGE. Y/M/D	OCCUPATION.	DATE OF DEATH.	CAUSE OF DEATH.	PLACE OF BIRTH.	NAME OF PARENTS OR HUSBAND.	INFORMANT.
				1850				
James Edward Wales	M	1 4 25		June 25	Consumption	Franklin	William & Mary E.	Jason Fisher
Philip Farley	1	1 6		Aug. 7	Brain Fever	"	Peter & Mary	"
Nathan Pond	Mr.	81	Farmer	Sept. 2	Dysentery	"	Unknown	"
James Baker	S.	89	"	Oct. 5	Lung Fever	Medfield	Unknown	"
Edward A. Norcross	M	5		Dec. 20	Typhoid Fever	Franklin	Rufus & Maranda	John Warfield
Herbert Lawrence		9		Oct. 25	Unknown	"	Amos & Harriet	"
*Eliza P. Moulton	Mr.	38		Jan. 10	Consumption	"	Mark D.	Jason Fisher
†Polly Nutter		53 3 9		Jan. 14	Disease of Spine	"	John	"
‡Rufus Bassett		53 8 6		Jan. 20	Brain Fever	Northbridge		John Warfield
§Sarah L. Hart		24		Jan. 27	Consumption	Appleton, Me.	John	"
§Eleazer Partridge		65		Mar. 8	Lung Fever	Franklin		Jason Fisher
§Rachael Pond	W	80		Mar. 13	"	Medway		"
¶	M	2 6		June 24	Brain Fever	Fall River	Tyler R. & Persis M.	"
¶Rebecca Pennell	W	63		July 28	Dropsy	Franklin		"
**Robert Shurtleff	Mr.	23		Aug. 15	Drowning	Middleboro		"
** Betsey Shurtleff		27		Aug. 15	"	Franklin	Robert	"
††Ann E. Horton		27		Sept. 1	Consumption	Warren, R.I.	Sanford	"
§Clarissa N. Ward	F	3		Sept. 20	Dysentery	Franklin	Edwin & Mary	John Warfield
††Frederick W. Boyd	M	1 1 8		Sept. 20	"	Springvale	Wm. & Betsey	"

Deaths in the Town of Franklin during the Year 1851.

NAME OF DECEASED.	S	AGE.	OCCUPATION.	DATE OF DEATH.	CAUSE OF DEATH.	PLACE OF BIRTH.	NAME OF PARENTS OR HUSBAND.	INFORMANT.
				1851				
Elizabeth Woodward	S.	60		Feb. 5	Consumption	Franklin	James & Louis	Jason Fisher
Alfred Knapp Ray	M	5		Feb. 17	4	"	James P. & Susan	"
Julia Blake	Mr.	81		Mar. 3	Consumption	Oberl. N. Y.	Timothy	"
Mary R. Wales		28		April 3	"	Medway	William	"
Ruth A. Whiting	W	79		April 9	"	Attleboro	Joseph	H. Coleman
Eugene N. Corbin	2	M		May 3	5	Franklin	Nelson & Nancy M.	Jason Fisher
Maria Amelia Dean	F	4 6		May 11	Dropsy on Brain	"	Luther & Maria A.	John Warfield
Thankful Gay	3	S.	19	May 20	4	Pawtucket, R.I.	David & Mary	Jason Fisher
Nancy Maria Gilmore		19		May 31	Consumption	Medway	Phelander S. & Nancy	"

*, * M, Male. F, Female. S, Single. W, Widow. Mr., Married. Wr., Widower. * Died in Boston, † Wrentham, ‡ Foxboro, § Medway, ¶ Wrentham, ** Wm. Gardner, Van. Alinon Blake, died in Fall River. *, Charlestown, **, Lynnfield, ††, New Bedford, ‡‡ Springvale. Place of interment, 1 Milford, 2 Wrentham, 3 Franklin City. 4 Inflammation of the Bowels, 5 Measles and Pneumonia.

Deaths in the Town of Franklin during the Year 1851.—(Continued.) Place of interment Franklin, unless otherwise indicated.

NAME OF DECEASED.	SEX	AGE. Y|M|D	OCCUPATION.	DATE OF DEATH.	CAUSE OF DEATH.	PLACE OF BIRTH.	NAME OF PARENTS OR HUSBAND.	INFORMANT.
				1851				
Mary Rebecca Wales	**F	3		June 1	Consumption	Franklin	Wm. & Mary R.	Jason Fisher[1]
Nancy Frost	S	34		June 14	"	**	Peter & Eliza	"
Belinda Fisher	Mr.	39		June 14	"			"
William W. Scott[1]	S	15		July 23	Billious Fever	Alstead, N.H.	John	JohnWarfield
Timothy Blake	Wr.	88	Shoe Maker	July 28	Old Age	Franklin	Lemuel & Ruth	Jason Fisher
Ezekiel Adams	Mr.	46	Cabinet Maker	July 31	Liver Complaint	Bellingham	Joel & Lois	"
Ann Elizabeth Fisher[2]	F	1	4	Aug. 8	Fever	Charlestown	George N. & Sarah L.	JohnWarfield
Mary G. Metcalf[1]	"	2		Aug. 25	Dysentery	Franklin	Alfred H. & Susanna	"
Roxanna Richardson	"	6 23		Sept. 4	"	"	Howard & Mary	Jason Fisher
Alfred P. Newell	M	2 1		Sept. 6	"	"	Hiram & Clara	JohnWarfield
— Ward		17		Sept. 7	"	"	Edward L. & Mary	Jason Fisher
Mary Rourke[3]	Mr.	28		Sept. 23	Consumption	Ireland	James	JohnWarfield
Marcus E. Chase	M	1 11 9		Sept. 24	Dysentery	Bellingham	Hiram & Matilda	Jason Fisher
Rachael Bullard	W	95		Sept. 29	Old Age	Wrentham	Elisha	JohnWarfield
Elizabeth L. King	F	5		Sept. 30	Dysentery	Franklin	David & Lucy	Jason Fisher
Warren Edmund Adams[4]	S	24		Oct. 26	Consumption	Medway	Joel P. & Julia A.	JohnWarfield
Francis H. Fisher	M	1 3		Nov. 12	Dysentery	Franklin	Walter H. & Emely	Jason Fisher
Percy Fisher	Mr.	60		Nov. 18	Diabetes	"		"
Jerusha Newell[5]	W	81		Nov. 26	Old Age	Cumberland	Jabez	
Patty Clark	Mr.	56		Nov. 13	ConsumptionBlood	Chester, Vt.		P. S. Bates
*Margarett Buffington	S	58		Jan. 30	Fever	Walpole	William	
†Ellen M. Fisher	"	24		Mar. 4	Consumption	Franklin	Willis & Caroline	
‡Joseph Pitcher	Wr.	81		April 24	Dropsy	Barnstable		JohnWarfield
*Leonard A. Arnold	Mr.	37		May 12	Consumption	Framingham		Jason Fisher
§Abigail H. Ladd	"	26		May 24	"	Franklin	Charles W.	"
‖Emeline Grover	"	39		Aug. 18	Fever	Walpole	Charles	"
¶Margarett Grover	F	11		Sept. 9	"	Foxboro	Chas. & Emeline	"
*Charles E. Scott	M	18 6		Sept. 25	Dysentery	Medway	George W. & Lucy	JohnWarfield
*Sarah Jane Buffington	"	7		Oct. 22	Canker	Franklin	Wm. & Margarett	Jason Fisher
¶Louisa King	Mr.	22		Dec. 31	Consumption	Winslow, Me.	Warren	JohnWarfield

*M male, F female, S single, Mr. married, W widow, Wr. widower. [1]Died Medway, [2]Savannah, Ga., †Barnstable, ‡Milford, §Milton, ‖Foxboro, *Canton, **Cumberland, R. I. ‡Place of interment Franklin City, [2]Charlestown, [3]Milford, [4]Medway, 5 Cumberland, R. I.

Deaths In the Town of Franklin during the Year 1852.—Interment in Franklin unless otherwise indicated.

NAME OF DECEASED.	SEX	AGE Y/M/D	OCCUPATION.	DATE OF DEATH. 1852	CAUSE OF DEATH.	PLACE OF BIRTH.	NAME OF PARENTS OR HUSBAND.	INFORMANT.
Roger Robinson	Mr.	30	Machinest	Jan. 2	1	Ireland	John & Jane	Jason Fisher
Alpheus Adams	"	66	Blacksmith	Jan. 9	Consumption	Franklin	Thadeus & Rachael	"
William Buffington	"	56/5	Farmer	Feb. 7		Lemington, Vt	Noah & Anna	"
Leonard Pond	"	85	"	Feb. 9	Old Age	Franklin	Benja. & Lois	"
Julia Ann Barden	F	30		Feb. 13	Consumption	Wrentham	Artemas	"
*Phebe Louisa Blake	F	/15		March 8	Lung Fever	Franklin	Elias & Mary A.	"
Edene Dean	W	88		March 13	Paralysis	"	Seth	"
Richard O'Niel	M	9		March 18	Consumption	"	Nicholas & Maria	"
Paul Clark	Mr.	81	Farmer	March 19	Fever	"	John & Ruth	"
Mary Rouke	F	1/6		March 24	Consumption	"	James & Mary	"
Walker	M	/14		March 24	Fits	"	Ozias & Sarah J.	"
†Sarah Peck	Mr.	68		March 30	Billious Fever	3	William	"
†Emeline Barrows	N	22/6		April 8	2	4	Alexd. & Charlotte	John Warfield
Herbert A. Jorden	M	2 /2/17		April 19	Dysentary	Franklin	George A. & Sarah	Jason Fisher
Clark	N			May 27	Whooping Cough	"	Paul B. & Abigail	"
Jane A. Daniels	N	19		May 31	Consumption	"	Albert E. & Olive G.	"
§Grace Carr	Mr.	63		June 22	Disease of Heart	Hancock, Vt	Daniel	"
Mary King	F	13		July 24	Scarlet Fever	Franklin	John & Erepta	"
Eveline Bemis	Mr.	19/5		Aug. 5	Consumption	"	Charles H.	"
Ella Maria Metcalf	F	1/5		Aug. 12	Dysentary	"	Otis F. & Lucy M.	"
Nathan Adams	Wr.	77	Farmer	Aug. 14	Consumption	"	John & Naomi	"
Herbert Wallace Metcalf	M	3		Sept. 4	Dysentary	"	Otis F. & Lucy M.	"
¶John Bayley Briggs	"	1/7		Sept. 5	"	"	Hiram E. & Deborah A.	"
Edmund L. Bemis	"	4/5		Sept. 12	Consumption	Bellingham	Chas. H. & Eveline	"
¶Olive Pond	W	60		Oct. 7	"	Franklin	Nathan & Polly Penniman	J. Warfield
Esmer A. Richardson	F	2/27		Oct. 7	Bowel Complaint	"	Howard & Mary	Jason Fisher
George S. Kilburn	M	3/8		Oct. 10	Dysentary	"	Warren A. & Betsey F.	"
Amelia K. Thayer	F	14		Oct. 20	Canker Rash	"	Nath'l & Caroline	John Warfield
Emma F. Dorr	"	1/10/5		Oct. 24	Dysentary	"	David S. & Hellen	Jason Fisher
Gilbert Gilmore	M	5				"	Philander S. & Nancy	"

* Wrentham, † Cumberland, R. I. ‡ Newton. § Medway, ‖ Attleboro. ¶ Holliston. 1 Inflammation of the Lungs. 2 Inflammation of Bowels. 3 Cumberland, R. I. 4 Rockland, Me. *., M male, F female, S single, Mr. married, W widow, Wr. widower.

FRANKLIN TOWN RECORDS—DEATHS.

Deaths in the Town of Franklin during the Year 1852.—(Continued.) Interment in Franklin unless otherwise indicated.

NAME OF DECEASED.	S	AGE Y/M/D	OCCUPATION	DATE OF DEATH	CAUSE OF DEATH	PLACE OF BIRTH	NAME OF PARENTS OR HUSBAND	INFORMANT
Rozina B. Paine	Mr.	40		Oct. 28	Erysiplas Fever	Bellingham	Hiram	John Warfield
Elizabeth A. Hubbard	S.	14 11 24		Nov. 17	Tyfoid	Franklin	Elisha & Amelia	John Warfield
Jabez Wright	Mr.	75	Farmer	Dec. 2	Asthma	Bellingham	Seth & Joanna	Jason Fisher
Joseph Gilmore	"	84	"	Dec. 6	Old Age	Franklin	David & Joanna	"
Frank Herbert Fisher	M	6		Dec. 11	Whooping Cough	"	Adin & Mary	"
*Amos Richards	Mr.	58		April 11	Fever	Winslow Me		
†Pardon E. Scott	"	31		Oct. 11	Consumption	Franklin		John Warfield
‡Ladora A. White	F	1		Sept. 11	Fits	1	Cyrus N. & Ruth P.	"
§Malinda Guild	Mr.	51		May 27	Consumption	Bridgewater	Hernon	"
‖J. Francis Atwood	"	34		Dec. 23	"	Middleboro	Francis & Elizabeth	Jason Fisher
¶Mary Metcalf	"	48		Feb. 17	"	Walpole	Elias	"

Deaths in the Town of Franklin during the Year 1853.—T. C. HILLS, Registrar.

NAME OF DECEASED.	S	AGE Y/M/D	OCCUPATION	DATE OF DEATH	CAUSE OF DEATH	PLACE OF BIRTH	NAME OF PARENTS OR HUSBAND	INFORMANT
Anna Fisher	S.	61		Jan. 22	Nervous Insanity	Franklin	Peter & Anna	J. Fisher
Elias Baker	Mr.	72	Farmer	Jan. 30	Diabetes	"	John & Molly	
Emmons Fisher	S.	22		Jan. 31	Consumption	"	Willard & Betsy	
Martha S. Southworth	F.	5		Mar. 14	Congestion of brain	Eastford, Ct.	Mason S. & Sophia L.	
Eunice Mann	S.	75		Mar. 30	Disease of the liver	Franklin	Nathan & Eunice	
Ida Delma Blake	F.	1 3		April 5	Teething	Wrentham	George L. & Abby F.	
Loani B. Gay	W	65 7		April 7	Consumption	Brookfield	Amos B.	
Nathan Metcalf	Mr.	88	Farmer	April 13	Old Age	Franklin	Barnabus & Rebecca	
Wm. Edwin Perriman	M	2 1		April 20	Erysipelas	"	Luke & Elizabeth D.	
George R. Metcalf	"	5		April 23	Dysentary	"	Richardson & Harriet	
**Harriet B. White	S.	22		June 7	Fever	Maine	Sewell & Belinda	
Hannah M. Daniels	Mr.	56		July 1	Scrofula	Croyden, N. H.	David W.	
††Elisha Hubbard	"	64	Farmer	July 18	Heart Complaint	Franklin	Joshua & Sarah	
Eveline Elizabeth Morse	F	3 7		July 18	Consumption	"	Aaron H. & Deborah E.	
Nath'l Emmons Adams	M	2 11 15		July 20	Dysentary	"	Peter & Clarisa D.	
Susan Marsh	Mr.	18		July 26	Fever	"	Lewis H.	
Clarabell Adams	F	1 5		Aug. 8	Dysentary	"	Peter & Clarisa D.	
Addison N. Pond	M	17		Aug. 10	Fever	"	Hiram & Joanna M.	

* Died in Canton, † Milford, ‡ Providence, R. I., § Central Falls, R. I., ‖ Aiken, S. C., ¶ Medway. Interment, ** Northbridge, †† Franklin, on his farm. 1 Providence, R. I. S. * M male, F female, S single, Mr. married, W widow, Wr. widower.

Deaths in the Town of Franklin during the Year 1853.—(Continued.) Interment in Franklin unless otherwise indicated.

NAME OF DECEASED.	C.S.	SEX	AGE. Y/M/D	OCCUPATION.	DATE OF DEATH.	CAUSE OF DEATH.	PLACE OF BIRTH.	NAME OF PARENTS OR HUSBAND.	INFORMANT.
					1853				
Shadrack Newell	*	M	2		Aug. 20	Dysentary	Franklin	Arnold J. & Eliza	J. Fisher
Adelaide L. Guild	*	F	3		Aug. 27	"	"	Albert & Lurena	J. Warfield
Abigail M. Richardson	S		29		Aug. 22	"	"	Elisha & Ruth	"
Frank E. Ware		M	1 1		Sept. 1	"	"	Benja. B. & Sally	J. Fisher
Margaret Marroon	S		17		Nov. 21	Consumption	Ireland	Patrick & Mary	"
Ellen J. Jorden		F	1 11 10		Oct. 10	"	Franklin	George A. & Sarah	J. Warfield
——Hamilton		M			Oct. 26	"		Wm. & Jane	"
Ruth Hammond		W	64		Dec. 4	Dropsy	Scituate, R.I.	Uriah	
Lysander Clark	1	Mr.	31	Boot Maker	Dec. 6	Consumption	Bellingham	Mason	
Andrew Simmons		Wr.	95	Laborer	Dec. 23	Old Age	Africa		
*Polly Kingsbury		W	70		Jan. 15	Consumption	Southboro	Joshua & Polly Fisher	
†Albine L. Dorr		F	4 17		March 8	Lung Fever	Franklin	David S. & Hellen B.	
‡Mary Hartshorn		S	29		April 24	"	"	Seth S. & Lydia	
*Albert S. Ware		F	1 2 19		May 5	Lung Fever	Wrentham	Lyman S. & Susan	
§Irene F. Norcross		W	48 11		May 5	Consumption	Franklin	Widow of Asa G.	
‖Prudence Knapp		Mr.	49		May 24	Cancer	Uxbridge	Melville	
¶Amos H. Allen		"	49 6 4		Aug. 18	Consumption	Franklin	Nathan & Hannah	
‖Mary O'Niel		F	1 12		Aug. 29	Dysentary	Cumberland	Nicholas & Maria	
†Olive Dunbar		Mr.	76		Oct. 16	Fever	Medfield	Simeon	
**Caroline Lewis		"	29		Oct. 20	Consumption	Wrentham	James	

Deaths in the Town of Franklin during the Year 1854.—Registered January, 1855.—T. C. HILLS, Registrar.

NAME OF DECEASED.	C.S.	SEX	AGE	OCCUPATION.	DATE OF DEATH.	CAUSE OF DEATH.	PLACE OF BIRTH.	NAME OF PARENTS OR HUSBAND.	INFORMANT.
					1854				
Alice Robinson		F	3		Jan. 13	Fever	Franklin	John K. & Hannah	
Margarett Jones		S	22		Jan. 30	2	Ireland	William	
Mary Kyle		Mr.	84		Feb. 3	Consumption	Rehoboth	Joel	
Mary Daniels		W	92		Feb. 7	Old Age	Wrentham	Patrick	
Mary Callaghan		"	52		Feb. 12	Consumption	Ireland	Erastus & Mary G.	
Harriet C. Adams		F	7		Feb. 17	Fever	Salem	San'l & Mahitable	
Alfred Ware		Mr.	67	Carpenter	March 11	Mortification	Wrentham	Wm. & Sophia	
Paul Earl	2	"	33	Farmer	March 29	Measles	3		

∴ M married, F female, S single, Mr. married, W widow, Wr. widower. *Died in Wrentham, †Medway, ‡Foxboro, §Aiken, S. C., ‖Cumberland, R. I., ¶Framingham, **R. I. 1 Interment at Bellingham. 2 Inflammation Bowels. 3 New Braintree.

Deaths in the Town of Franklin during the Year 1854.—(Continued.)

Place of Interment Franklin unless otherwise indicated.

NAME OF DECEASED.	SEX AND COND'TION	AGE. Y/M/D	OCCUPATION.	DATE OF DEATH. 1854	CAUSE OF DEATH.	PLACE OF BIRTH.	NAME OF PARENTS OR HUSBAND.
Arrabella A. Hartshorn	Female	1 25		Mar. 30	Consumption	Franklin	Edmund & Susan
Ellen F. Metcalf	"	5 2		April 10	Dysentary	"	Otis F. & Lucy M.
Reuben G. Pond	Married	41	Farmer	April 17	Typhoid Fever	Wrentham	Samuel & Catherine
Jonathan Hawes	"	81	"	May 21	Consumption		Jonathan & Mary
Michael Metcalf	"	51		June 3	"	Franklin	Nathan & Patty
Nancy Hills	Single	62		June 11	"		Jason & Polly
Polly Hills	Widow	87		June 23	Dropsy		Jason
Samuel Clark	Married	71	Farmer	July 2	"	N. Bridgewater	Samuel & Esther
Mary A. Blake	Female	5 17		July 5	Fever	Franklin	Erastus E. & Abby M. Baker
Henry N. White	Male	15 1	Bon't Presser	July 7	Typhoid Fever	Wrentham	Jason N. & Lucena
Wm. Stearns De Witt	"	1 2 1		July 12	Dysentary	Franklin	Alex'd F. & Martha
Jemima Wales	Married	76		July 16	Old Age	Milford	Otis
Emegene Cook	Female	3		July 18	Fever	Franklin	Lucian & Sarah
Ellis Scott	Male	3 18		Aug. 8	Consumption	"	George & Lucy
Emma F. Freeman	Female	4 10		Aug. 26	Dysentary	"	James M. & Mary
Elvia Cook	Single	19		Sept. 6	Consumption	"	Elias & Elvira
Josephene Norcross	"	18		Sept. 7	Scarlet Fever	"	Asa G. & Irene
Martha P. Whiting	Female	7		Sept. 10	Typhoid Fever	"	Daniel P. & Lydia
Josephene S. Winn	"	21		Sept. 13	Consumption	"	Otis & Lydia
Sarah Fisher	Single	18	Clerk	Sept. 28	"	"	Willard & Betsey
James T. V. Woodward	Married	35		Oct. 23	Typhoid Fever	"	Austin & Mary A.
Susan A. Gillmor	Single	22		Nov. 4	Dropsy Brain	"	Robert & Rebecca
Henry W. Adams	Male	2 6		Nov. 21	Consumption	"	Albert & Susan D. W.
Susan J. Wiggin	Female	1 6		Dec. 10		"	Shepherd & Jane
Ann Whitney	Married	35		Dec. 14	Dropsy	Pawtucket	Silas
Nehemiah Adams	Single	82	Farmer	Dec. 19	Consumption	Wrentham	Peter & Esther
Nancy Clark	Widow	74		Dec. 31		Roxbury	Nathan
Caroline Kingsbury	Married	50		Mar. 10	Old Age	Franklin	Fisher
*Remember Smith	Widow	85 11		April 15	Consumption	Mansfield	Moses
†Elias Metcalf	Married	53 10		April 7	"	Franklin	Timothy & Abigail
‡Sarah A. Hardy	"	28		April 11	Whooping Cough	Dublin, N. H.	Emmons M.
§Isadora F. White	Female	1 3 24				Providence, R. I.	Newell & Ruth

* Died in Bellingham. † Medway. ‡ Dublin, N. H. § Providence, R. I.

FRANKLIN TOWN RECORDS—DEATHS.

Deaths in the Town of Franklin during the Year 1854.—(Continued.) Place of Interment Franklin unless otherwise indicated.

NAME OF DECEASED.	SEX AND CONDITION.	AGE. Y/M/D	OCCUPATION.	DATE OF DEATH.	CAUSE OF DEATH.	PLACE OF BIRTH.	NAME OF PARENTS OR HUSBAND.
				1854			
*Charles C. Metcalf	Male	11 — —		April 24	Fever	Franklin	Erasmus B. & Ann S.
†Emma E. Clark	Female	5 — —		May 5	"	Natick	Wm. J. & Arlısa
‡Joan E. Wiggin	Married	31 — —		May 28	Consumption	Essex	Shepherd
§Asa Kingsbury	"	77 — —		June 30	"	Franklin	
§Waldo Wales	Male	1 7 —		Aug. 28	Dysentary	Bellingham	Geo. W. & Mary
‖Sylvester Richardson	"	1 1 —		Aug. 29	Canker	Holliston	Howard & Mary
§Ida Abby Wales	Female	3 — —		Aug. 31	Dysentary	Bellingham	Geo. W. & Mary

Deaths in the Town of Franklin during the Year 1855.

				1855			
Robert Gilmore	Married	66	Basket Maker	Jan. 6	Consumption	Franklin	Robert & Olive
George Cheney	"	"		Jan. 7	"		Lyman S. & Lizzie
Nancy Pond	Married	66	9	Jan. 17	Consumption	Wrentham	Lewis, 2d
Henry Wm. Nye	Male	8 — —		Mar. 28	Brain Fever	Franklin	Wm. & Eliza
Amy Pond	Married	65 — —		April 9	Consumption	Windham, Ct.	Martin
Harriet A. Bartlett	Female	3 — —		April 26	Lung Fever	Franklin	Wm. A. & Harriet
Henry B. Pond	Married	38	Male Spinner	May 1	Consumption		Martin & Amy
Chickery Shepherd	"	71	Farmer	June 15	"	Foxboro	John & Chloe
¶Harriet Thayer	"	27		June 21	"	Franklin	Obed P.
**Gilbert Lothrop	"	75		June 24	Brain Fever	Easton	Seth & Hannah
Laura Nason	Single	54	Straw Sewer	July 4	Consumption	Walpole	Jesse & Hannah
Nathan Gilmore	Married	76	Mason	July 16	Disease of the Brain	Franklin	William
††Nathaniel Follett	Single	23	Boot Maker	July 17	Consumption	Pawtucket, R. I.	Willard & Lydia
Edward S. Hills	Male	1 3 —		July 18	Dysentary	Franklin	Sanford & Mary C.
John Alby	Married	75	Shoe Maker	Aug. 11	Dropsey	Lynn	John
‡‡Mary Jane Emerson	Single	34	Straw Sewer	Aug. 24	Consumption	Hollis, N. H.	Wm. & Sarah J.
§§Hartford Leonard	Married	59	Blacksmith	Aug. 31	Dysentary	Foxboro	Jacob & Milly
‖‖Charles Keith	Single	22 4 15		Sept. 2	Consumption	Walpole	Charles & Nancy
Solomon P. Pond	Widower	89 6 —	Butcher	Sept. 10	Old Age	Franklin	Oliver & Anna
Albert P. Gilmore	Male	2 8 —		Sept. 16	Dysentary	"	Philander S. & Nancy
George W. Salley	"			Sept. 21	Cholera Infantum		James & Susan
Hannah Clark	Widow	72 11 —		Nov. 1	Consumption	Walpole	Eleazer & Jerusha

* Died in Lock, Texas, † Natick, ‡ Medway, § Bellingham, ¶ Walpole. ** Sharon, †† Wrentham, ‡‡ Hollis, N. H.
§§ Foxboro, ‖‖ Walpole.

Deaths in the Town of Franklin during the Year 1855.—(Continued.) Interment in Franklin unless otherwise indicated.

NAME OF DECEASED.	SEX AND COND'TION	AGE. Y/M/D	OCCUPATION.	DATE OF DEATH.	CAUSE OF DEATH.	PLACE OF BIRTH.	NAME OF PARENTS OR HUSBAND.
				1855			
Betsey F. Kilbourne	Married	28		Nov. 22	Consumption	Medway	Warren A.
Sylvia Ware	Single	66		Nov. 22	Typhoid Fever	Franklin	Jesse & Kezia
Jane Robinson	Widow	68		Nov. 25	Lung Fever	Ireland	?
Esther B. Warfield	Married	76		Nov. 25	Disease of the Heart	Franklin	John
Hiram Paine	Widower	41	Manufacturer	Nov. 28	Typhoid Fever	Mendon	
Jane Hollerin	Female			Dec. 28	Inflamation of Lungs	Franklin	Timothy & Hannah W.
Eliphas Lawrence	Married	71 4/21		Dec. 29	Typhoid Fever	"	
George Adams	Male	12 3		Dec. 29	Cancer	"	Ezekial & Susan
*Melville Knapp	Widower	61		Feb. 21	Dropsy		Moses & Peggy
*Sarah Cook	Single	25		March 10	Consumption		Galen
†William Makepeace	Widower	91 8		March 23	Old Age	Norton	Wm. & Ruth
‡Ellis Perry	Single	50		March 29	Accidental Fall	Franklin	Arnold & Betsey
§Olive C. Frost	Married	27		May 13	Fever		George W.
‖Jenny M. Woodward	"	23		Aug. 3	Childbed	Wrentham	Wm. H.
‡Simeon Dunbar	Widower	90		Sept. 23	Dysentary	Sharon	
$Harriet Partridge	Single	24		Oct. 15	Consumption	Franklin	Eleazer & Hannah
§John Robinson	Married	66		Oct. 16	Dropsy	Ireland	Roger & Jane
**Charles A. Barrows	Male	2 14		Oct. 27	Canker	Wrentham	Samuel & Cornelia

Deaths in the Town of Franklin during the Year 1856.

NAME OF DECEASED.	SEX AND COND'TION	AGE.	OCCUPATION.	DATE OF DEATH.	CAUSE OF DEATH.	PLACE OF BIRTH.	NAME OF PARENTS OR HUSBAND.
				1856			
Stephen Kingsbury	Married	73	Farmer	Jan. 30	Disease of the Heart	Franklin	Stephen & Abigail
Hannah D. Hills	"	47		Feb. 14	Typhoid Fever	Bridgewater	Theron C.
Esther Lewis	Widow	76		Feb. 26	Consumption	Gilmantown, N. H.	William
Willard Gay, Jr.	Single	33	Laborer	April 8	Dropsy	Camden, N. H.	Willard & Mary E.
Marshall G. Norcross	"	21	Book Keeper	April 22	Consumption	Franklin	Asa G. & Irene
Fanny Woodward	"	50		May 19	Dropsy	"	James & Elizabeth
1Chloe Richardson	Widow	81		June 18	Neuralgia	Walpole	Levi & Mary Lindley
2Dennis Sullivan	Widower	83	Laborer	June 27	Old Age	Ireland	Dennis
Sarah Newell	Single	20		June 30	Typhoid Fever	Franklin	Arnold J. & Eliza
Leonard B. Brown	Male	2		Aug. 16	Inflamation on Brain	"	Leonard & Mahitta
Jemina F. Daniels	Married	68		Sept. 6	Consumption	Holliston	Luke

*Died in Woonsocket, R.I., †Oxford, ‡Boston, §Medway, ‖Buffalo, N.Y., $Sharon, **Wrentham. 1 Interment Franklin City, 2 Blackstone. 3 July 18, 1863, removed to Holliston.

FRANKLIN TOWN RECORDS—DEATHS.

Deaths in Franklin during the Year 1856.—(Continued.) Place of interment Franklin unless otherwise indicated.

NAME OF DECEASED.	SEX AND CONDITION.	AGE. Y/M/D	OCCUPATION.	DATE OF DEATH.	CAUSE OF DEATH.	PLACE OF BIRTH.	NAME OF PARENTS OR HUSBAND.
				1856			
Seneca Hills	Married	60	Farmer	Sept. 27	Consumption	Franklin	Jason & Polly
Polly B. Sargeant	"	75		Oct. 10	Mortification	Spencer	Asa
Clarinda Pond	Single	19		Nov. 17	Typhoid Fever	Holliston	Cutler & Lydia
Hannah Blake	Widow	74		Nov. 24	Paralysis	Franklin	Solomon
Artemas Barden	Married	33	Farmer	Nov. 27	Typhoid Fever		David & Julia
Hannah Nason	Widow	80		Dec. 27	Consumption		Jesse
*Christiana Wales	Single	27		Jan. 24	Fits		Mason & Electa
†Simeon Clark	Widower	72		April 14	Disease of the Heart		Dyer & Rachael
‡James M. Cook	Single	32		April 19	Consumption		Galen & Sarah
†Edward C. Ware	Male	8		May 3	Drowned		Benj. B. & Sally
§Hannah H. Partridge	Widow	58		June 3	Lung Fever	Walpole	Eleazer
‖Marcus M. Holbrook	Single	20		June 5	Drowned	Milford	Ellis & Eliza
¶Frank Hubbard	Male	2		July 8	Cholera Infantum	Salem	Joshua G. & Emely
**Sybil Metcalf	Widow	82		July 29	Paralysis	Medway	Stephen
††Jenny Farrington	Female		1	Nov. 6	Canker	Boston	George & Cleopatra

Deaths in Franklin during the Year 1857.

NAME OF DECEASED.	SEX AND CONDITION.	AGE. Y/M/D	OCCUPATION.	DATE OF DEATH.	CAUSE OF DEATH.	PLACE OF BIRTH.	NAME OF PARENTS OR HUSBAND.
James L. Daniels	Male	2 3			Worms	Franklin	Amos F. & Lucena
Susanna Metcalf	Married	83			Old Age	Boston	William P.
Thomas Bacon	"	26 5 20	Teacher		Consumption	Franklin	Joseph T. & Mary A.
Cutler Pond	"	82	Farmer		Old Age	"	Timothy & Sarah
Julia Rockwood		68			Fever	"	Asa
Witham A. Laing	Male	7			Lung Fever	"	Robert & Nancy
Abbot Brooks Bacon	"	9			"	"	George W. & Julia
Hiram Pond	Married	58	Farmer		Consumption	"	Jem Otis & Sally
Carrie M. Walker	Female	3 6			"	"	William J. & Susan
John L. Fitzpatrick	Single	20 6	Boot Maker		Cancer	Boston	John L.
Ursula C. Fisher	Widow	60 8			Old Age	Charlton	Rufus & Ellen E. Bacon
Lephe Miller	Married	80 8			Consumption	"	Philip W.
Eueline Shepard	"	26			"	Franklin	William P.
Florence Pitman	Female	4 1			Dysentary		John & Delia

* Died in West Boylston, † Wrentham, ‡ Woonsocket, R.I., § Paxton, ‖ New Bedford, ¶ Salem, ** Bellingham, †† Boston.

Deaths in Franklin during the Year 1857.—(Continued.) Place of interment Franklin unless otherwise indicated.

NAME OF DECEASED.	SEX AND CONDITION	AGE. y/m/d	OCCUPATION.	DATE OF DEATH.	CAUSE OF DEATH.	PLACE OF BIRTH.	NAME OF PARENTS OR HUSBAND.
Catherine Bierden	Married	28			Fit	Ireland	John
Julia E. Ballou	Single	28			Palsy	Cumberland, R. I.	Thurston & Caroline
Calla Bullard	Married	76 2			Fever	Franklin	Amos
*George Cook	Single	19			Consumption	"	Galen & Sarah
†David M. Gay	Married	57 5 21			Apoplectic Fit	"	Timothy & Submit
‡Joseph James Clark	Single	29 6 1			Consumption	Pawtucket, R. I.	Joseph J.
§Abba A. Burlingame	Married	25			"	Franklin	Smith
‖John Nutter	"	62			"	Pawtucket, R. I.	John

Deaths Registered in Franklin, Norfolk County, during the Year 1858.—T. C. Hills, Registrar.

Place of interment Franklin unless otherwise indicated.   Informant Jason Fisher unless otherwise indicated.

DATE OF DEATH.	NAME OF DECEASED.	AGE. y/m/d	SEX AND CONDITION	OCCUPATION.	PLACE OF BIRTH.	NAME OF PARENTS OR HUSBAND.	CAUSE OF DEATH.
1858							
Jan. 27	Patty Lincoln	90	Widow		Mansfield	Widow of Wm.	Old Age.
Feb. 28	Phylena Daniels	71	Married		Norton	Wife of Joel	Lung Fever
March 18	Abigail Metcalf	80 2	Widow		Franklin	Widow of Nathan	Consumption
March 31	Silas Fisher	59	Single	Farmer	Wrentham	Leonard	Intemperance
April 26	Harriet F. Gay	5	Female		Franklin	Walter H. & Sally A.	Scarlet Fever
April 26	Asa Partridge	85 1	Married	Farmer	"	Eleazer	Consumption
April 27	Agustus Newell	23	Single	Laborer	"	Hiram & Clarissa	"
May 5	¶John Allen Hartshorn	1 18 6 27			"	Lewis & Nancy	
May 19	Hiram Newell	51	Married	Boat Builder	"	Dexter	Fits
May 27	Susan Fisher	84	Widow		"	Widow of Levi	"
June 25	Hannah G. Snow	1 6	Female		"	Cyrus B. & Victoria	Palsy
July 4	2 Ellen S. Long	37	Married		Ireland	Wife of John	Scarlet Fever
July 6	Janette Eliza Whiting	5	Female		Franklin	Wm. E. & Betsey A.	Consumption
July 24	2 Ellen Sullivan	36	Married		Ireland	Wife of John	Scarlet Fever
July 26	Caroline Fisher	66			Franklin	Wife of Willis	Consumption
Aug. 6	Grace Mabel Breck		8 26 Female			Elias & Julia	Cholera Infantum

*Died in Cumberland, R. I. †Attleborough, ‡Boston, §Bellingham, ‖Taunton. *Interment Franklin City, 2 Blackstone. ¶Informant Sam'l B. Scott.

FRANKLIN TOWN RECORDS—DEATHS. 177

Deaths Registered in Franklin, County of Norfolk, during the Year 1858.—(Continued.)
Place of interment Franklin unless otherwise indicated. Informant Jason Fisher unless otherwise indicated.

DATE OF DEATH.	NAME OF DECEASED.	AGE. Y|M|D	SEX AND CONDITION	OCCUPATION	PLACE OF BIRTH	NAME OF PARENTS OR HUSBAND	CAUSE OF DEATH.
1858							
Aug. 26	Jennie Frances Freeman	5|11	Female		Franklin	J. M. & Mary	Dysentary
Aug. 31	Levi Williams	86	Married	Laborer		Marmaduke	Consumption
Sept. 7	*Celia A. Daniels	34|2|10	Female		Swanzy	Wife of Jefferson	
Sept. 20	†Catherine Stullivan	3|2	Female		Franklin	John & Ellen	Cholera Infantum
Sept. 20	‡Ida E. Hartshorn	4|11	"		"	George E. & Eliza M.	
Oct. 24	§—— Metcalf	|1	"		"	Samuel W. & Eliza J.	
Oct. 24	§—— Metcalf	|1	"		"	Samuel W. & Eliza J.	
Dec. 21	David Ware	44	Married	Laborer		David	Consumption
Jan. 4	‖Eliza J. L. Allen	24|9	"		England	Wife of Alfred W.	
Mar. 13	¶Arnold Perry	73|5	Widower	Laborer	Bellingham	David	Palsey
April 27	**Annie E. Clark	28|5|6	Single		Lowell	Joseph J.	Consumption

Deaths Registered in Franklin during the Year 1859.—T. C. HILLS, Registrar.

DATE OF DEATH.	NAME OF DECEASED.	AGE. Y|M|D	SEX AND CONDITION	OCCUPATION	PLACE OF BIRTH	NAME OF PARENTS OR HUSBAND	CAUSE OF DEATH.
1859							
Jan. 1	Eliza F. Partridge	61	Widow		Franklin	Levi & Molly Fairbanks	Consumption
Jan. 2	Marcella Woodward	1|5|22	Female		"	Marcellas & Sarah	Canker Rash
Jan. 3	††Sarah Jane Fuller	29	Single		"	Moses & Mary	Consumption
Jan. 4	‡‡Matilda R. Richardson	80|6|20	Widow			3	Influenza
Jan. 18	§§Susan V. Whiting	16	Single		Cumberland, R.I.	Joseph B. & Phila	Shot by Jona. Wales
Jan. 18	Jonathan Wales	28	"	Farmer	Franklin	Otis & Jerusha, Jr.	Shot himself
Jan. 21	‖‖‖Wm. S. Richardson	1|17|10|9	"		"	Stephen W.	Consumption
Jan. 26	Louisa Knapp	63	Married		Wrentham	Abijah Clark	Typhoid Fever
Feb. 15	Eliza Ware	57	"		Franklin	Wife of Frederic A.	Lung Fever
Feb. 21	Simeon P. Adams	49	"	Boot Manu'fr	Pawtucket, R. I.	Alpheus & Acsah	Consumption
Mar. 7	Lydia Follet	2|46	"		Douglas	Nath'l & Lydia Jenks	"
Mar. 9	Sylvanus Thayer	73	Male	Blacksmith	Franklin	Thaddeus	Disease of the Bowels
Mar. 11	Marcellas Woodward	1	Married			Marcellas & Sarah	
	Ruth Cook	57				Joseph & Ruth Whiting	Fits, died instantly

*Interment, Franklin City; informant, S. B. Scott. †Interment, Blackstone. ‡Interment, Franklin City; informant, Saul B. Scott. §Interment, Medway. ‖Died in Medway; int't, Franklin City, Saul B. Scott. ¶Died in Wrentham. **Died in Boston; interment, Franklin City; informant, Saul B. Scott. ††Interment, Medway. ‡‡Interment, Franklin City; informant, S. B. Scott. §§Interment, Wrentham; murdered. ‖‖Interment, bellingham; suicide. 1 Interment, Franklin City; informant, Saul B. Scott. 2 Interment, Wrentham. 3 Stephen & Abigail Kingsbury.

Deaths Registered in Franklin during the Year 1859.—(Continued.)

Place of interment Franklin unless otherwise indicated. Informant Jason Fisher unless otherwise indicated.

DATE OF DEATH.	NAME OF DECEASED.	AGE. Y/M/D	SEX AND CONDITION.	OCCUPATION.	PLACE OF BIRTH.	NAME OF PARENTS OR HUSBAND.	CAUSE OF DEATH.
1859							
March 20	*Sarah A. Durney	18	Single		Ireland		Poison (Suicide)
March 25	†Susan Lawrence	75 11 23	Widow		Sharon	Widow of Eliphas	Old Age
April 11	Sarah Robinson	37	Married		Grafton, N. H.	John K.	
May 17	Archd. DeWitt	54			Oakham	Benja. & Olivia	Disease of Heart **
May 29	Alice Gilmore	9	Female		Franklin	Wm. D. & Harriet	
June 6	‡Albert T. Brown	23	Married		Wrentham	John	Heart Disease **
June 6	Annie M. Emerson	2	Female		Franklin	Elias P. & Mary S.	Dropsy on Brain
June 10	George Hall	65	Married		Attleboro	Ephraim	Consumption
June 22	§Jeremiah Desmond		Male		Franklin	Jere'h & Catherine	
June 27	Peter Fisher	72	Widower	Farmer		Peter & Anna	Paralysis
July 30	Emely Kimball	22	Single			Jonas & Mary	Consumption
Sept. 1	‖Abbie M. Kingsbury	19 5				Horatio & Adelia	Typhoid Fever
Sept. 3	¶Rhoda Dean	79	Widow			Sam'l & Mehitable Ware	Dropsy
Sept. 4	1 Betsey Adams		Married		Wrentham	Silas	Hemorage of Lungs
Sept. 6	Wm. Cady King	1	Male		Harvard	George & Lucy A.	Cholera Infantum
Sept. 8	2 Laura Ellen Stark	7 11 8	Female		Franklin	Z. J. Stark	Typhoid Fever
Sept. 18	Peter Frost	82	Married		Lynn, N. H.	Peter & Sarah	Suicide (Hanging)
Nov. 5	3 Betsey Metcalf	78 6 14			Milford	Whiting	Fever
Sept. 23	4 Hannah Stewart	74	Widow		Franklin	Asabel & Alphira Sands	Consumption
Oct. 15	5 Joseph Gilmore	57	Married	Farmer	Sudbury, Vt.	Joseph & Lucinda	"
Oct. 16	Marena Pond	72	Widow		Franklin	Abijah & Abigail Allen	Paralysis
Oct. 26	Sanford Ware	78	Married			Jesse & Kezia	
Oct. 30	Herman R. Blake	56	"			Robert & Abigail	Burn
Nov. 22	6 Francis Blake	33	"		Wrentham	Harvey & Betsey	Consumption
Jan. 26	7 Everett P. Frost	1 4	Male		Acton	George N. & Susan	Scarlet Fever
March 3	8 Julia A. C. Allen	2 11 22	Female		Foxboro	Alfred W. & Eliza J. L.	"
Sept. 2	9 Wm. H. Ware	9 11 10	Male		Franklin	Lyman S.	Fall
Sept. 13	10 Horace A. Wood	20 11 5	Single		Medway	Alonzo H.	Scarlet Fever

*Interment Medway. †Interment Franklin City, Informant S. B. Scott. ‡Interment Wrentham. §Interment Quincy. ‖Interment Franklin City, Informant S. B. Scott. ¶Interment Dedham. 1 Interment Medway. 2 Interment Franklin City. 3 Interment S. B. Scott. 4 Interment Sudbury, Vt. 5 Interment Wrentham. 6 Interment Medway. 7 Died in Acton. 8 Died in Medway, Interment Franklin City. Informant S. B. Scott. 9 Died in Wrentham, Interment Franklin City. Informant S. B. Scott. 10 Died in Sharon, Interment S. B. Scott.
**Died Instantly.

Deaths Registered in Franklin, Norfolk County, during the Year 1860.—T. C. HILLS, Registrar.

Place of interment Franklin unless otherwise indicated. Informant Jason Fisher unless otherwise indicated.

DATE OF DEATH.	NAME OF DECEASED.	AGE. Y	M	D	SEX AND CONDITION	OCCUPATION.	PLACE OF BIRTH.	NAME OF PARENTS OR HUSBAND.	CAUSE OF DEATH.
1860									
Jan. 12	Nancy Webber	75			Widow		Castine, Me.	Joseph&Betsey Hibbard	Paralysis
Feb. 5	Anna Pond	88			Single		Franklin	Oliver & Anna	"
Feb. 26	*Betsey Fisher	82	1	15	Widow		Wrentham	Samuel	Old Age
Mar. 15	†Orretta Blake	1	3		Female		Holliston	Francis M. & Maria E.	Consumption
Mar. 29	Maria Clark	56			Married		Gloucester	Abel Mann	
April 7	*Edward Clagg	35	11		Single	Weaver	England		Lung Fever
April 28	—— Day				Male		Franklin		Still Born
May 16	†Alonzo M. Leavitt	2					Dorchester	Joseph & Alsie	Congestion of Lungs
May 20	Hannah Foster	86			Widow		Franklin	Manoah & Melina	Old Age
June 5	Mary Ellen Stewart	3	8		Female		"	Jesse & Keziah Ware	Croup
June 17	John Broady	82			Widower		Oxford	Robert & Martha	Old Age
June 29	*Duty Ware	71	2	13	Married	Farmer	Wrentham	Oliver & Betsey	Gall Stones
July 5	*Hermon Guild	77	10	9	Widower	Cabinet Maker		Ebenezer & Molly	Chronic Bronchitis
July 6	Dorcas Fisher	87	9		Widow		Medfield	Edward Cleveland	Old Age
July 7	§Mary E. Gibson	3	2	23	Female		Sutton	Cornelius & M. C.	Croup
July 26	*Philip W. Miller	85	7	27	Widower	Farmer	Rehoboth	Philip & Roby	Old Age
July 27	Samuel Dore	26	9	1	Single	Boot Maker	Boxford	Benja. & Susan	Inflammation Lungs
Aug. 11	‖Mary Ryan	65			Widow		Ireland	John&Catherine Morey	Apoplexy
Aug. 24	Diana Ware	73			"		Mendon	Alex d & Patience Wilson	Disease of Stomach
Sept. 9	Betsey Lawrence	83	9		Single		Franklin	2	Old Age
Sept. 16	James S. Coombs	47	2	11	Married		New Bedford	John & Betsey S.	Dropsy
Sept. 16	Susan Fisher De Witt	4	27		Female		Franklin	Alex'd F. & Martha E.	Bowel Complaint
Oct. 1	*Walter Scott Bassett	8	11	2	Male			Oscar M. & Susan M.	Inflammation of Leg
Oct. 14	¶Nellie M. Crosby	26			Single		Machias, Me.	Jeremiah & Susan	Typhus Fever
Oct. 17	**Ruth A. Clark	76			Widow		Augusta, Me.	Job & Althea Springer	Fever
Oct. 26	††Ellen Conghlin	17			Single		Ireland	John & Catherine	Heart Disease
Dec. 1	‡‡Mary G. Darling	61	7	18	Married		Cumberland, R. I.	3	Hernia
Dec. 12	Mary Alice Robinson	1			Female		Franklin	Robert & Eunice	
Feb. 26	§§Hannah Kingsbury	81			Widow		Sterling	Wife of Asa	Old Age
July 26	‖‖Betsey Gay	80	11	14	"		Dedham	—— Savels	Cancer

* Interment Franklin City; Informant Saul B. Scott. † Interment Medway. ‡ Interment Dorchester. § Interment West Medway; informant Simon Whiting. ‖ Interment Blackstone. ¶ Orland, Me. ** Wrentham. †† Milford. ‡‡ Wrentham; informant Elias Blake. §§ Died in Medway; informant Franklin City; informant S. B. Scott. ‖‖ Died in Walpole. 1 Age 45 minutes. 2 Joseph Lawrence & Abial Ware. 3 Ebenr T & Rach d Crowningshield.

Deaths Registered in Franklin, Norfolk County, during the Year 1861.—T. C. HILLS, Registrar.
Interment in Franklin unless otherwise indicated.

DATE OF DEATH.	NAME OF DECEASED.	AGE. Y|M|D	SEX AND CONDITION	OCCUPATION.	PLACE OF BIRTH.	NAME OF PARENTS OR HUSBAND.	CAUSE OF DEATH.
1861							1
Jan. 30	*Calvin Peck	81 3 14	Widower	Carpenter	Royalston	a Daniel & Relief	Lung Fever
Feb. 1	Sabra M. Bullard	63	Single	House Work	Bellingham	b Elisha & Rachael	Pleuritis 5 days
Feb. 5	Sukey M. Bullard **	68 4 11	Married	"	Franklin	c Levi & Catherine Morse	Strangulation
Feb. 14	Archibald Robinson	1	Male			d Geo. H. & Jane	2
April 14	†Frederick B. Williams	3 1 14			Hopkinton	e Chas. H. & Mary J.	Consumption
April 14	‡Sarah A. Pillsbury	35 4 11	Widow		Piermont, N. H.	f Richard & Mary Underhill	Cancer & Dropsy
May 16	Samuel Ware	77	Married	Farmer	Wrentham	g Sam'l & Mahitable	Disease of Brain
May 16	Gracie Mary Emerson	1 1 7	Female		Franklin	h Ellis P. & Mary S.	Dropsy
May 28	Eunice M. Hardy	44 7 5	Married	House Work	Wrentham	i David D. & Abigail Tyler	Anaemia
June 21	Julia B. Springer	21		Straw Sewer	Springfield, Me.	j Elias & Julia Breck	Dropsy
July 8	Sally Bird	63 9 21	Single	Tailoress	Stoughton	k Sam'l & Sarah	Kick of Horse
July 29	§Horatio Nelson	54		Farmer	Castine, Me.	l Thoms. & Jane	Diorrhœa
Aug. 30	Clarrisa Ann Whiting	1 1 16	Female		Franklin	m Joseph M. & Clarissa A.	3
Sept. 15	Emory Davis Thayer	5	Male		Ashland	n Wm. M. & Rebecca	Hemorrhage of Navel
Sept. 23	Janette Stewart		9	Female		Franklin	o Robert & Martha	Phthisis
Sept. 29	Clarissa Newell	51	Widow	House Work	Cumberland, R.I.	p Harvey & Huldah Scott	Typhoid Fever
Oct. 3	‖Charles A. Pierce	14 3 20	Male		Augusta, Me.	q Jefferson & Ruth E.	Hypertuphy of Heart
Oct. 11	David Baker	79	Married	Farmer	Franklin	r Abigail & Esther	Scrofula
Oct. 23	Francis F. Fisher	34 9 23	Single		Medway	s Frederic & Sarah	Pluro Pneumonia
Nov. 10	Achsah Fisher	73	Married		Franklin	t Hanan & Mary Metcalf	Deliram Tremens
Nov. 21	Cephas Bullard	71 5 18	Widower		Bellingham	u Elisha & Rachael	Fever on Brain
Nov. 27	Elizabeth Davidson	1 1 14	Female		Franklin	v Wm. & Elizabeth	Typhoid Fever
Dec. 5	Almira M. Gay	25 11 3	Single	Straw Sewer	Easton	w Timothy & Julia	Consumption
Dec. 10	Achsah Billings	63	Widow		Bridgewater	x Nath'l & Phebe Thayer	Ossification of Arteries
Dec. 11	¶Willard Gay	83 4 8	Widower	Turner	Franklin	y Daniel & Hannah	4
Dec. 12	John Warfield	69		Farmer	Medway	z Timothy	Disease of Brain
March 20	—— Robinson	80 6 22	Male		Franklin	fi Abijah & Car.	Stillborn
June 20	—— Lincoln					fl John K. & Mary E.	"
						ff Wm. R. & Deborah	

*Interment Orange. †Hopkinton. ‡Piermont, N. H. §Castine, Me. ‖Wrentham. ¶W. Wrentham. 1 Pulmonary Congestion 4 days. 2 Inflamation of Throat, Retension Urine 3 days. 3 Typhoid Fever. Ulceration of Bowels. 4 Pulmonary Congestion. a Born in Rehoboth, b Bellingham, Wrentham, c Franklin, Wrentham, d Ireland, e Southboro, Hopkinton, f Piermont, N. H., g Wrentham, h Dedham, Attleboro, i Walpole, Wrentham, j Medfield, Augusta, Mo., k Stoughton, l Castine, Me., m Franklin, Norton, n Franklin, Dover, o Nova Scotia, p Cumberland, R. I., q Augusta, Me., r Franklin, Dublin, N. H., t Franklin, u Bellingham, Franklin, v Scotland, England, w Franklin, Walpole, x Easton, Taunton, y Bridgewater, z Franklin, fi Ireland, Middleboro, fl Franklin, Rome, Me. **M. M. Morse.

Deaths Registered in Franklin, Norfolk County, during the Year 1861.—(Continued.)

DATE OF DEATH.	NAME OF DECEASED.	AGE. Y/M/D	SEX AND CONDITION.	OCCUPATION.	PLACE OF BIRTH.	NAME OF PARENTS OR HUSBAND.	CAUSE OF DEATH.
1861							
March 4	*Mira Ursula Hart	3 6 11	Female		W. Medway	a Chas. E. & Julia A.	Canker Rash
March 6	*Susan M. Hart	10 10 23	"		Franklin	b Chas. E. & Julia A.	"
March 18	*Mary G. Morgan	16 6 1	Married		"	c Chas. E.& Julia A. Hart	"
April 14	†Anna Judson Bennet	9 24	Female		Foxboro	d Levi & Nancy	Lung Fever
July 21	‖Henry Hartshorn	16	Single	Clerk	Franklin	e Gilbert & Ellen	Drowning

Deaths Registered in Franklin, in the County of Norfolk, during the Year 1862.

Place of interment Franklin unless otherwise indicated.   Informant Jason Fisher unless otherwise indicated.

DATE OF DEATH.	NAME OF DECEASED.	AGE. Y/M/D	SEX AND CONDITION.	OCCUPATION.	PLACE OF BIRTH.	NAME OF PARENTS OR HUSBAND.	CAUSE OF DEATH.
1862							
Jan. 17	Lewis C. Brown	75	Male & M.	B. at Builder	Cumberland, R.I.	Elijah & Anna	Liver & Stomach
Feb. 3	§Elizabeth A. Ware	11 9 11	F. majored		Franklin	B. B. & Sally	Small Pox
Feb. 4	⁋Lucy M. Metcalf	58	Married	Dress Maker	"	Nahum & Lucy Daniels	Premature Child Birth
Feb. 15	§Sally Ware	41 1	"		Easton	Jonathan & Phebe Drake	Small Pox
March 3	Olive Whiting	73	"		Franklin	Jason & Olive Morse	Dropsy
March 25	Anna Whiting	80	Widow		Smithfield, R. I.	Daniel & Eunice Sayles	⁊
April 11	Jeremiah Claflin	73 2	Married	Carpenter	Hopkinton	Eli & Louis	Typhoid Fever
April 11	*Elmer L. Rockwood	8 3 27	Single		Franklin	Erastus & Louisa	Consumption
April 23	Theron C. Hills	53	Widower	Merchant	"	Joseph & Deborah	Phthisis
April 24	Abigail Hunt	45	Married		"	Willisk Caroline Fisher	Old Age
April 28	Nancy Gilmor	85	Widow		"	Joseph & Susan Fisher	Fever
June 16	Israel Pierre	67	Married	Carpenter	"	John & Mary	Consumption
June 17	Susan Lawrence	80 7 6	Single	Spinster	"	Amos & ——	Kidney Complaint
June 20	1 Harvey Hills	60	"	Don't Presser	"	Jason & Polly	Teething
June 26	2 Mary Ann Whitaker	4 20	Single		Wrentham	Lewis R. & Isabella	Consumption
June 28	3 Abigail Cheever	85	Married		Norton	Moses& Purley Grant	Smith Fever
June 30	Charlotte Fisher	68	"		Franklin	6 Alshaek Philema	8
July 3	Samuel R. Marsh	5 2	Single		"	Lewis H. & Sophia	Cancer
Feb. 24	4 Fanny C. Staples	53 3 8	Married	House Work	Cumberland, R.I.	Enos & Mercy Jilson	Lightning
July 31	4 Phillip T. Miller	47 11	"	Farmer	Franklin	Philip W. & Relief	

*Died in Medway. †Foxboro. ‡Webster, §Bellingham, ⁋Providence, R. I. *Removed to, interred in Natick, Nov. 28, 1865. 1 Died in Keene, N. H., 2 Wrentham. 3 Interment Wrentham.   4 Died in Franklin City, Interment Franklin City, Informant Saul B. Scott.   5 Interment Franklin City, Informant Saul B. Scott. 6 May 1879 removed to Haverhill.   7 Congestion of Brain, Paralysis.   8 Drowned by supposed violence, assault, bruises.   a Born in Portsmouth, N. H. Franklin, b Portsmouth, N. H., Franklin, c Portsmouth, N. H., Franklin, d Northbridge, Franklin, e Franklin.

Deaths Registered in Franklin, in the County of Norfolk, during the Year 1862.—(Continued.)

Place of interment Franklin unless otherwise indicated.

DATE OF DEATH.	NAME OF DECEASED.	AGE. Y|M|D	S|x	C|o|n	OCCUPATION.	PLACE OF BIRTH.	NAME OF PARENTS OR HUSBAND.	CAUSE OF DEATH.	INFORMANT.
1862									
Aug. 6	Caleb Fisher	93 9 26	M	Wr.	Farmer	Franklin	Hezekiah & Abigail	Old Age	Jason Fisher
Aug. 17	*Otis Corbin	74 5 25	M	Mr.	Stone Mason	Dudley, Mass.	Joshua & Rosa	Heart Disease	Nelson Corbin
Aug. 25	†Frederic N. Atwood	23 3 28	M	S.	Farmer	Middleboro	Jacob & Joanna	Typhoid Fever	7
Sept. 8	Abby Ware	73	F	Wr.		Bridgewater		Disease of Heart	Jason Fisher
Oct. 2	‡Lewis L. Miller	22 1 15	M	S.	Soldier	Franklin	John W. & Emily M.	6	Saul B. Scott
Oct. 6	Emma Lucinda Thayer	3	F			"	Wm. M. & Rebecca	Cholera Infantum	Jason Fisher
Oct. 9	§Herbert L. Lincoln	22	M	S.	Soldier		Manly & Fidelia	Wounded in Battle	"
Nov. 7	Ruth M. Atwood	59 9 14	F	M	House Keeper	Bridgewater	Cyrus & Ruth Snow	Disease of Stomach	"
Nov. 11	‖Bridgett Hutchinson	47 2	F	M	"	Ireland	John & Mary McClusky	Dropsey	8
Dec. 15	¶Willard C. Lawrence	38 7	M	M	Boot Maker	Milford, Ms.	Cephas & Betsy	Diabatis	9
Dec. 17	**Mary Dohority	40	F		House Keeper	Ireland	Michael & Margarete Hart		
May 16, 1854	††Joseph Laurene Larkin	10 12	M			Franklin	John & Mary A.	Spasms, Worms	Saul B. Scott
July 27, 1860	Walter Scott Stockbridge	11 5 15	M				Horatio, Jr., & DataAnn		John Larkin

Deaths Registered in Franklin, in the County of Norfolk, in the Year 1863.

DATE OF DEATH.	NAME OF DECEASED.	AGE. Y|M|D	S|x	C|o|n	OCCUPATION.	PLACE OF BIRTH.	NAME OF PARENTS OR HUSBAND.	CAUSE OF DEATH.	INFORMANT.
Sept. 9, 1862	‡‡Nancy G. Guild	48 2 26	F	Mr.	House Wife	Wrentham	Philip & Nancy Hancock	Consumption	10
Jan. 22, 1863	‡‡Frank A. Wilkinson	5 3 1	M			Franklin	Willard B. & Fannie S.	Diptheria	Wm. A. Grant
Jan. 23, 1863	Albert Warren Hills	14 4 19	M			Dover, N. H.	Joseph G. & Ellen		Jason Fisher
Feb. 3, 1863	Ichabud Dean	79	M	Mr.	Farmer	Franklin	Ichabod & Chloe	Paralytic	"
Feb. 10, 1863	Amelia T. H. Daniels	65 10 20	F	"	House Wife	Dedham		Consumption	"
Mar. 6, 1863	§§Otis Winn	46 10 21	M	"	Soldier	2	Peter & Laurena		S. B. Scott
Mar. 27, 1863	Mary Rockwood	11 17	F	S.		Franklin	Erastus & Louisa	Convulsion Fits	Jason Fisher
April 8, 1863	‖‖Margarett Hanlihan	38	F	Mr.	House Wife	Ireland	John & Mary McCarty	Child Birth	12
April 10, 1863	Hugh Gilliland	64	M	Wr.	Farmer	"	John & Sarah		Gilmore Miller
April 17, 1863	Alonzo M. Guild	1 21	M	S.	Soldier	3	Herman & Malinda J.		Saul B. Scott
April 20, 1863	Polly Pond	78 10	F	W.		Franklin	Moses & Lydia Morse	Old Age	Jason Fisher
May 1, 1863	Lysander B. Hills	67	M	Wr.		"	Joseph & Deborah	Disease of Lungs	Geo. W. Nason

* Interment Wrentham. †Middleborough. ‡Died in Georgetown, D. C., §Halttmore, Md. ‖Interment Forest Hills, Roxbury, Mass., ¶Milford, Mass., **Providence, R. I., ††Woonsocket. ‡‡Wrentham. §§Died in Alexandria, Va. ‖‖Interment Worcester. 1 Died in Central Falls, R. I.: interment Franklin City. 2 Birthplace Watertown, N. Y., 3 Smithfield, R. I. 4 Giles Leach & Mehitable Wilber. 5 Hezekiah & Elizabeth Turner. 6 Ball wound in thigh, Aug. 30, '62, at Bull Run. 7 Shadrack Atwood. 8 Thomas Hutchinson. 9 Cephas Lawrence. 10 Washington Pierce. 11 Removed to Natick, Nov. 25, '65. 12 John L. Fitzpatrick. *, **M male Mr. married, S single, W widow, Wr. widower.

Deaths Registered in Franklin, in the County of Norfolk, during the Year 1863.—(Continued.)

Place of interment Franklin unless otherwise indicated. Informant Henry Bemis unless otherwise indicated.

DATE OF DEATH.	NAME OF DECEASED.	AGE. Y|M|D	SEX AND CONDITION	OCCUPATION.	PLACE OF BIRTH.	NAME OF PARENTS OR HUSBAND.	CAUSE OF DEATH.
1863							
May 4	*Emma E. Judkins	22 3 15	Female	Teacher	Bingham	Stephen & Sarah	Congestive Fever
May 11	†Catherine Sulivan	4 1 12	"		Franklin	Wm. & Bridgett	Burned
May 12	‡Sylvia D. Fisher	58 1 6	Married	Housewife	Medon	Peleg & Lovice Wood	a
May 12	§Sally Hawes	91	Widow		Franklin	John & Naome Adams	Old Age
June 4	‖Betsey Clark	78 9 6	"		Foxboro	Preston & Betsey Jones	Eresipalis
June 4	¶Hattie E. Morse	4	Female		Franklin	Aaron H. & Deborah	Inflamation of Bowels
June 16	*Margaret O. Riley	1 5	"		"	James & Mary	Erysipelas
June 25	Benjamin Frost	53 2 25	Married	Boat Builder	So. Boston	Peter & Eliza	b
June 29	Nath'l G. Johnson	33	"	Boot Maker	Holliston	Nathaniel & Eunice	Phthisis
July 2	Josephine Knapp	2	Female		Franklin	Gilbert C. & Lucinda	Scarlet Fever
July 5	1 Ariel Cheever	90	11 Widower		Wrentham	Daniel & Abigail	Bronchitis
July 10	Jason Fisher	76	Married	Blacksmith	Franklin	Jason & Mary	Dropsey
Aug. 4	Nelly F. Lesley	4	Female	Farmer	Worcester		Cholera Infantum
Aug. 7	Sarah Ware	91	Widow		Bellingham	Mary	Old Age
Aug. 8, 1862	2 Herbert A. Frost	2 6 22	Male		Acton	Elisha & Lucretia Burr	Cholera Infantum
Aug. 11	Betsey Thayer	81 1 11	Widow		Norton	Geo. H. & Susan M.	Old Age
Aug. 19	Lois Adams	89 1 27	"		Franklin	Wm.& Ruth Makepeace	Chronic Diahrea
Sept. 12	3 Lucy Ann Scott	49 6 25	Married		Holliston	Billy & Sarah Ware	
Sept. 17	Frank J. Wadsworth	2 5	Male		Franklin	Levi & Lydia Mann	Congestion of Brain
Sept. 21	William H. Roblee	24 10 7	Married		Unknown	Joseph H. & Abbie L.	Consumption
Oct. 23	Jarvis H. Hills	65	"	Merchant	Franklin	John & Catherine	c
Oct. 30	Estella E. Roblee	8 15	Female			Joseph & Deborah	Serofula & L Complaint
Nov. 7	3 Lewis Hartshorn	71 6 27	Married	Farmer	Foxboro	Wm. H. & Aurelia E.	Typhoid Fever
Nov. 9	4 Fidelia E. Pond	1 8	Female		Providence	Silas & Betsey	
Dec. 15	Nellie E. Fisher	6 5 21	"		Franklin	Edwin J. & Emily V.	Congestive Scarlatina
Dec. 15	Ruth Hall	61 10 27	"	Housewife	Wrentham	Marsha'l W. & Ellen F.	
Oct. 14	5 Willie C. Metcalf	3 18	Male		Ashland	John & Lavina Alexander	Brain Fever
Nov. 5	6 Catherine Keef	1 3 9 5	Female		Wrentham	John C. & Sarah A.	Burned
Dec. 5	7 Lydia Hartshorn	63	"	Housewife	Middleboro	William & Mary	Old Age
Dec. 29	8 Davis Thayer	86	18 Male	Merchant	Mendon	Nathan'l & Susan	Age & Paralysis

*Interment West Waterville, Me., Informant Geo. W. Nason. †Interment Woonsocket, Informant Parent. ‡Died in Natick, Interment Franklin City, Informant Saul B. Scott. §Informant Geo. W. Nason. ‖Died in Foxboro, Informant Franklin City, Informant Saul B. Scott. ¶Interment Woonsocket, R. I., Informant James O. Riley. 1 Interment Wrentham. 2 Died in Acton. 3 Interment Franklin City, Informant S. B. Scott. 4 Died in Providence. 5 Died in Ashland. 6 Interment Woonsocket, Informant D. P. Whiting. 7 Died in Foxboro. 8 Informant Wm. M. Thayer. a Inflamation of liver and veins and dropsy of hart and kidneys. b Accidental wound of abdomen, perforation of intestines. c Rheumatic gout, chronic dysentary.

FRANKLIN TOWN RECORDS—DEATHS.

Deaths Registered in Frank
Place of interment Franklin unless otherwise

DATE OF DEATH.	NAME OF DECEASED.	AGE. Y|M|D	SEX AND CONDITION.	NAME OF PARENTS OR HUSBAND.
1864				
Jan. 3	*George W. Dean	38 5 6	Married M	Icabod & Hannah
Jan. 4	†Triphena Morse	62 4 29	Married F	m
Jan. 7	Loami Gay	19 5 19	Single F	Walter H. & Sally A.
Jan. 11	‡Amanda Newell	56 11 1	Married F	Ebenezer & Hannah Arnold
Jan. 11	§Ellen Brown Davis	12 8	Single F	John A. & Martha B.
	Albert Erastus Rockwood			
Jan. 27	‖Aldis Mc. Allen (Error	2 2 27	Male	Cyrus M. & Sarah M.
Jan. 31	¶Earnest Paine	3 2	Male	Stephen. Jr., & Sarah C.
Feb. 16	**Olney Scott	68 9 26	Married M	Chas. & Amy
Feb. 17	Austin M. Baker	4 8 25	Male	Erastus E. & Abby
Mar. 1	Sarah I. Treene	29 4 20	Married F	Alfred & Sarah L. Jordan
Mar. 1	††James Murphy	7	Male	Patrick & Ann
Mar. 4	Mary L. Richardson	28	Married F	
Mar. 7	‡‡Erastus Rockwood	50	Married M	Asa & Julia
Mar. 8	§§James Shepardson	74 7 13	Widower M	Isaac & Lucy
Mar. 24	Everett Marsh Green	1 9 18	Male	Henry M.& Margarett M.
April 3	‖‖Lucy Bullard	67 2 7	Married F	Jason & Marion Morse
April 15	1 Sarah C. Adams	31 6 20	Married F	Spencer & Eliza Tolman
April 26	Emeline Cook	27	Married F	Jason W. & Lucena White
April 26	2 Merede Drake	61 11 18	Widow F	Nathaniel & Phebe Thayer
April 29	3 Wm. Henry Adams	22	Male	Lyman & Sarah E.
May 9	4 Fred Mellen Benson	1 6	Male	Stephen S.& Elizabeth R.
May 17	Nelly A. Hall	3 10 4	Female	T. H. & Lucinda S.
May 27	Willie Alpheus Russegue	5 8 12	Male	Alpheus A. & Mary
June 14	Julia G. E. Springer	3 26	Female	William A. & Julia
June 17	Frank E. Hill	2 7	Male	William & Susan E.
June 19	5 Lydia P. Ray	77 11	Widow F	James & Lydia Paine
June 28	Ruth Borden	86	Widow F	Parker & Lucy
June 30	6 Thomas W. Mann	69	Married M	Moses & Allice
Aug. 6	7 Mary E. Crowell	1 18	Female	Chas. & Lydia F.
Aug. 11	8 James Hagerty	9 1	Male	Patrick & Mary
Aug. 13	Maggie Marsh Green	26 6 29	Married F	Zachariah & Agnes E. Webster
Aug. 29	Phila B. Hills	67 10 6	Widow F	John & Annie Brown
Aug. 29	9 Mary Loeza Richardson	11 14	Female	A. D. & Mary Loeza
Aug. 30	a Edith A. Darling	1 25	Female	Byron M. & Anna M.
Sept. 6	b Geo. W. Scott	43 11	Widower M	Lemuel & Ruth
Sept. 10	Hellen J. Metcalf	9 8 15	Female	Richardson & Hariet N.
Sept. 16	c Dennis Sulivan	6 3 26		Dennis & Margarett
Sept. 29	Rena F. Bullard	71	Married F	Levi & ———Fisher
Oct. 1	d Luther Gowen	82	Married M	John Gowen
Oct. 31	Ada E. Dean	2 8 30	Female	Geo. W. & Ellen E.
Nov. 20	e John Caulfield	63	Widower M	
Nov. 23	f Ann Carr	49 5	Married F	Ganet & Elizabeth Farrol
Nov. 30	f Mary Jane Gunning	16 10 21	Single F	Alfred & Mary
Dec. 10	Nancy Wadsworth	72 5 6	Single F	Joseph & Mary
Dec. 11	Emeline L. Wales	2 11 20	Female	William S. & Julia A.
Dec. 19	g Elmer E. Wales	3 9 10	Male	John D. & Adelaid
Dec. 27	h Amos Bullard	86 3 10	Widower M	Asa & Hannah
Dec. 31	i George Granger	9 4	Male	Edward & Catherine
Oct. 7	———Hood	1	Female	James & Annett
May 5	j Charles H. Wilson	18 8 19	Single M	Silas H. & Jenette
Sept. 19	k John M. Fisher	21 7 7	Single M	Weston & Margarett
Sept. 19	l Charles R. Adams	21 2 9	Single M	Peter & Clarissa

*Machinist. †Interment Franklin City, ‡Cumberland, §Haveril, N. H. ‖Died in Malden. ¶§Farmer, interment Franklin City. ‖‖Interment Franklin City, 1 Wrentham, 2 Stoughton, 3 Wren interment Franklin City, 8 Woonsocket, R. I., 9 Franklin City. a Died in Franklin City, interment socket, R. I. d Farmer. e Laborer, interment Woonsocket. f Died in Franklin City, interment Milford. Virginia, interment Battlefield, Virginia. k Died near Winchester, Va., interment battlefield. inflammation of the Stomach. o Wounded in the Battle of the Wilderness. p Wounded in the

FRANKLIN TOWN RECORDS—DEATHS.

lin for the Year 1864.
indicated. Occupation indicated in foot notes.

PLACE of BIRTH	CAUSE OF DEATH	INFORMANT	Birthplace of Parents.	
			FATHER.	MOTHER.
Franklin	Consumption	Henry Bemis	Franklin	Franklin
"	Cancer of Stomach	S. B. Scott	Attleboro	"
"	QuickConsumption	Henry Bemis	Franklin	Cumberland
Cumberland, R. I.	Hepatic	"	Cumberland	"
Piermont, N. H.	Typhoid Fever	"	Piermont, N.H.	Haveril. N. H.
Franklin	Hooping Cough	Henry Bemis	Franklin	Southboro
"	QuickConsumption	"	Burrillville, R. I.	Woonsocket
Cumberland	Mortification	Huldah Scott	Cumberland	
Franklin	Typhoid Fever	Henry Bemis	Franklin	Franklin
Wrentham	Phthisis	"	Coventry, R. I.	Barnstable
Franklin	Debility	"	Ireland	Ireland
	Congestion of Brain			
Franklin	Paralysis	Henry Bemis	Franklin	Franklin
Wrentham	Pneumonia	S. B. Scott	Cumberland	Attleboro
Franklin	Measles	Henry Bemis	Franklin	Plainfield, N.J.
"	Billious Fever	Saul B. Scott	"	Walpole
Foxboro	Child Birth	r	Foxboro	Chester, Vt.
Wrentham		Henry Bemis	Attleboro	Wrentham
Easton	Dropsey	[bury	Easton	Taunton
Franklin	Fits	Horatio Kings-	Bellingham	Foxboro
Millville	Inflammation of Brain	Saul B. Scott	Mendon	Medway
Medway	Croup	"	Dixfield, Me.	Needham
Franklin	Diptheria	A. A. Russegue	Benson, Vt.	Whiting, Vt.
"	Typhoid Fever	Henry Bemis	Augusta, Me.	Springfield, Me
Franklin	Lung Fever	"	Franklin	Foxboro
Smithfield, R. I.	Congestion of Lungs	"	Smithfield, R.I.	Smithfield, R.I.
Fall River	Old Age	"	Fall River	Fall River
Smithfield, R. I.	Dropsey	"	Smithfield	Smithfield
Medway, Mass.	Dysentary	Saul B. Scott	Islip, L. I.	S.Hampton, N. Y.
Franklin	"	Henry Bemis	Ireland	Ireland
Plainfield, N. J.	Consumption	"	Plainfield, N.J.	Rahway, N. J.
Upton	Dysentary	"	Newport, R. I.	Upton
Franklin	Cholera Infantum	Saul B. Scott	Franklin	Manchester, Ct.
Millville	" "	"	Millville	Attleboro
Bellingham	Pneumonia	"	Bellingham	Franklin
Franklin		Henry Bemis	Franklin	Providence
"	Dysentary	"	Ireland	Ireland
"	Old Age	"	Franklin	
"		"	Unknown	
"	Hydrocephelus	"	Franklin	Franklin
Ireland	n	Saul B. Scott		
"	Fits	"	Ireland	Ireland
Holliston	Consumption		"	"
Milton		J. H. Wadsworth	Milton	Dedham
Franklin	Canker Rash	Henry Bemis	Franklin	Pelham
"	Burning	"	"	Franklin
Holliston	Fever and Old Age	Saul B. Scott	Holliston	Mendon
Franklin	Canker Rash	Henry Bemis	Ireland	Ireland
"		"	Nova Scotia	Canton
Wrentham	o			
Franklin	p			
	q		Both in Franklin	

¶ Interment Cumberland. **Farmer, interment Cumberland. ††Interment Milford. ‡‡Merchant, tham, 4 Blackstone, 5 Smithfield, R. I. 6 Blacksmith, interment Smithfield, R. I. 7 Died in Franklin West Medway. b Died in Franklin City, Laborer, interment Franklin City. c Interment Woong Died in Pawtucket, R. I. h Shoe Maker, interment Franklin City, i Woonsocket, R. I. j Died in l Died near Winchester, Va., interment battlefield. m Benjamin & Hannah M. M. Foster. n Chronic Battle of Berryville. q Wounded in the Battle of Berryville. r Horatio Kingsbury.

FRANKLIN TOWN RECORDS—DEATHS.

Deaths Registered in Franklin,

Place of interment Franklin unless otherwise

DATE OF DEATH.	NAME OF DECEASED.	AGE. Y|M|D	SEX AND CONDITION.	NAME OF PARENTS OR HUSBAND.
1865				
Jan. 9	*James Coffield	1 7	Male	Daniel & Bridget
Jan. 17	†Thomas Sullivan	23 2	Single M	Cornelius & Mary
Jan. 23	‡Joseph J. Clark	60	Male M	Simeon & Betey J.
March 10	Carrie B. Watkins	9	Female	J. P. & Adelia A.
March 12	Olive Thayer	67 2 19	Widow F	David & Olive Whiting
March 16	Betey M. Dean	49 4 8	Single F	Ichabod & Betey
March 19	Sarah J. Clark	22 7 14	Single F	Chas. A. & Maria
March 30	Mary G. Adams	44 26	Married F	Frank K. & M. G. Powell
April 21	§Clarance B. Joslin	2 2 2	Male	John & Elizabeth
May 6	‖Willard Pond	72 4	Single M	Robert & Olive
May 20	Evelyn E. Metcalf	18 8 4	Single F	Alfred G. & Charlotte A.
June 15	Julia A. Bacon	33 9 25	Married F	Paschal P.&Elnora A.Brooks
July 21	Carrie B. Adams	20 2 28	Single F	Peter & C. D.
July 29	Mary Tobin	19 7 8	Single F	Robert & Mary
Aug. 11	¶Nathan Clark	23 2 5	Single M	Alfred & Polly W.
Aug. 13	Lizzie Ruth Conant	5 5	Female	Joseph P. & Ruth A.
Aug. 18	1 Hiram Knapp	78 4	Widower M	Moses & Margarett
Aug. 30	2 Maxey Fisher	80 18	Married M	Joseph & Susan
Sept. 1	3 Eva Alice Young	10	Female	William & Emely A.
Sept. 3	4 Elmer B. Daniels	1 8	Male	Amos F. & Lucrecea
Sept. 5	Hariet W. Thayer	31 3 22	Married F	Jeremiah &-- Richards
Sept. 29	Maria Cook	72	Married F	Abraham & Mary Cummings
Sept. 29	5 Edith M. Jordon	19 4 2	Single F	Geo. A. & Sarah L.
Sept. 30	6 David King	65 2 26	Single M	John & Margarett
Oct. 2	Lewis E. Wales	1 5 18	Male	Wm. & Julia
Oct. 6	7 James Gilmore	88 5 18	Married M	David & Joannie
Oct. 8	George King, Jr.	9 8	Male	George & Lucy A.
Oct. 11	Margarett Doherity	32	Single F	Philip & Sally
Oct. 24	8Nancy H. Hartshorn	57 3	Widow F	Ebenezer & Sarah Hawes
Oct. 27	9 Ward Adams	66 11 4	Married M	Nehemah & Mary
Oct. 31	Sarah A. Woodman	36 6	Married F	James & Sally Kenneson
Nov. 1	Julian B. Bacon	8	Female	George & Julia
Nov. 4	a Thomas Prior	74	Married M	David & Mary
Nov. 24	b Piam Bullard	77 6 4	Married M	Elisha & Rachael
Dec. 12	c Wm. D. Gilmore	35	Married M	Robert & Rebecca
Dec. 16	Julia M. Farrington	72	Married F	John & Polly Merrifield
Jan. 12	d Michael Prior	9	Male	Thomas & Catherine
Jan. 20	d Catherine Prior	6	Female	Thomas & Catherine
Jan. 23	e Joseph J. Clark	60	Married M	Simeon & Betey J.
Jan. 23	Deborah Hills	90 9	Widow	Solomon & Sibel Blake
Jan. 28	f Eddie Woodman	3 6	Male	Wm. & Sarah
Jan. 30	—— Jordon	24	Male	Albert L. & Oliranda
Feb. 4	Robert R. Hills	27 8 24	Male	Joseph & Mary
Feb. 12	g Chas. H. Bemis	36 2 7	Widower M	Henry & Nancy
Feb. 12	William A. Mann	7 4	Male	William & Sarah B.
Feb. 13	Hattie A. Darling	2 9 15	Female	Mayo C. & Lucy A.
Feb. 19	Mary Ann DeWitt	63 9 19	Widow F	Andrew & Mary Dunn
Feb. 20	Frank W. Daniels	1 10 22		J. W. & Hariet E.
Feb. 21	h Martha A. Thayer	31 9 16	Married F	Welcome B. & Ella Darling
March 10	Carrie B. Watkins	9 8		John P. & Delia A.
March 10	—— Daniels	2		Maney M. & Hariet N.
March 12	Olive Thayer	67 2 19	Widow F	David & Olive A. Whiting
March 18	Elma E. Crosby	3 7	Male	Reuben & Mary F.

*Interment Woonsocket. †Died in Franklin City, soldier, Interment Milford ‡Died in Foxboro, ¶Died in Warren, R. I., Soldier. 1 Farmer. 2 Farmer. 3 Interment Foxboro. 4 Died in Wrentham, 7 Farmer. 8 Interment Franklin City. 9 Died in Worcester, Farmer. a Laborer. b Farmer, Interment City. f Interment Natick. g Carriage Maker. h Interment Bellingham. ** See Return. †† Wash-

… FRANKLIN TOWN RECORDS---DEATHS. 187

Norfolk Co., during the Year 1865.

indicated. Occupation indicated in foot notes.

PLACE OF BIRTH	CAUSE OF DEATH.	INFORMANT.	Birthplace of Parents.	
			FATHER.	MOTHER.
Woonsocket, R. I.	Inflamation of Stomach	Saul B. Scott	Ireland	Ireland
Ireland	Consumption	"	"	"
Franklin	"	"	Franklin	Brimfield
"	Congestion of Brain	Henry Bemis	Hopkinton	Attleboro
Douglass	Erysipelas	"	Douglass	"
Franklin	Scrofula	"	Franklin	Franklin
"	Haemoptysis	"	"	Gloucester
Dunbarton, Vt.	Cancer in Stomach	"	Graftsburg, Vt.	Dunbarton, N. H.
Bellingham	Diphtheritis	Saul B. Scott	Cumberland	Scotland
Franklin	Unknown	"	Franklin	Franklin
"	**Pelvic Abrox	Henry Bemis	"	"
Henniker, N. H.	Consumption	"	Henniker, N. H	Alsted, N. H.
Franklin	Dropsey	"	Franklin	Franklin
Brooklyn, N. Y.	Typhoid Fever	"	Ireland	Ireland
Franklin	Gun Shot & Fever	"	Franklin	Bellingham
Wrentham	Congestion of Brain	"	Ipswich	Rowley
Franklin	Consumption	"	Franklin	Franklin
"	Paralysis	"	"	"
"	Dysentary	William Young	England	England
"	"	Saul B. Scott	Franklin	Berkley
Winslow, Me.	Consumption	Henry Bemis		
Ashbraham	"	"	Attleboro	Attleboro
Franklin	Phthisis Pulmonalis	Saul B. Scott	Coventry, R. I.	Utica, N. Y.
Scotland	Induration of Liver	"	Scotland	Scotland
Franklin	Dysentary	Henry Bemis	Franklin	Pelham, Me.
"	Old Age	"	"	Pelham
"	Disease of Bowels	"	Rochester	Middleboro
Ireland	Consumption	"	Ireland	Ireland
Wrentham	Melaena	Saul B. Scott	Wrentham	
Franklin	Diarhea			
Conway, N. H.	Typhoid Fever	Henry Bemis		Abington
Franklin	Consumption	"	Franklin	Kenica
Ireland	Consumption	"	Ireland	Ireland
Bellingham	Scherous of Pylores	Saul B. Scott	Bellingham	Franklin
Franklin	Consumption	Henry Bemis	Franklin	"
Holliston	"	"	Holliston	"
Ireland	Scarlet Fever		Ireland	Ireland
"	"		"	"
Franklin	Consumption	S. B. Scott	Franklin	Brimfield
"	Old Age	Henry Bemis	" (Me.	Franklin
"	Canker Rash	"	Kennebunkport,	Conway, N. H.
"		"	Franklin	Newport, R. I.
Sharpsburg, Md.	Consumption	"	St. Mary, Md.	††
Franklin	"	"	Weston	Sudbury
"	Canker Rash	"	Chesterfield, N.H.	Winthrop
"	"	"	Bellingham	Franklin
Shirly			Shirly, Mass.	Groton
Franklin	Congestion of Lung		Franklin	Franklin
"	Consumption		Bellingham	Bellingham
"	Congestion of Brain		Hopkinton	Attleboro
"			Blackstone	Franklin
Douglass	Erysipelas		Douglass	Attleboro
Franklin			Simsbury, Ct.	Franklin

Physician, Interment Franklin City. §Died in Franklin City, Interment Franklin City. ‖Farmer Interment Franklin City. 5 Died in Wrentham, Interment Franklin City. 6 Interment Franklin City. ment Franklin City. c Laborer. d Interment Roxbury. e Died in Foxboro, Interment Franklin ington Co., Md.

188 FRANKLIN TOWN RECORDS—DEATHS.

Deaths Registered in Franklin, Norfolk

Place of interment Franklin unless otherwise

DATE OF DEATH.	NAME OF DECEASED.	AGE. Y/M/D	SEX AND CONDITION	NAME OF PARENTS OR HUSBAND.
1865				
April 28	*Hattie E. Stanley	29 10	Married F	Eliasar & Marietta Harris
June 30	†Mary Underhill	78 8 10	Widow F	Wm. & Lydia Tarbox
Dec. 11	Mary Blanchard Fisher	8 9	Female	Sewell & Annie B.

Deaths Registered in Franklin,

1866				
Jan. 1	‡Willis Fisher	82 5 10	Married M	Joseph & Susanna
Jan. 7	§Richard Roche	34	Married M	Thomas & Elizabeth
Jan. 13	‖Avilda Sayles	78	Single F	Daniel & Eunice
Jan. 14	¶Willard Fisher	69 10 9	Married M	Caleb & Sarah
Jan. 17	**Ruth Bacon.	89 4	Widow F	
Feb. 18	Jemima Hall [land	55	Married F	Otis & Jemima Wales
Feb. 20	Cora Isabella Cleave-	5 6 4	Female	Lowell B. & Melinda S.
Feb. 23	††Charlotte A. Hancock	23 4 21	Single F	Silas & Mary J.
Feb. 24	‡‡Susanna H. Merrill	22 3	Single F	Abial & Mahetable
Feb. 25	§§Lewis H. Hawes	37 4 22	Married M	Nathan & Sylva
Mar. 8	‖‖Joseph Whiting	67 10 16	Married M	Joseph & Mary
Mar. 10	1 Louis Gardner Chapin	1 4 23	Male	George H. & Hellen S.
Mar. 20	2 James F. Follen	1 8	Male	Patrick & Mary
Mar. 25	3 Nancy Cook	86 4 20	Married F	Sam'l & Mary Cleaveland
Mar. 29	4 Sarah Ann Kingsbury	21 10 4	Single F	N. D. & S. G.
April 20	Experience Morse	95	Widow F	George & Sarah Adams
April 30	5 Nathaniel Thayer	71 9 21	Married M	Nath'l & Rhoda
May 5	Juliette Breck	44 10 25	Married F	Joel & Ruth A. Clark
May 10	6 John Shehan	55	Married M	Daniel & Mary
May 29	Olive D. Thayer	1 25	Female	Laprelate M. & Alice
June 14	7 Elisha Richardson	75 10	Married M	Elisha & Abigail
June 21	Cynthia Daniels	73 5 8	Single F	Joel & Mary
July 11	8 Ellen M. Bacon	27 9 28	Single F	James & Mary A.
July 23	9 Polly H. Gowen	75 3 9	Widow F	David & Mary Hartshorn
July 31	Everett Lincoln Hub-	14	Male	Sabin & Almira
Aug. 23	a Eleanor C. Morse [bard	46 10 24	Married F	George & Abigail
Aug. 27	Agnes Haggerty	2 23	Female	Patrick & Mary [ter
Aug. 28	Hannah Baker	69 10 1	Widow F	Benjamin & Hannah Fos-
Sept. 2	b Cyrus Allen	73 3 6	Married M	Abijah & Abigail
Oct. 5	Arthur Hill	2 4	Male	William & Susan
Oct. 7	Nancy Cleaveland	77 6	Married F	John & Anna Brown
Oct. 27	Caroline F. Dean	75 10 2	Married F	John & Caroline Fraucner
Oct. 27	c Sarah Lucretia Webster	43 4 7	Married F	Simeon & Esther Johnson
Nov. 6	d Mary A. Shepard	42 5	Married F	Daniel & Eunice Pond
Nov. 8	Susan E. Foster	22 4 11	Single F	Elisha & Lonesa
Nov. 15	Alinda Hathaway	1 5	Female	Charles B. & Eliza
Dec. 9	Clara Anna Fairbanks	1 11 5	Female	John L. & Eliza
Oct. 11	e Levi F. Morse	69 5 13	Married M	Levi & Katurah
Dec. 10	Lydia Fisher	67 1 11	Married F	Henry & Aruba Ellis
Dec. 9	f Goldsbury Pond	96 2 11	Widower M	Oliver & Anne
Dec. 24	Relief Shepard	75 3 22	Widow F	David & Abigail Gilmore
Dec. 27	g Wilber Ballon	59 6 10	Widower M	Daniel & Mary
Dec. 26	h Mary F. Metcalf	41 3 21	Married F	Elisha & Rena Bullard
Dec. 31	Sally Clark	80 9 9	Widow F	Nath'l & Phebe Thayer

*Interment Burrillville, R. I. †Interment Piermont, N. H. ‡Occupation Farmer. §Occu
**Interment Franklin City. ††Occupation Milliner, interment Bucksport, Me. ‡‡Occupation
‖ Interment Malden. 2 Interment Blackstone. 3 Interment Cumberland 4 Occupation
Interment East Cemetery, Franklin. 8 Occupation Teacher 9 Died in Webster. a Interment
pation Farmer, interment Franklin City. f Occupation Farmer. g Occupation Farmer, inter
Brain. k Congestion of Brain, l Softening of the stomach, m Neuralgia of Stomach & Bowels.
M. Daniels. s West River, Pictou.

FRANKLIN TOWN RECORDS—DEATHS.   189

County, during the Year 1865.--(Continued.)

indicated. Occupation indicated in foot notes.

PLACE OF BIRTH.	CAUSE OF DEATH.	INFORMANT.	Birthplace of Parents. FATHER.	MOTHER.
Blackstone	Consumption	H. Bemis	Burrilville	Burrilville
Piermont, N. H.	Old Age	R. Underhill	N. H.	Piermont
Franklin	Lung Fever	Henry Bemis	Franklin	Stockton, Me.

Norfolk County, in the Year 1866.

Franklin	Lung Fever	Henry Bemis	Wrentham	Franklin
Ireland	Lung Fever	John Murphy	Ireland	Ireland
	Old Age	Oren Sayles	Smithfield	Cumberland
Franklin	Consumption	Henry Bemis	Franklin	Hingham
Wrentham	Dysentary	J. T. Bacon		
Franklin	Consumption	Henry Bemis	Franklin	Medway
"	Diptheria	"	"	Douglass
Bucksport, Me.	j		Orland	Annapolis N.S.
Freeport, Me.	Depthera	"	Freeport	Freeport
Franklin	Consumption	"	Franklin	Townsend
"	k	"		Walpole
Walpole	Dipthera	"	Uxbridge	Franklin
Blackstone	"	"	Ireland	
Medway	Old Age	"		
Wrentham	Dipthera	Saul B. Scott	Franklin	Walpole
Franklin	Old Age	Henry Bemis		
"	l	"	Mendon	W. Medway
Augusta, Me.	Consumption		Wrentham	Augusta, Me.
Ireland	"	John Murphy	Ireland	Ireland
Franklin	Cholera Infantum	Henry Bemis	Douglass	s
"	Dyspepsia	o	Franklin	Franklin
"	Dropsey	Henry Bemis	"	"
Bellingham	Phthisis	"	Wrentham	Bellingham
Franklin	Caused by a fall	"	Franklin	Franklin
"	Liver Complaint	p	"	Oxford
Sherburn	"	q	Natick	Newhamshire
Franklin	Dysentary	John Murphy	Ireland	Ireland
	Chronic Diarhea	r	Franklin	Franklin
Franklin	Dysentary	Henry Bemis	"	"
"	Cholera Infantum	"		Foxboro
Upton	Inflamatory Fever	"	Newport, R. I.	Upton
Wrentham	Dysentary	"	France	Southbridge
Rochester, N. Y.	m	"		
Walpole	Consumption	"	Walpole	Medfield
Franklin	"	"	Holliston	Franklin
"	Scrofula	"	Taunton	Boston
"	"	"	Boston	Cumberland
"	Caused by a fall	"	Franklin	Franklin
Medway		Saul B. Scott	Medway	Walpole
Franklin	Old Age	Henry Bemis	Franklin	Franklin
Raynham	"	"	Raynham	Stoughton
Burrillville	Sudden, unknown	Anna Trask	Burrilsville	Burrilsville
Franklin	Erysipulus	H. Bemis	Bellingham	Franklin
Easton	Bronchitis	"	Easton	Easton

pation Farmer. ||Occupation Straw Braider, interment Bellingham. ¶Occupation Farmer. Seamstress, interment Freeport, Me. §§Occupation Bonnet Presser. |||Occupation Farmer. Straw Sewer. 5 Occupation Manufacturer. 6 Occupation Laborer. 7 Occupation Farmer, Sherburn. b Occupation Farmer. c Interment Painsville, O. d Interment Medway, e Occument Burrilsville. h Interment East Medway, i Isaac & Thankful Heaton, j Congestion of n Inflamation of Liver, o S. W. Richardson, p Adin D. Sargent. q Jeremiah Bullard, r Mancy

FRANKLIN TOWN RECORDS—DEATHS.

Deaths Registered in Franklin, Norfolk County,
Place of interment Franklin unless otherwise

DATE OF DEATH.	NAME OF DECEASED.	AGE. Y|M|D	SEX AND CONDITION.	NAME OF PARENTS OR HUSBAND.
1867				
Jan. 7	*Lucina H. Bacheler	29 1 16	Married F	Job M. & Hannah M. Knight
Jan. 21	†Ruth Fisher	72 2 22	Married F	Samuel & Ruth Guild
Jan. 31	Walter Lyman King	7 19	Male	George & Lucy
Jan. 4	‡Margaret Robinson	34	Married F	James & Catherine Burns
Feb. 4	§Charles E. Torry	3 4	Male	John F. & Clara M.
Feb. 13	‖James M. Ryon	46	Married M	James & Mary
Feb. 25	¶Joseph Morse	67	Married	Jason & Miriam
March 4	Georgiana King	9 3 18	Female	George & Lucy A.
March 6	1 Reuben Cook	90 2 7	Widower M	Silas & Joanna
March 19	2 Edward A. Gilmore	3 7 2	Male	George H. & Martha J.
April 1	Mary R. Nason	84	Widow F	Samuel & Sally Rockwood
April 8	Mary Carroll	21	Married F.	Thomas & Honora
April 13	3 Julia A. Dean	58 11 27	Single F	Ichabod & Betey A.
April 23	Susan Hill	31	Married F	Eli & Margaret White
May 16	4 Dennis Shehan	17 3	Single M	John & Honora
May 27	Martin Green	76 4 19	Married M	
June 30	Lucia Adelaid Stockbridge	24 1	Single F	Horatio & Data A.
July 4	Sarah C. Kellogg	1	Female	Chaey & Sarah C. Pierce
July 4	Ann Duffy	48	Married F	Cornelius & Bridget McMa-
July 22	7 Walter H. Allen	20	Male	Amos H. & Eliza C. [han
July 27	§ Nancy Hartshorn †	78 1 24	Single F	Silas & Betey
Aug. 10	8 Eliza W. Thayer	43 7	Married F	Joseph P.& Elizabeth Bassett
Aug. 14	Harvell Albert Caswell	1 22	Male	Andrew A. & Susan F
Aug. 15	Hartwell Adelbert Caswell	1 23	Male	Andrew A. & Susan F
Aug. 28	Millard L. Farr	1 6 2	Male	Parker R. & Abbie E.
Aug. 30	a Catherine Barry	45	Single F	James & Eliza
Sept. 9	b Edward Dohority	65	Married M	Edmond & Margaret
Sept. 22	Mary Houlihan	20	Single F	John & Margaret
Sept. 28	e Patrick Neylon	62	Married M	James & Nancy [ry
Oct. 3	Laura Blake	73 5 1	Widow F	Augustus & Chloe Mow-
Oct. 3	Hariet N. Daniels	30 7 2	Married F	Elias & Hannah Baker
Oct. 7	d Angaline Snow	62	Single F	Cyrus & Ruth
Oct. 7	e Reuben Crossley	38 7 20	Married M	John & Sarah
Oct. 23	Hannah W. Haskell	66 5	Married F	George & Mary Newell
Nov. 7	f Mary Colvin	60 11	Widow F	James & Lydia Paine
Nov. 28	Susan H. Marden	31 6 11	Married F	Thurston & Caroline Bal-
Dec. 29	g Seth L. Hartshorn	73 10	Male	David & Mary [lou
Dec. 27	Maria Gilmore	78 4	Widow F	Nathan & ———Dellen
Sept. 30, '66	h Isaac Hill	28 7 12	Married M	William & Maria
Feb. 17, '66	i Wm. H. Chase	39 7 12	Married M	Mason & Lurana

Deaths Registered in Franklin, in the County of Nor
[rah Kimball

1868				
Jan. 4	j Sophia C. Blake	64 10 14	Married	Geo. W. Littlefield & Sa-
Jan. 9	k Asa Sargeant	88 4 6	Widower	John & Persis (Newton)
Jan. 25	Achsa P. Adams	80 10 20	Widow	Simeon & Achsa Partridge
Jan. 31	Rena P. Gilmore	77 3 5	Married	" "
Feb. 7	l Solomon F. Morse	53	Widower	Henry & Mary
March 10	m Caroline B. Ware	74 4	Single	Oliver & Betey
March 21	n Richard Underhill	49 6	Married	Richard & Mary
March 25	Abijah Clark	82 11 20	Married	Abijah & Meletiah
April 20	o William Graham	65	Single	
May 2	p Perry Lewis	70 9 11	Married	Jeremiah & Rebecca
May 16	Mary Ann Gifford	40	Married	William & Rhoda

*Interment Northbridge. †Interment Franklin City. ‡Died in Wrentham. §Interment Franklin
3 Seamstress 4 Laborer, 5 Blacksmith. 6 Died in Woonsocket, 7 Died in Woonsocket.
in Uxbridge, e Livery Stable. f Interment Holden, g Died in Attleboro, Laborer, h Box Maker,
Cemetery, New York, k Farmer, l Interment Hopkinton, m Interment North Wrenth, n Rail-
disease of the brain.

FRANKLIN TOWN RECORDS—DEATHS.

in the Year 1867.—A. A. RUSSEGUE, Registrar.
indicated. Occupation indicated in foot notes.

PLACE OF BIRTH.	CAUSE OF DEATH.	INFORMANT.	Birthplace of Parents.	
			FATHER.	MOTHER.
Cumberland, R.I.	Typhoid Fever	Henry Bemis	Smithfield, R.I.	Newport, R. I.
Franklin	Paralysis Dropsy	Saul B. Scott	Franklin	Medway
"	Lung Fever	Henry Bemis	Rochester Mass	Middleboro,
Ireland	Phthisis	"	Ireland	Ireland [Mass.
Franklin	Consumption	Saul B. Scott	Sutton, Mass.	Medway, Mass.
Ireland	"	John Murphy	Ireland	Ireland
Franklin	Appoplexy	Henry Bemis	Franklin	Walpole
"	Inflamation, Brain	"	Rochester Mass	Middleboro
Cumberland	Old Age	[more	Cumberland, R.I.	Bellingham
Wrentham	Burn	George H. Gil-	No. Providence	Smithfield, R.I.
Franklin	Old Age	Henry Bemis		
Ireland	Typhoid Fever	"	Ireland	Ireland
Franklin	Pleuro Pneumonia	"	Franklin	Franklin
Mansfield	Puerperal Fever	"	Mansfield	Mansfield
Wrentham	Consumption	John Murphy	Ireland	Ireland
Barre, Mass.	Lung Fever	Henry M. Green		
Franklin	Pulmony Con-[sumption	Henry Bemis	Uxbridge, Mass	Uxbridge, Mass
"		"	Rehoboth	
Ireland	Gravel	John Murphy	Ireland	Ireland [R. I.
Franklin	Consumption	Henry Bemis	Union, Me.	Woonsocket,
	**	Saul B. Scott		
Barre, Mass	General Debility	Henry Bemis	Norton, Mass.	Barre, Mass.
Franklin	Stopage		Taunton	Milford
"	Cholera Infantum		" [N.H.	" [R. I.
"	Dysentary [fall		Westmoreland	Cumberland,
Ireland	Spinal Injury by	John Murphy	Ireland	Ireland
"	Disease of Brain	"	"	"
Boylston, Mass.	Disease of Brain	"	"	"
Ireland	Ulcer in Stomach	"	"	" [R. I.
Woodstock, Vt.	Liver Complaint	Henry Bemis	Smithfield, R.I.	Cumberland Hills,
Franklin	Dropsey	"	Franklin	Franklin
Bridgwater	Dysentary	"	Bridgwater	Norton
Simsbury	Lung Feever	"	England	England
Dover	Consumption	"	Dover	
Mendon	††	"	Mendon [R.I.	Smithfield, R.I.
Cumberland, R.I.	Inflamation of Liver	"	Cumberland.	Attleboro
Franklin	Dysentary	"	Franklin	Franklin
Providence, R. I.	Anasarca	"		
Elmore, Vt.	Throat Disease	Stephen Adams	Montpelier	Middlesex, Vt.
Medway	Consumption	S. W. Richardson	Somerset, Mass	Swansey, Mass.

folk, for the Year 1868.—A. A. RUSSEGUE, Registrar.

Boscowen, Me.	Tumer	Henry Bemis	Kenebunk, Me.	Dover
Spencer	Paralysis	Adin D. Sargeant	Leicester	Spencer
Franklin	Pneumonia	Henry Bemis		Unknown
"	Pleuro Pneumonia	"	Franklin	Franklin
Hopkinton	Dysentary	"	Hopkinton	Hopkinton
Wrentham	Consumption	"	Wrentham	Wrentham
Piermont, N.H.	"	"	Piermont, N.H	Piermont, N.H
Franklin		"	Franklin	Franklin
Scotland	Old Age			
Exeter, R. I.	Unknown			
	Old Age	Geo. R. Paine	Exeter, R. I.	Exeter, R. I.
Norton		Henry Bemis	Tiverton, R. I.	Middleboro

City. ‖Stone Mason. ¶Farmer. ‖ Farmer, Interment Cumberland, R. I. 2 Interment Wrentham. a Died in Brooklyn, N. Y. a Interment Milford. b Farmer. c Farmer, Interment Milford. d Died Interment Medway. i Died in Canaan, N. H., Mechanic, Interment W. Medway. j Interment Green Road. o Farmer. p Farmer, Interment Coventry, R. I. **Injury by fall down stairs ††Organic

FRANKLIN TOWN RECORDS—DEATHS.

Deaths Registered in Franklin, County of
Place of Interment Franklin unless otherwise

DATE OF DEATH.	NAME OF DECEASED.	AGE. Y|M|D	SEX AND CONDITION.	NAME OF PARENTS OR HUSBAND.
1868				[ter) Gay
May 17	*Elisa T. Nottage	47 3 22	Married	David & Betcy W. (Proc-
July 22	†Eleanor Sherburn	68 4 14	Single	William & Sarah
July 23	‡William Fehln	25	Married	Dennis & Mary
Aug. 10	Freddie H. Nason	5 10	Single	Albert D. & Annie
Aug. 12	Corilla Dexter King	8 8	Single	George & Lucy A.
Aug. 23	Catherine McNally	18 3	Single	Michael & Margaret
Aug. 30	§Eliphalet D. Hardy	75 4 15	Widower	Henry & Rachael D.
Sept. 19	Winnie Stevenson	7	Single	Perez & Julia
Oct. 10	Emma Louisa Corbett	1 3	Single	George S. & Nettie L.
Oct. 17	‖Nathan Staples	64 6	Married	Ezekiel & Dorcas
Oct. 19	Charles Hathaway	14	Single	Chas. B. & Eliza [aker)
Oct. 24	¶Ira Hayward	70 11 6	Married	Eleazer & Tabatha(Whit-
Oct. 31	1 Daniel Coghlan	48	Married	Dennis & Ellen
Nov. 1	Hanora Shehan	48	Widow	Dennis & Mary Kennedy
Nov. 9	2 George W. Nason	62 9 28	Married	Jesse & Hannah [ley
Nov. 13	Mary Connors	26	Married	Jeremiah & JohanaBuck-
Nov. 16	3 Albert Adams	60 10 24	Married	Alpheus & Achsa P.
March 8	Freddie Ellsworth Hubbard	4	Single	Sabin & Almira
Aug. 22	4 Electra S. Miller	68	Married	John & Ann Smith

Deaths Registered in Franklin, in the County of Nor

				[Dean
1869				
Jan. 25	5 David Dean [more	67 8 7	Widower	Richard & Colly(Hering)
Feb. 16	6 Abby R. Hayford Gil-	36	Married	John & Cynthia Hayford
Feb. 27	7 Robert Tobin	57	Married	Unknown
Feb. 10	8 Francis T. O'Brien	2 13		Timothy & Elizabeth
March 10	9 Joseph John Pitcher	18 6 2	Single	Jonathan & Mary
April 25	a Weston Fisher	72 4 5	Married	Richard & Hannah
May 13	Maria H.(Hills)Coombs	62 6 13	Married	Timothy & Olive
May 12	Susan A. M. Blake	24 6	Single	Jeremiah D. & Nancy N.
May 5	James W. Walker	11 8 16		Maria Kingsbury
June 20	Catherine (Keany) McGuire	94	Widow	John & Bridget Keany
June 23	d Thomas H. Putnam	69 11 11	Married	Thomas & Rosamond B.
July 4	jJohn Joseph Desmond	4 1		Jeremiah & Ann
July 4	Hariet A. (Fisher) Al-	27	Married	Walter H. & Emily P.
Aug. 27	e Ezra Daniels [drich	82 8 22	Widower	Nathan & Sarah (Smith)
Aug. 12	Harry Fisher	1 2 12		Gilbert C. & Emely
Aug. 29	William H. Stewart	1 10		Robert B. & Martha
Sept. 30	f Annie P. (Pickering)	21	23 Married	Simeon & Elizabeth
Sept. 23	g Alfred Darling [Curtis	76 6 4	Widower	Peter & Persis [bury
Sept. 23	g John H. Richardson	69	Married	Wilks & Matilda (Kings-
Oct. 9	Eudora F. Hills	22 10 8	Single	Sanford & Mary C. (Metcalf)
Oct. 13	Annie (Howe) Daniels	86 8 20	Widow	John & Susanna (Fairbanks)
Oct. 14	Ella Jane Morse	19 9 10	Single	Thomas D. & Sarah E.
Nov. 9	h Nattalie Langly	65	Married	
Nov. 4	Gertrude J. S. (Squire)	23 7 22	Married	Salman W. & Betsey J.
Nov. 4	HattieE.King [Davis	5 28		George & Lucy A.
Nov. 10	Lucy Daniels	65 11 10	Widow	Joseph & Mary(Page)Whiting
Dec. 2	i Albert D. Richardson	36 1 26	Married	Elisha & Hariet B.
Dec. 6	Mary B. Underhill	18 4 24	Single	Richard & Emeline
Dec. 7	Caroline Torry	4 2		John F. & Clara A.
Dec. 24	j Charles Francis Rich	5 2	5 Single F	Lemuel F. & Margaret
Oct. 3	Jeremiah Sullivan	1 1		Daniel & Julia
Oct. 15	k Nancy Daniels	87	Widow	

*Interment W. Medway. †Interment W Wrentham. ‡Died in Bridgwater, Laborer. §Shoe Agent, 4 Interment Providence, R. I. 5 Farmer, Interment West Dedham, 6 Interment E. Medway. ingham. c Interment Wrentham. d Trader, Interment Foxborough. e Farmer. f Interment Hol- Author. j Interment Dorchester. k Died in alms house, Franklin.

Norfolk, for the Year 1868.—(Continued.)
indicated. Occupation indicated in foot notes.

PLACE OF BIRTH.	CAUSE OF DEATH.	INFORMANT.	Birthplace of Parents.	
			FATHER.	MOTHER.
Weymouth	Liver Complaint	Daniel Wood	Weymouth	Braintree
Burn, N. Y.	Cancer	Geo. A. Gilmore	Newport, R. I.	Providence, R.I
Ireland	Consumption	John Murphy	Ireland	Ireland
Walpole	Cholera Infanton	Henry Bemis	Franklin	Franklin
Franklin	Diarrhea C.	Geo. King	Rochester	Middleborough
Ireland	Consumption	John Murphy	Ireland	Ireland
Bradford	Liver Complaint	Henry Bemis	Bradford	Bradford
Bellingham	Cholera Infanton	Henry W. Brown	Owington, Ky.	Walpole, Mass.
Franklin	Humor	Henry Bemis	Franklin	Cumberland
Cumberland		S. B. Scott		
Franklin	Canker	Henry Bemis	Taunton	Boston
Plainfield, N. H.	Old Age	"	Charlestown, N.H	Killingly, Ct.
Ireland	Cholic	John Murphy	Ireland	Ireland
"	Consumption	"	"	"
Walpole	Stoppage in Bowels	Henry Bemis	Walpole	Franklin
Ireland	Congestion, Lungs	John Murphy	Ireland	Ireland
Franklin	Paralysis	Gardner Adams	Franklin	Franklin
"		Sabin Hubbard	"	Oxford
Hartford, Ct.	Congestion, Brain	Saul B. Scott	Hartford, Conn	Hartford, Conn

folk, in the Year 1869.—A. A. Russegue, Registrar.

W. Dedham	Consumption	Henry Bemis	West Dedham	West Dedham
Medfield	"	"	"	Mendon
Ireland	Heart Disease	"	Ireland	Ireland [wick
Franklin	Inflamation, Lungs	John Murphy	New Brunswick	New Bruns-
Medway	Consumption	"	"	Ireland
Wrentham		Henry Bemis	Wrentham	Wrentham
Sherburn	"	"	Medway	Medfield
Wrentham	Consumption	"	Wrentham	Wrentham
Franklin	Fever, Perforation	"	"	Franklin
Ireland	Old Age [of Bowels]	John Murphy	Ireland	Ireland
Hartford, Ct.	Suicide	S. B. Scott	England	Washington,
Roxbury	Consumption	John Murphy	Ireland	Ireland [N.H.
Franklin	"	Saul B. Scott	Franklin	Wrentham
"	Old Age	Henry Bemis	Medway	Walpole
"	Cholera Infanton	"	Franklin	"
"		"	Pictou, N. S.	Pictou, N. S.
Milford	Typhoid Fever	"	Bellingham	Franklin
Cumberland, R.I.	Heart Disease	"	Un	known
Franklin	Typhoid Fever	Saul B. Scott	Franklin	Franklin
"	Pulmonary Con-	Henry Bemis	"	Alstead, N. H.
Marlbrough	Old Age [sumption	"	Marlborough	Attleborough
Framingham	Typhoid Feever	"	Natick	Lempster, N.H
Cumberland				
Canton, N. Y.	Typhoid Pneumo-	"		
Franklin	Diarhea [nia	"	Rochester Mass	Middleboro
"	Dropsey	"	Franklin	.
"	A Pistol Shot	C. A. Richards		
Chelsea, Vt.	Consumption	Henry Bemis	Piermont, N.H	Benton, N. H.
Franklin	Convulsions	S. B. Scott	Sutton	Medway
Boston	Scarlatina	Daniel Dugan	Isleborough Me	Ireland
Franklin			Ireland	"
	Old Age			

Maker, ||Farmer, Interment Franklin City. ¶Farmer. 1 Laborer. 2 Trader. 3 Died in Melrose, 7 Laborer. 8 Interment Milford. 9 Silversmith, Interment Milford. a Farmer. b Interment Belliston. g Farmer. h Interment Smithfield. i Resident in New Jersey and death in New York.

FRAKLIN TOWN RECORDS—DEATHS.

Deaths Registered in Franklin for the Year ending

Place of interment Franklin unless otherwise

DATE OF DEATH.	NAME OF DECEASED.	AGE. Y M D	SEX AND CONDITION.	NAME OF PARENTS OR HUSBAND.
1870				
Jan. 20	Myron A. Blake	6 22	Male	William A. & Jennie E.
Jan. 20	*Henry L. Jordon	2 10 20	Male	George W. & Alice J.
Jan. 10	*Alice J. Jordan	26	Married	Amos H. & Ireane Crocker
Feb. 8	†Emery Davis Thayer	29 27	Married	Lyman E. & Hariet
Feb. 5	‡Joel Guild	63	Widower	Samuel & Ruth
Feb. 27	§Elizabeth O. Brien	35	Married	Patrick & Elizabeth Lau-
Mar. 20	‖Catherine Sexton	3	Female	John & Bridget [gan
Mar. 16	Carry L. Brown	6		L. B. & Anne M.
April 27	Minnie A. Cobb	11 7	Female	Henry G. & Betsey T.
April 23	Albert H. Bonsall	2 10 11	Male	Wm. H. & Sarah A.
April 12	*A. D. Daniels	63 10 6	Female	Peter & Abigail
May 11	**William Whelden	47 6 6	Married	Joseph & Elizabeth [son
May 25	Mary J. Fisher	29 5 29	Married	John & Margaret Patter-
May 1	§Mary McIntee	83	Widow	Wm. & Mary Crawford
May 1	††Herman C. Benson	31 1 17	Married	Lovering & Susan
June 2	S. Samantha Daniels	40 3	Married	Saul B. & Susan P. Scott
June 6	Julius S. Davis	3 7 17		Edmond & Gertrude J.
June 3	Alice E. Gould	9 8		William H. & Nancy J.
July 10	Anne C. Fitzpatrick	35 19	Single	John L. & Margaret
Aug. 18	aWilliam W. Metcalf	51 4	Single	William & Sally
Aug. 8	George C. Thorne	9 16		James H. & Mary B.
Aug. 29	‡‡Asa Rockwood	83 5 4	Widower	Timothy & Sarah
Aug. 30	§§Timothy Gay	72 9 28	Married	Timothy & Submit
Sept. 22	——— Batchelder	4		Ira F. T. Lizzie
Sept. 7	Grace F. Blake	34 6 7	Married	Thaddeus & Hariet
Sept. 22	William Barnard	73 2 28	Married	[Shepardson
Sept. 8	Mary Elizabeth Murphy	18 4 19	Single	John & Eliza
Sept. 23	‖‖Edson M. Rhodes	29 9 16	Married	Johnathan & Almira
Oct. 5	——— Newell	1 5	Male	Albert J. & Betsey W.
Nov. 6	Isabella J. Gould	18 23	Single	Wm. H & Nancy J.
Dec. 4	Abigail Metcalf	75 7 22	Single	Wm. H & Patty
Dec. 11	Delia Maria Robinson	21 6 17	Married	Eathan & Serena Thayer
Dec. 21	Abby E. A. Vanarsdalen	43 11 25	Married	8
Oct. 6	1 Emely A. Stockbridge	27	Married	Simeon & Delia Stedmon
Nov. 9	2 Samuel W. Pond	43 9 8	Married	Paul D. & Huldah

Deaths Registered in Franklin, Norfolk County,

				[Adams
Jan. 15	3 Abigail Bullard	83 3 28	Widow	Obediah & Abigail
Jan. 23	4 Anna Josephine Cook	1 3 14		Joseph W. & Polly
Feb. 2	Elmer B. Foster	8 10 16	Male	Peter & Louise
Feb. 6	§Bridget Murry	11 5 16		Francis & Ann
Feb. 15	William F. Foster	1 21		Peter & Louese
Feb. 22	James Gillen, Jr.	1		James & Jennie
Mar. 9	Georgianna Foster	3 10 9		Peter & Louese
Mar. 12	Annie Frances Atwood	26 7 4	Single	Jonathan F. & Anna M.
Mar. 17	Susanna Clark	78 8 13	Widow	Joseph & Mary Wadsworth
Mar. 24	5 John T. Brock	24 7 3	Single	Sanford W. & Mary E.
April 10	Rebecca G. Gilmore	81 1 5	Widow	David & Rebecca McLane
May 1	6 Ellen Martin	70	Widow	Michul Hughs
May 24	7 Sidney Whiting	85 2 6	Widower	Asa & Mary
May 30	Bessie F. Fishop	11 12	Female	Horace & Betsey A.
June 4	Erepta King	71 9 1	Married	Wm. & Sabra Claflin

*Interment Dedham. †Painter, interment Norfolk. ‡Interment W. Wrentham. §Interment
‡‡Trader. §§Farmer, interment Franklin City. ‖‖Straw Worker, interment Sheldonville. 1 Inter
Woonsocket. 5 Interment Mendon. 6 Interment Worcester, 7 Mechanic, 8 Nickolas V. B. &

FRANKLIN TOWN RECORDS—DEATHS.

December 31, 1870.—A. A. RUSSEGUE, Registrar.
indicated. Occupation indicated in foot notes.

PLACE OF BIRTH.	CAUSE OF DEATH.	INFORMANT.	Birthplace of Parents.	
			FATHER.	MOTHER.
Medway	Bronchitis	Henry Bemis	Franklin	
Boston	Brain Fever	J. B. Baker	Medford	Dedham
W. Dedham	Heart Disease	Henry Bemis	Hanson	Dedham
Wrentham	Pneumonia	"	Medway	Wrentham
Franklin	Dropsey	E. Foster	Franklin	Medway
New Brunswick	Childbirth	John Murphy	Ireland	
Franklin		John Sexton		Ireland
"		Henry Bemis	Plainfield, Ct.	Providence, R.I.
"		"	Easton	Yarmouth
Cambridgeport	Hydrocephalus	"		England
Providence, R. I.	Consumption	"	New hampshire	Franklin
England		"		England
Johnson, R. I.	Consumption	"		Scotland
Ireland	Paralysis	John Dolan		Ireland
Upton	Consumption	Henry Bemis	Sturbridge	Orleans
Bellingham	9	"	Bellingham	Mendon
Terrehaut, Ind.	Scarlatina [Lungs	"	Canton, Mass.	Canton, N. Y.
Franklin	Congestion of	"	Greenfield, N.	Goshen, N. H.
Boston	Consumption	John Murphy		[H. Ireland
Franklin	Insanity	Henry Bemis	Franklin	Mendon
"	Cholera Infantum	"	Boston	Beverly
"	Erysipelas	"	Franklin	Bellingham
"	Dysentary	"		[Me.
"		"	West Gardner,	Hollis, N. H.
W. Brookville,	Erysipelas	"	Brookville,Me.	Frankfort, Me.
England [Me.	Dropsey	"		England
Franklin	Consumption	John Murphy		Ireland
"	Consumption	H. Bemis	Wrentham	Wrentham
"	Canker	"		Franklin
Goshen, N. H.	Inflamation	"	Goshen, N. H.	Goshen, N. H.
Franklin	Mortification	"	Franklin	Brookfield
Worcester	Typhoid Fever	"	Worcester	Northbury,
Jersey City	Dropsey	"		[Mass.
Cumberland, R.I.		[son]		
Franklin	Heart Disease	S. W. Richard-	Franklin	Medway

In the Year 1871.—A.A. RUSSEGUE, Registrar.

		[son]		
Medway	Congestion of lungs	S. W. Richard-	Medway, Mass.	Medway, Mass.
Franklin	Scarlatina	Henry Bemis	Wrentham	Woonsocket
Cumberland	Scarlatina	"	Scotland	Cumberland,
Hopkinton	Consumption	Francis Murray		Ireland [R. I.
Franklin	Scarlatina	Henry Bemis	Scotland	Cumberland
		James Gillen	Ireland	Liverpool
Cumberland, R.I.	Scarlatina	Henry Bemis	Scotland	Cumberland,
Franklin	Scrofula & Tubercle	"	Middleborough	Franklin [R.I.
Milton	Paralysis	"	Milton	Dedham
East Blackstone	Pleurisy & Fever	"	Wallingford,	Blackstone
Franklin	Consumption	C. M. Allen	Scotland [Vt.	Franklin
Ireland	Old Age	Patrick Smith		Ireland
Franklin	Old Age	Henry Bemis	Franklin	Franklin
"	Hydrocephalus	Emely E. Ames	Slatersville,	Cumberland,
Holliston, Mass.	Consumption	Henry Bemis	Holliston [R.I.	Medway [R.I.

Milford. ‖Interment Mount Auburn. ¶Interment Providence. **Awl Maker. ††Interment Upton.
ment So. Franklin, 2 Farmer, interment W. Medway, 3 Interment East Medway, 4 Interment
Eliza Garretson. 9 Inflamation of Stomach. a Died in Worcester.

FRANKLIN TOWN RECORDS—DEATHS.

Deaths Registered in Franklin, Norfolk
Place of interment Franklin unless otherwise

DATE OF DEATH.	NAME OF DECEASED.	AGE. Y	M	D	SEX AND CONDITION.	NAME OF PARENTS OR HUSBAND.
1871						
June 9	*Michael Murphy	55			Married	Cornelius & Margaret
June 9	James T. Healy	1	1	2		Timothy & Kate
June 13	†Silence H. Capron	77	1	3	Widow	Seth & Rhoda Harden
June 20	‡Warren Hills	71	2	5	Single	Jason & Polly
June 20	§Stephen S. Hawes	61	9	22	Married	Herman & Abigail
June 21	Benjmin Geo. Trevett					
June 22	‖Jennie Gillen	24	5	27	Married	Cornelius & Mary Ellard
June 30	Ruth Mann	78	2	5	Widow	James & Esther Buxton
Aug. 4	Michael McCue	52	9		Married	Patrick & Hanora
Aug. 5	Martin McCue	13	8	26	Single	Patrick & Bridget
Aug. 29	Julia Sullivan		1	21	Female	Daniel & Julia
Sept. 7	Emeline C. Underhill	47	8	7	Widow	Moses & Mary Mead
Oct. 9	¶Joel Daniels	84	3	25	Married	Joel & Mary
Oct. 10	Isabel Ford		5	10		Danil W. & Louisa S.
Oct. 22	Sylvia Newell	90	8		Widow	Elijah & Annie Brown
Oct. 30	1 Michael Murphy	20	5	10	Single	Michael & Johanna
Dec. 2	Juline Pond	66	10	15	Single	Goldsbury & Priscella
Dec. 5	2 Oliver Dean	88	9	17	Married	Seth & Edna
Dec. 8	Mary Lizzie Allen	4	10	17		Thomas B. & Martha M.
Dec. 12	Irving W. Gould	2	2	13		Joseph P. & Marrianna
Dec. 15	3 Maria Hardy	44	5	2	Married	Nathn'l H. & Sarah B.
Dec. 29	4 Francis Williams	66			Single	Levi [Cary
Sept. 26	5 George F. Foster	1	8	19		Peter & Loeza
Oct. 28	6 Abigail Harding	97	2	22	Widow	Moses & Elizabeth Huse
Oct. 3	Joseph Youson	1	5			Frank & Louesa

*Laborer.   †Died in Cumberland, R. I., Interment Cumberland, R. I.   ‡Farmer.   §Mason.
Cemetery.   4 Died in alms house, Bridgwater, Interment Bridgwater.   5 Died in Wrentham, Inter-

FRANKLIN TOWN RECORDS—DEATHS.

County, in the Year 1871.—(Continued.)
indicated. Occupation indicated in foot notes.

PLACE OF BIRTH.	CAUSE OF DEATH.	INFORMANT.	Birthplace of Parents. FATHER.	MOTHER.
Ireland	Consumption	John Murphy	Ireland	Ireland
Franklin	Lung Fever	"	"	"
"		Henry Bemis		[water
"	Stone in Bladder	"	Franklin	North Bridge-
Union, Me.	Hernia	"	Union, Me.	Waldoboro,
"		"		[Me.
England		James Gillen	England	England
Smithfield, R. I.	Diarhea	Henry Bemis	Smithfield	Smithfield
Ireland		John Murphy	Ireland	Ireland
Franklin	Heart Disease	"	"	"
"	Cancer		"	"
Benton, N. H.	Consumption	Henry Bemis	Peacham, Vt.	Peacham, Vt.
Franklin	Old Age	"	Franklin	Medway, Mass.
Wrentham	Whooping Cough	"	Boston	Boston
Cumberland, R. I.	Old Age	"	Cumberland	Cumberland
No. Wrentham	Consumption	John Murphy	Ireland	Ireland
Franklin	Aneurism	Henry Bemis	Franklin	Medway
"	Heart Disease		"	Franklin
"	Whooping Cough	"	"	"
"	Crebral Meninigitis	"	Boston	"
Kittery, Me.	Dropsey	"	"	Boston
		N. Leonard		
Wrentham		Saul B. Scott	Scotland	Cumberland
Royalston, Mass.	Old Age	A. B. Corbett		
Franklin		J. L. Fitzpatrick		Canada

‖Interment Old Cambridge. ¶Farmer. 1 Laborer. 2 Manufacturer. 3 Interment Forest Hill
ment Franklin City. 6 Interment Norfolk.

INDEX OF BIRTHS.

Abby—John, 14.
Adams and Addams— ——— 48, 76, 85; Abby, 43; Abby Maria, 59; Abigail, 9; Achsah Metcalf, 33; Ada Louesa, 72; Albert, 26; Alice Maria, 48; Alpheus, 17; Alvin B., 42; Amos, 22; Amos Shumway, 24; Anna Frances, 46; Annie Laurie, 72; Artemas, 21; Augustus Edwin, 39; Carabel, 53; Charles Partridge, 65; Charles Richardson, 41; Chloe, 20; Chloe Fales, 19; Cora Marion, 65; Cyrus, 11; Daniel, 10; Ebenezer Ward, 13; Edward Appleton, 45; Ellen Frances, 66; Ellen Maria, 47, 66; Elisabeth, 24; Emerson, 28; Emma Josephine, 80; Emma Sobriety, 57; Erastus, 32; Erastus Gardner, 54; Esther, 30, 31; Eunice, 18; Fisher, 13; Francis Stephen Coombs, 54; Frank Nelson, 79; Fred Adelbert, 63; Gardner, 30; Georgetta Idella, 68; Hannah, 11; Hannah Frances, 57; Hannah Jane, 51; Hellen Frances, 40; Henry, 54; Henry C., 42; Herbert, 63; Ida Jane, 75; Isabella Jane, 39; James, 14; James, Jr., 20; James Francis, 40; Jemima Aldana, 28; John Fisher, 23; John Mason, 20; John Quincy, 60; Jonathan, 18; Joseph, 17; Julia, 31; Layton Jenks, 29; Lois, 19; Lowell W., 42; Lucinda, 9; Lucy Maria, 30; Maria B., 42; Mary, 58; Mary Ann, 24; Meletiah, 10; Melvin Augustus, 83; Merriam, 43; Nancy, 13; Nancy Richardson, 23; Naomi, 14; Nathan, 29; Nathaniel Emmons, 52; Oliver Ellis, 22; Peter, 11, 28; Rachel, 9; Sabra, 16; Samuel, 13; Sarah Bacon, 24; Sibyl, 24; Susie Merrill, 69; Thaddeus, 9; Thomas Bacon, 20; Timothy, 12; Ward, 20; Welcom Farnum, 70; Whiting, 16; William Henry, 70; William Hoyle, 80; William Maddison, 27; William W., 42.
Aldis—Eunice, 10; Hette, 10; Sara, 10.
Allen—Abbie Maria, 84; Abigail, 12; Abigail Clarinda, 36; Abigail Partridge, 27; Abijah, 16; Adaline, 34, 38; Aldis, 22; Aldis Maxey, 71; Alfred, 19; Almira, 22; Asa, 11, 34; Bernice May, 49; Calista, 29; Charlotte Jane, 34; Cyrus, 16; Cyrus Milton, 38; Dorcas, 29; Edwin Francis, 34, 38; Ellera, 11; Emily, 34, 38; Fidelia, 27; Frederick, 38; George, 38; Hiram, 22; Hiram George, 34; Hiram Hazard, 38; Ira, 26; James, 38; Jane Amanda, 38; Jemima (see Mima); John, 35; John Partridge, 11; Laura, 27; Lucinda, 33 (2), Marena, 16, 34; Martha, 29; Mary, 10, 30; Mary Lizzie, 79, Maxey, 16. Mima Emeline, 75; Nancy Lavilla, 44; Samuel, 9; Sarah Metcalf, 82; Simeon, 11; Thomas Bacon, 38; Walter Hawes, 46; Willard Agustus, 38; William Henry, 61.
Atwood—Anna Frances, 43, Francis, 46.
Aull—John Edward, 58.

Bacon— ———, 61; Abigail, 14; Albert OrVille, 40; Alby Miranda, 36; Delia Emmons, 28; Ellen, 37; Francis Albert, 86; George, 37; Henry Metcalf, 57; Herbert Brooks, 61; Joseph Thomas, 26; Julian Burbank, 77; Sally, 19; Thomas Metcalf, 36.
Bailey—James, 15.
Baker—Abigail, 25; Abijah Richardson, 23; Anna, 13; Austin Metcalf, 67; Charlotte, 24; David, 12; David Parker, 30; David Erastus, 62; Elias, 24; Erastus Emmons, 34; Esther, 10; Jemima Jane, 29; Jenny Parker, 73; John Ellis, 24; Joseph Herbert, 59; Julia, 24, 32; Mary Agusta, 57; Olive Harding, 24; Polly, 24; Rhoda, 24, 28; Sally, 26.
Ballou— ———, 63; Adalina Agusta, 45; Adelia Amelia, 61; Arlon Alonzo, 65; Jessie Caroline, 61.
Barden—Artemas, 34, 62; Francis Irwin, 46; Harriet Louisa, 56.
Barnard—William, Jr., 36.
Barrons—Polly, 17; Warren, 17.
Barrows or Barrus—David, 74; Emeline Lucretia, 48; George Washington, 48.
Bartlett—Harriet Almira, 59; Herbert Eugene, 66; Lucy Rachael, 71; William Albert, 61.
Barton—Anson Fisher, 78; Charles Edward, 45; Clarence Edgar, 42; Ida, 75.
Bassett—Clarissa Mary, 49; Elizabeth

Maria, 58; Elizabeth Smith, 78; Frederick Newhall, 84; Harriet Eliza, 80; Josephine Francis, 62; Walter Scott, 53.

Batchelder— ——, 85.
Bates—Julitta Metcalf, 24.
Bemis—Charles Henry, 35; Elmond Leander, 54; Nancy Louisa, 38.
Benson—Austin Fletcher, 84; Jessie Harriet, 69.
Bent—Arthur, 87; George M., 85; Harry Archibald, 86.
Bezely—Eliza, 24.
Billings—Enoch, 12; Nanna, 11.
Black— —— 58.
Blake— —— 52, 61; Abigail, 30, 31; Adelaid Maria, 41; Albert A., 40; Alvin, 17; Anna Eudora, 87; Augustus Mowry, 31; Austin, 20; Austin Judson, 33; Benjamin, 32; Bessie M., 66; Caroline, 32; Caroline Amelia, 40; Caroline Elizabeth, 38; Charles Bradley, 78; Charles Fisher, 30; Charles Robert, 18; Ednah Elvera, 43; Edward Augustus, 43; Eliza Ann, 37; Ella Iantha, 51; Ellen Agusta, 50; Flora Augusta, 69; Francis, 20; Francis Ann, 39; George A. A., 41; George Lewis, 38; George Lowell, 41; George Warren, 28; George Washington, 21; Harriet L., 40; Harriet Rachel, 35; Henry A., 40; Herman Miller, 35; Ida Delma, 53; James Herbert, 59; James M. A., 47; Joel Nelson, 26; John Warren, 16; Julia Ann, 38; Laura Ann, 43; Laura Emely, 71; Laura Matilda, 35; Lewis, 28; Lewis Addison Edward, 83; Lois, 36; Louisa Eveline, 41; Mary Jane, 33; Mary Louisa, 49; Mary Park, 33; Melancey Maria, 36; Meranda, 19; Nancy Maranda, 38; Nancy Meranda, 37; Nettie Metcalf, 75; Oramel Bradley, 37; Persis Maria, 45; Phebe Louisa, 41; Robert, Jr., 21; Roxana, 23; Samuel Andrew, 35; Sarah Matilda, 38; Seth Albert, 69; Solomon, 11; Stephen Mann, 25; Susan Malinda, 38; Susanna Morse, 26; Walter Francis, 75; William Adelbert E., 39.
Blele—Augustus, 87.
Bonsell—Albert Henry, 84.
Bosworth—Josephine, 58.
Bowditch—Bass, 9; Jonathan, 10; Mary, 11; Sophey, 12.
Boyd—Abigail Fisher, 24; Amos Hawes, 24; Betsey Willard, 19; George Edwards, 27; Juliana, 24; Oliver Dean, 24; Patty Whiting, 20; Polly, 15, 18, 21; Sally, 24; William Bradbury, 21.
Boyden—Betsey, 25; Caroline, 25; Calvin G., 34; Clarissa Ann, 25; Hannah, 32, Henry Newel, 32; James

Allen, 29; Julia Maria, 28.
Braden—Ida, 76.
Braley—Collins, 16; Lydia, 16; Nancy, 16.
Brayman—Francis Uriah, 50.
Breck or Brick—Grace Mabell, 63, Lucinda, 22.
Briggs— —— 52, 63; Cora Almira, 79; Cornelia Elizabeth, 49; Darius, Jr., 15; George Anna, 74; Lillia Mary, 86; Norman H., 72.
Brown— —— 61; Achsah Emeline, 44; Allison Sargeant, 43. Amelia Wilmarth, 47; Annie Amanda, 55; Edward Osgood, 44; Ella, 65; Elvira Ballou, 73; Flora Arletta, 82; Hellen Augusta, 44; Henry S., 47; Jabez Allen, 44; Jane Augusta, 60; John Woods, 44; Julia, 44; Leonard, 58; Lydia Ballou, 72; Mary Louisa Fisher, 43, 44; William Henry, 44.
Buckley or Burkley— Ann, 60; Daniel, 73, 79; Francis, 69; James, 76; Jeremiah, 62; William, 57.
Buffington—Clarissa Ann, 35; Ellen Maria, 37; Sarah Jane, 37.
Bullard — —52; Arbe, 17; Artemas Brown, 33; Asa, 34; Carrie Annetta, 54; Catharine Fisher, 36; Clarisa, 33; David Whitney, 26; Edward, 25; Electa, 32; Elezer Thompson, 28; Emeline, 35; Emerson Newel, 33; Irena Amanda, 51; Jane Menerva, 42; John, 15; Joseph Newel, 29; Joseph Warren, 34; Julete, 42; Julia, 31; Lyman, 13; Maria W., 39; Martha, 37; Mary C., 39; Mary Fisher, 33; Milletiah, 9; Phylete, 43; Pruda Maria, 35; Rena 36; Samuel Agustus, 46; Samuel Morse, 31; Sene, 15.
Burkley- See Buckley.
Burlingame - —— 54.
Burns- Edward, 84; Ellen Tracy, 81; Margaret Ann, 85; Mary Margaret, 84.
Burr—Laura Josephine, 49; Liberty Warren, 37; Sarah Orrilla, 37.

Canney—Charlote Abby, 77.
Capron—George Oliver, 61; Lillie May, 85.
Carpenter—Ella Hortense, 75; Freddie Albert, 64, 76.
Carr or Karr—Isadora, 86; William Henry, 55.
Cass—Frederick Nelson, 75; Walter Leroy, 77.
Castello or Costello— Catherine, 62; Ellenor, 63; Henry, 55; James, 58; Julia, 58; Thomas, 60.
Caswell—Hartwell Adelbert, 79, 80; Harville Albert, 80.
Chamberlain — Aldana Elizabeth, 51; Madora, 66.

INDEX—BIRTHS. 201

Chapman—Frederick Palmer, 78.
Chase—William Allison, 56.
Cheney— —— 59; Frank B., 61.
Chilson—Annie Dette, 83.
Claflin—Alonzo Robinson, 45: Calvin, 38; Calvin Samuel, 34; Florence 87; George Walter, 40; Josephine M., 76; William Henry, 34.
Clap—Harmon, 10.
Clark or Clarke— —— 53, 55, 58, 60, 75; Abigail Hawes, 36; Abijah, 16; Adaline, 21; Alfred, 33; Alfred, Jr., 49; Alice Augusta, 81; Ann Eliza, 46; Barnum, 17; Baxter, 17; Caroline Ada, 63; Charles Willard, 30; Clinton M., 79; Daniel Penniman, 21; Dyar Gilbert, 30, 33; Eleanor Jennette, 67; Elizabeth L., 41; Ellen Malinda, 39; Elton Orlando, 81. Erastus, 24; Esther, 10; Ezekiel Hall, 25; Franklin, 9. Frederic Clarence, 67; Gilbert, 33, 36; Horatio Kingsbury, 25; James Dawson, 25; John, 3d, 17; John Day, 26; Joseph Emerson, 72; Joseph Jones, 24; Lanson, 21; Laura, 21; Lois, 19, Mary, 23, 29, Mary C., 67; Mary Hawes, 26; Melatiah, 16; Melinda, 21; Mercy Richardson, 44; Nancy, 21, 30, 33; Nancy Melinda, 24; Nathan, 18, 41; Nathan, Jr., 23; Nellie Deeta, 84; Olive, 12; Paul, 9; Paul Baxter, 25; Preston Hawes, 24; Rachel, 17; Relief, 17; Sally, 28; Samuel, 11; Theron Edmund, 25; Willard, 33; William Edda, 62; William Emmerson, 26.
Clarry or Clary—Ellen Jane. 81; Thomas, 74; William Patrick, 81.
Clay—Aaron, 9.
Cleaveland, Cleavland or Cleveland— ——, 51: Addison, 22; Albert, 23; Alden Bradford, 28; Cora Isabelle, 69; Edwin A., 39; Evelyn, 43; Francis Augusta, 40; Frank Earnest, 65; George Preston, 21; Hannah, 22; Lowell, 29, Mary——, 48, William Metcalf, 57.
Cobb—Bessie Jane, 79; Charles Arther, 80; Hattie Mabel, 76; Leander Partridge, 22; Luther, Jr., 22; Minnie Adele, 83.
Coeyman—Willard Melville, 86.
Coffee—Calesta, 62; Warren, 50.
Coffield—Elizabeth Agnes, 82.
Colburn—David Gage, 25.
Cole—Ugene R., 43.
Coleman or Colman—Harvey, 13; Sally, 14.
Colgan—James Joseph, 87; Sarah Ellen, 80.
Colvin—Abby Melvina, 53, Abner James, 70; Zachariah, 50.
Combs—John Bridges, 24; Theophilus Clark, 26.

Condon—Lyons B., 74.
Conger or Congor— ——, 55, 58; Adie, 73; Carrie Elizabeth, 65; George, 61.
Conlin—Mary E., 76.
Connelly, Connolly or Conoley—Ellen, 69; Margarett, 76; Mary Ann, 61; Patrick, 72.
Connors—Joanna, 82.
Conoley—See Connelly.
Cook— ——, 55; Adelbert Osmond, 52; Agnez, 68; Alfred, 19; Amasa, Jr., 19; Anna Josephine, 86; Betsey, 23; Caroline, 71; Charles Madison, 29; Clayrasa, 10; Elbridge Gerry, 29; Elizabeth E., 65; Ellen Eliza, 70, Ellis Levi, 74; Frank Smith, 86; Freddie Elbridge, 82; Galen, 21; Josephine, 47; Lucy, 26, 29; Lydia Thompson, 69; Martin, 38; Mary Emony, 57; Maxey, 29; Milton, 29; Miranda, 23; Philena Amantha, 45; Pliny, 21; Sally, 21; Salvanus Scott, 23; Samuel, 21; Samuel S., 40; Sarah Maria, 36; Walter, 87; Walter Eugene, 77; Whipple, Jr., 23; Willie Almon, 86; Winneford, 63; Winslow, 23.
Cooledge—Lucy Caroline, 58.
Coombs—See Combs.
Cooper—Adelaide, 87; Amy Estelle, 86.
Corbett—Ellen Elizabeth, 87; Emma Lonesa, 82; George Sumner, 46; John James, 71; Mary Ann, 66; Stephen Howard, 25.
Corbin— ——, 76; Ada Frances, 70, Ada Louise, 70; Charles Henry, 60; Clara Maria, 55; Etta Amelia Barney, 77; Eva Augusta, 80; Minnie Mary, 77; Sarah Nellie, 65.
Costello—See Castello.
Cotton—Annie M., 81; Willie Austin, 67.
Coughlin—Daniel, 82; John, 71.
Covell—Daniel C., 42; Lucy A., 42.
Crooks—Annie Leonora, 76, John, 12; Marquise Metcalf, 24.
Crosley or Crossley—Elmor Ellsworth, 71; Florabelle, 66.
Crowley—James, 80.
Crowningshield—William, 67.
Cullin—Michael, 87.
Cummings—Albert Banbridge, 33; Eliza Ann, 49; Eugine, 52; Jeremiah, 51.
Cushing—David, 12; Hannah, 12, Marques Delefyette, 12; Pyam, 12.
Cushman—Mary, 48.
Cutlar or Cutler—George Stillman, 25; Jatham Clark, 22, Jemima, 18; John Hudson, 22; Samuel Guild, 24.

Daniels— ——, 68, 77; Abigail Clap, 22; Ada Francis, 41; Albert Barton, 55; Albert Early, 26; Almira Augusta, 37; Amariah, Jr., 14; Amos Fisher,

28; Anna Maria, 71; Benjamin Franklin, 37, Betsey, 18; Betsey Ann, 28; Caroline Matilda, 37, 52; Caroline Melita, 26; Charlene, 66; Charles Adams, 35, Charles Fisher, 30; Charlotte, 38; Clarissa Marie, 37; Cora Jane,67; Cynthia, 16; Cyrus. 11; Darvin Joseph, 29. David. 11; David Wood,19; Dexter Ward,22; Dorcas,11; Edward Francis, 66; Edwin, 38; Elisabeth, 10; Eliza, 35; Eliza Jane, 31; Eliza Partridge, 23; Ella Baker, 84; Ella Georgette, 50. Ellen Mariah, 36; Ellsworth Nalum, 73; Ernest Darwin. 77; Eunite, 9; Ezra, 13; Fisher, 19; Frank Wheaton, 74; Gardner Fisk, 59; George Warren, 45; Hannah, 23; Harriet Adaline, 38; Harriot Louisa, 29; Hattie Adelia, 75; Henry, 18, Henry Fisher, 49; Henry Metcalf, 35; Henry Smith, 39; Hiram Abiff. 29; Ida Marian, 59, Jane A., 39; Janette Phipps, 52; Jemima Leland. 27; Jerome Starkweather. 41; Joel, 13; Joseph Hills, 35; Julia Maria. 20; Juliann, 37; Kezia, 16; Laura Eveline, 56; Laura Melissa, 55; Lewis, 29; Lucelia Adalaid, 43; Lucy, 21; Lucy Gilbert, 36; Luke, 13; Martha Carpenter, 29; Martha E., 39; Mary Ann, 28, 84; Mary Clap, 29; Mary L., 39; Mary Leola. 72; Medora Ame, 65; Nahum Ward, 23; Nathan. 4th, 44; Nathan Anson, 59; Nellie Adelaide. 70; Olive, 16; Olive Sanford, 68; Oscar Jefferson, 81 Pliny. 20; Sabin Allen, 35; Sally. 14; Seth, 17; Sophia Phidella, 37; Squire Geo. Warren Lafayette, 34; Susan Fisher, 26; Susan Maria. 46; Thomas Jefferson, 22, 34; Unity Mira, 21, Waldo. 36; Walter Elmer. 74; William Haven, 38; William Henderson, 28. William Loren, 62; Willis George, 26.

Darling—Anna Louisa, 85, Betty, 13; Eddie Jefferson, 86; Hettia Ann, 56; Ida, 59; James, 81; Jesse, 67, 74; Leroy Armond, 61; Mary Jane, 80; Nellie Colburn, 79; Sarah Elizabeth, 62.

Davidson—Elizabeth Sarah, 70; Fanny Emely, 72; Frank, 85; George J., 85; Hellen Joanna, 65; Jane Elizabeth,76.

Davis—John Alonzo, 77.

Day— ——, 69; David, 11; Ebenezer. 11; Ernest Walter, 84; Jonathan, 11.

Dean—Abigail,9, 10; Abigail Daniels,26; Ada E., 72; Arther Adams,82; Betsy, 11; Charles, 84; Charles I., 40; Charlotte F., 40; Cyrus, 12; Edgar C., 63; Edmund Clark, 43; Eliza Ann. 26; Emma Grace Luthera,57; Gardner A., 40; George, 77; George Anna, 67; George W., 40; Hannah M., 40 (2);

Ichabod, 12; Julia Adams, 26; Luni A., 59; Maria Amelie, 46; Mary, 18; Oliver, 12; Silvester, 14; Tryphena, 13; William A., 40.

Deforge—Henry, 79.

Dennie—John, 69.

Desmond—James. 60; Jeremiah, 65; Joanna, 69.

DeWitt— ——, 71; Susan Fisher, 68; William Sternes, 55.

Doherty, Dohrity or Dougherty— ——, 63; Bridget, 85; Mary Ann, 82; Mary Eliza, 86; Phillip, 78.

Dolan—Mary Ann, 72.

Dorr—Aline Leroda, 54; Harriet Maria. 49.

Dougherty—See Doherty.

Dudley—Jane, 45.

Dugan or Dugen— ——, 75; Mary Elizabeth, 83.

Dunbar—Charles Leeds, 33; James Clark. 33; John Allen, 33; Mary Ann, 33; Susanna Matilda, 33; William Lewis, 33.

Dunn—Caroline Pamelia, 38; Charles Andrew, 85; Sarah Elisebeth, 38.

Dunton—Evelyn Amelia, 43; Henrietta Catherine. 85.

Earle—Martha Ella, 56.

Eaton—George Alfred, 74.

Ellis—Abigail Hunt, 30; Almira, 18; Charlotte Sophia. 32; Deborah Fairbanks, 24, 28; Elihu, 14; George Payson, 16; Henry Orville. 30; Levi, 11; Luther, 12; Lydia, 10; Maria Bloomfield, 28; Meranda. 14; Preston, 22; Rhoda Partridge, 28; Simeon, 26, Timothy, Jr., 22.

Ely—Sarah Jane, 43.

Emerson—Annie Maria, 62; George Ellis, 46; Gracie Mary, 68.

Emmons—Deliverance, 11; Diodate Johnson, 9; Erastus, 14; Martha, 10; Nathanael, 9; Sarah, 13; William, 12.

Engley—Arvilla Adams, 37; Elon Erastus, 38; Orlando Sweet, 35.

Erwin—Margaret, 57.

Esty—Frances Ann, 37.

Everett— —— 76; Frank A., 73; Eugene Ellsworth, 74.

Fahan—Mary Ellen, 81.

Fairbanks—Abigail, 17. Adin B., 49; Asa, 3d, 18; Caroline, 15; Clara Anna, 77; Eliza Jane, 78; Ellen Maria. 82; Jerusha. 13; Julitta, 14; Sarah, 22.

Fales—James Emers, 36; James Emerson, 36.

Farley—Rosanna, 52.

Farnum—Sarah Lucina, 59.

Farr—Lucella Frances, 66; Millard Lincoln, 78; Theodore Parker, 60.

Farrington—Dolly Ware, 15; Elijah

INDEX—BIRTHS. 203

Dalphon, 15; Fradrack, 15; John, 13; Sylvanus Warren, 32; William Williams, 32.
Farris—William Henry, 60.
Fay—Maria Louisa, 39.
Featherston—Julia, 57.
Feeley, Feely or Felee—Anna, 73; Charles, 82; Hannah, 82; Joanna Maria, 80; Julia Maria, 80; Margarett, 84; Mary, 75; Patrick, 83; Timothy, 77, 85.
Fergeson— —— 63.
Ferren—William Franklin, 53.
Fisher— —— 40, 57, 66, 74; Abby, 42; Abigail, 17, 19; Abigail Bacon, 29; Abigail Ursula, 27, (2); Abigail Whiting, 21; Abijah, 14; Adaline, 23; Adin, 20; Albert Rockwood, 35; Alexander Metcalf, 17, 36; Amelia or Melia,25; Amos, Jr.,17; Annie R.,87; Arthur Lewis, 59; Betsey, 17, 40; Caroline, 27; Caroline Fairbanks, 32; Charles,21,71; Charles Frances,50; Charles Lovell, 27, Charles Martel, 20; Charles Richmond, 30; Charles Sewall, 33; Charles Willis, 30 31; Charlotte, 24; Clara, 40; Clary, 19; David, 14, 23, 26; David Baker, 24; Daniel Cowel, Jr., 20; Edmond Tyler, 39; Edwin Allen, 32; Eliab, 10; Elial, 38; Elinor, 30; Eliza, 35; Eliza Ann, 32; Eliza Jane, 30; Eliza Tileston, 22; Ella Maria, 57; Ellen Maria, 34, 37; Emeline,29; Emily Harris,39; Erasmus Pond, 32; Eugene Gilbert, 51; Eunice, 20; Evelyn Eliza, 41; Francis Herbert, 54; Frank Herbert, 80; Frederic, Jr., 17; George, 14. 40; George Henry, 51; George Marshall, 66; George Nelson, 28; George Perkins, 28; George Washington, 31; Gilbert Clark, 35; Hannah, 20; Hariet A., 41; Hariot, 14; Harlow, 18, 27; Harman Cleveland, 19; Harriet Metcalf, 35; Harvey, 18, 27; Hellen Augustus, 83; Henry, 38; Henry Pelton, 78; Herman, 15; Hermon Maxey, 32; Irena, 22; Isabelle Louisa, 60; James, 35; James Ferdinand,34; Jason,13; Jemima,15; Joanna, 15; Joann Hopkins,32; John, 12; John Hancock, 27; John Lewis, 48; John Murry,75; John Warren, 29; Joseph, 15; Joseph Hawes, 34; Joseph Warren, 31; Julia, 11, 15; Julia Frances, 37; Julius, 19; Lewis, 12, 27; Lewis Leprilete, 34; Lewis Whiting, 17, 27; Levi Clark, 25; Louisa, 27; Louisa Jane, 31; Lucy, 23; Lucy Ann, 36; Lucy Baker, 22; Lucy Cobb, 40; Lurana, 27; Mabel, 77; Mareah Abbot, 32; Maria Ann, 27; Mariah Richardson, 34; Marshall Warren, 37; Martha Emmons, 37; Martha Jane, 45; Mary, 13, 14, 48; Mary Adaline, 28; Mary Ann, 41; Mary Blanchard, 77; Mary Ida, 26; Mary Jane, 40; Mary Louisa, 34; Matilda Emily, 30; Maxey, 13; Melia or Amelia, 25; Melinda, 30; Milton Metcalf, 25; Moses, Jr., 19; Nabby Whiting, 27; Nancy, 16, 24, 37; Nancy Maria, 30; Nathan Austin, 19; Nathaniel, 18, 27; Nathaniel, Jr., 15; Nathaniel Emmons, 21, 27; Nathaniel Horace, 33; Nellie, 62; Oliver Gilbert, 29; Patty, 18; Paul Metcalf, 32; Perez, 11; Peter, 13; Preston Willard, 50; Rachel Emeline, 34; Rena, 17; Rufus Albert, 41; Ruth, 14; Sally, 14; Samuel Biram, 15; Sarah, 39; Sarah Ann, 36; Sarah Hawkins, 28; Sarah Jane, 33; Sewell, 38; Smith, 24; Susan, 30, 31; Susan Matilda, 33; Susanna, 29; Thomas W., 40; Walter Harris, 27; Walter Merrifield, 39; Warren, 26; Weston, 40; Whiting, 14; Willard, 19; William Henry, 35, 38; William Lewis, 32; Willis, 12.
Fittspatrick or Fitzpatrick—Gerrard, 53; Julia Allice, 73.
Fitzgerald—Julia, 81.
Fletcher—Josephene, 69.
Flinn— —— 60.
Foley—Abby A.,72; Frederick Thomas, 80.
Follen—Susan, 67.
Follett—Arravesta, 50; Arravilla, 50; Eldora A., 43; Manning Adelburt,63.
Force—Lucinda Ware, 20.
Ford—Mary, 83; Nannie Jane, 82; Patrick, 78; Thomas Francis, 79.
Foster— ——— 45; Alice Ann Maria, 86; John Francis, 83; Susan Emily, 43; William, 20.
Franklin—Emma Louesa, 77.
Freeman—Emma Frances, 57; Jennette F., 65; Julia Arabella, 54.
Fros.— ——56; Harriet Agusta, 62.
Fuller— ——— 68; Abner Gilbert, 26; Asa Metcalf Baker, 28; Elizabeth Cutler, 30; George Newell, 31; George Warren, 86; Gilbert, 37; Mary Ann, 35; Nancy Cutler, 30; Sarah Jane, 36; Stephen Burton, 29; William Fisher, 28.
Galvin—Ellen, 86.
Garvin—James Henry, 70; Thomas, 60.
Gary—Louisa, 23; Lucinda, 23; Nancy, 23.
Gay— ——— , 56; Abby Maria, 48; Abigail, 19; Abigail Sumner, 24; Adelaid Forsena, 84; Amor Bacon, 13; Anna Agusta, 52; Ann Frances, 39; Charles, 66; Charles Herbert, 40; Charlotte Bacon, 27; David Morse, 26; Edgar Adelbert, 82; Edward, 14;

Edwin Lafayette, 39; Eldana Melinda, 39; Ellen Maria, 37; Emeline, 40; Frank Ellsworth, 79; George Edwin, 52; Harriet Frances, 55; Henry Wilks, 39; Isadora Susan, 43; Joseph Lewis, 48; Leoma, 43; Levi Lewis, 43; Lucina Pinkney, 51; Marietta Butridge, 55; Mary, 19; Mercey Bacon, 30; Nancy, 26; Nancy Melvina, 40; Nelson, 26; Oliver Dean, 59; Rufus Putnam, 14; Thomas Pinkney, 31; Timothy, Jr., 19; Timothy Ellis, 41; Walter Harris, 29.

Gibson—Fred Valentine Cornelius, 82; Lyman Henry, 74, 76; Mary Frances, 62.

Gifford—Ada Eldora, 82; Frank, 77; Joseph F., 74; Lena Mary, 80.

Gillmor, Gillmore or Gilmore— ——, 50, 58, 71; Abigail Charlotte, 28; Adalade M., 40; Adaline Jane, 28; Adelia Robbins, 28; Albert, 31; Albert Greene, 33; Albert James, 47; Alfred Farrington, 71; Annie Mary, 65; Betsey Rebekah McL., 36; Caroline Anstice, 45; Caroline Ormelia, 34; Charles Willard, 34; Charlotte Amanda, 33; Charlotte Louisa, 30; Chauncey Fuller, 84; David, 17; Edward Allen, 74; Edward H. Robbins, 31; Ellis, 67; Emeline Ann, 72; Francis Henry, 34; George Albert Green, 41, 43; George Robert McLane, 30; Harriet Francis, 30; James, 12; James, Jr., 14; James Partridge, 31; Jenny Lousea, 77; Joseph, 16; Joseph Hills, 38; Louisa R., 40; Lowell, 32; Lucinda Adams, 30; Lurana, 34; Martha Laura, 41; Mary Ann Bancroft, 38; Mary Arabella Stewart, 45; Metcalf, 37; Molly, 17; Nance, 11; Nancy Fales, 26; Nancy Maria, 38; Nathan, 10; Nathan Otis, 19; Olive, 13; Olive Maria, 31; Olive Rebekah, 34; Pashance, 12; Robert, Jr., 14; Rufus, 14; Sally, 14; Samuel Tirrel, 28; Sanford, 12; Sarah Ann, 33; Susan Adelia, 37; Theron Gilbert, 46; William, 15; William Davis, 36; William Ellis, 34; William Smith, 38.

Going or Gowen—Artemas Warren, 27; Blanche Lillian, 85; Charles, 30; Edward Lester, 84; George Metcalf, 29; Horace, 32; Horatio Kingsbury, 26; John, Jr., 17; Louisa Marena, 29; Luther, 18; Mary Ann, 25.

Gordan, Gorden or Gordon—Abby, 85; James, 82; Jenny Lind, 57; John, 79; Sarah Maria, 47; Susan Edna, 56.

Gorton—Frederick, 76.

Goss—Albert Horace, 86.

Gould—Alice Elizabeth, 83; Irving Wadsworth, 84; Joel, 9; William H., 77.

Gowen—See Going.

Graham—Thomas Nilson, 41.

Granger—George, 60; Henry, 56, 59; Mary Ann, 54; Nannona, 74; Sarah, 62.

Grant—Edith Martha, 71.

Gray—Frances Elizabeth Smith, 38.

Green or Greene—Abby Jane, 48; Ellen Maria, 41; Everett Marsh, 72; Fred Holbrook, 68; Henry Martin, 31; Job Herbert, 49; Lois Anngenette, 34; Lydia Avy, 45; Martha Emeline, 53; William Henry, 67.

Greenwood—Betsey C., 34; John Henry, 83.

Grow—Nellie Carrie, 70.

Guild— ——, 71; Ada Marinda, 65; Adelaide Louisa, 51; Benjamin, 21; Benjamin Haden, 36; Benjamin Haven, 44; Betsey, 16; Caleb Mason, 26; Charles E., 40; Charles II., 40; Chloe, 27; Cyrus, 16; Earl Bradford, 54; Ebenezer, Jr., 16; Elizabeth E., 40; Elvira Louisa, 35; Erastus, 31; Esther, 15; Harriet F., 40; Ida Malinda, 65; Isabel B., 40; Joel, 24; John, 15; John Edmund, 24; Joseph Grafton, 44; Julia, 20; Lewis Adrean, 35; Liewis, 12; Loisa, 26; Lorinda Ann, 31; Lucy, 15; Lucy Cutler, 29; Lydia, 18; Martha Louisa, 44; Mary Elizabeth, 44; Nancy, 22; Phebe, 16; Polly, 20; Rachel, 21; Ruth, 21; Samuel, Jr., 16; Sukey, 23; Timothy, 16.

Gurney—Marion Gertrude, 82; Paul Eugene, 69; Richard Elbridge, 65; Sarah Caroline, 46.

Hagerty, Haggarty, Haggerty or Higgerty—Charles, 73; James, 69; Thomas L., 72; William James, 81.

Hall—Abigail Charlotte, 38; George Gardner, 39; Harriet Bowditch, 39; Jane Elizabeth, 38; John Hiram, 34; Mary Ann Gillmore, 38.

Hallerin, Hollarin or Hollerin—Ellen, 58; James, 59; Jeremiah, 74; John, 61; Margaret, 69; Timothy, 66.

Hamilton— ——, 56; Almeda Elizabeth, 53; Charles Henry, 49; Edward Francis, 51; George, 54; Herbert Eugene, 51; William, 46.

Hancock—Charles I., 72; Sarah Jane, 78; Susan, 28.

Harding—Betsey, 21; Bulkley Adams, 29; Charles Lewis, 28; Elisha, 19; Eliza Ann, 31; Fisher Hartshorn, 27; George Warren, 30; Harriot, 22; Irene Francis, 32; Joseph, 21; Lewis, 16; Lucy, 13; Nabby, 21; Nancy Maria, 32; Nancy Williams, 31; Olive, 23; William Curtis, 29.

Hardy—Grace Maria, 54; Sanford Cary, 58.

INDEX—BIRTHS. 205

Harris——— ———, 71; Elisha Joseph, 67; Eva Frances, 63; James Dyer, 42; Malinda, 56; Mary Shephard, 45, 46;

Hart——— ———, 60; Abigail Ann, 46; Alexander Ezra, 48; Benjamin Andrew, 57; Caroline, 48; Ella Jane, 53; Frances Lavina, 56; George Eugene, 61; Joseph Jackman, 54; Martha Adalma Caroline, 51; Susan Maria, 51.

Hartshorn or Hartshorne ——— ———, 48, (2); Arrabella Ada, 57; Colburn, 9; Ebenezer, 9; Elbridge Preston, 29; Ellen Josephine, 67; Flora Gertrude, 74; Frank Eugene, 45; George, 31; George E., 39; Gilbert, 30; Henry D., 40; Ida Elizabeth, 65; Isabella Ida, 57; Julia, 35; Mary, 32; Mary Josephine, 43; Olive A., 39; Polly, 15; Seth Lawrence, 17; Walter, 37.

Haskell——— ———, 44; Clarrinda Pond, 35; Eleanor Amanda, 32; William Turner, 35.

Hattien—Eliza Eveline Holbrook, 33.

Hayward or Haywood—Claudius Drusus, 12; George Warren, 40.

Hawes or Haws——— ———, 61; Abel, 13; Abigail, 18, 19, 37; Abijah, 16; Ada A., 53; Amelia, 29; Amos, 18; Beriah, 16; Calvin Milton, 38; Edward, 37; Esther Adams, 36; Eugene, 50; Fanny, 23; Ichabod, 13; Jemima, 16; Joab, 16; Joseph, Jr., 18; Josiah, 22; Julia Eliza, 39; Kezia, 11; Levi, 16; Lewis Henry, 37; Mary 16, 17, 36; Mary Jane, 37; Matthias, 16; Meletiah Everitt, 18; Moses, 18; Nathan, 21; Nathaniel, 29; Peter, 18; Preston, 22; Sally, 25; Samuel Partridge, 9; Sara, 14; Sukey Sumner, 21; Susa, 18; Susanna, 22.

Hawkins—James Fisher, 34.

Haws—See Hawes.

Haywood—See Haward.

Hazard—Charles Granville, 53; Hannah Frances, 50.

Healey or Healy—James Timothy, 85; John Collins, 77; Mary, 81.

Heaton—Abigail Hills, 30; Brainard, 26; Charles Hamilton, 48; David, 21; Ellen Josephine, 44; George Dean, 34; Hermon, 14; Huldah, 14; Isaac, 15; Isaac Erving, 24; Lynda, 18; Millie, 18; Nathan, 10; Noah, 10; Olive, 18, 19; Ruth, 44; Salle, 13; Sally, 13; Samuel, Jr., 20; Sinai, 11; Syntha, 11; William Albert, 33.

Hewes or Hews—James Harvey, 23; John, 74; Virgil, 18; Virgil Hammond, 20.

Higgerty—See Hagerty.

Hill or Hills——— ———, 67, 68, 70, 71, 76; Abba Isabella, 46; Alberton Metcalf, 53 (note); Betsey Pond, 19; Beulah, 10; Caroline, 24; Carrie Eva, 82; Carrie Matilda, 74; Charles Frances, 77; Charles R., 81; Ede, 12; Edgar Franklin, 82; Edward Sanford, 57; Elias, 12; Elias Ware, 22; Ella, 73; Ella Augusta, 50; Ervin Loyd, 60; Esther, 10; Eudora Frances, 47; Francis S., 40; Frank Sheredin, 77; George Henry, 43; George W., 40; Harriet Adelade Elizabeth, 41; Harriot, 31; Harvey, 22; Hendrick Sanford, 52 (see note); Ichabod, 10; Jarvis Harlow, 20; Jemima, 10; Jennie Elizabeth, 66; Jenny Gilmore, 75; Joanna, 12; Jonah, 10; Joseph Gilmor, 32; Lewis, 17; Lillian Frances, 80; Louisa Maria, 31; Lucy Ann, 71; Lysander Blake, 19; Mary Amanda, 73; Melissa Blake, 31; Micah, 10; Molly, 10; Nabe, 10; Nancy, 15; Olive Gilmore, 23; Polly, 23; Seneca, 19; Seth Rockwood, 35; Susan Maria, 39; Theron Clement, 26; Warren, 20; William, 37; William Elleot, 36; William Warren, 70.

Hilton—Evelyn E., 67.

Hitchcock—Lois Bailey, 32.

Holbrook—Edwin N., 84; Emely Smith, 81.

Hollarin or Hollerin—See Hallerin.

Hollihan, Hulihan or Hullihan——— ———, 74; Ellen, 71; Thomas, 67.

Holmes—Ellen Maria, 50; Ida Janette, 63; Louisa Ann, 47.

Hood——— ———, 76; Batha Idilla, 86; Jannie, 80; Lizzie Anna, 77; Marrietta, 83.

Hopkins—Elisha, 46.

Hosie—Mary Irene, 81.

Howard—Abby, 68; Edmund Francis, 46; Franklin Everett, 76; Henry Morton, 82; Mabel E., 73.

Hoyt—Rosetta, 54; Rosina, 54.

Hubbard or Hubbart—Abigail, 24; Adin Sargeant, 56; Eben, 22; Elisha, 20; Elizabeth Amelia, 39; Ernest Eugene, 70; Everett Lincoln, 78; Freddie Ellsworth, 82; Joshua George, 39; Sabin, 33; William Edwin, 34.

Hulihan or Hullihan—See Hollihan.

Hunt Edward Eugine, 52.

Hunting—Edmund, 33; Eliza, 37; Horatio, 32; Juliet, 37.

Ingraham—John, 54.

Inman—Althena M., 58; Elmira W., 41; Susan A., 47.

Johnson—Sally Walker, 33; Thomas Francis, 87.

Jones—Abigail, 22; Adams, 21; Bathsheba, 21; Edward Davis, 27; Mary Dahm, 28; Phillip, 71; Sarah Eda, 38; Timothy Ellis, 21.

FRANKLIN TOWN RECORDS.

Jordan, Jorden or Jourdan— ——60;
Albert Lewis, 41; Alfred Almond, 53;
Alfred Harris, 41; Alice Iantha, 53;
Alton Alden, 57; Alvira Wood, 35;
Charles Andrew, 85; Charles Henry,
69; Clarence Edmond, 74; Edith Minerva, 47; Edwin Arnold, 41; Ellen
Frances, 49; Emma Frances, 77;
Herbert Alden, 51; John Warren, 56;
Samuel Harris, 43; Sarah Jane, 41;
Sarah Louisa, 43; Walter Earnest, 67.
Josely or Joslin—Frederic Weston, 68;
Mitty Sarah, 70; Myrtie Elmina, 78.
Jourdan—See Jordan.

Karr—See Carr.
Keefe—William Edward, 83.
Kelly—Francis, 86; James Martin, 81.
Kelsey—Carlos Franklin, 51; Ezra
Warren, 49.
Kilburn or Kilburne—Arthur Warren,
69; George Samuel, 54.
Kimball—Clarissa, 42; Edmond, 42;
Emily, 42; Martha, 50; Nancy Maria,
46; Susan, 42.
King— —— 73, 76 (2), 81; Albert
Newel, 36; Charles Jackson, 36;
David Addison, 79; Edwin, 41; Elizabeth Eldon, 61; Esther Matilda, 78;
Frances Eddy, 72; Frederick Henry,
86; Georgeanna, 63; George Washington, 36; Harriet, 41; Hattie E.,
83; John Adams, 36; Lucy Maribel,
74; Mary, 41; Mary Lucy, 55; Theodore Dexter, 85; Walter Lyman, 79;
William Claflin, 36; William E., 67;
William Warren, 85.
Kingsbury—Abial, 13; Abigail, 14;
Abigail Maria, 40; Abner Ellis, 33;
Almira Hart, 26; Asa Cutler, 24;
Benjamin, 14; Caleb Blake, 20;
Charlotte Helen, 33; Charlottee Sabins, 20; Clarisa Elizabeth, 33;
Ebenezer Lawton, 27; Emery E., 39;
Fisher Adams, 27; Flora Agnsta, 44;
George Allen, 39; George Daniels, 36,
38; Horatio, 10, 27; John Haven,
31; Luther, 9; Maria H., 39; Marion
Adella, 49; Mary E., 46; Mary Fisk,
27; Matilda, 9; Nathaniel Davis, 33;
Olive, 14; Orion Smith, 22; Polly
Fisher, 33; Samuel Allen, 17; Sarah
Ann, 43; Stephen, 11; Susan Fisher,
38; Theodore Turner, 18; Willard, 16.
Knapp—Alfred, 17; Emilia, 29; George
Washington, 20; Gilbert Clark, 28;
Hiram, 17, 31; Josephene Gilbert, 70;
Julia Sequestra, 34; Matilda Gertrude, 77; Matilda Hawes, 32; Melville, 17; Peggy, 17; Polly, 19; Susan,
31; Sylvia Lucretia, 30.

Laing—Charles Walter, 66; William
Archibald, 61.

Lannon—See Lennon.
Larkin—Edward, 61; Henry, 58; John,
69; Joseph Lawrence, 56; Lawrena
Nigh, 77; Lawrence H., 76; Margarett
Clara, 72; Mary Darcy, 73.
Lathua—Marcetta, 27.
Lavan—Michael S., 77.
Lawrance or Lawrence—Adelaid E., 42;
Addison Clark, 24; Almira, 30; Almon, 17; Amos Turner, 32; Anna,
16; Anson, 21; Armeliah, 19; Asa
Whiting, 20; Caroline, 28; Charles
C., 42; Daniel Sanford, 18; Ebenezer,
17; Eleazer Hills, 14; Eliphoz, 12;
Eliza, 22; Ellis S., 72. Esther, 18;
Eunice, 16; George Leprilette, 31;
Hannah 14; Harlow, 19; Harriet
Agusta, 54; Herbert, 52; Jabez
Fisher, 25; Jairus, 30; Joseph, 13;
Joshua, 12; Julia, 15; Nathan, 15;
Palmy, 16; Polly, 18, Pudy, 16;
Ransom, 14; Susanna 27; Victoria,
44.
Lee—Israel, 10; Sarah, 10.
Legg—Allemar, 12; Ferdinand, 16;
Julia, 16, 76.
Lemon—James, 76.
Lannon or Lennon—Charles, 82; Margaret, 79; Patrick, 72; Thomas Joseph, 86.
Leonard—George Shaw, 39; Mary
Louisa, 39.
Lesure—Charles Francis, 83.
Lethbridge—Abigail, 14; Claracy, 12;
Clementinie Sabins, 20; Fardanand,
9; Hephzibah, 15; Jerusha, 13;
Nama, 16; Poly, 9; Richard, 13;
Sabem, 13; Sally, 19. Samuel, 3d, 14;
Susanna, 10; Susanna Candon, 25;
William, 11.
Lewis— —— 58 (2).
Lewitt—Elone, 13; Stephen, 14.
Lincoln— —— 70; Alice Jennette,
55; Arther Llewellyn, 79; Charles
G., 67; Charlotte F., 40; Clarence
Decator, 62; Edwin Ruthvien, 37;
Franklin Hamilton, 37; Herbert J.,
86; Herbert Lafayette, 40; Julia
Aurelia, 34; Manly, 19; Manly DeValence, 34; William Russell, 32.
Linett—Peter, 15; Susanna, 16.
Lombard—Annie Randall, 81; Wendell
Bennet, 83.
Lucior—Celina Praxide, 83.
Lynch—Ellen, 76; Margaret, 84; Timothy, 80.

Maguire—Francis P., 82.
Makepeace or Makepease—George Lamont, 21; Polly, 20; William, Jr., 18.
Man or Mann— —— 58, 63; Alden,
71; Betsy, 14; Chloe, 11; Cynthia
Plan, 29; Eldod, 10; Elias Watts,
18; Elizabeth Ann, 78; Emeline

Copps, 27; Esther, 11; Eunice, 9; Harriet Emily, 30; Hellen Agnes, 85; Horace, 19; Jemima, 10; John Rollins. 45; Jonathan Edwards, 50; Lydia Bishop, 20; Mary Emmons, 76; Nathan, 13; Patty, 15; Polly, 12; Rebeccah, 13; Rosalinda, 13; Seneca, 11; Sewell Rollins, 47; Stephen, 16; Synthe, 13; Thomas Stanley, 14; William Davidson, 82.
Marjen—Caroline Eliza. 50; Earnest Ballou. 62.
Marrs—Susan Elizabeth, 54.
Marsh—Edna Eliza, 74; Frank Pierce, 55; Mary Ella Isadora. 45; Samuel Robertson, 62.
Marsten or Marston— —— 66; Willis Eugene, 59.
Martin—Maryeth Maranda, 58.
Maxey—Emma Jane, 50.
McCarty— Eugene, 74; Hellen, 53; Jeremiah, 69.
McClusky—Philip II., 85.
McCue— —— 67; Martin, 63; Winnie, 69.
McFarland or McParland Bridget, 80; Celia, 73; Daniel, 85; Edward, 59; James, 66; Margaret. 76, 81; Mary Ann, 62; Philip Hews, 70.
McMann—Peter, Jr., 78.
McParland—See McFarland.
McWails—John, 18.
Mec—Thomas, 49.
Merrifield or Merryfield—Aaron, 17; Alanson, 21; Emma Frances, 51; Marshal Gardner, 31; Mary Meranda, 55; Willis, 23.
Merrill—Alvah Morrison, 57.
Merryfield—See Merrifield.
Metcalf— —— 49, 58, 66 (2), 71; Abby Harding. 55; Abigail, 18; Abigail Harding, 18; Abigail Laurinda, 29, 38; Abigail Richardson, 26; Abijah Whiting, 22; Achsa, 15; Ada Edwina Serres, 87; Adelbert Alvah, 52; Adeline, 54; Albert, 24; Alesford, 11; Alfred, 34; Alfred G., 39; Alfred Harding, 30; Alice. 69; Alice Isadora, 46; Allen, 23; Anna Frances, 45; Artemas, 17, 19; Artimas Gilbert, 20; Asa, 13; Austin, 31; Bathsheba, 20; Bathsheba Crane,. 22; Betsey Whiting, 34; Caroline, 24; Charles, 25; Charles C., 41; Charles Edwards, 33; Charles Herman, 33; Eben, 15; Ebenezer Torrey, 27, 38; Eleanor Amelia, 33; Electa, 19; Eliab, 12; Elial, 37; Elias, 20; Eliel, 24; Elizabeth, 21; Ella Maria, 52; Ellen Frances, 55; Elvira, 15; Emaline Betsey, 27; Emeline Whiting. 36; Erasmus B., 33; Erastus Lovel (l). 28, 68; Evelina Eudora, 46; Fisher, 24; George Dwight, 59; George Earnest, 56; George Nelson, 39; George Richardson, 53; George Wildes, 63; Gilbert Dean, 25; Hannah, 20; Harriet Elizabeth, 41; Harriot, 31; Harvey, 14; Herbert Wallace. 50; Hiram, 27; Horace Preston, 31; James, 3d, 22; Jonathan, Jr., 24; John Calvin, 20; John George, 24; John Whiting, 50; Joseph Harding, 22; Joseph Whiting, 25; Judson, 10; Julia, 19; Juliana. 31; Julitta, 15; Junia, 17; Laura. 27 (2); Lois, 9, 10; Louesa Adelaid, 73; Lucretia, 32; Marquis, 15; Martha Miller, 37; Mary, 12, 19, 33; Mary A., 47; Mary Ann, 27; Mary Anna, 59; Mary Dawson, 22; Mary Elizabeth, 38; Mary Gilbert, 52; Mary Robinson. 22; Melea, 15; Melenda, 15; Michael, 22; Michael Edmund, 39; Miletiah, 27; Milton, 14; Miranda Newman, 28; Nahum Fisher, 47; Nancy, 18, 26; Nancy Allen, 28; Nathan, Jr., 20; Nellie Elizabeth, 61; Olive, 19; Olivia, 17; Otis Fisher, 32; Patta, 15; Patty, 23; Paul, 19; Peggy, 15; Persis, 15; Polly, 10, 16; Prudence Fercry, 13; Richardson, 30; Roxey, 25; Salla, 10; Samuel, Jr., 27; Sarah Amelia, 39; Sarah Emeline, 66; Sena, 16; Susanna, 15; Theron, 12; Timothy Augustus, 31; Whiting, 9; Willard, 10; Willard Fisher, 77; William, 15; William Pitt, Jr., 23; William Sumner, 55; William Torry, 38; William Warren, 32.
Millard—Joseph, 10; Thankful, 10.
Miller or Muller— —— 51, 61; Abijah Thurston, 19; Alice Oretta, 74; Alonzo R., 47; Arthur Orenzo, 74; Charlotte, 31; Charlotte Levina, 65; Edward Howe, 46; Elkanah, 22; Erastus Darwin, 27; Francis G., 40; Frank Ellsworth, 75; Ferdinand Holton, 24; Georgiana Parker, 41; Gillmore, 30; Hannah B., 40; Hannah Fales, 20; Hariet Gilmore, 72; Herman Blake, 32; Horace G., 41; Jesse, 20; Jesse, Jr., 27; Jesse T., 41; John L., 40; John Warren, 25; Joseph, Jr., 21; Julim Laureal, 23; Levina, 25; Lewis Gillmor, 36; Lewis L., 40; Lewis Leprilete, 20; Louisa Darwin, 39; Mary Eliza, 40; Nancy, 22; Nathan Rockwood, 53; Olive, 65; Rachel Johnson, 27; Rufus, 17; Sally, 22; Waldo Suarrow, 29.
Mitchel—Lillie Agusta, 69.
Monroe or Munroe—Charles Edward, 64; Mary Emily, 45.
Morley—Ellie Jane, 84.
Morrill—Nathaniel, 26.
Morrison—Charles Edward, 75, 79; Edwin, 62.
Morse—Aaron, 18 (2); Adelbert Hart-

well, 76; Albert Mory, 38; Angelia Josephine, 41; Annie Loueza, 78; Arabella Jane, 41; Bertha Florence, 85; Bradford Fisher, 39; Caroline, 24; Charles Edson, 34; Darius, 18; David Thurston, 26; Earnest Munroe, 70; Eddy Lincoln, 84; Edith, 65; Elmer Lugene, 78; Emily Frances, 66; Esther, 17; Eveline Elizabeth, 55; George Fisher, 38; George Lincoln, 34; George Washington, 22; Granville, 41; Hannah, 11; Harriet Eliza, 67; Harvey, 16; Hellen Lousi, 82; Hervey Wilton, 29; Horace Smith, 32; James, 32; James Hewins, 23; Janette Marion, 57; Jason, 15; Joel Johnson, 34; Joseph, 20; Levi, 25; Levi Fisher, 19; Lois, 17; Louisa Franklin, 34; Lucius Adelbert, 41; Lucius Quintus Cincinatus, 33; Lucy, 18; Lucy Harding, 23; Lydia, 25; Mabel Ermina, 69; Mabel Harriet, 68; Mary Jane, 33; Maybelle, 67; Moses, 18; Obed Daniels, 25; Olive, 14, 26; Polly, 15; Rhoda, 25; Samuel, 9; Samuel Augustus, 34; Sarah Evelyn, 62; Sukey, 15.

Mulcha—Hannah, 57.
Muller—See Miller.
Munroe—See Monroe.
Murdock—Clarence Frank, 85; Eva, 82.
Murphey or Murphy—Agnes, 58; Ann Jane, 54; Catherine, 67; Dennis, 57; Ellen, 57, 61, 65; George, 55; John, 57; Julia, 57; Margaret (e), 51, 59; Mary, 54; Mary Eliza, 63; Michael, 69, 71; Patrick, 74; Patrick Francis, 75; Sarah, 78; Thomas Henry, 60.

Nason—Adelbert Merrill, 60; Albert Davis, 41; Charles Melvine, 40; Claretha Hannah Elizabeth, 85; Ella Gertrude, 72; George Warren, 40; James Henry, 40; Jesse Leonard, 40; Mabel Frances, 78; Millard, 62; Oramel, 52; Preston Clark, 48; Walter Leroy, 69; William Emmons, 40; Willie Oscar, 57.
Nelson—Sally, 24.
Newell— ———,47,56,85; Abby Ella, 80; Agusta Hiram, 42; Alfred Peck, 50; Edwin, 53; Ellen Frances, 42; Eugene Preston, 48; Francis, 44; Frederic, 44; James Edward, 65; Nelson Erwin, 47; Olney Pierce, 42; Ready Clinton, 59; William Henry, 49.
Nickolson—Mary Grace, 87.
Norcross—Asa Greenwood, 25; Cornelia Aregelia, 41; Edward Agustus, 45; George Alexander, 40; Josephine, 39; Marshall Greenwood, 39; Martha, 39; Silas Thayer, 25; Silvia, 25; Warren Fisher, 36.
Noyes—Hellen Emergene, 53; Henry Eugene, 53.
Nye— ———, 49; Charles Francis, 69; Emma Eliza, 55; Henry William, 47; Herbert Willis, 47; Nathan Cleveland, 61.

O'Brien or O'Brine—Henry, 54; John Thomas, 80; Margaret Ella, 81; Thomas, 81.
Ogden—John Elmer, 71.
O'Neal—Richard, 52.
O'Riley—Mary Isabelle, 68.

Packard— ———, 54.
Paine—Elias Addison, 34; Estella Maria, 69; George Stanley, 63; Lillian A., 67.
Parkhurst—Horace Hamilton, 31; Jotham, 20; Otis Torry, 31.
Partridge—Abigail Harding, 23; Alibeans, 10; Allen, 22; Amelia Bassett, 41; Amos, 11; Apollos, 11, 14; Asa, 31; Charles, 36; Charles Henry, 68; Charlotte, 34; Clarissa Prentis, 30; David, 11, 14; Dianthe, 29; Edmund Francisca, 43; Edwin, 37; Eleazer, 11; Elias Anson, 30; Elisabeth, 14, Eliza Jane, 35; Elmira Diantha, 36; Emily 25; George Brown, 35; George Ithamar, 34; George Seth, 45; Hannah, 10; Harriet Keith, 36; Harriet Maria, 34; Ithamar, 11, 32; John Wheeler, 32; Julia Ann, 34; Julitta Richardson, 29; Kezia, 11; Mary Bassett, 32; Mary Clark, 24; Mehetabele, 11; Nancy, 21; Nathan, 13; Pairle, 11; Rhoda, 14 Sabara, 12; Sally Putnam, 32; Sylvia Pond, 29; Timothy Agustus Warren, 28; Walter Fernando, 48; Willie Hall, 85.
Pelton—Mary Ophelia, 79.
Penniman—Charles, 36; Hannah, 36; Joseph Henry, 55; Martha Lavina, 53; Silas, 36.
Perkins—William Isaac, 73.
Perrigo—Charles, 21; Clarinda, 21.
Perriman or Perryman—Edward, 52; Elizabeth Esther, 58.
Perry—Asa Terrel, 39; Aurela, 20; Ellis, 23; Emeline Hannah, 39; Joel, 18; Josephine Aurela, 35; Patience, 18; Timothy, Jr., 18; Waldo Cutler, 22.
Perryman—See Perriman.
Phipps—Elbridge Moulton, 38; Eliza, 34; George Gardner, 39; Harriet Newel, 34; Martha, 28; Martha Warren, 29; William, Jr., 28.
Pierce—Addison Daniels, 41; Adeline N., 47; Alfred John, 38; Charles Stilman, 41; Edwin Merrill, 45; Ellen Elizabeth, 59; Emma Grace, 78; Franklin Dexter, 80; George Washington, 41; Israel, 18; Israel Ferdinand,

INDEX—BIRTHS.   209

41; James Gilmor, 33; John, Jr., 15;
John Edwin, 41; Joseph, Jr., 17;
Joseph Kimball, 37; Julia Ann, 32;
Marion Roseline, 76; Mary Jane, 49;
Nancy, 15; Susan Almira, 41; Washington, 25; Willard, 20.
Pike—Irene Milllard, 68.
Pitman—Ada Cordelia, 63.
Pond— ———, 58; Abbot Sequard, 55;
Abel, 35; Abigail, 11, 16; Addison
N., 41; Adela, 26; Adelia Maria, 35;
Aider A., 72; Albert Richardson, 35;
Alexander Gillmore, 37; Alfred, 23;
Alfred Daniels, 33; Almira Louisa,
41; Almira Lovering, 38; Alvin
Davis, 37; Amanda, 20; Amory, 38;
Anna, 9; Apollos, 14; Arnold Rawson, 30; Arthur Addison, 65; Asa, 12,
28; Asa Aldis, 17; Austin Davis, 28;
Baruch, 10; Benajah, Jr., 23; Benjamin, 3d, 14; Benjamin Davis, 22;
Betsy, 13; Bradford Henri, 50; Calley, 11; Calley Dexter, 27; Caroline,
30, 33; Caroline Goldsbury, 25; Catherine, 13; Charlotte Maria, 37; Clarinda, 19; Clarissa Ann, 26; Cyntha,
20, 22; Daniel, 14; Edene, 11; Edmond Fisher, 34; Edmond Sanford,
35; Edwards, 30; Edwin Calvin, 39;
Elbridge, 27; Eleanor Dorcas, 81;
Eli, Jr., 22; Eliab Metcalf, 31; Elihu,
18; Elihu, Senior, 30; Elihu, Jr., 30;
Elisabeth Gillmore, 25; Eliza Alice,
53; Elizabeth,30; Elizabeth Augusta,49;
Eliza Jane,39; Eliza Pitman,25; Ellen,
39; Ellen Maria,75; Ellen Maria Aldana 54; Emily, 30; Erasmus,20; Erastus
W., 40; Estelle Louisa, 52; Esther,
23; Francis Wheeler, 36; Frank Davis, 64; Fred Edwin, 70; George Leland, 32; George Otis, 37; George
Samuel, 46; Gilbert C., 35; Gillmore,
24; Girtrude Darling, 56; Goldsbury,
Jr., 19; Grace, 21; Grace Sumner,
64; Hannah, 20; Hannah Cutler, 26;
Hannah Marion, 35; Harmon, 16;
Harriet A., 36; Harriet Jane, 41;
Harriet Maria, 35; Harriet, S., 39;
Henry, 18; Henry Bowen, 30; Henry
Fisher, 64; Henry Johnson, 24; Hiram, 16, 20; Huldah, 31, 35; Increase
Sumner, 21; Isabel, 33; Jabez, 9;
James Hiram,38; James Preston, 21;
James Sullivan, 30; Jane Elizabeth,
38; Jane Maria, 31; Jarvis, 19; Jem
Otis, 19; Jeremiah Metcalf, 11; John,
Jr., 11; John Fairbanks, 20; John
Richardson, 30; Joseph Park, 30; Judith, 13; Juliana Metcalf, 33; Juline,
22; Justin, 15; Justin Eli, 31; Kezia,
16; Kezia Gould, 25; Laura L., 75;
Laureta, 16; Levi, 20; Lewis, 15;
Louisa Maria, 42; Lucinda, 13; Lydia,
22; Lydia Ellis, 33; Lyman,
23; Lyman Partridge, 26; Malchiah Addison, 37; Malchiah, 13;
Mariantinette, 23; Martha Atkins,
46; Martha Washington Aldana, 36;
Martin, 12; Mary 16, 23; Mary Jane,
37; Mary Martha, 70; Matilda Earle,
59; Mayo, 19; Melesent, 16; Meranda,
18, 25; Merinda, 17; Metcalf, 9;
Metcalf Everett, 45; Milletiah, 25;
Name, 10; Nathan Clark, 19; Nathaniel Hammon, 37 (2); Nathaniel
O., 36; Nathaniel Ogden, 26; Olive,
11, 13; Olive Celestina,35; Partridge,
20; Paul Dexter, 12; Perez, 12; Polly,
12; Polly Boyd, 18; Polly Hill, 35;
Prentice, 25; Prise, 11; Rachel, 20,
21; Rachel Maranda, 38; Rhoda, 11;
Robert, 14; Ronina, 18; Roxeena, 17;
Ruth, 11; Sally, 21, 24, 37; Samuel,
24; Samuel Metcalf, 9; Samuel Willis, 35; Sarah, 16, 31; Sarah Maria,
29; Sena, 17; Silvia or Sylvia, 19,
32; Sumner, 21; Susan B., 40; Susan
Malinda, 38; Sylvia or Silvia, 19, 32;
Theodore Asa, 50; Timothy, 33; Timothy Lealand, 17; Vesta Almira, 52;
Wellington, 31, 35; Welton Adelbert,
69; Willard, 15, 21; William, 21;
William Henry, 28, 39, 40, 56; Wilton
A., 73.
Pratt—Elisha Partridge, 13; Elizabeth
Maria, 29; Jenner Lewis Sweeting,
34; Spencer Atkinson, 26.
Prue—Casmere, 83; Edwin, 83; Elizabeth, 81; Ella Frances, 81; George
Edward, 82; Henry, 83; John Sherman, 80.

Rahala—Mary Ann, 59.
Rand ———, 40.
Rardon, Reardon or Riadon—Catherine
Marion, 75; Jeremiah, 71; John, 67,
William, 79.
Rawson—George Sylvester, 32.
Ray—Alfred Knapp, 52; Amanda Malvina, 2d, 35 (2); Edgar Knapp, 43;
Eliza Ann,35; Horace Warren, 35;
James Francis, 46; Sarah Anjuline,
35; William Francis, 57.
Razee—Arthur Wilmot, 63.
Reardon—See Rardon.
Remick— ———, 62; George B., 67;
Minnie Ann, 76.
Rhodes—Edmund Francis, 51; Emily
Jane, 47.
Riadon—See Rardon.
Rich—Anna Rosetta, 84; George Edmond, 80.
Richards—George Lewis, 50.
Richardson— ———, 47, 74; Abigail,
9, 19; Abigail Haven, 36; Abigail
Mary, 33; Albert Dean, 37, 73; Albert Milton, 32; Albretto Erastus, 51;
Asa, 19; Baruch, 12; Betsy, 13; Ce-

phas Holbrook, 37; Charles Addison, 36; Charles Eugene, 47; Charlotte Gillmore, 31; Clarissa Day, 29; Daniel, 15; Delea, 15; Eleanor Blake, 25; Eliab, 14; Elijah, 12; Eli Milton, 24; Elisha, 14; Elisha Fisher, 30; Eliza Ann, 22; Ella Jane, 48; Elona, 26; Emelina Meleta, 29; Erastus, 21; Esmereld, 54; Ezekiel, 16; George Lowel, 25; George Warren, 33; Harriet Maria, 41; Harriet Phipps, 60; Harrot Newell, 30; Henry B., 42; Henry Bullard, 44; Hephzibah Bacon, 13; Horace Augustus, 30; Jemima, 12; John Haven, 22; Johnson Ellis, 22; John Warren, 39, 76; Juletta, 28; Julia Ann, 33; Lidia, 14; Marcus, 16; Mary, 38, 39, 79; Matilda Kingsbury, 34; Maud Louise, 68; Mehetable, 17; Meranda, 19; Moses, 16; Nance, 10; Nancy Mann, 24; Olive, 19; Oliver, 10; Rena, 14; Rosa, 17; Ruth Mariah, 27; Sabra, 17; Salla, 10; Stephen Wilkes, 27; Susanna, 9, 16; Thomas, 18; Violetta Paolina, 49; William Edmund, 51; William Stephen, 40, 83; William Tyler, 31.
Riely or Riley—Albert James, 81; Francis Thomas, 85; Margaret O., 74; Mary Maria, 54; Sarah Ann, 60; William P., 83; William Patrick, 86;
Robbins—Lewis, 11; Marcus, 11.
Robenson or Robinson— ——, 58, 62, 70; Alice, 57; Archabaid, 67; Claracy Ann, 79; Elizabeth Miller, 57; Ephraim, 54; Fanny, 62; John Quincy, 49; Mary Alice, 70; Samuel, 10; William Franklin, 49; Zenas Edward, 18.
Roblee—Estella, 74.
Rockwood— ——, 45, 55, 56; Abigail, 10; Abijah Thurston, 31; Albert Erastus, 75; Albert William, 69; Anna Mabel, 83; Asa, 13; Asa Phillips, 29; Benjamin, Jr., 12, 23; Bradly Mortimer, 72; Edmond Joel, 41; Elroy Wales, 70; Erastus, 28; Erastus Daniels, 39; Eugene Morse, 49; Hannah, 13; Hannah Jane, 35; James, 32; Jerusha, 23; Julia Etta, 49; Julian, 30; Julius Thurston, 78; Lucius Osborne, 46; Mary, 11; Mary Ann, 28; Mary Louisa, 44; Mathan Miller, 36; Medora Abbie, 85; Mehitabel, 23; Nathan, 20; Olive, 13; Salla, 12; Samuel, 23; Sarah Jane, 37; Seth, 23; Susanna Bailey, 34; Timothy, Jr., 17; William, 35.
Rourk—Mary, 52.
Royals— ——, 62.
Ruggles—Arthur Leslie, 69; Susan, 31.
Russegue—Francis Alonzo, 46; George Meaker, 60; Henry Elmore, 52; Willie Alphens, 65.
Russell—George Randolph, 86.

Ryan or Ryon—John, 75; Margarett, 60.
Salley or Sally—George N., 66; Herbert Edmond, 75; James G. W., 59.
Sargeant or Sargent—Hariet Ada, 77; Leander Darwin, 42.
Sayles or Sayls— ——44; Anna, 17; Arial, 10; Ariel, 26; Avilda, 13; Caleb Warner, 29; Catherine A., 41; Daniel, Jr., 17; George L., 41; Joanna, 41; John, 17; Josiah, 17; Juliana, 20; Latinus V., 41; Levina, 15, 17; Loui, 9; Lycurgus, 41; Nabby, 19; Nahum, 26; Olive A., 41; Oren, 26; Richard, 11; Sarah Ann, 28; Selah, 17; Smith O., 41; Stephen, 17; Thomas Wilson Door, 41; Uvilda, 17; Willard, 15.
Scammel or Scammell—Dana, 54; Hellen Stearns, 58.
Scofield—Bridget, 79.
Scott—Burnside Winfield, 72; Chandler Leville, 28; Charles, 48; Charles Harrison, 28; Ellis, 57; Estella Amanda, 51; George Henry, 45; Henrietta T., 42; Julia Ann, 30; Malvina Viana, 49; Maria Angenette, 30; Mercy Ray, 66; Otis, 28; Welcome Earnest, 85; Willard Ellis, 48.
Sexton—Bridget, 77; Catherine, 80; James Henry, 82.
Shay—Frances Abby, 62; Hannah Elizabeth, 54; Joseph Daniel, 80; Michael Edward, 68.
Sheen or Shehan—Catherine, 60; Cornelius, 71; Daniel, 53; Ellen, 65.
Shepard—Addie Mary, 80; Louis Addison, 85; Martha Almira, 79.
Shepardson—Catherine Elizabeth, 42; Charles Kingsbury, 83; Harriet Ellen, 87.
Sherman—Lillian Frances, 77.
Slocomb or Slocum—Julia, 9; Lewis, 9; Philo, 10; William, 14.
Smalley—Louisa Jane, 37.
Smeedy, Smida or Smiddy—Charles, 79; Ellen Frances, 80; Henry, 83; Mary Elizabeth, 75, 76.
Smith— ——68, 72; Elias, 12; Elisabath, 12; Emeline Frances, 49; Frank, 70; Georgiana Emily, 45; James, 12; Lysena Clark, 26; Molly, 12; Sally Anjalina, 24; Sarah, 12; Sarah Adeline, 45.
Snow— ——58; Cyrus Herbert, 46; Hannah Gertrude, 62; Ruth Alice, 51; Viola Antonette, 53.
Springer—Julia Gracie Evelyn, 70.
Standish—George Mayo, 54.
Staples— ——73; Carrie Ellen, 61; Charley Albert, 82; George Edwin, 84; Hariet E., 73; Nathan Amos, 66; Walter Addison, 74.

INDEX—BIRTHS.

Stewart— ———— 61; Charles Lyman, 55; George Edwin, 72; Hatty Ann, 80; Jane, 71; John James, 73; William Henry, 81.
Stockbridge—Adelaid Frances, 84; Bertha Atwood, 78; Charles Elliot, 47; Lucia A., 75; Walter Scott, 50.
Sulivan, Sullivan or Sulliven—Annie Maria, 78; Cate J., 81; Catherine, 62, 65; Cornelius Daniel, 81; Daniel, 71; Daniel Edward, 86; Dennis, 52, 65; Eliza Jane, 69, 76; Emma Francis, 72; Hariet F., 74; James Patrick, 79; Jeremiah, 84; Joseph H., 82; Julia, 86; Lanar, 57; Margaret Lizzie, 71; Margarett, 61; Maryann, 59; Mary Ann, 79; Michael Henry, 68; Nellie, 87; Sarah Elizabeth, 85; Thomas, 56; William Andrew, 54.

Taft—Daniel Warren, 68.
Taylor—Bartholomy Foster, 17; Benjamin, 15; Isabella, 16; James, 15; Lucius, 15; Melea, 15; Salome, 19.
Teehan—William, 67.
Thayer—Adaline, 23; Addison Richard, 67; Adelbert Davis, 51; Asa Clark, 27, 28; Betsey Ann, 32; Charles Edwin, 32; Charlotte Lavina, 61; Clarissa, 23; Davis, 29 (2); Deborah Burril, 28; Eliza, 28; Ella M., 79; Ellen Frances, 60; Elmer Jerome, 76; Emma Lucinda, 72; Evelina Villers, 29; Ezekiel Austin, 25; Fisher Daniels, 28; Frederick L., 83; Herbert Whiting, 65; Isolin Frances, 49; Jonathan Wails, 23; Mary Ann Taft, 34; Mary Eliza, 72; Orrella, 26; Pamelia, 28; Richardson, 27; Sally, 28; William Makepeace, 32.
Thomas—Adelbert Morris, 66; Charles Agustus, 58; Edgar Austin, 60; William Clarence, 56.
Thompson— ———— 63; George Frederic, 58; George R., 41; Harriet Zeolide, 60; John Richardson, 31; Julia, 65; Moses Everett, 29; Peruda Adaline, 32.
Thorn—George Henry, 86.
Thurston—Abigail Thayer, 29; Alfred, 32; Bathsheba, 34; Caleb, 11; Daniel, 12; Daniel Brintnell, 28; David, 12; Eliza Maria, 25; Eunice Susan, 29; George Newell, 30; Gilbert Rhodney, 28; Harriot, 26; Harriot Saphrona, 27; Henry, 32; Hiram, 31; Jonson, 19; Julette, 14; Julia, 23; Lewis, 35; Louisa Marion, 36; Luke, 12; Maria, 31; Mary Sumner, 26; Nahum, 15; Nancy, 10, 25; Paul, 13; Perlina French, 21; Philo, 17; Saphony Alexander, 25.
Tiletson— ———— 55.
Tolman—Alice Leonora, 56; Carrie Mitchel, 60.
Torrey, Torry or Tory—Caroline, 83; Ebenezer, 27; George Baxter, 36; Harriot Byron, 20; John, Jr., 27; John Laurel, 36; John Winthrop, 82; Sally Richardson, 27.
Tower—Levi Howard, 86.
Treen—George W., 59.
Tufts or Tuffts—Emma Henrietta, 46; Frances Elizabeth, 50.
Turner—Calvin, Jr., 24; Harvey, 18; Hattie Mabel, 80; Miranda, 24; Olive, 19.

Underhill—Issadora, 56; Myron R., 56.

Vannet— ————, 61.

Wadsworth or Wardsworth— ————, 66, 72, 78; Alvah Chapman, 81; Joseph, 70; Joseph H., 34; Marth Ella, 83; Mary, 32.
Wails or Wales— ————, 71; Abigail Adams, 39; Abigail Olive, 42; Adelbert, 67; Amos Sanford, 45; Charles Alfred, 28; Ellen Augustus, 43; Elmer Ellsworth, 70; Elmira Frelove, 33; Frances Orinda, 46; Freloye Fairbanks, 29; George French, 28; Gertrude, 83; Gilbert Adams, 49; Hannah, 22; Harriot, 28; James, Jr., 23; James, 65; James Edwin, 50; Jemima, 26; Joanna Alden, 33; Jonathan, 10, 39; John Davis, 39; Julia Ann, 39; Lavina Frances, 55; Manerva Ann, 79; Marianna, 50; Mary Francis, 82; Mary Holbrook, 39; Mary Rebecca, 52; Mason, 21; Oen Otis, 39; Olive Fairbanks, 23; Otis, 10, 22; Polly, 23; Rachel, 12; Ruth, 21; Violetta Amanda, 02; William Henry, 30, 59; Willard, 23; Willis, 25.
Walker—Charles Edmund, 63; Martha Emma, 78; Mary Ann, 80; Mary Mann, 25, William J., 62.
Wall—Thomas, 52.
Ward— ————, 53; Edward Herbert, 56.
Ware— ————, 47; Alfred, 13; Amasa, 10; Betsey, 25; Clarinda, 9; Edna Jane, 65; Edward Cary, 49; Elbridge Gerry, 31; Elizabeth Adelaid, 51; Ella Agusta, 47, 48; Elvira, 25; Ema Frances, 50; Emeline, 31; Emma Eugene, 43; Envira, 11; Esther, 23; Frances Zebiah, 44; Frank Eldon, 54; Frederick A., 18; Gilbert Adams, 31; Hannah A., 23; Harvey, 12; James Edson, 37; James Ervin, 45; Jesse, 10; John Aldis, 18; Levina Miller, 35; Louisa Amelia, 41; Lucretia Burr, 25; Matilda Maria, 35; Moses, 10; Nabby, 25; Nathan, 26; Olive Daniels, 33; Olive Metcalf, 29; Persis, 26; Philander, 14; Phinehas, 19; Poly, 9;

Rhoda Ann, 60; Sabin, 28; Samuel Gilbert,33; Sanford,11; Sarah, 12; Sarah Smith, 36; Silvea, 14; Susa, 15; Violette Pauline,56; Warren, 11; Willard Adams, 29; William Henry, 50.
Warfield—Abijah Baker, 32; Ebenezer Ellis, 32; Esther Baker, 22; Harriot Atwood, 32; Mary Elizabeth, 41; Sarah Hellen, 40.
Warren—Mary Elizabeth, 83.
Watkins—Etta Ophelia, 85; Henry E., 86.
Weatherhead— — ——, 51; Lizzie Maud, 84.
Webb—George Matherson, 73; Sarah Louisa, 62.
Wescott—Edward Wilson, 48.
Weston—George Hary, 86.
White—Almira, 50; Anna Warren, 21; Betsey, 21 (2); Eliel Metcalf, 16; Elihu, (Jr.,) 9, 26; Elijah, Jr., 21; Ella Jane, 78; Japheth, 23; Jemime, 20; Luther, 9; Lyman Partridge, 24; Nathan, 19; Polly, 24; Sabra, 23; Sally; 18; Susanna, 20 (2); William, 18, 21; William Gardner, 45.
Whiticker—Charles Frederick, 73.
Whiting— ———, 40, 57, 63 (2), 67, 68, 71; Abigail, 22, 27; Asa, Jr., 18; Charlotte, 14; Claragene Harding, 48; Daniel Peter, Jr., 26, 35; Daniel W., 40; Elisabeth, 27; Eliza, 25; Eunice, 10; Flavius Ballou, 52; George Bridgely, 53; George Washington, 26; Hannah, 20; Horace Truman,35; Isabelle French, 62; Jairous, 22; Jairus Bradford, 36; James Munro, 35; Jane,35; Janette Eliza, 55; John, Jr., 16; John Brooks, 35; Joseph, 4th, 20, 44; Joseph Blake, 25; Josephine Ellen, 43; Joseph Milton, 27; Lucy, 22; Lydia Adaline, 43; Lydia Blake, 27; Marietta, 58; Martha, 33; Martha Briggs, 48; Mary, 13, 35; Mary Maria, 38; Nancy Jane, 52; Nathan, 19; Nathaniel, 21; Olive,39; Pelatiah, 10; Peter, 3d, 25; Polly, 19; Rebeca McLaine, 15; Rosanna Pitman, 37; Ruth Adams, 21; Salla, 12; Sally P., 22; Sukey, 21; Sydney, 13; Sidney Sandford,27; Thomas Edwin, 36; Willard Clark, 31; William Boyd,36; William Eustis, 38; William Joseph, 60; Zeolide Elizabeth, 38.
Whitney—Charles Henry, 50.
Wiggin or Wiggins—Edward Agustus, 63; Elizabeth Janette, 48; Ellen Laura, 68; George Arthur, 61; Jacob Edward, 45; Susan Joanna, 55.
Wightman—Horace, 36; Sarah, 36.
Wilkinson—Frank Agnstine, 63; Malon E., 72; Willard Lincoln, 69.
Williamas or Williams— ———, 50; Anna M., 73; Asa, 9; Cali, 10; Isabella A., 59; Polly, 13; Rolla, 68.
Winn or Wynn— ———, 77; George Otis, 61; Josephene S., 58.
Wiswall—Lowell Maddison, 58.
Witherell—Lillian Mabel, 80.
Wolford or Woolford—Emery,61,75, 76; Martha Fransena, 73; Nellie M., 66; William Francis, 51.
Wood—Abigail, 16; Alonzo Hills, 25; Asa Whiting, 31; Ebenezer Partridge, 12; Elias Pinckney, 34; Elisabeth, 9; Eliza Guild, 22; George, 39; George Leonard, 31; Horace Austin, 28; Horatio, 16; Ichabod Hawes, 25; Levi Williams, 27; Lois, 11; Lucinda, 37; Mille Farrington, 24; Owen, 37; Polly Adeline,32; Silence, 11; Susanna Torry, 31; Warren, 25.
Woodman—Hattie, 74; Jennie C., 77; Sarah Ann, 63; Wilber Blossom, 56.
Woodward—Abigail Crane, 32; Alfred Allen, 36; Almera, 12; Austin, 15; Caroline Louisa, 37; Elizabeth, 15; Elizabeth Preston 36; Ellen Matilda, 37; Elsie Colwell, 36; Elvira, 13; Fanny,26; Harriot Elvira, 32; Harvey,17; James Thomas Voax, 31; Joseph, 13; Joseph Addison, 32; Marcella, 62; Marcellus, 66; Preston, 26; Sarah Marcella 69; William Henry, 36.
Woolford—See Wolford.
Wright—Johanna, 23; Larnard, 9; Polly, 29; Solomon, 18.
Wyckoff—Hariet Talcott, 79.
Wynn—See Winn.

Young—Carrie Howard, 77; Daniel Herbert, 85; Edgar Atwood, 80; Henry Edwin, 78; Susan E., 67.
Youso—Joseph, 87.

MARRIAGES.

Abbe— Miriam, 125.
Adams—Abigail, 93, 95; Aldana L., 106; Alpheus, 96; Alvin B., 125; Amanda M., 138; Amos, 97, 104; Asa, 108; Aurelia Eunice, 127; Belinda, 105; Bella F., 135; Betsey, 95, 96; Caleb, 94; Chloe F., 100; Christiana, 131; Cyrus, 95; Daniel, 95; Emerson, 105; Esther, 92; Eunice, 92, 101; Experance, 107; Ezekiel, 105, 106; Francis J., 126; Gardner, 109; George, 107; George Albert, 140; Hanna, 95; Hellen Francis, 129; Henry C., 132; Henry S., 133; Horace N., 113; Isabella J., 124; James, 93, 96; James O., 129; Jasper, 92; Joel, 99; John, 96, 109; John W., 96; Lizzie M., 129; Louise M., 123; Lucy, 109; Lydia A., 132; Lyman, 131, 136; Macy, 94; Maria B., 119; Mary, 108; Mary Ann, 105; Moses, 90; Nathan, 94; Nathaniel, 107; Obadiah, Jr., 104; Peter, 109; Rachael, 93; (or) Rachel, 90, 108; Ruth, 108; Sally B., 120; Sarah B., 106; Sibyl, 97; Silas, 120; Simeon P., 105; Timothy, 94; Ward, 107, 122; William, 89, 99; William, Jur., 96; William Gardner, 126.
Ainsworth—Edwin, 116.
Albe, Albee or Alby—Abbie Jane, 129; Hannah, 95; Hattie E., 125; Jemima, 95; Nathaniel, 95.
Alden — Ebenezer, 94; Eunice, 93; Spooner, 98.
Aldis—Sally, 93.
Aldrich—Charles M., 134; Seneca, 93; William, 105.
Alexander—Abby E., 121; Samuel, 109.
Allen—Abigail P., 104; Amos, Dr., 96; Amos H., 102, 103; Charles, 101; Charlotte E., 133; Clarinda, 102; Cyrus, 102; Duty, 107; Eliza W., 112; George, 93; Hannah, 92, 100; Hannah M., 132; James W., 140; John K., 119; John Partridge, 94; Lucinda, 110; Marena, 106, 121; Mary, 89; Melzar W., 134; Polly, 95; Samuel, Capt., 99; Thomas B., 127.
Alley—Betsey, 116; John, 97.
Andrews—Charles W., 134.
Angles—Anna, 139.

Armington—Julia A., 118, 123; Kittie, 131; Lydia, 129.
Armsby—Anna, 107; Persis, 107; Silas, 92.
Arnold—Daniel, Jr., 105; Leonard A., 105; William A., 140.
Atwood—J. Francis, 110; Shadrach, Dr., 105.
Ayers—Rebecca, 107.

Bacon—Abby M., 118; Delia E., 106; Emily J., 134; George W., 118, 134; Joseph, Capt., 95; Lois, 96; Lydia, 108; Mary, 91; Ruth, 94; Sarah, 93, 102; Seth, 94; Sula C., 97; Thomas, 108; Thomas M., 121.
Baker—Abigail, 105; Charlotte, 103; David, 95; David P., 116; Elias, 96, 105; Erastus E., 118; Esther, 90; Hannah, 91; Jemima J., 110; John, 89; Julia, 97, 121; Mary A., 110; Polly, 96; Rhoda, 96, 104.
Balcom—Abil H., 110; Mary S., 110.
Baldwin—Elizabeth, 129.
Ballou—Abby A., 119; Almira, 110; Amy, 96; Caleb W., 122 (note); Carrie N., 124; Ellen F., 133; Eliab P., 138; George W., 120; Laurinday A., 106; Oren E., 130; Warrin J., 106; Wilson C., 122.
Barber—Addie M., 131; George N., 115.
Barden—Artemas, 117, 119; David, 97; Julia, 104; Louisa, 106.
Barrows—Adaline A., 132; Emeline L., 109.
Bartlett—Annet, 129.
Barton—Albert, 138.
Basset or Bassett—Abigail, 106, 109; Mace, 96; Oscar M., 113; Rufus, 101; Sally, 98.
Bates—Eliza L., 122; Leuretia, 95; Lyman, 96.
Battle or Battles—Polly, 97; Silence, 90.
Baylies—Prince, 94.
Bear—Thomas, 95.
Becket—Lucy, 100.
Beckwith—Charles, 130.
Bemis—Charles H., 117; Louise N., 125; Theodore S., 106.
Bennet- Charles L., 134; William, 92.
Benson—Stephen S., 125.
Bent—George O., 135; Wilmer D., 135.
Bethell—Richard D., 130.

Bigelow—James, 109.
Billings—Mary E., 126; William Frank, 138.
Black—Almira, 118.
Blackington—Aaron, 93.
Blackman—Submit, 90.
Blake—Abigail, 94, 95, 105, 114; Abraham, Jr., 92; Anjinette, 109; Augustus M., 110; Austin, 101, 138; Barnum, 106; Calvin, 93; Charles G., 106; Charles H., 133; Chloe, 92; David P., 101; Ebenezer, 94; Edwin E., 104; Elias, Jr., 105; Fannie A., 136; Francis M., 119; George A. A., 128; Hannah, 122; Hepzebah, 97; Herman, 102; Jason, 92; Julia A., 119; Laura M., 124; Levi, 106; Lois, 100; Lucia M., 136; Luther, 105; Martha, 95; Mary L., 109; Mortimer, 106; Olive, 91, 107; Oramel B., 123, 140; Phillip, Dea., 93; Polly B., 105; Robert, Jr., 94, 102; Samuel, 91, 93; Sarah, 93, 97; Sibbel, 95; Solomon, Jnr., 96; Timothy, 108; Willard N., 114; William A., 127; Willing, 92.
Blanchard—Louiza, 101.
Blandine—Enoch, 97.
Bliss—Henry A., 128; Thomas, 96.
Borden or Bordon—Hope T., 130; Martha J., 128.
Bowen—Charlotte E., 127; Enoch, 114; William, Rev., 103.
Boyd—Bethuel, 92; Betsy W., 101; Juliann, 102; Willard, 93.
Boyden—Amos, 91; Betsey, 102; Caroline, 104; Clarissa, 105; Comfort, 107; Julia M., 104; Olive, 101; Pamela, 104.
Boyle—Agustine B., 117.
Boynton—Roxana, 120.
Bradford—Fanny, 112.
Bradshaw—Diodat, 94.
Brayton—Randall T., 104.
Breck or Brick—Charlotte, 96; Julia, 125; Maria, 105; Rebecca, 136, see Brock.
Brett—Georgie E., 136.
Brick—See Breck.
Briggs—Betsey, 107; Darias, 92; Darwin T., 114; Jacob, 95.
Brintnell—Bathsheba, 95.
Britton—Mary J., 136; William E., 140.
Broady—Joh. 102.
Brock—Albert L., 136.
Brooks—Julia A., 118.
Brown—Daniel, 136; George A., 133; George F., 121; Hannah, 92; James O., 102; Leonard, 106; Luceau B., 130; Phila., 101; Silvina M., 134; Susan E., 110.
Brownell—Julia, 100.
Brunswick—Hyman, 103.
Bryant—John M., 127.
Buffington—Amelia C., 110; William, 102.
Bullard—Agustus H., 114; Amos, 94; Anna, 91; Cephas, 99; Clarissa, 98, 116; Elisha, 100; Eliza A., 122; Emerson N., 115; Jerusha, 90; Joseph, 98; Mariah, 102; Mary, 112; Mary T., 114; Olive, 107; Plam, 99; Ruth, 98; Samuel M., 110; Silas, 104.
Bumpus—Lemuel E., 139.
Burnam—Jeremiah, 105.
Burrington—Lester Lorenzo, 134.
Butler—Lois, 91.
Butman—Warren, 131.
Butter—Ruth, 106.
Butterworth—Matilda, 99; Nancy, 99.
Buxton—Roxana, 122.

Cadmas—William B., 128.
Cahoon—Mehitable J., 114.
Campbell—Henry, 97.
Canny—Ella G., 132.
Capron—Sanford T., 133.
Carleton or Carlton—Sarah Reading, 103; Turzah, 102.
Carlow—Lottie, 140.
Carlton—See Carleton.
Carpenter—Charles H., 119; Job, 95.
Casper—Charlotte, 103.
Cass—Anson L., 128.
Chamberlain—Ellen, 113; Prudence, 102; Sarah J., 125.
Chapin—George H., 128; Rufus, 116.
Chase—Abigail, 93; Alexander, 118; Bowers S., 112; Hiram, 113; Marietta, 139; Sabil M., 110.
Cheever—George, 100.
Cheney—David, 105; Mary, 103.
Chilson—Anna, 95; James O., 129; Martha W., 113.
Claflin—Calvin, 124; Fanny, 104; Jeremiah, 106.
Clark—Abby H., 113; Abijah, 90, Jr., 101, Jur., 96; Adeline, 106; Ann Eliza, 139; Antionette S., 137; Benjamin, 90; Betsy or Betsey, 94, 104, 108, 109; Betsy W., 130; Charles E., 132; Charles T., 106; Dyer, Jr., 92; Elijah, 105; Elizabeth, 91; Erastus, 109; Erastus O., 129; Esther, 113; Ennice, 89; Ezekiel W., 112; Hannah, 94; Hermon F., 124; Hiram, 103; John B., 124; Lois, 98; Lucy Jane, 129; Mary, 90, 102, 107, 109; Mary R., 126; Nancy, 104; Nancy Melinda, 104; Nathan, 92, 95; Nellie M., 134; Olive, 97; Parmelia, 92, 101; Paul, Jnr., 96; Prudence, 105; Rachel or Rachael, 93, 107; Rhoda T., 109; Ruth, 90; Sally, 93, 102; Simeon, 108; Stephen A., 98; Susan, 124; Sussanna, 97; Sylvester, 104; William G., 117.
Cleaveland, Cleavland or Cleveland Bela, 95; Dorcas, 93; Hellen S., 128; Mary, 105; Nancy, 104, Mrs., 110;

INDEX—MARRIAGES. 215

Nathan, 97; Sophia B., 113.
Clegg—Mary Ann, 132.
Cleveland—See Cleaveland.
Cobb——, 134; Ida M., 139; Luther, 107.
Cole—Caroline P.. 131; Hellen G., 129: Jonathan, 127.
Collins—Catherine, 129; James, 127: Sarah, 92.
Colvin—Geo. Anna M.. 134.
Comestock or Comstock—Nathan, Jr., 103; Sarah, 126.
Comey—William M., 132.
Comstock—See Comestock.
Connor—Anthony. 134.
Converse—Maria E., 119.
Cook—Abby W., 128; Abijah, 111; Amasa, 107; Amory B., 102; Barton F., 134; Betsey, 103; Ellen A., 131; Hannah A., 120; Hiram, 103; Horase, 95; Jerusha, 93; Josepine A., 136; Julia A., 131; Lucian A., 119; Lucy, 103; Lucy A., 122; Maranda, 102; Mary, 107 (2); Mary Ann W., 106; Orinda H., 116; Peacy B., 104; Reuben, 104; Samuel, 101; Samuel S., 122, 131; Sukey P., 104; Winslow, 126.
Coolidge—Caleb L., 110; James. 106.
Coombs—Stephen A., 120.
Cooper—Pliny E., 137.
Corbet or Corbett—George S., 134; James S., 106.
Corbin—Daniel O., 128; Julia, 129; Sylvenus W., 133.
Corson—David W.. 132.
Couillard—Annie M., 140.
Covill—David, 105.
Cowell—Willard G., 141.
Craig—Hariet M., 133.
Crane—Bathsheba, 107; Cyrus R., 130.
Crocker—Jeremiah, 89.
Crooks—Beriah. 99; George A., 131; John. 96.
Cross—Samuel. 125.
Cullam—Gerrat, 139.
Cummings—Sarah, 105.
Curtis—Emma S., 132; William W., 133.
Cushing—Hannah, 95; John, 106: Sally, 93; Samuel, 94: Selah, 96.
Cutler—Catherine, 108; James, Jr., 113: Simon. 107: Susanna, 108.
Cutting—Abby A., 119.

Daggett—Hannah, 108; Olive. 107.
Daily—Dennis F.. 137.
Daniels—Abigail, 91. 102: Adams, 106; Albert E., 102: Amariah, 91: Asa, 89: Betsey A., 110; Caroline M.. 113: Charles F., 110; Cloe, 107; David, 93. 102; Dorcas, 94: Eliza, 111: Eliza J., 110, 120; Eliza Jane, 110: Ellen M., 121: Elsa, 99: Fisher,
101; Hannah, 108; Harriet L., 106; Henry, 100; Henry M., 111; Jemima L., 124; Jesse, 90; Joel, 90, 124; Joseph, 93; Julia A., 109; Julia M., 99; Juletta, 91; J. Wheaton. 122: Keturah, 89; Lucius W., 127; Lucy M., 112: Luke, 123; Mancy M.. 135; Martha E., 123; Mary, 90, 92; Mary Ann. 105; Mary L., 139: Nathan, Jr., 91, 101: Peter, 95: Sally, 96, 99; Simeon. 91: Thomas J., 126; Unity, 95; Waldo, 115.
Darcy—Bridget. 128.
Darling—Alfred O., 120; Anna M., 139; Assa, 97; Eli, 90; Ellen E., 120; Eunice, 89, 109; Fenner, 132; Laretta W.. 109; Lucina A., 133; Lydia E., 117; Lyman C., 130; Mayo C., 122; Nathan E., 135; Peter, 90.
Dart—Allen E., 134.
Davidson—John Howe, 138.
Davis—Orlando J., 120; Samuel, 97.
Day—Joseph P., 136; Nancy, 92.
Dean or Deane—Abigail, 95; Addie A., 138; Calvin, 100: George W., 120; Ichabod, Capt., 103, Jur., 95; Jarvis, 99; Julia, 108; Oliver, 135; Rena, 91; Seth, 90.
Devrant—Hannah, 99.
DeWitt—Horace S., 125; Martha M., 120.
Dickerson or Dickinson—Edward F., 112; Hanson E., 115.
Dilburr—Maria, 99.
Dillings—Agnees, 130.
Doherety, Doherty or Dougharty—Celia. 120; Edmond, 128; Michael, 139.
Dolley—Lydia Ann, 125.
Dolliff—Anson D., 121.
Dolliver—Albert H., 136.
Dougharty—See Doherety.
Douglass—Minnie M., 138.
Dove—Benjamin, 103; William, 135.
Downe—Anna S., 109.
Dowson—James. 94.
Doyle—John, 138.
Drake—John, 114.
Draper—Bebee, 117.
Duffy—John, 137.
Dugan—Daniel, 127.
Dunbar—Charles, 101; Joseph, 120.
Dunn—Alexander, 104; Lucy, 108 (2).
Dupee—Elias, 104.
Dyer—Sarah A., 127.

Eames—Eliphalet, 119.
Earle—Mary M., 116; Nancy S.. 118.
Eaton—Edwin, 104.
Edwards—Betsey, 99.
Ellis—Abel. 95; Deborah F., 110; Esther, 89; Joseph, 107; Levi, 98: Lois, 90; Luther, 109; Lydia. 95, 108; Miranda, 97; Morse, 99; Preston. 104: Royal, 108; Sally, 96; Sarah,

108.
Ely—David, 105.
Emerson—Ellis P., 110.
Emmons—Martha, 98; Mary, 98.
Engley or Ingley—Betsey, 109; Lucy L., 105; Orlando S., 129.
Esty—Hannah, 134.
Everett—Leonard F., 120; Melatiah, 99. or Meletiah, 107; William F., 136.

Fairbanks — Asa, 90; Billings, 108; Caroline, 97; Jerusha, 96. John L., 126; Julitta, 96; Lucy, 96; Melcent, 90; Olive, 92; Sarah, 104; Willard, 94.
Fales—Annie E., 135; Emerson, 104; James, 108; John, 92; Samuel 2d, 101; Sarah, 89; Shubael, 95.
Farr—Parker R., 121.
Farrington—Aaron, 89; David, 103; Emely C., 117; Harriet M., 122; Julia A., 117; Lewis, 92; Martha J., 120; Preston M., 115.
Fearhum—Fidelia, 101.
Feel—Eliza F., 114.
Fichem—Samuel, 100.
Fisher—Aaron, 91; Abby, 106; Abigail, 92, 100, 108; Abigail B., 109; Achsah, 117; Adeline, 103; Adin, 102; Amos, 107; Asa, 90; Caleb, 93, 106; Caroline, 103; Charles M., 101; Daniel, 92; Daniel C., 96, Jr., 105; Edmond T., 131; Eliza B., 117; Eliza J., 103, 106; Ella F., 135; Emeline, 106; Esther, 102; Eunice, 89; Gilbert C., 115; Hannah, 103; Hariet A., 134; Harlow, 112; Hezekiah, Lt., 91; Irine, 103; Jason, 96, Jur., 98; Jemima, 91, 98; Jennie M., 141; John, 90; John H., 105, 118; John J., 103; Julia F., 116; Julius, 102; Katurah, 92; Levi, 90, 97; Lewis, Esq., 97; Louisa, 104; Louisa J., 116; Lurana, 92; Mary, 90, 93, 96 (2), 101, 107; Mary Ann, 128; Mary Emma, 136; Mary J., 131; Maxey, 97; Melinda, 115; Molla, 102; Moses, 91; Nancy, 93, 106; Nathaniel, 101; Olive, 90; Patty, 100; Pegge, 90; Perez, 96; Peter, Jur., 98; Prissilla, 108; Rachael, 91; Rachel E., Mrs., 106; Rena, 100; Rhoda, 91, 92; Rufus Albert, 140; Ruth, 97; Samuel, 91, 103; Samuel R., 100; Sarah J., 115; Seth, 108; Smith,109; Susa,93; Susan, 106; Susan M., 130; Timothy, 91, Jr., 92, 93; WalterM., 136; Weston, 100; Willard, 116; Willis, Lt., 97, Esq., 124.
Flanders—Mardie E., 132.
Fletcher—William, 110.
Follett—Albert E., 135; Betcey, 97; Joshua G., 132.
Folsom—Nettie M., 132.
Forbes—Daniel H., 110.

Ford—Francis, 139.
Forrist—Martin C., 102.
Foster—Benjamin, 93, 106; Elias, 94; Elisha, 103; George Warren, 139; Hannah, 105; Jane, 135; Martha E., 130, 137; Rhoda, 104; Tryphena, 101.
Frail—Nathan W., 137.
Frankein—Asa M., 133.
Franklin—Hartford H., 110.
Freeman—Phebe, 94.
Frost—Benjamin, 124; George H., 121; Susan, 131.
Fuller—Ada, 131; Andrew S., 135. Asa, 89, 97; Betsey, 103; George N., 133; Mary A., 115; Rachel, 102; Simeon, 100; Susie A., 132; William F., 105.
Furbush—Asa B., 101.

Gammell—Joseph L., 135.
Gaskell—George N., 139; William, 106.
Gasken—Della C., 139.
Gates—Charles E., 107.
Gay—Amos B., 97; Anna A., 140; Edward, 100; Ellen M., 110; Henry W., 124; Nancy, 101; Samuel E., 117; Solomon, 107; Thomas, 91; Timothy, 90, 104; Walter H., 106; Wilkes, Jr., 104; Willard, Esq., 98.
George—Gilbert B., 113.
Getchell—Hester A., 136.
Gifford—Stephen T., 137.
Gilbright—Mary, 137.
Gillmor, Gillmore, Gilmor or Gilmore—Abigail C., 93; Abigail C., 105; Adelia R., 105; Adeline J., 104; Albert J., 131; Apollos, 94; Chloe D., Mrs., 110; David, Jur., 90; Edward R. H., 110; Elizabeth, 92; George H., 128; George R., 104; Harriet F., 106; Helen R., 115; James, 2d, 98; James P., 110; John, 107; Joseph, 90, Jur., 99; Joseph F., 101; Lucinda A., 127; Martha A., 133; Mary, 89, 91; Mary Ann, 103; Mary Ann W., 103; Mary A. S., 128; Nancy, 95, 105; Nancy M., 105; Nathan, 93; Olive, 109, Mrs., 98; Patience, 96; Phebee, 92; Philander, 104; Rebecah, 91; Robert, 90, Lt., 99; Rufus, 96; Sally, 93; William, 93, 109, 2d, 104; William D., 122.
Glidden—Abigail B., 105.
Gline—Phineas, 98.
Goddard—Samuel, 92.
Goldthwart—Thomas, Jr., 103.
Gould—Almira C., 113; Joseph P., 134.
Govis—John, 107.
Gowen—Asa, 95; Charles, 110; Charles R., 137; Clara Isabel, 140; Luther, 97, 101.
Granger—Mary Ann, 139.
Grant—Abby, 116; Alpheus C., 105; Betsy, 98; John E., 127; Joseph, 126; Lydia, 107; Mary C., 114; Mary H.,

INDEX—MARRIAGES. 217

114; Olvia S. C., 120; Samuel W., 111.
Grantham—Thomas E. H., 132.
Graves—Mary J., 135.
Green or Greene—Angenette L., 116; Caroline, 121; James G., 100; Mary E., 133.
Greenlaw—Theopilas, 118.
Greenwood—Seneca A., 119.
Gridley—Lucinda, 102; Oliver, Jnr., 99.
Griffin—Harriet A., 123.
Grover—Andrew, 113; George W., 134; Molly, 92.
Groves—Debby, 89; Genette, 96.
Guild—Amey, 109; Cyrus, 98, 99; Ebenezer, Ju'r, 97; Edwin A., 138; Hannah L., 119; Illeone E., 136; James A., 109; John, 96; Joseph G., 136; Julia E., 110; Lydia, 98; Mary Elizabeth, 119; Ruth, 98; Samuel, 107; Susan, 104; William H., 128.
Guile—Nancy, 102.
Gurney—William A., 123.

Hager—Rose, 89.
Hall—Camillas, 2d, 105; Clarra, 131; Edward, 90; George, 102; Horace B., 103; Maryann G., 114.
Hallet—Mary E., 115.
Hamilton—Rebecca, 118.
Hammond—Edson Dana, 115; Sally, 93.
Hancock—Daniel Merrill, 103; Harriet, 110; Nancy, 109.
Harding—Abigail, 89; Amos, 91; Asa, 107, 109; Betsey, 95; Elisha, Dr., 100; James, Esq'r, 96; Joseph, 99; Lewis, 97; Mary, Mrs., 89; Molly, 89, Nancy, 97; Nancy M., 114; Olive, 94.
Hardy—Eliphalet D., 127; Julia A., 110; Nellie C., 125.
Harrington—Isaac, 99; Lucy A., 133.
Harris—Charles, 90; Harriet A., 121; Lydia, 127; Walter, Rev., 91.
Hart—Aaron, 93; Alexander, 113; Alexander L., 114, 117; Charles E., 109; Ella J., 137; William G., 137.
Harishorn—David, 91; Gilbert, 109; Henry A., 139; Irene, 97; Nancy, 100; Olive A., 126; Polly, 101; Seth L., 99.
Harvey—Ezra, 89.
Harwood—Levi L., 105.
Haskel, Haskell or Haskill—Eleanor A., 109; Olive, 98; Samuel, Jnr., 99.
Hastings—Thadens, 94.
Hathaway—Benjamin, 99.
Hatten—Mary, 106; Willard, 101.
Haven—Eunice, 93; Polly, 94.
Hawes or Haws—Abigail, 100, 102; Amelia, 100; Amos, 107; Charles, 104; Eleanor, 93; Elijah F., 133; Elvira, 110; Elvira S., 127; Esther, 89; Ichabod, 108; Jemima, 90; Joel, 108; Joseph, Jr., 92; Josiah, 103; Levi, 92;

Lonesa C., 135; Mary, 95, 98, 102; Meletiah, 90; Sarah, 93, 96; Solomon, 93; Susanna, 90.
Hawkins—Aaron C., 102; Hezeziah, 103; Sally N., 106.
Hayford—Harvey, 98.
Hayward or Heywood—Elbridge, 125; Hannah, 108; Ira, 105; Nahum, 108.
Healey or Healy—Henry W., 139; Timothy, 129.
Heany—Margaret, 134.
Heath—Almira B., 114; John C., 137.
Heaton—Charles H., 140; Henrietta, 140; Huldah, 97; Joseph, 91; Melansa G. M., 129; Nellie J., 136; Olive, 98; Patty, 107; Ruth, 95; Sally, 99; Samuel, 102.
Hefford—Susan, 119.
Henna—Lizzie A., 134.
Herrick—Loami B., 97.
Hewitt—Eliza, 100.
Heywood—See Hayward.
Hide or Hyde—Leonard, 98; Polly, 108.
Higgins—Caroline N., 118; William D., 118.
Hill or Hills—A. Arabella, 138; Abigail, 90; Albert H., 123; Anna, 90; Ann P., 105; Asa, 96; Elliot, 102; Frank S., 126; Isaac. 125; Jarvis H., 101; Jason, 92; Jesse, 92; Joel, Capt., 102; Jones, 90; Joseph, 89, Capt., 93; Kate M., 137; Leonard, 90; Lewis, 100; Lois, 107; Lysander B., 100; Martha C., 105; Mary H., 101; Meelissia, 110; Molly, 93; Moses, 94; Noah, 90; Olive G., 102; Persis, 106; Sally, 98; Seneca, 100; Theron C., 104; William, 103, 122; Ziba, 89.
Hixon or Hixson—Asa, Rev., 103; Clarissa, 107; Edward H., 114; Esther, 91; Hepzibah, 108; Mary, 91.
Hodgers or Hodges—Betsey, 98; Mary S., 115.
Hoffses—Emerson W., 137.
Holbrook—Abigail, 102; Amariah, 107; Cephas, 99; Eliab, 97; Jesse, 107; Lydia, 92; Meletiah, widow, 94; Nahum, 95; Phineas, 107; Sabin, 110; Samuel, 107; Seth, 100; Zebiah, 107.
Holden—Elmira, 135.
Holmes—Ebenezer N., 112; Kesia, 91.
Holt—Lillian Augusta, 126.
Hood—Alllee, 128; James, 129.
Hooker—Sarah, 119.
Hooper—Dorcas V. L., 118.
Hopkins—Lizzie, 139.
Horr—Nathan, 103.
Horton—David, 99; Mary W., 102.
House—George W., 122.
Howard—Elizabeth, 138; Sylvester E., 124.
Howe—Elbridge, 109; William H., 135.
Hoyt—Ellen, 117.

Hubbard—Abigail, 106; Amelia T., 123; J. George, 117; Nathaniel T., 139; Sabin, 113; Susan, Mrs., 110; William E., 113.
Hucker—Catherine, 91.
Hunt—Joel E., 109; Samuel, 119.
Hutchings—Francis L., 118.
Hyde—See Hide.

Ide—Betsey, 97; Daniel, 93; Jacob, Rev., 98.
Ingley—See Engley.
Inman—Bathsheba, 102; Seth, 109, 112.

Jackson—Anna, Mrs., 102; William, 100.
Jacobs—Joseph C., 127.
Jardin—Mary E., 139.
Johnson—Charles E., 140; Nathaniel G., 125; Obadiah K., 114; Persis, 102; Stephen C., 109; Willard, 101.
Jones—Esther, 90; Flora A., 137; John, 108; Timothy E., 114.
Jordan, Jorden or Jordon—Albert L., 127; Edwin A., 138; Ellen F., 138; Evelyn C., 117; George A., 110; Horatio A., 125; Samuel H., 131.
Joslyn—Mary E., 130.

Keith—Emily J., 115; Prudence, 103; Warren, 95.
Kelly—Anna J., 131.
Kelsey—Giles C., 114.
Kemp—Nancy, 124.
Kenyon—Jonas, 137.
Kideler—Thomas, 106.
Kimball—Jonas, 105; Moses, 106.
King—Edwin H., 123; Harriet E., 122; Warren N., 119; William F., 128; William Francis, 126.
Kingman—George F., 116.
Kingsbury—Abeil, 96; Abigail, 100; Benjamin, 107; Beriah, 93; Caleb B., 100; Cyrus, 91, Elizabeth, 92; George A., 140; Helen C., 113; Horatio, 105; John, 107, 123; Joseph, 96; Katherine, 96; Maria H., 124; Mary A., 105; Susanna, 91.
Kingsley—Edward, 139.
Kingston—Mary E., 135.
Kitteredge or Kittredge—Jacob, 111, Dr., 102.
Knap or Knapp—Alfred, 99; Emilia, 109; Hiram, 98; Melville, 98; Peggy, 96; Polly, 99; Susan, 110; Sylvia L., 109.
Knox—Margaret, 128.
Kollock—Ebenezer, 94; Sarah, 94.

LaCroix—James, 115.
Ladd—Charles W., 113.
Laing—Robert J., 118.
Lambert—Elizabeth, 100.
Lane—Sarah, 103.

Lasure or Lesure — John F., 131; Simeon, 103.
Latin Ville—Abbie B., 137.
Laurence or Lawrence—Almira, 106; Amos, 108; Anna, 100; Beriah, 93; Caroline M., 130; Cephas, 92; David, Jr., 92; Ebenezer, 89; Elizabeth, 109; Elizabeth L., 131; Eliza E., 121; Eunice, 93; Hariet Augustus, 140; Isabella L., 112; Jairns B., 109; Joseph, 90; Julia, 97; Laura Ann, 128; Laura Annie, 126; Marietta L., 103; Mary, 91; Ozias, 93; Prudence, 98; Ransom, 98; Sarah J., 134; Susan, 103.
Lawton—George W., 100.
Lee—Alfred B., 98.
Legg—Abner, 89; Joshua, 89.
Leland—Frank, 97; Jeremiah, 93; Rebecca W., 132.
Leonard—Hartford, 116; Hartford P., 120.
Lesure—See Lasure.
Lethbridge—Abigail, 97; Hepzibah, 99; Jerusha, 98; Sally, 89, 99; Susanna, 94; Sussanna, Mrs., 98; William, 97.
Levenseller—Margaret, 100.
Lewis—George R., 121.
Lewitt—Peter, Jnr., 98.
Lievett—Peter, 90.
Lincoln Julia A., 110; Manly, 101; Manly D., 117; Martha E., 126; Mary Elizabeth, 137; Mille, 97; Morris, 101; Patty, 102; William, 92; William R., 115.
Lindley—Chloe, 96; Molly, 92; William, 104.
Linkfield—Adeline M., 124.
Linniken—Eli J., 132.
Linsey—Clarra A., 133.
Long—Dennis, 140.
Lorden—Joanna, 127.
Louffborough—Louisa B., 114.
Lovel—David, 90.
Lovering—Rebekah, 91.
Lovett—Asahel F., 126.
Lozell—Daniel, 109.
Luke—Fanny A., 128; Mary A., 125.

Mac———See Mc.
Maine—Susan, 130.
Makepeace—Mary, 100; William, 93.
Manchester—William N., 139.
Mann—Annie, 97; Betsey, 100; Billy, 90; Cynthia, 97; Elias, 89; Hannah, 120; Margaret, Mrs., 102; Nancy, 93; Rebeca, 98; Richard, 97; Rosalinda, 97.
Marden—Eliza, 125; George R., 137.
Marsh—Lewis H., 109; Olive, 106.
Martin—Jane, 105; John, 132; William H., 118.
Mason—Eliza, 119.
Mayo—Adaline B., 121; Eliza J., 138.

INDEX—MARRIAGES. 219

Mayshaw—Henry, 131.
McCallam—Granville, 116.
McDearmont—James, 133.
McDonald—Kate, 135.
McDougall—Allen W., 140.
McGee—Bridget, 122.
McGuire—Bernard, 135.
McHugh—Bridget, 139, Rosa, 139.
McKean—Nathan, 110.
McLane—David, 91; Rebecca Gillmore, 99.
McMullen—Rosa, 133.
McParland—Hugh, 120.
McPherson—See Pherson.
Merchant—Henry, 129.
Meriam—Joseph, Capt., 102.
Merifield or Merrifield—Aaron, 100; Jemima, 95; John, 89.
Messenger—Eli, 95; Lucius, 102; Nancy L., 115.
Metcalf—Abby L., 123; Abijah, 93; Achsah, 90, 106; Addison, 100; Allice I., 136; Alvah, 116: Asa, 90. 91; Betsey W., 116; Calvin, 92; Edmond M., 128; Elias, 104. 110; Elvira, 97; Emeline M., 126; Emeline W., 119; Erasmus B., 109; Erastus L., 106; F. Leslie, 136; Haman, 103; Hanan, 89; Hannah, 108; Harlet E., 128; Hiram, 115; James, Jr., 89, Dea., 98; Jarusha, 89; Jeremiah, 107; Jessie, Dea., 100; Joanna W., 116; John, 114; John C., 124, Dr., 102; John Wilson, 103; Jonathan, 108; Juliana, 109; Julitha, 90, or Julitta, 99; Martha, 108, 134; Martha M., 127; Mary, 100; Mary C., 122; Medora A., 122; Meletiah, 89; Melia, 100; Michael, 102, 117; Molly, 89; Nathan, 91, 97; Olive, 101; Otis, 112; Patty, 91, 96, 118; Paul, 108; Pelatiah, 100; Persis, 97; Richardson, 110; Sabra, 92; Samuel, 107, Jr., 106; Sarah, 124; Sena, 99; Stephen, Jr., 104; Titus, 90, 93.
Millard—Pruella Addie, 138; Samuel, 100.
Miller—Charlotte, 106; Gillmore, 109; Hannah B., 130; Hannah F., 101; James D., 112; Jesse, 93, 109; Levina, 103; Lorenzo, 109; Mary J., 137; Nancy, 102; Posidonius L., 130; Rachel Johnson, 103; Rufus, 99; Sally, 102; Thankful, 95.
Monroe or Munroe—Caleb C., 125; Charlotte H., 128.
Montgomery—Clarra E., 136; Frances J., 128.
Moore—Barnard, 114.
Morse—Adelia M., 117; Caroline, 104; Darius, 107; Eliakim, 97; George Washington, 102; Granville, 129; Hannah, 96; Horace S., 110; James, 94, 98; Jason, 91, 107; Joseph, 92;

Levi, 92; Levi F., 101, 130; Louisa F., 113; Lucy, 99; Lydia, 104; Mary B., 109; Mehetable, 94; Olive, 97; Polly, 96, 98; Rhoda, 92, 101; Ruth, 107; Samuel, 96; Sarah, 92, 101, 109; Susa, 99; Walden, 92.
Moses—Joseph, 110.
Moulton—Eunice, 109; Grainville W., 140.
Mumle—Dory, 103.
Murphy—Mary, 123.
Murray—Mary, 127.
Nason—Charles M., 117; Elijah, 102; Elisabeth, 101; George W., 103, 104; Jesse, 94; Jesse L., 125; Preston C., 133.
Neel—Augustus, 108, 109.
Newel or Newell—Albert I., 130; Anna B., 128; Ellen F., 125; Eva A., 132; Jabez, 93; Lucien B., 132; Nelson C., 132; Olney P., 131; Sylvia A., 117.
Newgent—John, 135.
Newton—Molly, 89.
Nichols—Charles E., 131; Roxy, 101; Sarah E., 111.
Nickleson—Huldah, 99.
Norcross—Asa G., 103; Clarissa, 111; Martha, 124.
Nottage—Annie, 137; John S., 138.
Nutter—John, 100.
Nye—Caleb T., 113; Susan, 111; William, 111.

Paddock—Lydia, 99.
Page—Polly, 107.
Paine—Joseph A., 110; William, 97.
Parcus—Moses, 91.
Park—John, 113.
Parker—Jeremiah, 108.
Parkhurst—Susanna, 97.
Parnel—Benjmin, 94; Polly, 94.
Partridge or Partrige—Aaron, 94; Achsah, 96; Addie, 135; Asa, 94; Benjmin, 94; Catherine A., 112; Edmond F., 132; Eleazer, Jur., 96; Elias, 93; Elisha, 89; George H., 135; George I., 110; Hannah, 102; Harriet M., 112; Hiram, 110; Joel G., 105; Kezia, 92; Lois, 93; Lydia A., 116; Miriam, 91; 100; Nathan, 98; Philete, 91; Phinehas, 100; Rena, 98; Sally, 104; Salome, 91; Samantha, 104; Simeon, 90; Susan J., 115; Sylvester, 92; Timothy, 96.
Patch—Abigail Cornelia, 98; Renselaer, 121.
Payson—Betsy, 94; Edmond, 97; Mary, 96; Nancy, 95; Samuel, 99.
Pebbles—James T., 115.
Peck—Nancy, 96; Sarah M., 110.
Peirce—See Pierce.
Pennell—Calvin, 98.
Penniman—Daniel, 109; Nathan, 101; Roxana, Mrs., 111; Sena, 95.

Perham—Chloe D., 109; Watee D., 101.
Perkins—Frank, 134; Shepherd, 99.
Perrigo—James G., 136.
Perry—Arnold, 95; Asa D., 106; Mary, 96; Patience, 101; Ruth Davis, 99; Waldo C., 102.
Pettee—Hannah, 107.
Pettis—Betsey, 110; Nancy M., 105.
Pherson—J. W. M., 118.
Phetteplau—Henry M., 120.
Philips or Phillips—Hattie L., 131; Sarah, 107.
Phips or Phipps—Eliza, 110; Harriet, 110; Jedediah, 101, 104, 105; Maria, 110; Martha W., 106.
Pickering—Addison, 132; Addison H., 123; Annie R., 133; William R., 131.
Picket—John, 138.
Pierce—Alfred J., 132; Annie, 99; Barnam C., 130; Emma M., 134; Ferdinand I., 129; George W., 139; Jenna Maria, 136; John, 91, 104, Jur., 100; John Edwin, 130; Nancy, 98; Ruth, 92; Susan A., 132.
Pike—Abbie M., 135; Louisa, 101; Nahum, 98.
Pillsbury—Harriet A., 126; Marion L., 124.
Place—Nathan, 97, 99.
Plimpton—Beriah, 108.
Plummer—William E., 133.
Pond—Abagail or Abigail, 90, 94, 103; Abijah M., 109; Adela, 99; Alexander D., 115; Alfred, 104; Alfred W., 129; Alson, 98; Amanda, 99; Anna M., 110; Ann Maria, 125; Apollos, 91; Barzilla, 90; Benajah, 108; Benjamin, Jur., 95, 3d, 108; Betty, 93; Calley, 94; Charlotte, 109; Clarinda, 98; Cynthia, 100 (2); Darius, 107; Dinah, 91; Ede, 94; Edena, 90; Eli, 98, Jur., 102; Eliab M., 112; Elihu, Jr., 102, Esq., 106; Eliza, 126; Elizabeth, 111; Eliza L., 127; Ellen Miria, 123; Erasmus, 101; Erasmus A., 117; Eunice, 92; George R., 111; Goldsbury, 108; Hannah, 108; Hannah C., 103; Harriet N., 121; Henry E., 114; Huldah, 92; Increase Sumner, 102; Inez E., 140; James H., 128; James P., 100; Jane E., 112; Jem Otis, 93, 104; Jeremiah M., 96; John C., 136; Jonathan, Jr., 106; Joseph, 89; Juline O., 130; Justin, 99; Kezia, 92; Lavina, 89; Lois, 92; Lucinda, 97; Margarett, 89; Maranda, see Mi; Martha A., 114; Mary, 108; Mary A., 140; Mary H., 111; Mary J., 117; Melatiah or Meletiah, 90, 93; Meranda, see Mi; Milcha, 94; Mime, 108; Miranda, 99, E., 105, R., 118; Nathan, 91, 93, 106; Olive, 96; Oliver, 108; Otis, 107; Polly B., 101; Rachel, 91; Rebach, 90; Robert, Jr., 89; Ruth M., 105; Sammel, 95; Sarah, 108; Sarah G., 117; Sarah Maria, 106; Susan M., 121; Susanna, 90; Timothy, 108; Timothy L., 100; Willard, 98; William, 108.
Potter—Jennie, 133; Mary Ann, 129.
Powers—Simeon, 106.
Pratt — Abigail, 107; Amanda, 130; Anna, 100; Caroline Fayette, 103; Jeremiah, 91; Spencer, Dr., 95, 101.
Preston—John Bowers, Rev., 94.
Price—Peter, 133.
Puffer—Timothy, 89.
Pushee—John, 99.

Rae—Susan C., 138.
Rand—James S., 109.
Randall—Oliver, 113.
Rathburn—Benjamin, 97.
Rawson—Gordon, 105.
Ray—Francis B., 119; James P., 110.
Raymond—Lucy, 99; Susan, 99.
Reed—Susanna, 94.
Remick—Susan A., 135.
Revere—Thomas, 91.
Rhodes—Maria Lonesa, 140.
Rice—Benjamin F., 120; Henry, 98.
Rich—Mary, 98.
Richards—Francelia E., 125; Rebecca W., 112.
Richardson—Abigail, 97; Albert M., 112; Amasa, 91; Amos, 92; Clarissa, 109; Daniel, 108; Delia, 98; Eleanor, 100; Eli, Jur., 96; Elijah, 96; Elisha, 97; Elisha F., 113; Emeline M., 105; Erastus, 112; Forada, 91; Fremont M., 140; Henry Bullard, 137; James, 108; Jemima, 95; John H., 101; Julia, 94; Julia Ann, 115; Lonesa M., 140; Lydia, 91; Maria, 100; Mary A., 114; Mehitabel, 94; Nancy, 95; Nancy A., 126; Olive, 89; Persis, 108; Polly, 94; Rena, 96; Sally, 89, 94; Samuel, 92; Seeva, 91; Stephen W., 112; Susanna, 90; Timothy, Jr., 93; Warren A., 119; William T., 110; Ziba, 108.
Ripley—Benjamin W., 103.
Robbie or Roby—Edwin A., 104; William Henry, 127.
Robbins--Aquilla, 89; Jesse, 92; Molly, 90; Olive, 90.
Robertson—John, 103.
Robinson or Robinsson—Ebenezer W., 106; George H., 119; Jane, 119; Joel, 93, Major, 93; John K., 126; Lucy Ann, 106; Percy, 90; Sarah T., 112.
Roblee—Aurelia E., 130.
Roby—See Robbie.
Rockwood — Abijah T., 110; Asa, 98; Benjamin, 91; Edmond J., 128; Elisha, 89; Erastus, 105; Erastus D., 123; Ennice, 91; Joseph, 95; Mary, 102;

INDEX—MARRIAGES. 221

Mehitabel, 100; Nathan. 101; Peggy, 102; Samuel. 89; Susan B., 119; Susanna, 95; Timothy. 107; William. 124.
Rogers—Edwin R., 136.
Roix—Mary A., 140.
Round or Rounds—Asa R., 136; Daniel H., 138; Emma, 92; Lois, 96.
Ruggles—Jeremiah, 89.
Russegue—Francis A., 138.
Russel or Russell—Hepzibah, 97; Lucy, 98; Martha L., 133; Thomas J., 136.
Ryder—Sarah Irving, 134.

Sampson—Calvin, 99; Lizzie E., 133.
Sanford—Elisha, 108.
Sanger—Charles H.. 122.
Sargent or Surgeant—Almira, 113; Asa. Jr., 131; Susan, 106.
Savage—Anna, 137.
Sawin—Isaac, 99.
Sawyer—Samuel, 130.
Sayles—Anna, 95; Duty, 99; Joanna, 120; Kate A., 124; Selah, 94.
Scamitton—Anna S., 131.
Scott—Allice L., 134; Estella A., 136; Huldah, 138; Lemuel, 98; Lizzie A., 125; Lucinda L., 115; Oceanna A., 129; Ophelia H., 132; Otis, 98; Ruth, 112; Susan M., 113; Sylvia, 101; Victoria M., 116; Welcome, 94; Willard, 110; Willard E.. 137; William. 94.
Seavey—George W.. 116.
Seekel—Benjamin G., 112.
Shaw—Francis A., 118; Sarah, 99; William P.. 118.
Shepard or Sheperd—Addison S., 128; William P., 119.
Shepardson—Catherine E., 129; Grace F., 123; Joseph E., 129; Thaddeus H., 135.
Shepherd—See Shepard.
Shields—Janitt, 106; Thomas R.. 127.
Shipy—Hopkins, 102.
Shumway—Mary, 112.
Shurtleff—Robert, 116.
Siload—Ebenezer, 91.
Simmonds or Simmons—Andrew, 100; William C., 136.
Simons—Mary W., 103.
Simpson—Leander, 98.
Skinner—Abigail. 103; Zenas, 109.
Sloan—James C.. 130.
Slocom, Slocomb or Slocum—Abby B.. 119; Charles E., 109; Joshua. 108 (2); William, 96.
Small—Amelia J., 127; Matilda, 113.
Smith—Calvin, 104; Calvin M., 121; Catharine, 95; Esther, 89; Gains, 90; Joann, 101; Luthera. 130; Maria, 137; Maria B., 109; Mary, 94. 101; Miriam, 107; Olive, 96; Polly, 108 (2); Sarah, 91; Susan P.. 104; William D.. 124.

Snow—Cyrus B., 116; Deborah, 104; Hannah D., 104; Homer V., 126; Ruth M., 101.
Southwick—Sarah M., 132.
Southworth—Jedediah, 125.
Sparhawk—Cynthia, 107.
Spaulding—Harriet E., 120.
Spear—Jenny, 95.
Springer—William A.. 125.
Stanley—Osmyn A., 121, 134.
Stanton—Thomas, 102.
Staples—Amos W., 121; Bridget, 137; Nathan, 128.
Stearns—A. Janette, 121; George A.. 131.
Stedman—Emely A., 127.
Stevens—Elisha, 97.
Stewart—Robert A., 138.
Stimpson—Mary, 138.
Stockbridge—Francis M., 127.
Stockwell—Jonathan, 108; Jr., 108.
Stricklin—John, 97.
Stubbs—Josiah H., 140.
Sullivan—Mary, 138.
Sumner—Ossian, 124.
Sunderland—Hannah, 117.
Surgeant—See Sargent.
Swazey—Patience, 94.
Sweet—Polly, 103; Sullivan. 103.
Swift—Susan H., 133.

Taft—Alonzo M., 135; Eli, 92; Esther, 103; Mary A., 140.
Taylor—Hattie A., 140; Isreal W., 115; James, 91; Simeon, Jr., 114.
Tenney—John W., Dr., 103.
Thain—Thomas, 102.
Thayer—Alexander, 115; Alice, 102; Benjamin, Jur., 95; Benjamin C., 138; Betsey Ann. 116; Caroline, 115; Charlotte M., 126; Cushman, 99; Davis, Jr., 115; Deborah B., 104; Eliza, 101; Emely J.,121; Isoline F., 140; James, 96; Julia, 97; Laprelate M., 128; Larned, 94; Martin, 95; Mary, 100; Nancy E., 118; Nathaniel, 92; Obadiah Allen, 93; Obed B., 116; Patty, 95; Peter, 95; Phila, 108. Roxana. 101; Susan, 101; William M., 112.
Thomas—George H., 118.
Thompson—Alice J., 131; Clara D., 127; David, 94, 113; Ebenezer, 91; Edwin, 116; Hannah T., 110; Hellen M., 125; Huldah, 108; John R., 109; Julia. 98; Lewis, 103; Lucy, 93.
Thurston—Abigail T., 105; Daniel, 95; David, 97; Elizabeth, 89; Eliza M., 103; Esther, 96; Julia, 98; Louisa Marion, 115; Lucretia, 91; Luke, 97; Miranda, 104; Molly, 90; Nancy 94, 104; Philo, 99; Rachel, 98; Vina, 93.
Ticknor—Howard M., 129.
Tiffany—Harriet, 103; Huldah, 110;

Patty, 92.
Tillinghast or Tillinghest—Caroline, 103; Frederick A., 137.
Tingly—Martin V., 129.
Titus—Olney, 93.
Tobine—George A., 125.
Tonn—Solomon, 91.
Torrey or Torry—John, 103; Jun'r, 94; John F., 131; Mary, 94; Nancy, 99.
Tower—Jason, 139; Lydia H., 126.
Tracy—Deborah D., 115.
Turner—Calvin, 107; Sally, 108.
Tuson—Martha M., 138.
Twichell—Chloe A., 104.

Underwood—George M., 117.

Vay—Edith Mc. E., 140.
Voax—Emeline H. B., 103.
Vose—Alfaretta A., 135; Ebenezer S., 118; Ellen B., 131; Harriet, 116.
Vox—Mary Ann, 100.

Wadsworth—George F., 137; George M., 126; Joseph H., 123; Seth, 101; Susan, 101.
Walls or Wales—Abbie O., 123; Abby, 121; Abiram W., 106; Amos A., 104; Clive Fairbanks, 100; Harriet S., 107; James, Jr., 101; Jemima, 105; Joanna, A., 114; John, 95; John D., 122; Jonathan, Jr., 95; Julia A., 113; Marianna, 134; Otis, 95; Rachel, 95; William H., 118, 123; Willis, 104.
Wakefield—Mehetable, 94.
Walker—George M., 120; John H., 127; John S., 117; Natalia, 100.
Wallace—George E., 121.
Waller—Polly, 107.
Ward—William S., 131.
Ware—Alfred, 98, 117; Amariah, 93; Amos, 91; Arival P., 114; Asa, Jnr., 96; Betsey A., 118; Betsy, 103; Clarinda, 94; Daniel Addison, 103; David, 96, Jr., 110; Elias, 89; Elizabeth C., 114; Frederick A., 101; Frederic Augustus, 125; George H., 140; Gilbert A., 106; Hannah, 93; Hiram, 124; Jabez, 92; Lois, 99; Louisa, 137; Lyman P., 105; Lyman S., 110; Mary, 89; Mary A., 128; Melia, 91; Miranda, 101; Nathan, 110; Olive, 94; Olive D., 113; Olive M., 106; Preston, 98; Rhoda, 94; Robert H., 119; Samuel, Jur., 99; Sarah A., 122; Violetta P., 136.
Warfield—Abijah B., 111; Ebenezer E., 106, 109; Esther B., 104; Harriet A., 110; Nellie S., 127; Sarah Hellen, 127, note;
Warren—Emmerson F., 130; Sally Ann, 114.
Watkins—John P., 129.

Watson—Susan A., 137; Susan S., 137.
Weatherhead—Louesa J., 134; Saphrona, 89.
Webb—Ann, 140.
Webber—Sarah A., 117.
Weeden—Charlotte Emeline, 103.
Wells—Jonathan, 96.
Wescott—Jerome, 110.
Weston—Edward G., 139.
Wheeler—Berthenia E., 120; Jane, 101; Perssis, 96; Polly, 100.
Wheelock—Elijah, 97.
Whelden—Amelia L., 139.
Whipple—Lucretia, 104; William G., 105, 110.
Whitaker or Whitiker—Emma Jane, 127; James G., 126; Mary A., 120; Richard, 103.
White—Asa, 116; Charlotte A., 123; Eliab, 90; Elijah, 107; Elmira, 109; Emeline, 122; Lyman, 95; Lyman P., 105; Nathan, 108; Rufus F., 134; Sally, 108; Susan A., 122.
Whiting—Abigail, 105; Adelaid B., 122; Asa, 101; Jr., 89; Benjamin, 95; Benjamin W., 122; Betcy, 93; Charlotte, 90; Daniel, 104; Elias, 110; Elisabeth, 89; Eliza, 104; Esther, 92; Hannah, 91, 92; Helen B., 106; Jairius, 103; John, 90; John B., 134; Joseph, 107; 3d, 94; Louesa M., 130; Lydia, 94; Mary, 93, 94; Mary E., 124; Mary N., 115; Matilda D., 126; Peter, Jur., 95; Polly, 100; Sally P., 101; Seth, 94; Sidney, 97; Sukey, 92, 100; Willard C., 106; William E., 116.
Whitiker—See Whitaker.
Whitney—Nancy, 112.
Whittemore—Sarah A., 113; William, 106.
Wiggin—Hannah A., 105.
Wight—Abner, 92; Nathan, 89.
Wilbar—Ruth, 97.
Wilder—Marshall P., 105, 121.
Wilkinson—James W., 136.
Williams—Charles E., 137; Jane F., 138; Levi, 104; Margarette, 90; Samuel, 90; William, 90, 122.
Wilmarth—Apollos, 106; Benjamin, 89.
Wilson—Arathuse, 109; Charles, 124; Hariet M., 128; James B., 121.
Winslow—Harriet N., 112.
Winn—Lucina, 109; Sarah L., 110.
Wiswell—Betsey, 107.
Witherell—Polly, 97.
Witt—Alexander C., 100; Archibald C., 100.
Wood or Woods—Alonzo H., 105; Betsey, 104; Ebenezer Partridge, 96; Elizabeth, 95; Harriet B., 105; John, 102; Lucy, 93; Sarah, 96; Silvia D., 105; Susan, 110; William E., 122.
Woodbury—Mary A., 136.
Woodman—James Frank, 140; William,

133.
Woods—See Wood.
Woodward—Alfred, 101; Almira, 99; Amos P., 126; Austin, 100; Elizabeth C. N., 105; Elizabeth P., 118; Ellen M., 116; Harvey, 101; James, 90; Lucretia, 102; Marcellas A., 122; Melissia H., 109; Nathan, 107; Preston, 101; Rachel, 95; William H., 120.
Wright—Carline M., 101; Chloe, 90; David, 108; Jabez, 100; Jerusha, 98; Joanna, 97; Mahitable, 124; Molley, 107.

Young—Lewis, 104; Thersa, 139; William S., 123.

DEATHS.

Adams or Addams—Abigail, 161, or Abigail, 143, 144; Achsa P., 190; Albert, 192; Allice Maria, 166; Alphens, 169; Asa, 149; Betsey, 153, 178; Carrie B., 186; Charles R., 184; Chloe, 149; Clarabell, 170; Daniel, 147, 149; Elizabeth, 156; Esther, 148, 152; Ezekiel, 168; George, 145, 174; Hannah, 145; Harriet, 154, 165; Harriet C., 171; Henry W., 172; Ithamer, 161; James Dea., 155; Joel, 157; John, Ens'n, 145, Jr., 145; Julia, 152, 164; Layton Jenks, 152; Lois, 183; Mary, 144, 149, 150; Mary G., 186; Mary Jane, 155; Moses, 148; Nancy, 144, 154; Nancy R., 153; Nathan, 169; Nathaniel, 150; Nathaniel Emmons, 170. Nehemiah, 172; Noami, 145; Peter, 143, 146; Rebeckah, 154; Rachel, 153; Sarah, 147; Sarah C., 184; Seth, 145; Simeon P., 177; Susan, 149; Thadeus, 154; Timothy, 143; Ward, 145, 186; Warren Edmund, 168; Whiting, 164; William, 154; William Henry, 184; William Maddison, 149.
Aldice or Aldis—Esther, 153; John, 143.
Aldrich—Harriet A. (Fisher), 192.
Allen—— 160, 161; Abigail, 144, 150, 154, 156; Abijah, 155; Aldis Mc., 184; Alfred, 153; Amos H., 171; Calista, 153; Charlotte Jane, 153; Cyrus. 188; Dinah, 150; Eliza J. L., 177; George, 157; Hannah, 162; Hiram George, 153; John, 150; Juletta, 165; Julia A. C., 178; Mary, 155; Mary Lizzie, 196; Maxey, 145; Samuel, 144; Walter H., 190.
Alley—John, 173; Rosalinda, 163.
Appleby—Seth, 164.
Arnold—Leonard A., 168.
Atwood—Annie Frances, 194; Frederick N., 182; J. Francis, 170; Ruth M., 182.
Bacheler or Batchelder—— 194; Lucina H., 190.
Bacon—Abbot Brooks, 175; Abigail, 143, 148; Amos, 143; Chloe, 147; Deborah, 144; Elen, 156; Ellen M., 188; Hipsabah, 143; Joseph, Dea., 159; Julia A., 186; Julian B., 186; Lydia, 146; Mehitable, 154; Ruth 188; Seth, 152; Theophilus, 144; Thomas, 144, 175; Capt., 146; Jr., 146.
Baily—Susanna, 157.
Baker—Abijah, 143, 153; Austin M., 184; David, 180; Elias, 170; Esther, 146; Hannah, 188; James, 167; Jemima, 162; John, 150; John Ellis, 155; Julia, 156; Molly, 151; Olive, 150; Phebe, 152; Sally, 155 (2).
Balcom—Abel, 159.
Ballou—— 162; Julia E., 176; Mary Ann, 156; Wilber, 188.
Barden or Burden—Artemas, 175; Julia Ann, 169; Mary, 153; Olive, 156. See Bordon.
Barnard—William, 194.
Barry—Catherine, 190.
Barrows—Charles A., 174; Emeline, 169.
Bartlett—Harriet A., 173.
Bassett—Mary, 156; Rufus, 167; Walter Scott, 179.
Batchelder—See Bacheller.
Bear—Thomas, 150.
Bemis—Charles H., 186; Edmund L., 169; Eveline, 169.
Bennett—Anna Judson, 181.
Benson—Fred Mellen, 184; Herman C., 194.
Billings—Achsah, 180.
Bird—Sally, 180.
Bishop—Bessie F., 194.
Blake—— 143; Abigail, 156; Beriah, 154; David, 156; Eliza Ann, 156; Eunice, 150; Francis, 178; Grace F., 194; Hannah, 145, 175; Herman R., 178; Ida Delma, 170; Ira, 165; Julia, 167; Kezia, 145; Laura, 190; Louisa Jane, 160; Maddison, 165; Mary, 145; Mary A., 172; Mercy, 148; Myron A., 194; Oretta, 179; Patromelia, 147; Phebe Louisa, 169; Philip, Dea., 157; Robert, 146; Solomon, 153, 158; Sophia C., 190; Susan A. M., 192; Susanna Day, 153; Susanna Morse, 149; Sybil, 153; Timothy, 168; Waittn, 156; William Gardner Van Almon, 167.
Blanden or Blandin—Enoch, 164; Milly, 156.
Bonsall—Albert H., 194.
Borden—Ruth, 184. See Barden.

INDEX—DEATHS. 225

Bowditch—Mary, 144.
Boyd—Frederic W., 167; Hannah, 155; Hugh, 144; John, Col., 154; Willard, 163.
Braley—Roger, 146; Ruth, 150.
Breck, Breek, Brick or Brock—Anna, 166; Grace Mabel, 176; John T., 194; Jonas, 152; Judith, 158; Juliette, 188.
Brewster—Peggy, 158.
Brick—See Breck.
Briggs— ——— 163; John Bayley, 169.
Broady—Anna, 164; John, 179.
Brock—See Breck.
Brown—Albert T., 178; Carry L., 194; Edwin L., 166; Leonard B., 174; Lewis C., 181.
Buffington—Margarett, 168; Sarah Jane, 168; William, 169.
Bullard—Abigail, 194; Amos, 184; Artemas Brown, 154; Calla, 176; Cephas, 180; Elisha, 156; Irene A., 166; Joseph Warren, 154; Julia, 154; Lucy, 184; Piam, 186; Rachael, 168, or Rachel, 159; Rena F., 184; Sabra, 180; Sukey M., 180.
Burden—See Barden.
Burlingame—Abba A., 176.

Cady—Letisa, 152.
Callaghan—Mary, 171.
Capron—Silence H., 196.
Carr—Ann, 184; Grace, 169.
Carrol—Mary, 190.
Caswell—Hartwell Adelbert, 190; Harvell Albert, 190.
Caulfield—John, 184.
Chamberlaine or Chamberlin—Ellen E., 164; Harriet, 164.
Chapin—Louis Gardner, 188.
Chase—Marcus E., 168; William H., 190.
Cheeney or Cheney—George, 173; Wm. Henry Harrison, 158.
Cheever—Abigail, 181; Ariel, 183.
Claflin— ———, 162; Calvin, 155; Jeremiah, 181; Lois, 157; Louisa, 156; Roxeena, 153.
Clagg—Edward, 179.
Clark— ———, 169; Abijah, 165, 190; Annie E., 177; Asa, 147; Jr., 144; Benjamin, 144; Betey, 183; Daniel Penniman, 147; Dyar, 147, 152; Dyar Gilbert, 153; Elizabeth, 148; Ellen Melinda, 164; Emma A., 173; Esther, 146, 149, 153; Hannah, 173; Horatio, 149; Huldah, 150; John, 146; John Day, 149; Joseph J., 186 (2); Joseph James, 176; Judith, 143; Kate, 148; Lanson, 146; Lysander, 171; Maria, 179; Melinda, 146; Millie, 147, or Milly, 156; Nancy, 156, 172; Nathan, 165, 186; Patty, 168; Paul, 169; Peggy, 151; Phebe, 155; Rachel, 151;
Rhoda, 156; Ruth A., 179; Sally, 146, 188; Samuel, 152, 172; Sarah J., 186; Simeon, 175; Stephen A., 151; Susanna, 194.
Cleaveland, Cleavland or Cleveland—Cora Isabella, 188; Francis Augusta, 158; George P., Capt., 157; Hannah, 163; Henry, 156; Louely, 157; Nancy, 188; Polly, 151; Susan, 156.
Cobb— ——— 152; John Franklin, 148; Minnie A., 194; Polly, 151.
Coffield—James, 186.
Coghlan—Daniel, 192.
Cole— ——— 163.
Colvin—Mary, 190.
Conant—Lizzie Ruth, 186.
Connors—Mary, 192.
Cook—Anna Josephine, 194; Elvia, 172; Emegene, 172; Emeline, 184; George, 176; James M., 175; Joanna, 154; Lucy Ann, 158; Maria, 186; Nancy, 188; Reuben, 190; Ruth, 177; Sarah, 174.
Coombs or Cooms—James S., 179; Maria II. (Hills), 192; Sarah T., 157.
Corbet—Emma Louisa, 192.
Corbin—Eugene N., 167; Otis, 182.
Coughlin—Ellen, 179.
Crooks—John, 144.
Crosby—Elma E., 186; Nellie M., 179.
Crossley—Reuben, 190.
Crowell—Mary E., 184.
Cummings— ——— Mr., 158; Abraham, 158.
Cunliff—Abigail, 162.
Curtis—Annie P. (Pickering), 192.
Daniels— ——— 186; A. D., 194; Adams, 153; Amariah, 157; Jr., 155; Amos, 143; Amelia T. H., 182; Annie, 192; Betsey, 147, 149; Celia A., 177; Cynthia, 188; David, 143, 144, 153; Dexter Ward, 147; Elizabeth, 143 (2), 144, 157; Elmer B., 163; Eunice, 154; Eunice A., 157; Eunice Ann, 159; Ezra, 192; Mrs., 136; Frank W., 186; George W., 155; Hannah, 147; Hannah M., 170; Hariet N., 190; Henry, 147; Mrs., 146; Hepzebah, 147; James L., 175; Jane A., 169; Jemima F., 174; Joel, 157, 196; Joseph, 154; Joshua, 146; Julia, 144; Kezia, 145; Lucy, 156, 192; Magdalen, 143; Mary, 146, 151, 171; Miliah, 151; Molly, 143; Nancy, 192; Nathan, 145, 158; Peter, 161; Phylena, 176; Sq. Geo. Warren Lafayette, 153; S. Samantha, 194; Sarah, 157; Seth, 144; Simeon, 148; Sophia, 161; Susanna, 154; Unice, 154; Unity, 152.
Darling—Alfred, 192; Amasa, 153; Edith A., 184; Hattie A., 186; Mary G., 179.
Davidson—Elizabeth, 180.

Davis—Charlotte, 160; Ellen Brown, 184; Gertrude J. S. (Squire), 192; Julius S., 194.
Day — ——— 179; Ebenezer, 143; Henry, 149.
Dean—Abigail, 143, 153; Ada E., 184; Betey M., 186; Betsey, 153; Caroline F., 188; Chloe, 152; David, 192; Mrs., 163; Ebenezer, Capt., 151; Edene, 169; George W., 184; Hannah, 147, 156; Ichabod, 151, 182; Julia A., 190; Maria Amelia, 167; Oliver, 196; Rhoda, 178; Seth, Ens., 156; Tryphena, 149; William, 158.
Desmond—Jeremiah, 178; John Joseph, 192.
DeWitt—Archibald, 178; Mary Ann, 186; Patty, 156; Susan Fisher, 179; William Stearns, 172.
Doah or Dorr—Alline L., 171; Emma F., 169; Lucretia, 146.
Doherity or Dohority—Edward, 190; Margarett, 186; Mary, 182.
Dorr—See Doah.
Dove—Samuel, 179.
Drake—Merede 184.
Drown—James, 150.
Duffy—Ann, 190.
Dunbar—Olive, 171; Simeon, 174.
Dunton—Eveline A., 163; Joel, 165.
Durney—Sarah A., 178.

Earle—Paul, 171.
Eddy—Sally, 154.
Ellis—Deborah, 150; Elihu, 144; Joseph, 148; Mary, 148; Meletiah, 144; Sarah, 150; Simeon, 148; Timothy, 147.
Emerson or Emmerson — Annie M., 178; Gracie Mary, 180; Mary Jane, 173.
Emmons—Deliverence, 143, 149; Diodate Jonson, 143; Erastus, Maj., 151; Martha, 155; Nathaniel, 143; Rev., 158; Sarah, 152.
Everett—Abijah, Dr., 147.

Fairbanks — Abigail, 148, 164; Asa, Capt., 148; Jr., Capt., 147; Billing, 148; Clara Anna, 188; Gideon, 143; Juletta, 160; Molly, 159; Warren, 154.
Fales—Mary, 144; Thankfull, 154.
Farley—Philip, 167.
Farr—Millard L., 190.
Farrington or Ferrington—David, 156; Henry, 164; Jenny, 175; John, 145; Julia M., 186; Otis, 154; Patience, 152.
Fechem—George, 149.
Fehin—William, 192.
Fenno—Andrew, 166.
Ferrington—See Farrington.
Fisher — ———, 162, 163, 166; ———

Widow, 151, 158; Aaron, 155; Abigail, 144, 145, 148, 149; Abigail Whiting, 146; Achsah, 180; Alexander Metcalf, 155; Amos, 148; Ann Elizabeth, 168; Anna, 143, 170; Asa, 160; Belinda, 168; Betsey, 150, 158, 163, 179; Caleb, 182; Caroline, 164, 176; Charles, 147; Charles Willis, 151; Charlotte, 181; Clara, 156; Clare, 158; Daniel C., 157; Darius, 157; David, 147; Dinah, 149; Dorcas, 179; Eleazer, 147, 151; Elial, 156; Ellen M., 168; Emmons, 170; Esther, 153; Francis F., 180; Francis H., 168; Frank Herbert, 170; George, 166; Hannah, 145; Harriet, 151, 163; Harry, 146, 192; Harvey, 149; Hezekiah, Lieut., 148; Irene, 159; Jabez, 155; Hon., Esq., 147; James, 149; Jason, 152, 183; Jemima, 144; Joanna, 152; Joanna Hopkins, 152; John, 144; John M., 184; John Warren, 152; Joseph, 145, 151; Leonard, 158; Levi, 161; Lewis, 161; 3d, 149; Lucius W., 159; Lurana, 147, 155; Lydia, 188; Mariah Abbot, 152; Martha, 159; Mary, 147 (2); 148, 157; Mary Adaline, 150; Mary Blanchard, 188; Mary J., 194; Matilda Emely, 151; Maxey, 186; Nabby Whiting, 149; Nancy, 154, 156; Nancy Maria, 151; Nathaniel, 149, 155; Jr., 145; Nathaniel Horace, 153; Nellie E., 183; Paul Metcalf, 153; Peletiah, Esq., 154; Perez, 168; Persis, 156; Peter, 157, 178; Rachel, 155; Rhoda, 145; Richard, Mrs., 158; Ruth, 190; Salina, 155; Sarah, 148, 172; Sarah H., 157; Silas, 176; Susan, 158, 176; Susanna, 166; Sylvia D., 183; Timothy, 165; Mrs., 149; Ursula C., 175; Vina, 147; Warren, 149; Weston, 192; Willard, 188; Willis, 188.
Fiske—Sarah, 156.
Fitzpatrick—Anne C., 194; John L., 175.
Follen—James F., 188.
Follet or Folletl— ———, 165; Lydia, 177; Nathaniel, 173.
Ford—Isabel, 196.
Foster—Ehmer B., 194; George, 158; George F., 196; Georgianna, 194; Hannah, 179; Susan E., 188; William F., 194.
Freeman—Emma F., 172; Jenny Frances, 177.
Frost—Benjamin, 183; Everett P., 178; Herbert A., 183; Nancy, 168; Olive C., 174; Peter, 178.
Fuller—Elizabeth, 151; Sarah Jane, 177.

Gates—Charles, 166; Harriet S., 164.
Gay—Abigail, 146; Almira M., 180; Betsey, 179; Charles, 166; David M., 176; Deborah B., 162; Edwin La-

INDEX—DEATHS. 227

fayette, 157; Ellen, 163; Harriet F., 176; Loami, 184; Loami B., 170; Mary, 149; Nelson, 148; Rachel, 153; Thankful, 167; Thomas, 159; Thomas Pinkney, 152; Timothy, 154, 194; Wilkes, 161; Willard, 180; Willard, Jr., 174.
Gibson—Mary E., 179.
Gifford—Mary Ann, 190.
Gillen—James, Jr., 194; Jennie, 196.
Gilliland—Hugh, 182.
Gilmor, Gillmore, Gillmor or Gilmore —————— 152, 163; Abby R. Hayford, 192; Albert, 151; Albert Green, 154; Albert P., 173; Alice, 178; Charlotte Louisa, 151; Chloe, 159; David, 155; Mrs., 150; Edward A., 190; Elizabeth, 153; Gilbert, 169; Israel, 145; James, 186; Lieut., 147; Joseph, 170, 178; 3d, 152; Lucy, 150; Maria, 190; Molly, 157; Nancy, 181; Nancy Fales, 149; Nancy Maria, 167; Nathan, 173; Olive, 147; 161; Rachel, 154; Rebecca G., 194; Rena P., 190; Robert, 173; Dea., 149; Samuel, 161; Susan A., 172; Willard, 155; William, 145, 158; 3d, 152; William D., 186.
Goings, Gowen, Gowens or Gowin— Elvira, 152; John, 145; Luther, 184; Lydia, 144; Maxcy Allen, 147; Polly H., 188.
Goldsbury—Eunice, 145.
Gould—Alice E., 194; Irving W., 196; Isabella J., 194; Joseph, 148; Kezia, 145.
Gowen, Gowens or Gowin—See Goings.
Graham—David, 158; Sophronia L., 161; Thomas Nilson, 159; William, 190.
Granger—George, 184.
Grant—Rachel, 158.
Green or Greene—Everett Marsh, 184; Hannah, 149; Maggie Marsh, 184; Martin, 190.
Grooves—Ephraim, 148.
Grosvenor—Molly 152.
Grover—Emeline, 168; Margarett, 168.
Guild—————— Widow, 148; Adelaide L., 171; Alonzo M., 182; Ebenezer, 152; Dea., 145; Hermon, 179; Joel, 194; John, 153; Lucy Cutler, 152; Lydia, 151; Malinda, 170; Nancy G., 182; Olive, 150; Samuel, Dea., 158.
Gunning—Mary Jane, 184.

Hagerty or Haggerty—Agnes, 188; James, 184.
Hall—George, 178; Jemima, 188; Nelly A., 184; Ruth, 183.
Haltien—Eliza Eveline Holbrook, 153.
Hamblet—————— 150.
Hamilton—————— 171.
Hammond—Ruth, 171.
Hancock—Charlotte A., 188.

Harding—Abigail, 147, 196; Elisha, 150; Jr., 149; Fisher Hartshorn, 149; James, 157; Louis, 164; Lucy, 145; Ruth, 149.
Hardy—Eliphalet D., 192; Eunice M., 180; Maria, 196; Sarah A., 172.
Hart—Caroline A., 166; Caroline M., 163; Charles E., 163; Martha A., 166; Mira Ursula, 181; Sarah L., 167; Susan M., 181.
Hartshorn—————— 163; Arrabella A., 172; Betsey, 166; David, Maj., 158; Mrs., 157; Henry, 181; Herbert A., 164; Ida E., 177; John Allen, 176; Lewis, 183; Lewis W., 165; Lydia, 183; Mary, 171; Nancy, 190; Nancy H., 186; Seth L., 190; Silas, 152; Walter, 155; William T., 161.
Haskell—————— 161; Clarinda P., 161; Hannah W., 190; Laura, 162; Samuel, Mrs., 159; William Turner, 156.
Hastings—————— 149.
Hathaway—Alinda, 188; Charles, 192.
Haulihan or Houlihan—Margarett, 182; Mary, 190.
Haven—Olive, 154.
Hawes or Haws—Abigail, 144; Amos, Capt., 147; Beriah, 151; Edward, 155; Eunice, 146; Hannah, 146, 147, 156; Jonathan, 172; Joseph, 155; Ens., 151; Julia Eliza, 157; Kezia, 144; Levi, Dea., 157; Lewis H., 188; Mariah, 143; Mary, 144; Milatiah, 148; Nathan, 145; Nathaniel, 145; Pamelia, 157; Polly, 151; Preston, 147; Sally, 183; Stephen S., 196.
Hawkens—Sarah, 151.
Haws—See Hawes.
Haywood—Ira, 192.
Healy—James T., 196.
Heaton—————— Mrs., 160; —————— widow, 147; Abigail Hills, 151; Harman, 145; Isaac, 145, 146; Julia, 148; Lydia, 146; Nathaniel, 144; Noah, 144; Samuel, Mrs., 150; Sinai, 144; Synthe, 144; William, 143.
Hill or Hills—————— 158, 162; Abigail, 162; Albert Warren, 182; Arthur, 188; Betsey, 146, 153; Beulah, 143; Deborah, 186; Edward S., 173; Elias, 143; Eliza, 155; Eudora F., 192; Frank E., 184; Hannah D., 174; Harriot, 152; Harvey, 181; Isaac, 190; Jarvis H., 183; Jason, 154; Joseph, 153; Capt., 150; Lysander B., 182; Margarette Ann, 164; Maria, 153; Micah, 143; Nancy, 172; Phila B., 184; Polly, 148, 172; Robert R., 186; Seneca, 175; Susan, 190; Theron C., 181; Warren, 196; William E., 156.
Holbrook—Marcus M., 175.
Hollerin—Jane, 174.
Holmes—Dorcas, 149.
Hood—————— 184.

Horton—Ann E., 167; Caleb, 165; Martha, 153.
Houlihan—See Haulihan.
Howard—Huldah, 150.
Hubbard—Abigail, 143; Eben, 147; Elisha, 170; Elizabeth A., 170; Everett Lincoln, 188; Frank, 175; Freddie Ellsworth, 192; Joshua, 144, 153; Sarah, 160.
Hunt—Abigail, 181.
Hunting—Horatio, 153.
Hutchinson—Bridgett, 182.

Ide—George, 165; Mary, 157; Ruth, 148.
Inman—Elmira, 158; Elmira W., 160.

Jackson—Molly, 151; William, 152.
Johnson—Nathaniel G., 183; Samuel C., 154.
Jones— ——— 163; Abigail, 147; Adams, 146; Joanna, 158; Margarett, 171; Therece, 154.
Jordan, Jorden or Jordon— ——— 186; Alfred Harris, 159; Alice J., 194; Edith M., 186; Ellen J., 171; Henry L., 194; Herbert A., 169.
Joslin—Clarance B., 186.
Judkins—Emma E., 183.

Keef—Catherine, 183.
Keith—Charles, 173.
Kellogg—Sarah C., 190.
Kilburn or Kilburne—Betsey F., 174; George S., 169.
Kimball—Edmond, 158; Emely, 178.
King—Charles, 157; Corilla Dexter, 192; David, 186; Elizabeth L., 168; Erepta, 194; George, Jr., 186; Georgiana, 190; Hattie E., 192; Louisa, 168; Mary, 169; Sarah, 153; Walter Lyman, 190; William Cady, 178.
Kingsbury—Aaron, 145; Abbie M., 178; Abigail, 151; Asa, 173; Caroline, 172; Daniel, 144; Ebenezer Adams, Capt., 158; George D., 155; Hannah, 179; Horatio, 148; James, 152, 155; Mary Fisk, 150, 153; Polly, 171; Sarah Ann, 188; Stephen, Capt., 148, 174; Timothy, 153; William Henry, 153.
Knap or Knapp—Hiram, 186; Josephine, 183; Louisa, 177; Matilda H., 162; Melville, 174; Moses, Maj., 148; Peggy, 158; Prudence, 171.
Kyle—Mary, 171.

Ladd—Abigail H., 168.
Laing—Witham A., 175.
Lane—Ammariah, 143.
Langly—Nattalie, 192.
Larkin—Joseph Laurene, 182.
Lawrence—Anna, 163; Betsey, 179; Daniel, 149; David, 145; Ebenezer, 146 (2); Eleazar Hills, 145; Eliphas, 174; Esther, 166; Herbert, 167; Joseph, 157; Joshua, 144; Rebecca, 148; Seth, 145; Susan, 178, 181; Thomas, 143; Willard C., 182.
Lawton—Cynthia, 155.
Leavitt—Alonzo M., 179.
Lee—Ruben, 144.
Leland—Anna H., 166.
Leonard—Betsey, 162; Elizabeth, 158; Hartford, 173.
Leprilete—Deborah, 153.
Leshure—Duluna, 155.
Lesley—Nelly F., 183.
Lethbridge— ——— Mrs., 151; Caleb, 143; Clarissa, 149; Ferdinand, Dr., 149; Hipzibah, 144; James, 148; Jerusha, 156; Nancy, 145; Samuel, 147, 150.
Lewis—Caroline, 171; Esther, 174; Perry, 190.
Lewitt—Eione, 144.
Lincoln— ——— 180; Hannah, 151; Herbert L., 182; Jabez, 145; Patty, 176; William, 151.
Littlefield—Elizabeth, 161.
Long—Ellen S., 176.
Lothrop—Gilbert, 173.
Lumbert—Jabez, 154.

Mackeny—Jeremiah, 143.
Makepeace—Mary, 157; William, 174.
Mann— ——— 163; Abial, 152; Asa, 151; Chloe, 164; Cynthia, 162; Dolly, 148; Eldod, 143; Elias, 154; Elias W., 155; Elisha, 145; Esther, 144; Eunice, 156, 170; Jonathan E., 166; Mary, 155; Nathan, 151 (2); Dea., 143; Rebekah, 157; Ruth, 196; Seneca, 144; Stephen, 148; Susan, 157; Susanna, 147; Thomas, 148; Thomas W., 184; William, 143; William A., 186.
Marden—Susan H., 190.
Marroon—Margarett, 171.
Marsh—Mary, 162; Samuel R., 181; Susan, 170.
Martin—Ellen, 194.
McCue—Martin, 196; Michael, 196.
McGuire—Catherine (Keany), 192.
McIntee—Mary, 194.
McNally—Catherine, 192.
Merrifield—Ann M., 165; Mary, 153.
Merrill—Susanna H., 188.
Metcalf— ——— 165, 177 (2); Abial, 147; Widow of, 143; Abigail, 155, 158, 176, 194; Abigail G., 156; Abigail Lanrinda, 156; Abigail Richardson, 149; Abijah W., 157; Albert, 157; Alfred, 156; Allen, 148; Amelia, 166; Artemas, 146 (2); Asa, 155; Betsey, 178; Charles C., 173; Charlotte, 152; Ebenezer, Dr., 146; Jr., 146; Electa, 165; Elial, 155, or Eliel,

INDEX—DEATHS. 229

145; Elias, 172; Ella Maria, 169; Ellen F., 172; Emeline Betsey, 150; Esther, 146; Eunice, 147; Evelyn E., 186; George R., 170; Hannah, 145, 149; Hanon, 159; Hellen J., 184; **Herbert Wallace**, 169; James, Dea., 147, 159; Jonathan, 149, 162; Jr., 152; Jonathan, widow of, 147; Joseph Whiting, 150; Judson, 144; Julia, 146; Laura, 149; Lucy M., 181; Mary, 152, 154, 170; Mary A., 159; Mary F., 188; Mary G., 168; Michael, 172; Milly, 155; Milton, 148; Nancy, 148; Nathan, 170; Olive, 163; Patty, 148, 153; Paul, Dr., 145; Peggy, 145; Polly, 146; Prudence, 158; Rebecka, 146; Roxy, 149; Ruth, 144; Sally, 157; Samuel, 160; Sarah, 158; Susanna, 175; Sybil, 175; Timothy, 150; Timothy Augustus, 156; Willard, Mrs., 158; William Haven, 159; William W., 194; Willie C., 183.
Miller—Electra S., 192; Hannah, 158; Horace G., 161; Jesse, Jr., 146; Jesse T., 159; Joseph, Dea., 155; Julius L., 154; Lephe, 175; Lewis L., 182; Nathaniel, 166; Phillip T., 181; Philip W., 179; Rhoda, 159; Thankfull, 153.
Mitchell—John, 165.
Morgan—Mary G., 181.
Morse— ——158; ——Widow, 146; Aaron, 146, 157; Anna, 154; Darius, 158; Jr., 155; David, 143; David T., 157; Eleanor C., 188; Ella Jane, 192; Esther, 145; Eveline Elizabeth, 170; Experience, 188; Hattie E., 183; Hervey Milton, 150; James, 154; Jason, 155; Joseph, 190; Keturah, 148; Levi, 155; Levi F., 188; Lois, 143; Lydia, 153; Merriam, 161; Moses, 145; Obed, 155; Olive, 145, 148; Patty, 153; Samuel, 144, 146; Samuel Augustus, 154; Sarah, 151; Solomon F., 190; Susan Blake, 149; Susanna, 143; Triphena, 184.
Moulton—Eliza P., 167.
Murphy—James, 184; Mary Elizabeth, 194; Michael, 196 (2).
Murry—Bridget, 194.

Nason—Freddie H., 192; George W., 192; Hannah, 155, 175; Jesse, 162; Laura, 173; Mary, 160, 161; Mary R., 190.
Nelson—Horatio, 180.
Newell— ——165, 194; Alfred P., 168; Amanda, 184; Agustus, 176; Clarissa, 180; Hiram, 176; Homer, 158; Jerusha, 168; Sarah, 174; Shadrack, 171; Sylvia, 196.
Neylon—Patrick, 190.
Nickerson—The Widow, 150.
Norcross—Asa, 152; Asa G., 159; Cornelia Angeline, 160; Edward A., 167; Elizabeth, 156; Irene F., 171; Josephene, 172; Marshall G., 174.
Nottage—Elusa T., 192.
Nutter—John, 176; Polly, 167.
Nye— ——164; Henry William, 173.

O'Brien—Elizabeth, 194; Francis T., 192.
Ockinton—William, 145.
O'Niel—Mary, 171; Richard, 169.

Paine—Earnest, 184; Hiram, 174; Rozina B., 170.
Partridge—Abigail, 151; Achsah, 151, Asa, 176; Eleazar, 156, or Eleazer, 167; Elizabeth, 144; Eliza F., 177; Hannah, 157; Hannah H., 175; Harriet, 174; Ithamer, 147; Joseph, 165; Julia, 144; Lois, 149; Mehitable, 144; Nathan, 153; Peggy, 145; Phineas, 162; Polly, 165; Simeon, 153.
Peck—Calvin, 180; Oliver, 158; Sarah, 169.
Pennamin—Nathan, 158.
Pennell—Rebecca, 167.
Perriman—William Edwin, 170.
Perry—Arnold, 177; Aurelia, 152; Ellis, 174; Mary, 153; Simeon, 156.
Phinney—Eliza, 164.
Phipps—Fanny, 160; George Gardner, 156; Lydia, 156; Martha, 149; Rhoda, 155.
Pickering—Eber, 152.
Pierce—Addison D., 161; Charles A., 180; Israel, 181; John, Mrs., 155; Joseph, 151; Julia Ann, 153; Mary, 161; Nancy Melinda, 157.
Pillsbury—Sarah A., 180.
Pitcher — Joseph, 162, 168; Joseph John, 192; Thankful, 166.
Pitman—Florence, 175.
Pond— ——162; Abel, 144; Abigail, 143 (2); Addison N., 170; Alfred, 164; Alfred Daniels, 154; Amos, 153; Amy, 173; Anna, 150, 179; Baruch, 143; Benjamin, 145, 148; Caroline, 148; Clarinda, 158, 175; Cutler, 175; Daniel, 145; David, 143; Edmond Sandford, 154; Elbridge, 157; Eli, 147, 166; Eliab, 147; Elihu, 163; Senior, 151; Elisha, 146; Dr., 148; Elmira, 155; Erasmus, 154; Esther, 163; Fidelia E., 183; Goldsbury, 188; Mrs., 161; Hannah, 149, 150, 154; Hannah Marion, 154; Harriett A., 161; Henry, 147; Henry B., 173; Hermon, 145; Hezakiah, 152; Hiram, 175; Huldah, 151; Ichabod, 144; Irene, 152; Jabez, 143; James Otis, 159; Jarvis, 146; Jemima, 147, 156; Jeremiah M., 154; John, 152; Juline, 196; Justin, 159; Widow of, 163;

Leonard, 169; Louisa, 162; Malelah, 147; Marena, 178; Margaret, 148, 157; Mary, 147, 150; Mary Louisa, 157; Mehitabel, 144; Merinda, 146; Metcalf, 143; Miletiah, 149; Nancy, 173; Nathan, 167; Ogden, 155; Olive, 155, 169; Oliver, 146, 149; Oliver N., 161; Paul D., 159; Pennuel, 143; Phebe, 143; Polly, 144, 182; Rachel, 157, or Rachael, 167; Rebecca, 147; Reuben G., 172; Robert, 157; Ruth, 156; Sally, 154; Samuel, 147, 153; Samuel W., 194; Sarah, 146, 150, 151; Sena, 146; Solomon P., 173; Syvia, 150; Timothy, Lieut., 155; Timothy L., Capt., 157; Wellington, 160; Willard, 160, 186; William, 159; William Henry, 150; Ziba, 158.
Pratt—Elizabeth, 152; Lewis, 148; Solomon Hewes, 144; Spencer, 151.
Prior—Catherine, 186; Michael, 186; Thomas, 186.
Puffer—Gilbert, 150.
Putnam—Thomas H., 192.

Rand———, 158.
Rawson—Lucy, 150; Nancy, 150.
Ray———, 162; Alfred Knapp, 167; Chloe, 151; Eliza, 151; Eliza A., 162; Gilbert Ruel, 162; Horace Cook, 150; James, 154; Joseph, 164; Lydia P., 184; Robert, 162; Sally 152; Selina, 154.
Redwood—Nancy, 158.
Reed—Alexander, 147.
Rhodes—Edson M., 194; Emma Jane, 163.
Rich—Charles Francis, 192.
Richards—Amos, 170; Elenor, 166; Martha, 164; Sarah, 166.
Richardson—Abigail, 151, 154; Abigail M., 171; Albert D., 192; Amasa, 157; Betsey, 148; Charlotte, 151; Chloe, 164, 174; Eli, 154; Capt., 152; Elisha, 146, 188; Eliza B., 161; Elona, 148; Emely F., 166; Esmer A., 169; George Warren, 153; Horace, 156; Jemima, 144; John, 148; John H., 192; John Wilkes, 159; Julia, 150; Louisa P., 165; Lydia, 155, 158; Mary, 150, 157, 158; Mary L., 184; Mary Loeza, 184; Matilda R., 177; Mehitable, 157; Melita, 161; Roxanna, 168; Ruth, 154; Sylvester, 173; Timothy, Mrs., 150; William S., 177.
Rierden—Catherine, 176.
Riley—Margaret O., 183.
Robinson———, 180; Alice, 171; Archibald, 180; Delia Maria, 194; Jane, 174; John, 174; John Alden, 163; Margaret, 190; Mary Alice, 179; Roger, 169; Sarah, 178; Sarah H., 162.
Roblee—Estella E., 183; William H., 183.
Roche—Richard, 188.
Rockwood——, 162; Albert Erastus, 184; Anna, 158; Asa, 194; Jr., 152; Benjamin, 144, 149; Elmer L., 181; Erastus, 184; Hannah, 149; Hannah Jane, 154; James, 153; Julia, 175; Julia Ann, 157; Mary, 182; Mary Ann, 158; Mehitabel, 148; Nathan, Jr., 164; Peggy, 164; Ruth, 149; Sally, 156; Samuel, 146; Sarah, 154; Seth, 152; Silence, 154; Timothy, 158; Jr., 146.
Rouke or Rourke—Mary, 168, 169.
Ruggles—Jacob, 151.
Russegue—Willie Alphens, 184.
Ryan or Ryon—James M., 190; Mary, 179.

Salley—George W., 173.
Sargeant—Asa, 190; Polly B., 175.
Sayles—Avilda, 188.
Scott—Charles E., 168; Content, 147; David, 162; Ellis, 172; George W., 184; Lucy Ann, 183; Olney, 184; Pardon E., 170; William W., 168.
Sexton—Catherine, 194.
Shaw———, Mr., 157.
Sheehan or Shehan—Dennis, 190; Hanora, 192; John, 188.
Shepard or Shephard—Chickery, 173; Emeline, 175; Mary A., 188; Relief, 188.
Shepardson—James, 184.
Shephard—See Shepard.
Sherburn—Eleanor, 192.
Shurtleff—Betsey, 167; Robert, 167.
Simmonds or Simmons—Andrew, 171; Patrick, 165.
Skinner———, 160; Zopher, 159.
Slocomb—Peda, 143.
Smalley———, 157.
Smith—Christopher, 156; Diadama, 151; Oliver, Jr., 146; Polly, 151; Remember, 172.
Snow—Angaline, 190; Catharine, 164; Cyrus, 180; Hannah G., 176; John, 165; Lizzy A., 161; Ruth, 165.
Southworth—Martha S., 170.
Springer—Julia B., 180; Julia G. E., 184.
Stanley—Hattie E., 188.
Staples—Fanny C., 181; Mary, 150; Nathan, 192.
Stark—Laura Ellen, 178.
Starkie—Esther, 165.
Stewart—Hannah, 178; Janette, 180; Mary Ellen, 179; William H., 192.
Stevenson—Winnie, 192.
Stockbridge—Emely A., 194; Lucia Adelaid, 190; Walter Scott, 182.
Sulivan or Sullivan—Catherine, 177, 183; Dennis, 174, 184; Ellen, 176; Jeremiah, 192; Julia, 196; Thomas,

INDEX—DEATHS. 231

186.

Taft— —— 160.
Taylor —Melea, 145.
Thayer—Amelia K., 169; Asa, Capt., 150; Betcy, 183; Davis, 150, 183; Eliza W., 190; Emory Davis, 180, 194; Emma Lucinda, 182; Evelina Viller. 150; Fisher, 162; Hariet W., 186; Harriet, 173; Margaret G., 159; Martha A., 186; Mary Ann, 158; Nathaniel, 153, 188; Olive, 186 (2); Olive D., 188; Rhoda, 165; Sally, 149, 153; Susan M., 161; Sylvanus, 177.
Thompson—Eleazer, 149; Electa, 154; George R., 161; Keziah, 154; Prudence, 151.
Thorne—George C., 194.
Thurston—Abijah, 149; Bathsheba, 154, 164; Caleb, Col., 158; Charlotte, 157; Charlott Louisa, 150; Chloe, 145; Daniel, 161; Dea., 144; David, 149; Elizabeth, 147; Eunice Susan, 151; Harriot, 148; Harriot Saphrona, 150; Henry, 152; Hiram, 152; Julia, 151; Leviey, 159; Maria, 151; Mary, 152; Rachel, 154; Saphony Alexander, 149; Susanna, 155.
Tobin—Mary, 186; Robert, 192.
Torrey or Torry—Caroline, 192; Charles E., 190; Hannah, 145.
Treene—Sarah I., 184.
Trevett— Benjmin George, 196.
Tucker—Betsey, 151; Ebenezer, 152; Luisa, 152; Sally, 152.
Tufts—Frances Adora, 165.

Underhill—Emeline C., 196; Mary, 188; Mary B., 192; Richard, 190.

Vanarsdalen Abby E. A., 194.

Wadsworth—Frank J., 183; Mary, 156; Nancy, 184; Nancy Stone, 156.
Walls or Wales—— 166; Abigail, 164, 166; Christiana, 175; Elmer E., 184; Emeline L., 184; Frances O., 164; Freelove, 152; Ida Abby, 173; James, Capt., 155; James Edward, 167; Jemima, 172; Jonathan, 177; Mrs., 148; Lewis E., 186; Mary R., 167; Mary Rebecca, 168; Ruth, 146; Sarah A., 166; Waldo, 173; Willard, 158.
Walker— —— 169; Carrie M., 175; James W., 192.
Wallace or Wallis—Chancey, 150; Charlotte, 161; Pliny, 150.
Ward— —— 168; Clarissa N., 167.
Ware— —— 163; Abby, 182; Abial, 158; Albert S., 171; Alfred, 153, 171; Amariah, 159; Benjamin P., 150; Betsey, 152; Billa, 152; Caroline B.,

190; Chloe, 157; Clarissa, 150; David, 158, 177; Diana, 179; Duty, 179; Edward C., 175; Eleazor, 160; Eli, 156; Eliza, 177; Elizabeth A., 181; Elvirah, 144; Emeline, 158; Eunice, 165; Frank E., 171; Hannah, 145, 153; Harvey, 144; Hepzebah, 146; Jabez, 147; James Edson, 156; Jemima, 156; Jerusha, 160; Jesse, 149; Jr., 146; John Aldis, 146; Kezia, 152; Lucretia, 160; Mahitable, 155; Mary, 145; Oliver, 151; Phinehas, 146; Lt., 153; Poly, 143; Sabin, 166; Sally, 157, 181; Samuel, 155, 180; Samuel Gilbert, 154; Sanford, 178; Sarah, 155, 183; Susanna, 150, 156; Sylvia, 174; Tamar, 152; Willard Adams, 150, William H., 178.
Warfield— —— 148; Ebenezer E., 165; Esther B., 174; John, 180.
Watkins—Carrie B., 186 (2).
Watson—Cynthia, 156; George, 166; Samuel, 156.
Webber—Nancy, 179.
Webster—Sarah Lucretia, 188.
Wescott—Almira, 166.
Wheldon—William, 194.
White—Betsey, 146; Harriet B., 170; Henry N., 172; Isadora F., 172; Jerusha, 149; Ladora A., 170; Nathan, 159; Susanna, 146; William, 146.
Whipple--Comfort, Mrs., 159.
Whitaker or Whittacar — Mary Ann, 181; Richard, 157.
Whiting— —— 158, 159; Anna, 181; Asa, 145 Caleb, 144; Charlotte, 159; Claragene, 164; Clarissa Ann, 180; Elizabeth, 151, 153, 157; Hannah, 146; Horace Freeman, 156; Janette Eliza, 176; Joseph, 143, 159, 188; Dea., 154; 2d, 149; Lydia, 145; Martha P., 172; Mary, 144; Nathaniel, 147; Olive, 156, 181; Peddy, 148; Pelatiah, 148; Peter, 150; Dea, 147; Ruth A., 167; Seth, 155; Sidney, 194; Susan V., 177.
Whitney—Ann, 172.
Whittacar- See Whitaker.
Whittemore—Martha, 157.
Wiggin—Joan E., 173; Susan J., 172.
Wilkinson—Frank A., 182.
Williams—Francis, 196; Frederick B., 180; Jerusha, 144; Levi, 177; Mabell, 155; Salla, 144.
Willson or Wilson—Abiah, 154; Beckah, 156; Betsey, 157; Charles H., 184; Jane, 144.
Winn—Josephene S., 172; Otis, 182.
Wiswell—Dexter F., 165.
Wood or Woods—David, 155; Hannah, 154; Horace A., 178; John, Jr., 155; Lois, 151; Silena, 147; Spencer, 145.
Woodman—Eddie, 186; Sarah A., 186.
Woodward—Anna, 148; Austin, Mrs.,

158; Elizabeth, 167; Elvira, 150; Fanny, 174; Hannah, 157; James, 149; James T. V., 172; Jenny M., 174; Kezia, 148; Lois, 160; Marcella, 177; Marcellas, 177; Nathan, 157; Jonathan, 145; Rebecha, 146; Seth, 155; Susanna, 147.

Wright — Jabez, 170; Joanna, 158;

Young—Eva Alice, 186.
Yousoo—Joseph, 196.

www.ingramcontent.com/pod-product-compliance
Lightning Source LLC
Chambersburg PA
CBHW021821230426
43669CB00008B/828